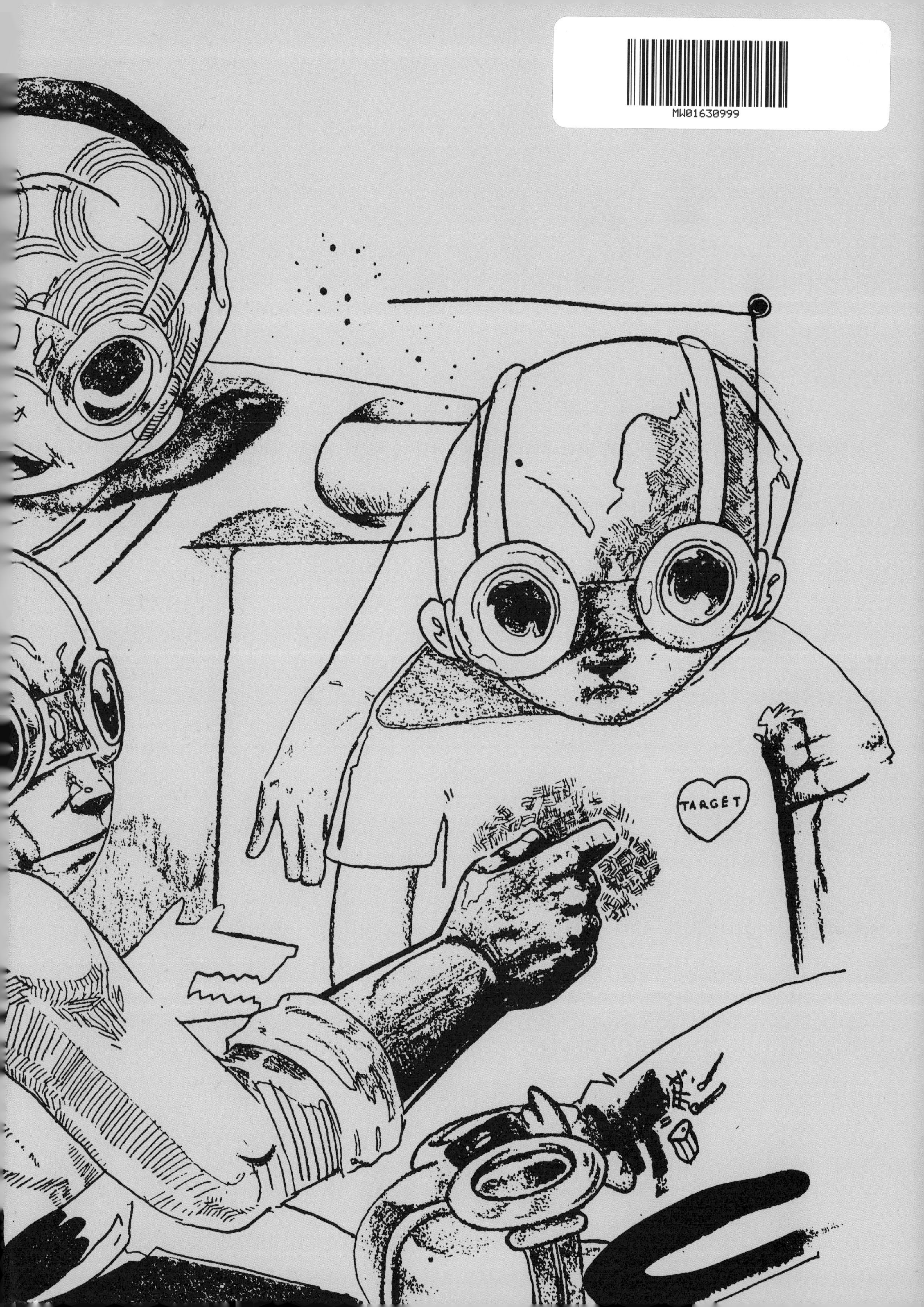
TARGET

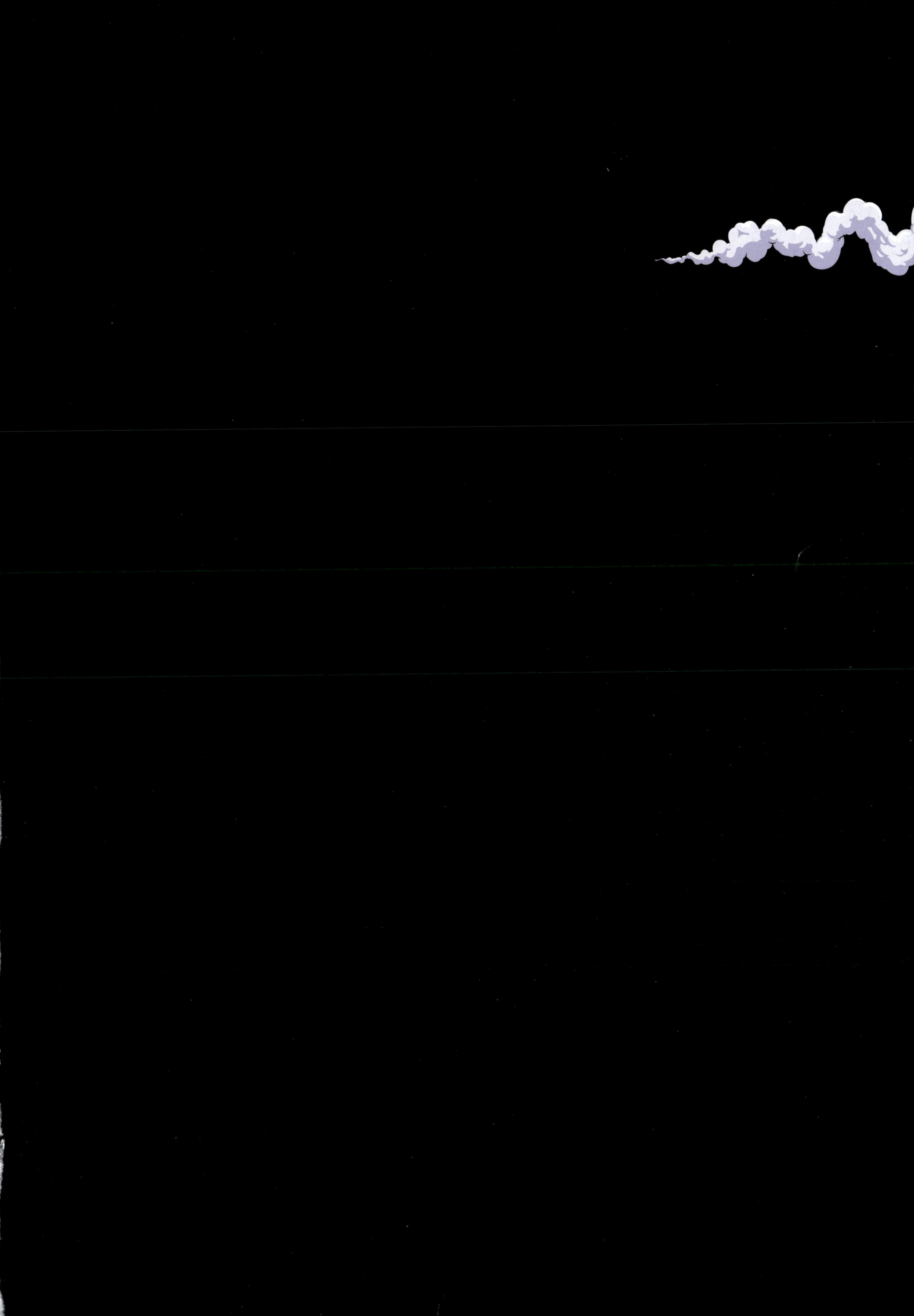

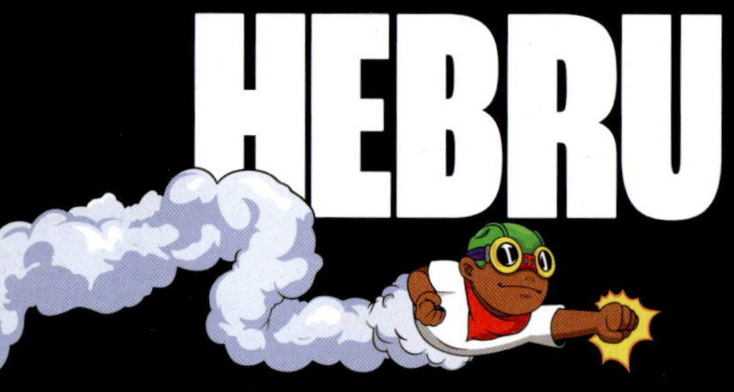
HEBRU

BRANTLEY

First published in the United States of America in 2022
by Rizzoli International Publications, Inc.
300 Park Avenue South New York, NY 10010
www.rizzoliusa.com

Text contributions by Hebru Brantley, Michael "Killer Mike" Render, Carlo McCormick, Lupe Fiasco, Derrick Adams, Bisa Butler, Kevin "Coach K" Lee, Don C, Charles Shepard, Derek Collins

For Hebru Brantley:
Editor: Rhea Fernandez
Editorial Coordination: Marika Shishido Dato
Design Coordination: Janay Everett

Graphic Design by Oliver Munday & Paul Spella

For Rizzoli:
Publisher: Charles Miers

Editor: Ian Luna
Project Editor: Meaghan McGovern
Design Coordination: Olivia Russin
Production Manager: Barbara Sadick
Copy Editor: Mimi Hannon
Proofreader: Erin Sheehy

The Editors and Rizzoli would like to thank Rhea Fernandez, Oliver Munday, Marika Dato, Paul Spella, and Janay Everett. We would like to express our deepest gratitude to Hebru Brantley.
—Ian Luna

Printed in Singapore

2022 2023 2024 2025 2026 / 10 9 8 7 6 5 4 3 2 1

ISBN: 978-0-8478-7219-0
Library of Congress Control Number: 2022939353

Visit us online:
Facebook.com/RizzoliNewYork
Twitter: @Rizzoli_Books
Instagram.com/RizzoliBooks
Pinterest.com/RizzoliBooks
Youtube.com/user/RizzoliNY
Issuu.com/Rizzoli

HEBRU BRANTLEY

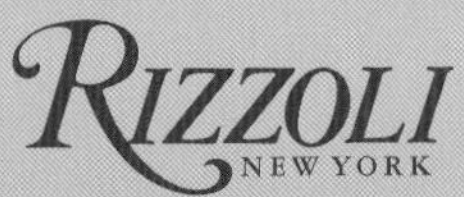

TABLE OF CONTENTS

SUPER KIDS, COLOR CORRECTION, AND THE POWER OF POP

A FOREWORD BY CARLO McCORMICK

The word "wonderful" might at first seem to be a hackneyed term for describing the art of Hebru Brantley, but wonder—as in the sense of wonder, of marvel and curiosity—is indeed the fantastic and inexplicable joy that animates his work. Here, by the nature of the subject and the gaze of innocence it evinces, we are transported to the magical imagination and impersonations of childhood, to a make-believe that is at once particular yet utterly universal. It is a preternatural embodiment of dreams and identity so pure that we cannot help but respond in kind. Brantley's subjects are kids, caught in the act of realizing something about themselves and transfigured by the potency of actualizing their inner truth; they remind us of what life can be before the limitations of growing up and knowing better constrain possibility and potential. To see the world through the eyes of a child is to know both how difficult we have made it for so many of us and how much better it can be.

Falling in love with Hebru's cast of beguiling characters is simple and natural enough; this is the very kind of art where we may rightly ask, "What's not to like?" But in this instinctual fascination lie complex questions posed by the characters' innately ulterior personae. Yes, we immediately recognize these captivating personages, as familiar as our own kin or the kids down the street, but by the very nature of their coloration we have to ask why we haven't quite seen them this way before. Hebru Brantley will readily admit that the genesis of his figures is lodged in the startling absence of people who look like him and inhabit a world that resembles his own that he enjoyed in the fictions of his youth. That abrasive discontinuity between fantasies and the appearance of ordinary life feels like the grit in the oyster, a discomfort that produces a pearl.

Because we all deal with culture on a kind of macro level, the very recent but still unfinished business of considering work by artists of color, and including representations that are not so obviously white and polite, may appear to many like some sort of belated correction. Perhaps it is, but on the micro level, when you ask artists like Brantley why they paint what they do, the answer is pretty straightforward: because they never got to experience the pictures and fictions that represent their reality. Sure, there is a politics to this, but let's not confuse this with political art, which has a valid but very different agenda and rhetoric. There is plenty of need for art that confronts all the inequities and injustices we have long lived with, but there remains a fundamental place for a more basic reimagining, something not unlike the way youthful minds imagine their own thrilling futures, a presentation of what we would like to see.

The great exploits of Modernism are well behind us; let us leave them to the museums where they belong. We now live in a postmodern paradigm where we no longer expect art to shock us with a disruptive difference, so it is well time for us to understand that creating what we desire in the voids of omission is already subversive. For too long have we made the happiness and innocence of white kids a kind of Norman Rockwell fetish, picturing children who do not look like that as somehow more knowing and adult, less capable of innocence and joy. Brantley's art is the great remix of contemporary cultural strategies at work, where the sounds of play and laughter are not the privilege of the few but a chorus of the many. Iconic in their broad accessibility, Brantley's most endearing and enduring characters—Flyboy, Lil Mama, and Phibby—are all the more real to us because they come directly from the artist's lived experience.

The ingenuousness of children has long been held as sacrosanct, and the protection of that safeguarded domain has had its own power dynamic of representation, typically bordering on censorship. Back in 1954, a psychologist named Frederic Wertham published a book, *Seduction of the Innocent*, in which he decried comic books as the cause of juvenile delinquency, blaming crime comics (including superheroes like Superman, who was in his mind un-American, or Batman and Robin, who he saw as gay partners), to such a populist uproar that Senate hearings ensued and the industry was forced to regulate its content. Since then, we've seen cartoons, video games, and now even recognized literary classics come under the reactionary specter of alarm, scrutiny and banishment. This of course (along with the import genres of Manga and Anime) is the legacy to which the art of Hebru Brantley firmly

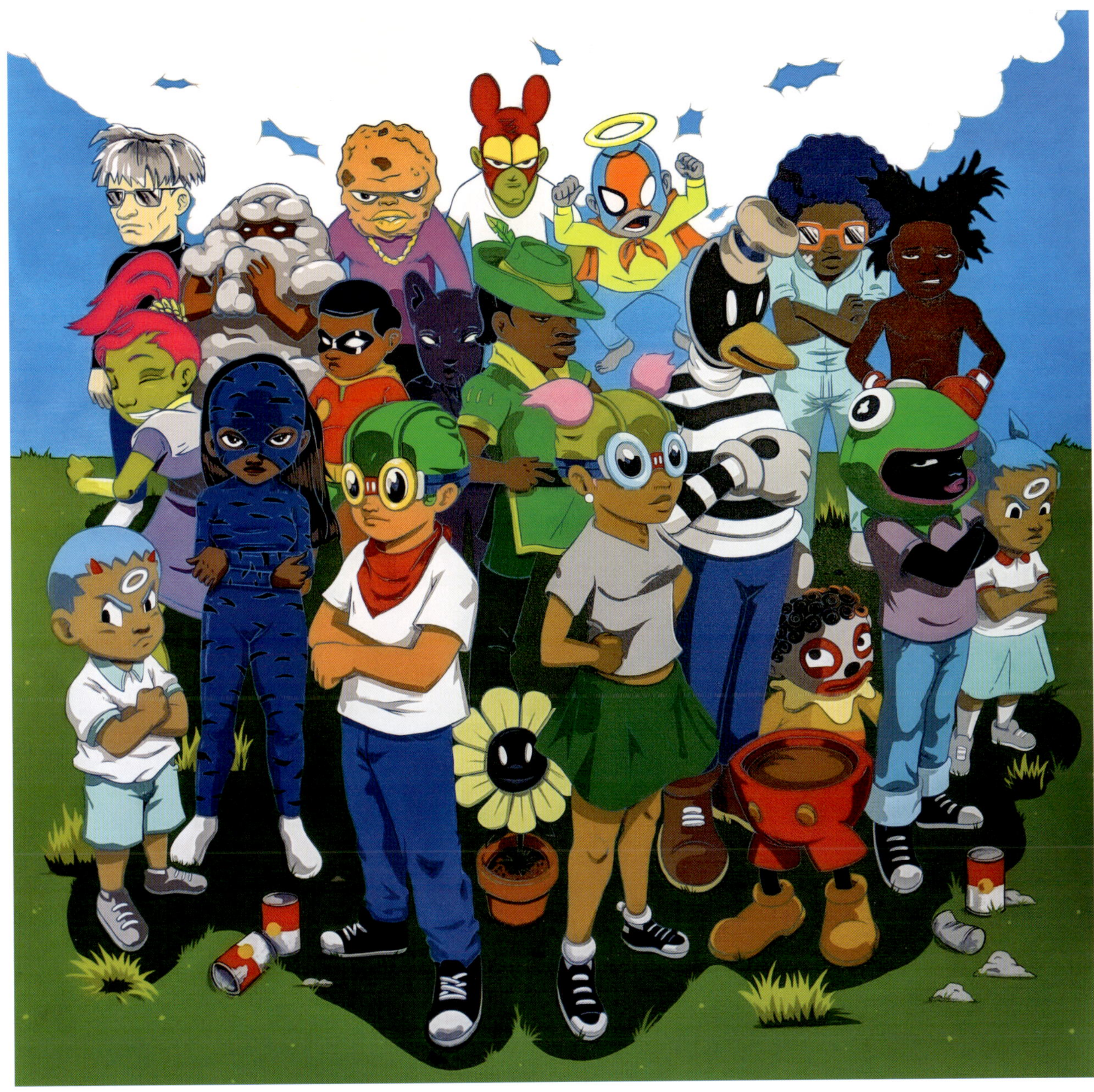

The Family
Mixed media
on canvas
48 x 49 inches
2020

belongs. Today, parents bemoan the screen-time of their children, whereas when I was young, they told us TV was rotting our brains, but this is your mind on pop, and it is, as it's always been, a place of free-fettered imagination and creativity.

A self-confessed comic book and cartoon fan—and what is more, an avid collector of comic and cartoon artifacts and toys, which is a whole further level of commitment—Brantley is a contemporary master of this vernacular visual language. By embracing this explicitly populist mode of storytelling, Brantley reminds us that art can still communicate with a directness and accessibility that too often gets muddled in rhetoric of art world discourse. His too is a complicated inheritance, and when he shares his knowledge of the long racist history within some of our most beloved cartoons from the likes of Disney and Warner Brothers, we may understand his work is not just about what we see but what we do not see.

Eschewing the tropes of traditional narrative, leaving interpretation to the individual viewer, Brantley's most recognizable figures—such as Flyboy, who is a distillation of his own childhood aspirations (discretely coded in the reminiscence of Tuskegee Airmen) and Lil Mama, who he explains is an amalgam of all the younger aunts and fierce women he knew growing up—are deeply personal yet profoundly communicable. And for all the ways his art reflects upon our shared history, it is drawn from the evolution of comic figures and muralism, infused with a contemporary urban flavor that locates us in cultural time as well in our own time—bringing us all to our better selves where children still play and aspire for a world of shared humanism and agency.

CAN'T STOP, WON'T STOP

MICHAEL "KILLER MIKE" RENDER IN CONVERSATION WITH HEBRU BRANTLEY

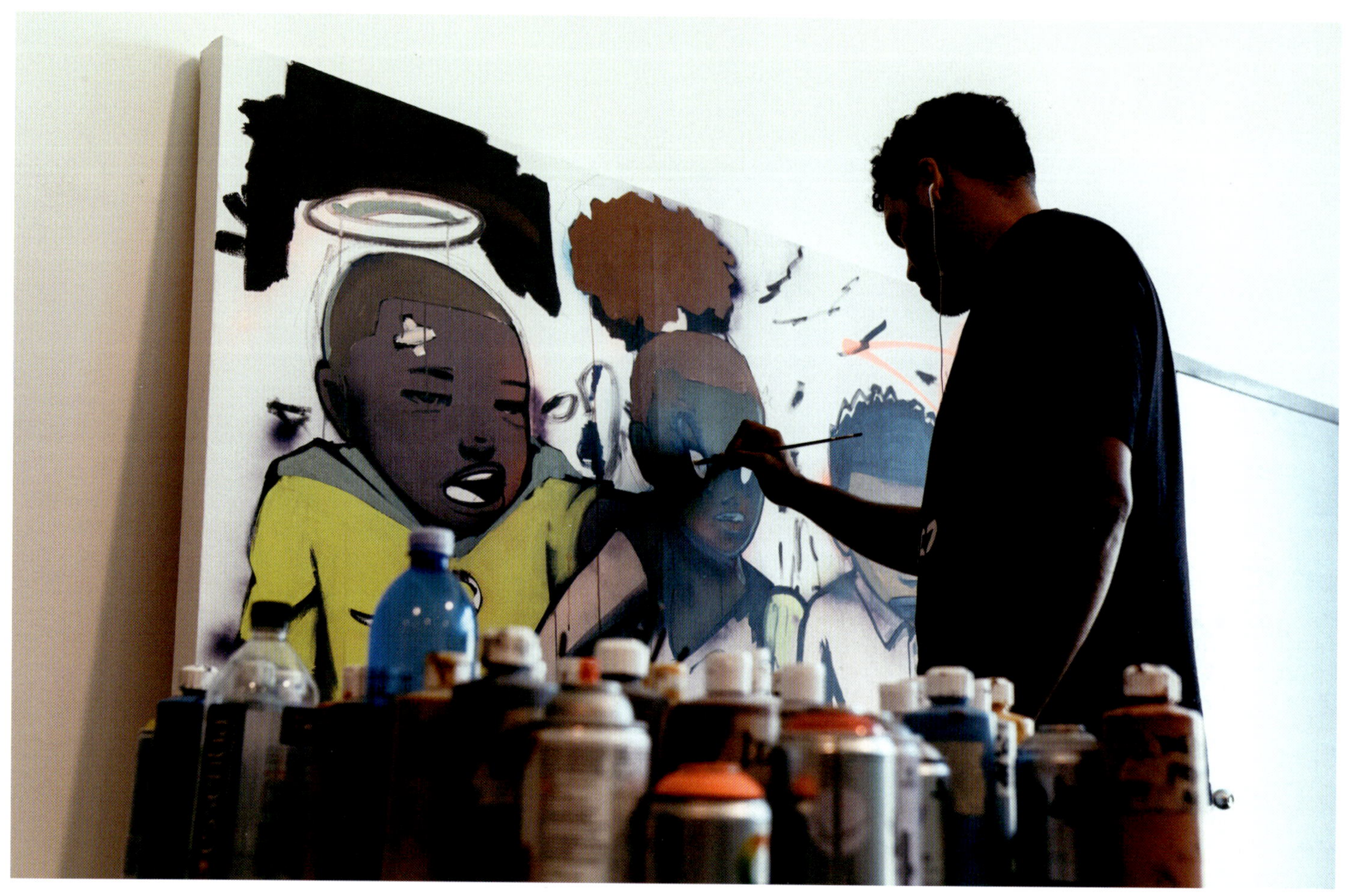

KM: So, Hebru, first of all, thank you for sitting down and talking with me. I appreciate you. I, like everybody else in the art world who really loves art, caught wind late, so the prices went up. And I want to say congratulations. Yesterday's price ain't today's.
HB: Thank you very much.
KM: But let's go back to a moment in time. Let's go to the origin of your most famous characters, the first you breathed life into. And that's Flyboy and Lil Mama. You did it back in the day on a legal pad. How did those characters come to you? What brought them to fruition, out of your imagination?
HB: I've always been a heavy doodler. I come from the old-school era of real hip-hop, where it was rapping, b-boying, you know, graffiti culture. I come from the black book era, so every sketch went in the black book, and I just got used to doodling. I love to draw and not really think about what I am creating. That's kind of how a version of Flyboy came to be. It was, just through sketching. The one time I happened not to have a sketchbook around, I grabbed the first thing that I could draw on, which was the back of a legal notepad.
KM: I'm a believer in the power of doodling. I don't know if I'm very good. I know I've doodled a lot. I have a character with eyebrows and a nose and a smile that kind of represents the inner 9-year-old me that refuses to die. In matters of Flyboy, where does he come from? Is it representative of you? Is it representative of someone you know? What brought Flyboy to fruition, your earliest work with him and what are you trying to express? And has your understanding evolved as you've evolved as an artist?
HB: Yeah, I think Flyboy came from a place where I was trying to figure out what I was saying as a visual artist. A lot of my early works were a little heavy-handed, and I think it kind of gave people pause. It was one of those things where I felt that [style of work] might have just been one part of me, but it wasn't the whole thing. And so I challenged myself to do something that felt more me, felt more a piece of who I was.

I was looking at my loves: hip-hop, animation, comics, manga, all of that. I was also really into graffiti culture. And using characters as I once had to create narratives was something that I got back into doing. I wanted to do it in a more elevated fashion. So, I looked back on the history of the Tuskegee Airmen, and I felt at that time—and this was before there was a movie—that there was such an immense responsibility on these young brothers. There was an immense pressure. Strangely, for me as a student taking this all in, it seemed that there was this unexpected freedom of being able to fly. When you fly, it makes things small, and you feel that you have a God's-eye view of the world, and just thinking about how powerful that sentiment could be at a time when you were seen as less than half a human. It kind of arrived from there.

As I started to think about Flyboy more, I thought, how do I do this in the context of an art show? And I started thinking about Charles Schulz and Peanuts, and how he used these characters to speak through him, of his anxiety, how he saw social ills, and how they were the conduit for that. I wanted to do the same thing with Flyboy.

To the last part of your question, Flyboy is me. Flyboy is my son. Flyboy is more than me, more than my son, but I think that is where it starts. And then over the years, it's taken shape and become symbolic of Black men, Black joy and Black spirit, which is really beautiful to see.

KM: What's dope is my family's from Tuskegee. There's a tremendous amount of pride in being a Tuskegeean and having a family rooted out of there, not only for the university, but because of the Airmen. You know, we recently lost one of the last Tuskegee Airmen. And besides being young men, because they were young when they went into the military, besides being educated men, you can't be a fool flying a plane, they were some fly motherfuckers, man. Like, they literally look cool.

And Flyboy, he looks cool. As a character, whether sculpture or on a canvas, he looks cool. And I notice that a lot of times, he and other characters have the same stance or motif—a lot of times it's a heroic stance almost. When you talked earlier about being too heavy-handed, sometimes it's the artist, whether it's music or genre of art, because you keep embracing hip-hop, and I'm so thankful to hear that. Hip-hop is not just niggas singing and dancing, right? Hip-hop is writing, whether it be graffiti in art form, it is DJing, it is b-boying—which is the dance—and it is rapping, far down the list. So, before I ever wanted to be a rapper, I thought I was going to be an artist, but I didn't have spray paint and trains to go find. I thought I was going to be a b-boy. I was too chubby to breakdance. My mom wouldn't buy me turntables. So, I ended up rapping.

But as you get to be a rapper, you want to take on all the world, you want to tell everybody all the problems. The power of hip-hop is the personalization of problems. It wasn't that hip-hop spoke on every world issue. It's humanizing it by saying, this is how it affects me. And I noticed a lot of times, the motifs when you paint Flyboy and others, it's a very heroic stance, so it's almost like self-encouragement. So, instead of saying the world is bad, everything forgets me, Flyboy stands in opposition, almost, to it.

There's a very hope-filled thing about it. Could you talk about that? Is that a purposeful thing that you're doing in terms of how you paint the characters, how you model them in terms of 3-D, and the impression you want to give people?

HB: I don't know whose quote this is, but "be the change you want to see in the world." For me, I'm not always at my best. I feel like I'm 50-50 most days. You know, hit or miss—I can go either way. Sometimes I need those pep talks, and I don't know where they're going to come from, but I'm hoping the universe will send them to me. Needing a shot of inspiration at times. I wanted to project to people in the way that these kids stand, and the way that these kids are sort of facing head on, and instill that hope, to instill that sense of empowerment over power.

KM: So, there is a personal factor, then.

HB: Yes, absolutely. Absolutely.

KM: And oftentimes, they feel like characters that could be a part of a bigger story...It's almost like when you're a kid and you're playing in the yard, but in your mind, you're fighting that battle right in your front yard, and you're the baddest, most badass soldier in the world. Are your characters part of a bigger story, and if so, what's the story, if you can give us that? And do you mean for the work to encourage other people as it encourages yourself?

HB: The intention was always to put the characters in a narrative. Whatever I was trying to thematically say, also hid the subtext within the work. But it wasn't until after a couple shows where I really started to understand what participants and viewers felt. And more than anything, I think hearing what they felt helped me understand what I was doing and what the purpose of it really was, because I feel like sometimes you create in a bubble, and I didn't have the luxury of always having a sounding board around me.

These were personal things that I was doing and creating, but they took hold and started to inspire. Honestly, the time that I became fully aware of what this was and the intention behind it was when this little nine-year-old girl came up to me at my second or third show. First of all, her father was like, "yo, she doesn't talk." She had had some type of traumatic situation happen to her. She didn't really talk to me, and she said a few words, but she handed me a Flyboy and a Lil Mama that she made out of Play-Doh. And her father was like, "I told her we were going here earlier this week, and she's been working on these all week. Whatever this is, it caught her mind. It caught her attention." And I think from that point, it was like, holy shit, this thing has real power to it, that I didn't even realize in its creation.

KM: Back to Charles Schulz. It really hit me, like, the Peanuts I can remember being young, watching, waiting for the Peanuts special to come on. I wanted to know Linus, in relation to Charlie Brown, in relation to Lucy, in relation to Snoopy, or the other characters. I wanted to know, what was that world like that they were living in? How was it similar to mine?

It seems that with Flyboy and Lil Mama, they live in a world that is constructed in a very personal way, in your head and heart. And other people see it and identify with it. Like, I didn't have to see it twice for me to get it. This wakes up all the nine-year-old imagination in me. It wakes up the *Akira* fan in me. It wakes up all the Peanuts in me. It wakes up my love of things that are now, that's not old and antiquated, but just art that is being and created right now. What is the world like that you're drawing from that you've brought those characters in? And are there other characters? Will there be more? Will the universe expand as you've gotten older? Do you imagine more? What's that world like that's in your head that we don't get to see, that brings these characters out?

HB: It's kind of a loaded question, because I think the world of the characters that people get to see in the galleries and that context is an exaggerated version or extension of my world, of our world. One of the biggest painter influences for me was Norman Rockwell. His version of America wasn't my version of America—

KM: —Hold on. Now, you named Charles Schulz. I'm a big Charles Schulz fan. I literally resisted naming Norman Rockwell, because I was like, if I've got this Black thing going here and all I'm talking about is white artists, somebody's going to get mad and say, well, why you ain't talk about Ernie Barnes? Why you haven't mentioned Basquiat?

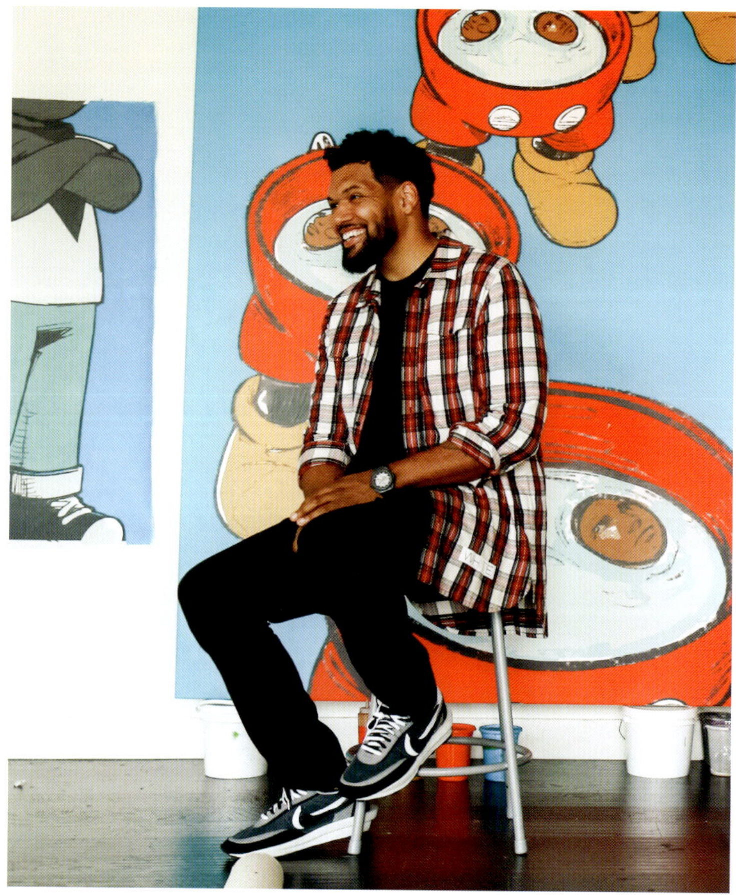

Well, let me tell you something. Norman Rockwell is one of my absolute most favorite artists because of the truth he conveyed. The truth that he conveyed when that little girl is sitting outside the principal's office with the black eye. The truth that he conveyed is to me beyond race, ethnicity, sexual orientation. It was simply a human truth of—that's my youngest daughter. She's just a tough-ass little chick. So, hearing you say Rockwell, man, you done warmed my heart. I'm not going to keep interrupting. But I've just got to—fuckin' salutes, man.

HB: I appreciate it, man. Everybody has a different version of America. So, that's one way of conveying Flyboy or Lil Mama. It's the comic-book guy in me. It's the graphic novel, science fiction reader, where I've spent several years developing a real story, a real world, a real place. But that's sort of adjacent to the fine-art world. But even the fine-art world, there's other characters like Phibby, who is a kid that dons this green sort of Kermit type of helmet—

KM: That's like Linus with his blanket.

HB: Mm-hmm. It also kind of came out of a place of being really frustrated with the way in which we are allowed to participate…Referring to us Black folks, a dark-skinned Black man has to think about the way in which he engages. And so, from that, I just thought from a satirical standpoint, what happens when you put some fuckin' loud-ass green Kermit hat on, you know what I mean, to be acceptable and to be seen as less than, and not be taken as seriously. And, oh—it's palatable now. So, it kind of started from that space, too, of just being really, really frustrated with that narrative.

KM: You handled it beautifully. There is the famous story of Shaquille O'Neal when he was at LSU and a marketing professor telling him he's unmarketable because he's big and he's Black, which was him projecting, "I'm afraid of you, so I assume other people will be, too."

HB: One hundred percent.

KM: And Shaq saying he went back home that night to his dorm and said, you know, I'm going to be marketable. And Shaq, man, Shaq is literally on every commercial on TV ever. Happy birthday to the god Shaquille O'Neal. But he is on everything from Dollar General to how to lift weights to get your chest big.

HB: IcyHot, he got everything.

KM: Yeah, like, for real, man. Shaq is the new Ed McMahon. When we were younger, it was like, Ed McMahon made you trust everything. Shaquille O'Neal is that now.

But OK, let me ask you, what's your process, rather, from start to finish, when you're creating a new work? Are you still working in the medium of physical paints and canvas, or are you strictly digital now? And if it starts digital, how does it translate into the physical when you start going into sculptures? You know, what some people would call "toys" because we like comics and stuff, you're making sculpture. And it absolutely is beautiful. What's the process of getting from an idea to a sculpture?

HB: Sure. I still try to stay as true to the old ways as possible. So, it's always pencil to paper first, with a physical sketch. And then transferring that to digital sometimes, figuring my way through a palette. But the end result is always painting on canvas. And so, even now in the NFT era, it's hard to fully grasp at times not having the physical plane.

KM: I don't believe in nonphysical things. Azealia Banks says how can you own music and you can't physically hold a CD. When she said, if they cut off your streaming service or Apple cuts off or if Spotify, or if at that time Tidal—and then you really think about it, my children don't know the pleasure, except for my oldest child, of opening a record, of appreciating the artwork.

So, you're saying that, "as an artist, it's important for me when people talk about art to understand that there's a process, there's an idea process, there's an experimentation process, there's an 'I see it clearly' process, and then putting brush to canvas or putting pen to paper or putting wax in a mold, that to me, that validates what this shit costs on the other side, because a lot of toil went into it, a lot of blood, sweat, and tears."

HB: Yeah, and you should be able to feel that, you know? I think even if I go from large-form sculptures to smaller forms, again, what some might call toys, for me that's still time and dedication to understanding the form. That's a whole other level of comprehension because you're not in 2-D anymore. I think it's super important to always hold true to the principle.

KM: Yeah, seeing Darth Vader as a Lego toy truly let me know art is real. I never imagined Vader as a Lego. So, if ever I get to see any of your work done in Play-Doh, just know I'm buying every cent in the goddamn store. No resales. We're driving the price up.

What separates your work from some of the other artists that are creating in the same spaces? I could tell you as a fan a half dozen things that I love about it, but is there a purposeful thing that you're going towards, because we know that with Flyboy and Lil Mama, they're radically different from, say, like, what a KAWS is doing. We know his characters, we know what's inspired him, we've read his interviews, we see him. But you don't travel the path of imitating what's out there. You created something very specific to you, very specific to where you're from. It speaks from the place you're from and resonates with others because the truth really is not bound by color, class, or other things.

But you have found your own space within this space. What are the things you purposely did to separate you from a half-dozen other artists that deal in the space of comic influence, that deal in the space of creating sculpture that may be more modern or a toy or even anime-based? What makes you different, man?

HB: I think experience, right? Where I'm from, how I grew up. I grew up, man, in that weird time, and you know that time, where being smart was to be ridiculed. To want to do better was to be a nerd. To read comic books, you might as well just go ahead and cast yourself off the island. But for me it was always being able to navigate what was traditionally not cool, as opposed to what was. And, man, it's like, I want to inject my personal experience into everything that I do. And I'm not those other guys. I'm not KAWS. I love all of those guys, you know what I mean? And their work obviously has a huge place within the whole conversation. But I think for me, the biggest thing is, man, I'm a 6-foot-8 Black man from the South Side of Chicago.

KM: But, man, you, unlike other artists from the South Side of Chicago or from the west side of Atlanta, you've managed to put it all together and present it in such a real and authentic way that it never feels contrived. For young artists that are going to read this, everyone goes through a period of contrivance. You know, I was trying to make a krump song when me and T.I. just looked at each other, and he was like, man, we not no krump rapper. Know what I'm saying?

HB: Right.

KM: So, I was just like, just let me put lyrics over a krump beat. What would you say to a young artist to push them through where they are? What would be your advice to say to them, "you've got to keep doing this," or "you've got to find this," because you seem to have done it and balanced it well.

HB: I think the biggest thing, man, is just to ask yourself—sort of an honesty check—is this truly you? Is this something that you think is dope, or are you doing it because you think somebody else thinks it's dope? There weren't many me's out there that I could look at and say, "Oh, yeah, no, so that's how you do it," besides, like, a Kerry James Marshall. There's serious dudes, contemporary, figurative Black artists in the space.

KM: Fahamu Pecou is someone we both know.

HB: Oh, absolutely. Can't forget Fahamu. And again, even in those days of figuring it out, like, Fahamu's got his canvas set up to my left. I've got a canvas on the right. And Fahamu had his vision I think early. He had his coming to Jesus moment with the art gods, and they said, this is your path. That's how we became friends. I was so enamored with what he was doing. I was like, holy shit, this dude, he's speaking another language. He's also speaking to all the shit that I love.

KM: But the question is in there because you didn't bite.

HB: Right.

KM: You didn't bite. You didn't swag swipe. And it's not obvious you were influenced by it, from an artistic standpoint. The fact that you carved your own way and path I think is one of the things that as an artist a lot of times you're just too scared or nervous to do. And you end up doing a variation of what's out. What makes you—do you still love doing this shit? Because it appears you still do. And where does the drive to create new shit come from once you've become successful like you are?

HB: I absolutely love doing it. I think that the drive always comes from outdoing myself. I'm sure like for you, brother, you've got rhymes on rhymes and ideas on ideas, and it's really just a race against the clock at this point. How much of this shit can I get out before my time is up?

KM: That's real. That's a brilliant thing. If more human beings moved from that space, we might be in a better place. How much of this shit can I get out before my time is up? And that translates to how much time can I spend thinking about this shit? How much time can I spend giving love to my woman and children? How much time can I spare for me?

HB: Yes.

KM: How much time can I give to fans on an earnest, everyday basis? That's something I think artists have that a lot of other people don't understand, because there's a sense of urgency and a need. You can't spend too much time—like, my old art teacher, Mr. Murray, said, "Son, no art piece is ever finished. It's just abandoned by the artist." And I've thought about that.

HB: Absolutely right.

KM: So, you abandon that piece, and then you move on to the next. It's a part of leaving one piece, the propulsion to the next. Like you said, competing with outdoing yourself, like the next Flyboy move gotta be better. The next one just gotta—you gotta blow their minds even more. You still work from that hip-hop-ass arrogant ego space? I hope you do.

HB: Yes, I do. Yes, Lord.

KM: That's that shit, man.

KM: That's what I'm talking about, man. That's what I'm talking about. The fact you refer back to hip-hop so many times, too, I've really got to tell you, is going to have me smiling the rest of my days because hip-hop is something that's style-based. So, what would you call your style? What is it? Because you're not just doing a painting. You have a brand. It's known for merchandise. Shit overlaps. If I'm a kid that cannot afford your painting, I can fuck around and afford one of the small runs of statues or a keychain or something. I can afford something. And it seems that you've mastered a certain balance.

HB: I mean, that's by design. You know, like, I look at artists like Warhol. Warhol never got monetized—let's say that. Not monetized, but participate in the sort of bastardization or commercialization of his work, right?

KM: You can go into Forever 21 and get a Warhol-like T-shirt, absolutely. I understand exactly what you're saying.

HB: That's my point. I really saw what Shepard Fairey did and how Shep was able to galvanize all of these different people and different cultures under iconography, solely under iconography. And that emblem and that logo meant something different to everybody. And so, for me, it's very similar. I want people to have access to the things that I create on different levels and to share that because, that's how information is going to be spread beyond just you posting some shit up. Man, I can't tell you how many times a kid has mentioned something to their parents about a hoodie or a shoe collab or something I've done, and then the parents are like, whoa, whoa, whoa, like, who is this? This shit is dope. Again, relationships upon relationships are built like that.

KM: What's crazy about Shepard is, Shepard probably made more money off the face of Andre the Giant than Andre the Giant or professional wrestling, because it invokes wrestling nerds like my cousin. It invokes a stoic, weird, wild face for street artists. You're actually bringing shit to the game. You've made it even cooler, dare I say, than some artists. And you've referred to hip-hop. Like, do you—like, nigga, how long you been cool? Because you've mastered this cool shit.

Look, man, my non-bio dad is 6-foot-7. One of my best friends is 6-foot-8. So, you've got big guys, it's not always easy to pull off cool. You pull off cool, you really do. You exude a certain energy. You command a room when you're in it.

HB: You know what's funny, man? I really appreciate that. I really appreciate that. I don't consider myself cool at all, but thank you, brother.

KM: If you could summarize the essence of each of the main characters—Flyboy, Lil Mama, and Phibby—with a couple words each, what would they be? Let's start with Phibby. Let's start from the back. Phibby in a few words.
HB: Shit. That is tough. Phibby. Defiant.
KM: Defiant.
HB: Yeah. I think maybe defiant, shy—he's a walking contradiction, so I'm trying to think of words that contrast.
KM: I've known some shy kids that were terribly defiant. They'll stand their shy ass in that corner, and they won't move if they don't agree with the move until you bring out their favorite jam
HB: That's true. No, that's real. Flyboy's my Mickey Mouse. I think there's just the leadership, I think an innate leadership quality, which is always I think a word that comes up. And then Lil Mama, I would just say brilliant. I don't know if this is reductive, but I would also say feisty.
KM: Yeah., I'm celebrating my 15-year-old. And she—those two words. She's feisty, and she's brilliant, to the point where she made the honor roll, and one year she slapped the shit out of one of our friend's nephews. And you know what? If you grew up on the South Side of Chicago and south side of Atlanta, you might need those skills as a woman, you know?
HB: Absolutely. Absolutely. And that's where she comes from, you know? Like, man, I grew up on the low end of Chicago, and in my, like, seven-block radius, there were no boys that were my age. Everybody was either older or, like, you know, the niggas that just refused to leave their mama's house or their grandmama's house. But then all the girls were close to my age. And, man, they were some of the toughest little hood chicks. I mean, the Kool-Aid in the hair. And that's why a lot of times Lil Mama's hair is that pink.
KM: Yeah, because it's the wash.
HB: It looks just like girls dyeing their hair with—
KM: It starts red, and then it washes out a little bit. Absolutely. You ever heard of Paul Frank?
HB: Yeah, absolutely.
KM: What were you like as a kid? Because you seem to be—I think that if you never let, say, the 9-to-12-year-old in you die, if you keep that age alive—I always say keep the 12-year-old alive—that happiness will find you always. I don't know if you'll get rich. I don't know if you'll do everything. But you'll get to do more of the things you want to do than most people, and you'll have a life rich in experiences and influence if you've never let that 12-year-old in you die.
HB: I agree.
KM: You know, 12 is somewhere between—I didn't know if I liked titties or G.I. Joe more, but I knew they were both important to me.
HB: This is some crazy shit, Mike. Twelve was the exact age, right, the exact age where it was like, I can sell all my Ninja Turtles to my homeboy so that I can buy a Wu-Tang album.
KM: Exactly! That's what I'm saying. My basement is the basement right now of a 12-year-old. There are toys and sneakers and—so, as a child, we had some similar experiences. You gave a shit about Wu-Tang, and you knew you still liked Ninja Turtles. Which, quietly, I haven't seen this visually acknowledged, but I always felt something, like Donatello, Rafael, them being named for artists is a big part of what made me a fan. I'm going to just say to whoever thought of that, you really opened it, because as kids you go look shit up. You're like, what the fuck does this name mean? Michelangelo, you know what I'm saying? That's my name, too.

So, whoever did that one, I always think that art, although street art or hip-hop art or Pop art or Modern art oftentimes is written off as low-hanging fruit, but the ability to make people think and question I think has been one of the more beautiful things about that type of art, whether it was Rockwell in his day with advertising or Warhol with painting the Campbell's can, or Flyboy standing defiantly against all of it, you know?

Did you visit the museum as a kid? And I say that because I sit on the board of the High Museum with Fahamu and with a few other people like Coach K (Kevin Lee), who has an impressive art collection. And I know in Atlanta, we're one of the few museums where 50 percent of the people that visit the High Museum are Black people. So, it's an honor for me to serve on that board.

But did you go to the museum as a kid? And is there a painting that sticks with you or stuck with you from that experience? And do you think a museum should be a part of education in terms of elementary or primary school?
HB: Well, I had a single mother. She didn't have no time to take me to a museum. My grandmama wasn't going to take me to no museum. That was on the North Side of Chicago. So, I only got to go either with friends' parents or—White friends' parents or—
KM: Or public school.
HB: —on school trips. And the dope thing about Chicago—and I've talked about it before a lot. But even just going north—like, my school was on the North Side, and so I got to leave the South Side, which a lot of brothers don't. But Chicago , we've got a Picasso statue. We're known for some dope shit. So, seeing that stuff, and then that juxtaposed with Jesse Jackson's Rainbow Coalition—
KM: —First started by Fred Hampton. Let's make sure that's known.
HB: Yes, 100 percent. You're absolutely correct. But being around there during the week, the South Side and obviously every Black kid is familiar with the iconic art that somebody in their neighborhood did of Malcolm, Martin, Medgar Evers, whoever. That was really a big part when I was a kid of, one, seeing public art, and then when I finally got to the galleries, it was cool, but it didn't hit me as hard as, like, the public art. Also, the public art just worked its way into my subconscious. I would pass the shit all the time, and that's how I found out how to get around town. The art would be my landmark.
KM: It's amazing. One of my more proud moments was seeing Fahamu get to do the Martin Luther King train station in downtown Atlanta. And he did these legs that looked as though—you could look at the legs and it looked like someone's ascended in flight. Public art is important. And this is for all the politicians, mayors out there. It's important because it finds children where they're at, and it inspires them right there. I can remember going to the High Museum as a kid, and I got it and understood it. And some of the same kids that were with us that had loved going to the zoo a few months before were standing there like, what the fuck am I looking at, because they didn't understand all the blank space behind the walls, all the negative space, was supposed to pull you in toward the art. They didn't understand you were supposed to step to it, read it, look at it, think about it, step back, walk around. They didn't get the whole experience. And they weren't taught to.

But when art met us, all of us kids, no matter where we were, we knew that painting of John Lewis was right there. And who was John Lewis? And then you look it up, and it meets you where you are. And it's amazing that you say that. It's amazing that it affected you that way, because I didn't think of that until that moment. But the street art, even when I was a kid it brought me deeper into art because it met me right where I was. It didn't require that I had to travel to meet it or see it.

Who were your heroes as a kid, and who are your heroes today?

HB: My heroes as a kid were, honestly, artists and world builders. So, like, anyone from—shit, I mean, Lucas, George Lucas.

KM: So you're a *Star Wars* guy?

HB: Oh, my God, yeah. It's in the DNA. You know, Lucas, Spielberg, those guys. But then even, you know, on the art front, Todd McFarlane and Jim Lee. You know, they did the comics. Spawn—

KM: Oh, Spawn. So, you're a Spawn reader.

HB: —and X-Men. Yeah, I used to love Spawn. And the '80s Pop movement. Definitely Basquiat was a huge, huge influence on me and I think on most young Black creatives.

KM: And your mom, a single mom, working hard, couldn't maybe take you on those excursions, but was an encourager. I think a lot of times, that's the difference between success and failure with people. Do they have encouragers? My mom didn't know what the hell I was doing in the studio, but she was like, you come back from this, say you're happy, then more studio for you. Now, I'm not going to pay for it, but I'm going to listen to these wack-ass records you play for me until you get good. And then I'll be telling the truth when I say I like it, baby. But so, your mother was an encourager. What was her name?

HB: My mom, her name was Pamela Roberts. So, she was one of 14, man, came from a real big family from Kentucky.

KM: Ms. Pam was from Kentucky. Thirteen siblings.

HB: She was the one that read everything. And I thank God for that, because my mom was just really informed. Before the Internet, before them days, she'd come out with the paper and the magazine articles. She was always putting stuff in my path. I remember being a kid—you know, we were talking about Ninja Turtles, and my mom was like, "Hey, baby, I don't know if you've heard about this black-and-white graphic novel that these guys created with artists' names." And I was like, "No." And I went to the comic shop: "Hey, y'all got something called Ninja Turtles?" It sounded dope. You know what I'm saying? And then it wasn't shit like the cartoon that came out a few years later, which was obviously for kids. She was the one that put Pop art in front of me. She was like, "I know you're spending every dime you get on comics and buying basketball cards and shit. Look at this." This is how you can take those loves and merge it, you know what I mean?

It was like seeing Roy Lichtenstein do comic-book strip panels, seeing Warhol using Superman panels, and shit like—it was like, oh, I can do this, and it's art? So, yeah.

KM: That's dope. Shouts out to his family. She did it. She did a hell of a job. I'm a believer in readers, as my grandmother was a reader and believed in it.

What inspires you today? Is it the visuals or the music that inspires you? What gets you in a creative vibe?

HB: I think more so than anything, it probably would be music, because music's 80 percent of what is sort of pumping around me when I'm creating. But, yeah, it's music, old and new, it's music, man. It could be a line from a not-so-well-known artist to a note. But, yeah, I always say when I create, it's like somebody working out, right, like you play the type of music when you need to get in your bag at the gym, you're going to play that stuff that gets you up there. And when you're just going through the motions, you might play some stuff that's a little bit more introspective. And

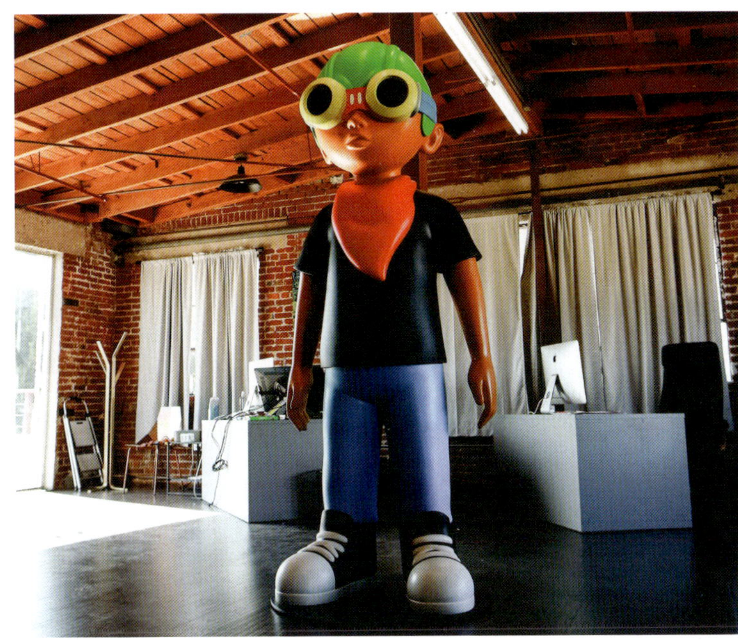

so, I think that that's sort of how I dictate the playlist in the space from jazz to hip-hop to old soul. I'm a pretty eclectic brother.

KM: I think you're worthy to hang in the hallways of the High Museum. So, I'm definitely going to bring that up in a meeting or two or three.

HB: I appreciate that. Word.

KM: And I think we have an amazing museum, but you have seen museums across the world. My wife surprised me with a trip to the Louvre when we were in Paris. For those that don't know, I wear jewelry in a very Ghostface-type way, all right? I'm either very no-jewelry and just a pendant of my mother, Denise, who was also an artist, a florist. Or I have a huge pendant of the Nike of Samothrace, which is in the halls of the Louvre and just sitting there. And I walked up to it there, and I have my chain on, and I'm looking at the statue that I can't figure out how to steal, because I want it in my backyard. But it's on my neck, and then people start to recognize me, and they see I'm wearing the chain, and it turns into an event of sorts.

I love that my wife took me there. I love that museum for that. So what museum invokes an emotion out of you just being there? Is it MoMA? Is it the Schomburg Center for African American History in Harlem? Is it the museum in Chicago? Which one means something to you?

HB: I think that's a really good question. It's kind of a mix, a 50-50 bag. I think the Art Institute of Chicago, just because it's my hometown and it was the first museum I ever went to, but I also have to say the High because the High was the first museum that actually allowed me to see Fahamu. I spent so many of my formative years in Atlanta, I was there for seven and a half years.

And I'm not saying that just because you're on the board, but again, it has sentimentality to it. I took my son, say, maybe, right before the pandemic, but I hadn't been in years. I spent so much time in and around that building, and I don't know, it just holds a lot of sentimental value.

KM: Last question, I would love to know what are you most proud of, and what do you intend to do in the next 10 years?

HB: I'm most proud of my three children, my babies. And in the next 10 years, man, I think is just growth, in all ways—fatherhood, creating, and I want to get some of these films out and do some bigger art exhibitions around the world. Can't stop, won't stop.

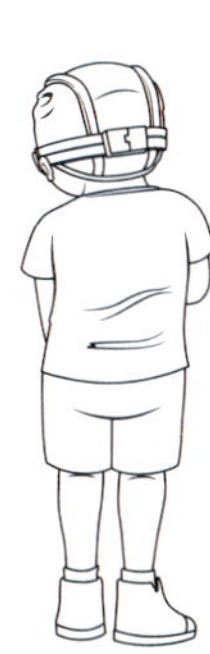

COLOR

ONE:

ARTWORK

FLYBOY

FLYBOY

*. FLYBOY, SKY BOY, CHI BOY. DIE BOY, SIGH BOY,
WHY BOY?, MY BOY, CRY BOY, EYE BOY, DRY BOY,
SLY BOY, LIE BOY, DENY BOY. DO NOT COMPLY BOY,
SUPPLY BOY, BUY BOY, HIGH BOY, RELY BOY, PIE BOY,
PASTRAMI ON RYE BOY, 2 WINGS AND A THIGH BOY,
MILD SAUCE ON MY FRY BOY, YELLOW #5 DYE BOY,
THE DEVIL LEVEL NIGH BOY, KISS YO ASS GOODBYE BOY,
MASAI BOY. BUSINESS IN DUBAI BOY, BRIDGE OVER THE
RIVER KWAI BOY, RICKSHAW THROUGH THE BUSY STREETS
OF MUMBAI BOY, ALL AROUND THE WORLD AND BACK
WITH NO DEGREE FROM U OF I BOY, LIVE TO SEE
25 BOY, MIND YA BUSINESS DON'T EVEN TRY TO PRY BOY,
WON'T GET THE JOB WHY EVEN APPLY BOY, CAN'T WEAR
NO SUIT AND TIE BOY, WHO AM I BOY? AS I WAIT
ON YOU TO REPLY BOY, I SAY KOMPAI BOY, TAKE A
SIP OF THIS CHAI BOY, WATER MY BONSAI BOY,
AND INHALE THESE TREES LIKE I'M TRYING TO SEE
HALIE SELASSIE I BOY, CHICAGO IN JULY BOY,
EL DORADO PARKED OUTSIDE THE Y BOY, WAIT A MINUTE.
YOU ARE I BOY!!! HI BOY OR BETTER YET
WASSUP MAN?

LUPE FIASCO,
2015

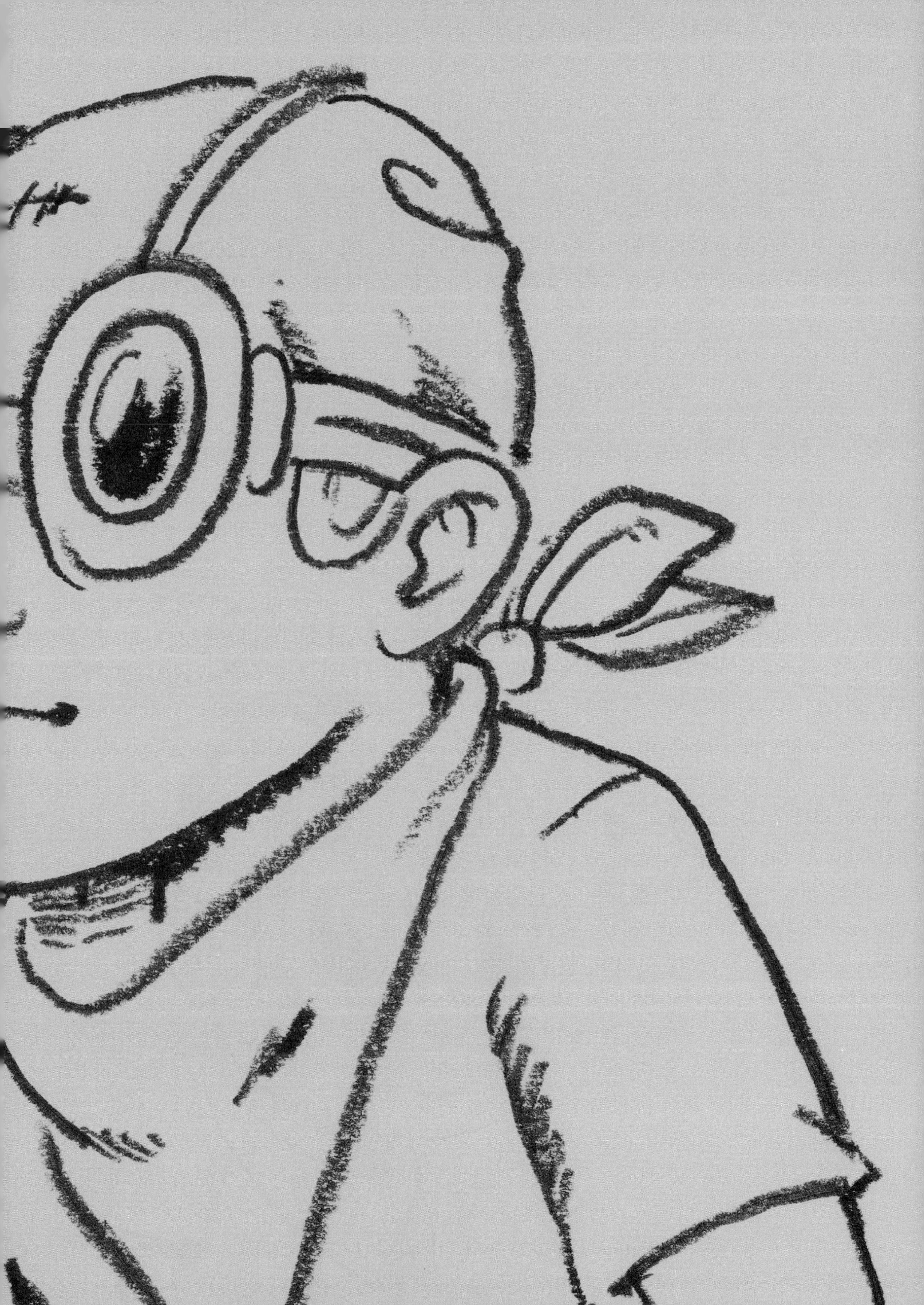

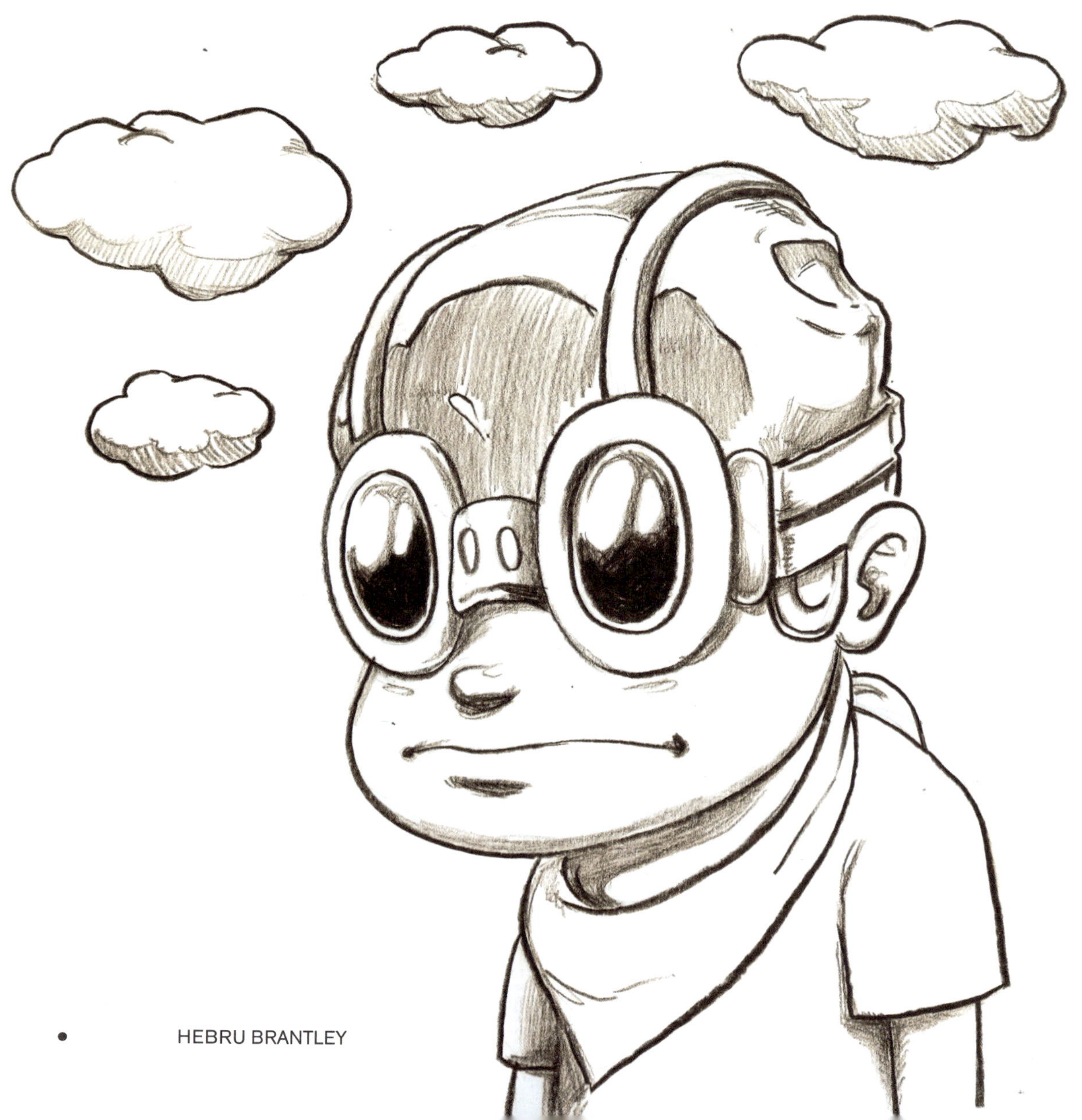

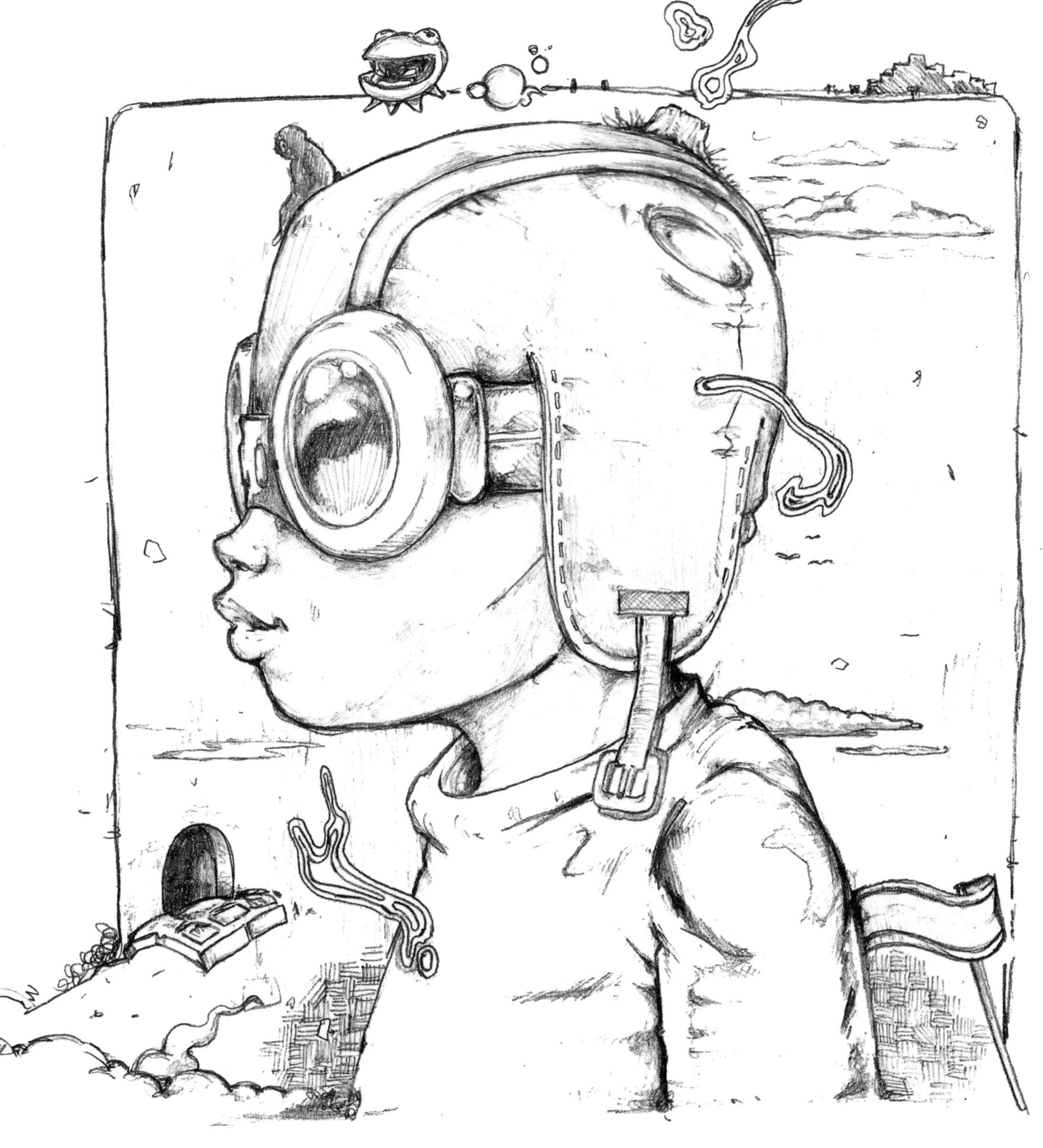

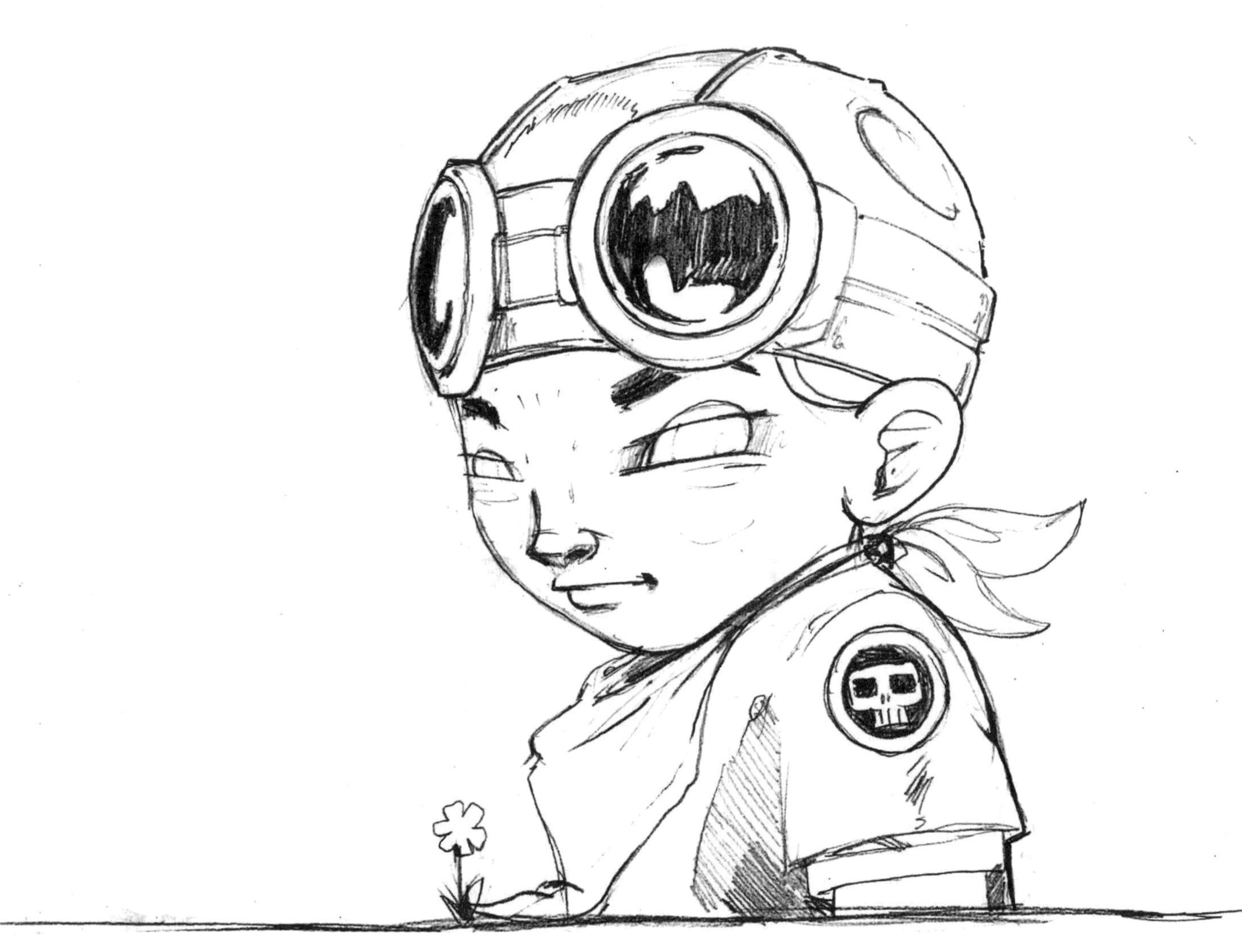

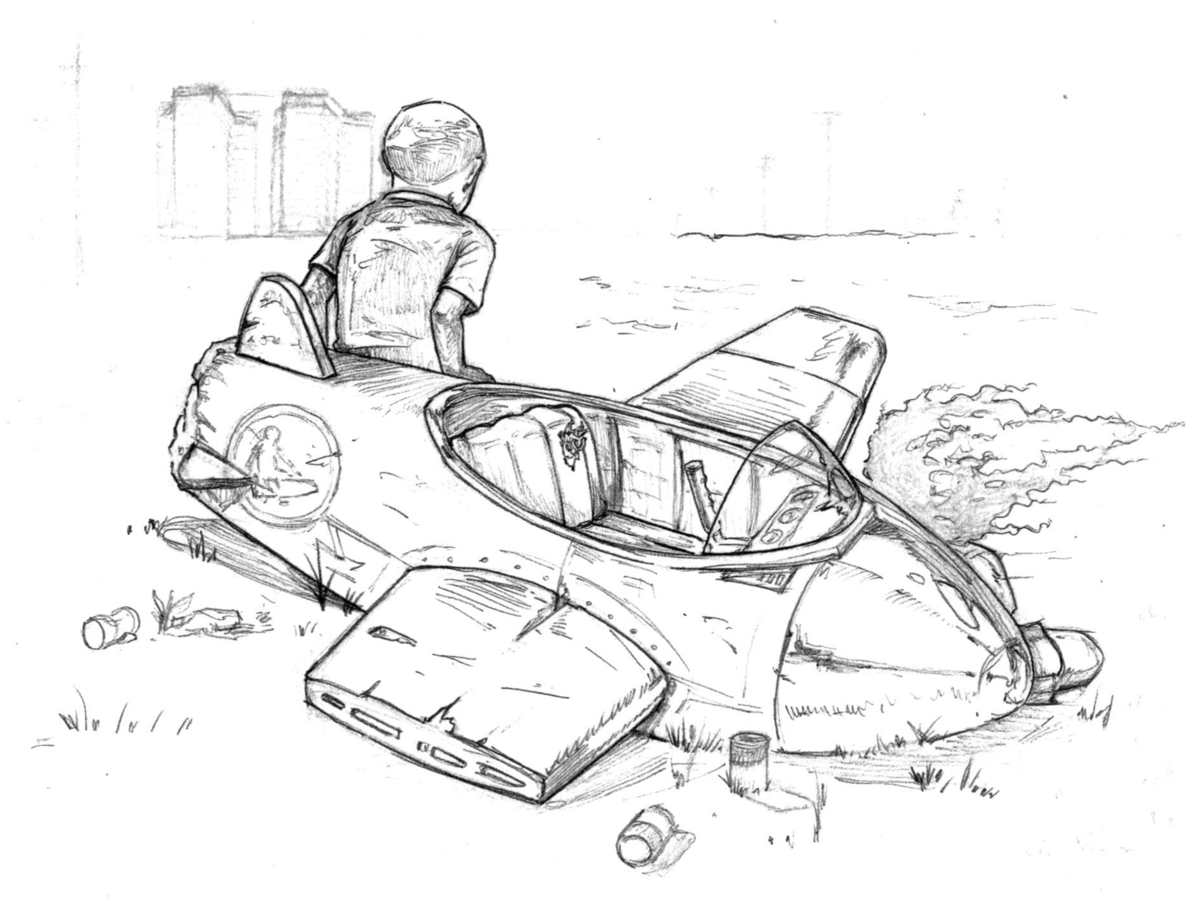

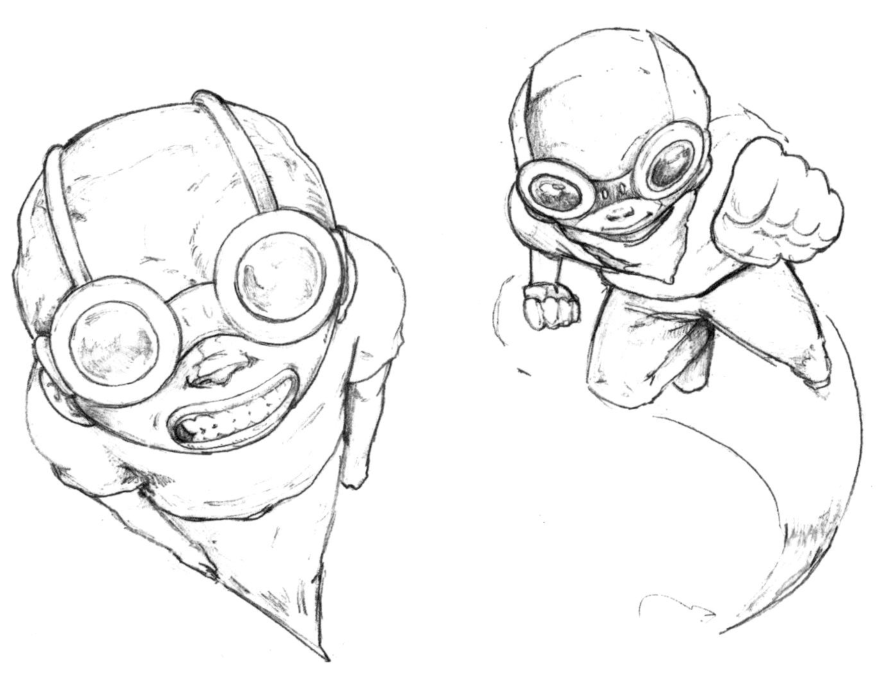

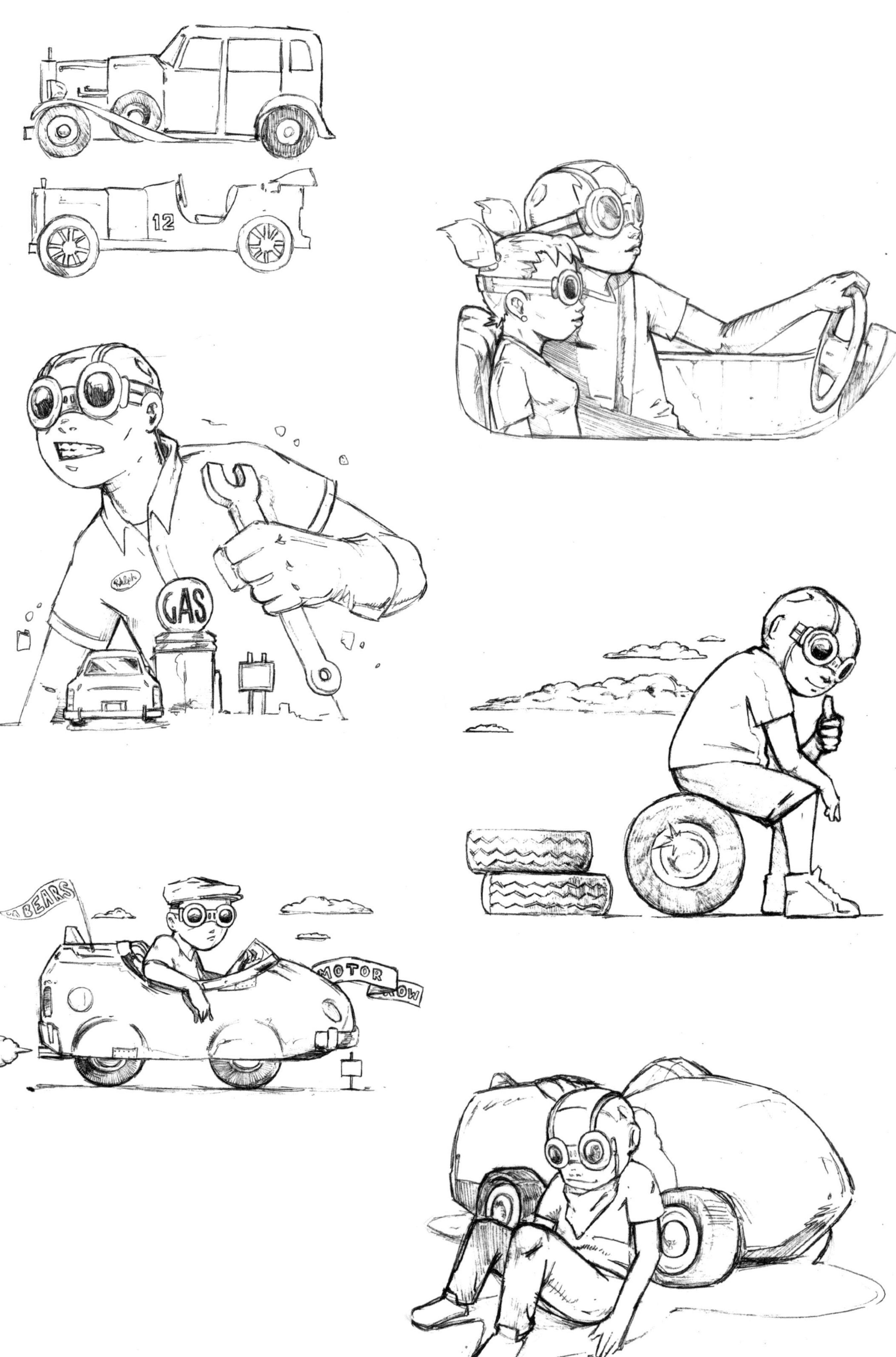
12
GAS
BEARS
MOTOR

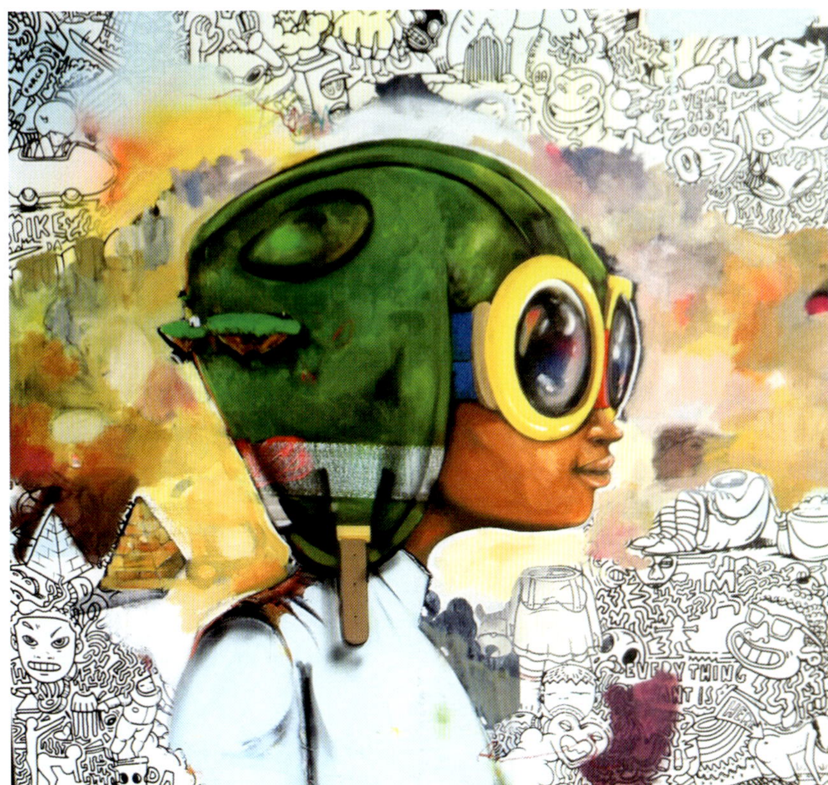

It's Getting Harder to Smile
Oil and acrylic pen
on canvas
2012

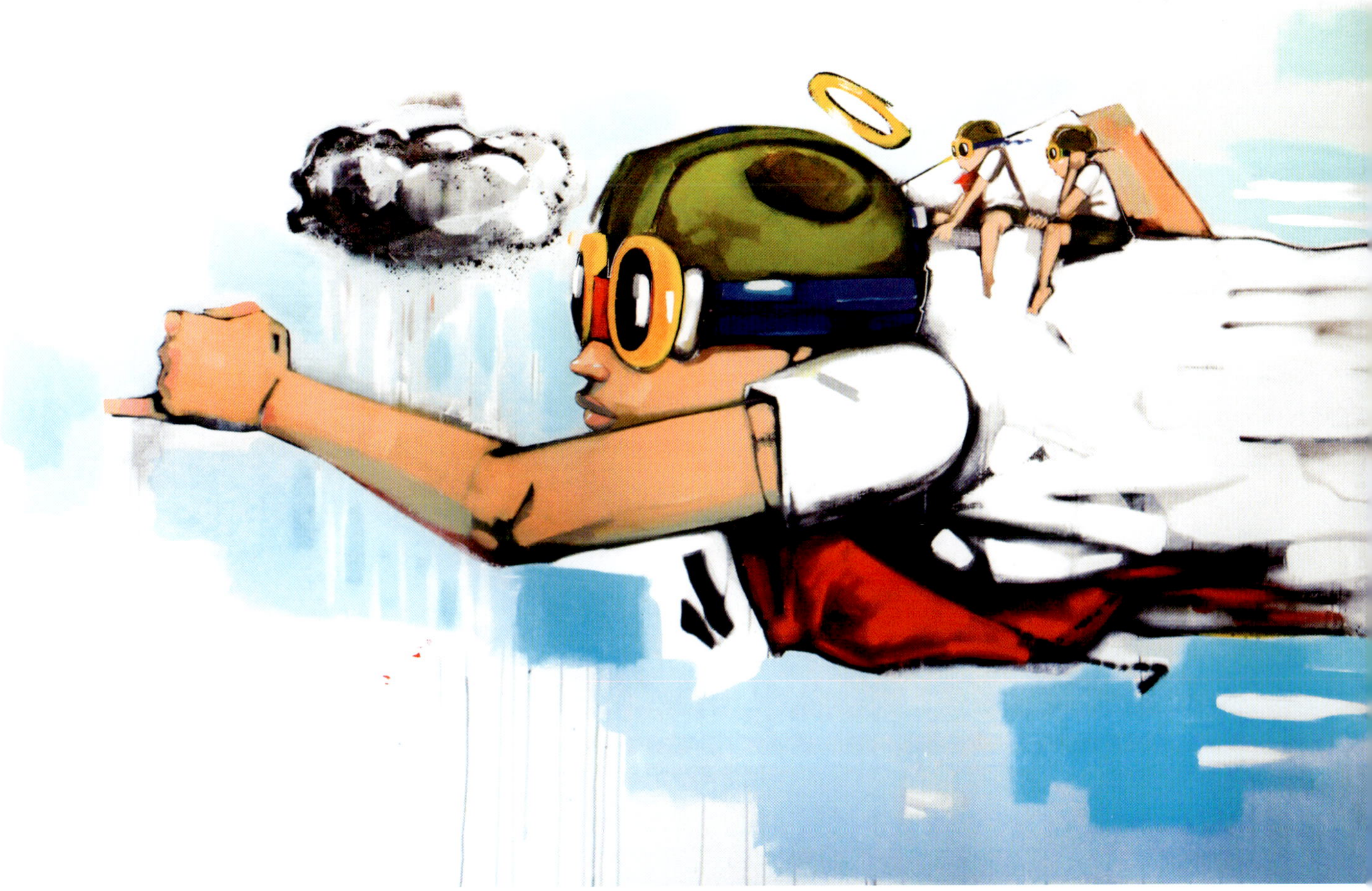

Riding High
Mixed media
on canvas
2013

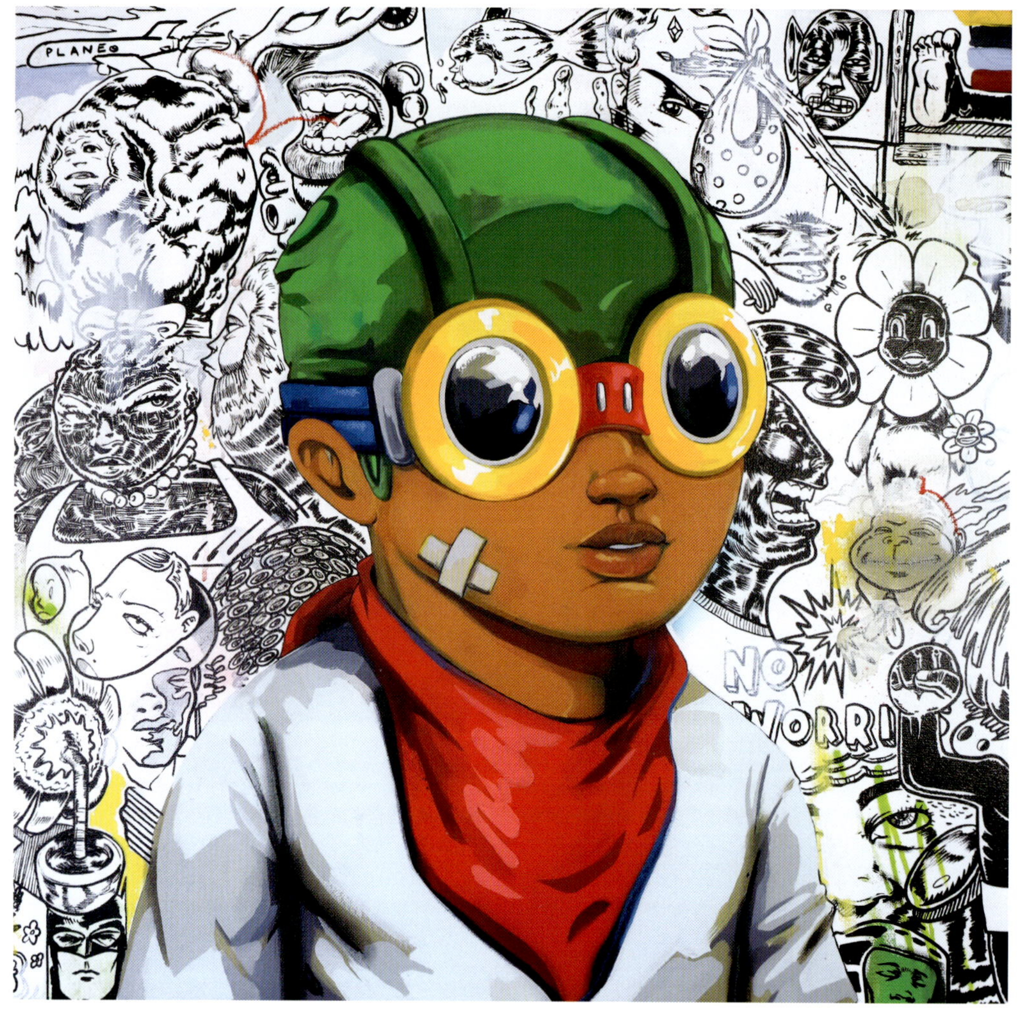

Trying to Catch a Leprechaun
Mixed media
on canvas
30 x 30 inches
2020

M.A. Barnes
Mixed media
on canvas
54.25 x
54.25 inches
2017

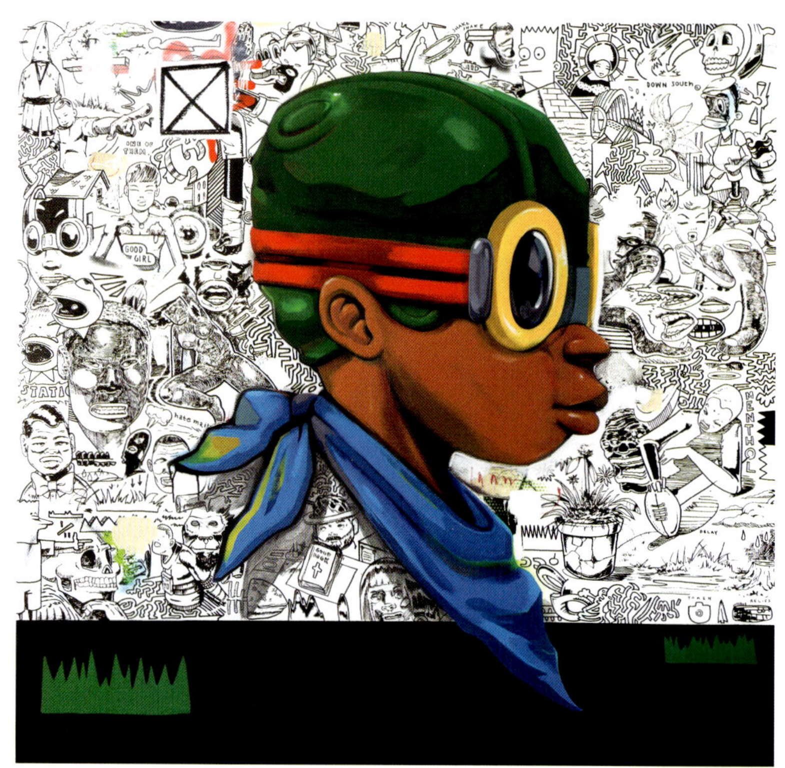

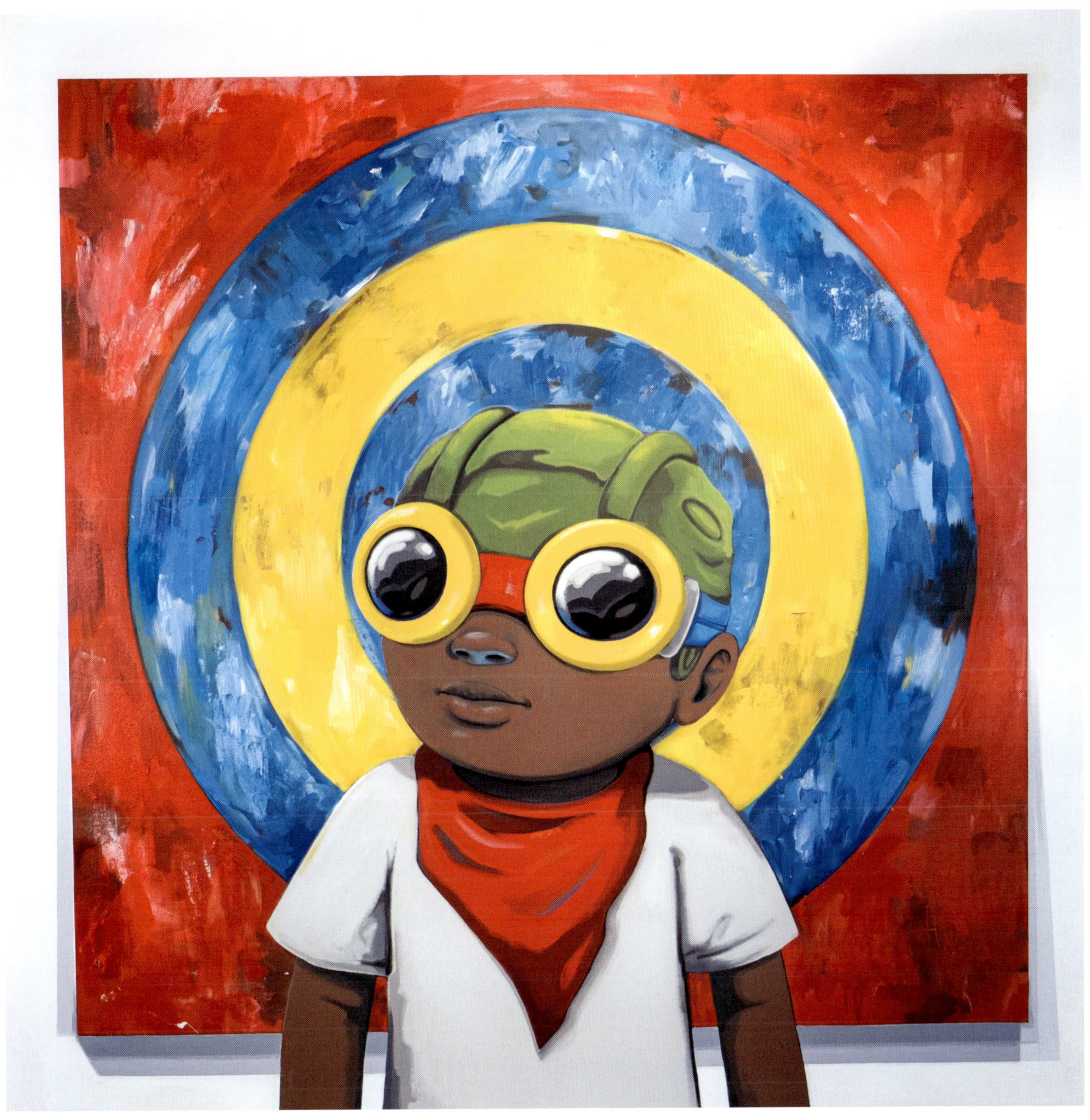

Jasper's Target
Acrylic on canvas
52 x 52 inches
2020

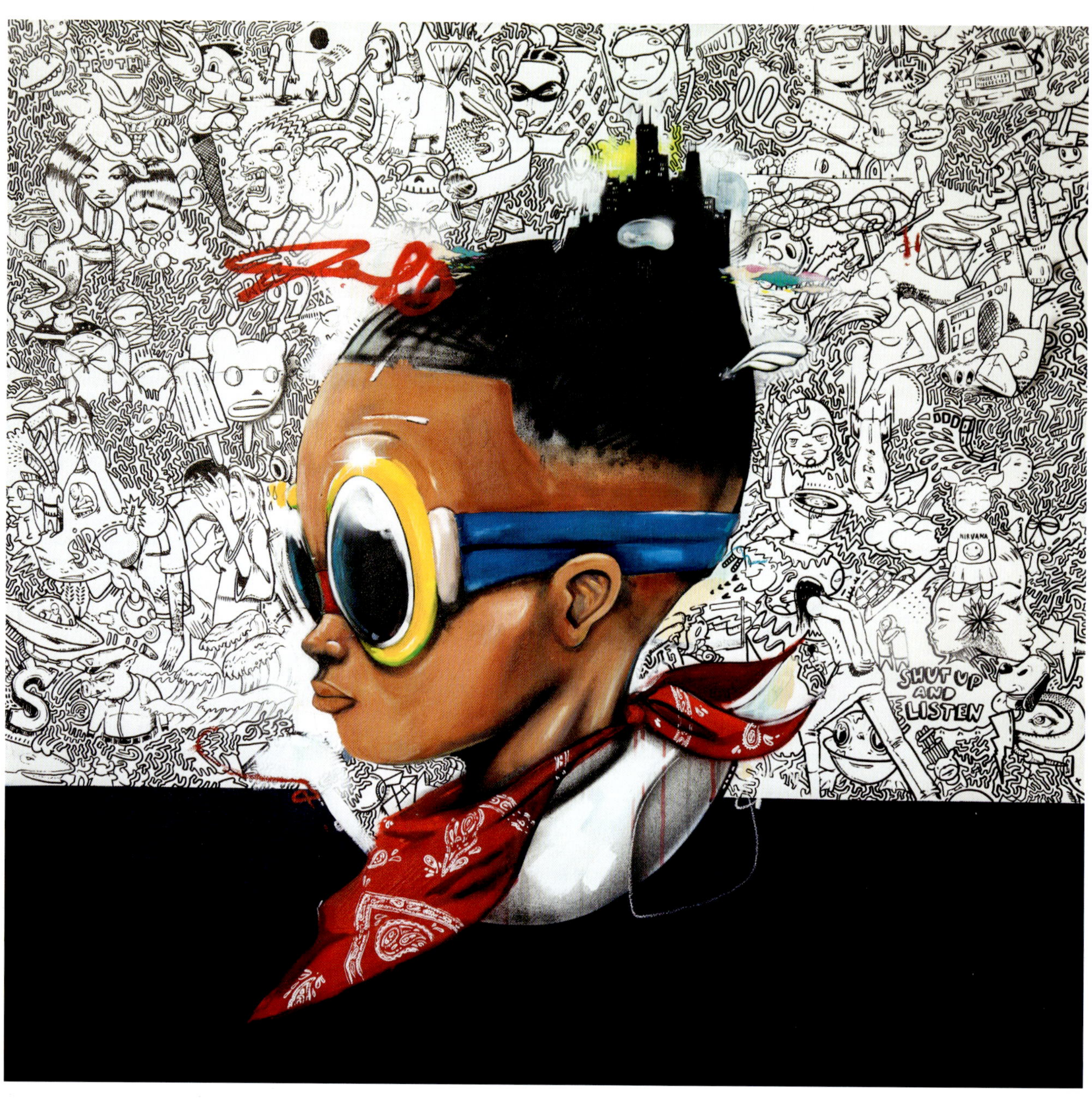
TRUTH
SHOUTS
hello
XXX
SHUT UP
AND
LISTEN

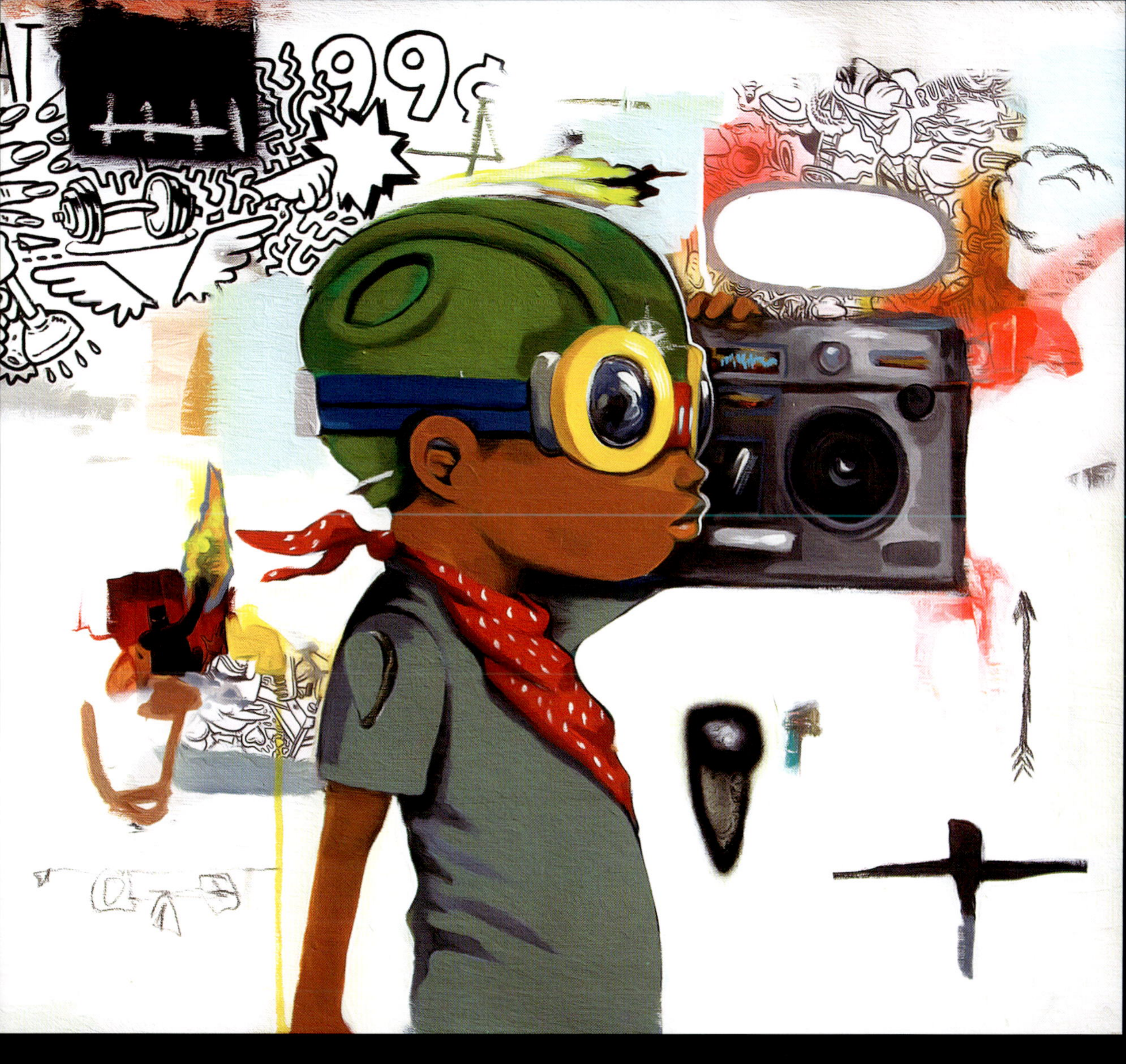

(Opposite)
Lollapalooza 20th Anniversary
Mixed media

(Above)
Radio (Dilla's Last Song)
Mixed media

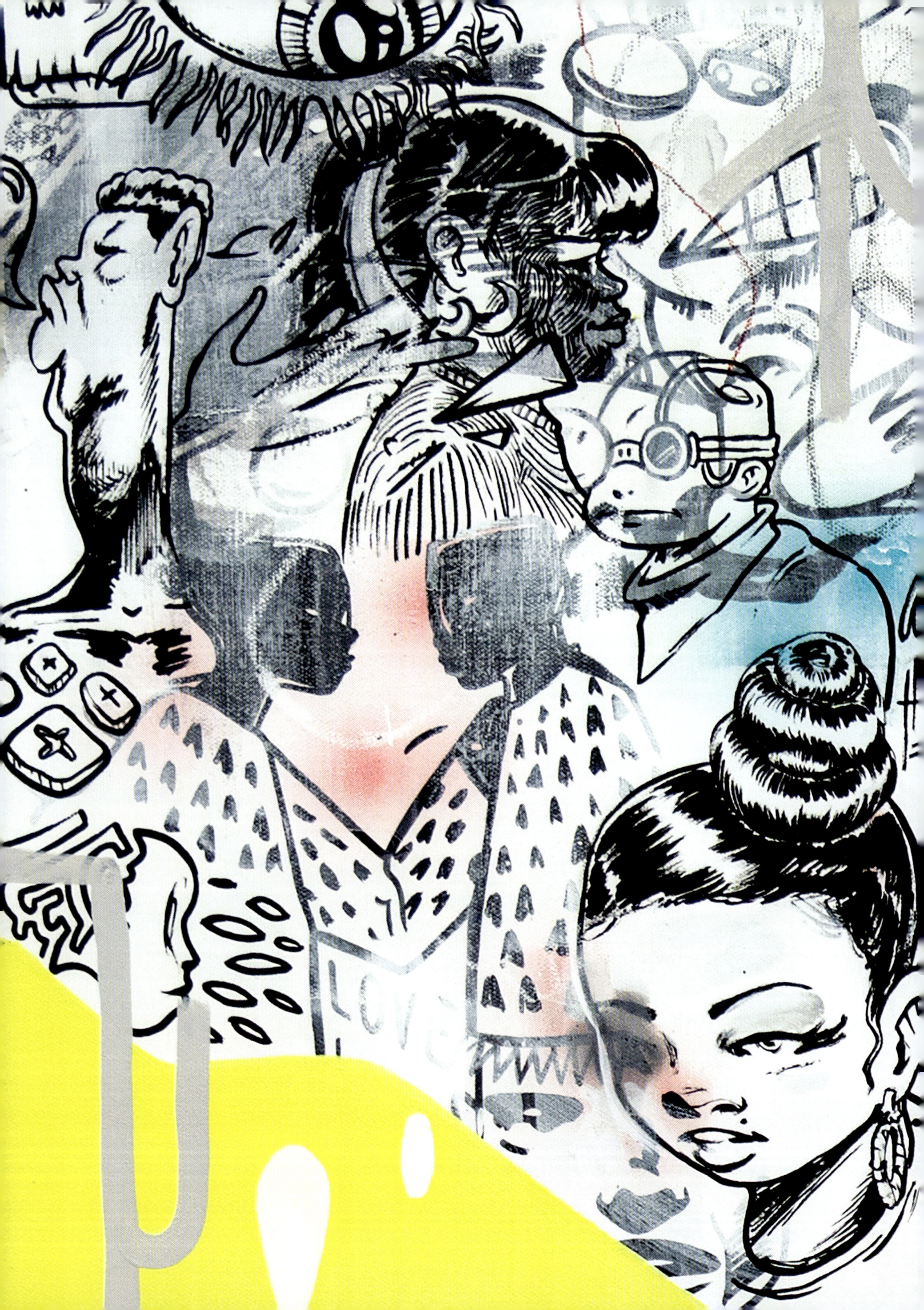

(Opposite and below)
Untitled
Acrylic on canvas
48 x 60 inches
2019

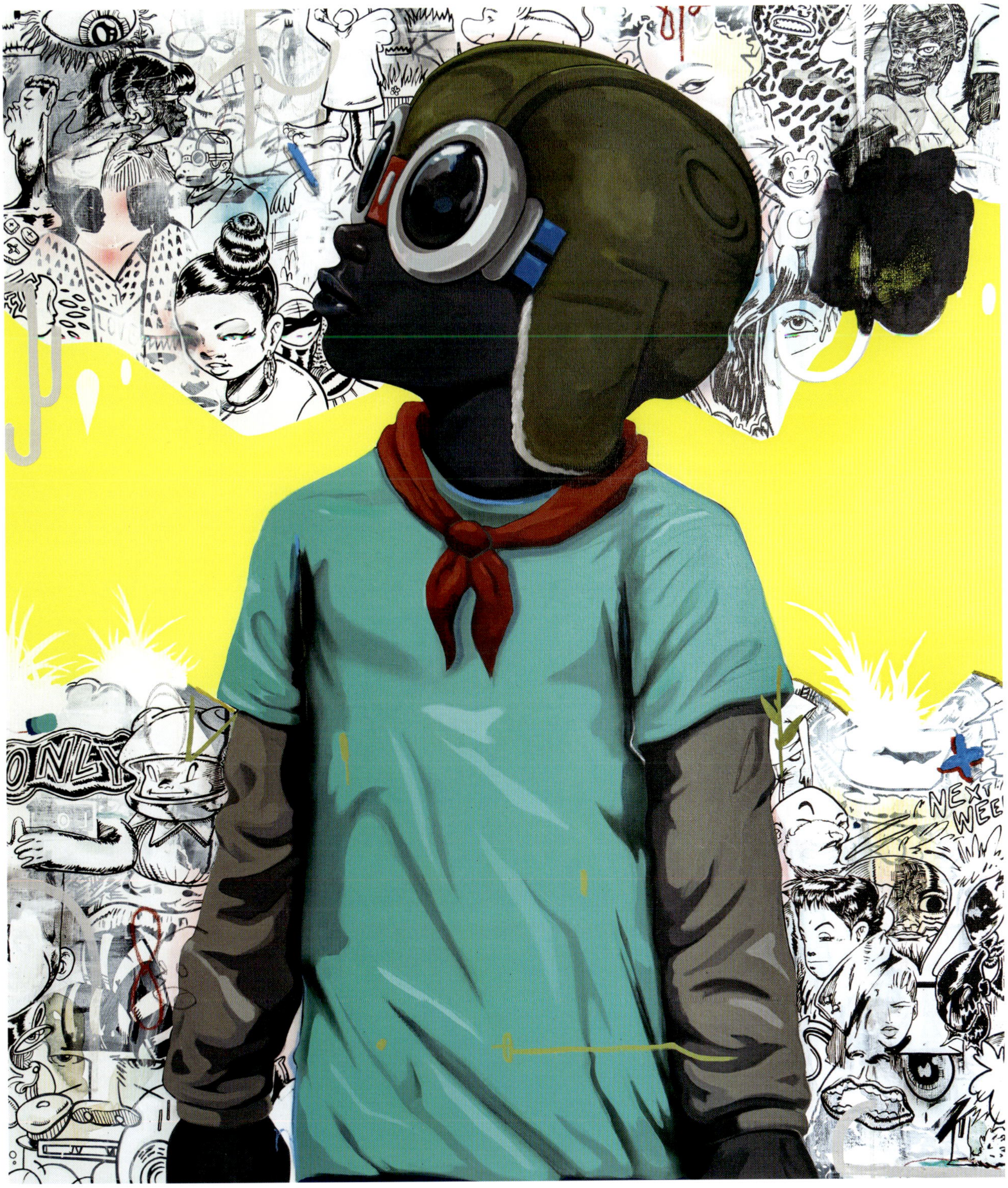

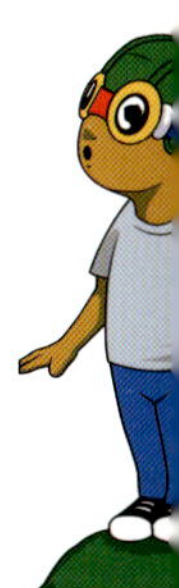

(Opposite above)
Suddenly
Mixed media and
diamond dust
on canvas
47 x 63 inches
2017

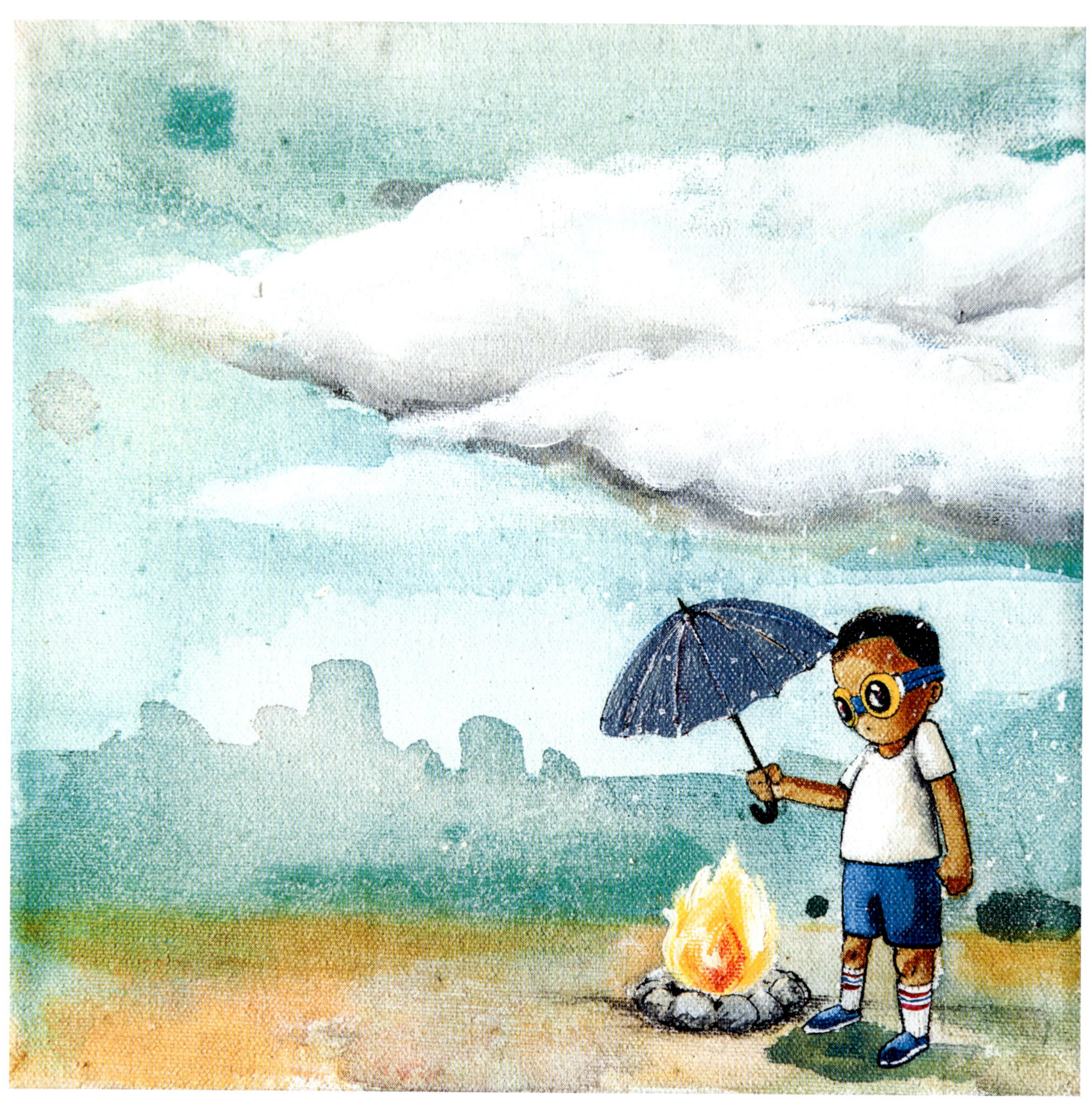

Protection
Mixed media
on canvas
2014

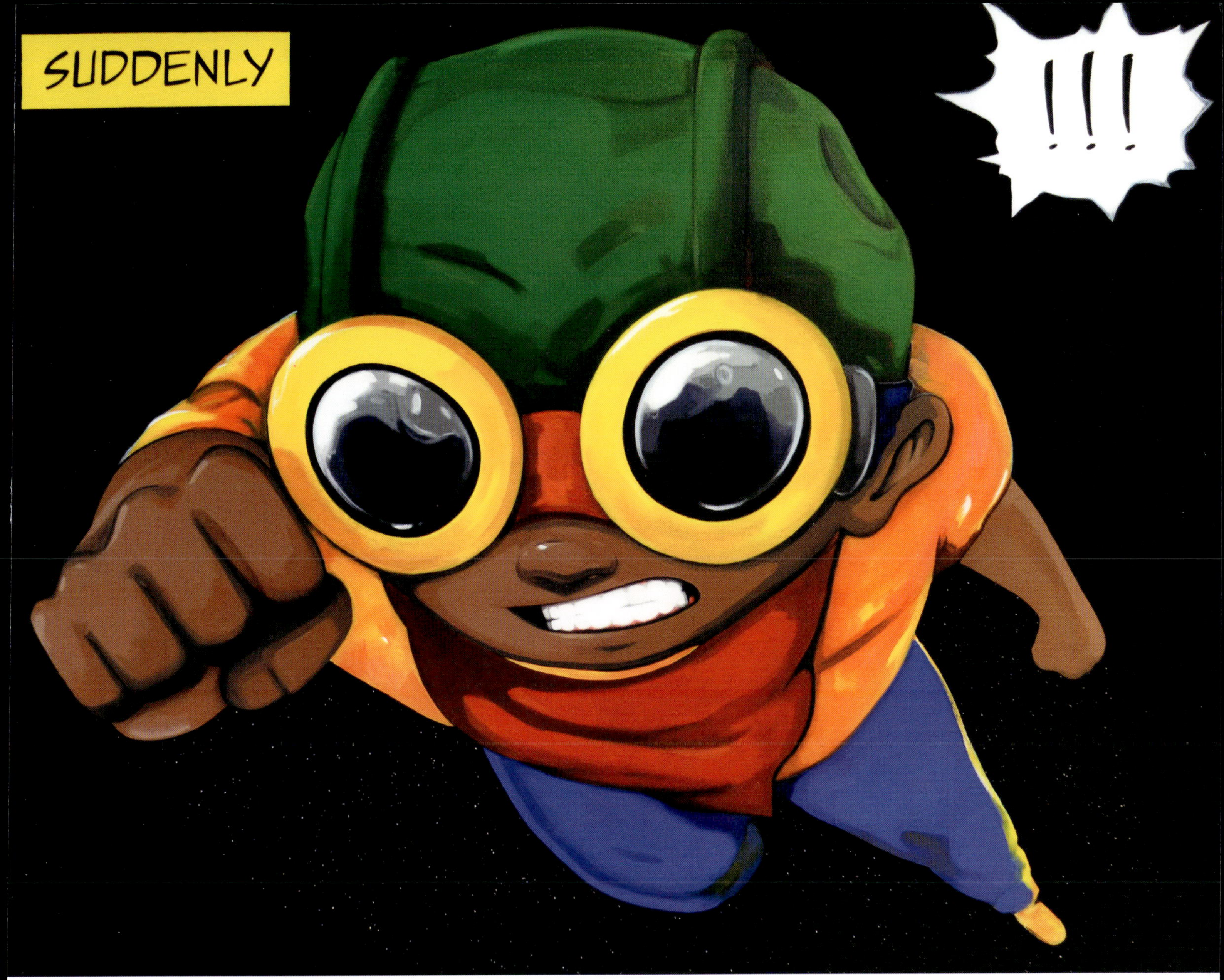

(Left)
Boom Bastic
Acrylic and diamond dust on canvas
12 x 12 inches
2016

(Right above)
Lucky Star
Mixed media on canvas
60 x 48 inches
2016

(Right below)
Who?
Mixed media on canvas
36 x 48 inches
2019

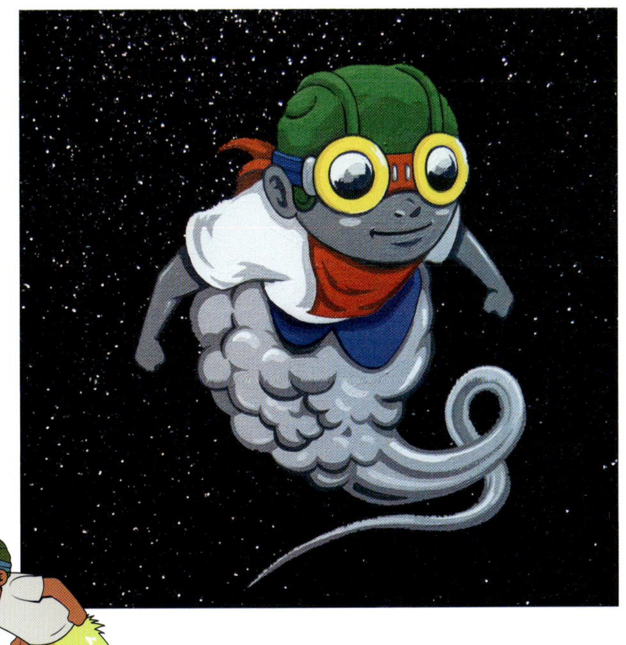

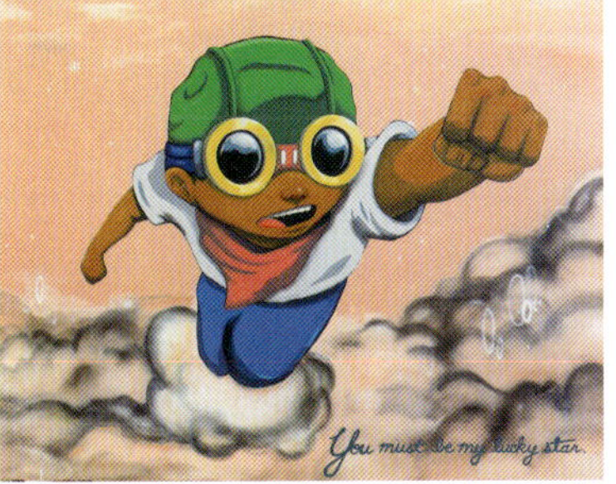

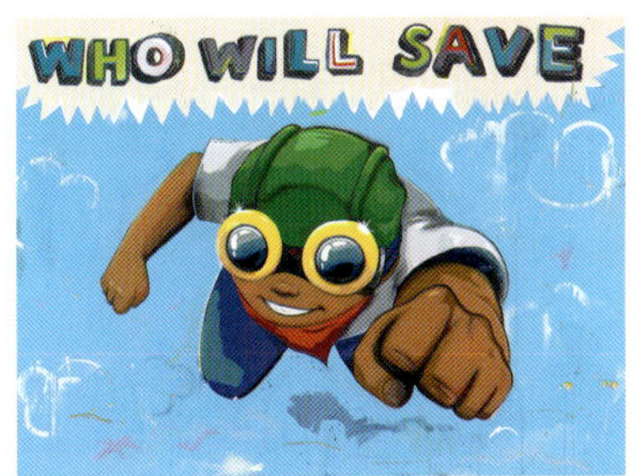

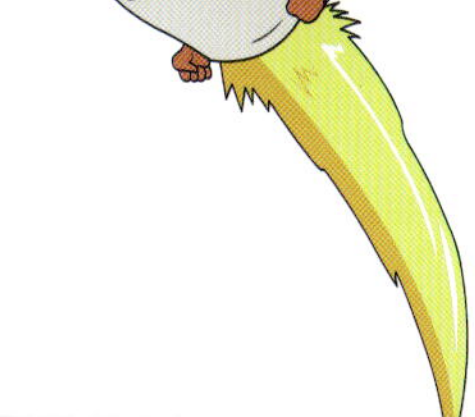

(Below)
Spirit of the North Star (Sleep Is the Cousin of Death)
Mixed media and
diamond dust on canvas
2014

(Opposite, from top)
Midnight Marauders
Oil on canvas
90.5 x 63 inches
2014

R.I.P., 2020
Acrylic, oil and
spray paint on canvas
36 x 36 inches
2020

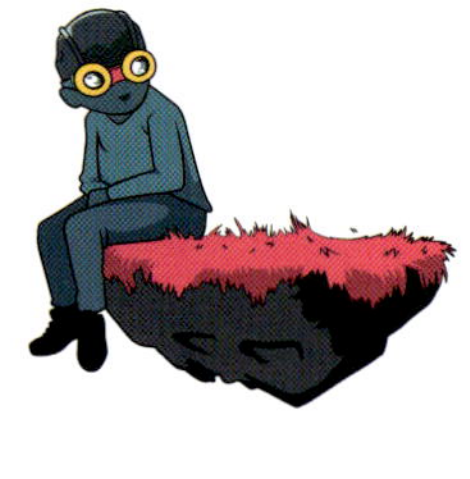

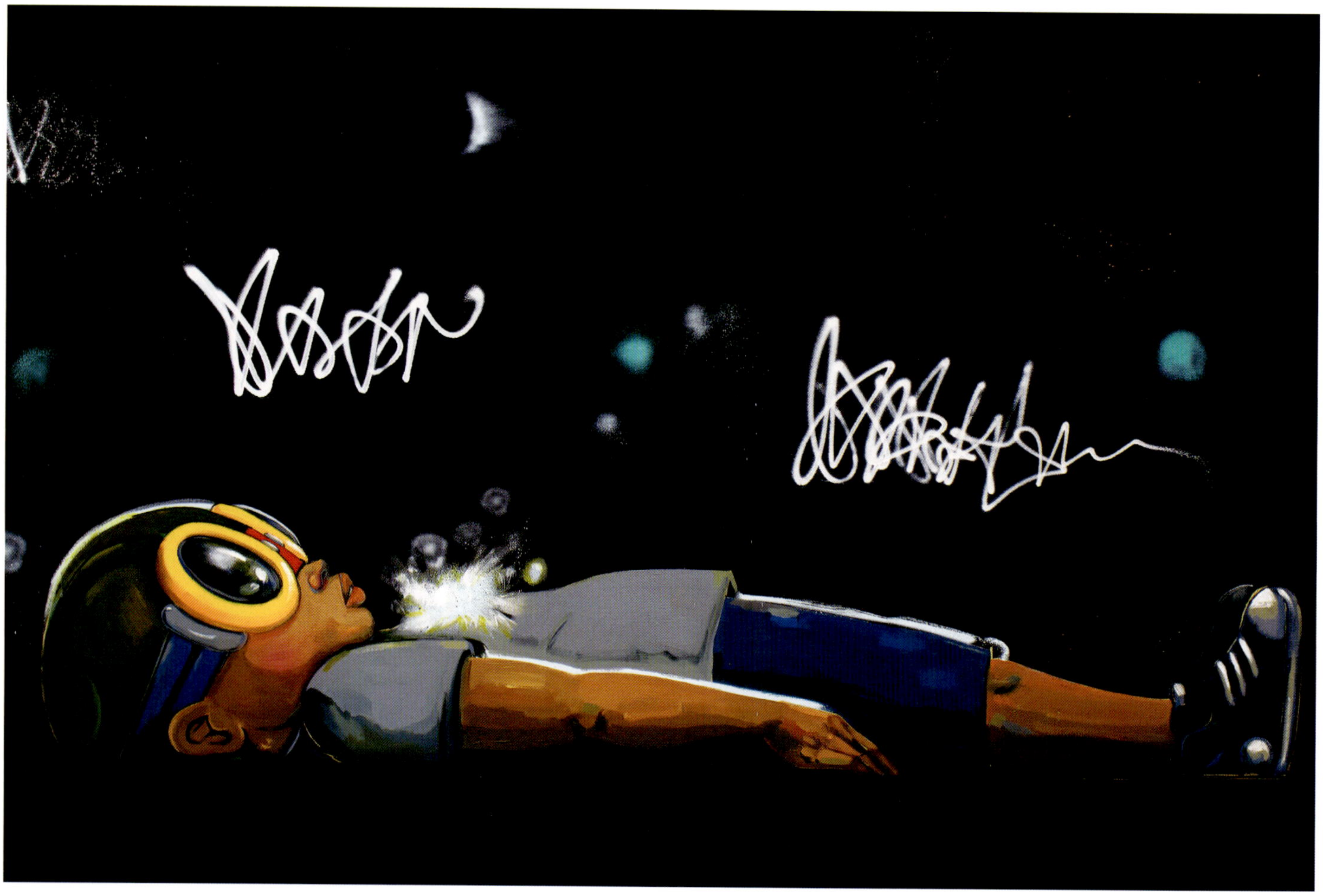

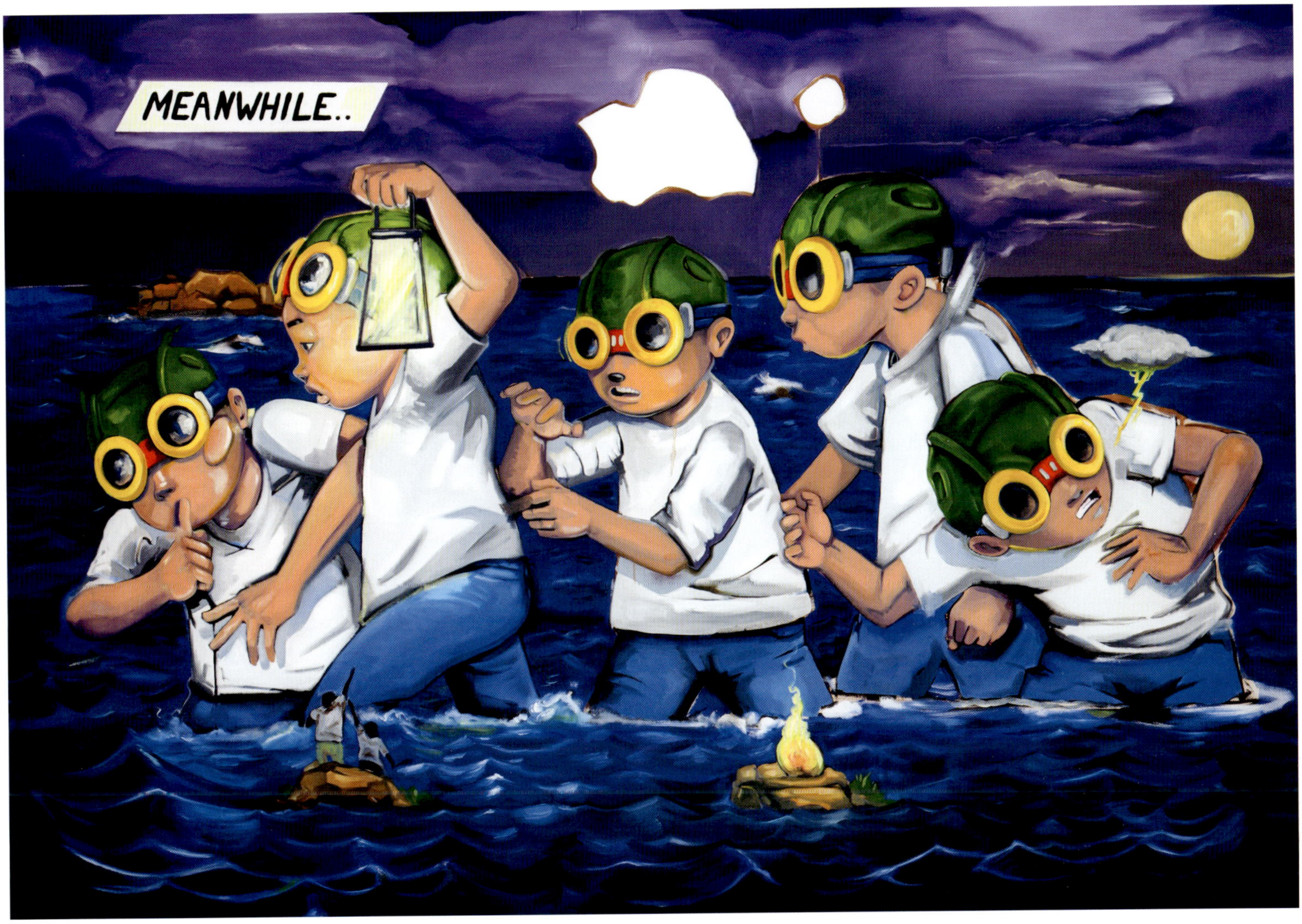

MEANWHILE..

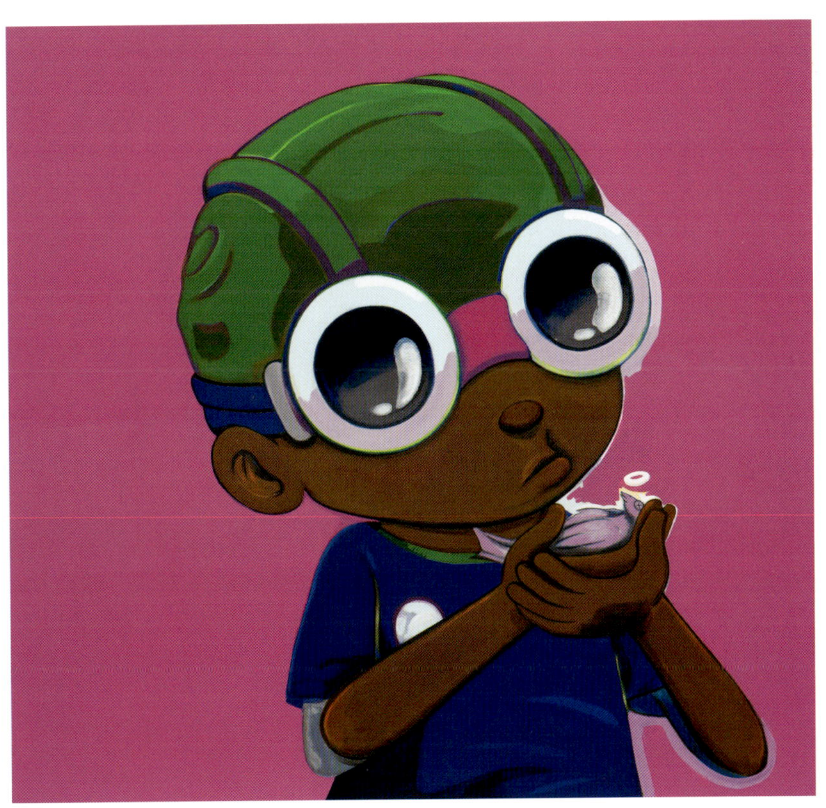

Night Flight
Mixed media
on canvas
44 x 36 inches
2021

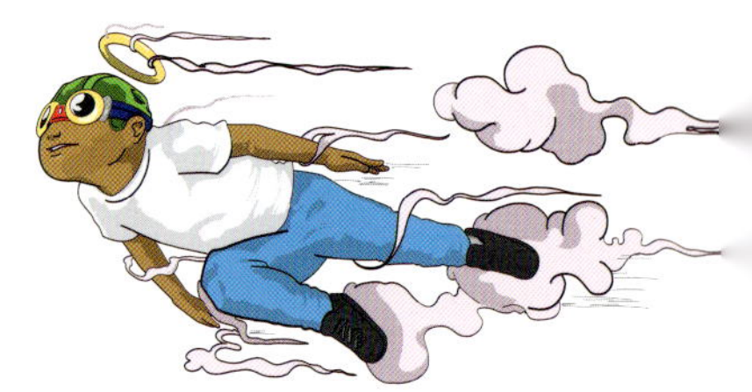

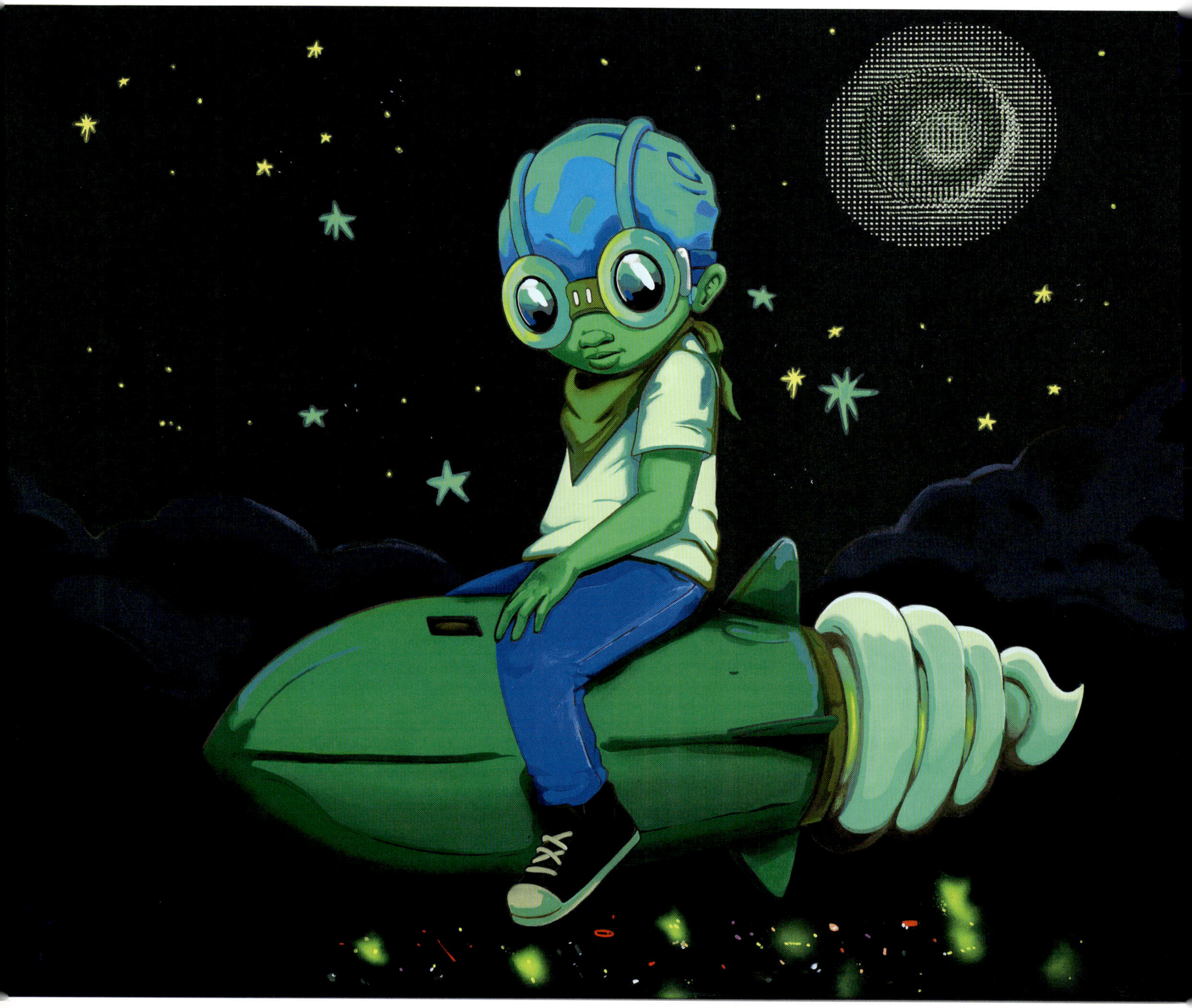

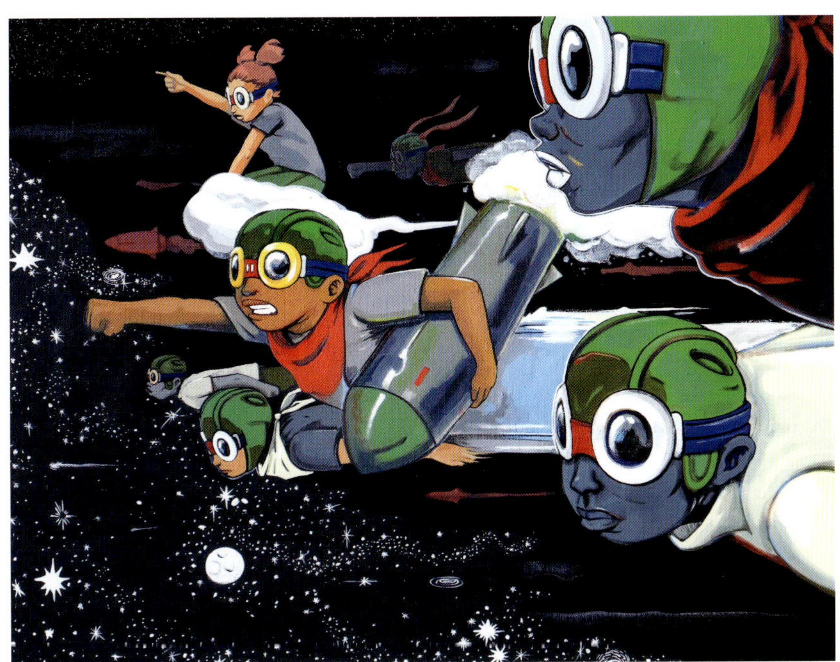

(Left)
Where Only Few Have Seen
Mixed media and diamond dust on canvas
30 x 24 inches
2020

(Below)
Escape The End
Mixed media and diamond dust on canvas
66 x 48 inches
2020

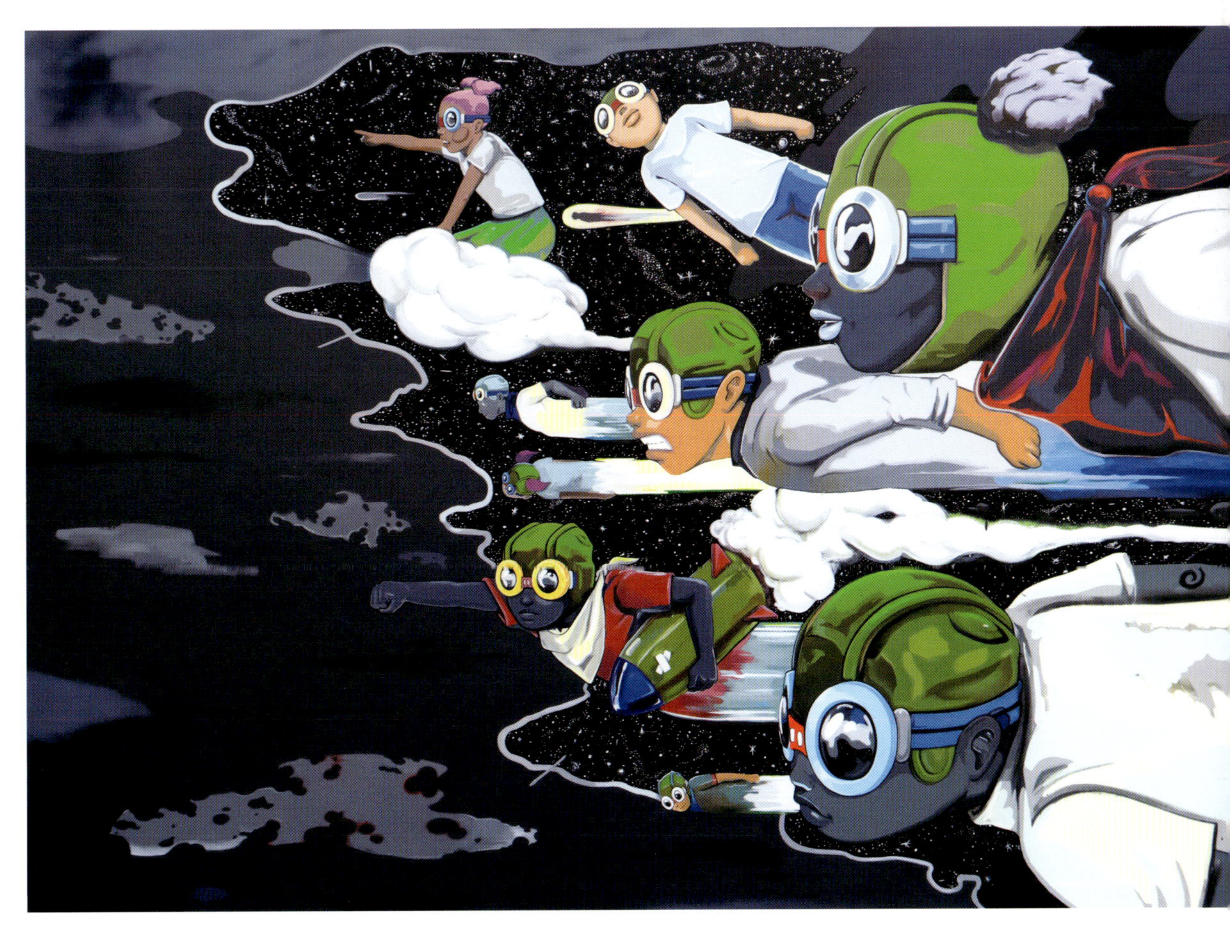

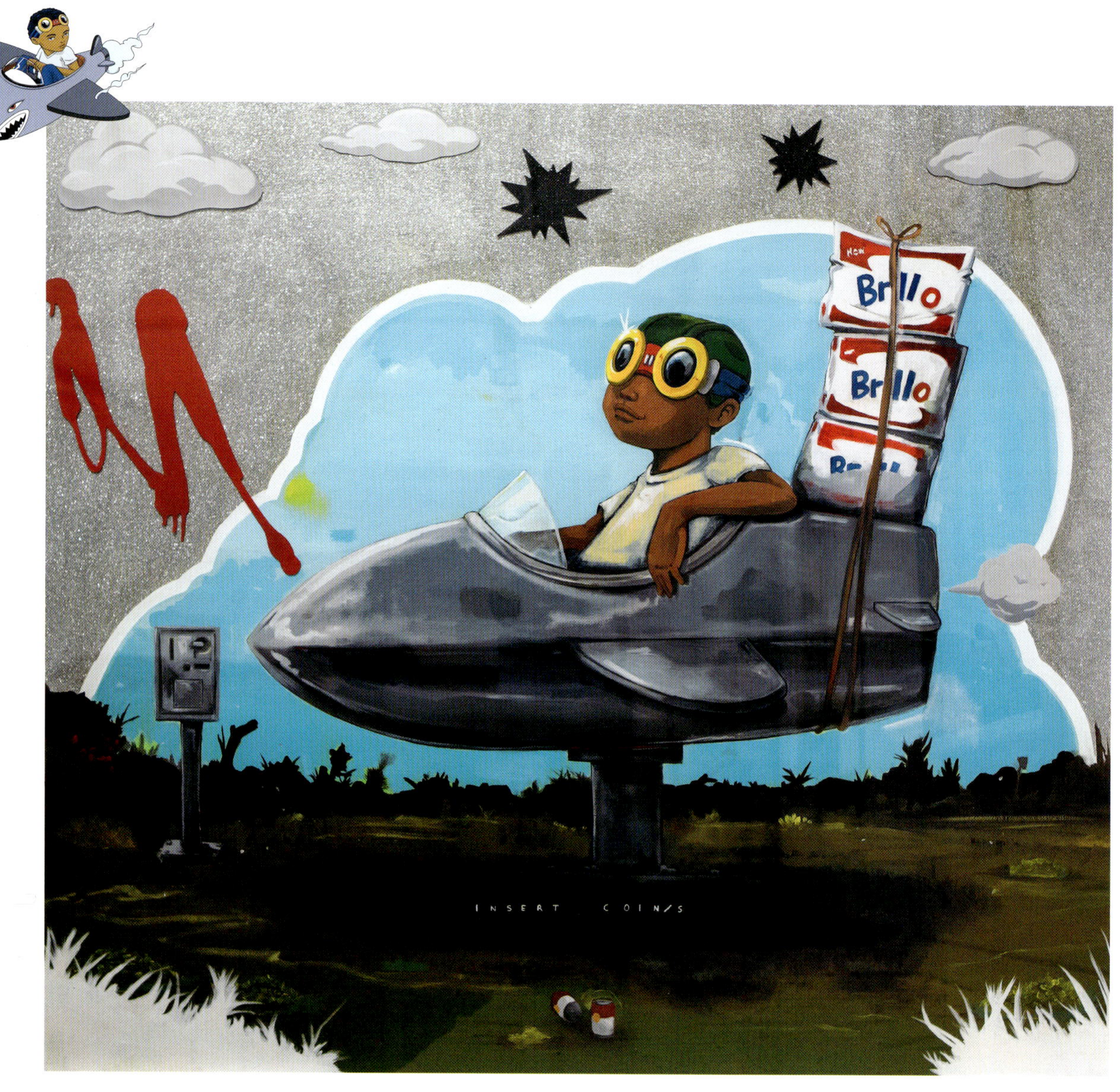

(Above)
Free from Personal Restraint
Mixed media and diamond dust on canvas
59 x 54 inches (framed)
2017

(Opposite, above)
Dive Bomber
Mixed media on canvas
30 x 30 inches
2017

(Opposite, below)
I'm Ok For Now
Mixed media on canvas
36 x 36 inches
2020

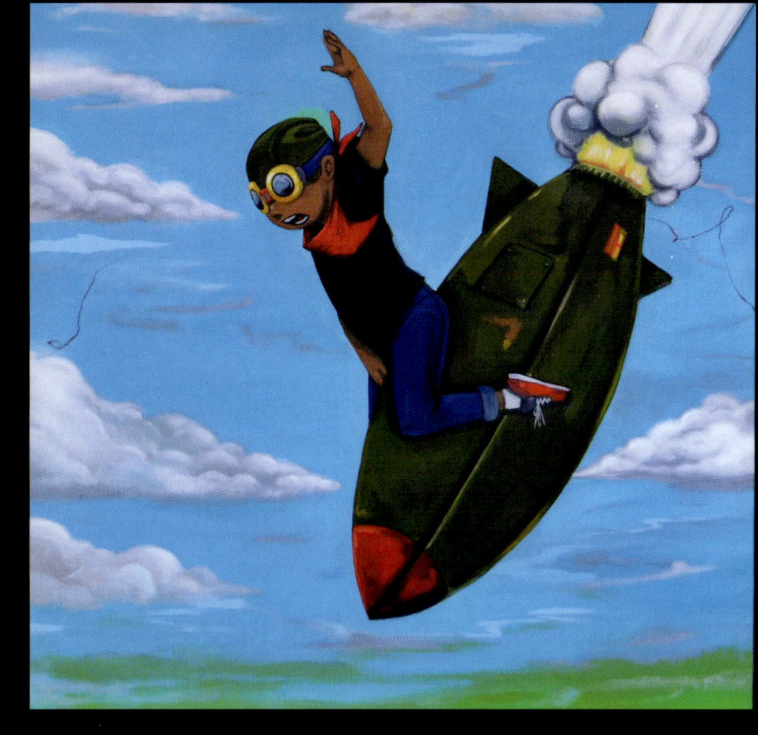

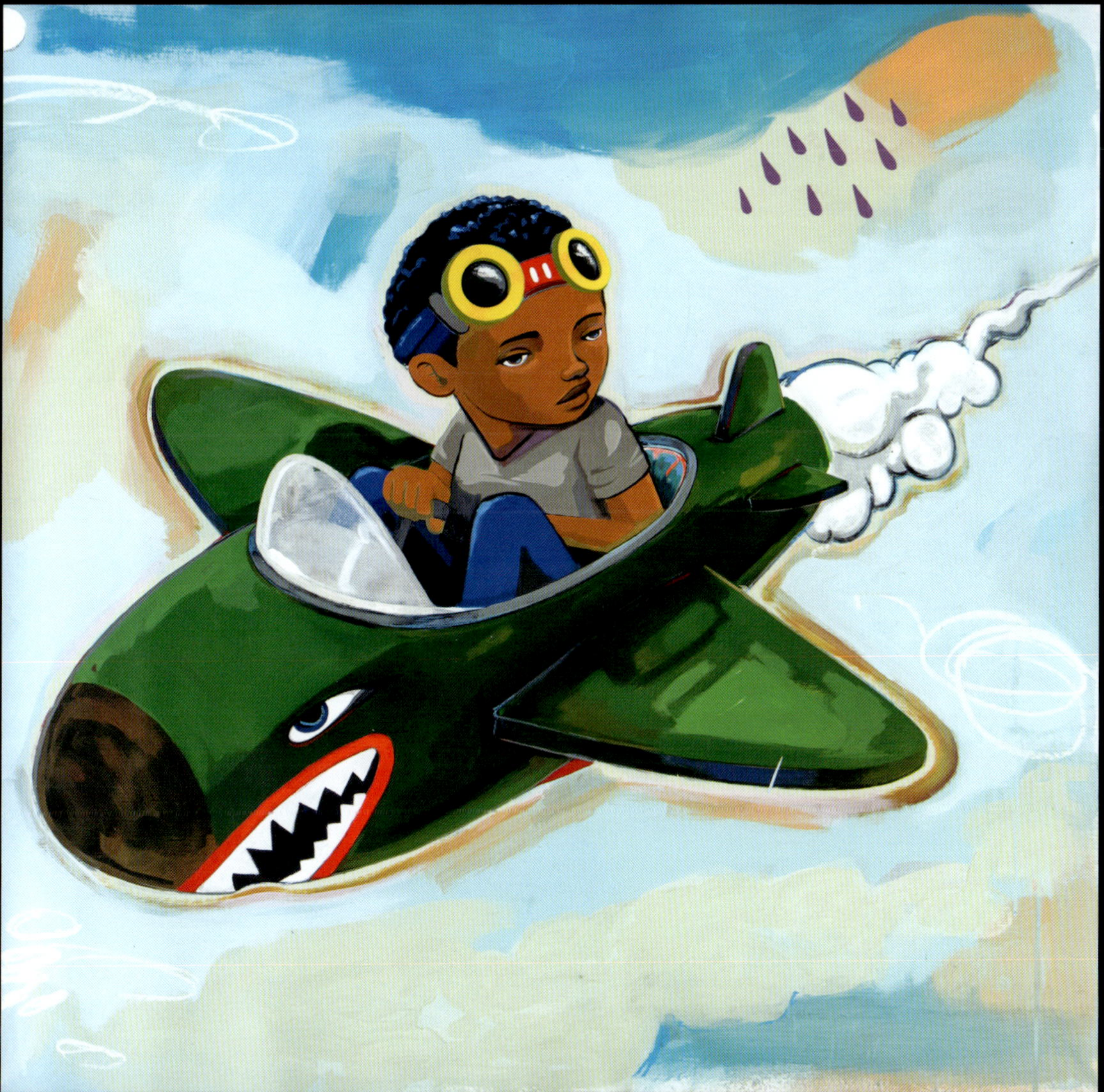

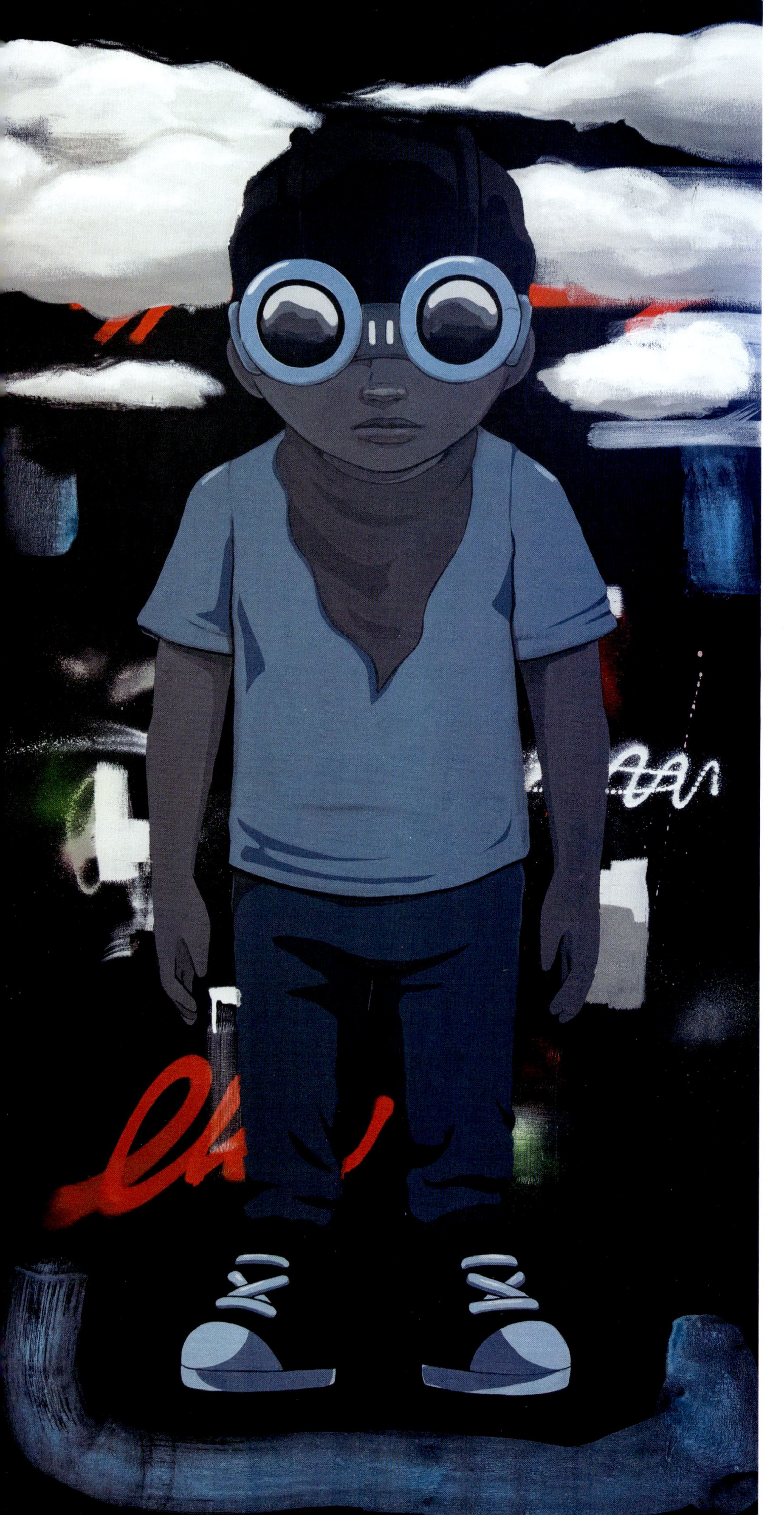

(Right)
Prospect 21
Mixed media
on canvas
48 x 48 inches
2020

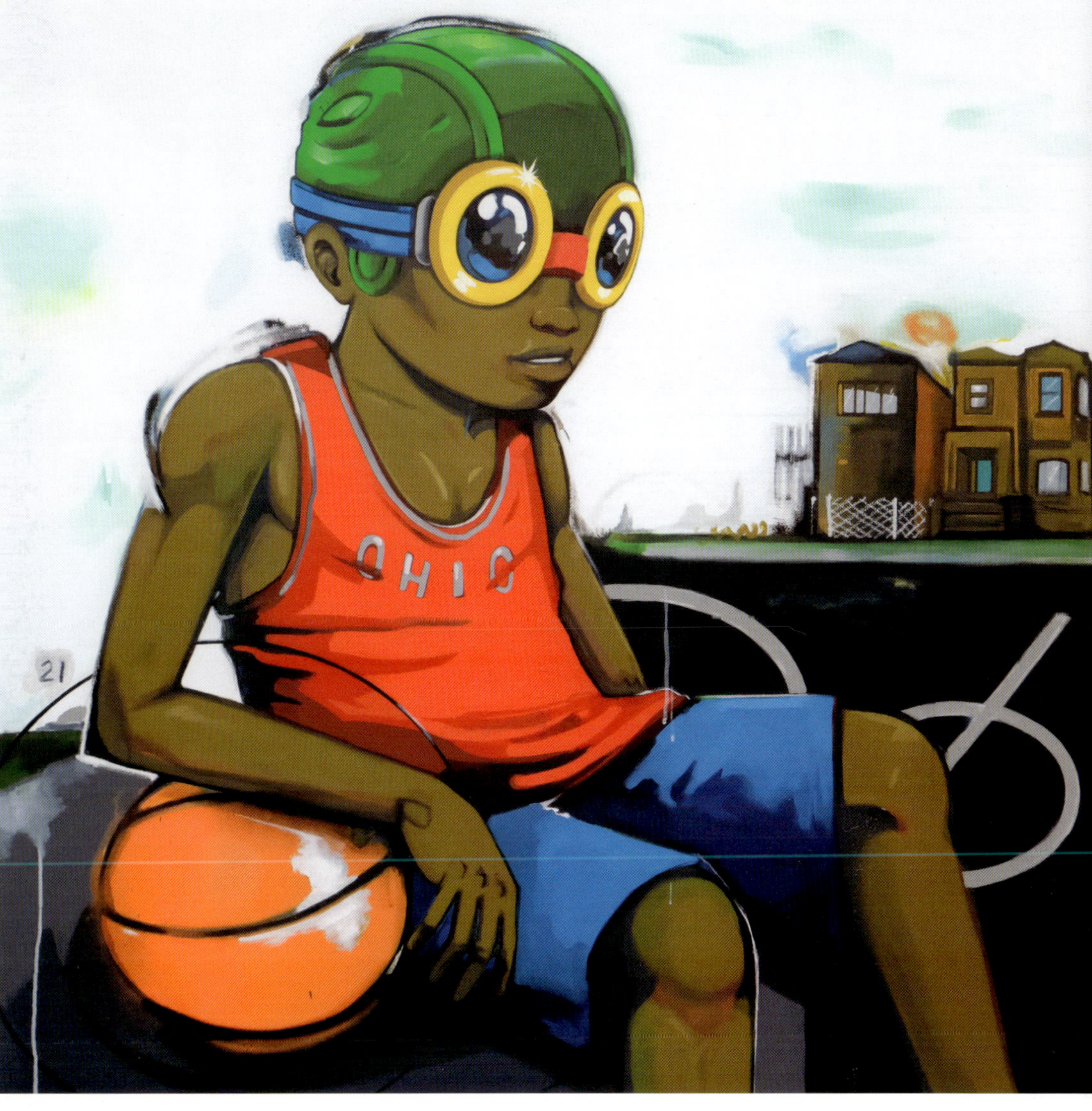

(Below)
Untitled
Mixed media
on canvas
2013

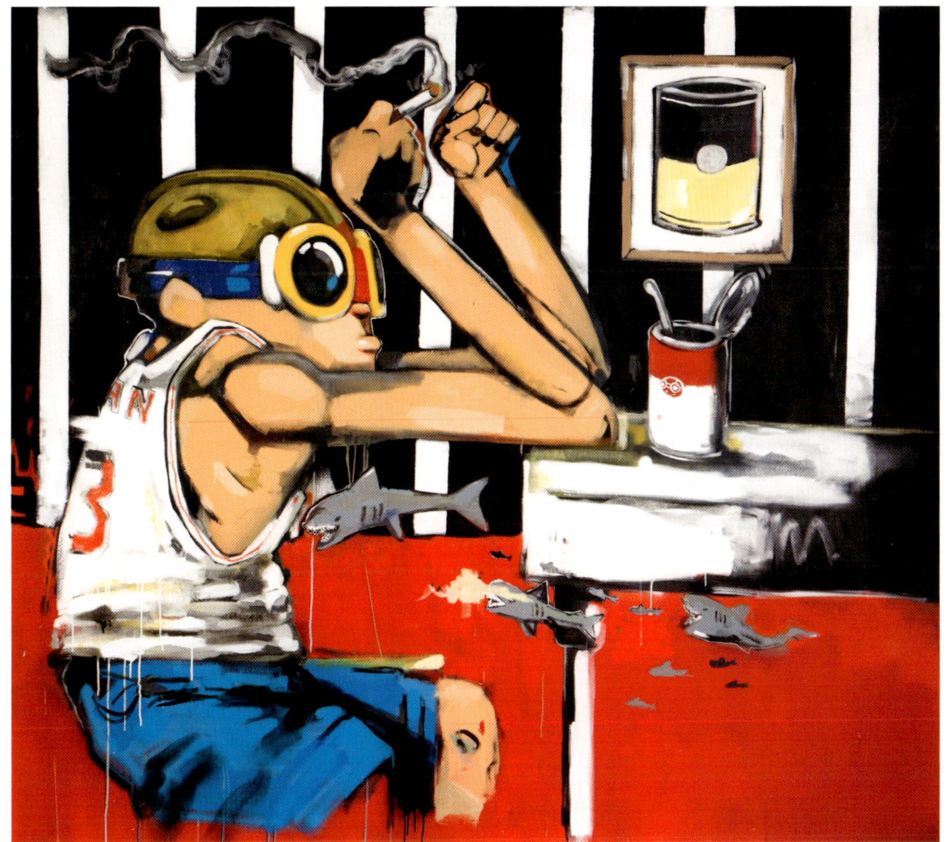

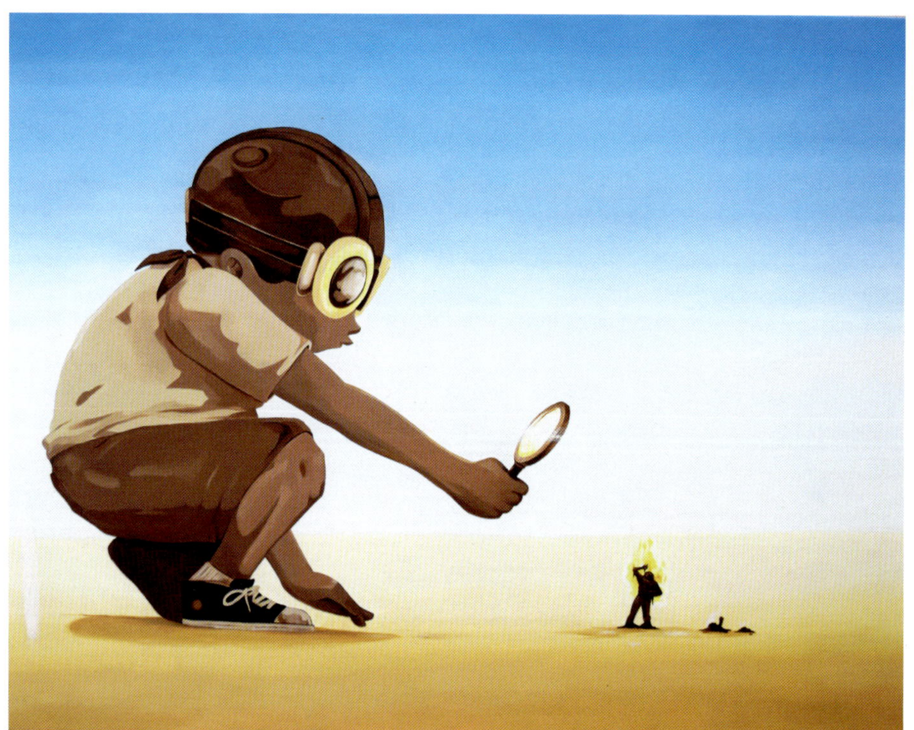

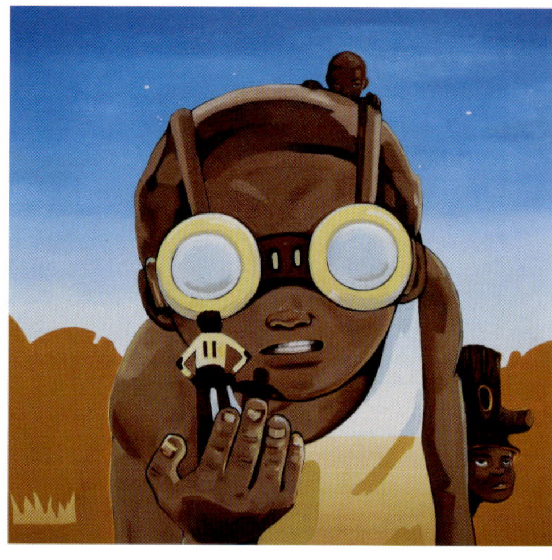

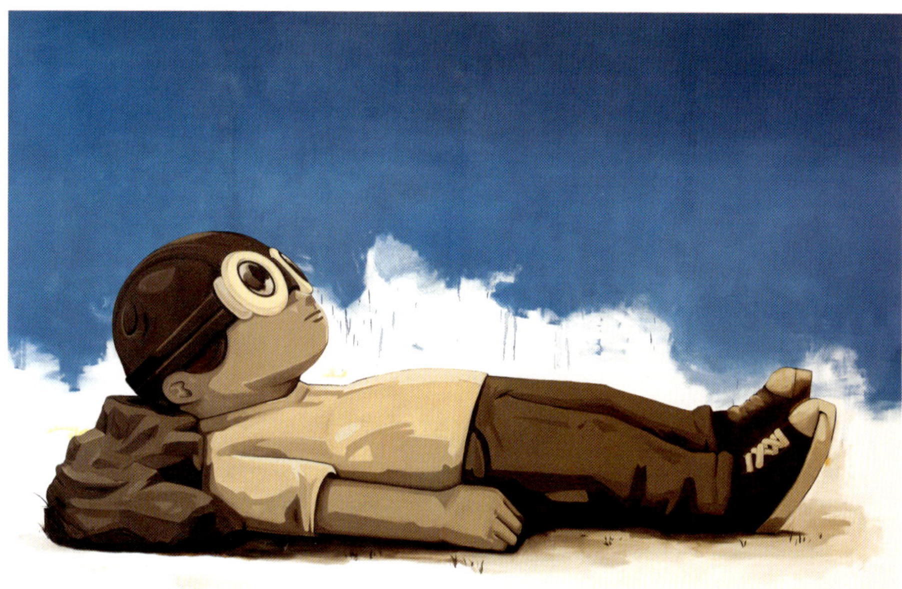

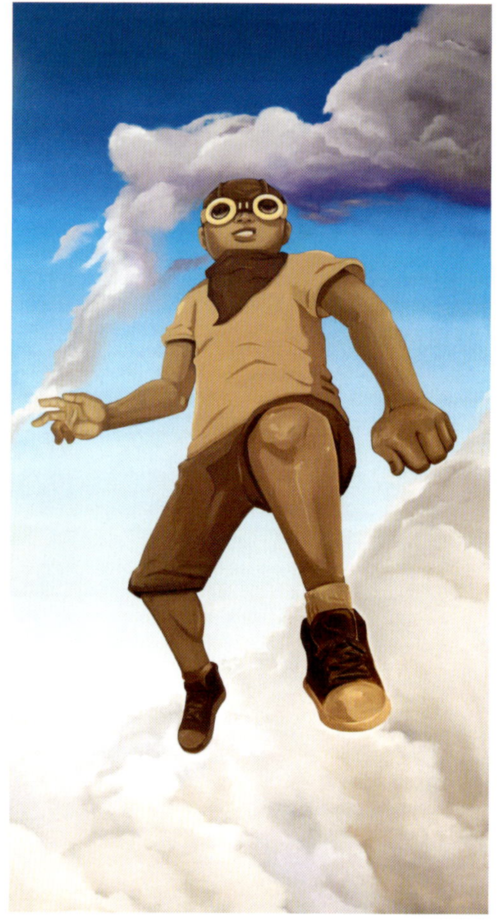

(Above, clockwise from top left)

Fried
Oil on canvas
46 x 58 inches
2018

Crowded
Oil on canvas
33 x 32 inches
2018

Escalators
Oil on canvas
49 x 97 inches
2016

Sleep Is the Cousin of Death—Epilogue
Oil on canvas
130 x 84 inches
2017

(Opposite, clockwise from top left)

Flyboy as Parade Float
Oil on canvas
34 x 31 inches
2018

Yes Lord Ego
Mixed media on canvas
30 x 30 inches
2017

Little Big Head
Oil on canvas
36 x 36 inches
2018

Boy on Rocket
Oil on canvas
48 x 48 inches
2018

Until Next Payday
Oil on canvas
62 x 48 inches
2017

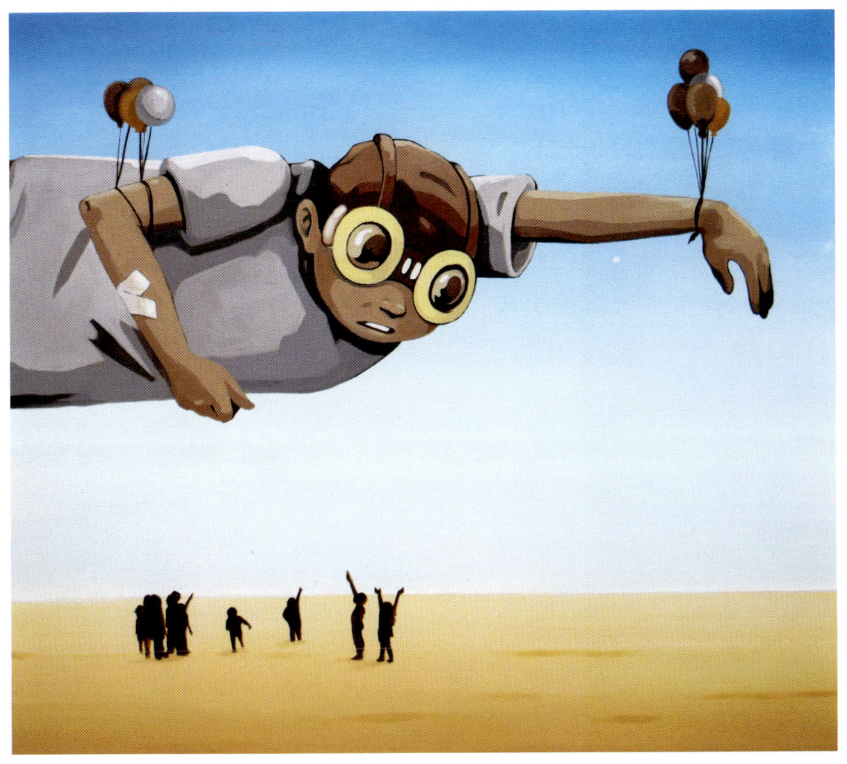

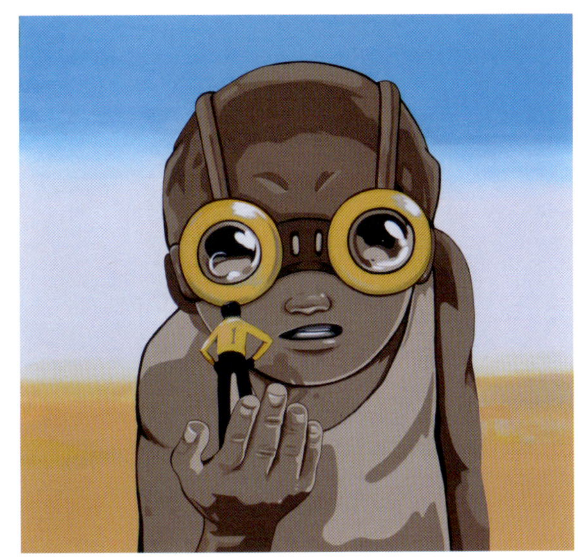

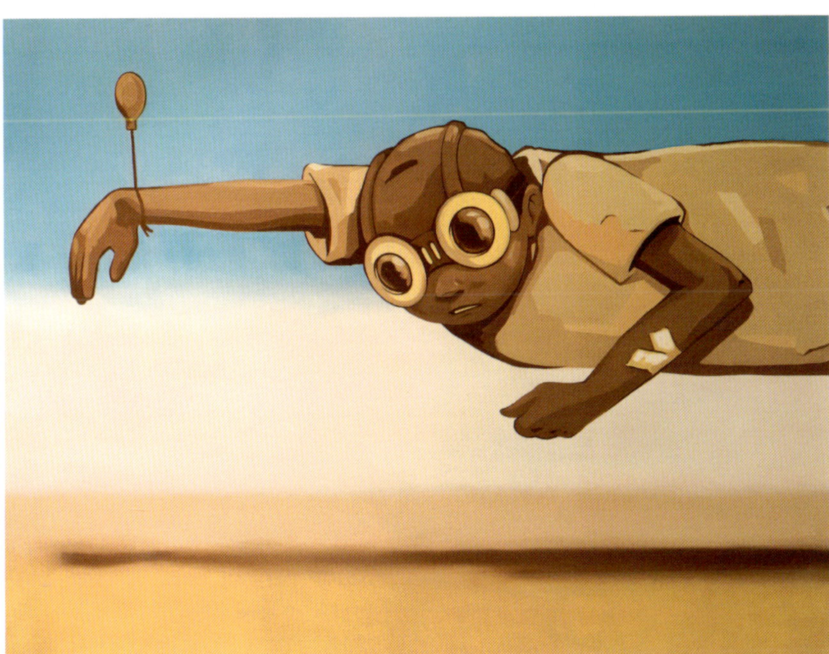

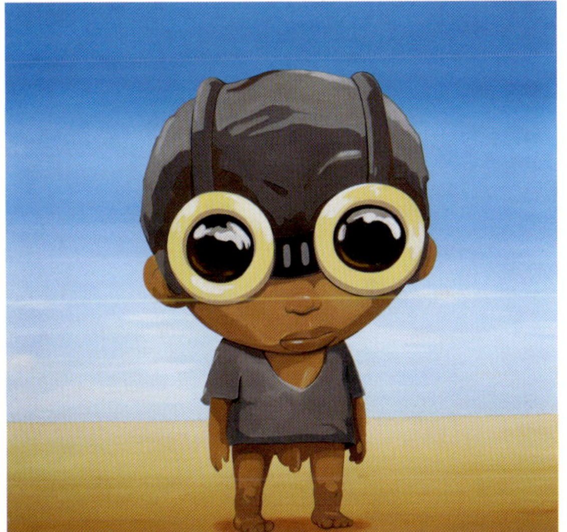

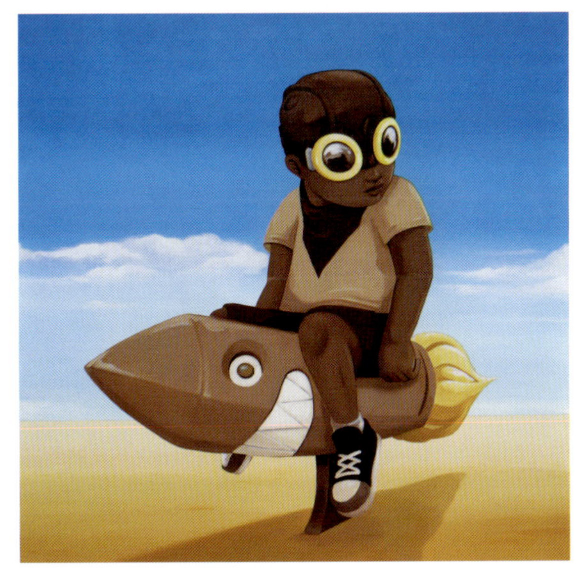

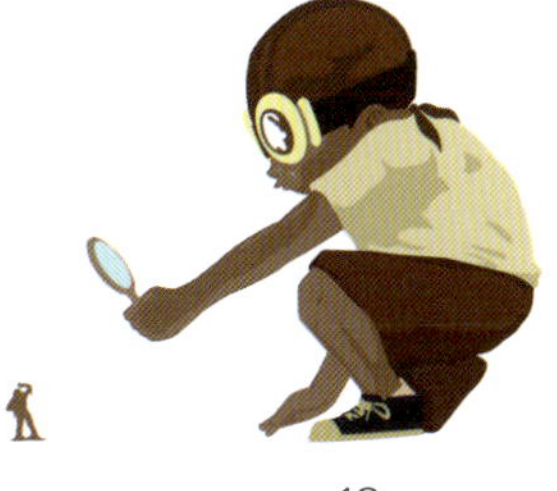

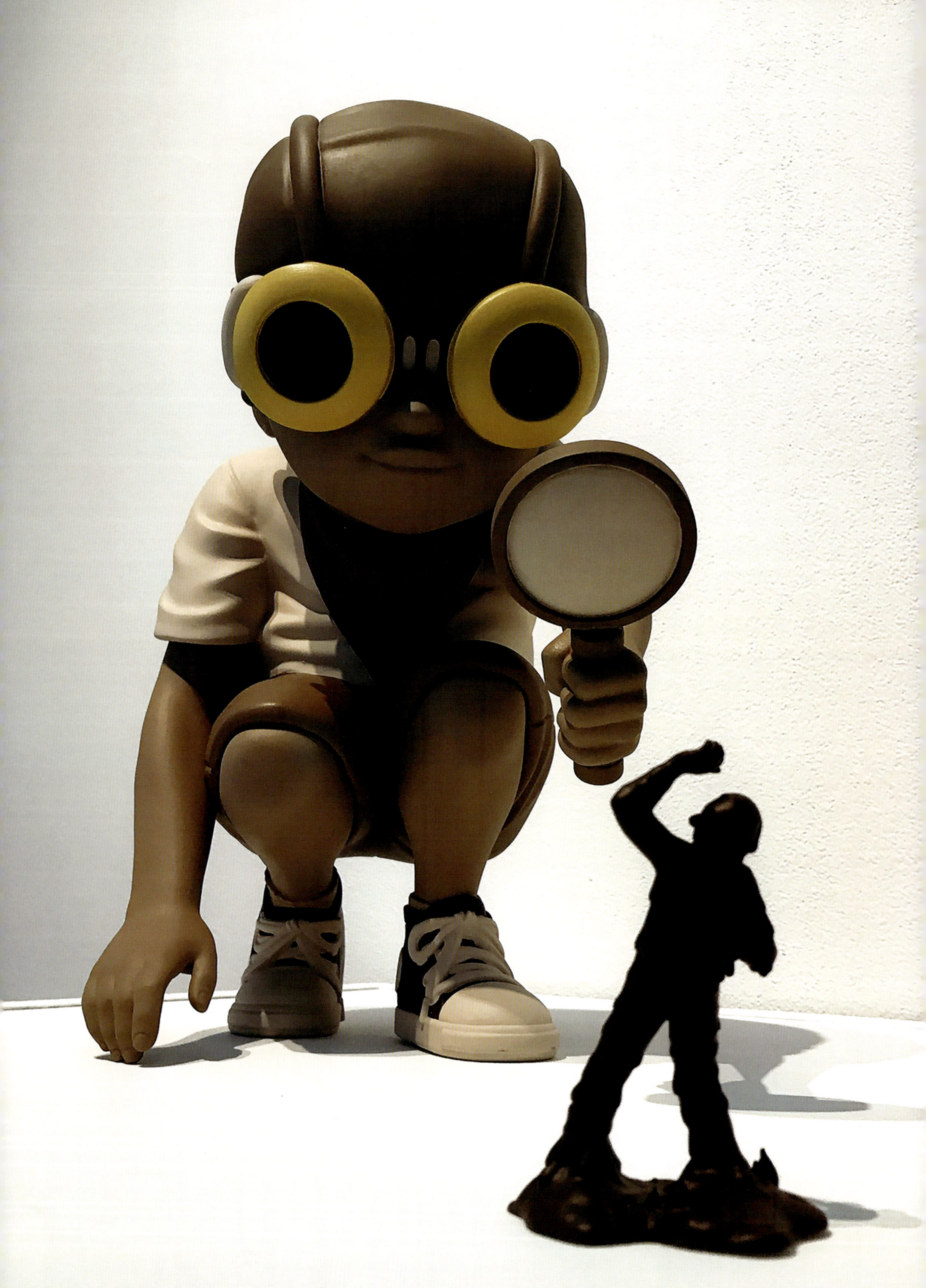

(Opposite)
Flyboy "Fry" (Sepia Edition),
Resin
2017

(Right)
Flyboy "Fry" (Gloss Black Edition),
High-gloss painted impact resin
2017

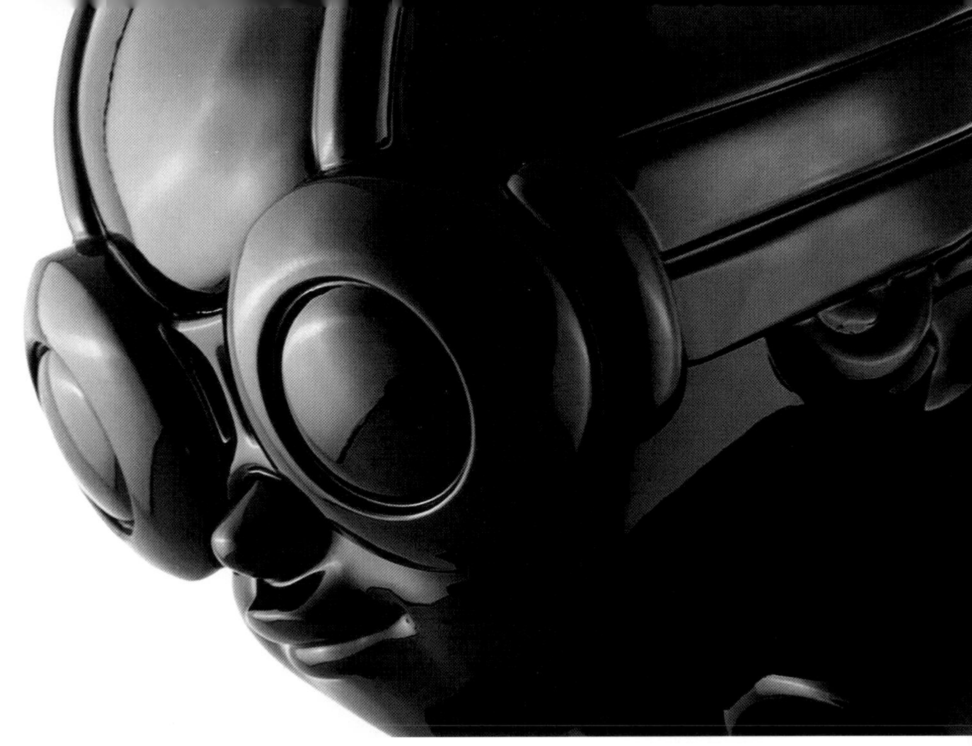

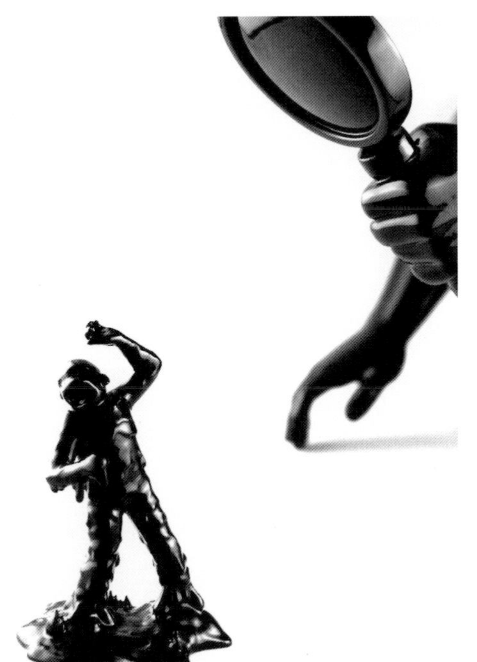

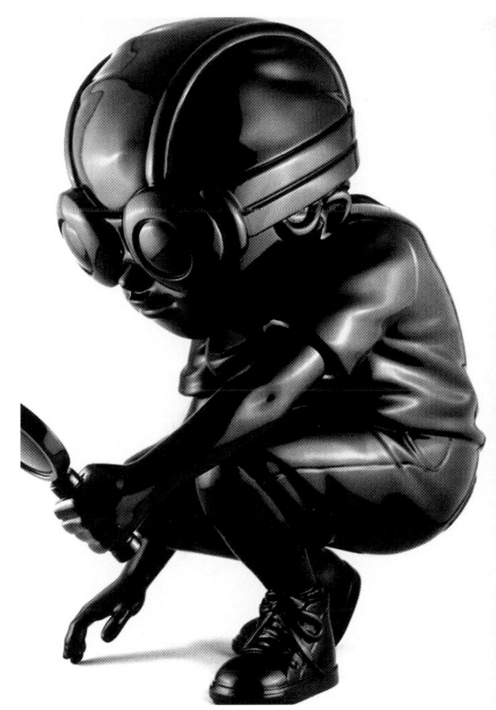

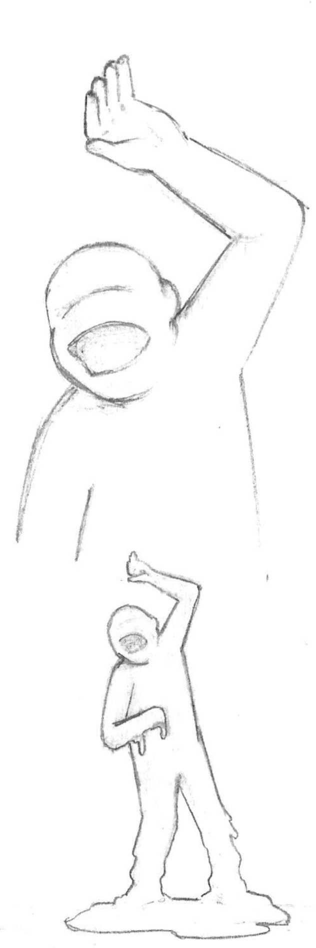

There is a charm to all of Brantley's characters that betrays a deeper, more serious set of themes. By immersing the viewer in a playful, comically crisp and seductive world, Hebru makes you think you're merely in for a joyride. It's fun. And the more you look, the more you wonder what his protagonists are doing—each seems thoroughly engrossed in a mission of exploration or discovery, or absorbed in thought, posing for the viewer or bemused, reflecting upon something to which the viewer isn't quite privy.

It's this elusive quality that I find so magnetic about Hebru's art. His narratives are never complete. Sometimes smiling, smirking, deadpan, occasionally contorted in anger or wonder, or looking royally self-satisfied, in his portraiture emotions swirl up to but still lurk somewhere beneath the surface. Sometimes there is a moodiness or melancholy that's hard to define. More often, what captures the attention is the sense of a character's confidence, poise, intense focus, determination, triumph, or sheer joy. No one really seems lost in their world, confused, or interrupted—and yet his characters are kid-heroes, who otherwise might be. Everyone seems to know what they're doing. Everyone seems to have a plan, is up against something big, or already on their way to victory. Many characters are rendered in a bright, saturated color palette and set against more muted backgrounds, highlighting this feeling of certainty. What also breaks through Hebru's canvases is an unshakeable sense of a new Black identity—not a nostalgic recovery of a lost one, but a fresh one coined universally from the fearlessness of youth, whose spirit soars unapologetically.

The emotional effect is immediate, and it's why his work has such a powerful crossover appeal, traversing nations and boundaries, people and generations. Hebru's art is as hot in the US as it is in Asia, and it's hot among traditional collectors and newer ones alike. He's also serious about crossing genres into collaborative merchandising—inspired as he is by Warhol, the feverish Basquiat, and Haring. From basketball to gin, sports gear to apparel, Hebru draws inspiration from Pop Art's pioneering, commercial genre-bending in the '80s. He also taps the street artist's anti-elitist impulse to reach people by making the city his canvas and his art accessible.

Ultimately, it's the energy—it's all about the Flyboy energy coming off his paintings, coming out of his sculptures and radiant figurines that just makes his art so irresistibly cool.

—DEREK COLLINS, DEAN OF THE FACULTY OF ARTS AT THE UNIVERSITY OF HONG KONG, SENIOR CONSULTANT FOR PHILLIPS ASIA

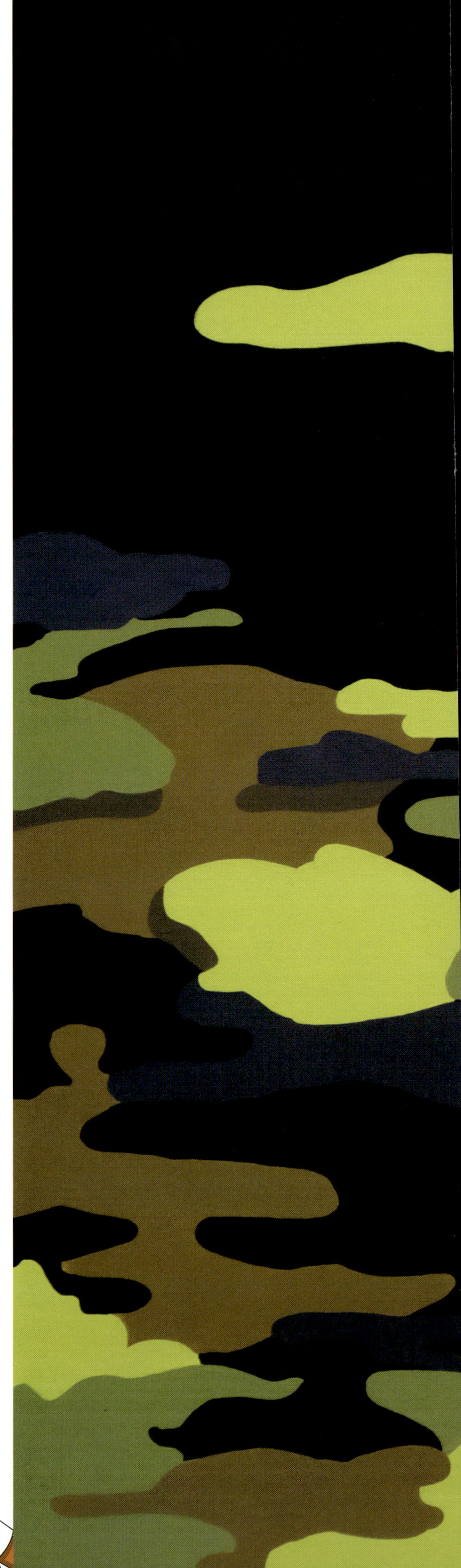

Ein Camo (Cause I Don't Wanna Be A "Remember Him"), Mixed media on canvas, 30 x 30 inches, 2020

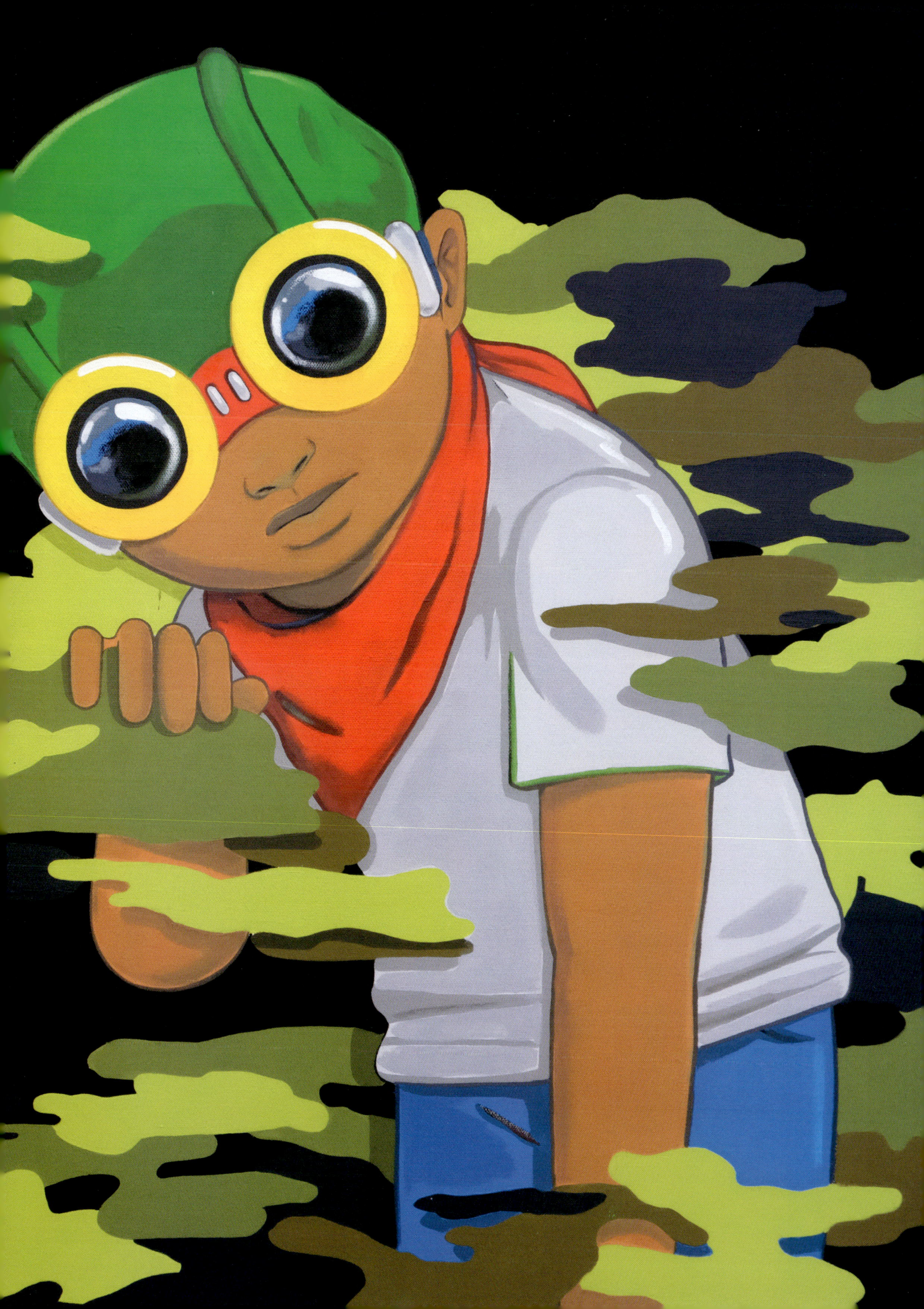

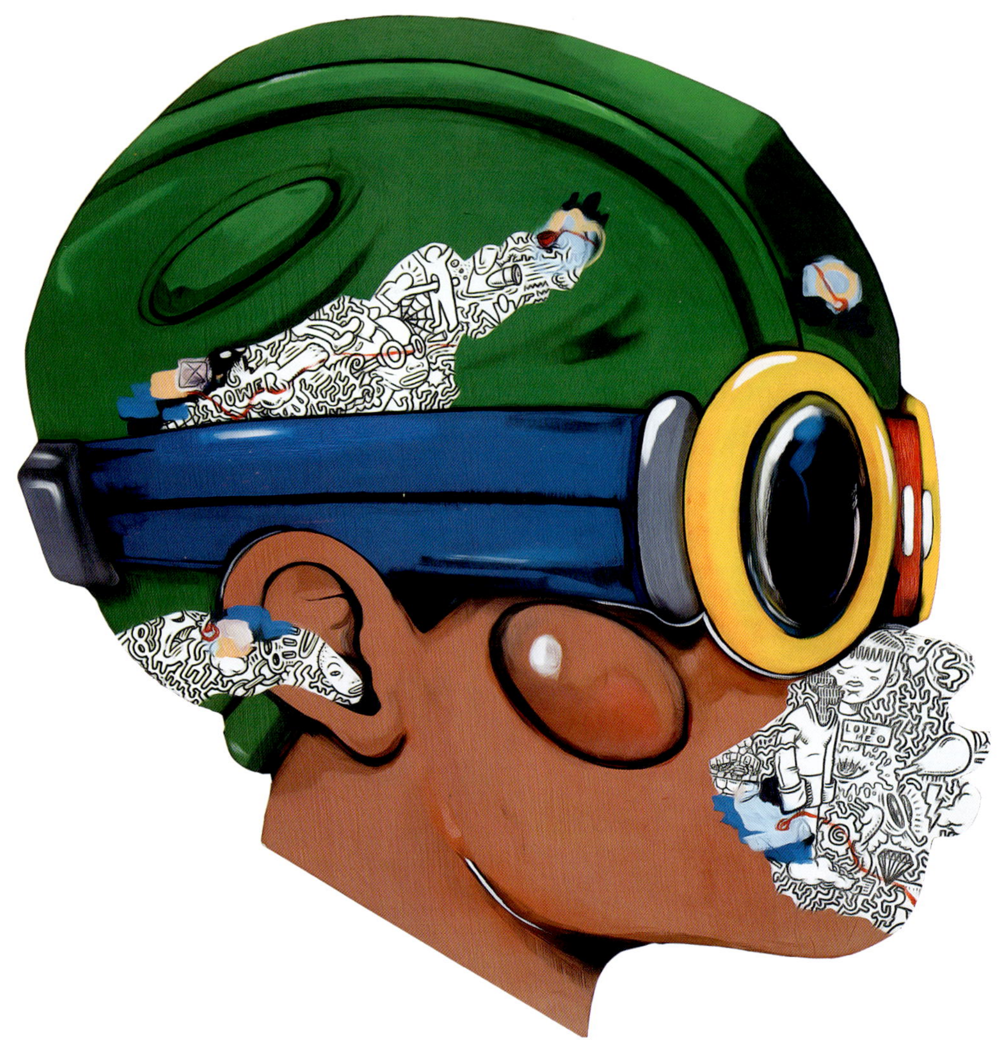

The Profile

Mixed media on canvas, 42 x 42 inches, 2013

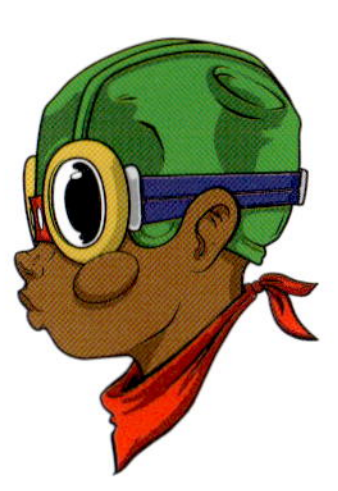

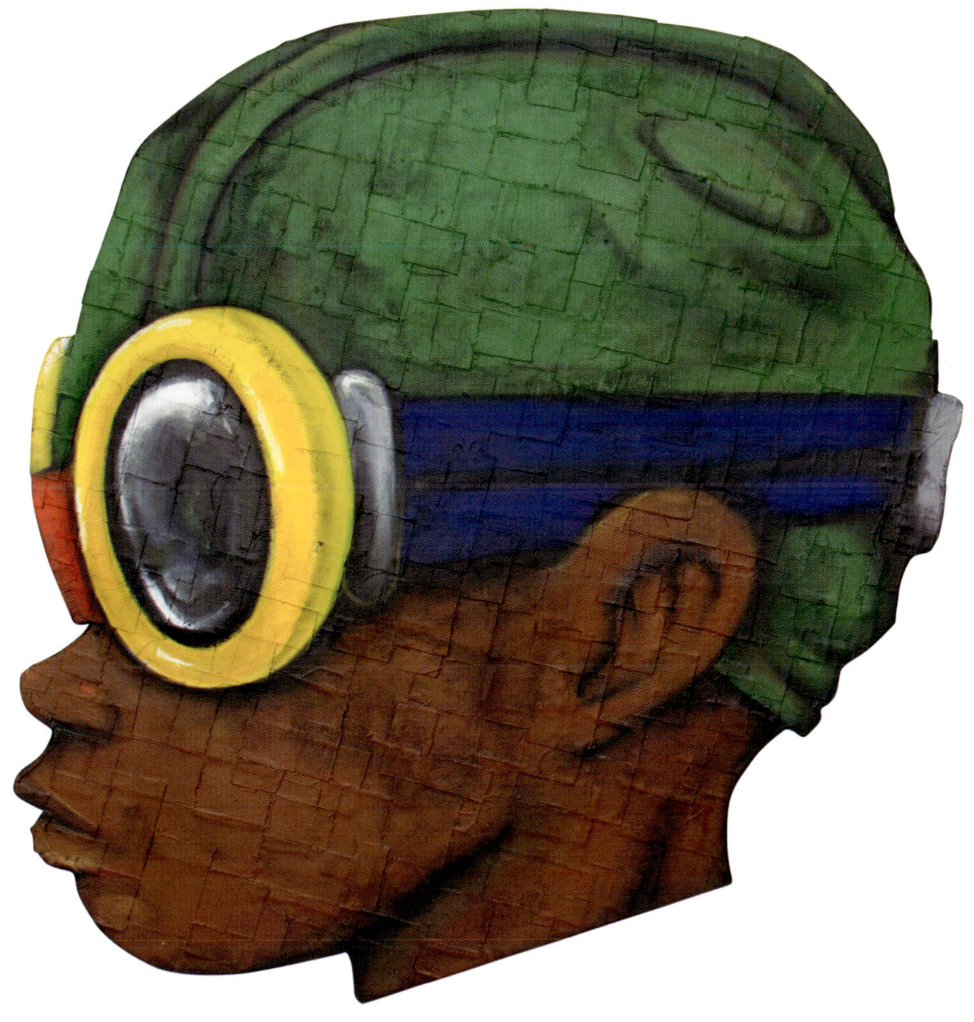

Stonewall Jackson

Mixed media and canvas on wood, 42 x 42 inches, 2016

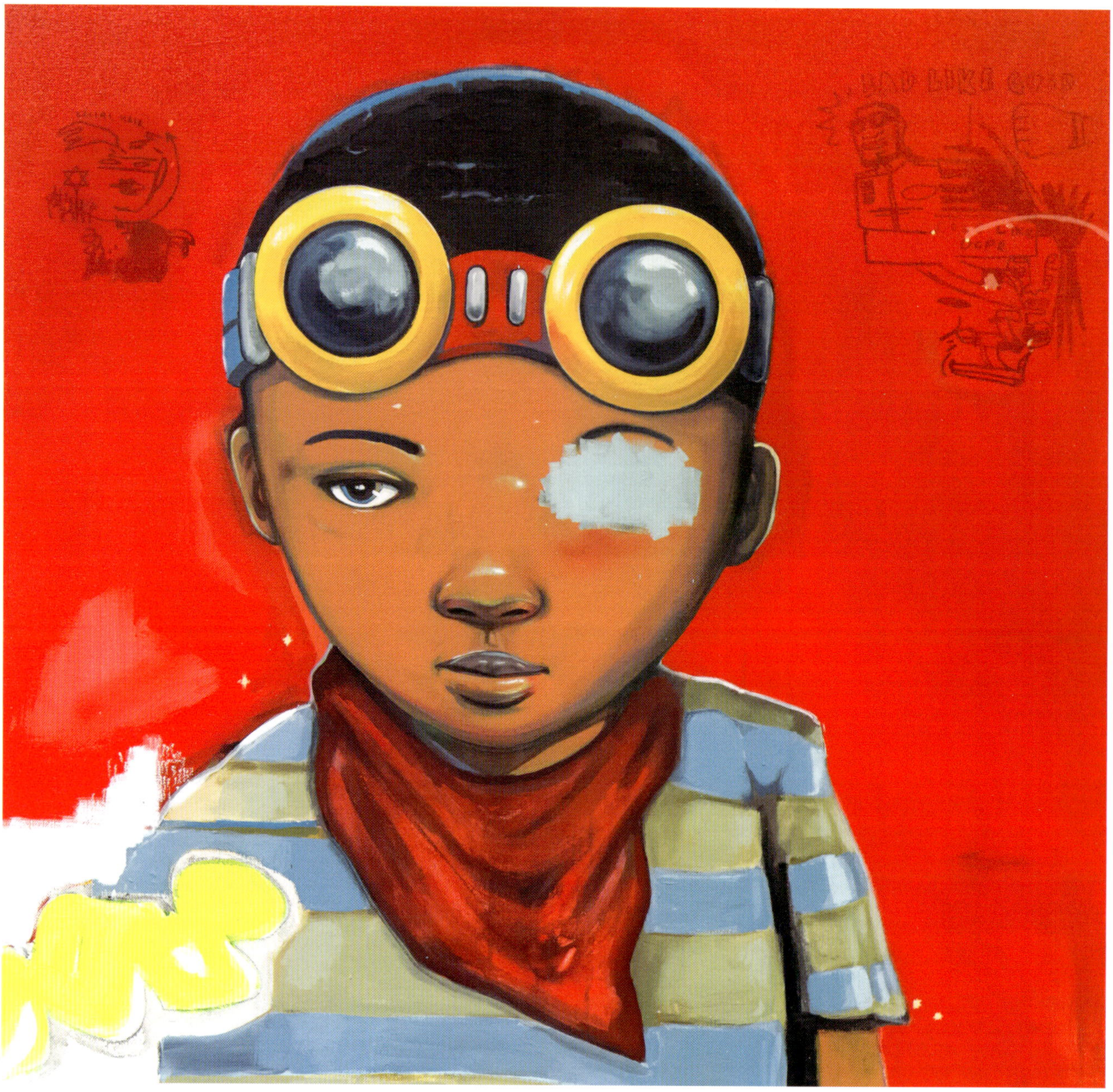

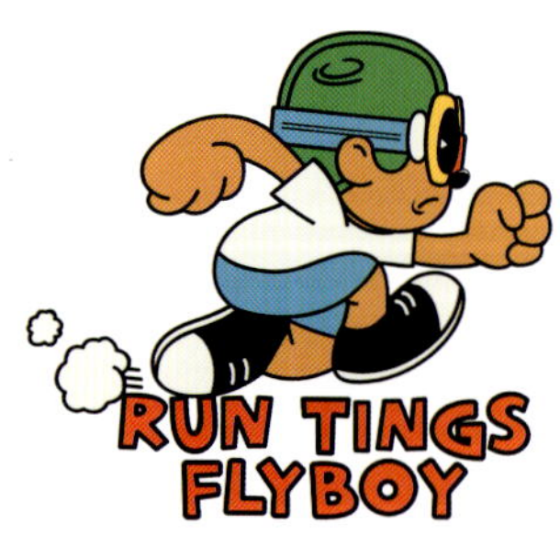
RUN TINGS
FLYBOY

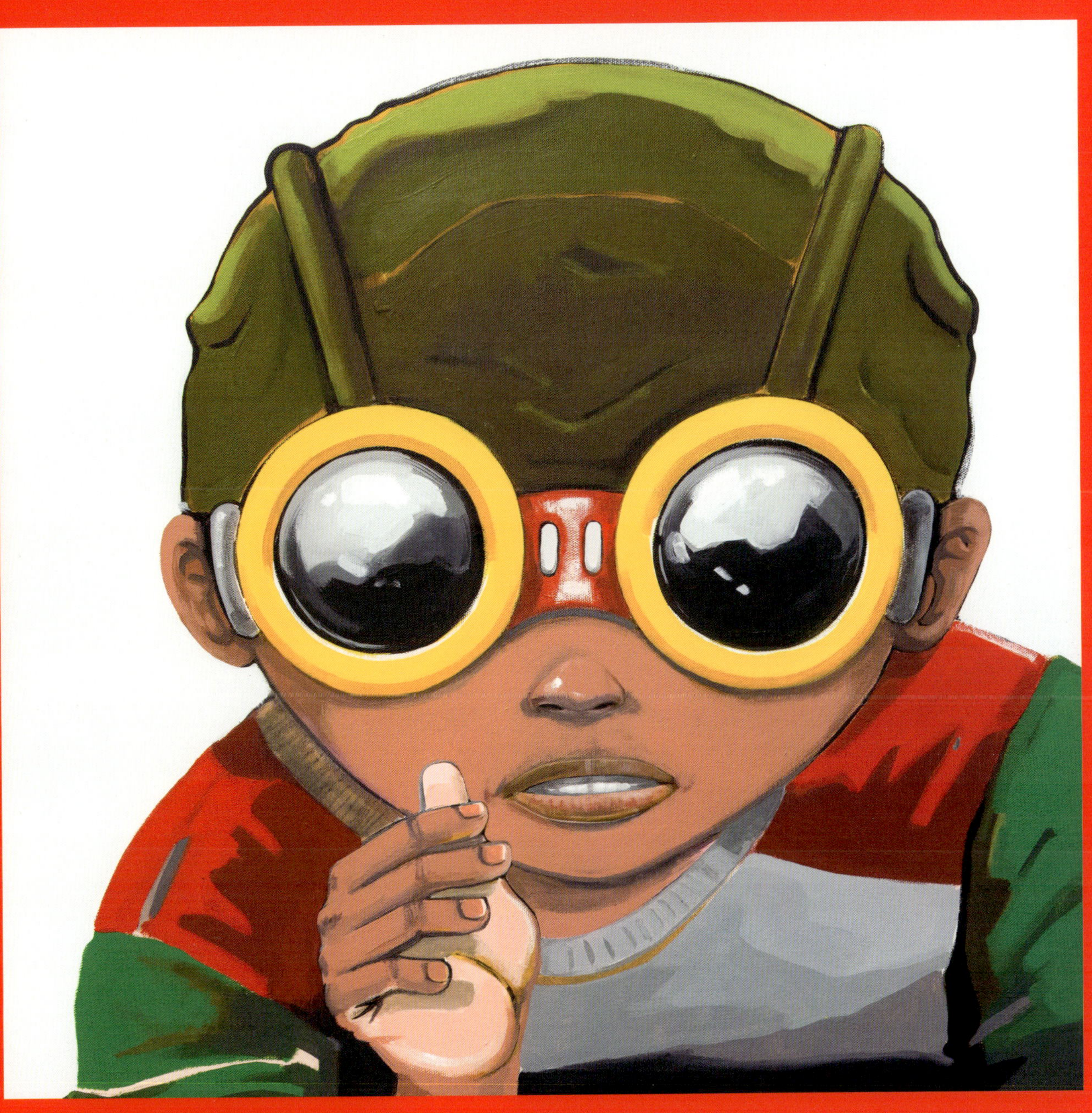

(Opposite)
Blood Is a Crip (Stolen)
Mixed media on canvas
30 x 30 inches
2016

(Above)
The Gauntlet (Arm Wrestling)
Mixed media on canvas
24 x 24 inches
2016

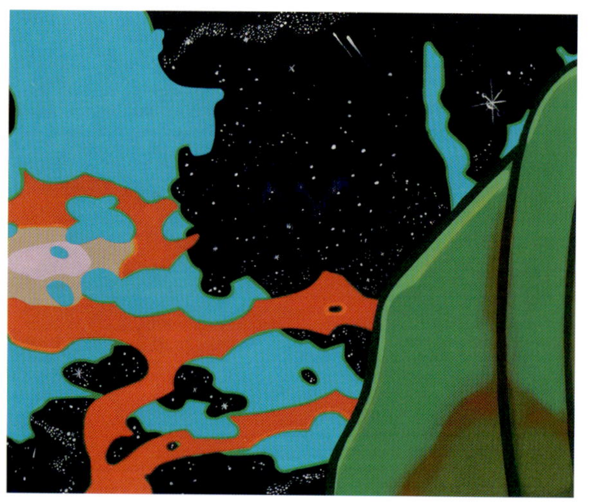
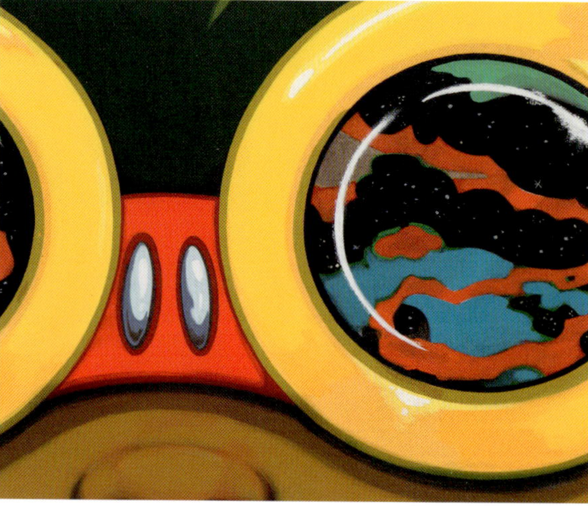
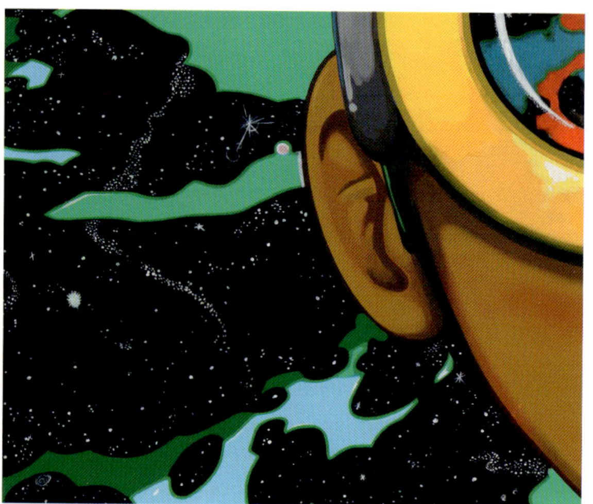
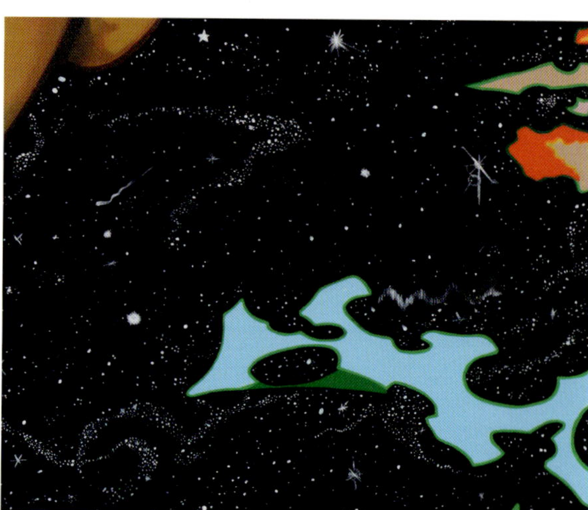

"HEBRU BRANTLEY'S WORK SPEAKS TO YOU IN A VERY UNIQUE WAY. HE HAS A BEAUTIFUL WAY OF TAKING YOUTHFUL BLACK CHARACTERS AND PRESENTING THEM WITH SUPER POWERS THAT WERE HANDED DOWN FROM THEIR ANCESTORS."

—KEVIN "COACH K" LEE

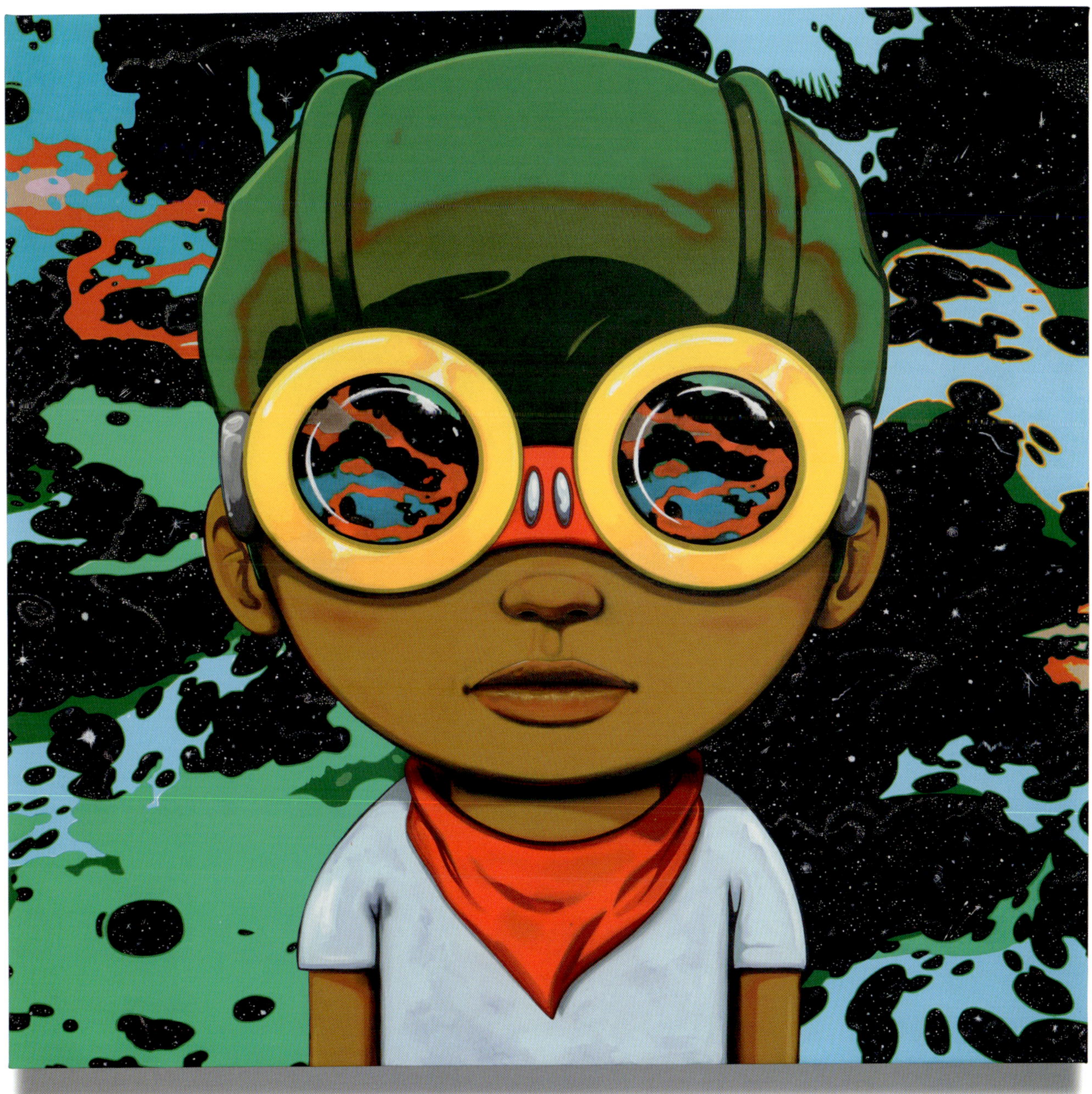

Space Is the Place

Mixed media on canvas, 70 x 70 inches, 2021

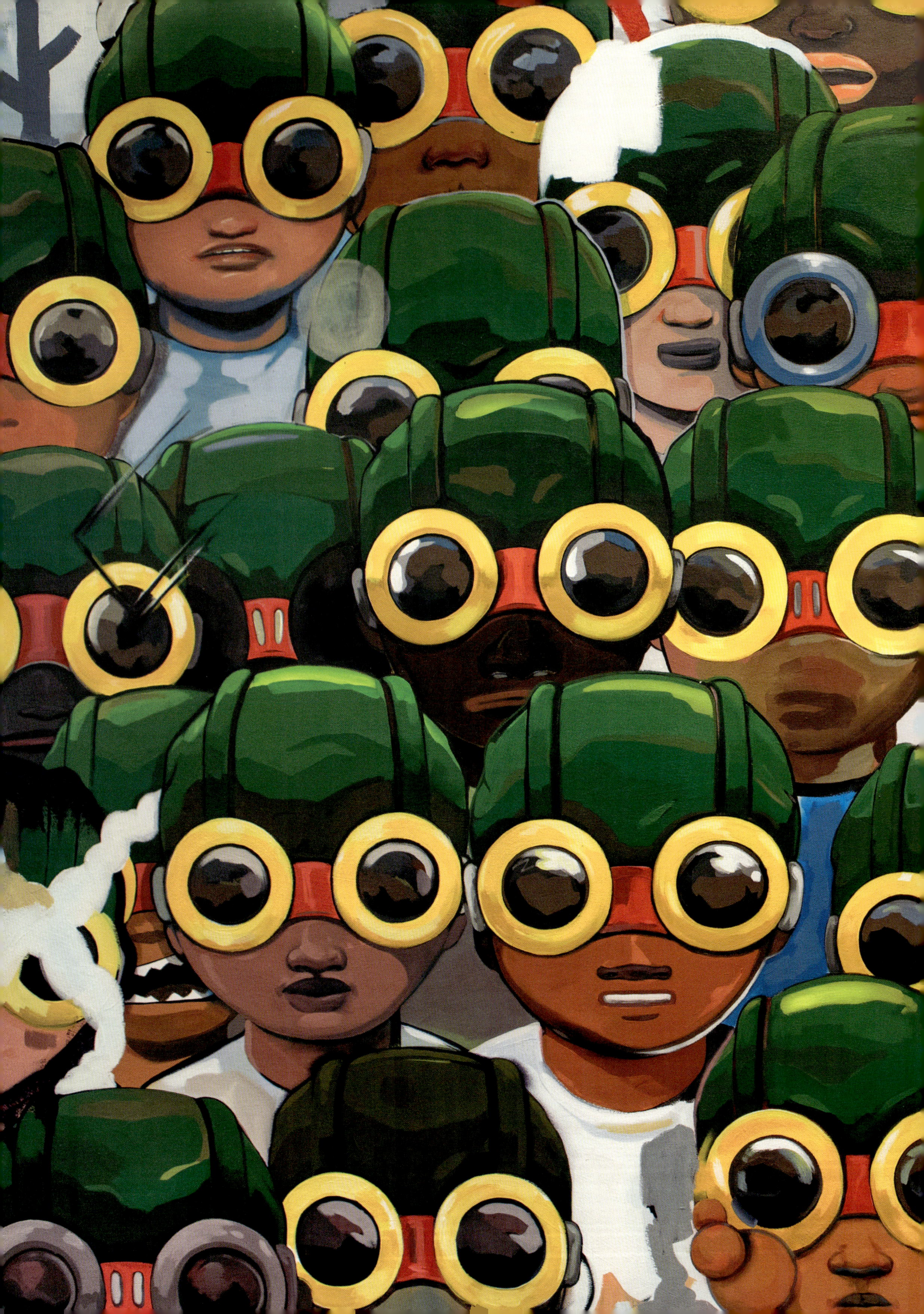

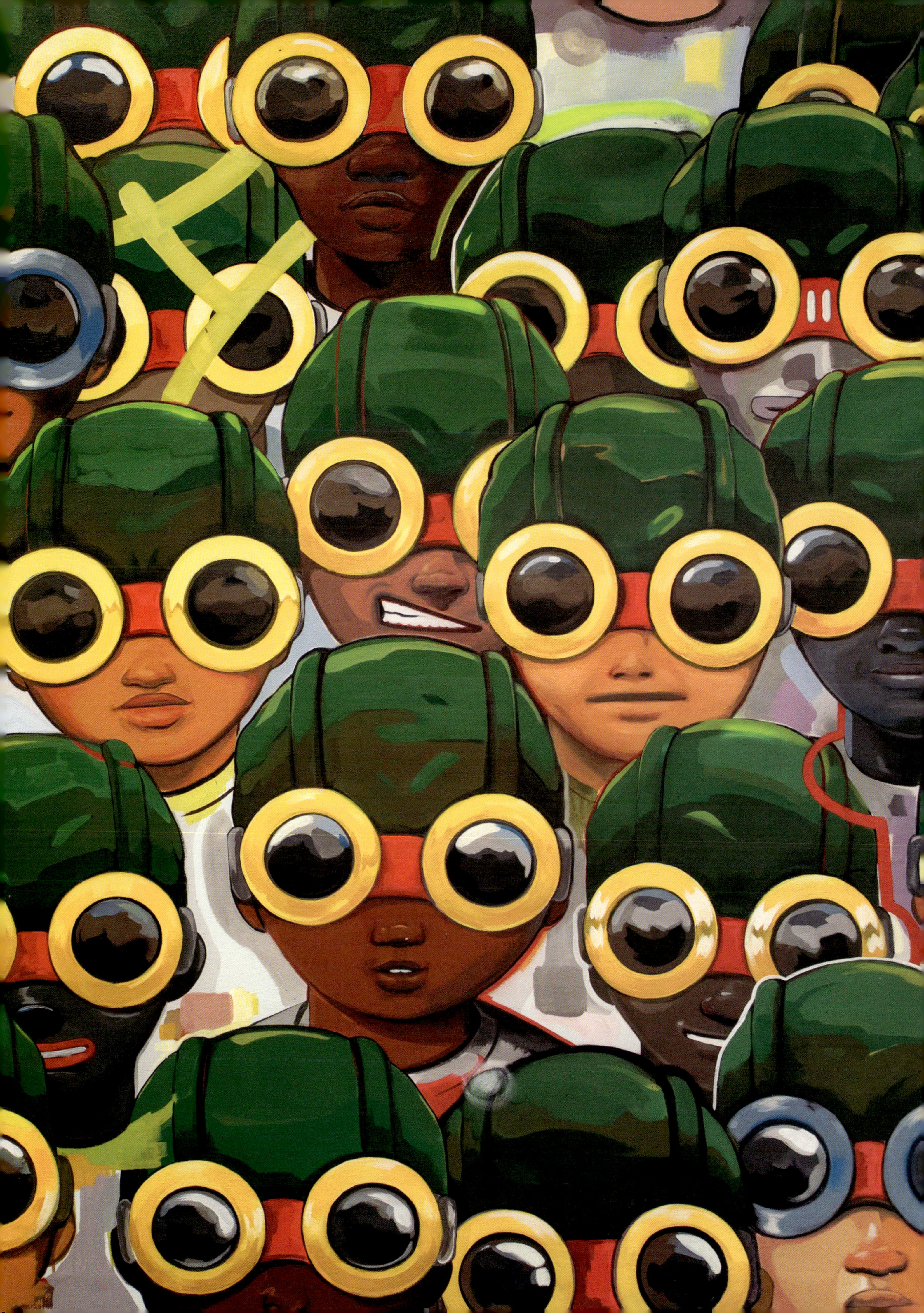

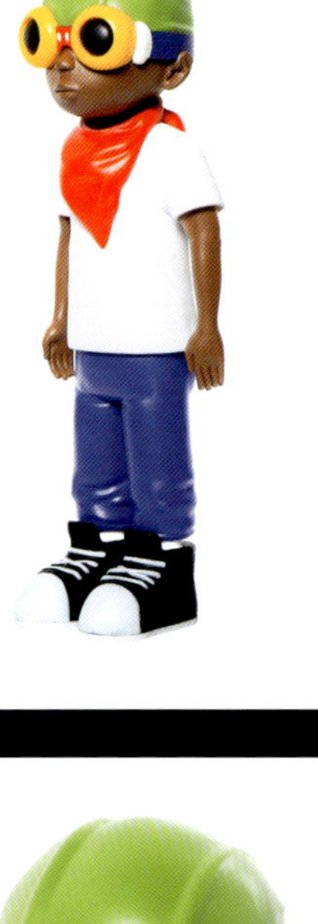
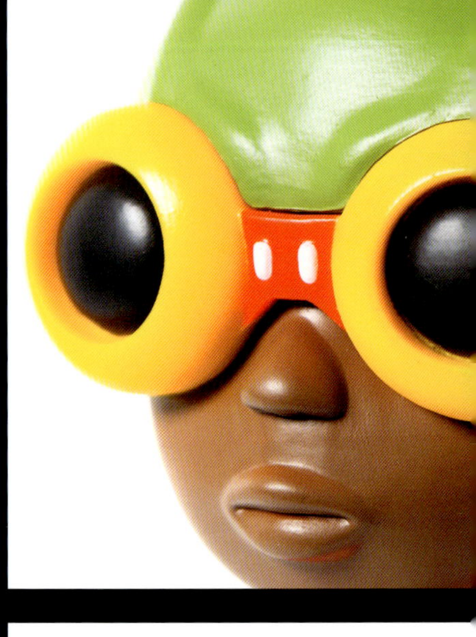
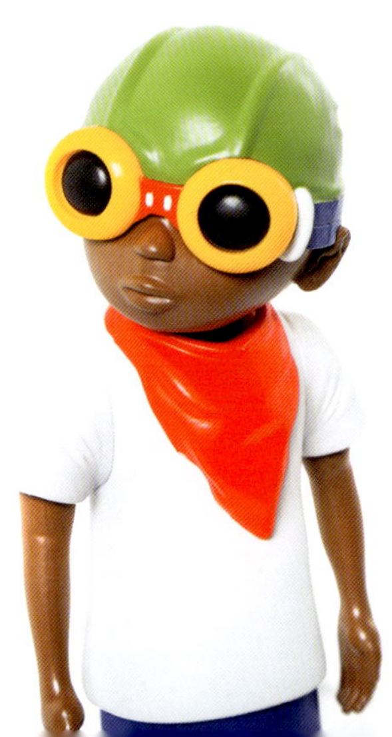
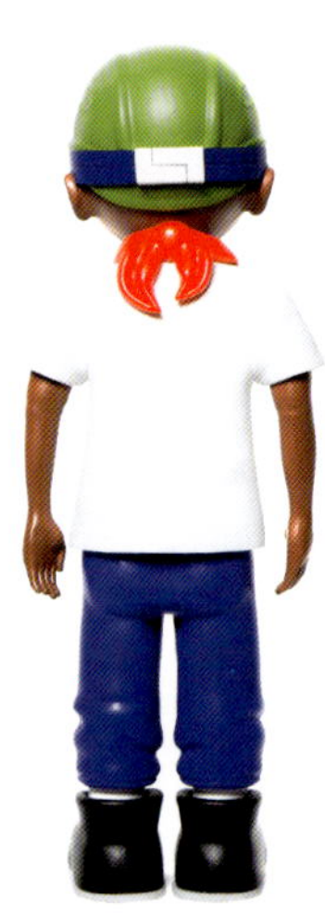

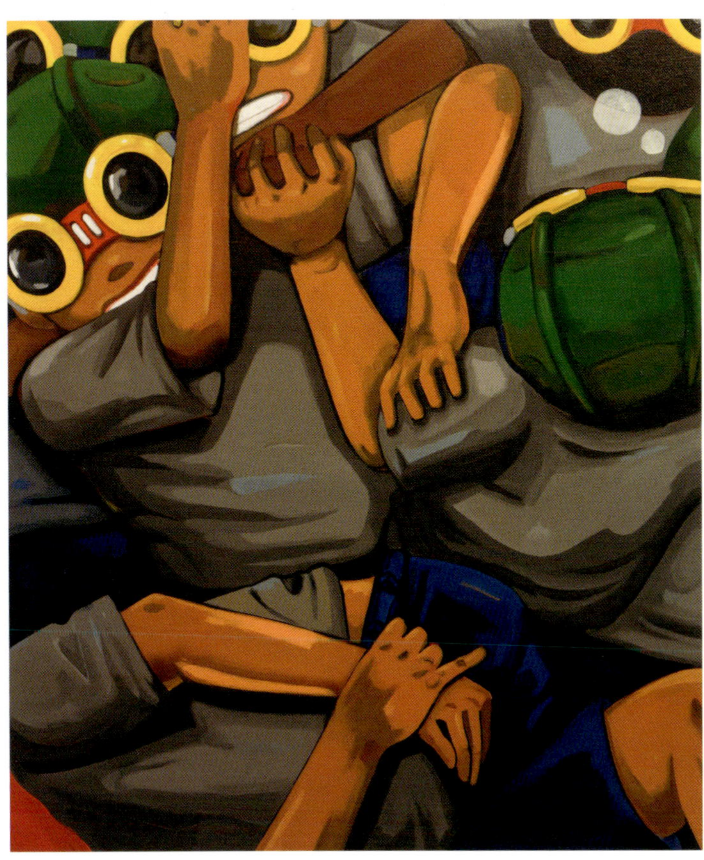

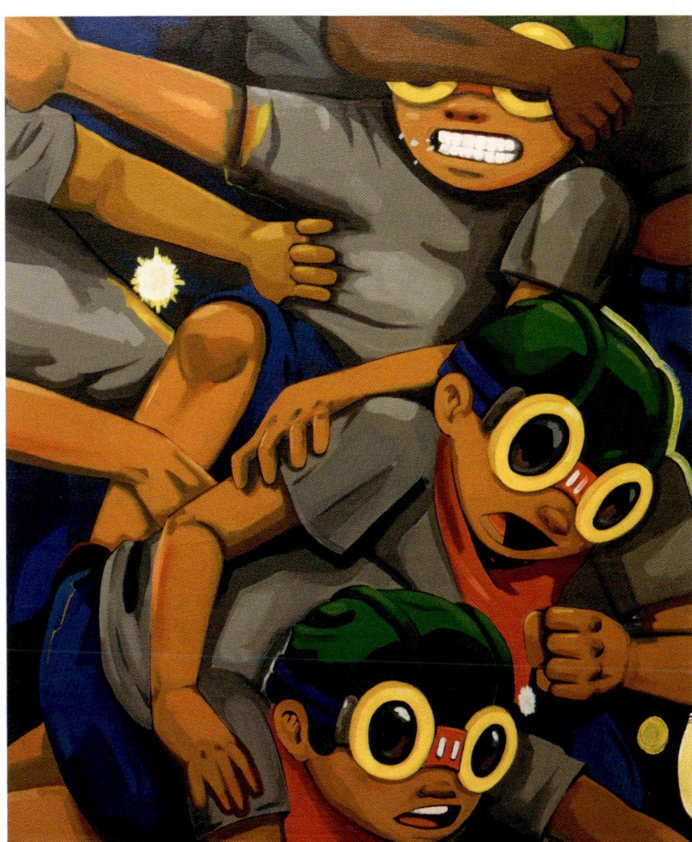

(Above, from left)
A Rare Look: Anderson Cooper's Coverage on the Barrel Pt. 1
Mixed media on canvas
28 x 34 inches
2017

A Rare Look: Anderson Cooper's Coverage on the Barrel Pt. 2
Mixed media on canvas
28 x 34 inches
2017

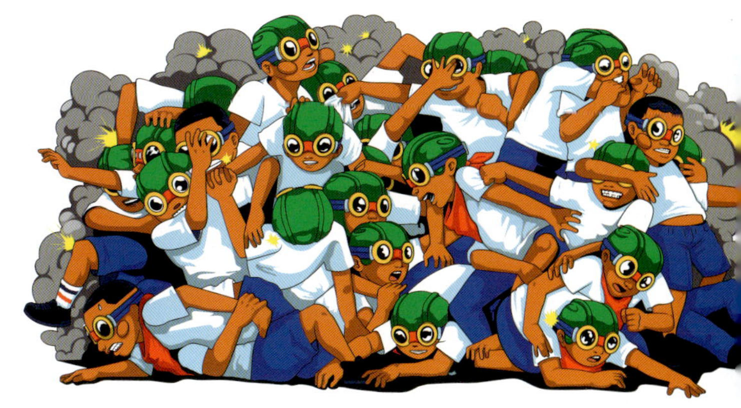

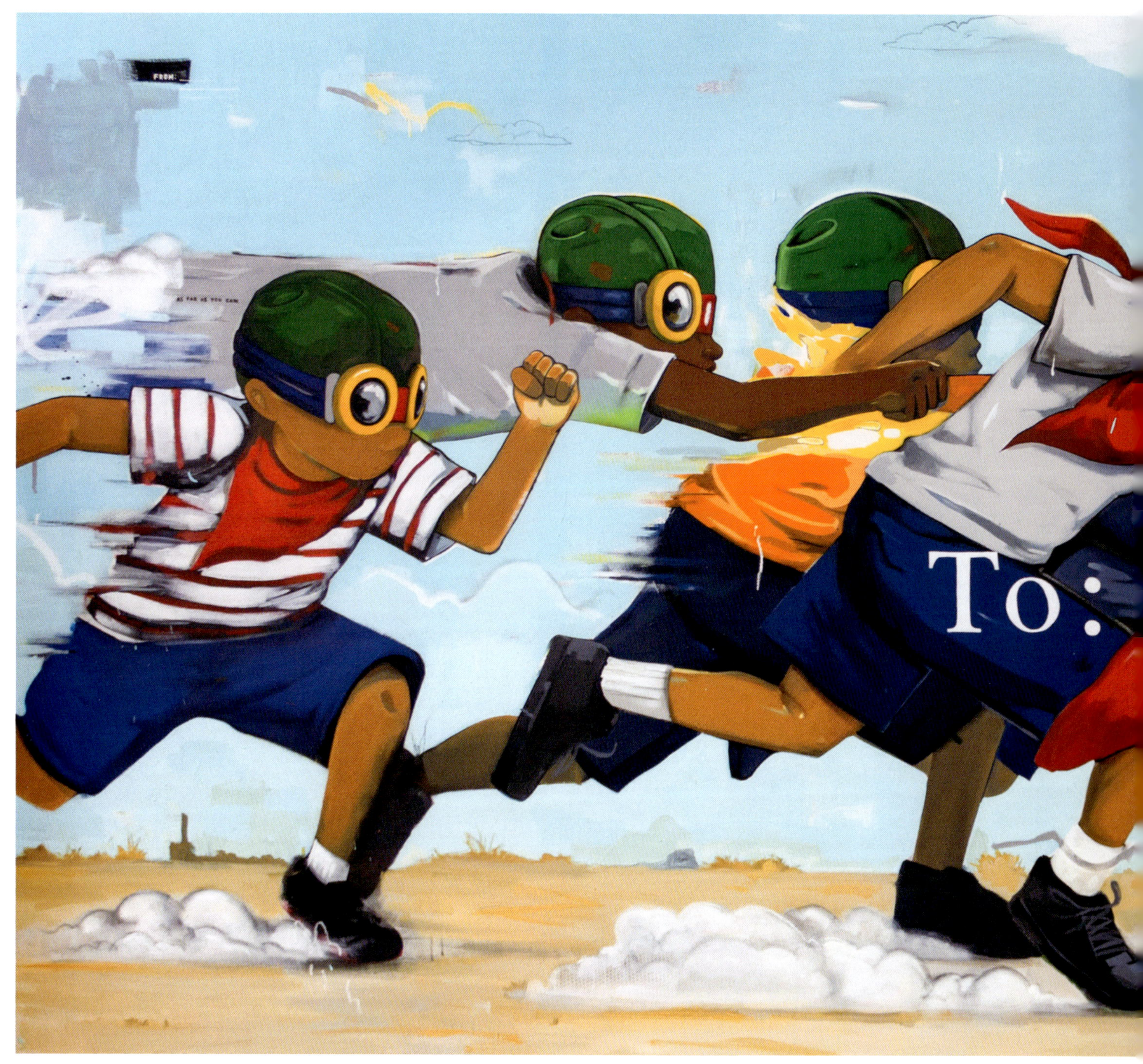

Run, Boy

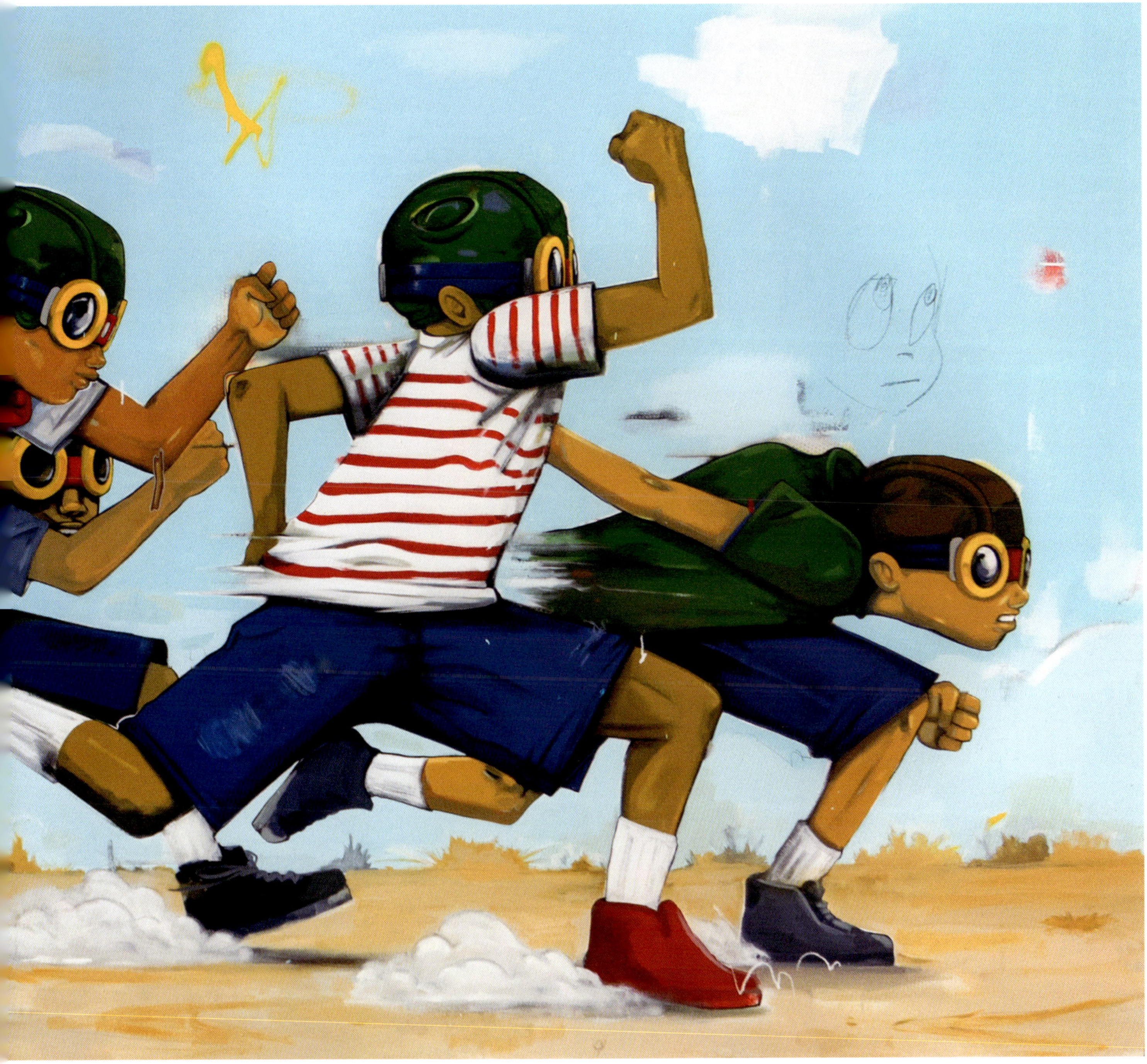

Mixed media on canvas, 144 x 64 inches, 2016

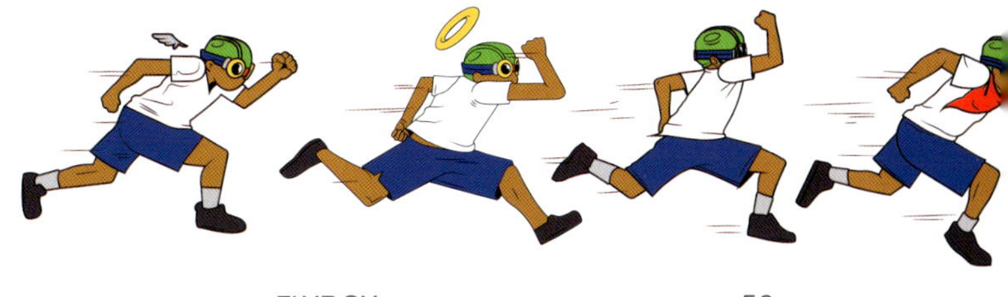

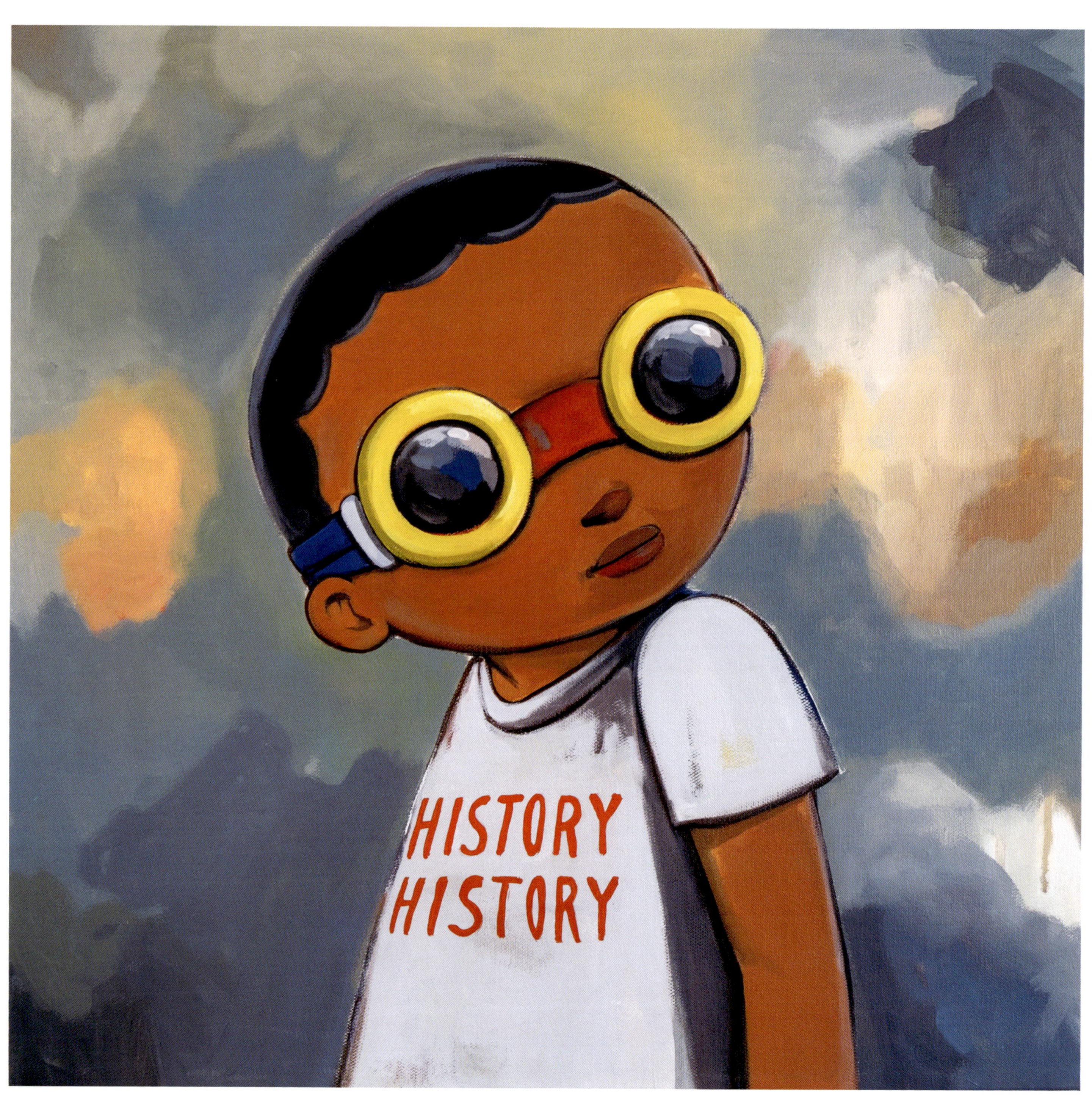

History Repeats

Mixed media on canvas, 20 x 20 inches, 2018

(Below)
I'll Be out in a Minute
Colored pencil on paper
11 x 14 inches
2019

(Right)
Fuck 'Em
Colored pencil, pastel, and graphite on paper
11 x 14 inches
2020

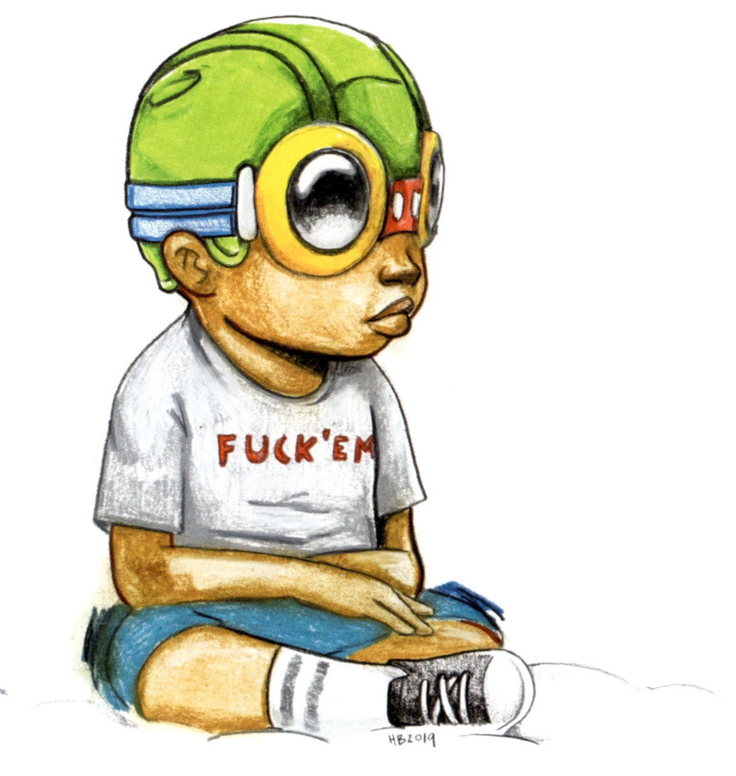

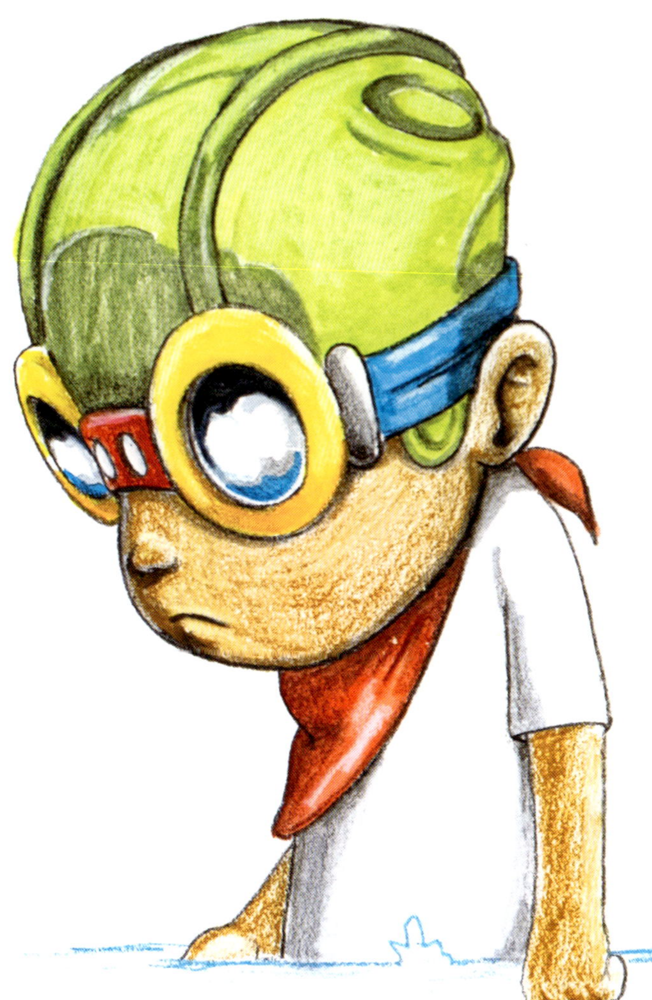

Lack of Faith Or No Trust
Colored pencil on paper
11 x 14 inches
2020

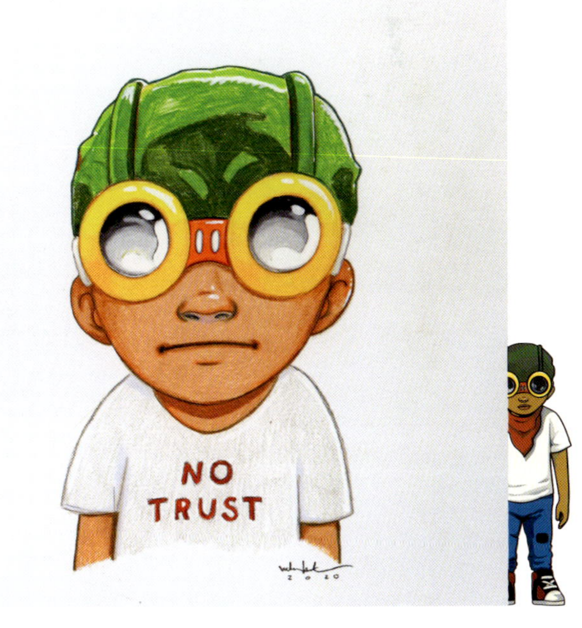

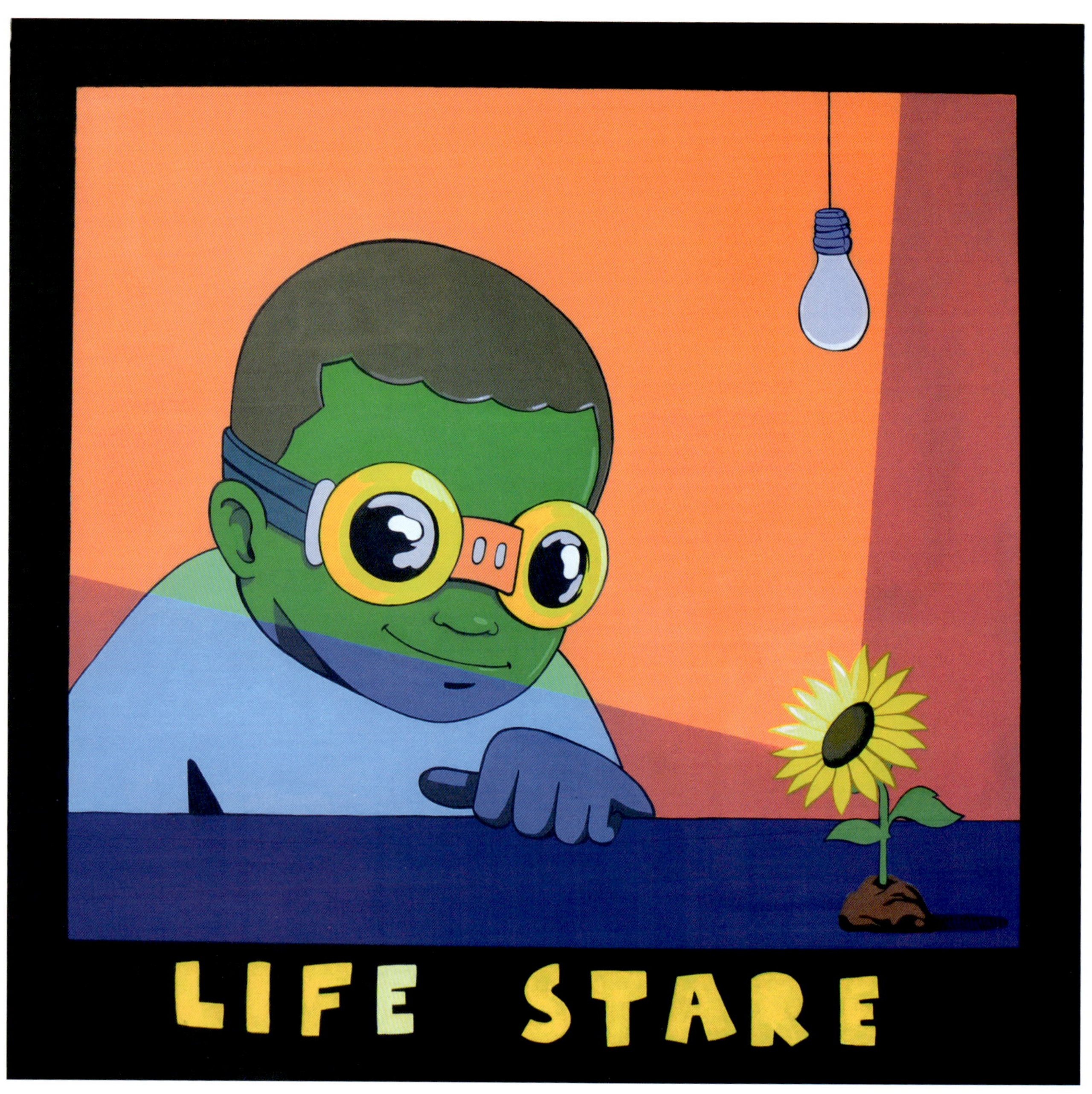

Life Stare

Mixed media on canvas, 32 x 32 inches, 2018

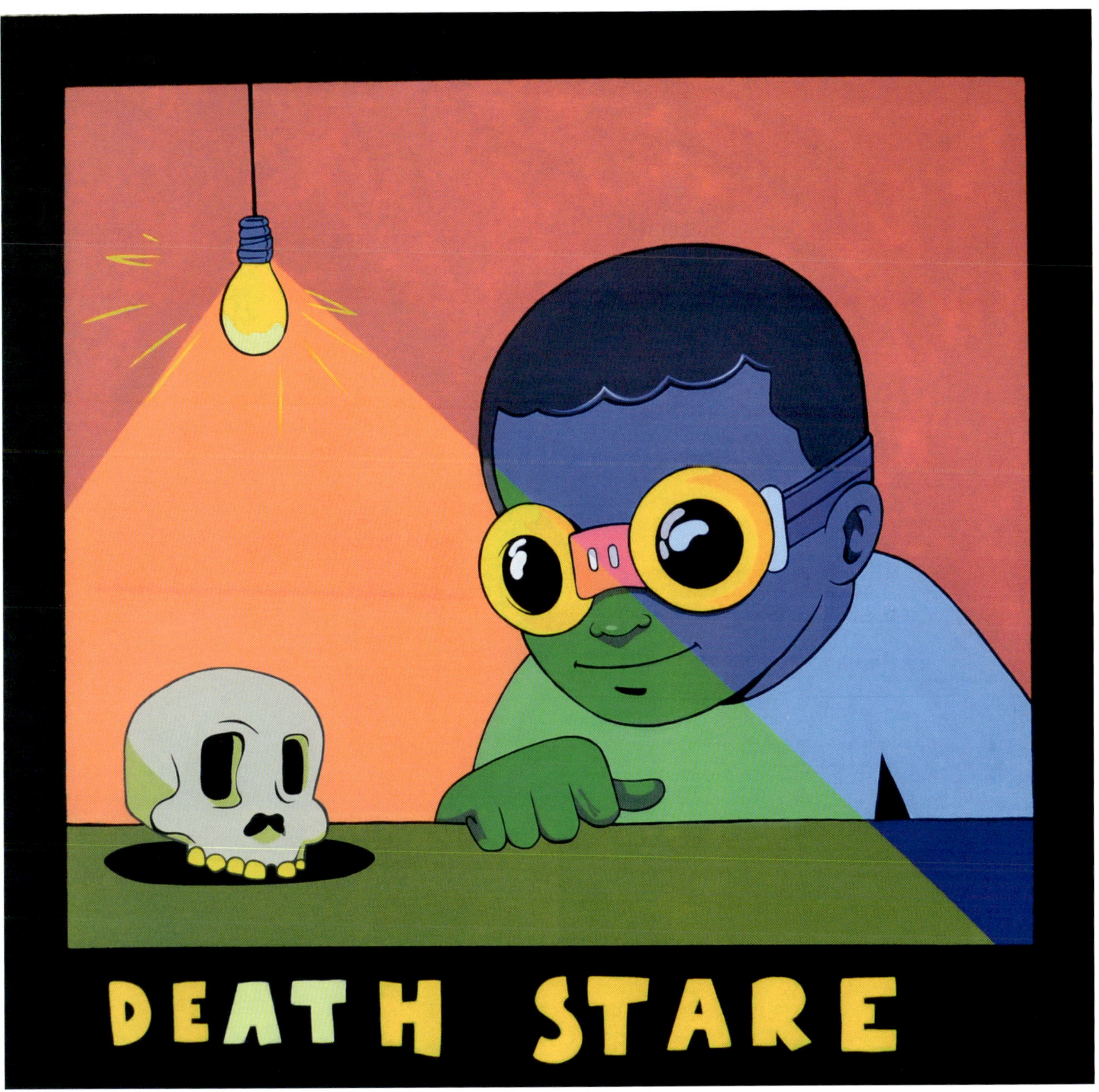

Death Stare

Mixed media on canvas, 32 x 32 inches, 2018

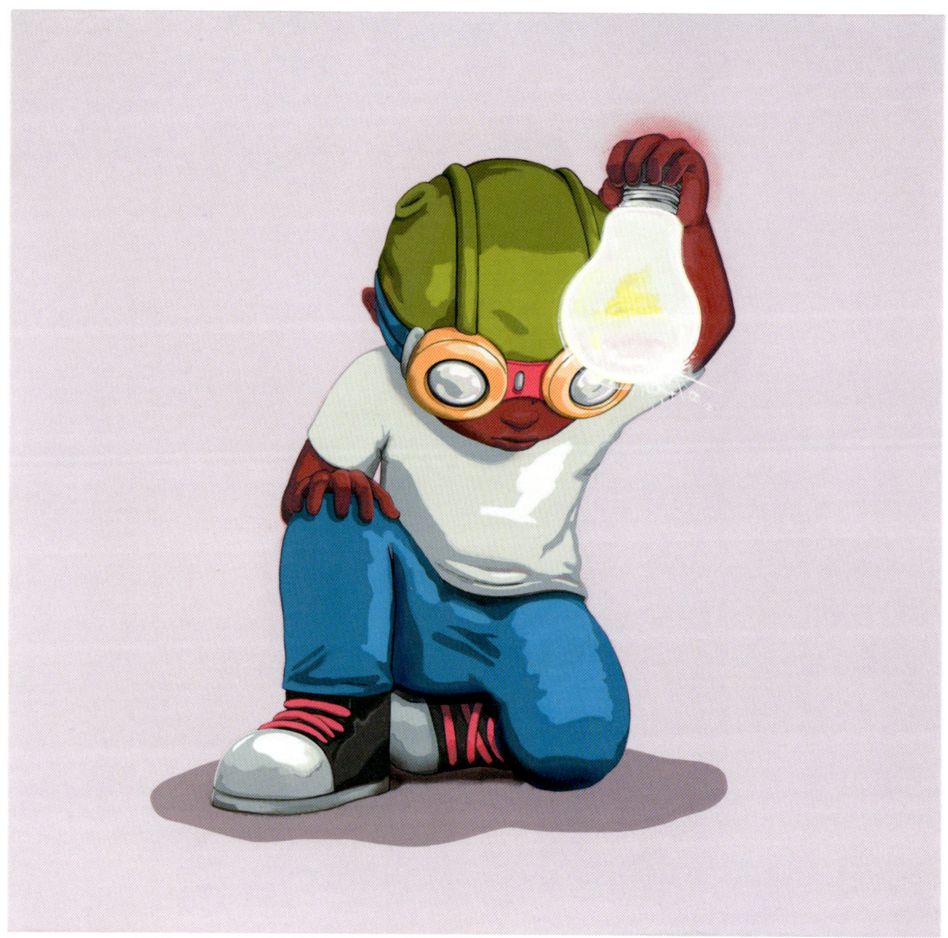

(Above)
The Ultra Lumen Pt. 1
Mixed media on canvas
48 x 62 inches
2021

(Right)
The Ultra Lumen Pt. 2
Mixed media on canvas
48 x 48 inches
2021

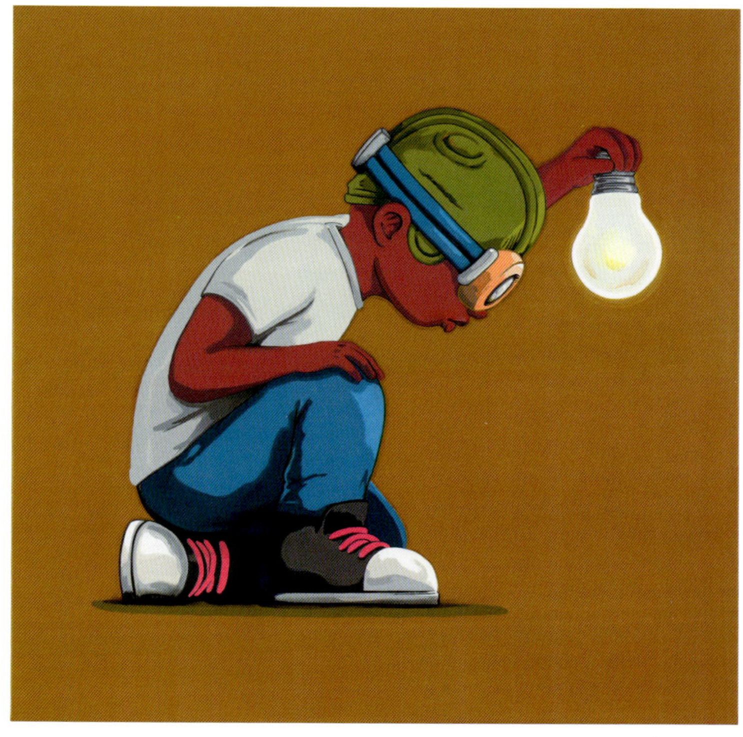

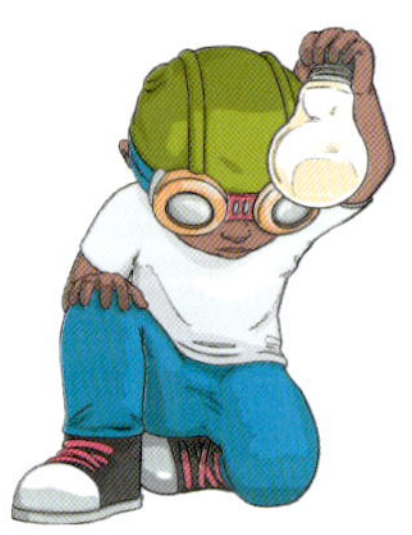

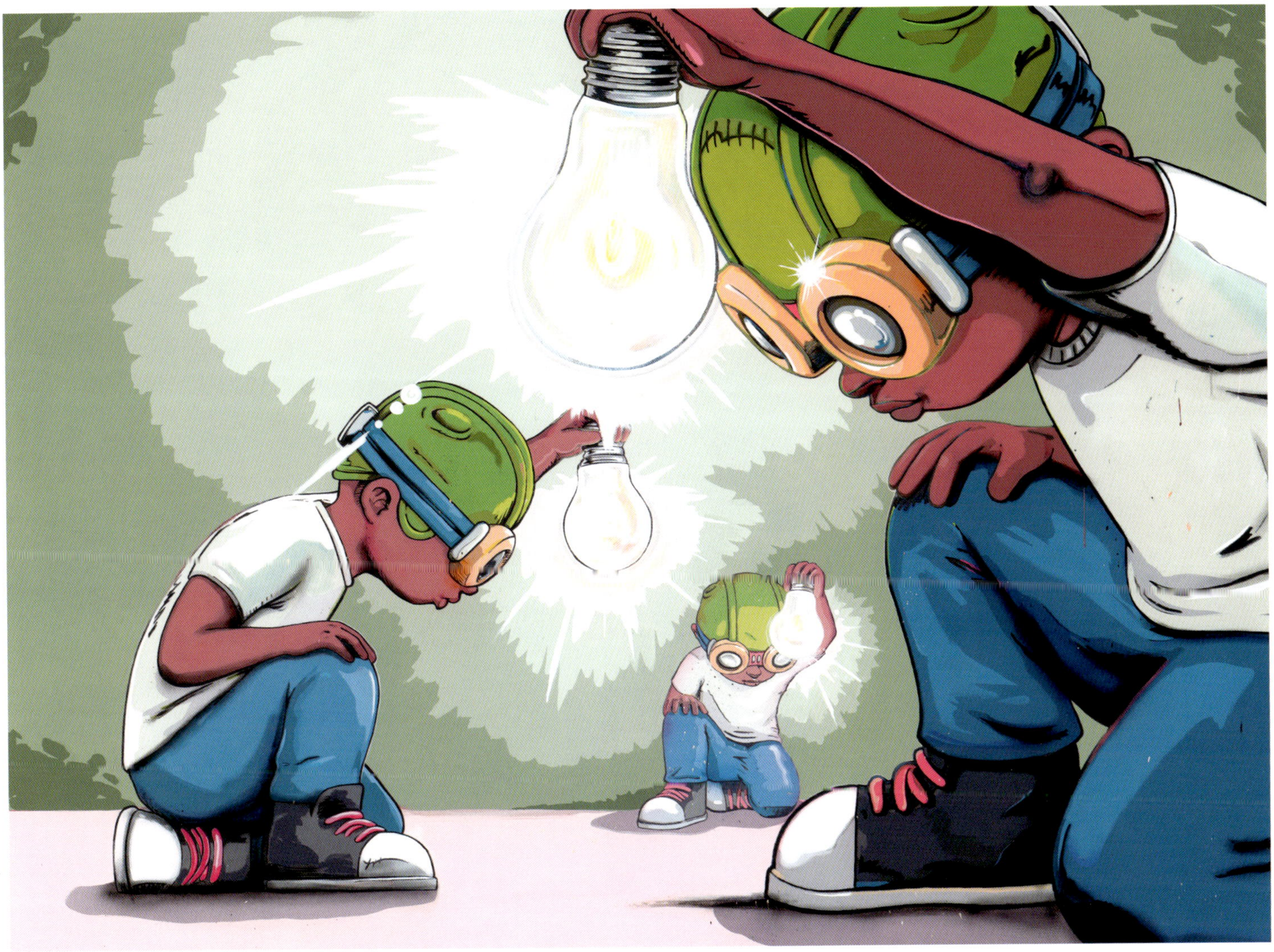

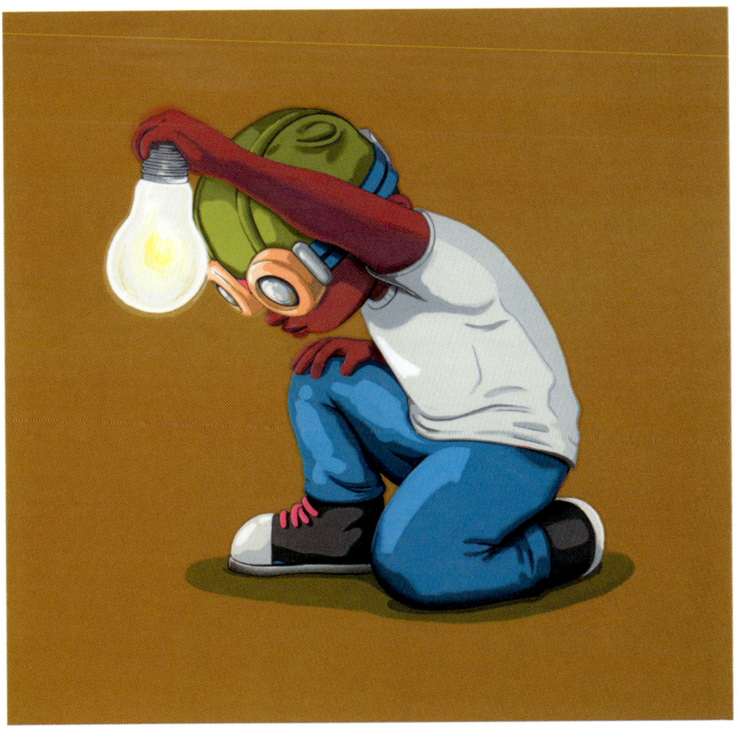

(Left)
The Ultra Lumen Pt. 3
Mixed media
on canvas
48 x 48 inches
2021

(Above)
Lumenaires
Acrylic, pastel,
and spray paint
on canvas
80 x 60 inches
2021

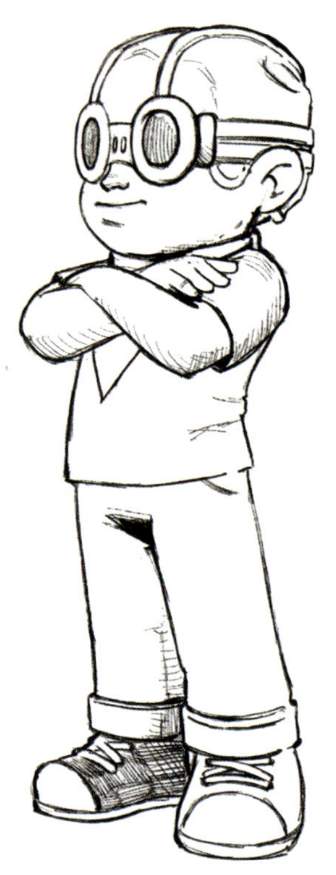

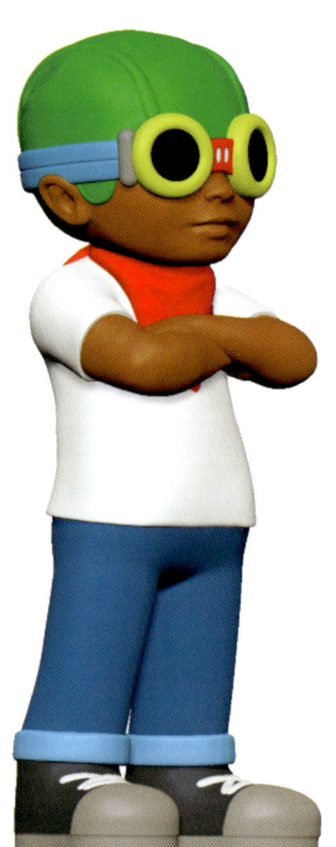

(Opposite) ***Last (Great) Debate***

Mixed media on canvas, 36 x 48 inches, 2020

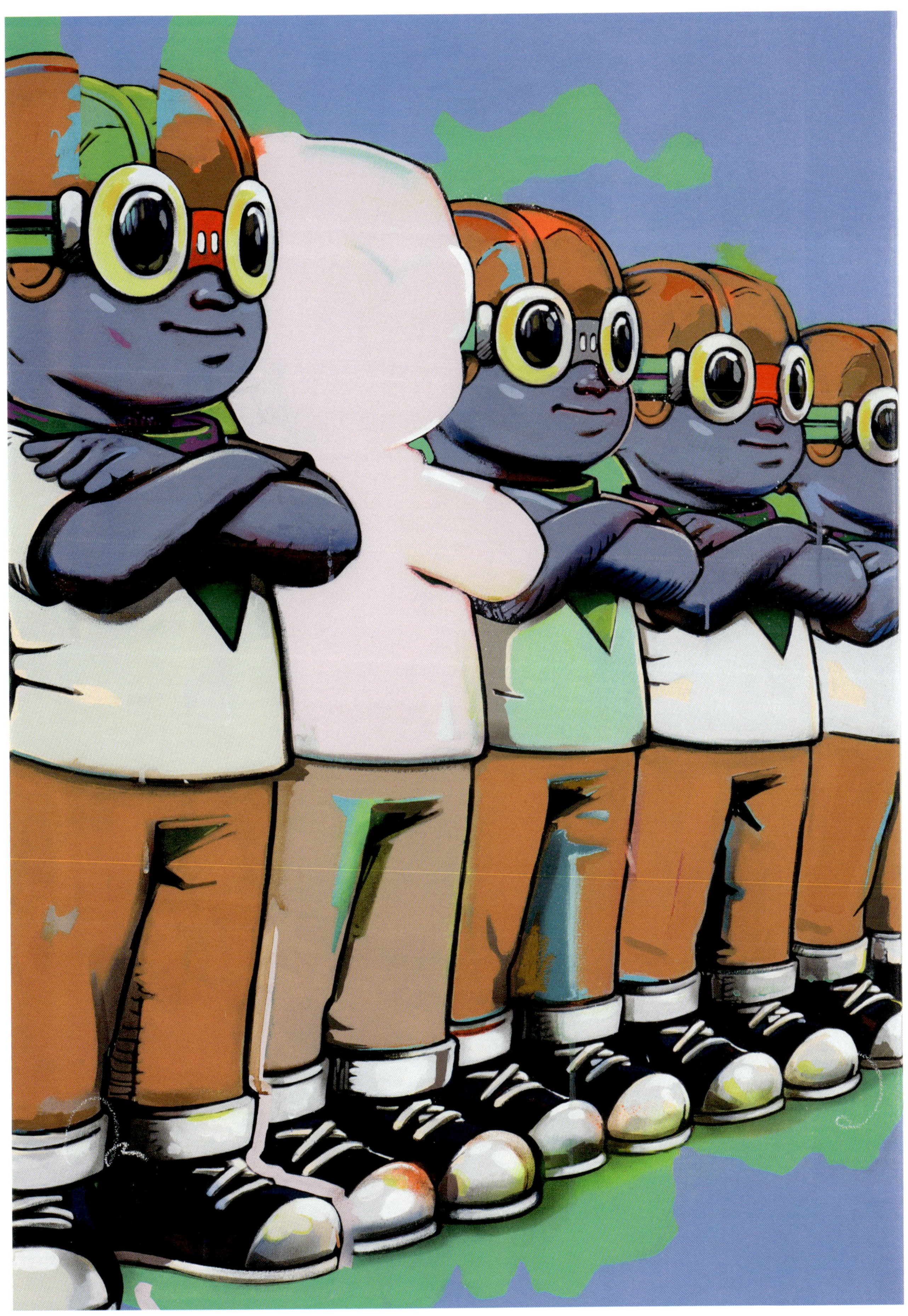

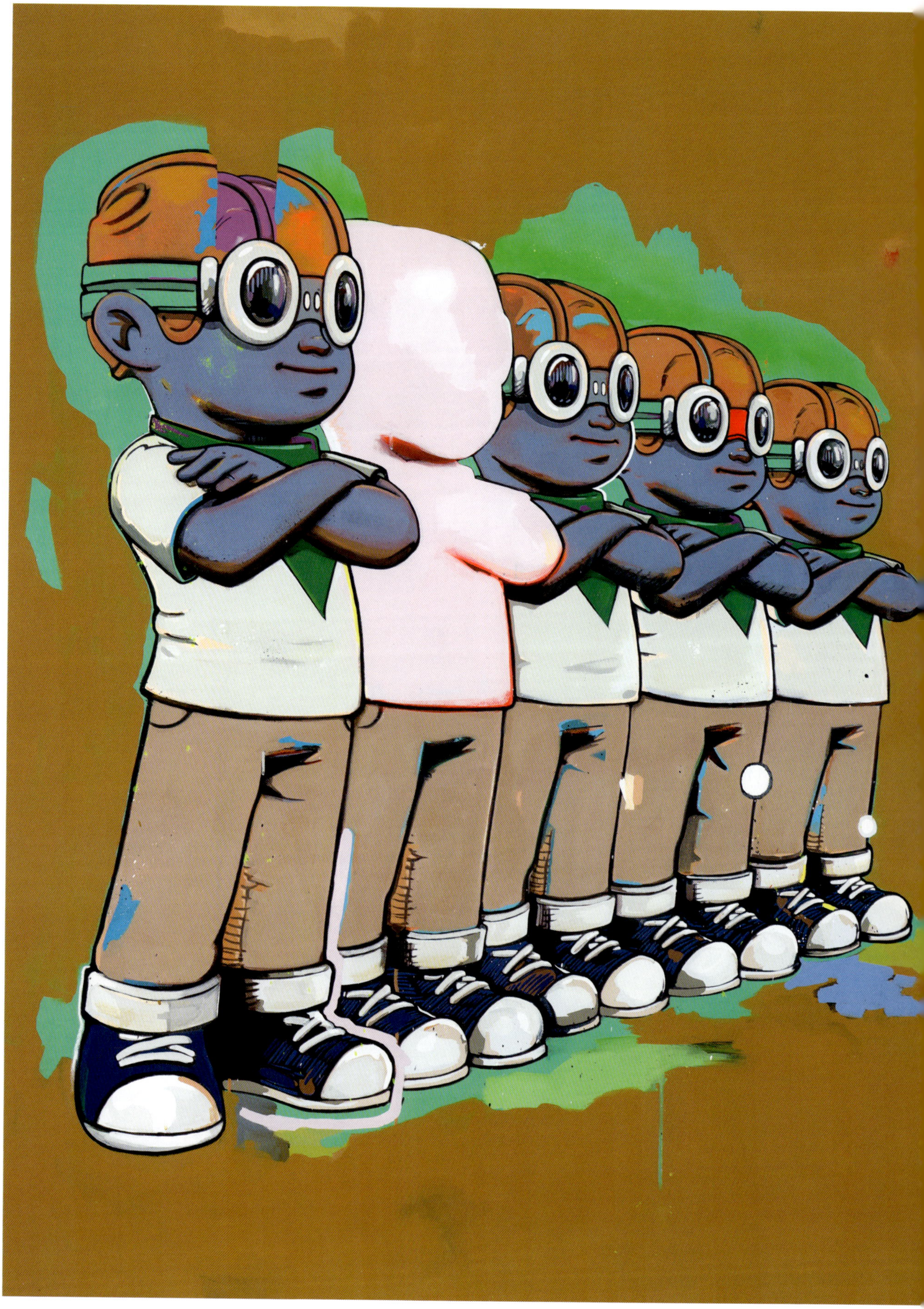

Special Episode of the Great Debate

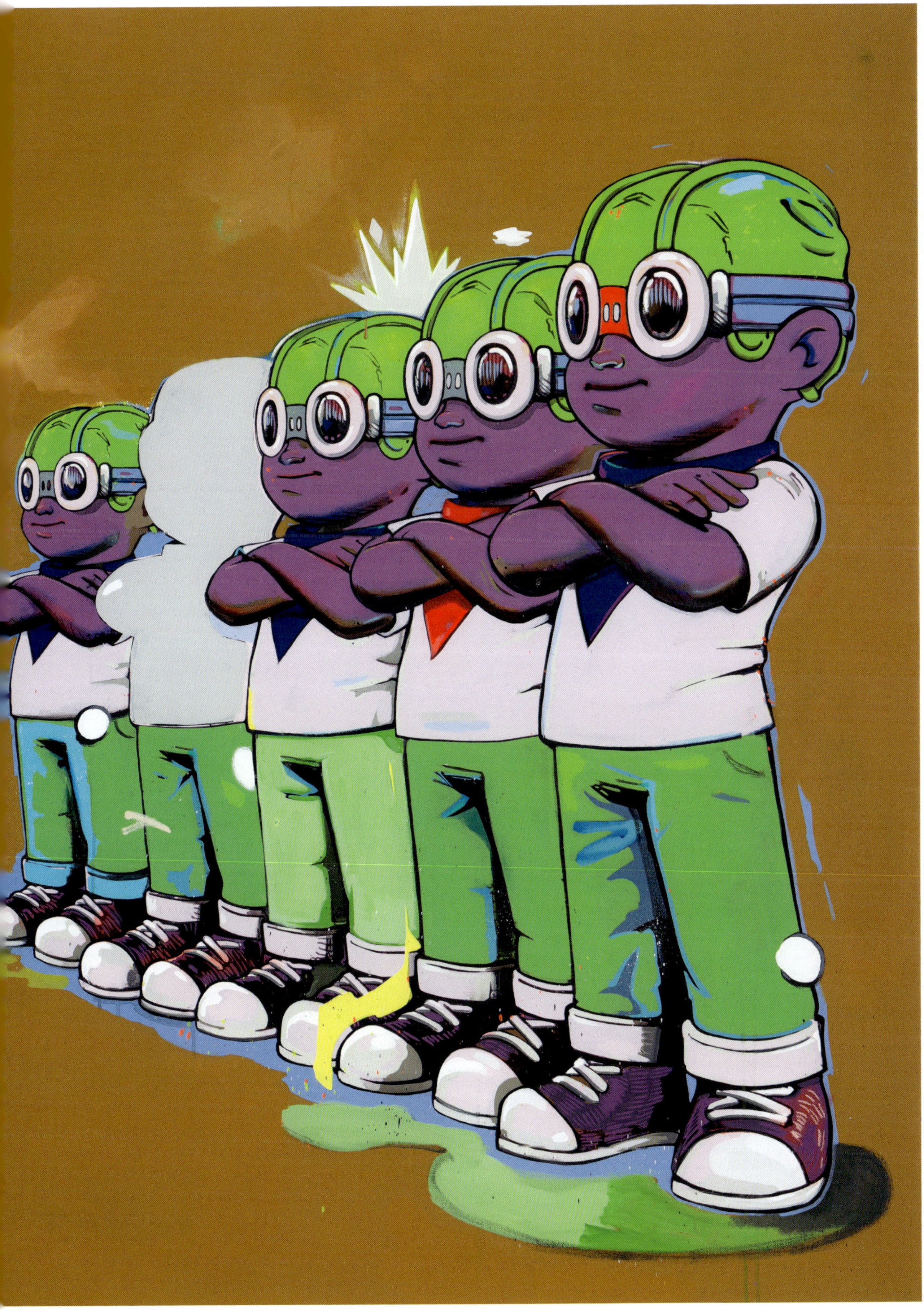

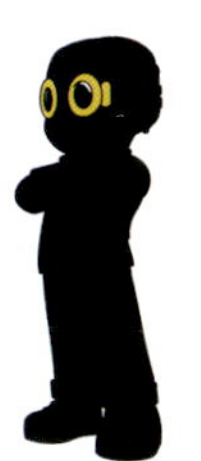

Mixed media on canvas, 85 x 65 inches, 2021

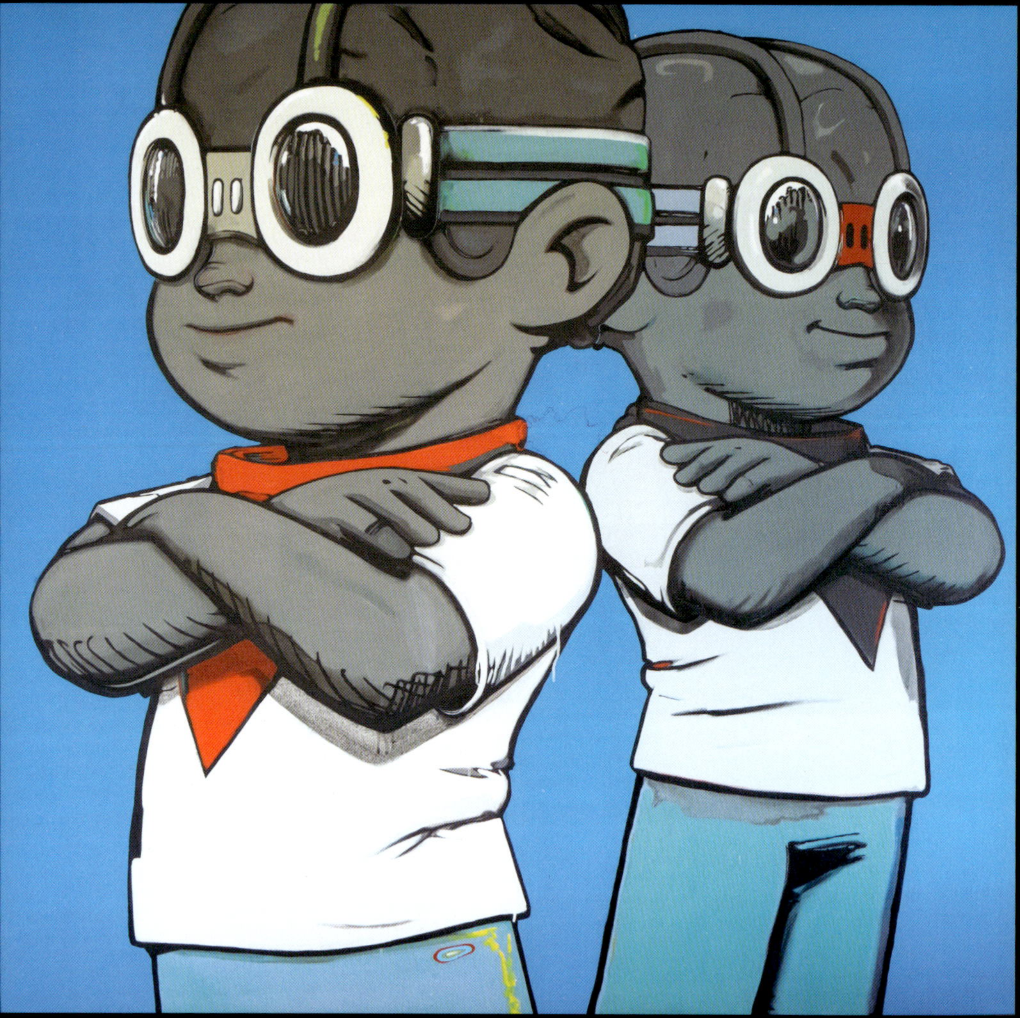

(Above)
Black Boys with Arms Crossed
Mixed media
on canvas
60 x 60 inches
2019

(Right)
Great Debate (Bboy Stance)
Mixed media
on canvas
40 x 48 inches
2019

(Opposite)
Solo
Acrylic on
canvas
48 x 60 inches
2020

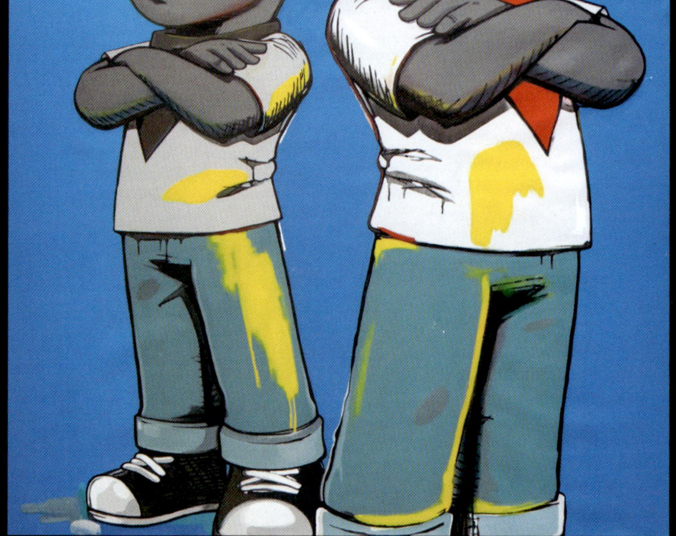

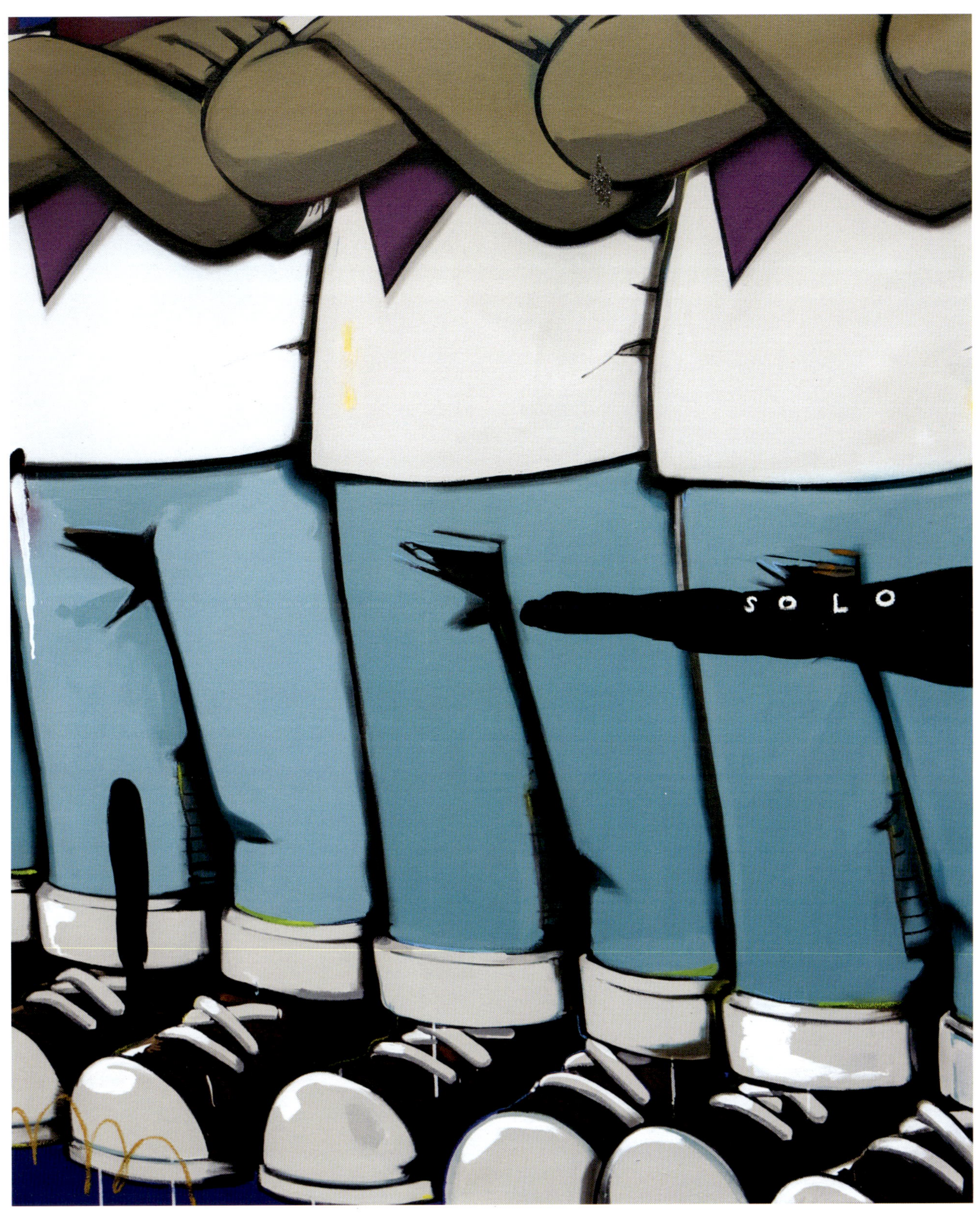
SOLO

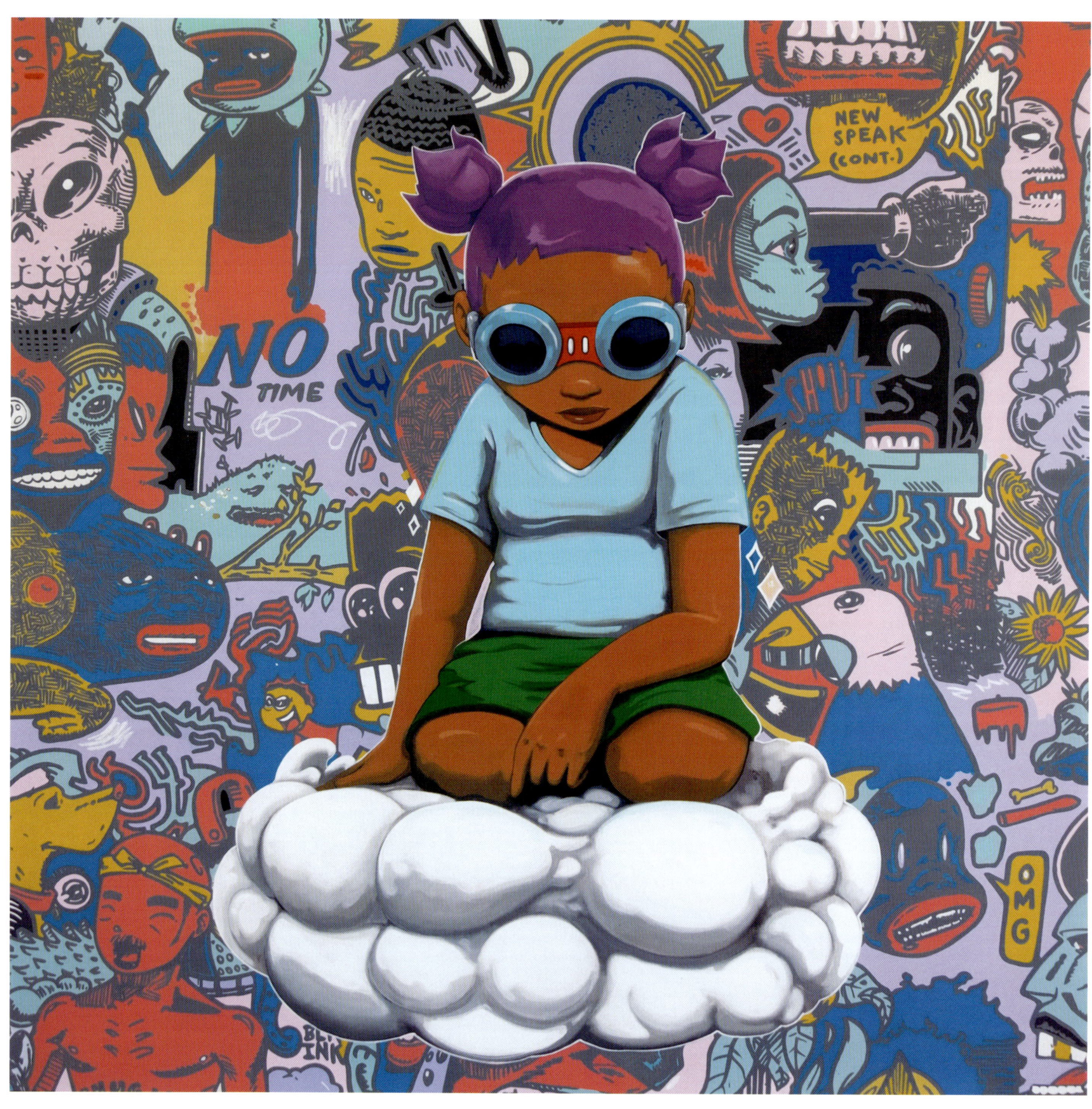

Lil Mama
as Gaia
MIxed media
on canvas
50 x 50 inches
2019

LIL MAMA

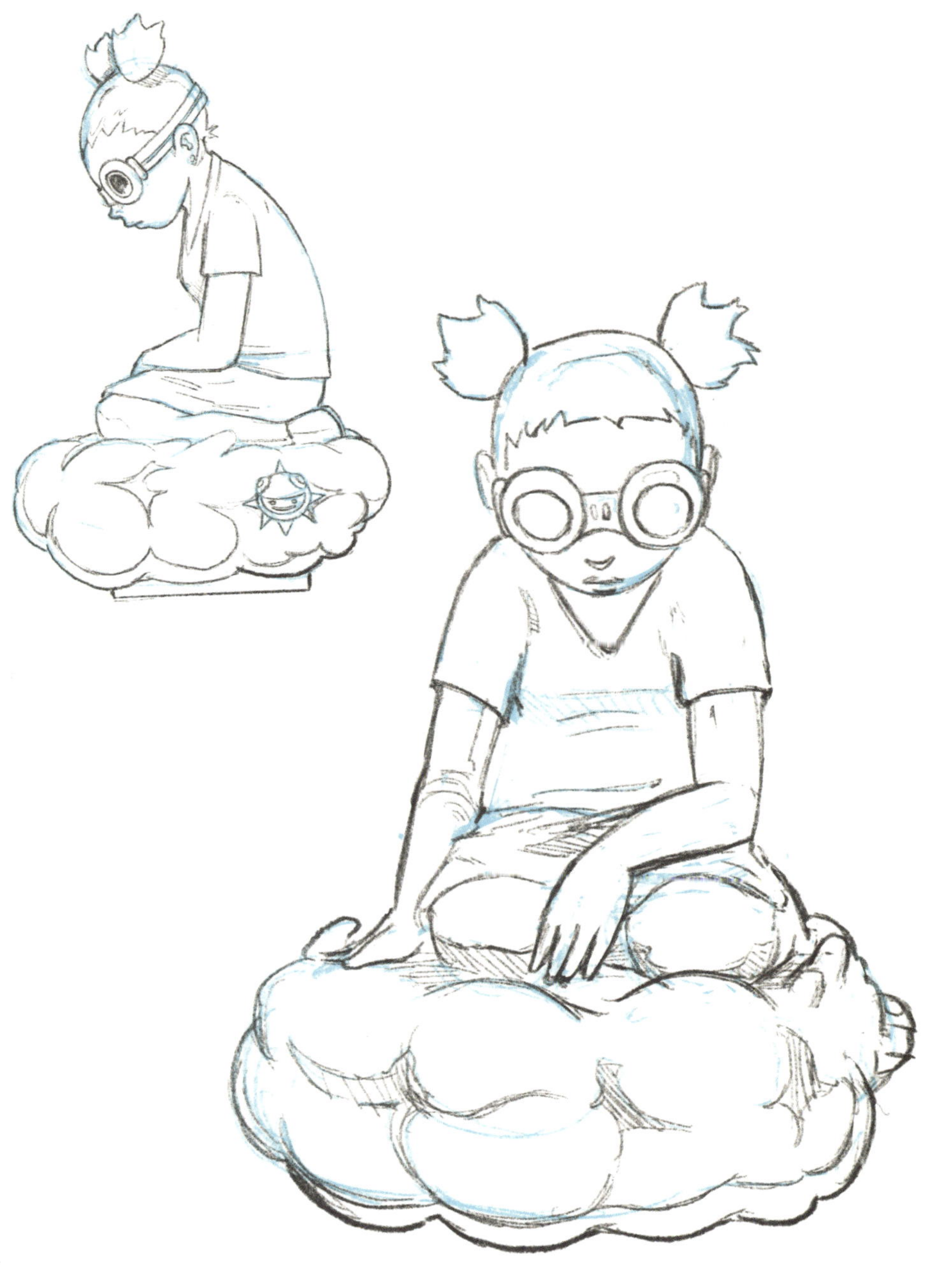

Who are Flyboy and Lil Mama? They're the readers. They embody what it is to dream and imagine. To have that feeling of being a kid with limitless potential. We get that beat out of us as we get older, and I wanted to encapsulate that feeling. It was not so much about building characters but about capturing a feeling. You put the goggles on and you're transported. Yesterday's losers are today's CEOs. As a kid (tall, Black, from Chicago) I wasn't expected to be into the things I was. I wasn't allowed to dream or have an imagination beyond what I was. I masked myself in order to not be labeled weird. It was taboo to be into art. Social media has given weight to art and the artist. But hell no, when I was young it wasn't cool to be into things. You got dogged out for having an imagination. Flyboy and Lil Mama are part of my own personal iconography.

—HEBRU BRANTLEY

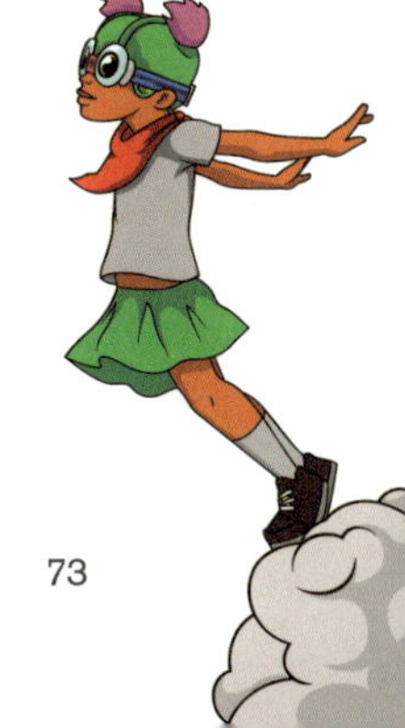

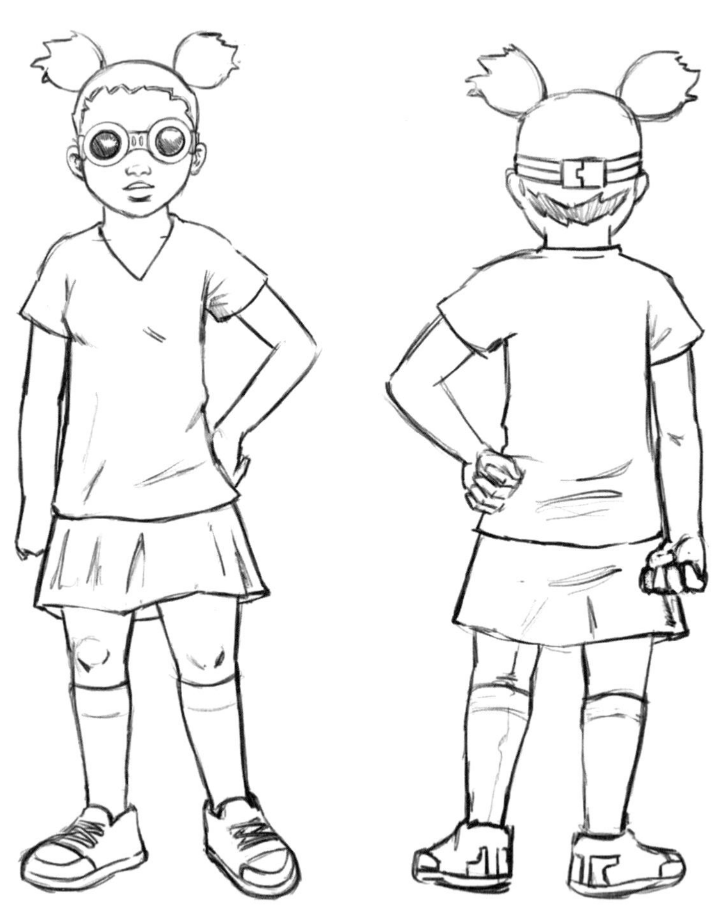

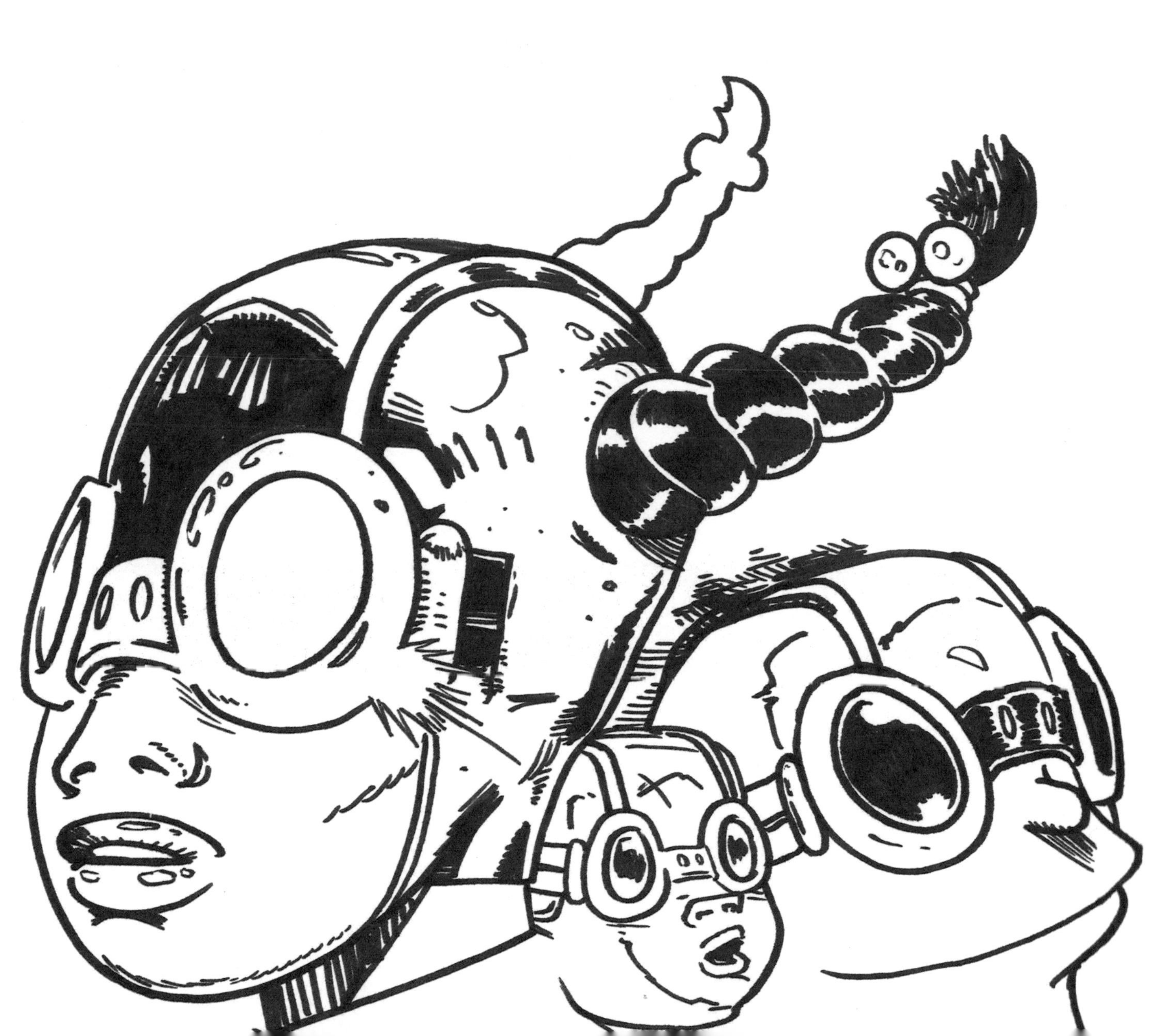

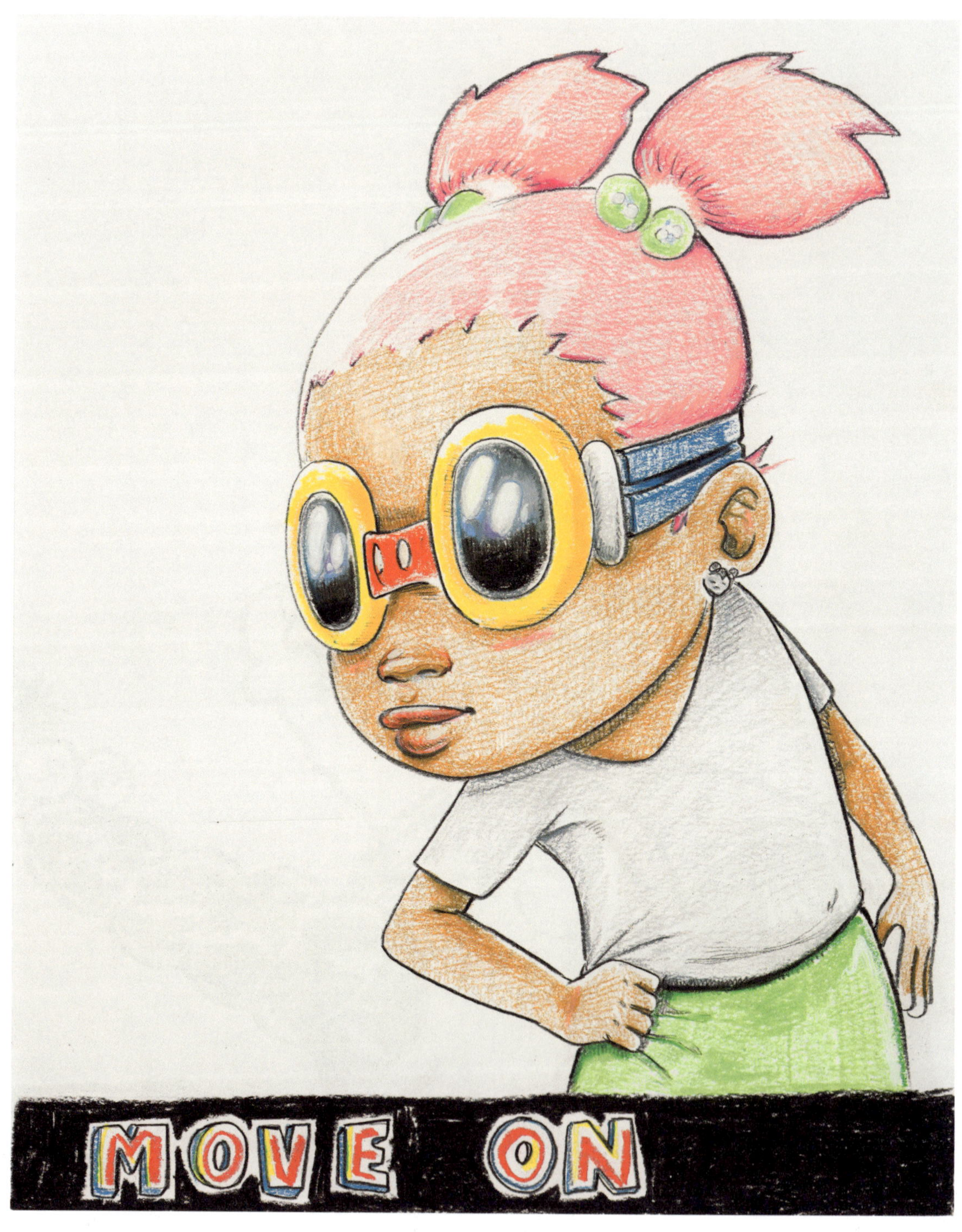
MOVE ON

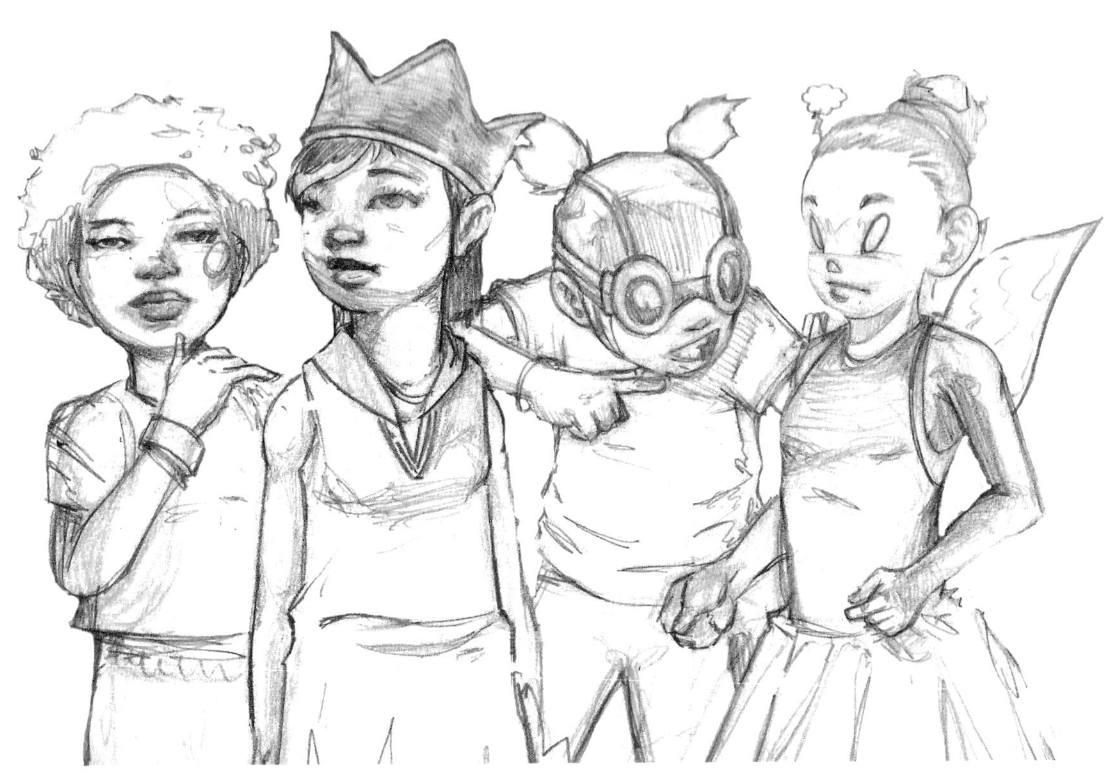

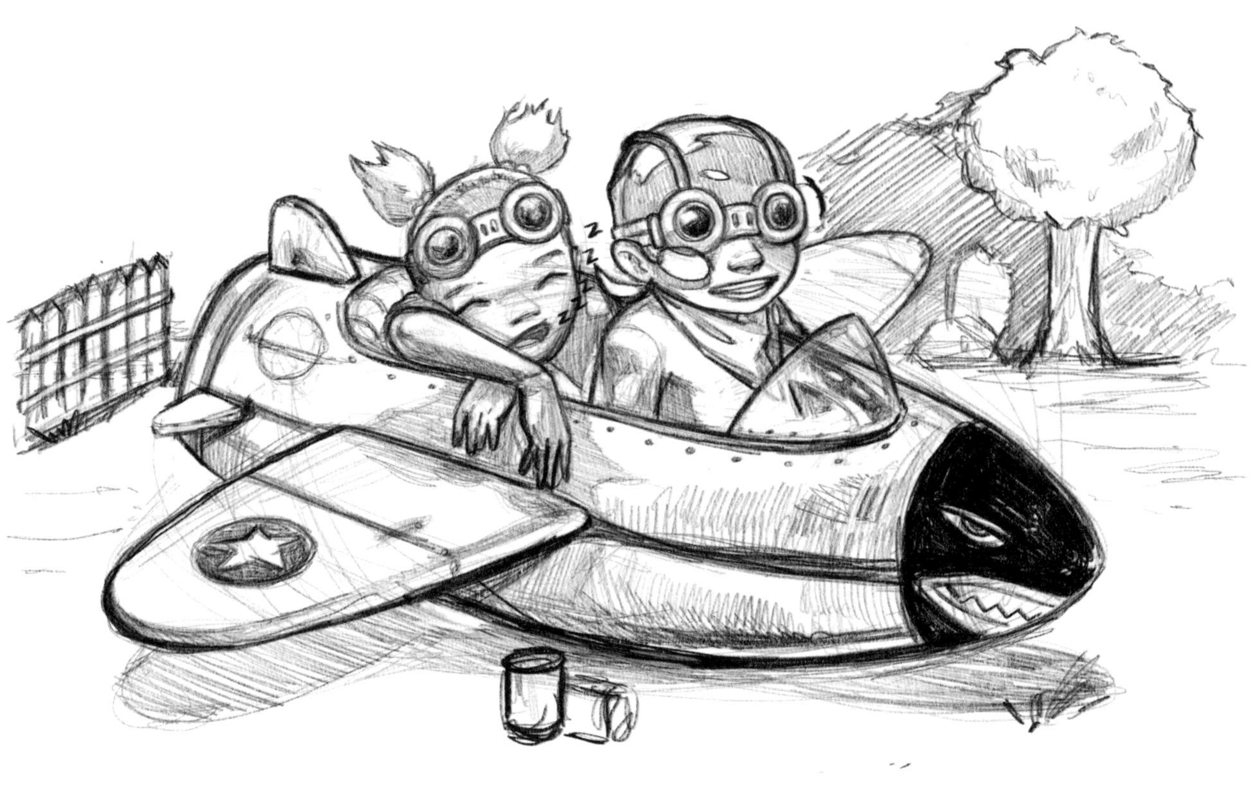

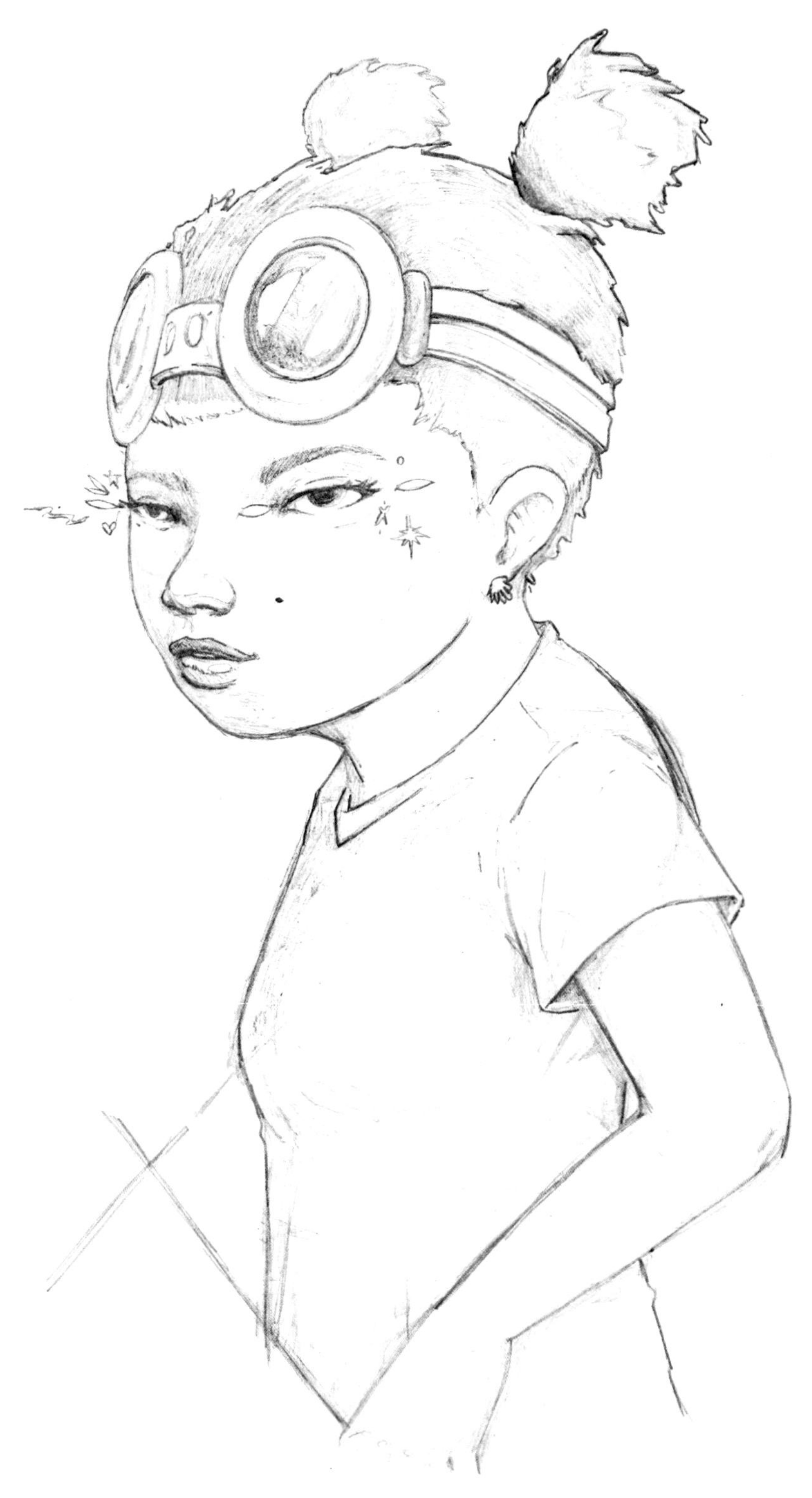

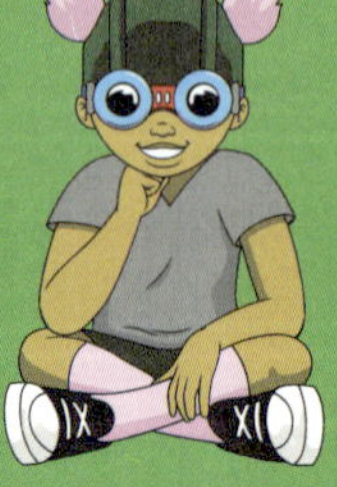

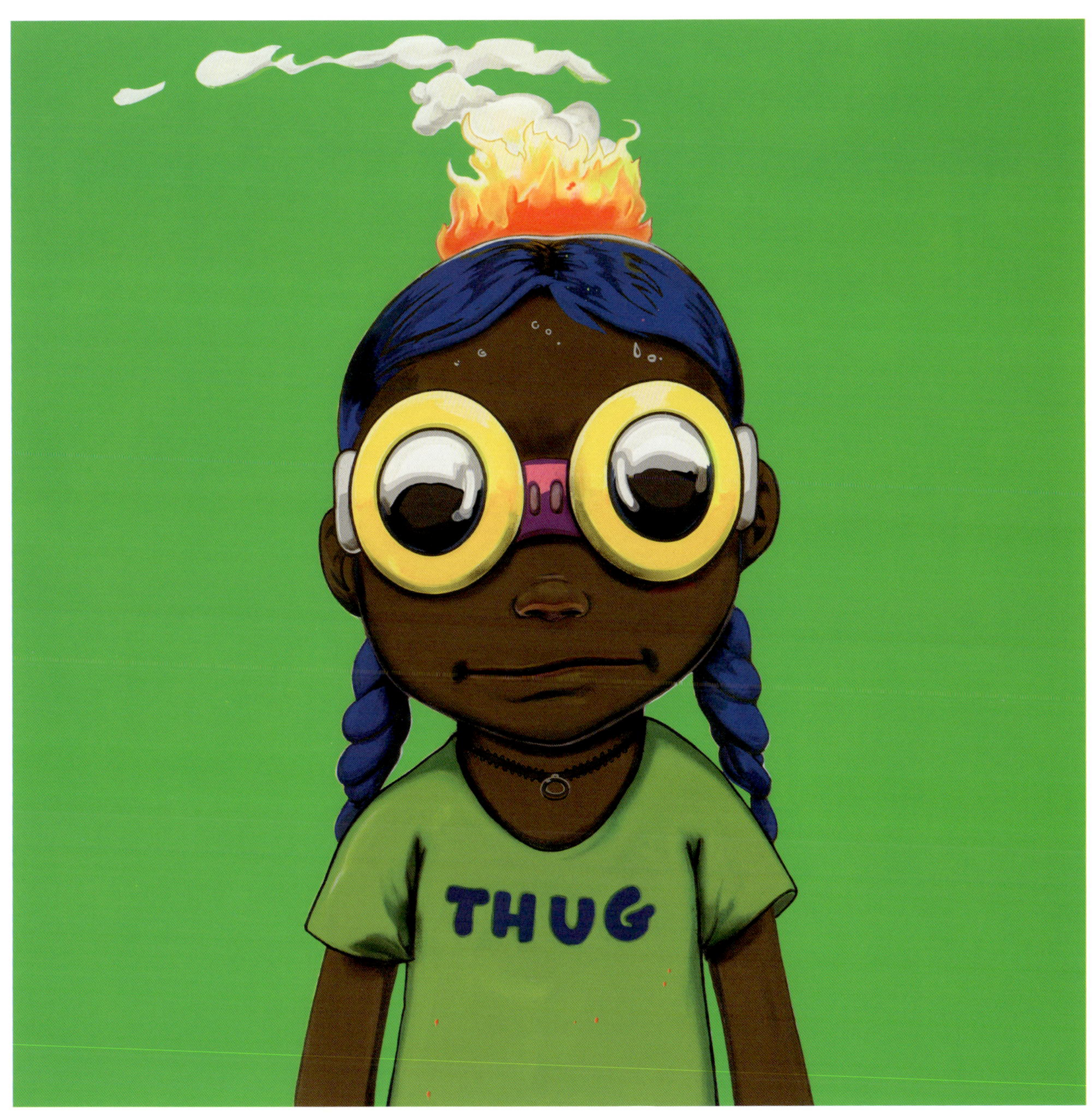

I'm Fine, Why'd You Ask Pt. 2
Mixed media
on canvas
36 x 36 inches
2021

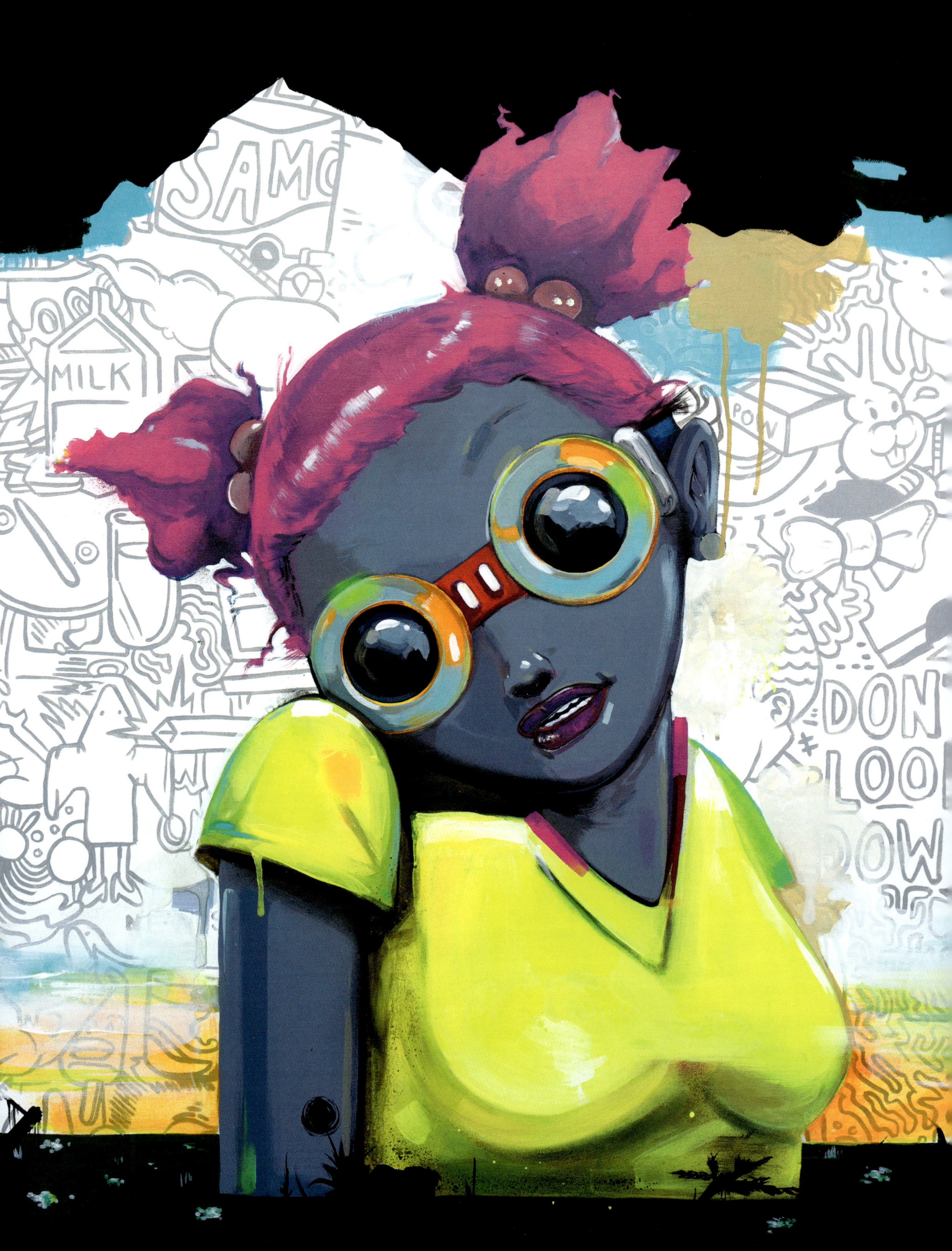
SAM
MILK
DON
LOO
DOW

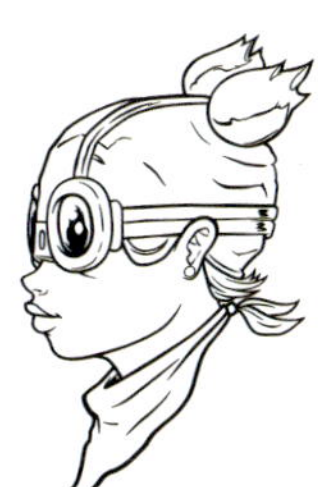

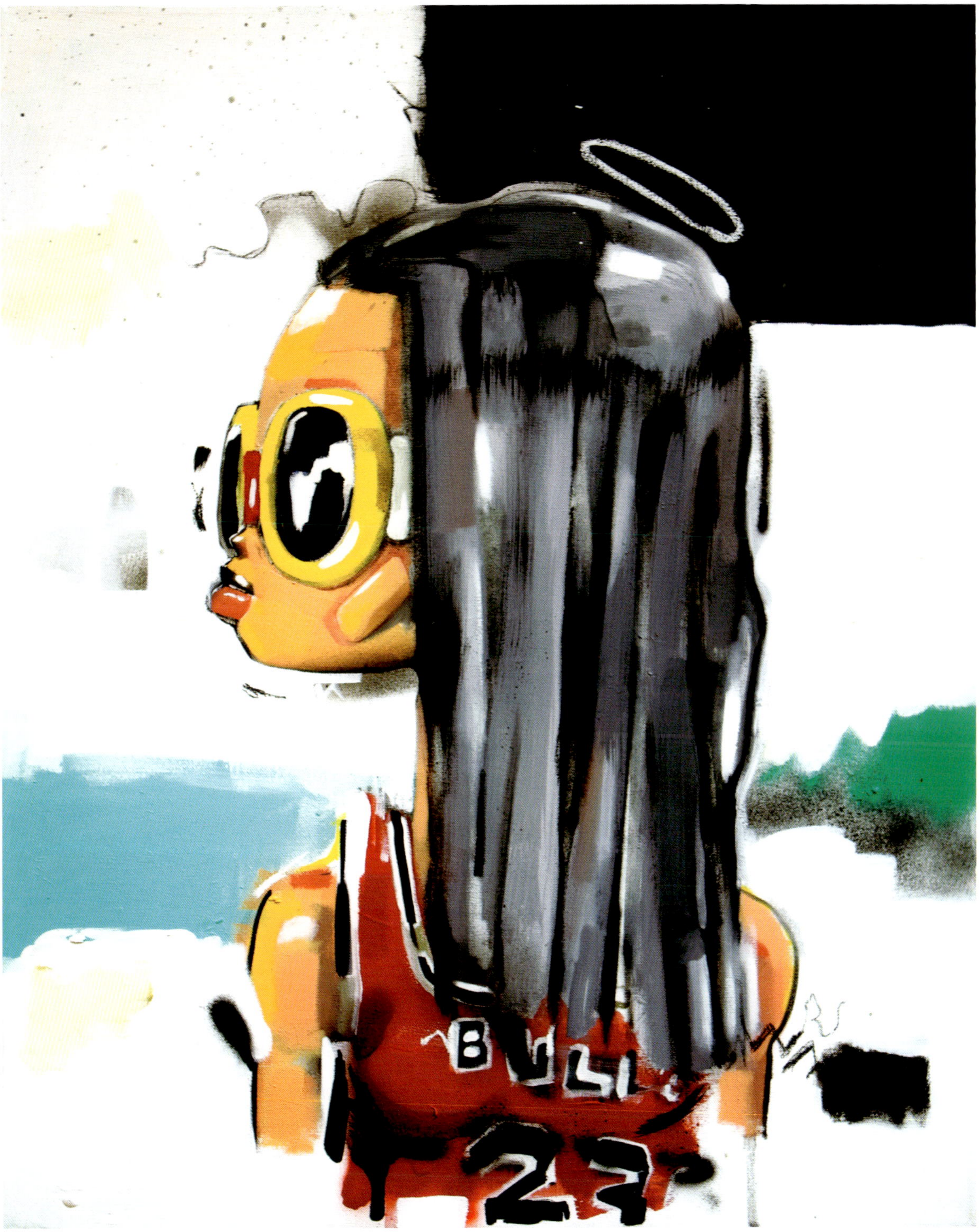

(Opposite)
No Gardens Pt. 2
Mixed media
on canvas
30 x 40 inches
2016

(Above)
Just Hold On
Mixed media
on canvas
2013

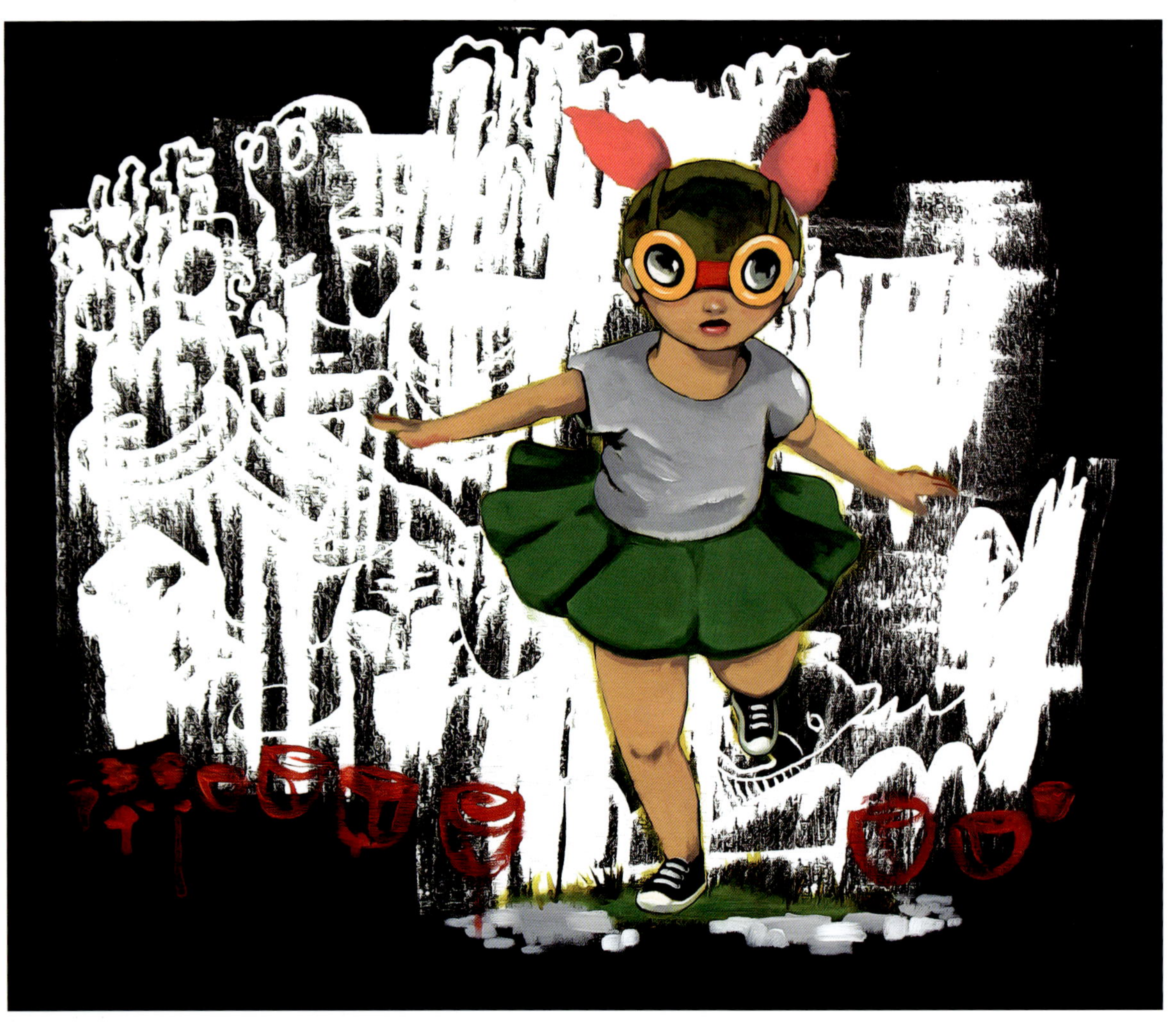

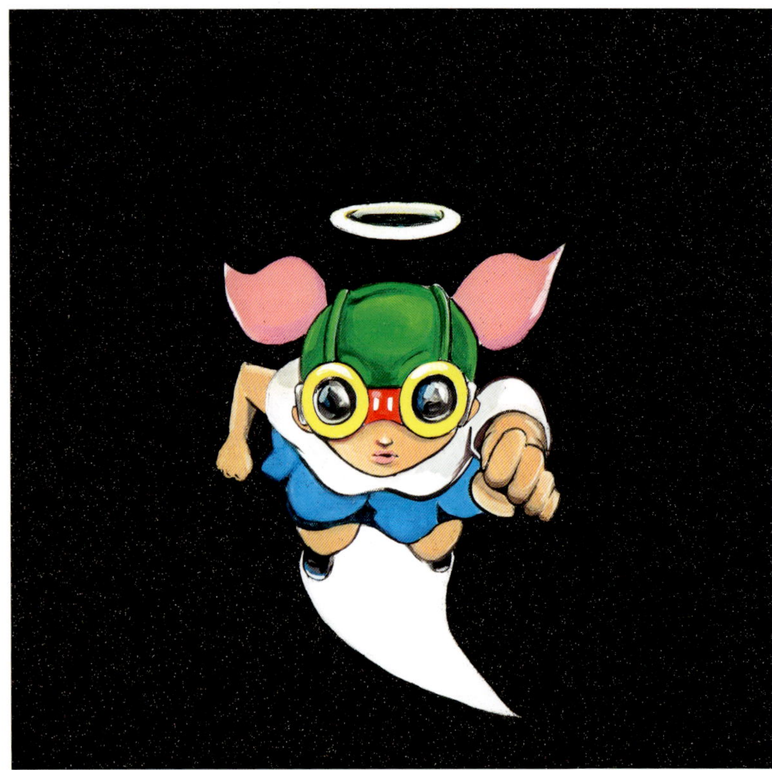

(Above)
Little Miss Sunshine
Mixed media on canvas
2014

(Left)
Charge
Oil and diamond dust on canvas
2013

Another Girl, Another Star
Mixed media
and diamond dust
on canvas
24 x 48 inches
2016

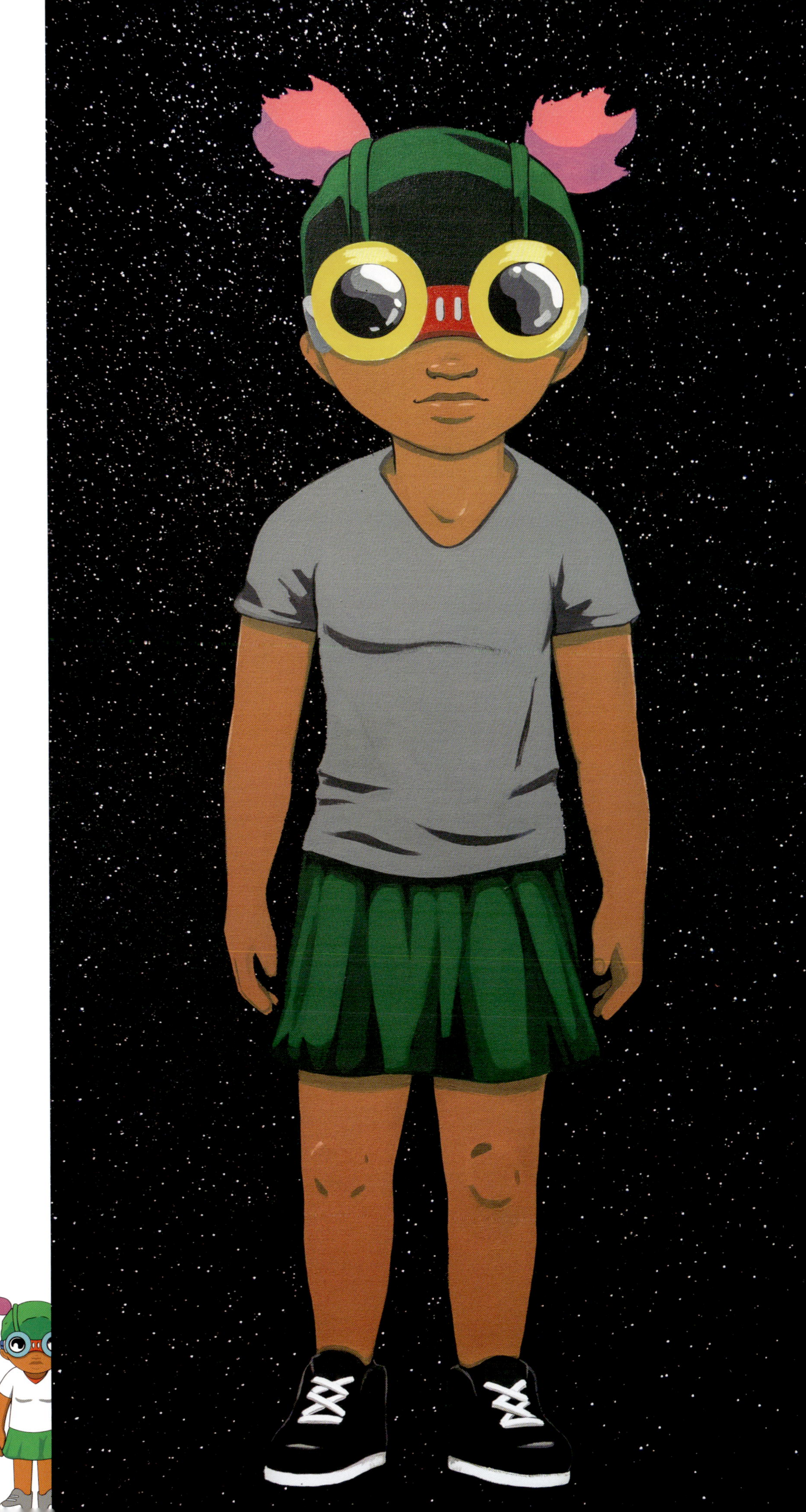

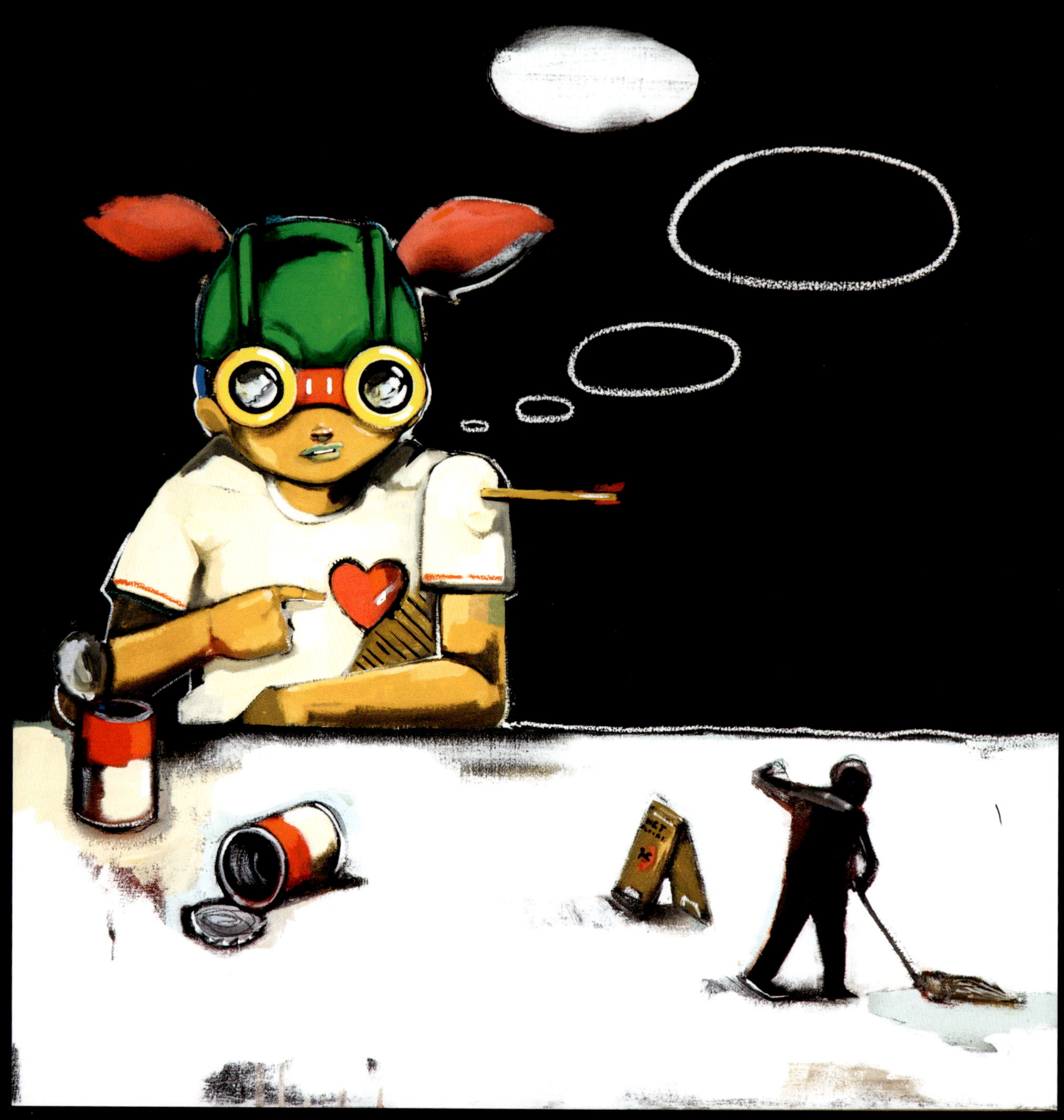

After Love
Mixed media
on canvas
30 x 30 inches
2014

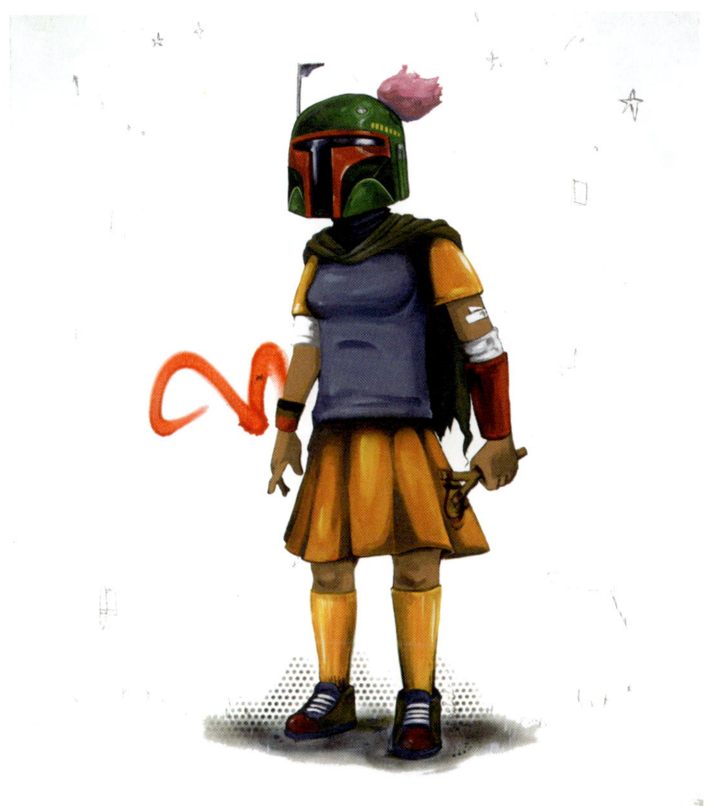

Fett
Mixed media
on canvas
30 x 22.5 inches
2016

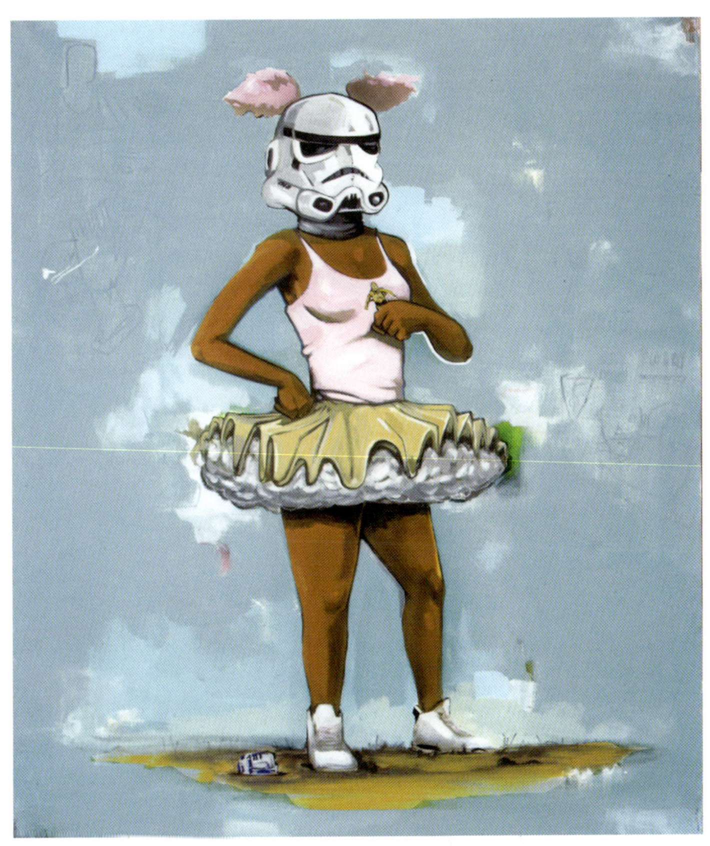

These Aren't the Droids...
Mixed media
on canvas
30 x 22.5 inches
2016

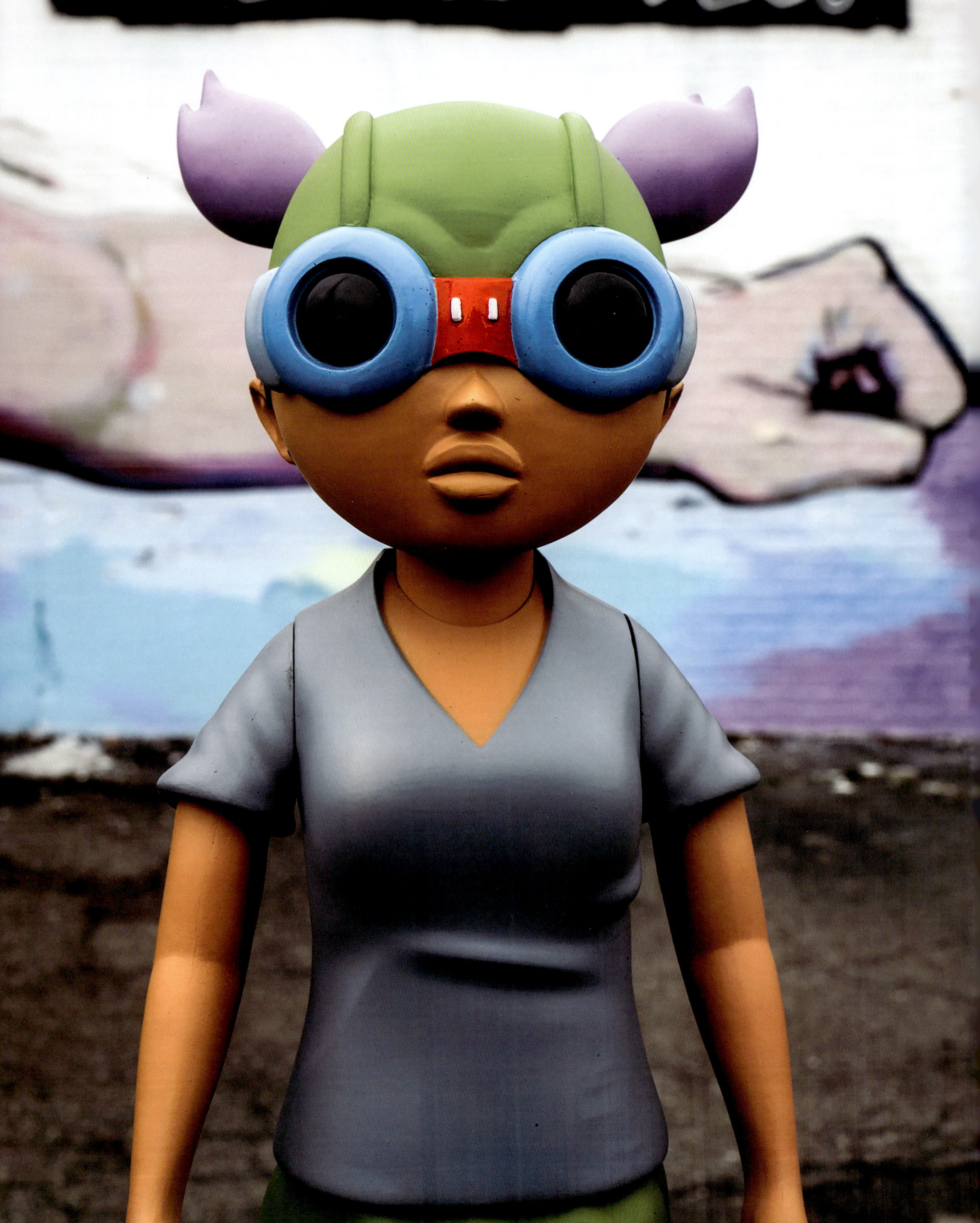
BLK GRL FLY.

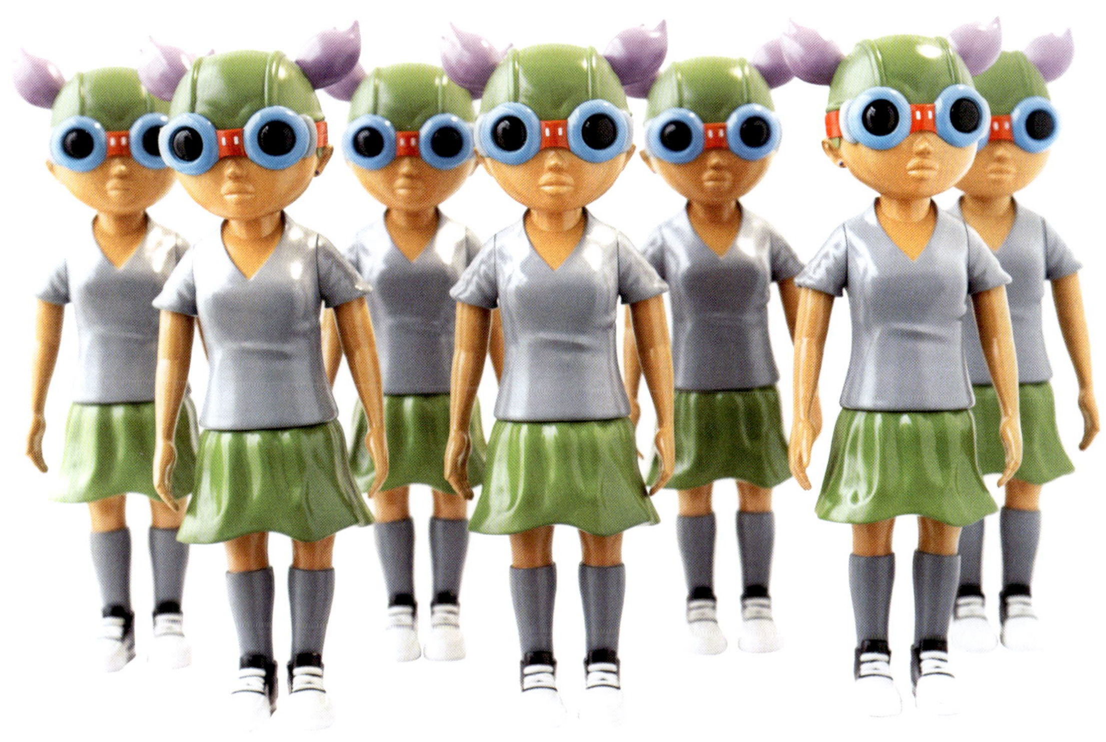

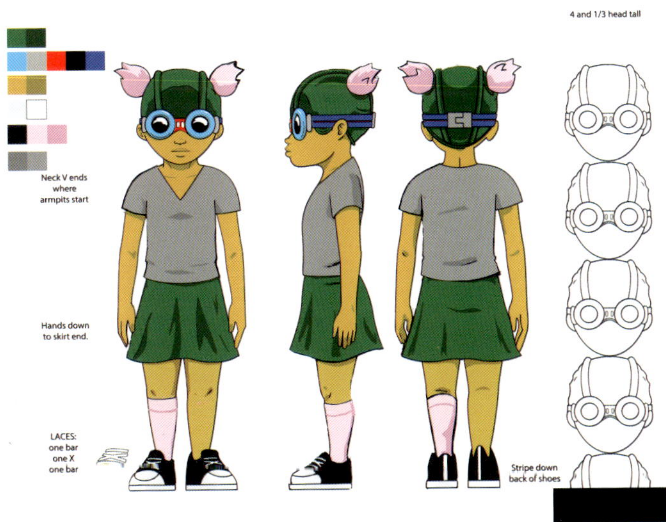

Lil Mama first-edition figure in matte and candy paint. Edition of 1,000, released in 2016.

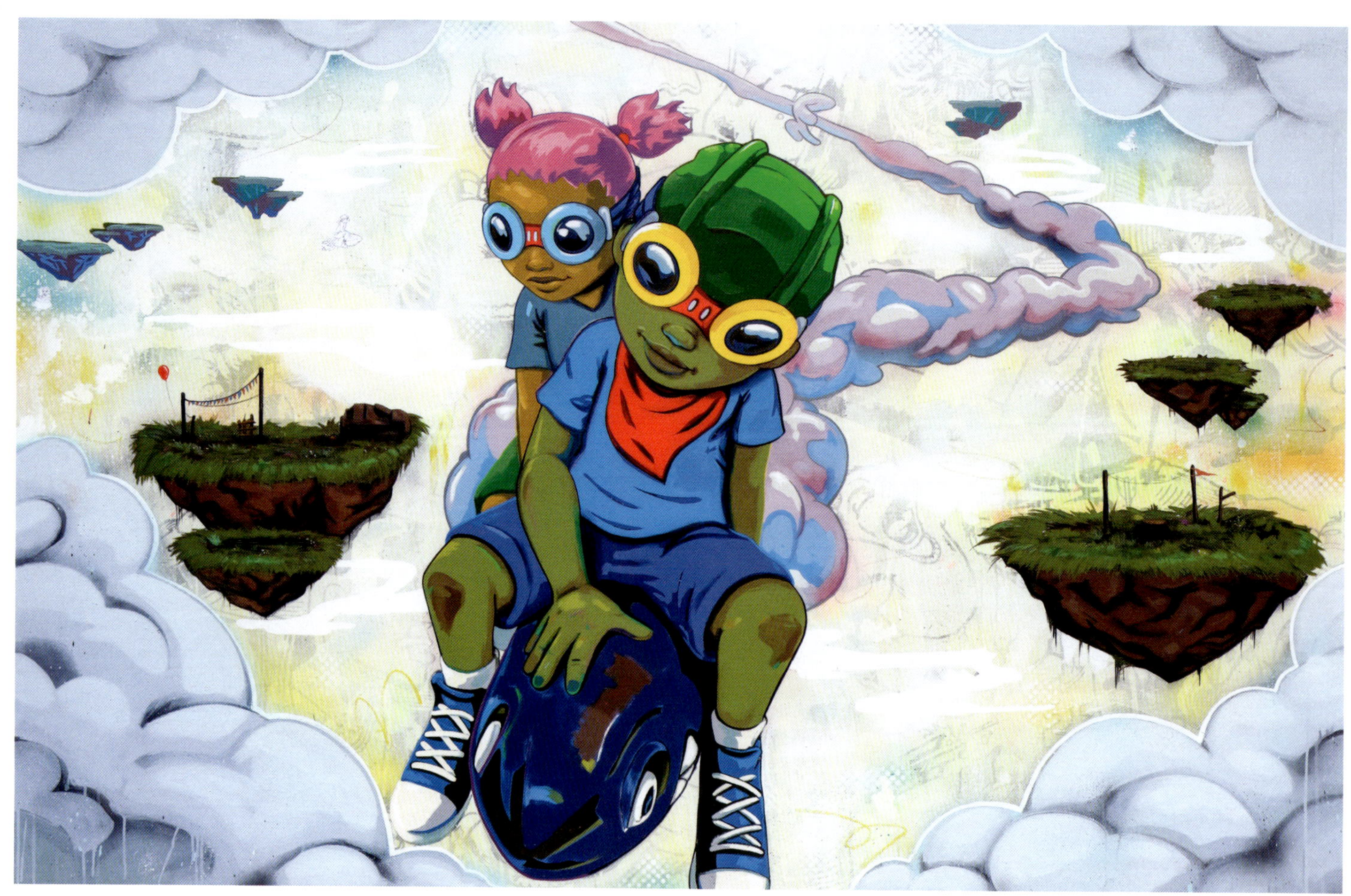

On to the Other Side
Mixed media on canvas
48 x 72 inches
2020

"HEBRU BRANTLEY IS A MAKER OF WORLDS. HE HAS CREATED AN ALTERNATE REALITY WHERE THE NEW MASTERS OF THE UNIVERSE ARE YOUNG AFRICAN AMERICAN CHILDREN. HEBRU NOT ONLY GIVES HIS CHARACTERS AGENCY BUT PUTS THEM IN POSITIONS OF POWER AND INVITES US TO EXPLORE THEIR WORLD; THE MEEK HAVE INHERITED THE EARTH AND IT IS MAGNIFICENT."

—BISA BUTLER

(Right, from top)

Untitled
Mixed media
on canvas
30 x 30 inches
2020

Best of Luck
Mixed media
on canvas
36 x 36 inches
2017

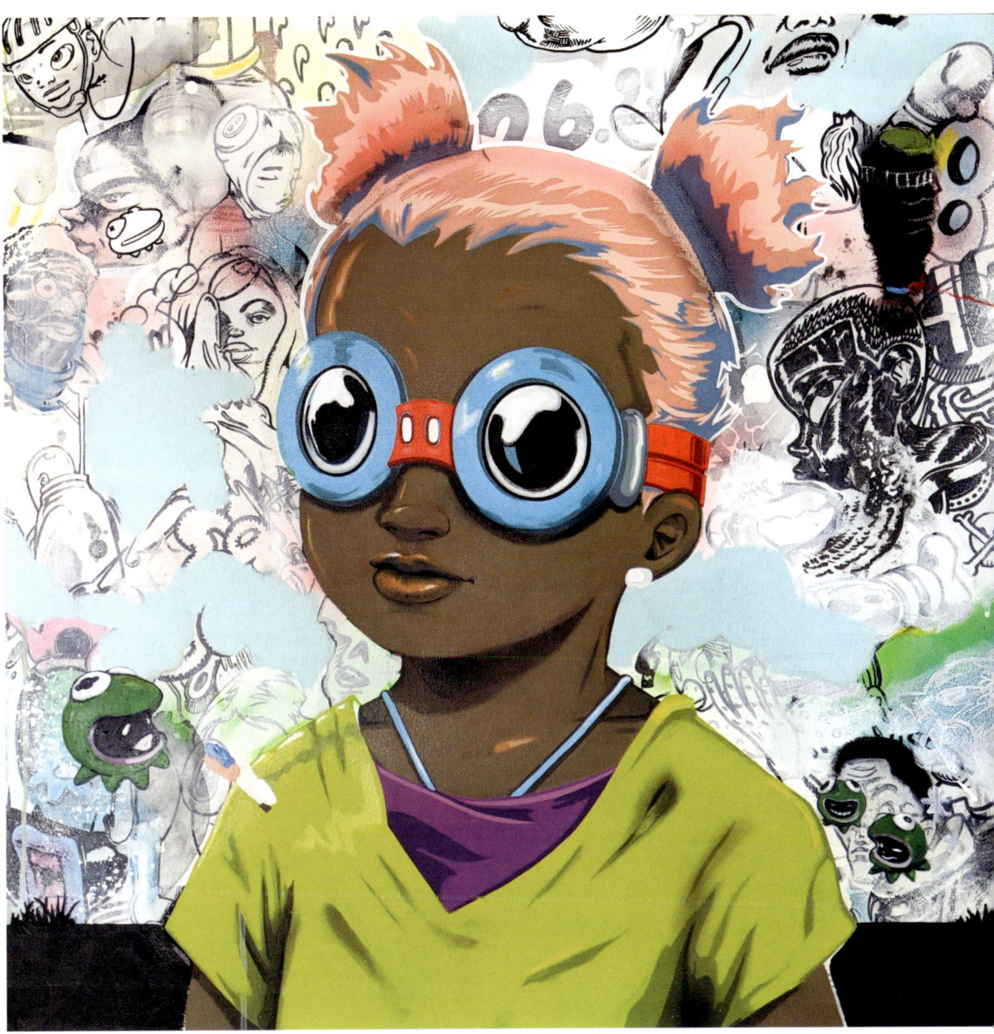

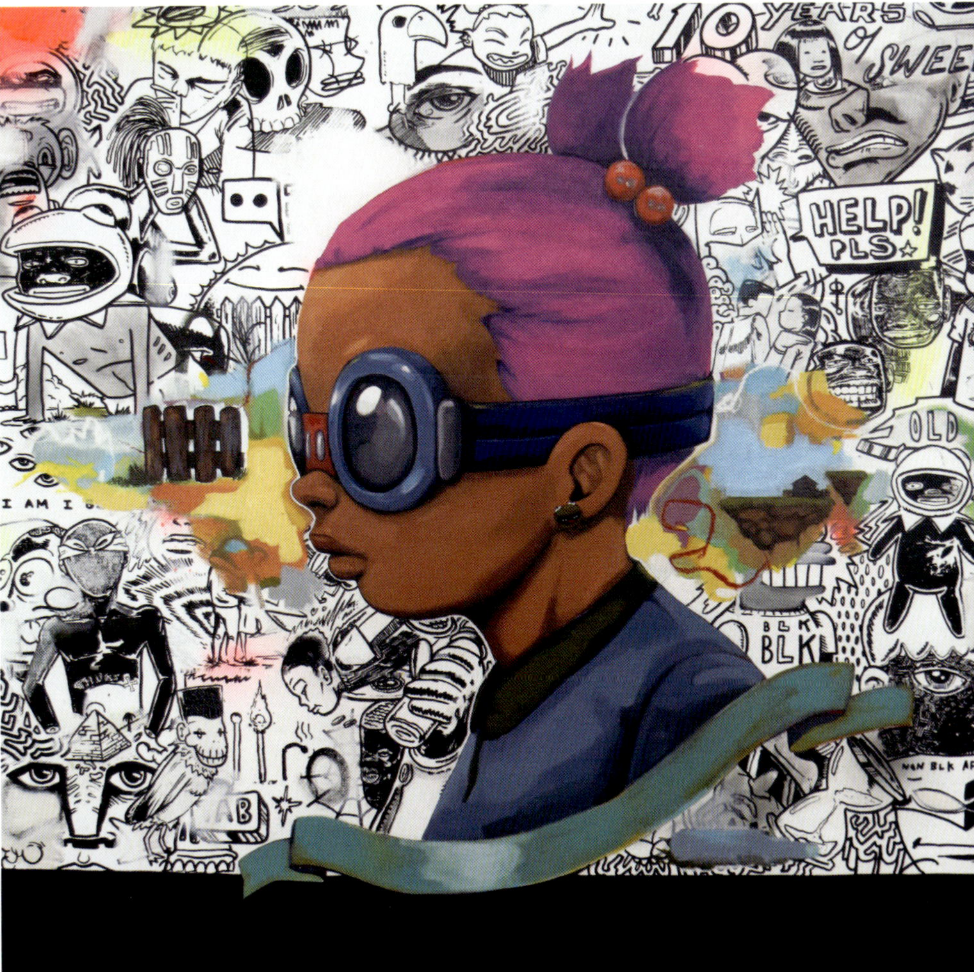

"LIL MAMA"

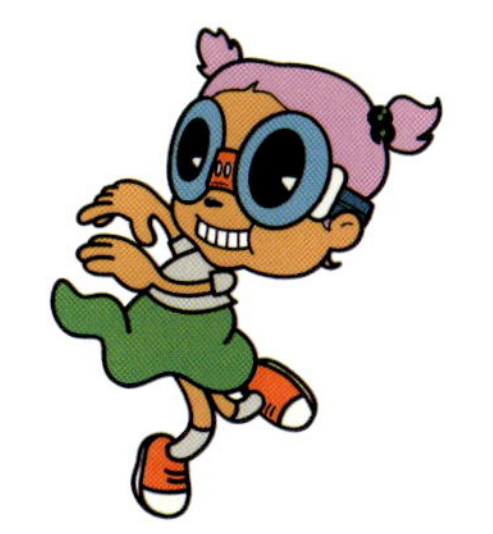

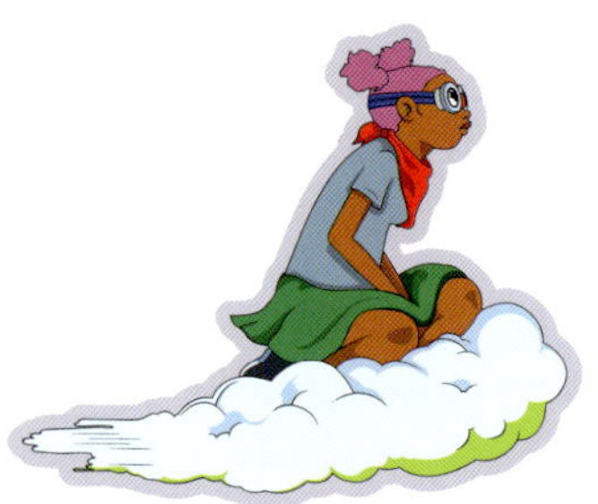

For Her + She
Mixed media
on canvas
34 x 28 inches
2017

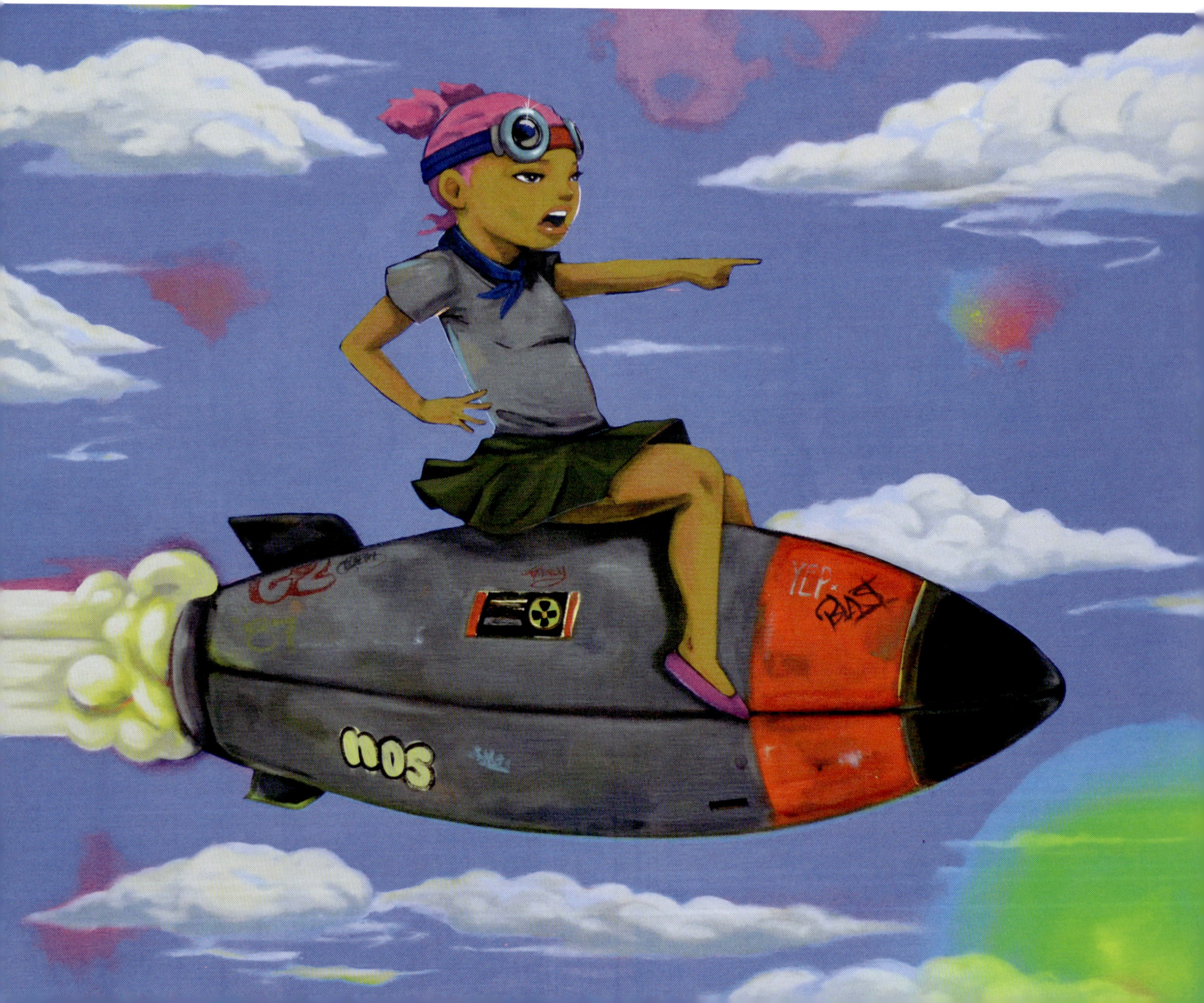

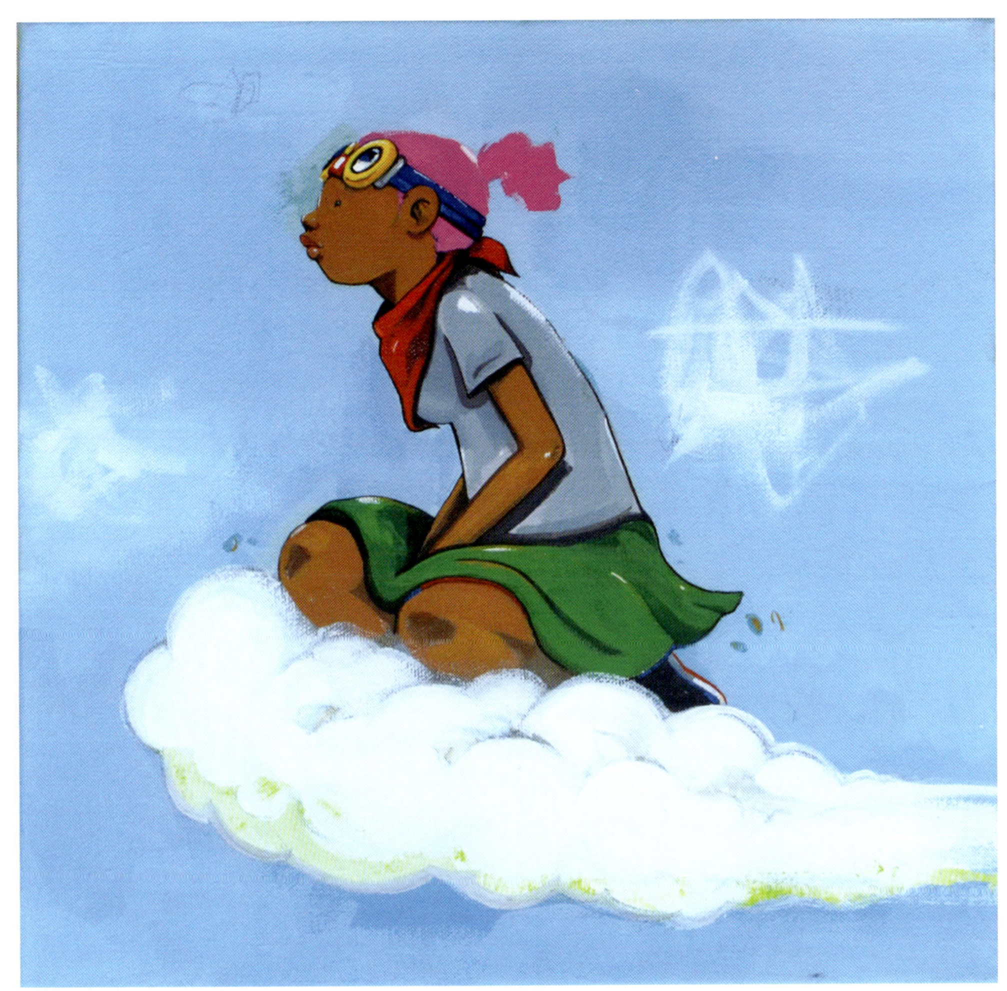

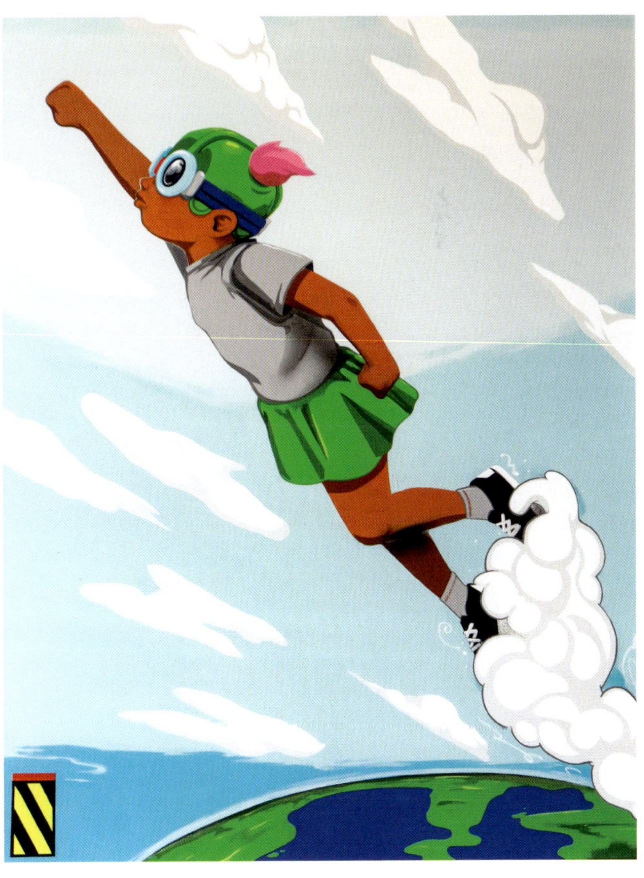

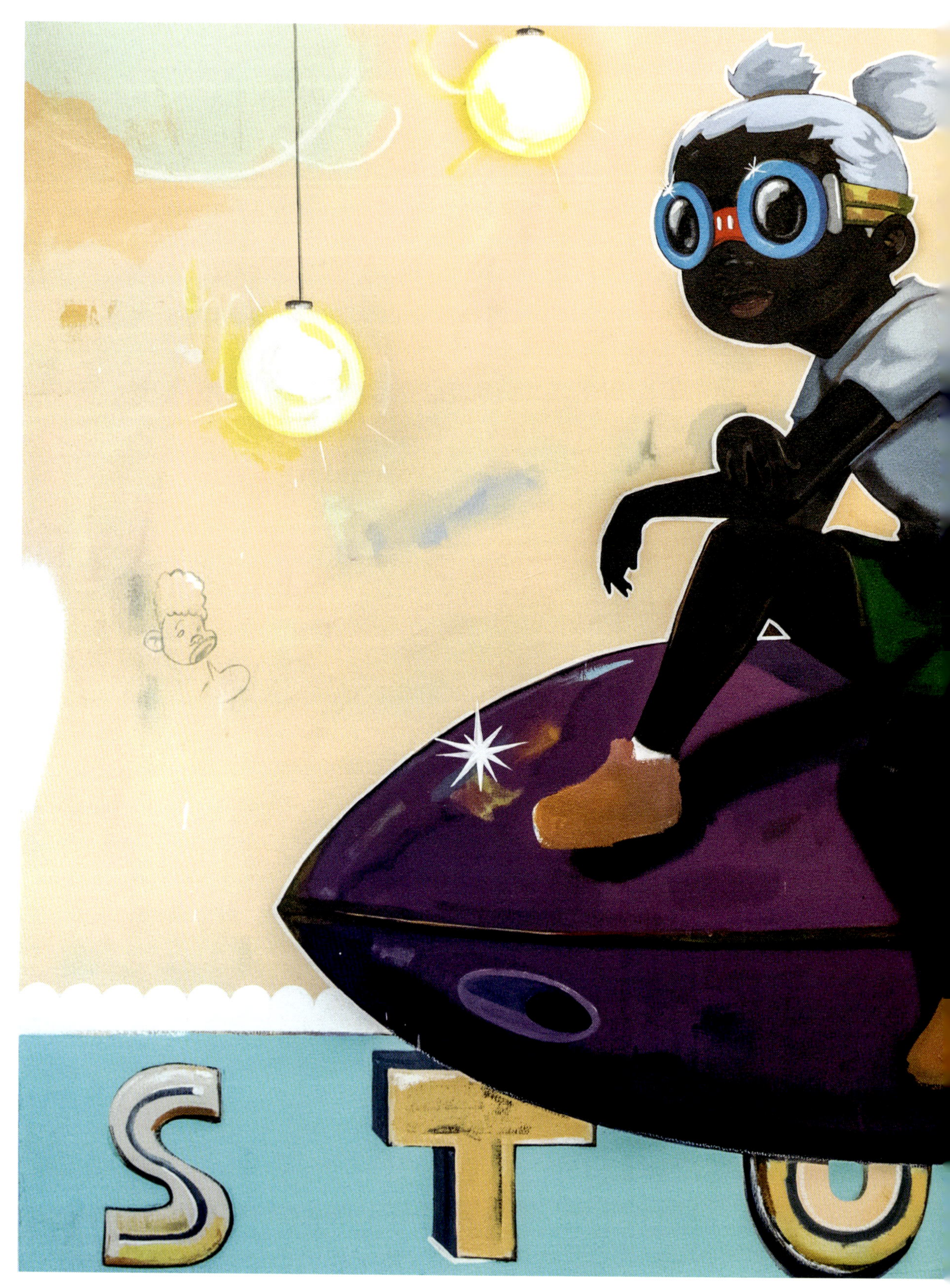

Stunt (Fresh off the Lot)

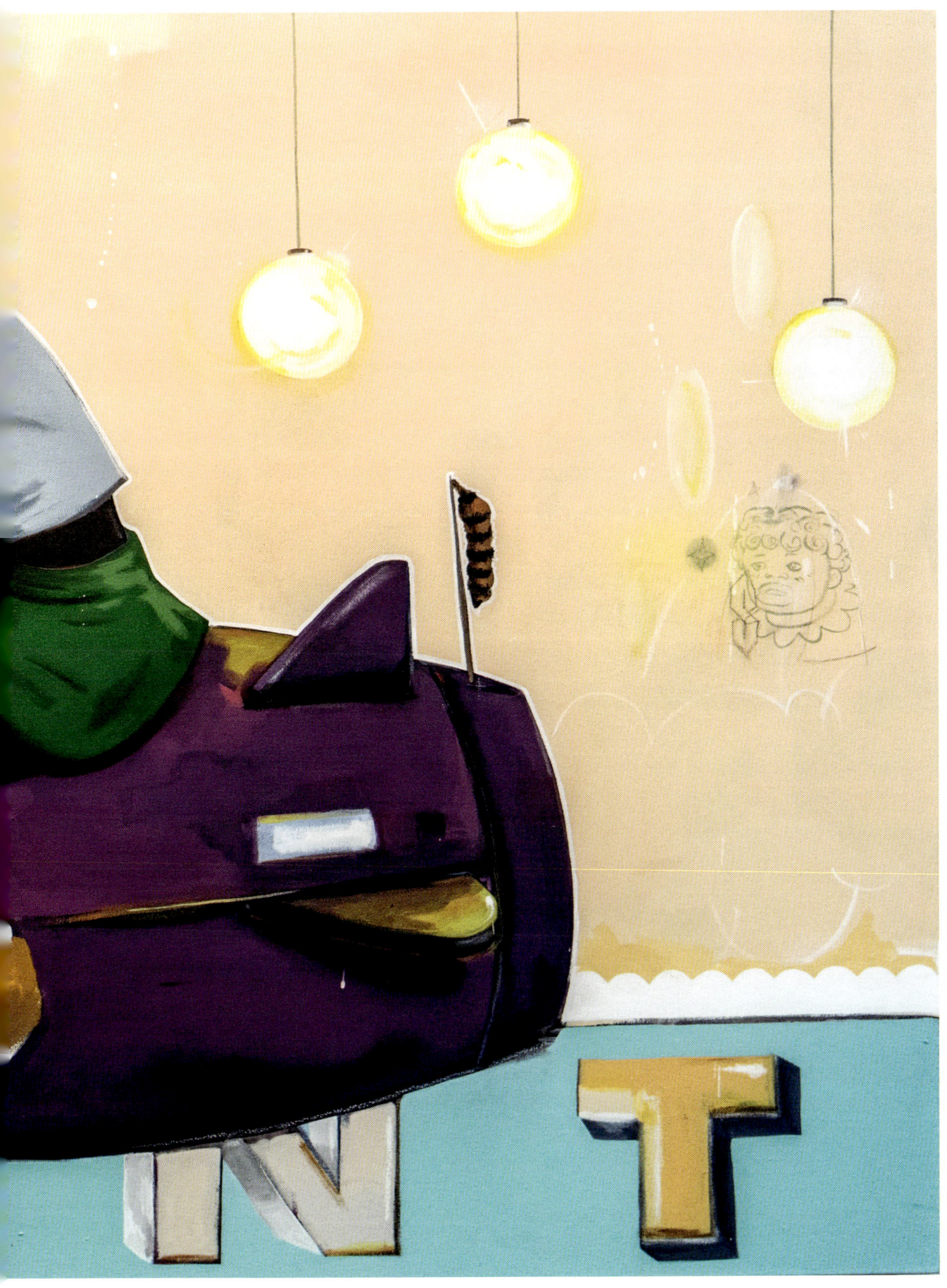

Acrylic on canvas, 62 x 42 inches, 2019

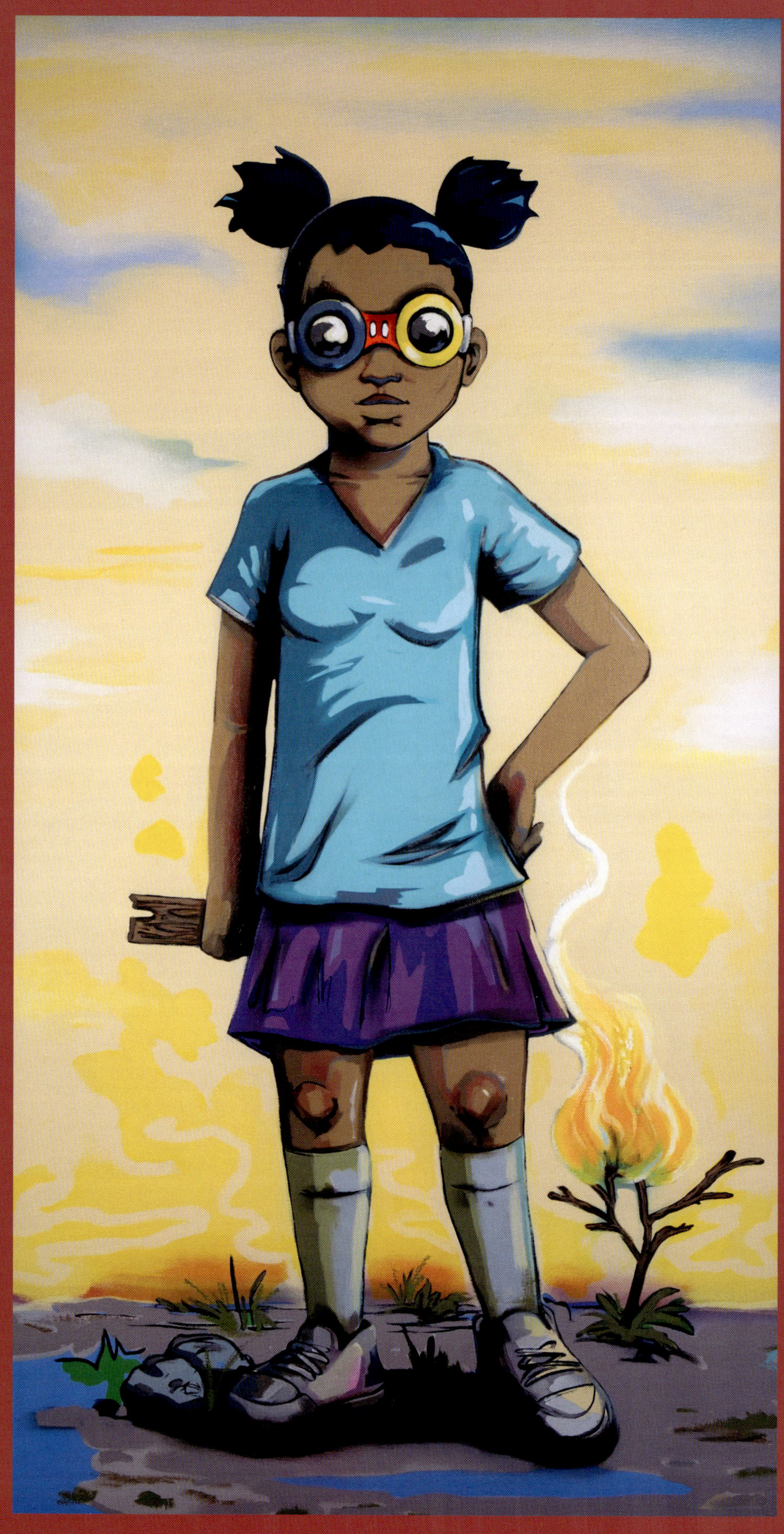

Little Girl, Pink
Mixed media
on canvas
27 x 55 inches
2019

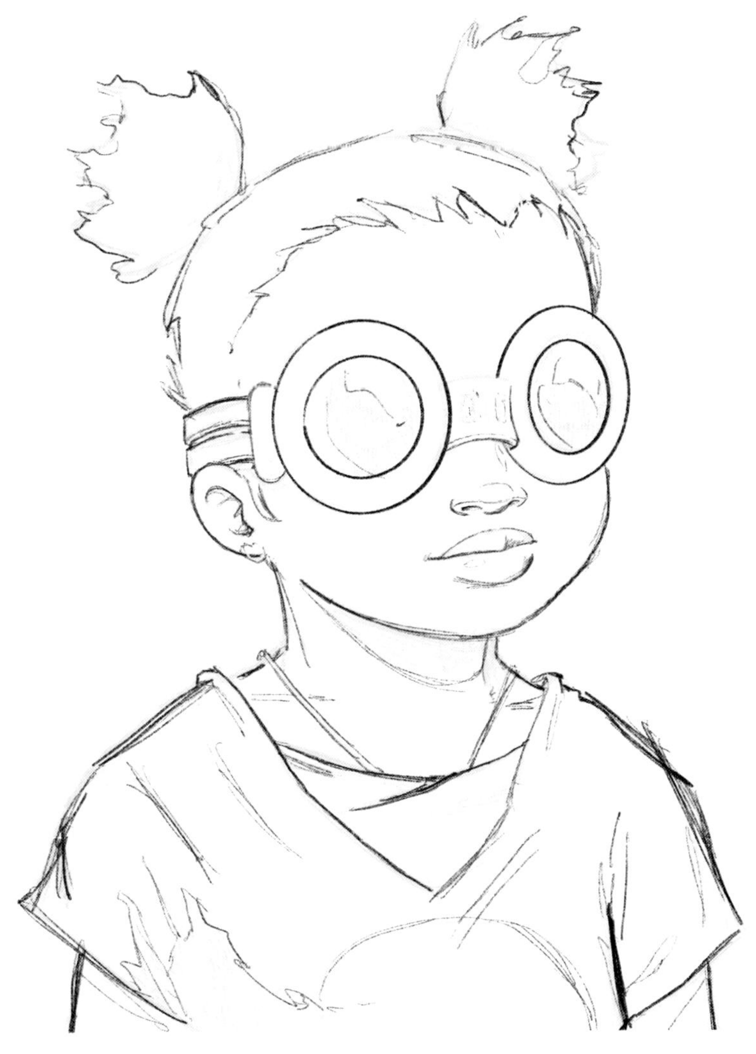

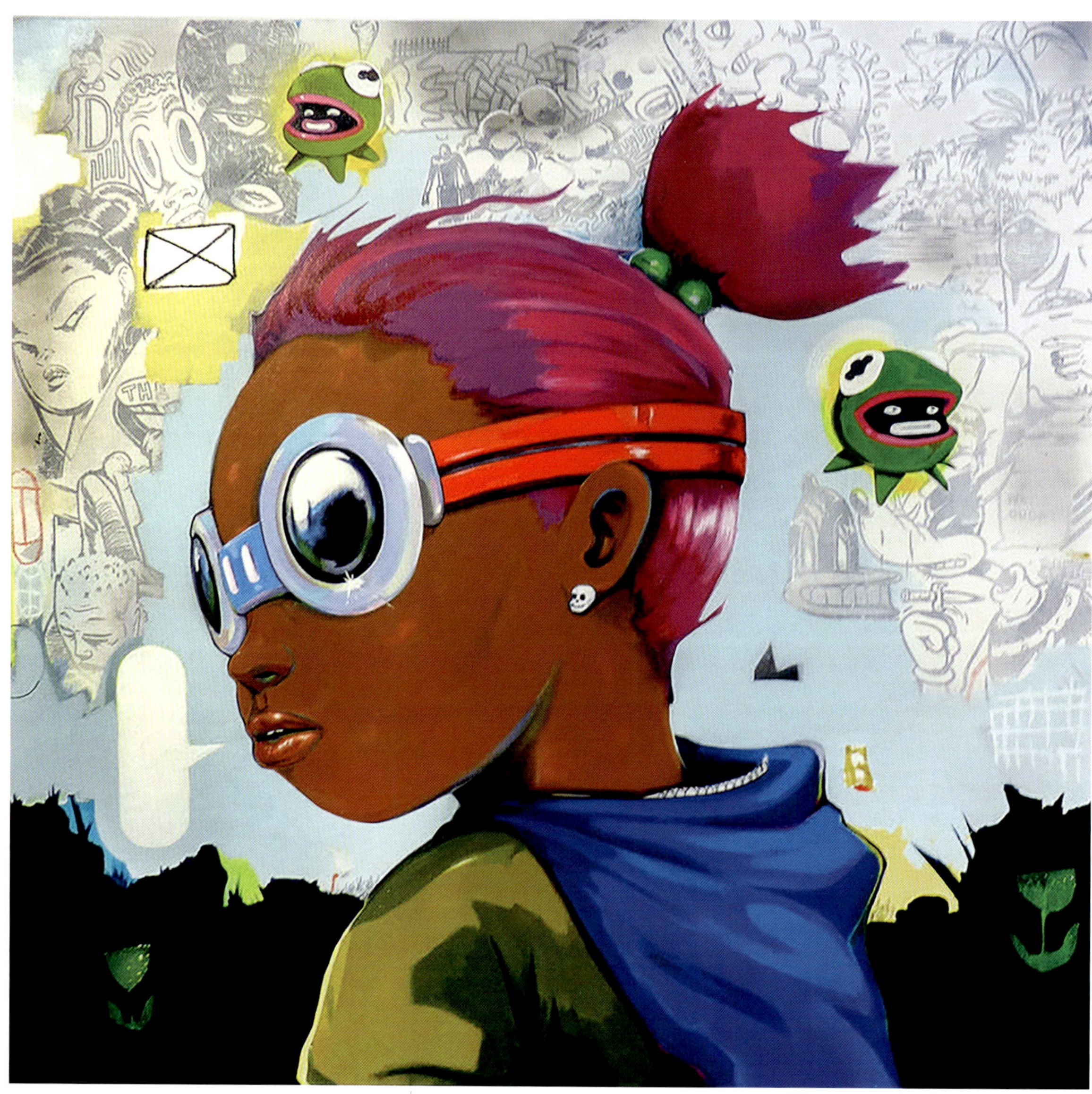

Why I Oughta
Mixed media
on canvas
36 x 36 inches
2018

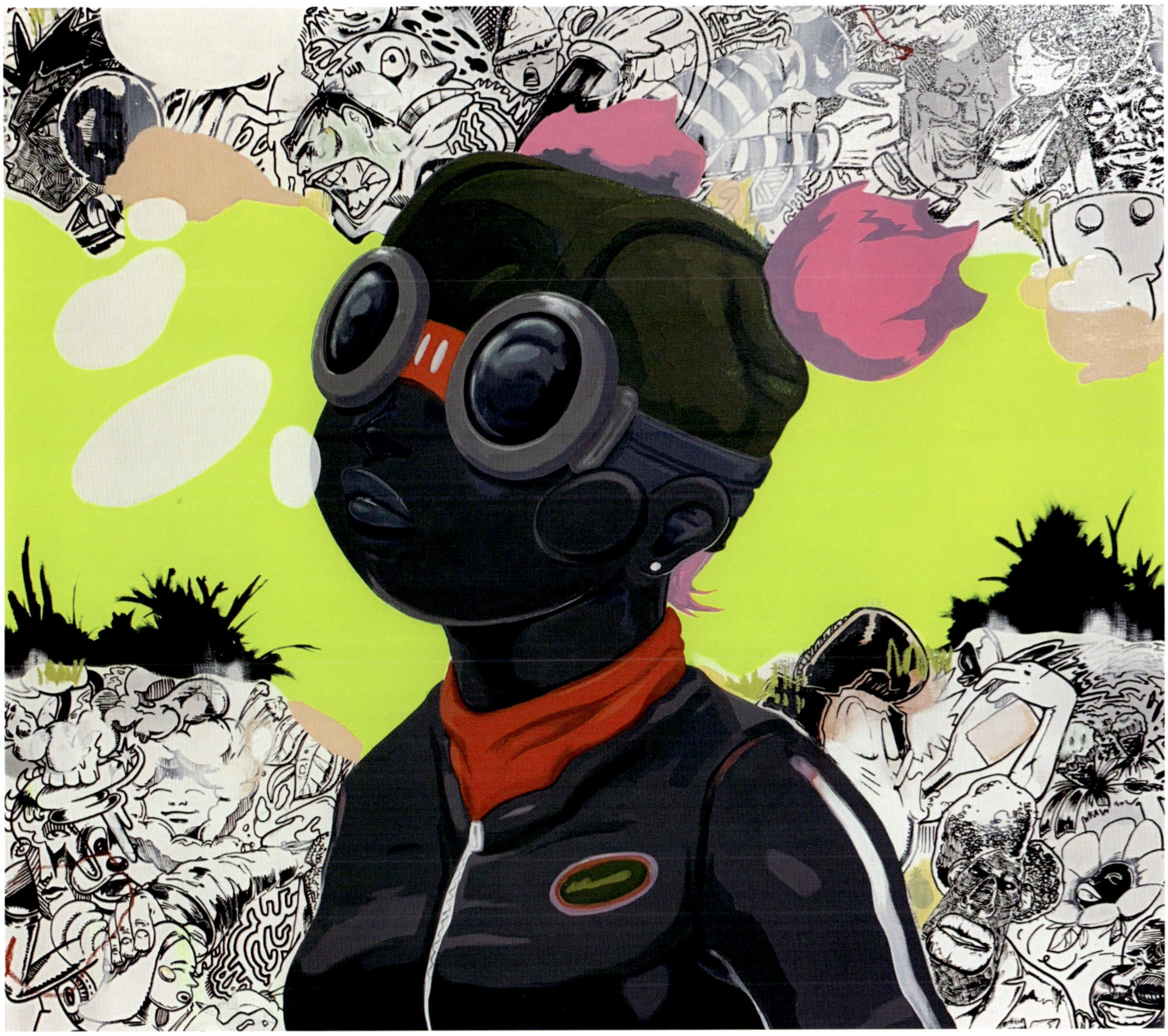

A Whisper Grows
Acrylic on canvas
36 x 36 inches
2019

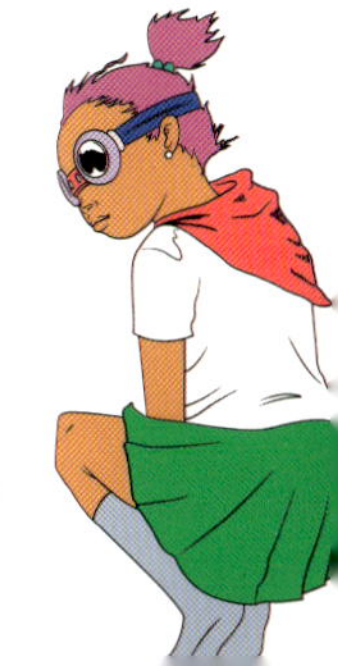

(This page)
Gaia
Black marble
24.8 x 17.3 x
18.1 inches
Edition of 8
2021

(Opposite)
Gaia
White marble
24.8 x 17.3 x
18.1 inches
Edition of 8
2021

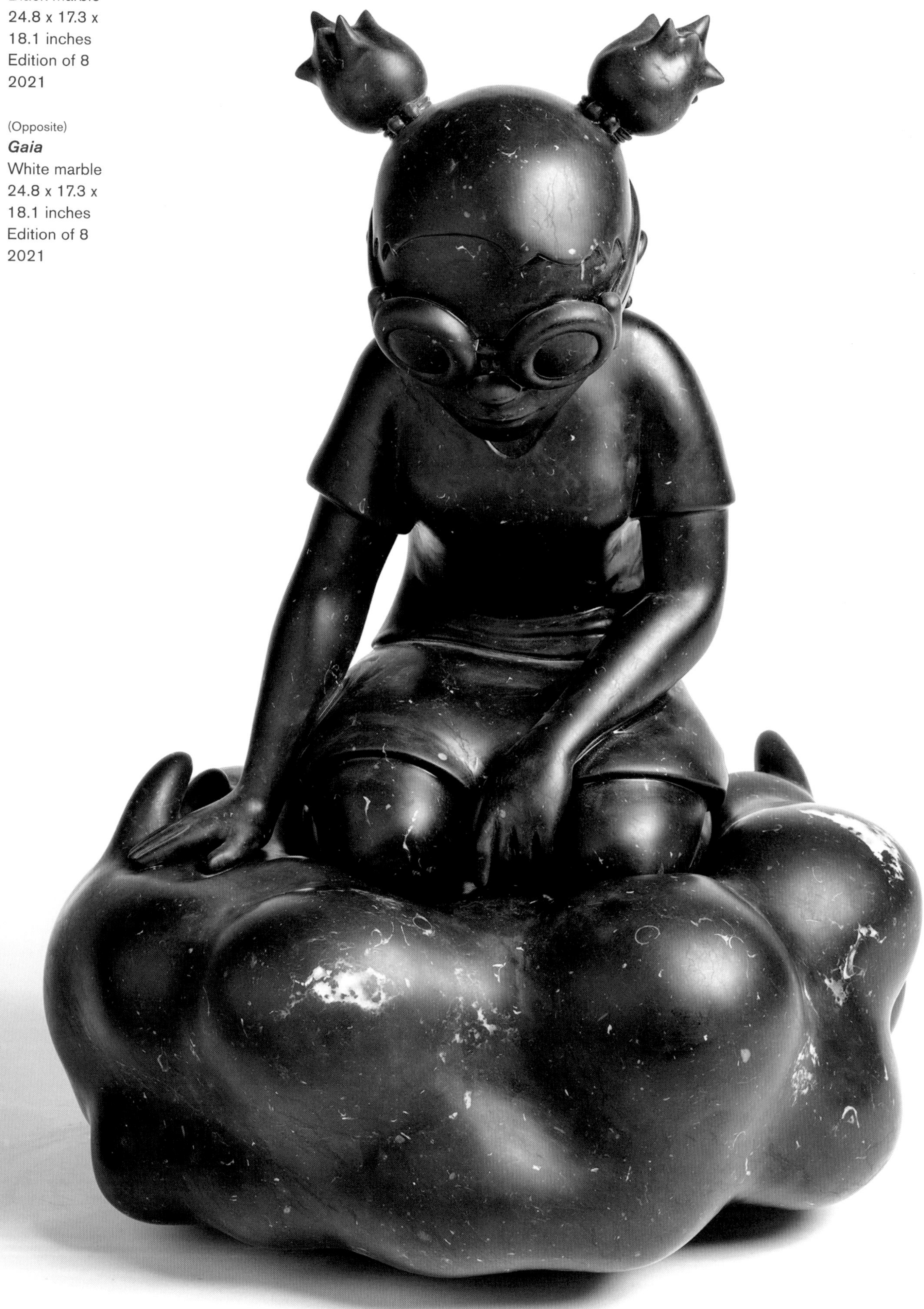

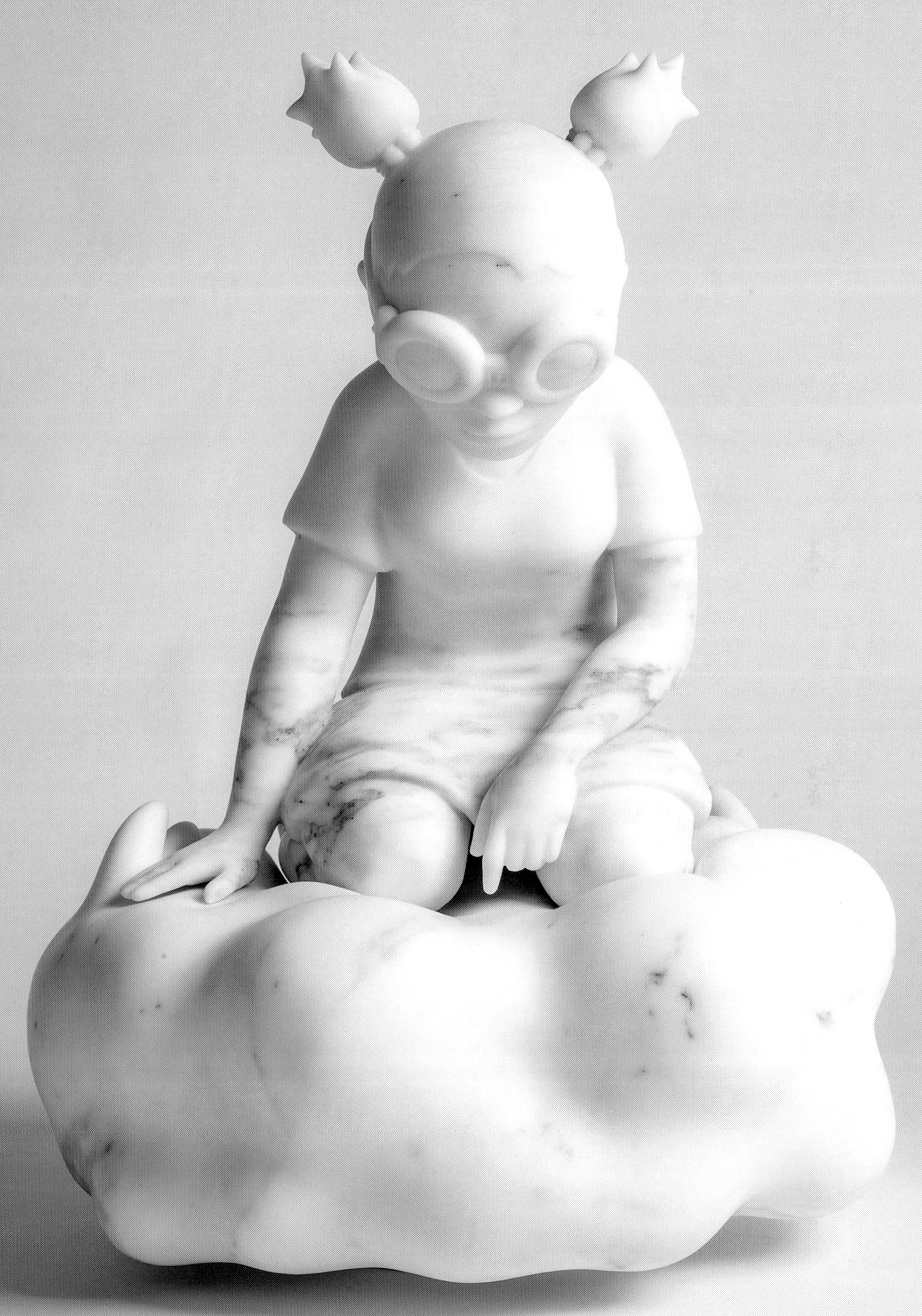

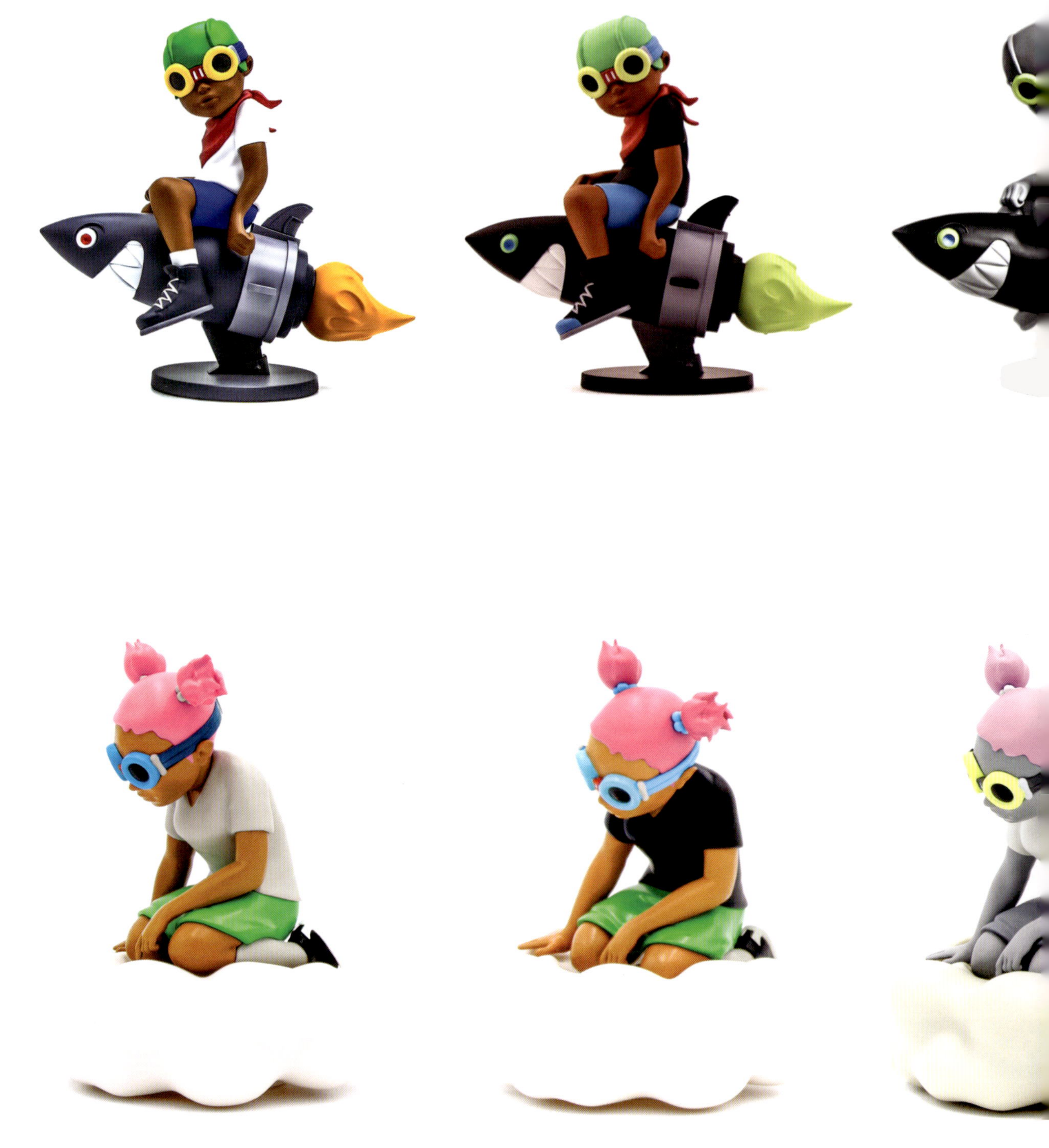

(Above) ***Beyond the Beyond,*** Hebru Brantley x BBC vinyl figure, all colorways, 8.5 inches high, 2017

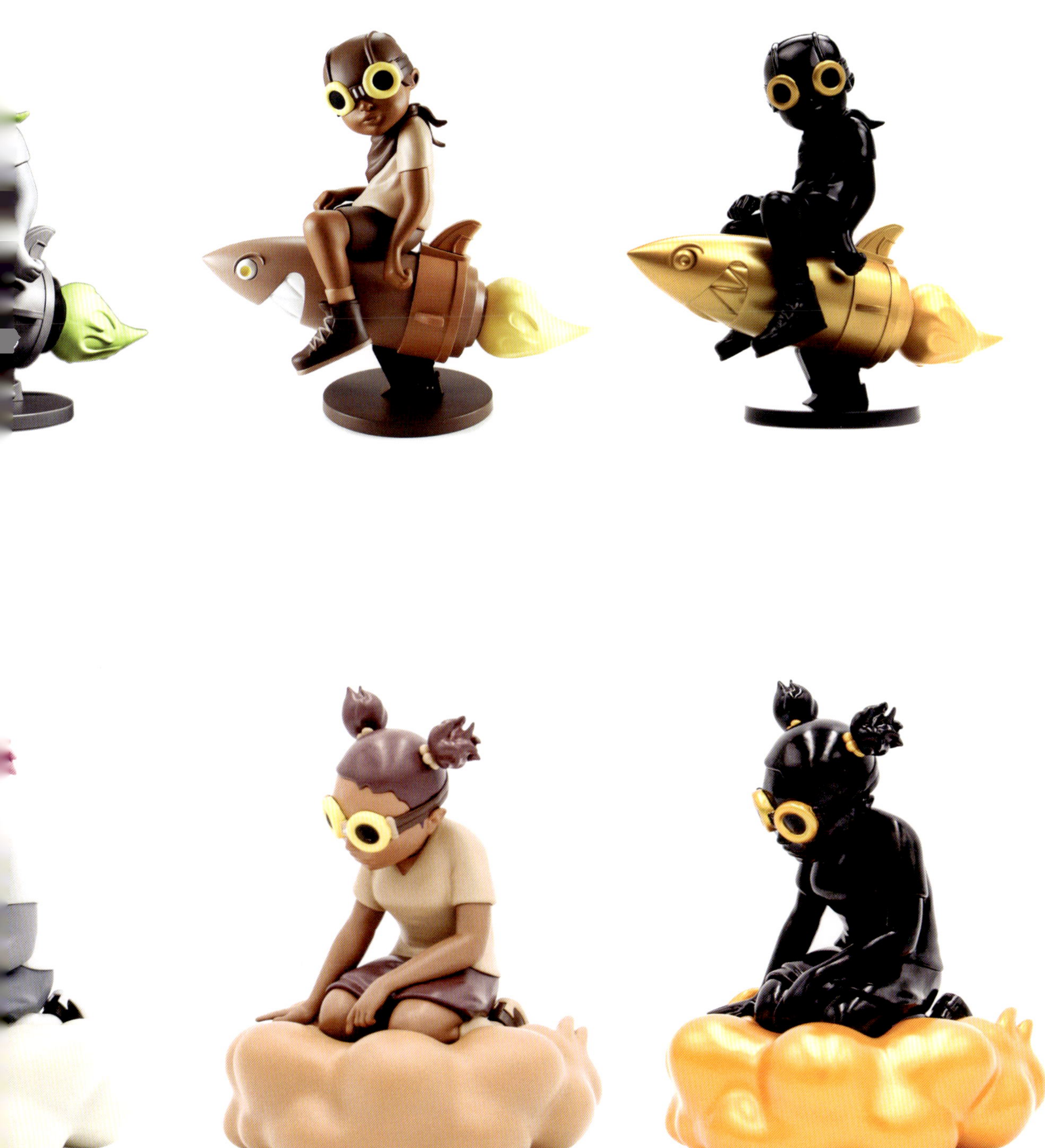

(Below) ***Lil Mama as Gaia,*** Hebru Brand Studios vinyl figure, all colorways, 7 inches high, 2021

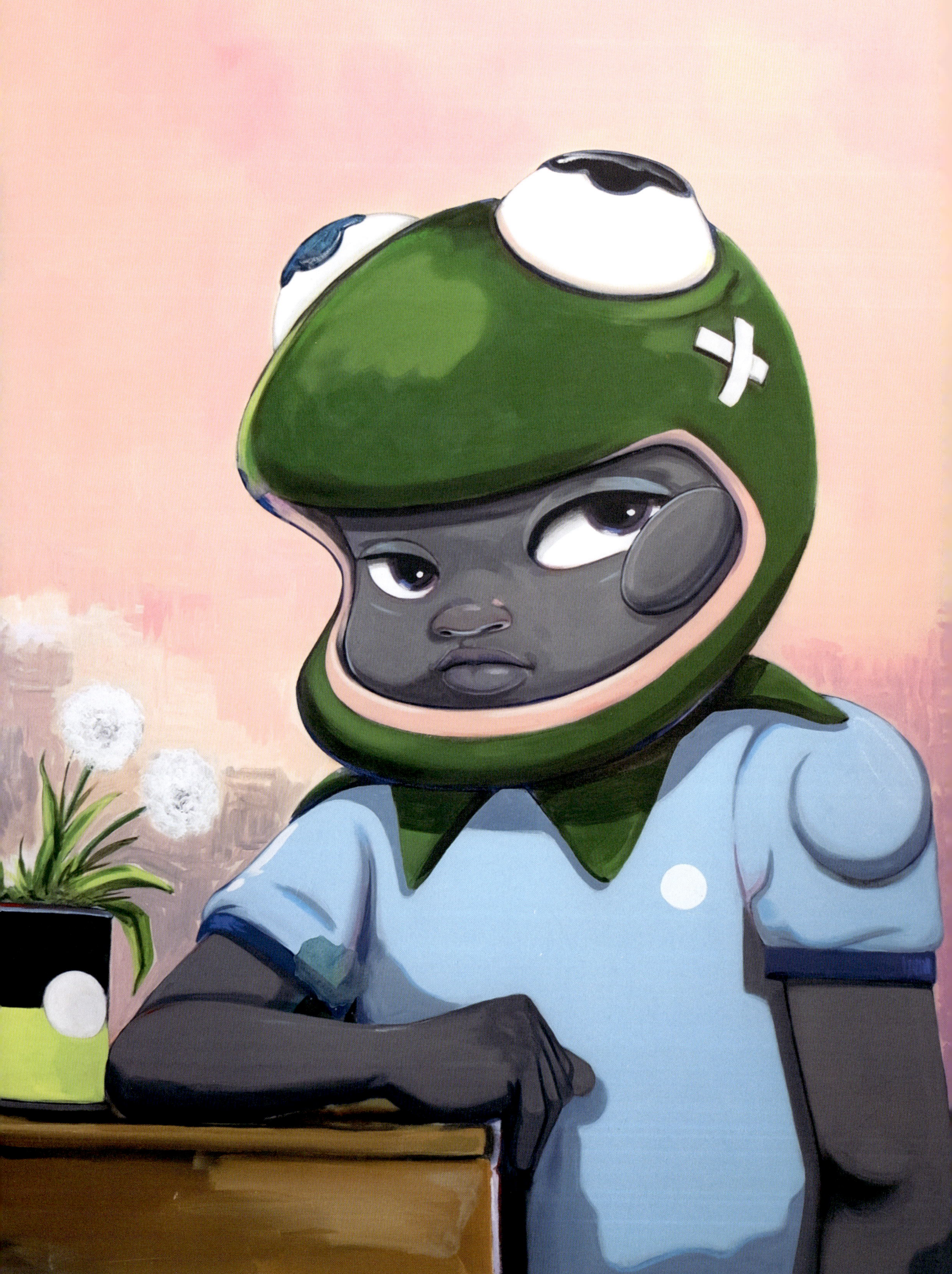

PHIBBY

"These characters were created first, and appreciated and grew a fandom strictly off the aesthetics—people were coming to see the artwork, not knowing the narrative, the backstory, the origin of the character but identifying with the essence of who that character was to a point where they felt like a part of their journey was being told through these paintings and I was speaking directly to them."

—HEBRU BRANTLEY

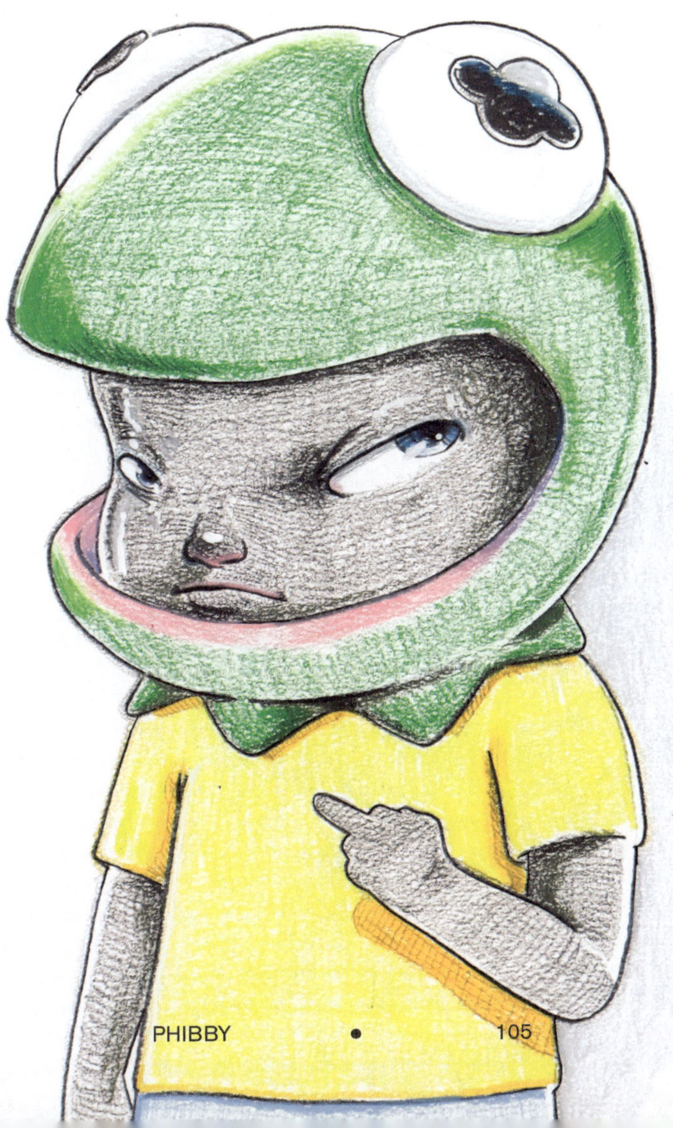

(Opposite)
Grade
Acrylic, spray paint,
and pastel on canvas
30 x 40 inches
2020

(Right)
This Is for You
Wax pastel
on paper
11 x 14
2020

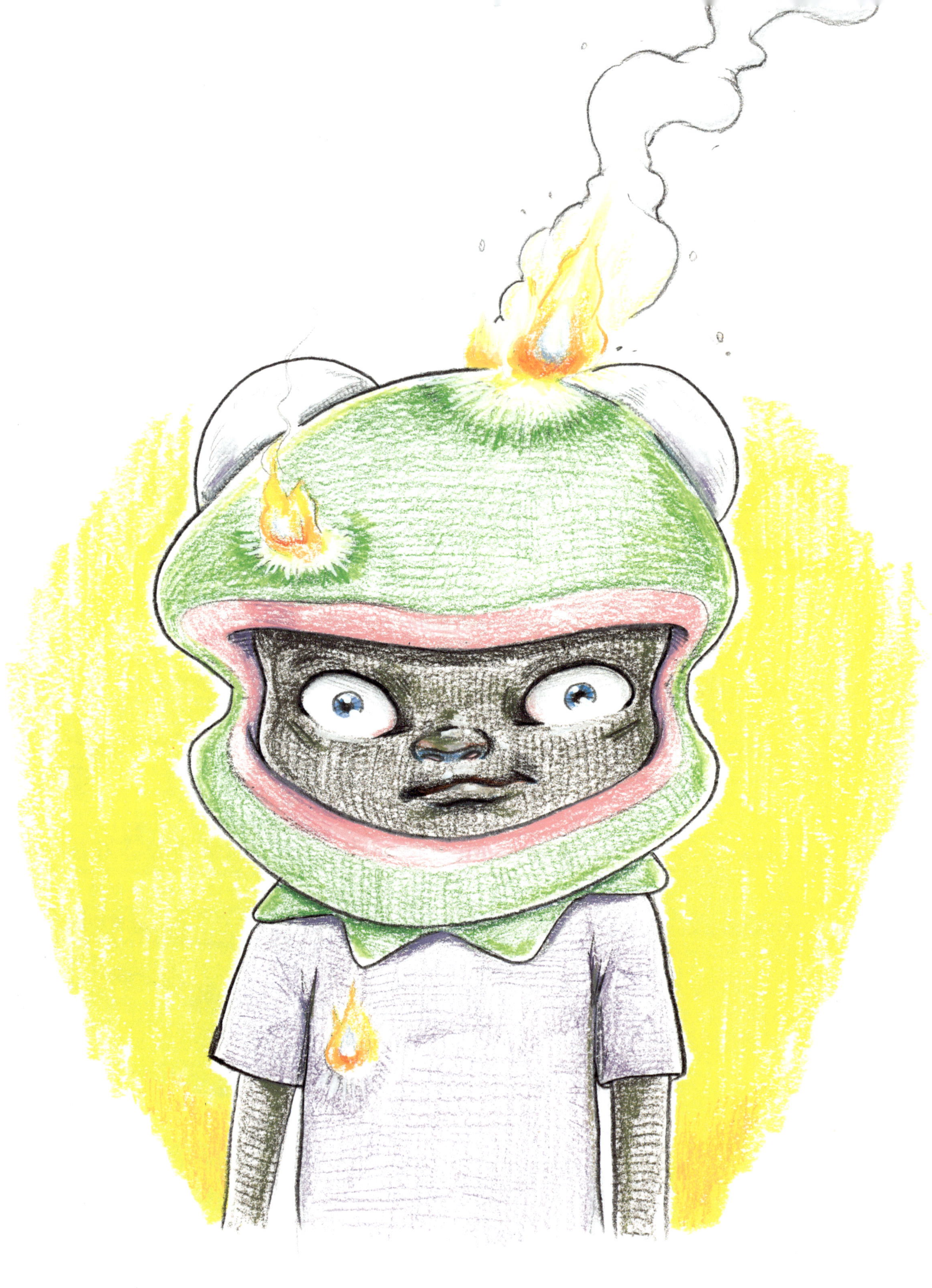

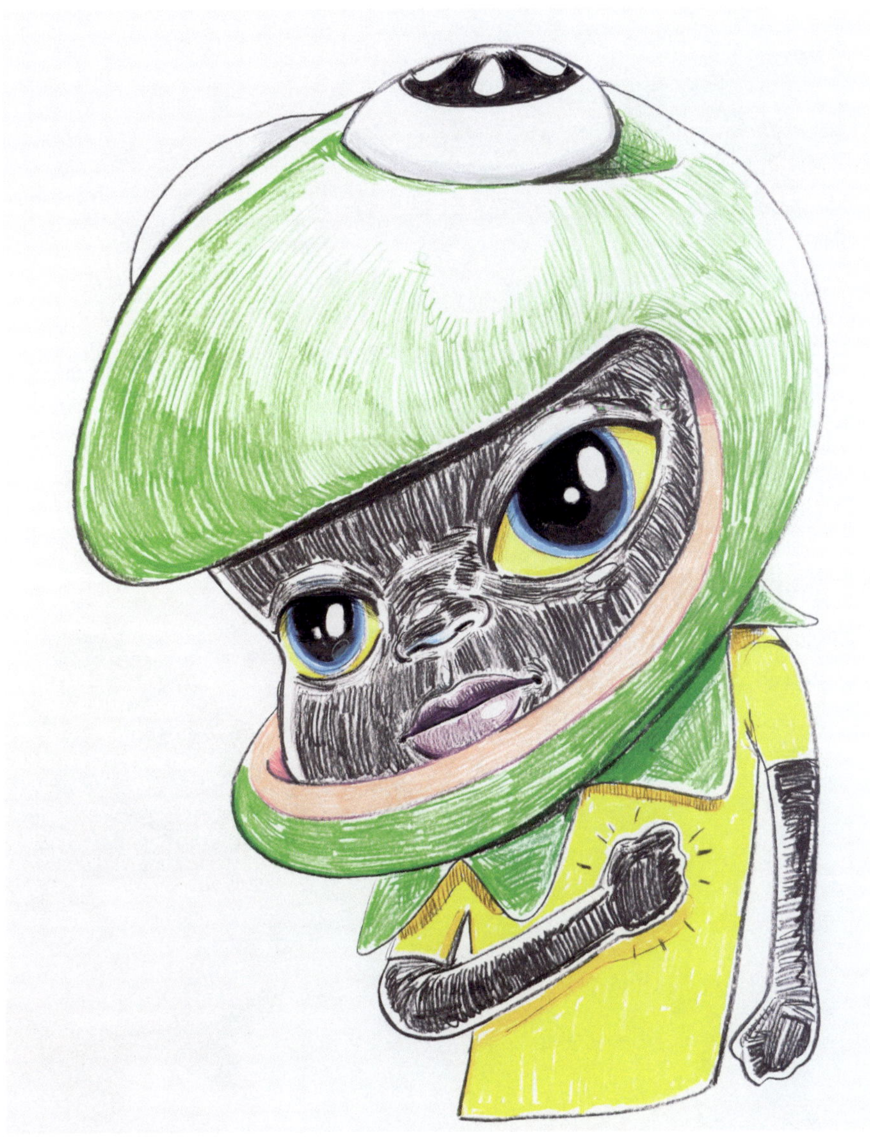

(Opposite)
I'm Fine Why'd You Ask
Mixed media
11 x 17 inches
2020

(Above)
Pound Yah Chest (Means All Is Love)
Wax pastel
and colored pencil
on paper
19 x 24 inches
2020

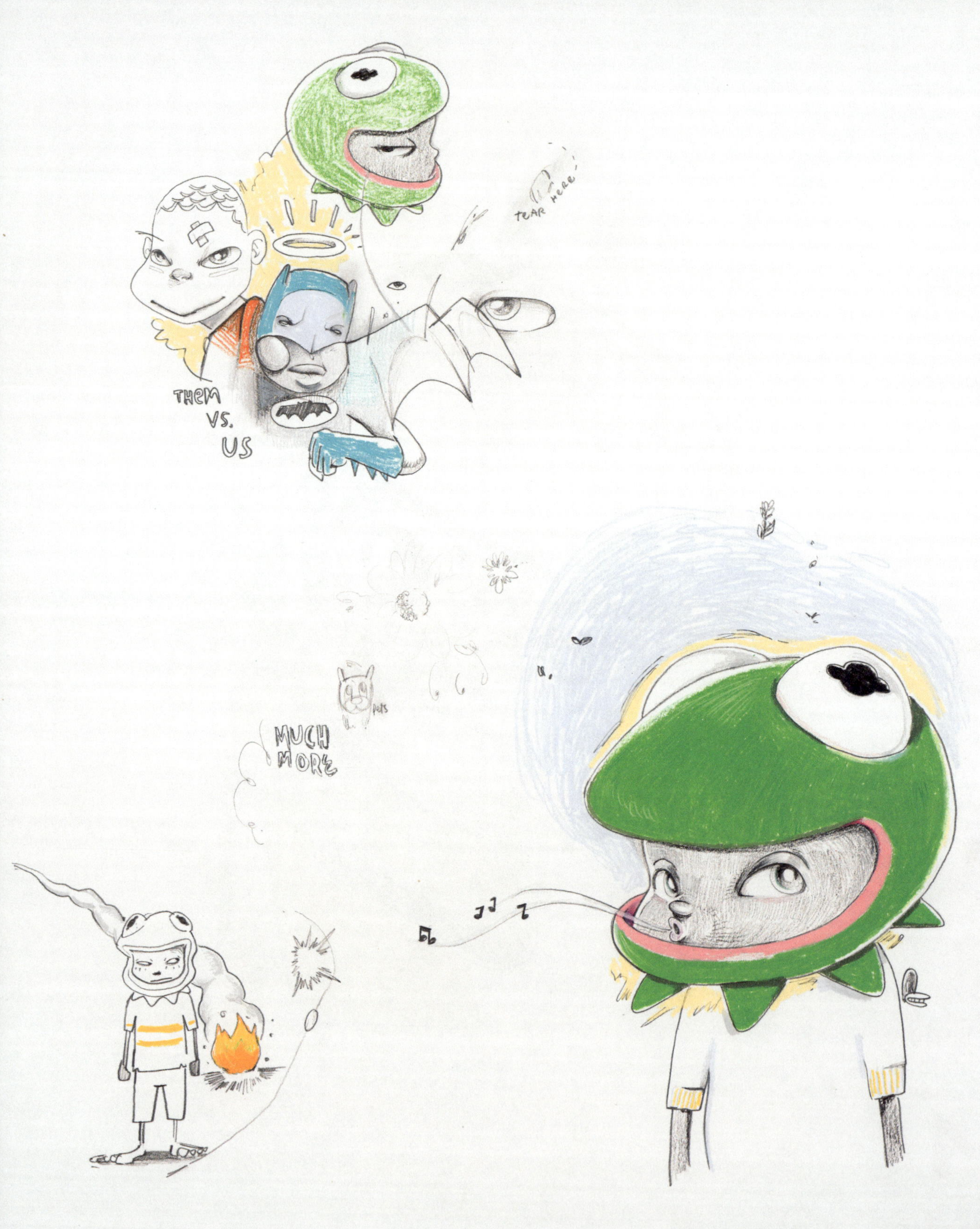
TEAR HERE
THEM VS. US
MUCH MORE
HEBRU BRANTLEY

(Opposite)
They'll Try and Break You
Mixed media
on paper
19 x 24 inches
2020

(Right)
Rogues
Wax pastel, colored
pencil, and paint
marker on paper
19 x 24 inches
2020

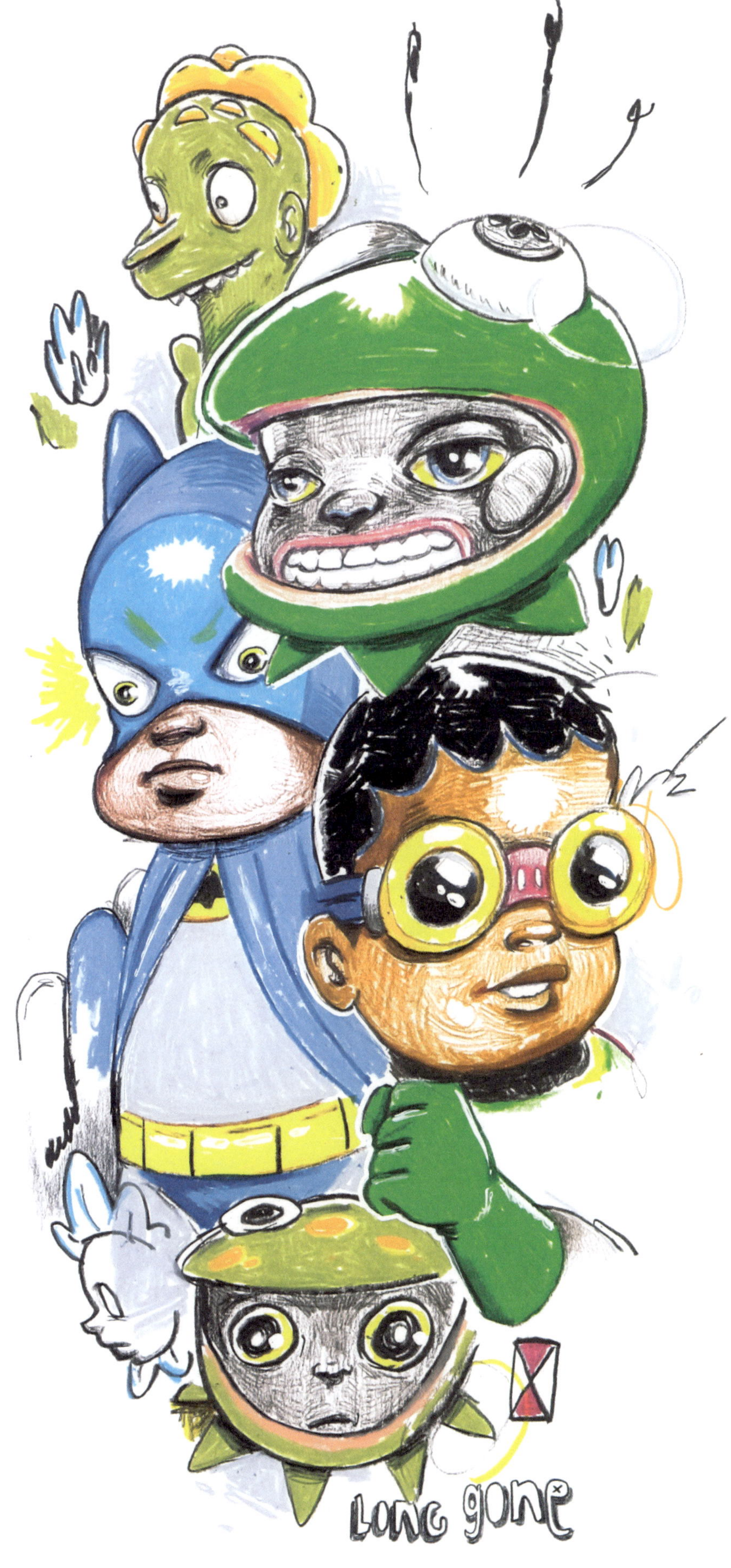

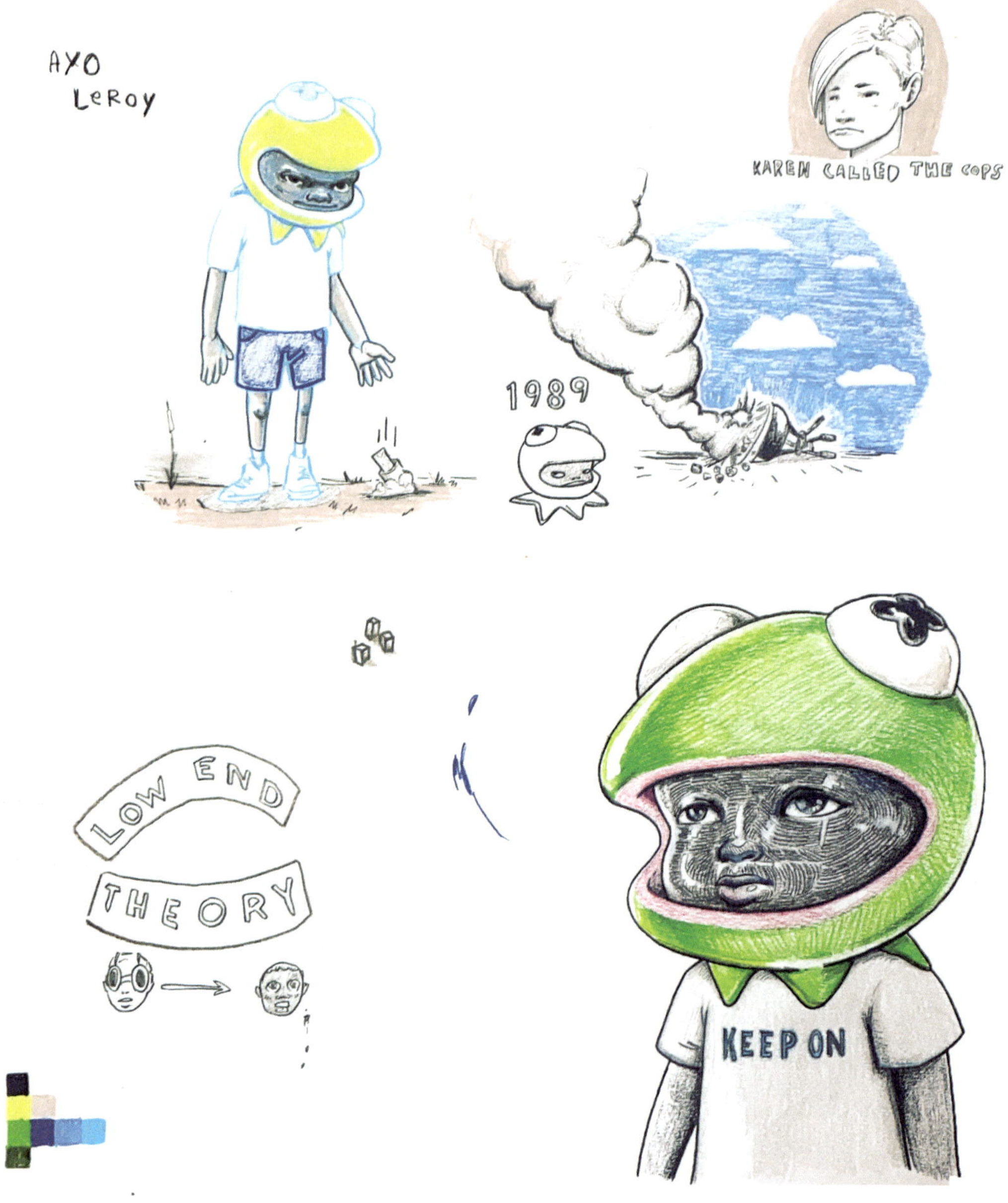
AYO
Leroy
KAREN CALLED THE COPS
1989
LOW END
THEORY
KEEP ON

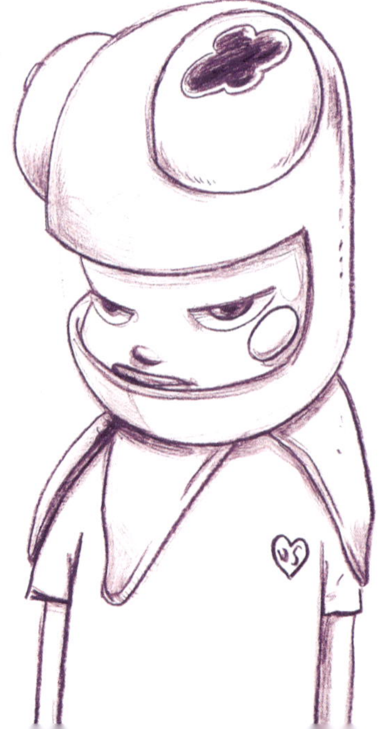

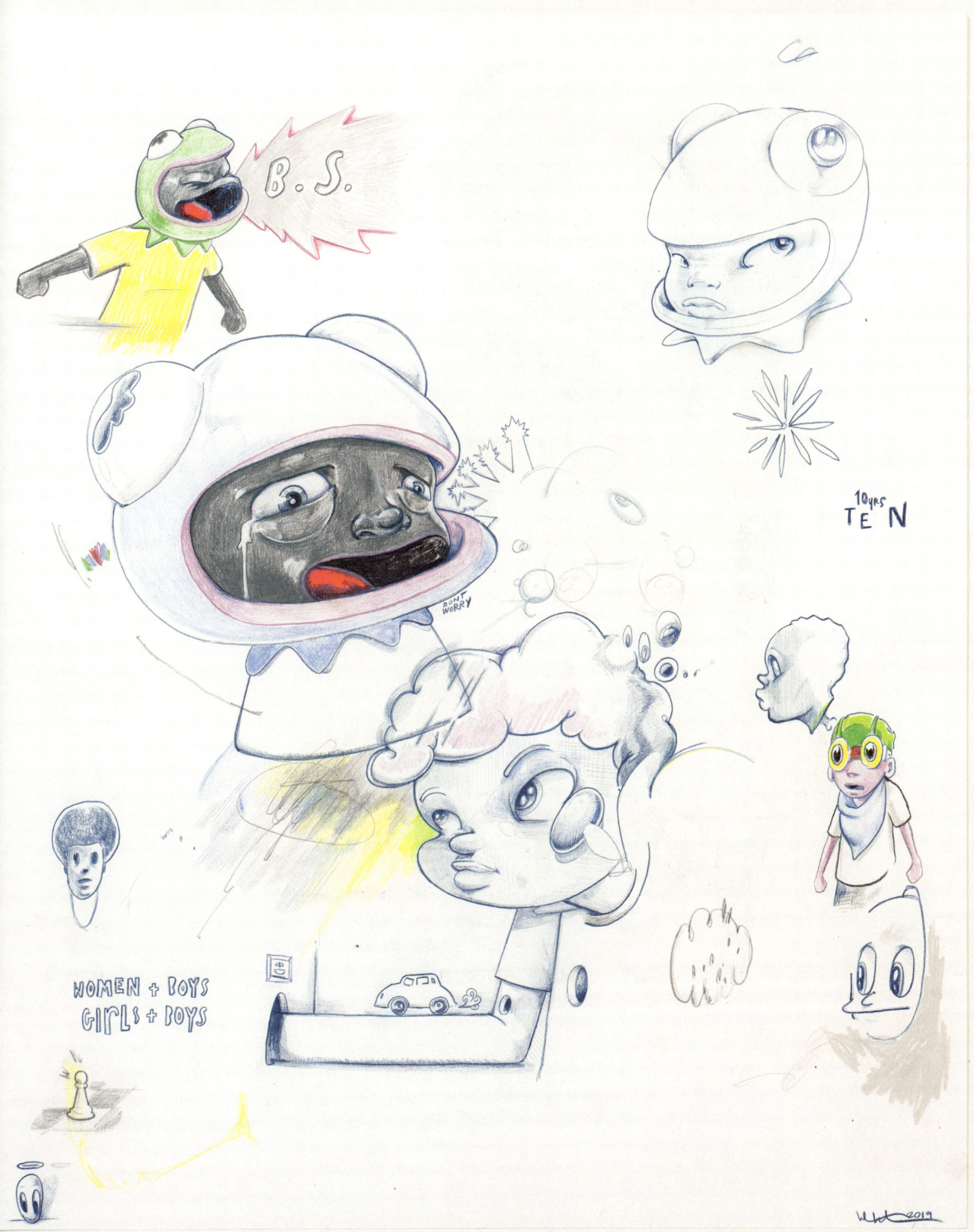
B.S.
10yrs
TEN
DONT WORRY
WOMEN + BOYS
GIRLS + BOYS

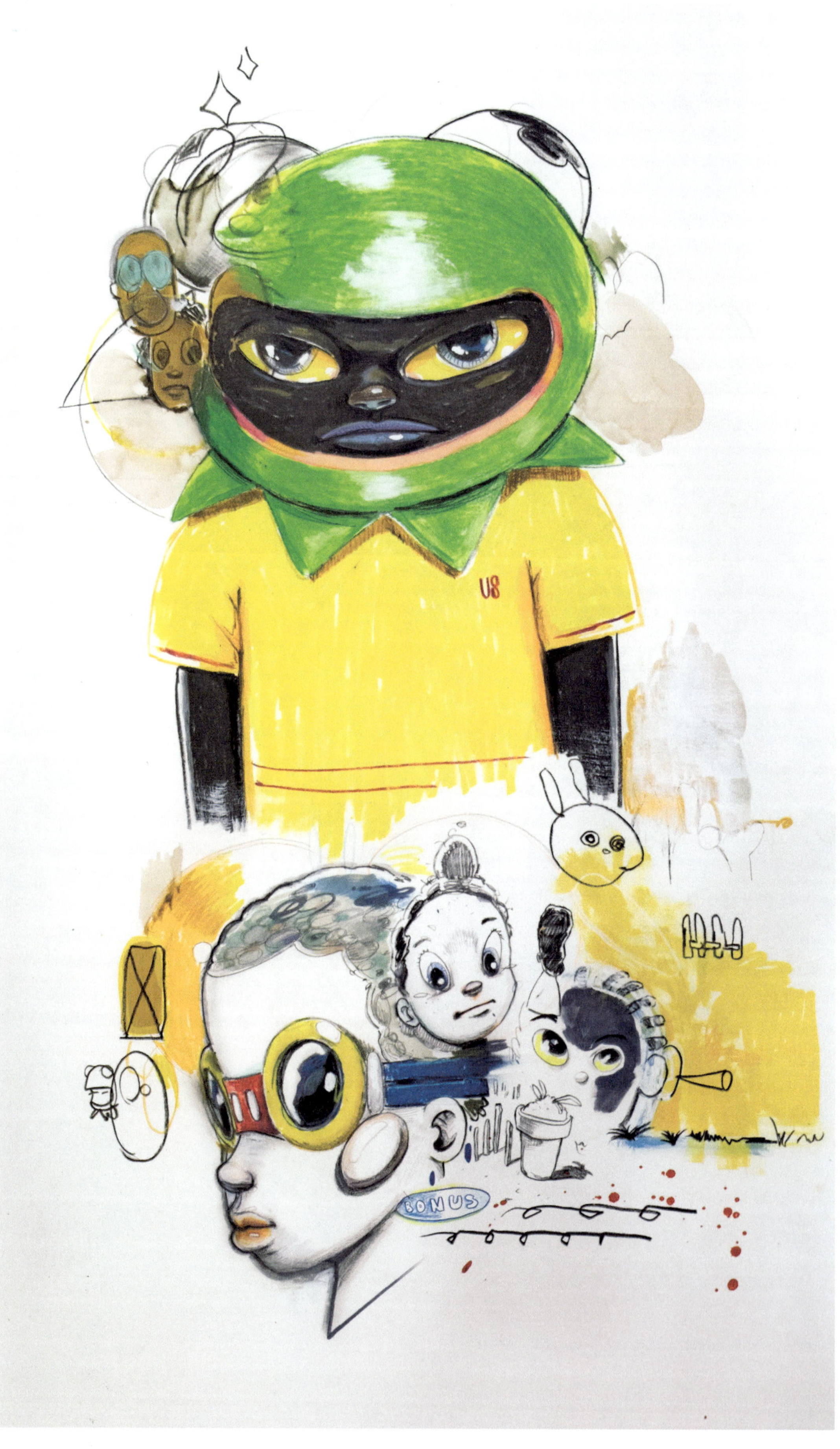
U8
BONUS

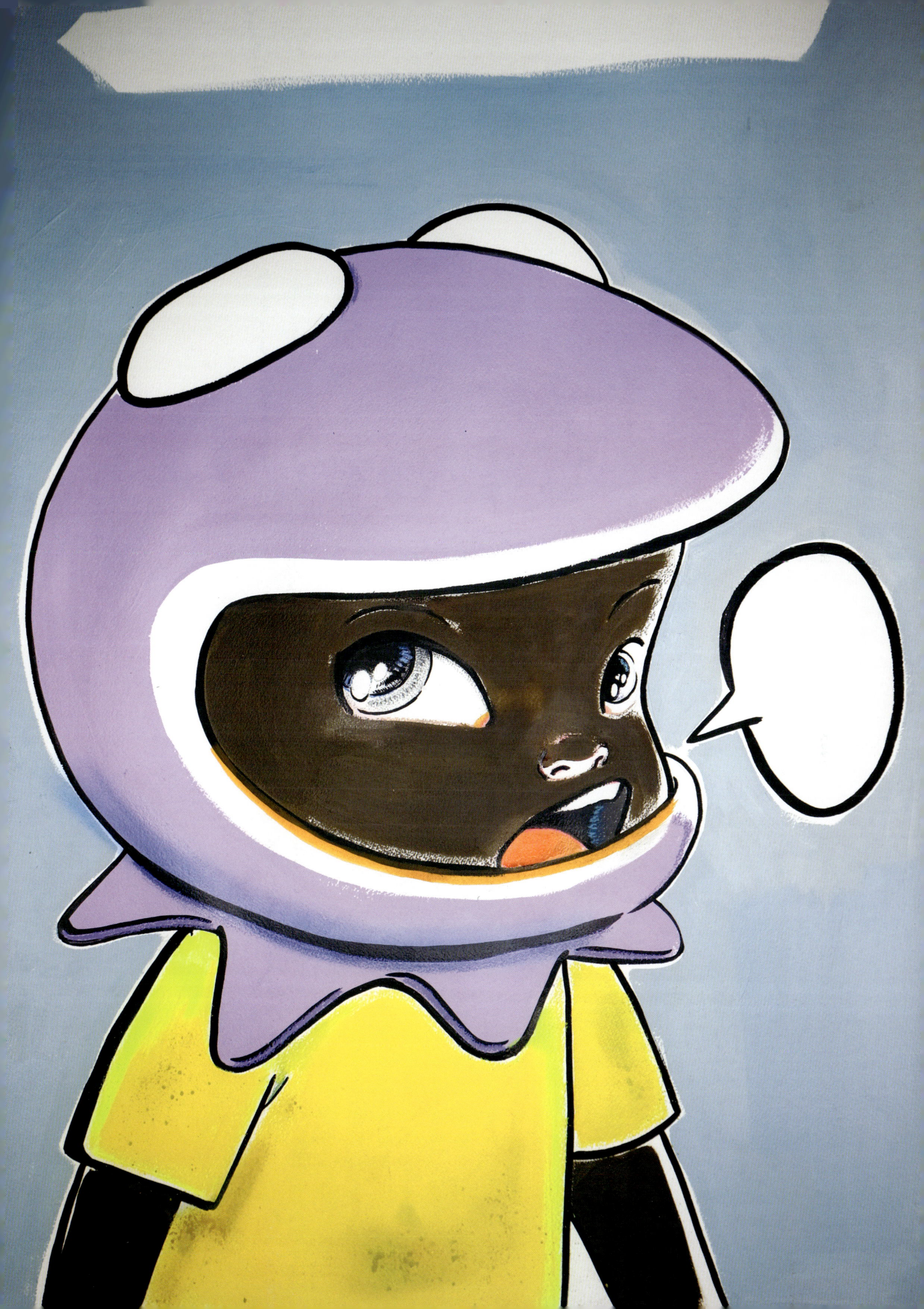

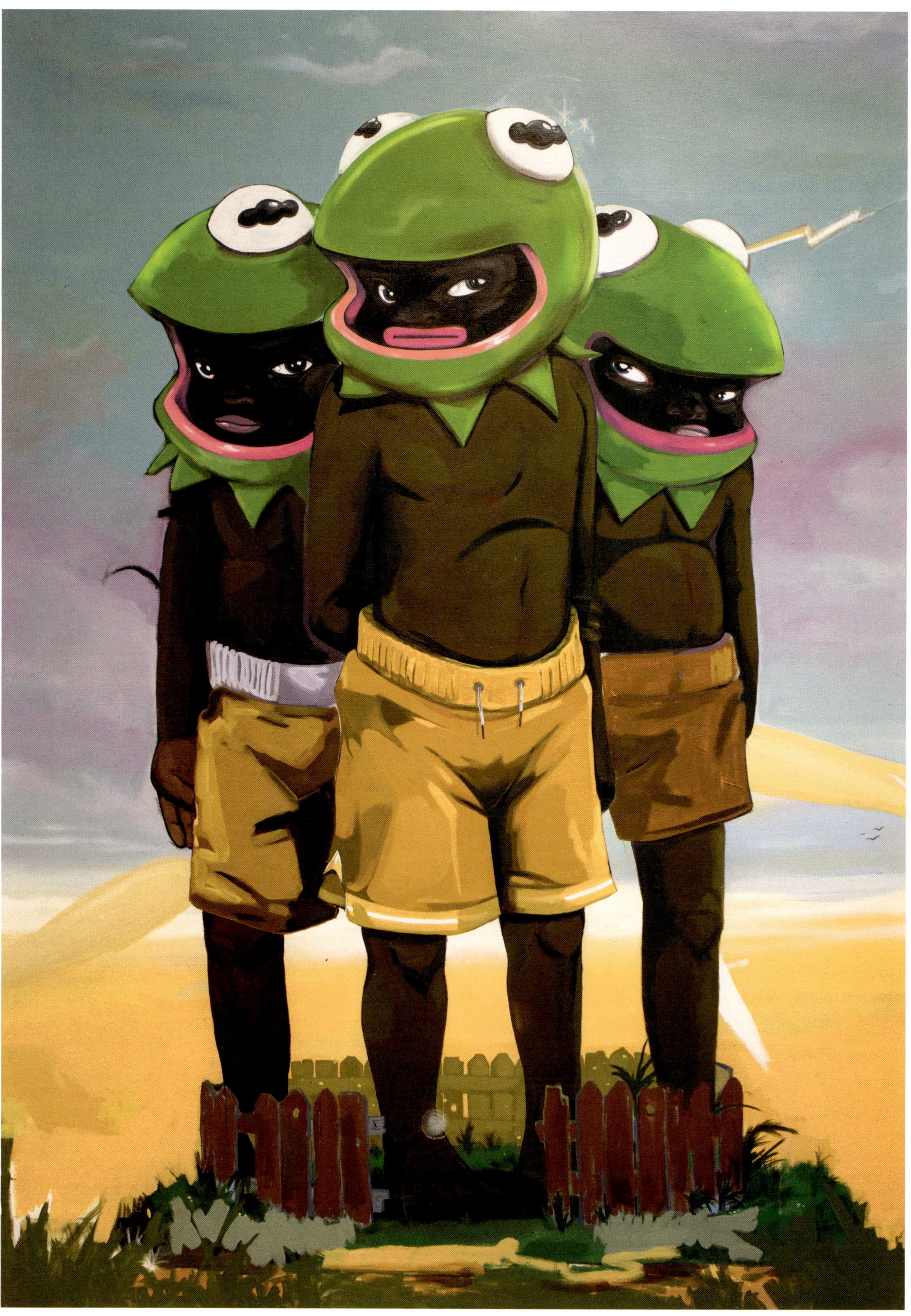

(Opposite)
There Was No Mention of Sports
Mixed media
on canvas
50 x 72 inches
2017

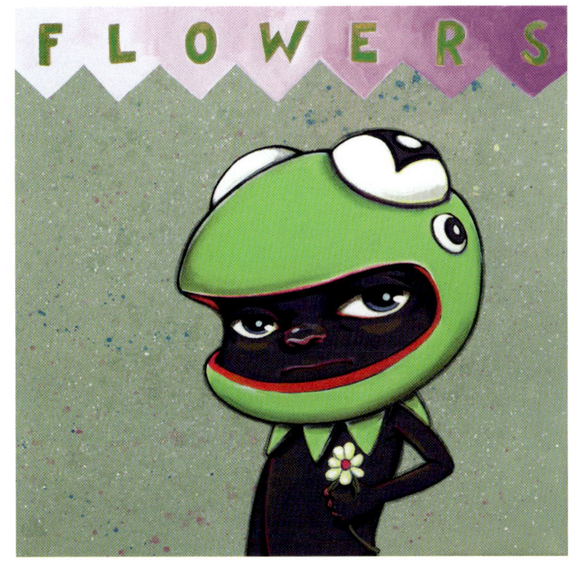

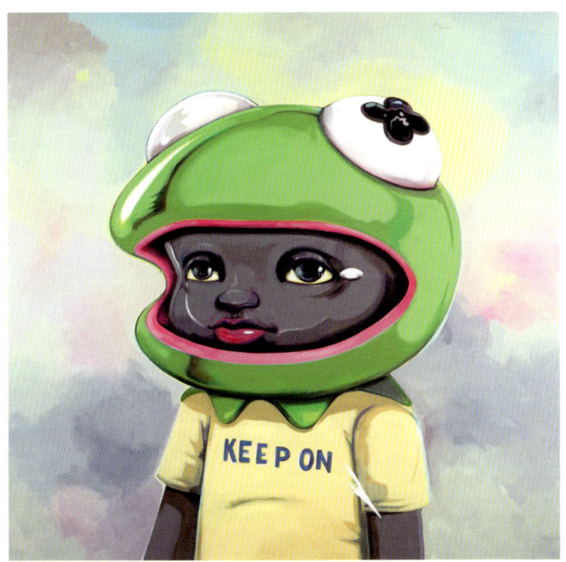

(From top)
One Fresh Flower
Acrylic and pastel
on canvas
20 x 20 inches
2021

Keep Keepin' On
Acrylic, pastel,
and spray paint
on canvas
72 x 72 inches
2020–2021

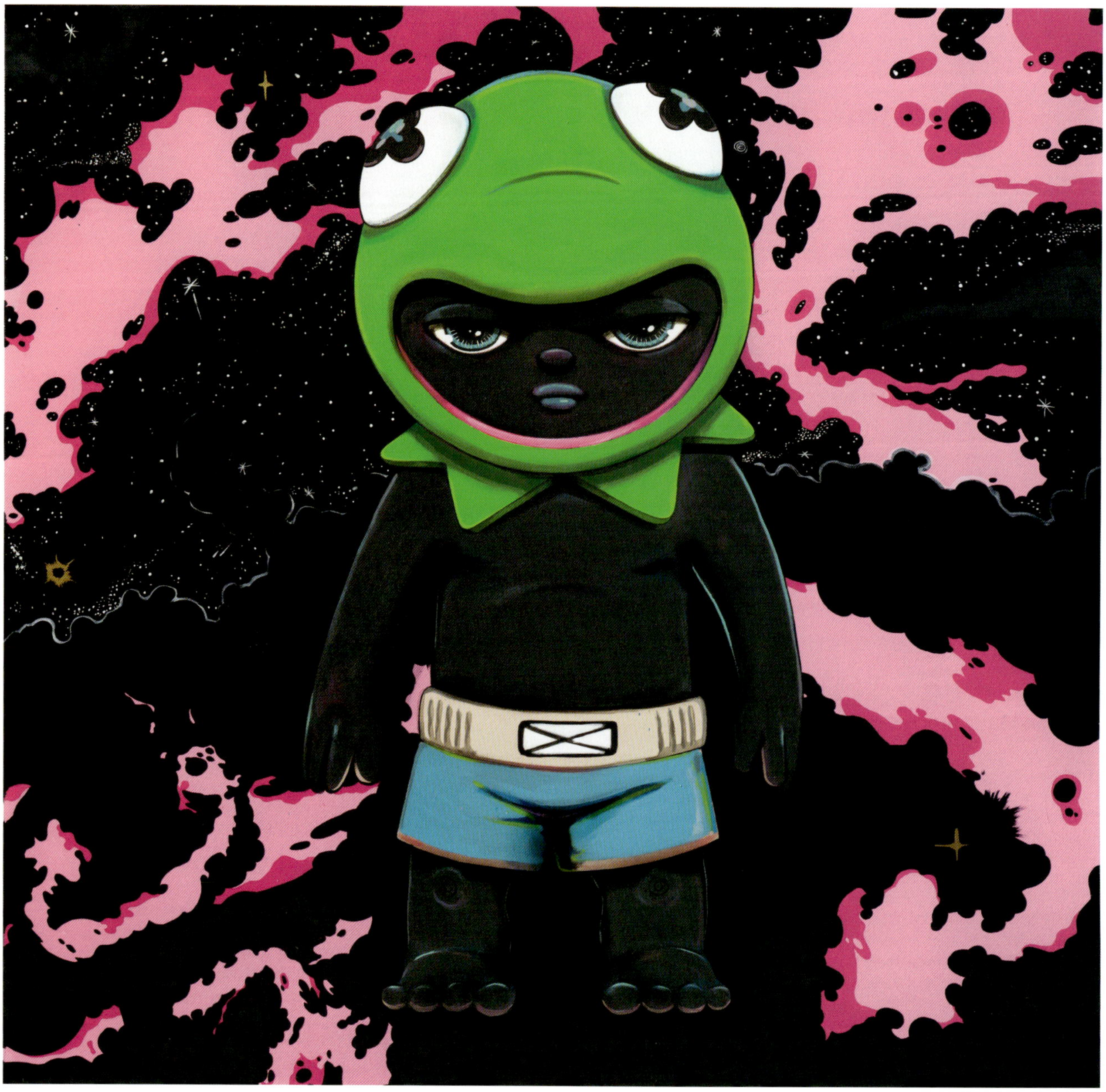

(Above)
Futr Futur
Mixed media
on canvas
36 x 36 inches
2017

(Opposite)
Smile
Acrylic on wood
18 × 24 inches
2018–2019

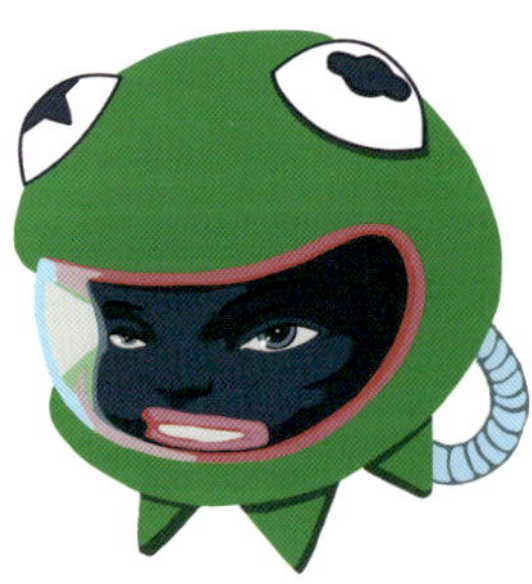

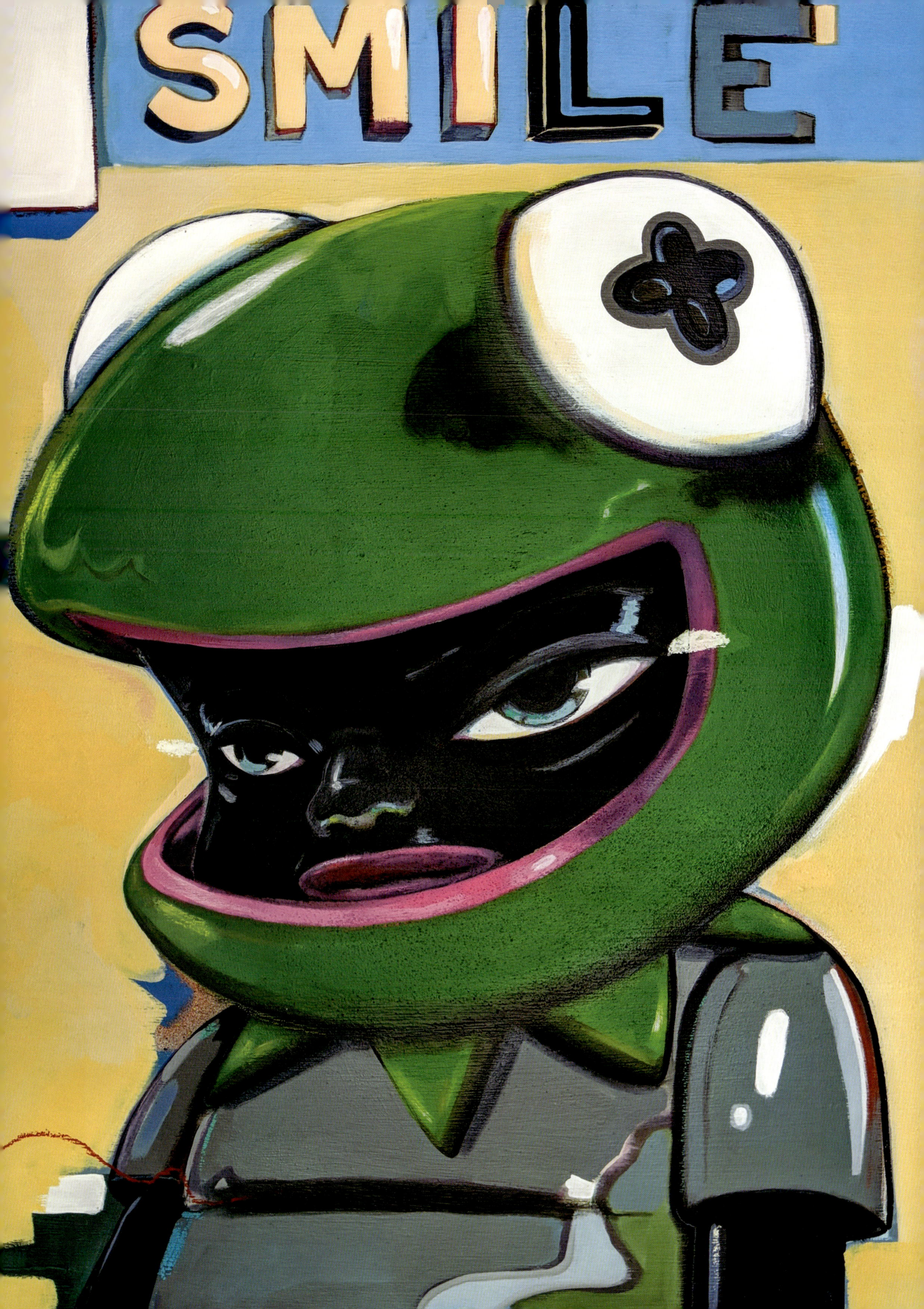
SMILE

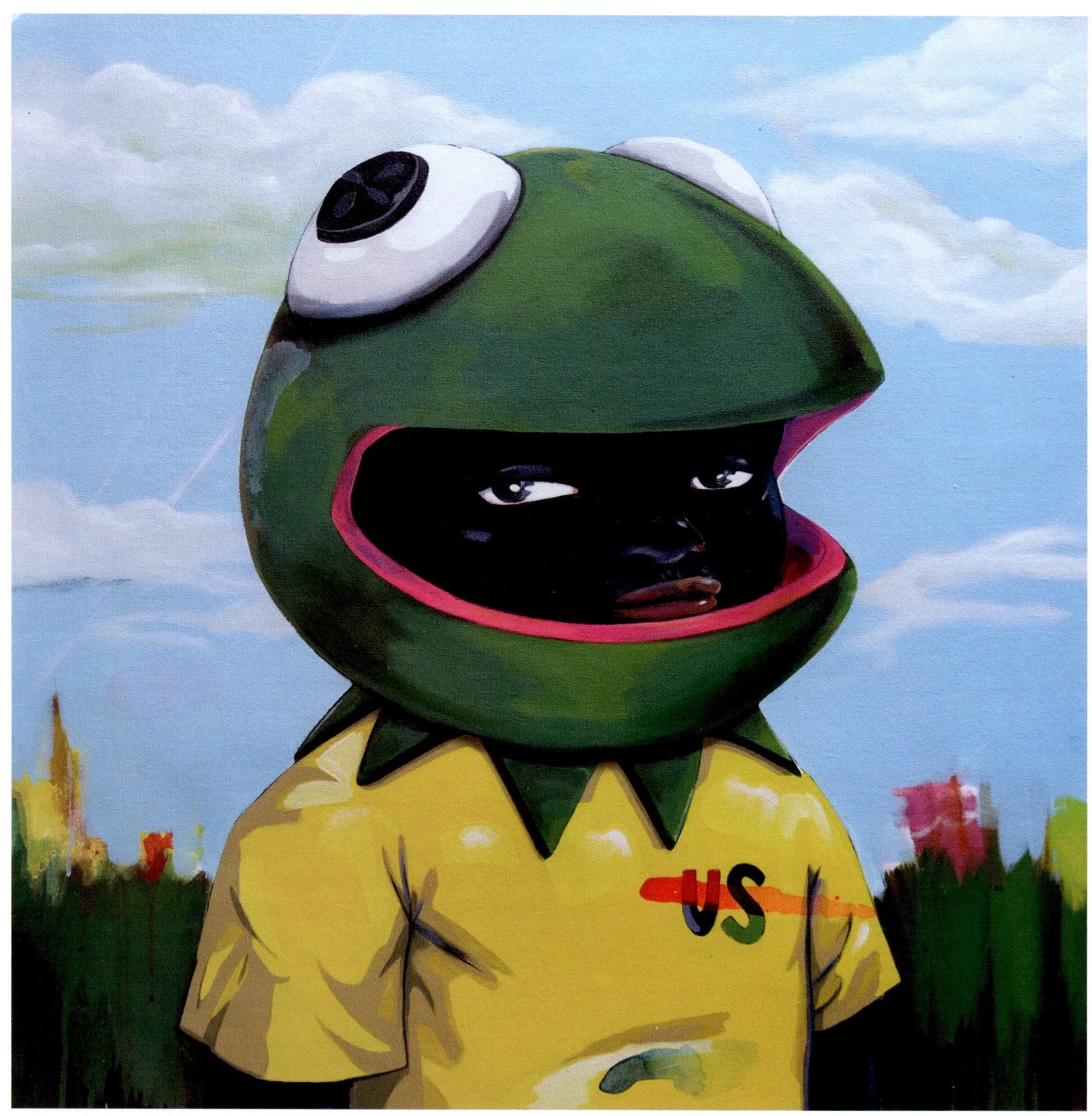

(Above)
Untitled
Mixed media
on canvas
30 x 30 inches
2020

(Opposite)
Paying
Homage Pt. 1
Oil and acrylic
on canvas
48 x 58 inches
2019

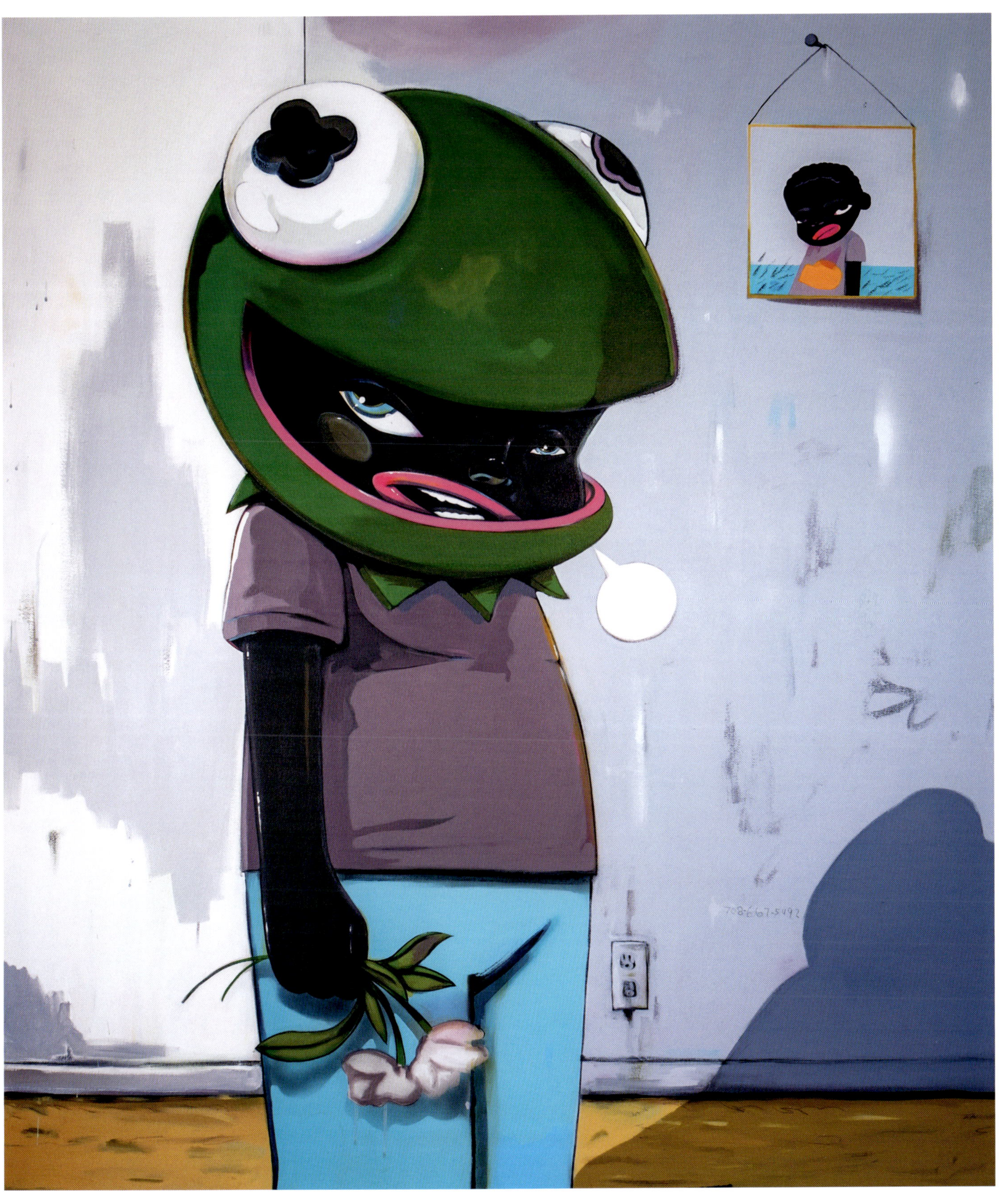
708-667-5492

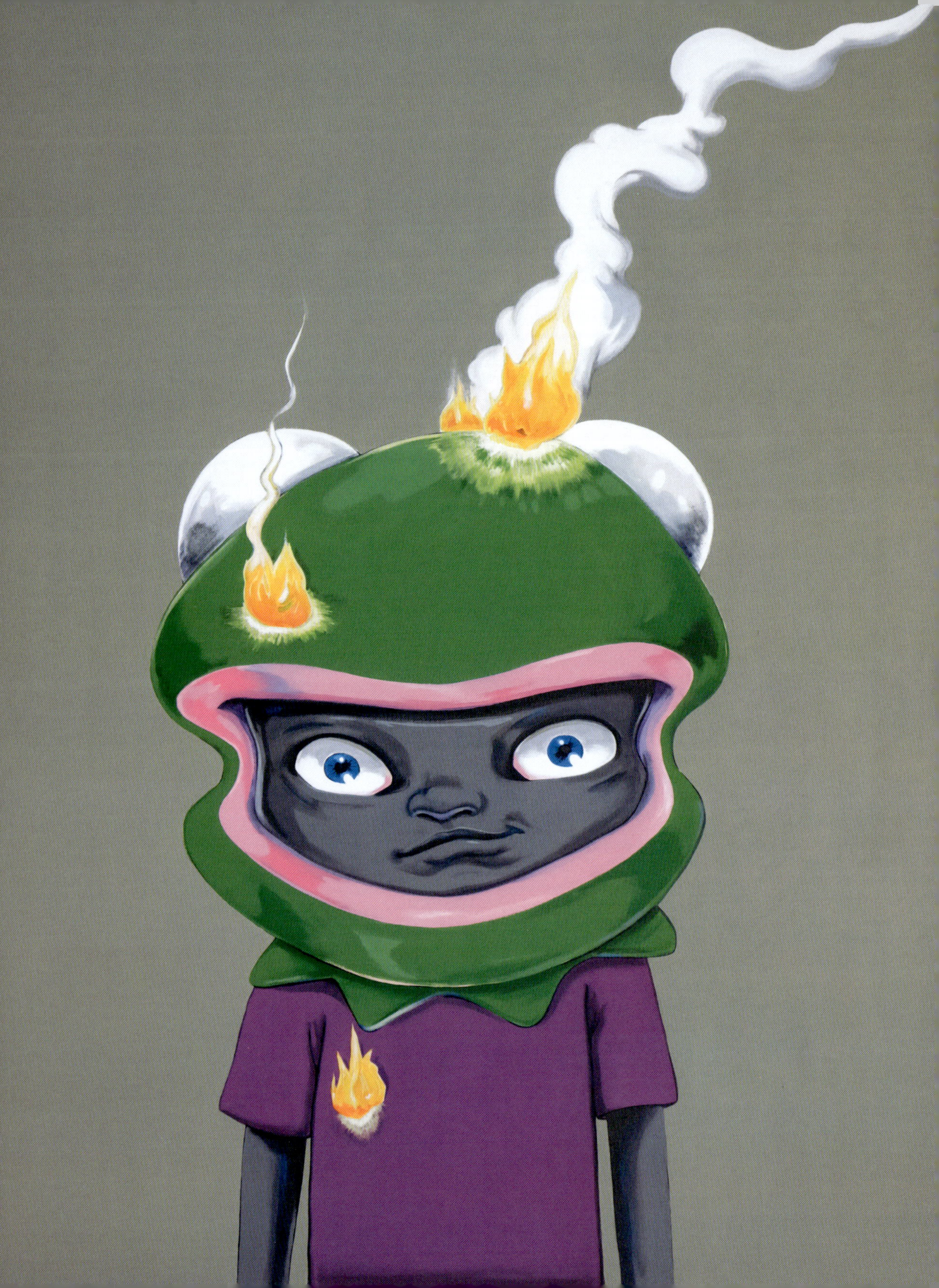

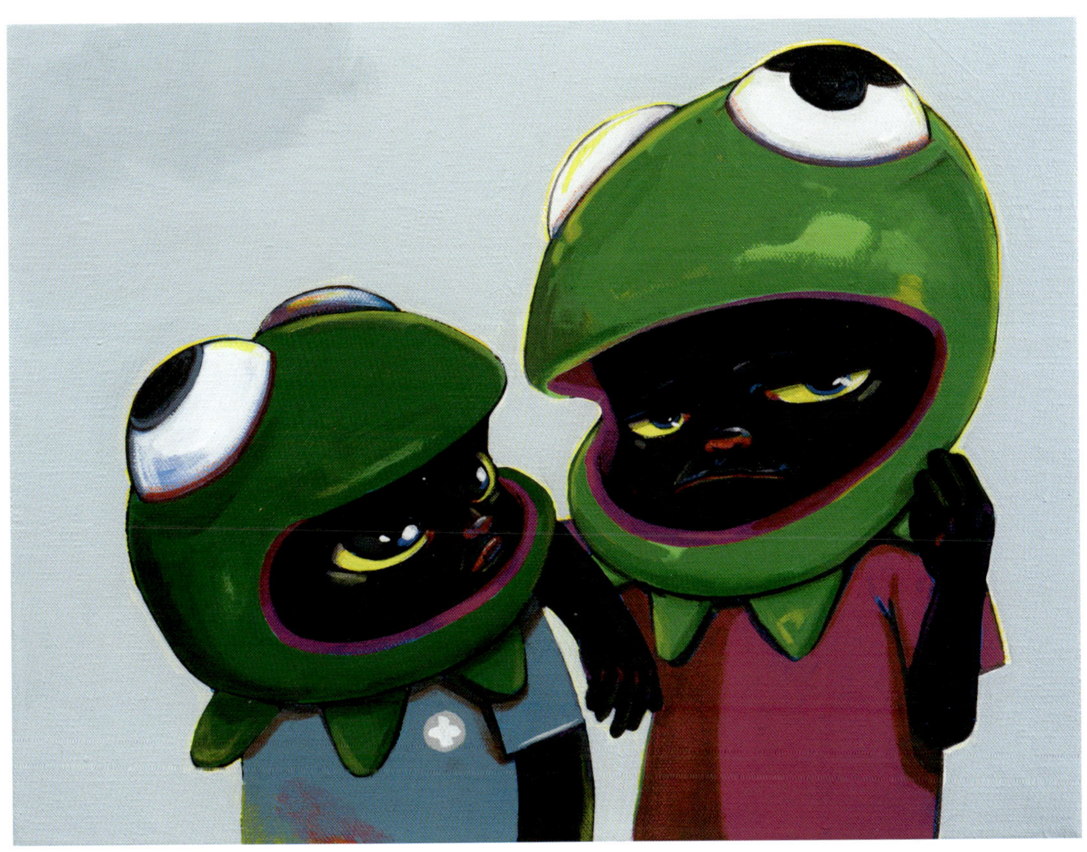

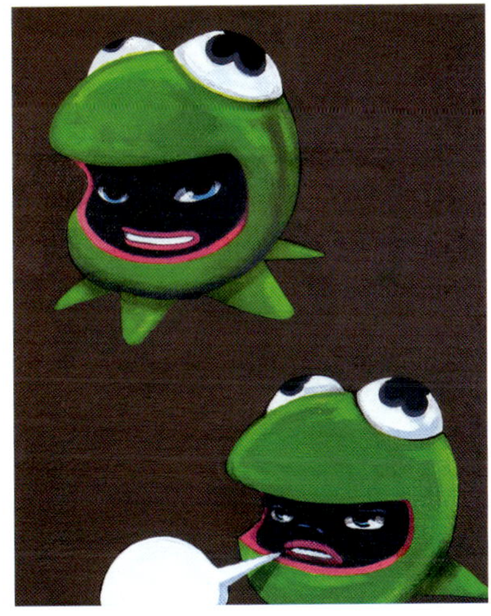

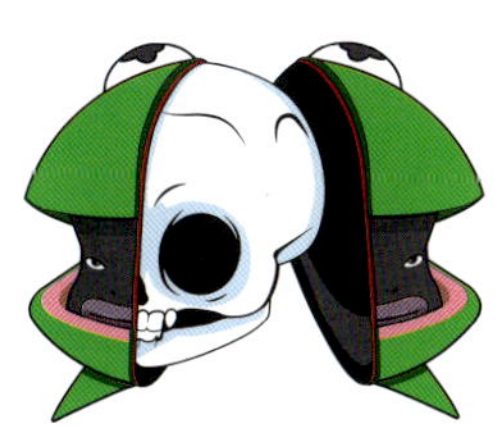

(Opposite)
No I'm Fine, Why'd You Ask?
Mixed media
on canvas
44 x 60 inches
2020

(Top)
Lessons on Life #204
Mixed media
on canvas
11 x 14 inches
2019

(Bottom)
These Two
Mixed media
on canvas
8 x 10 inches
2018–2020

No Ghost in the Wild
Mixed media
on canvas
30 x 30 inches
2020

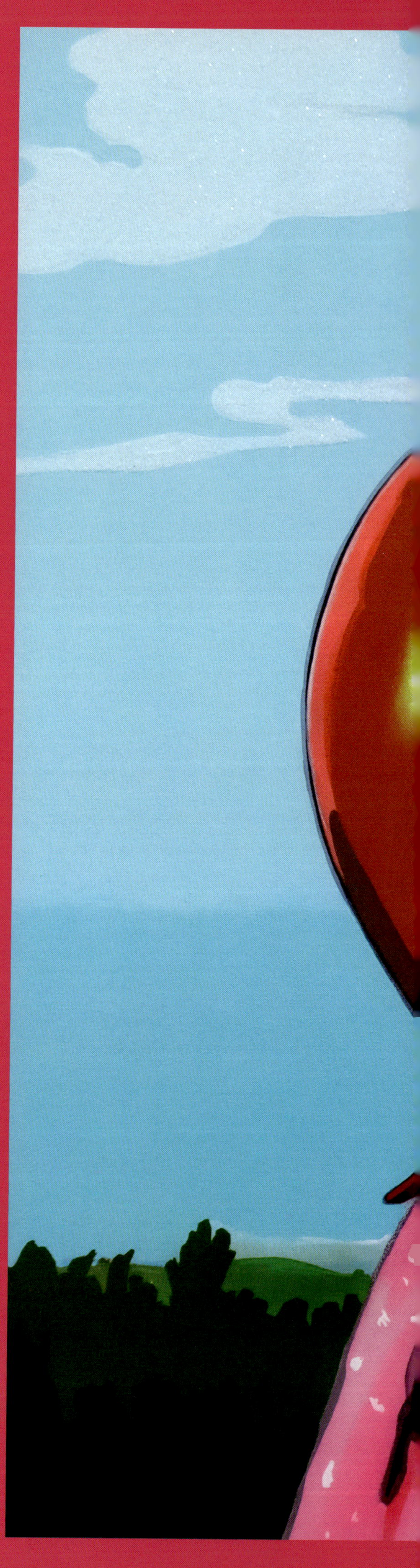

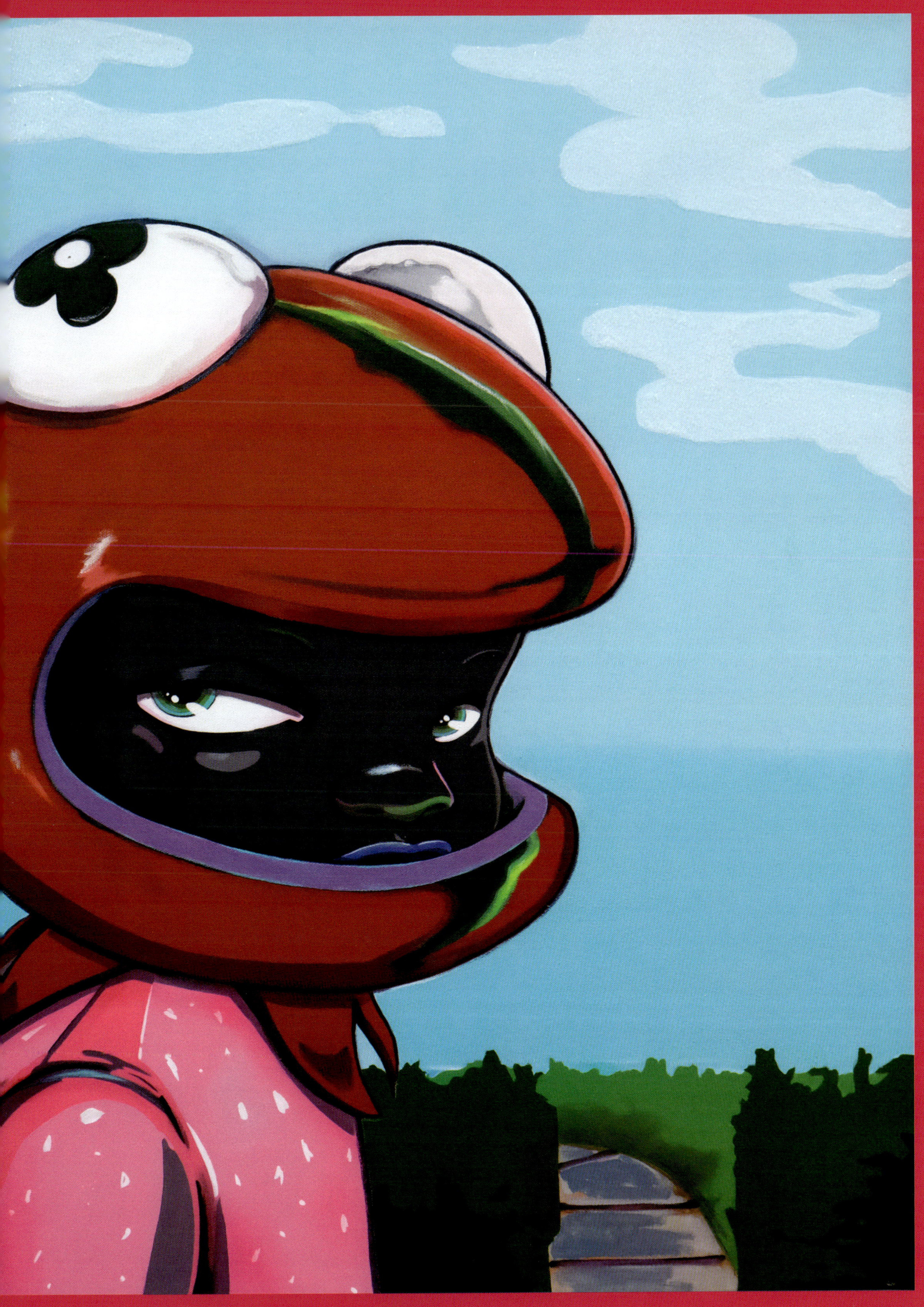

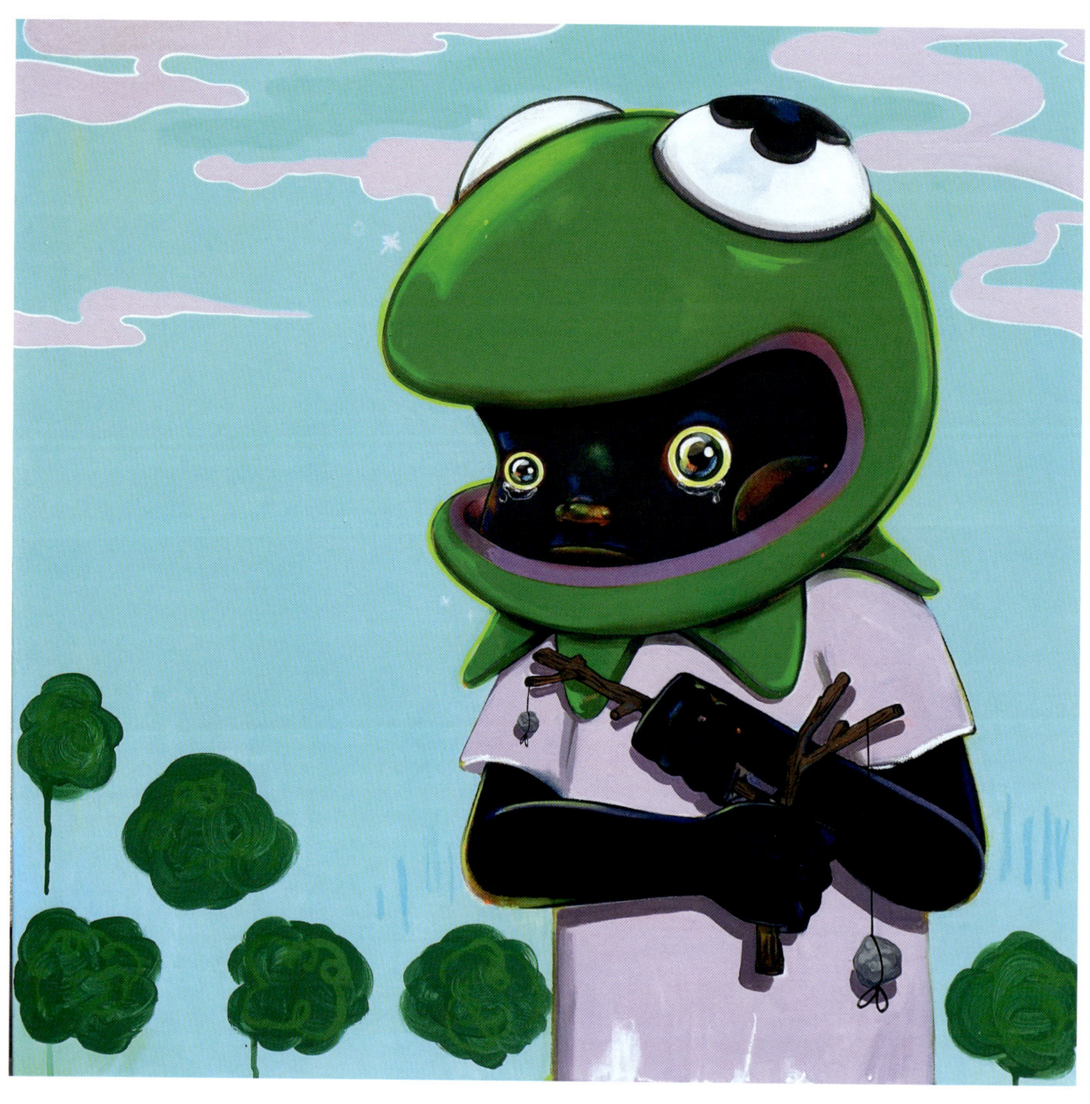

(Above)
Sticks & Stones
Mixed media
on canvas
30 x 30 inches
2021

(Opposite)
Into the Wild
Mixed media
on canvas
36 x 36 inches
2020

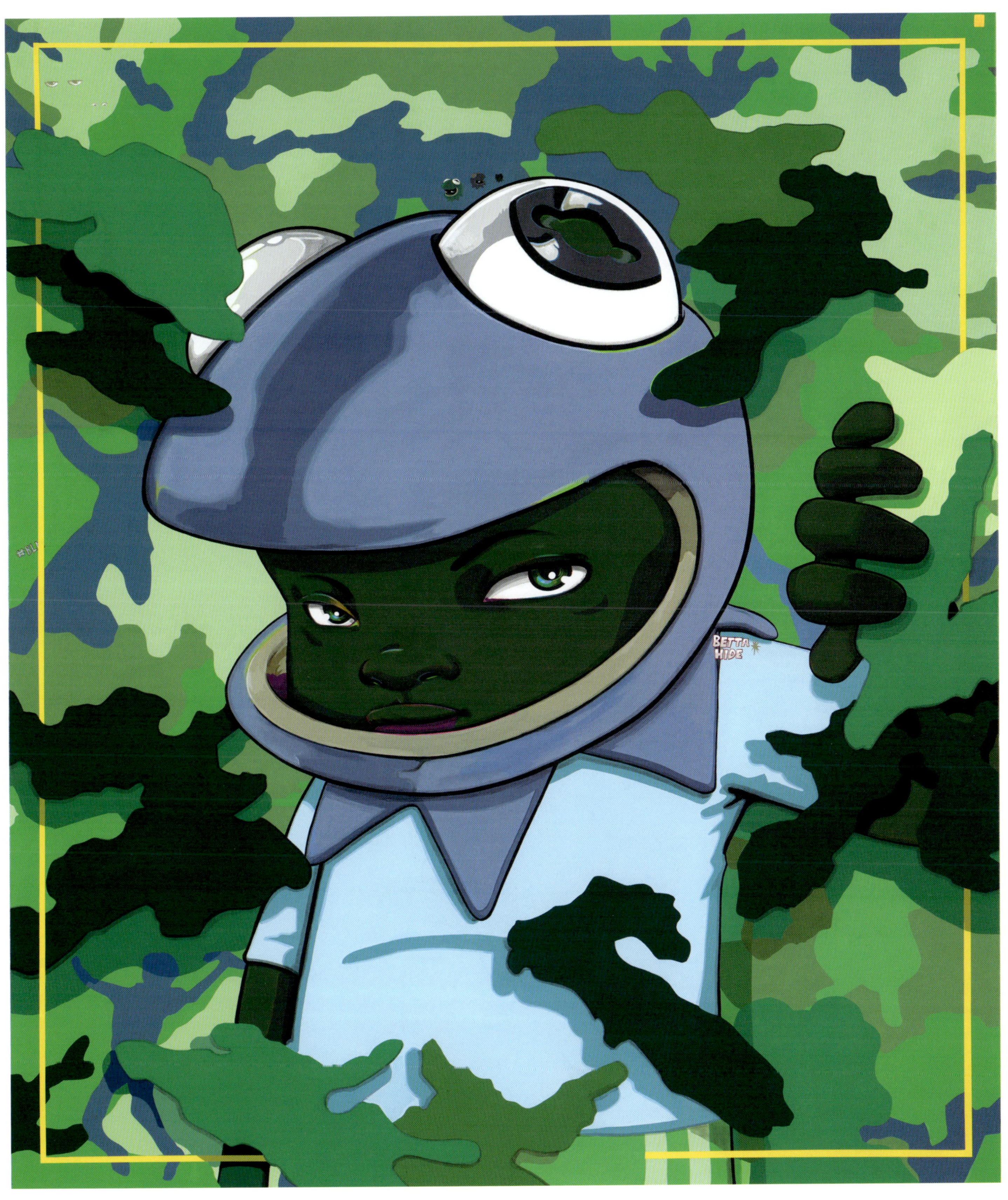
BETTA
HIDE

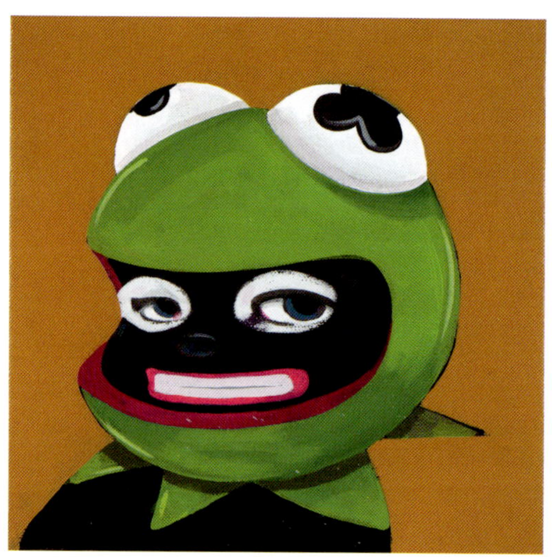

Smile
(Through the B.S.)
Mixed media
on canvas
8 x 8 inches
2020

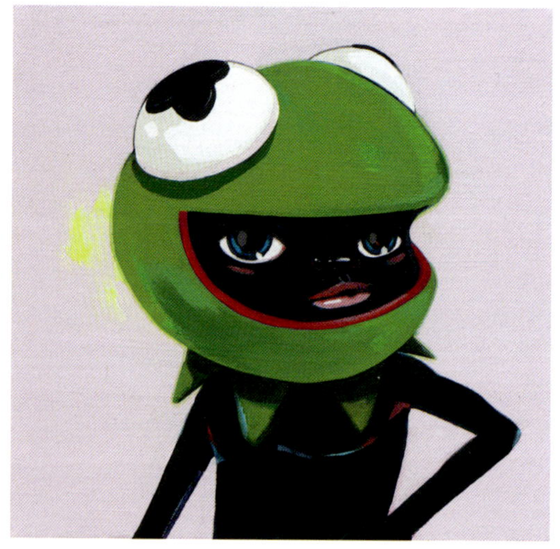

Lilac Phibby
Mixed media
on canvas
10 x 10 inches
2020

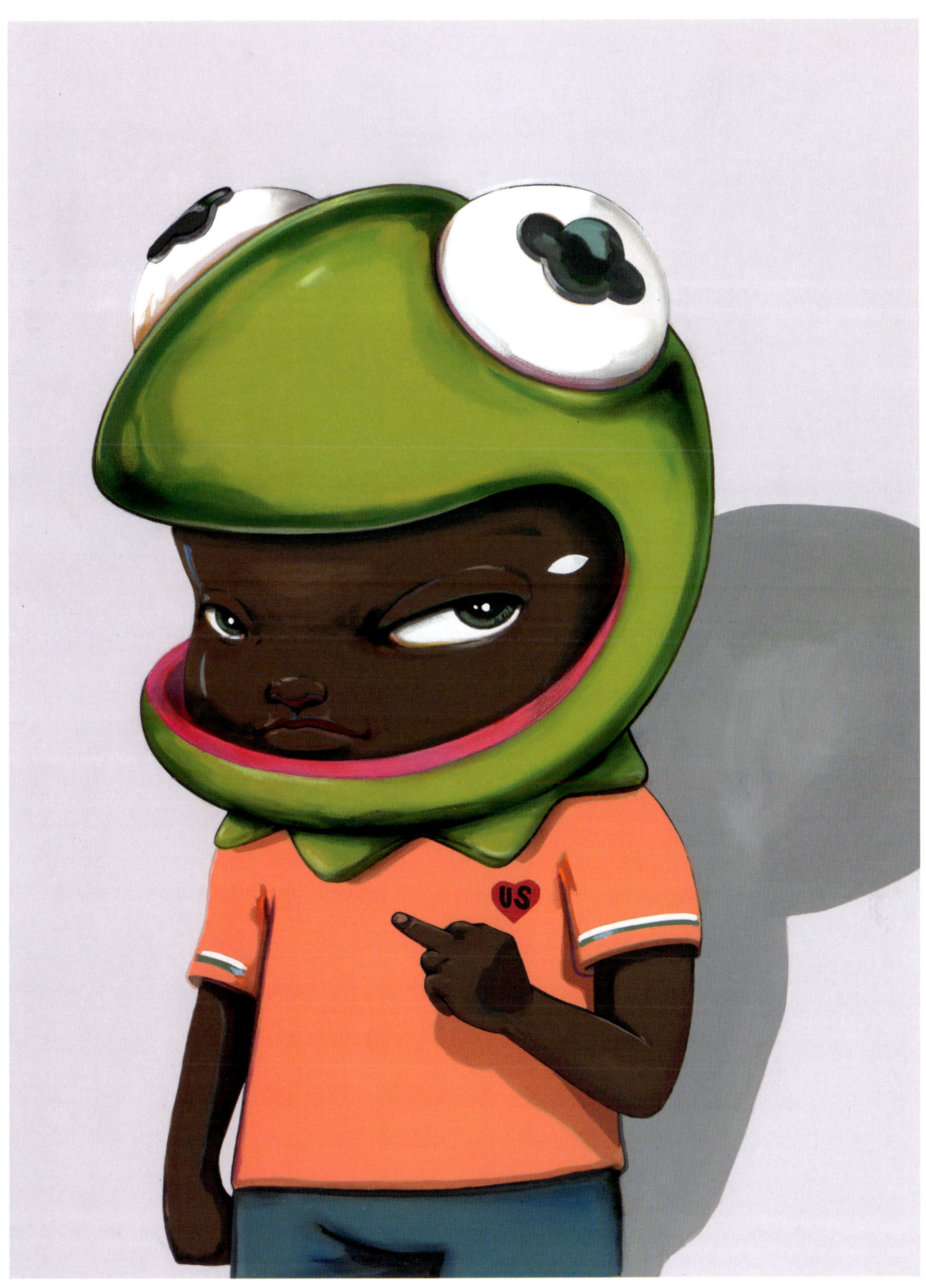

If You Against Us, This Is for You
Mixed media
on canvas
36 x 50 inches
2020

(Below)
Free Advice
Mixed media
on canvas
18 inches diameter
2019–2020

(Opposite)
Never Wrong
Mixed media
on canvas
30 x 30 inches
2020

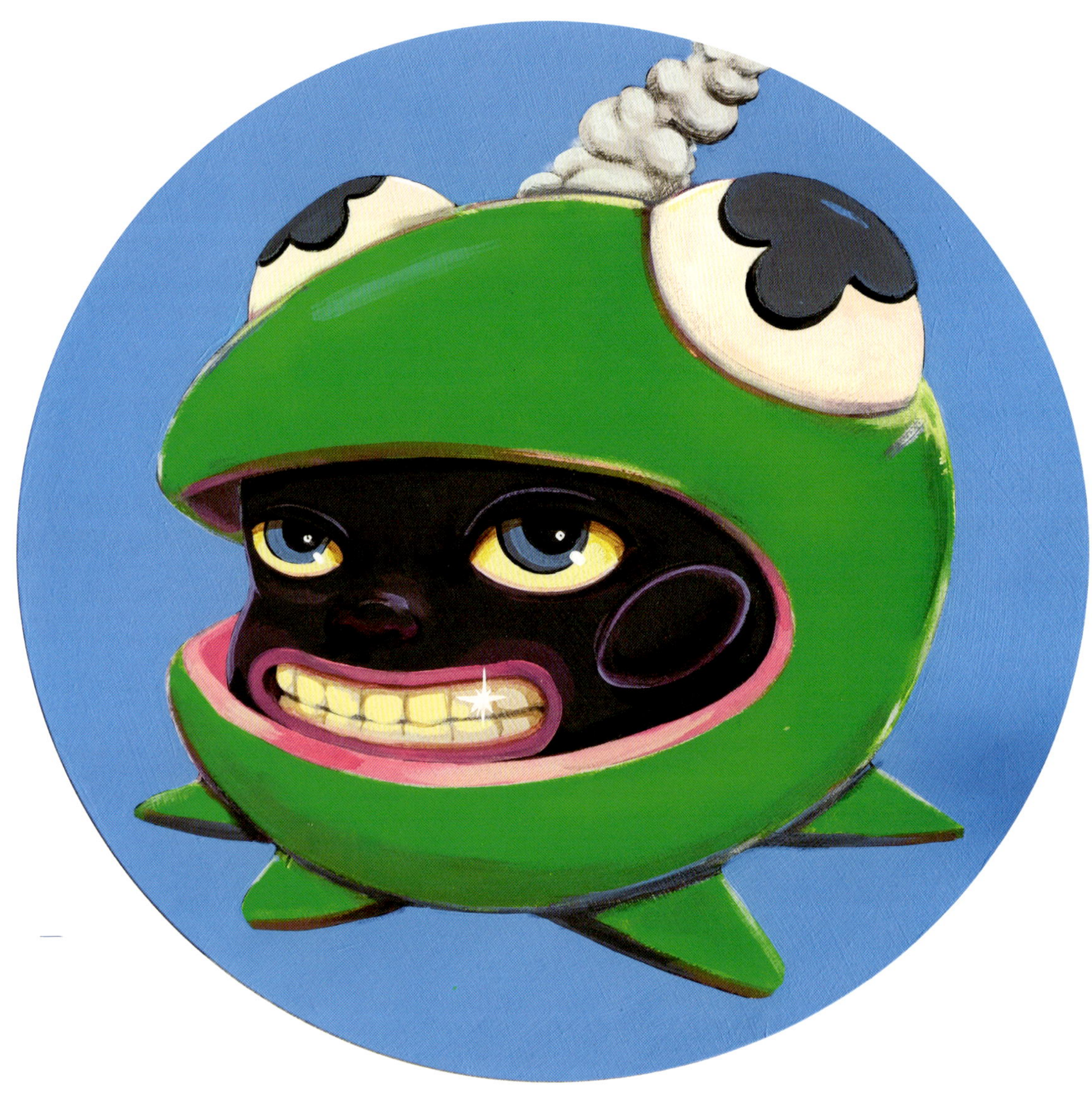

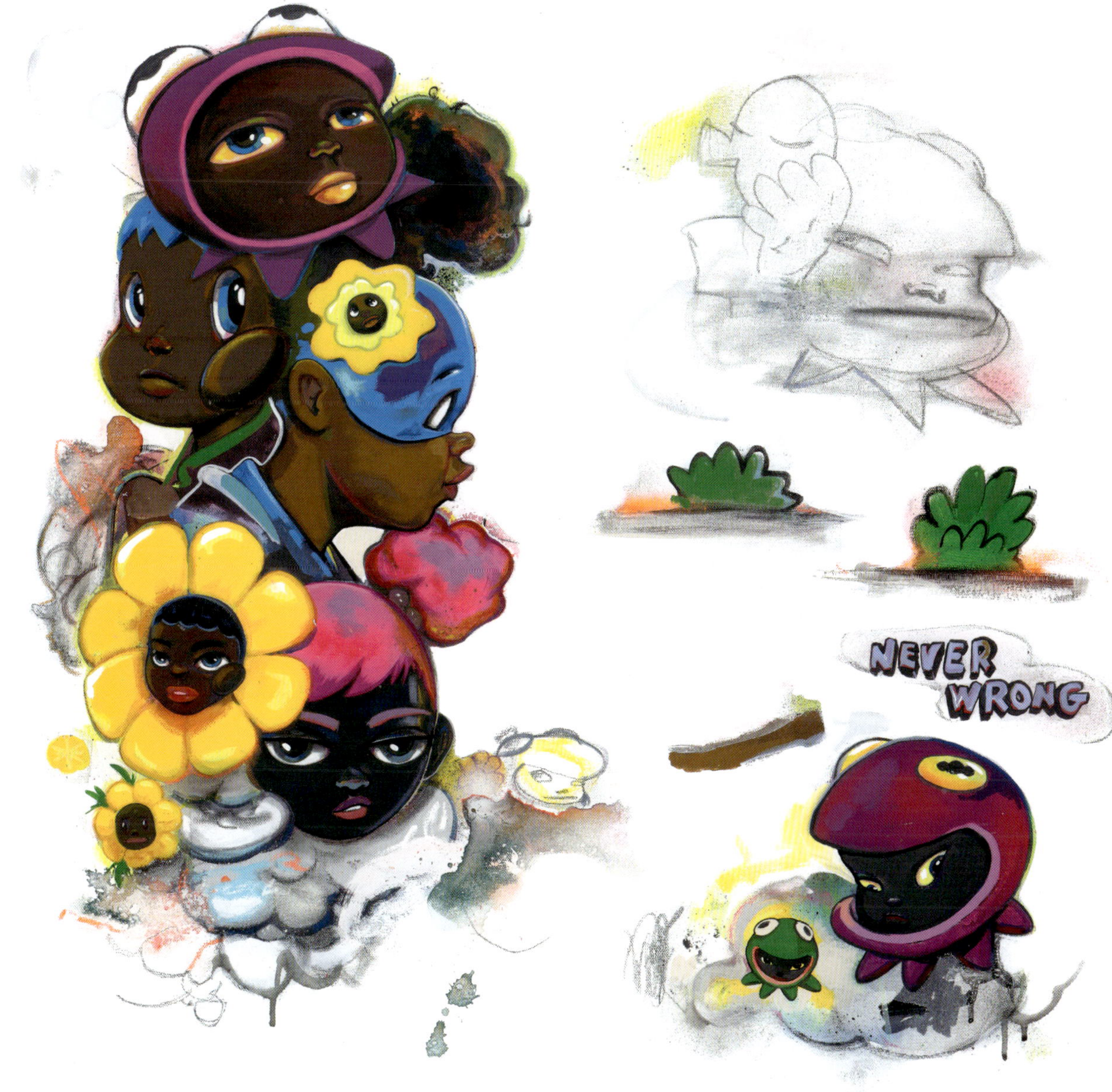
NEVER
WRONG

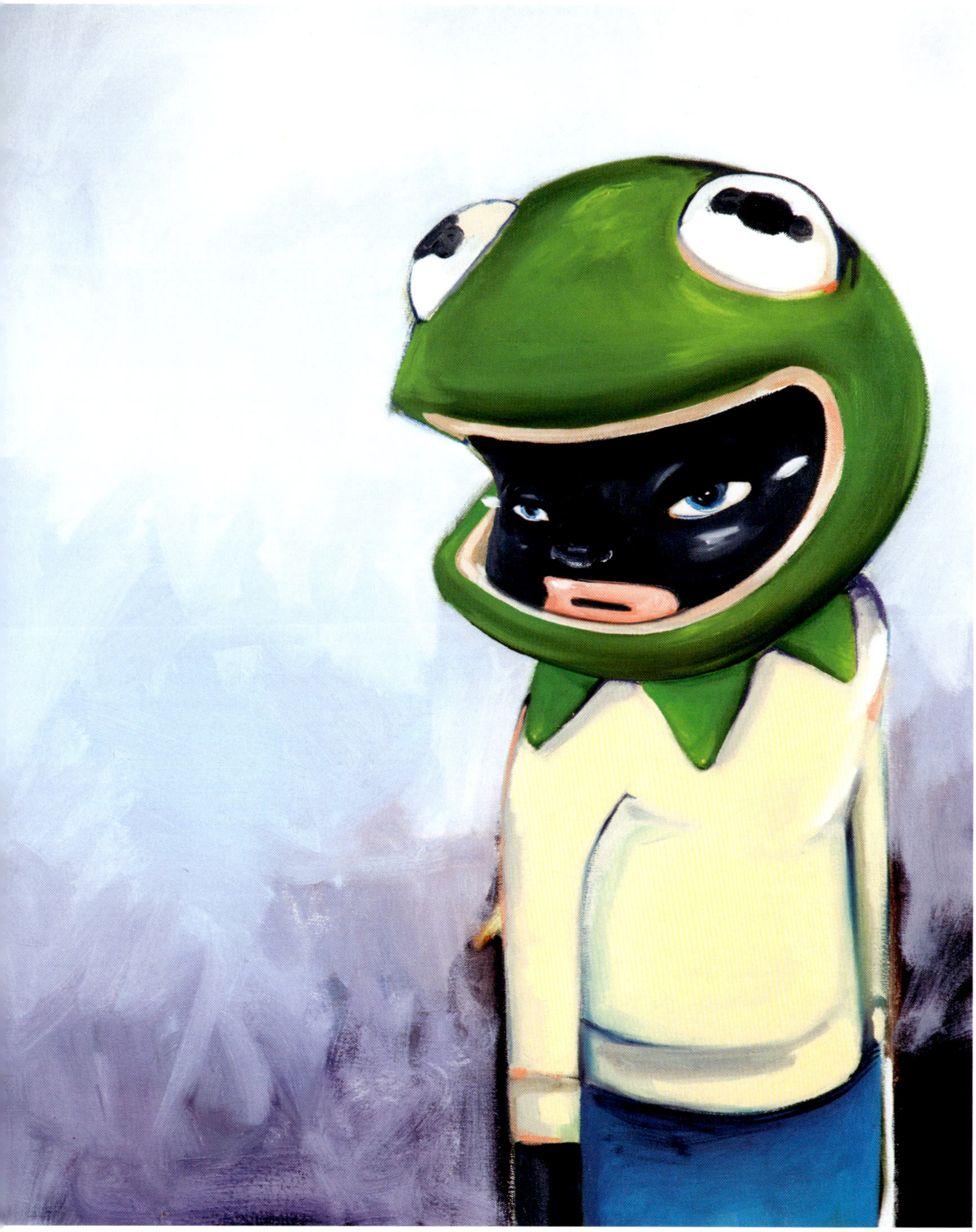

(Left)
Untitled
Oil on canvas
24 x 30 inches
2014

(Below)
No Worries
Mixed media
on canvas
28.5 x 34.5 inches
2017

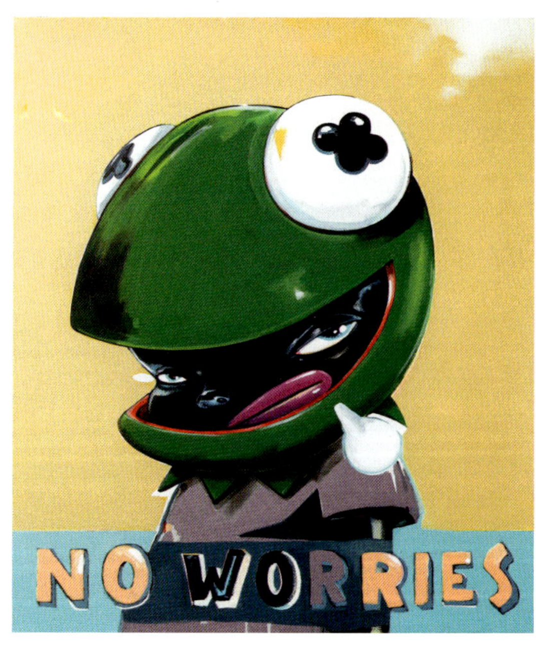

Dark Fiction
Fiberglass and
enamel paint
30 x 30 x 30 inches
2021

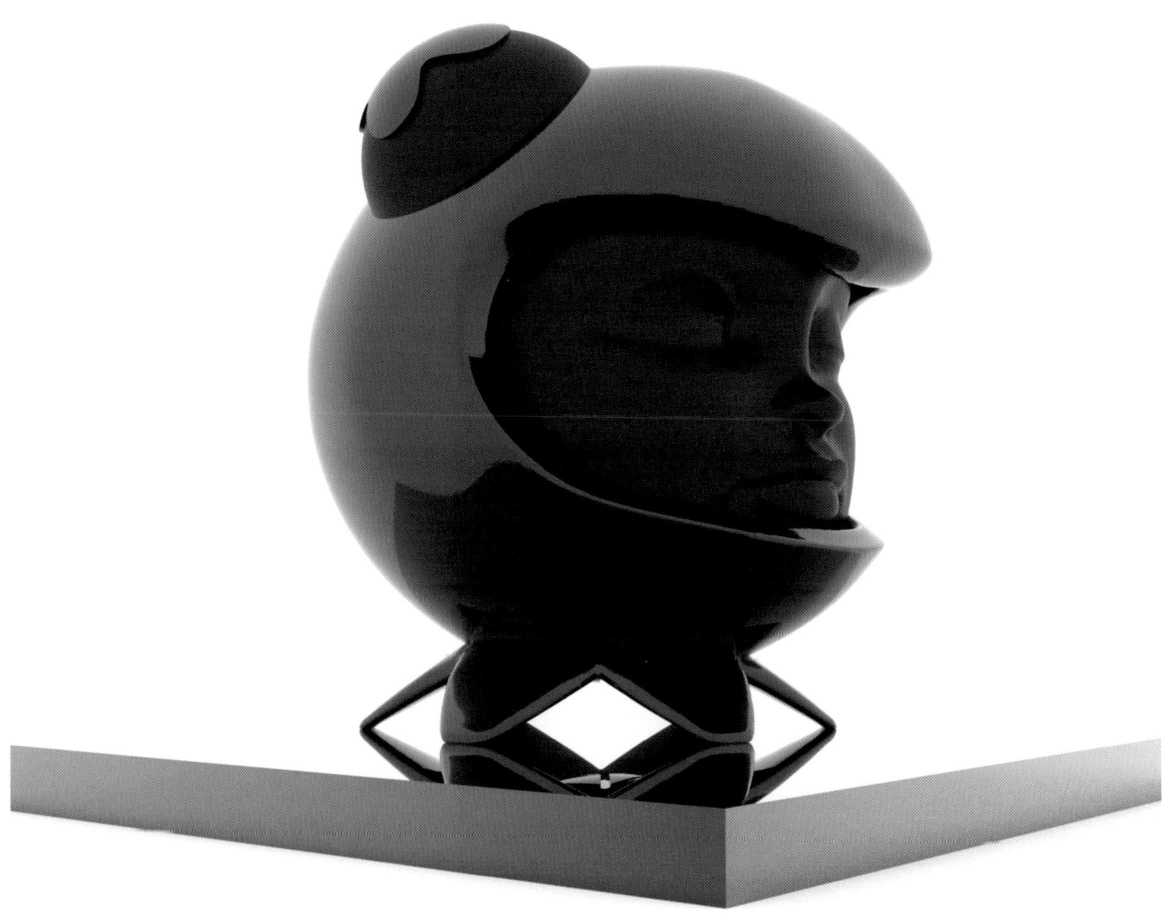

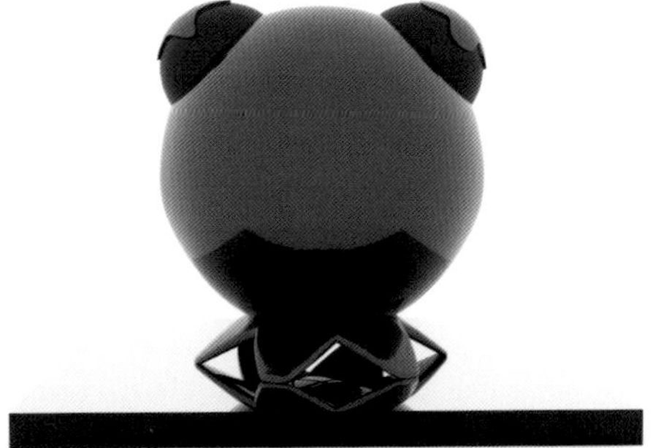

3 the Hard Way
Bronze sculpture
with satin paint finish
14.2 x 5.1 x 4.7 inches
2020

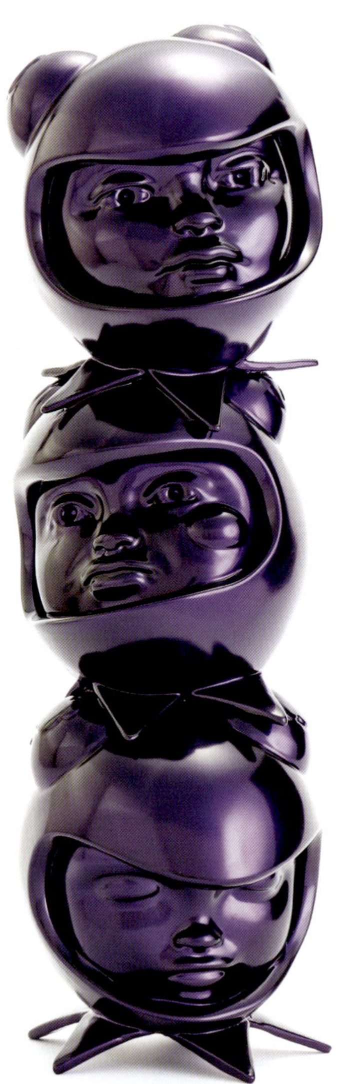

Phibby
Bronze sculpture
with painted finish
6.4 x 15.75 x
6.18 inches
2022

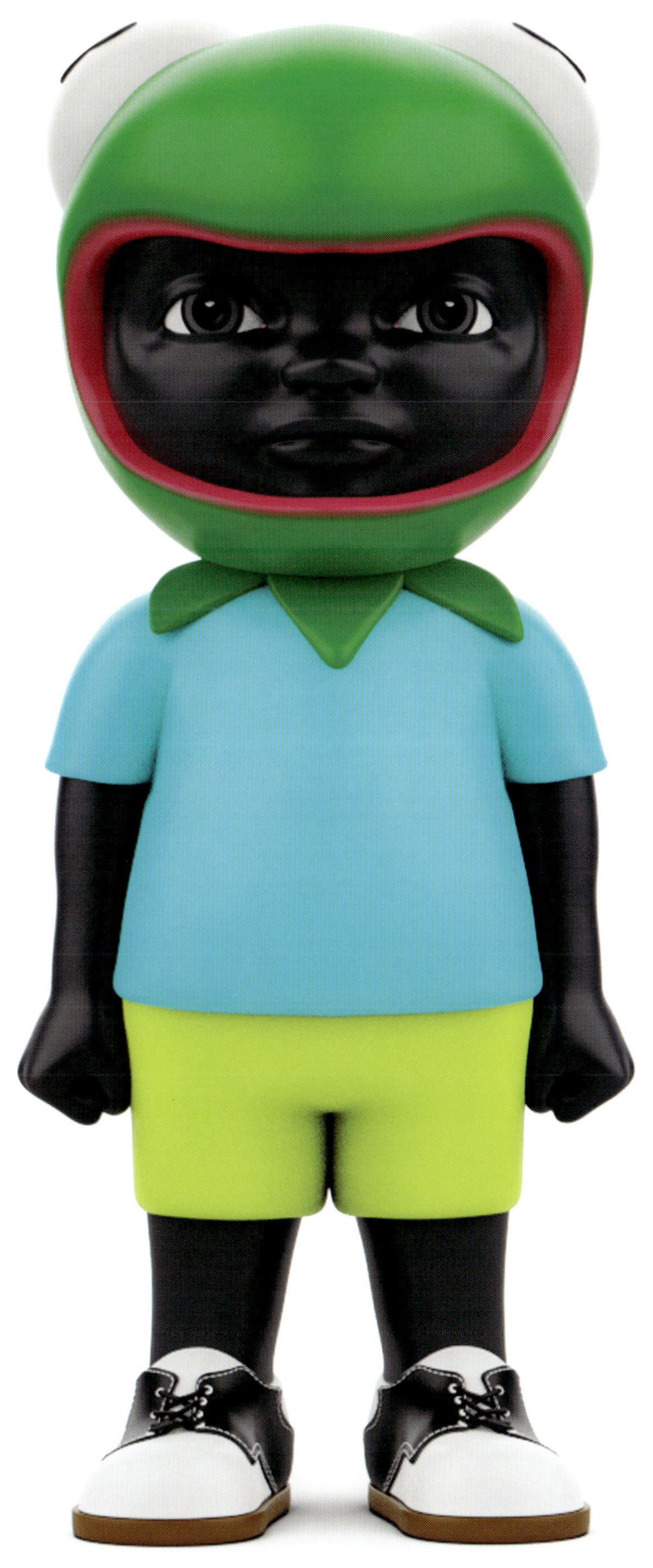

OTHER WORKS

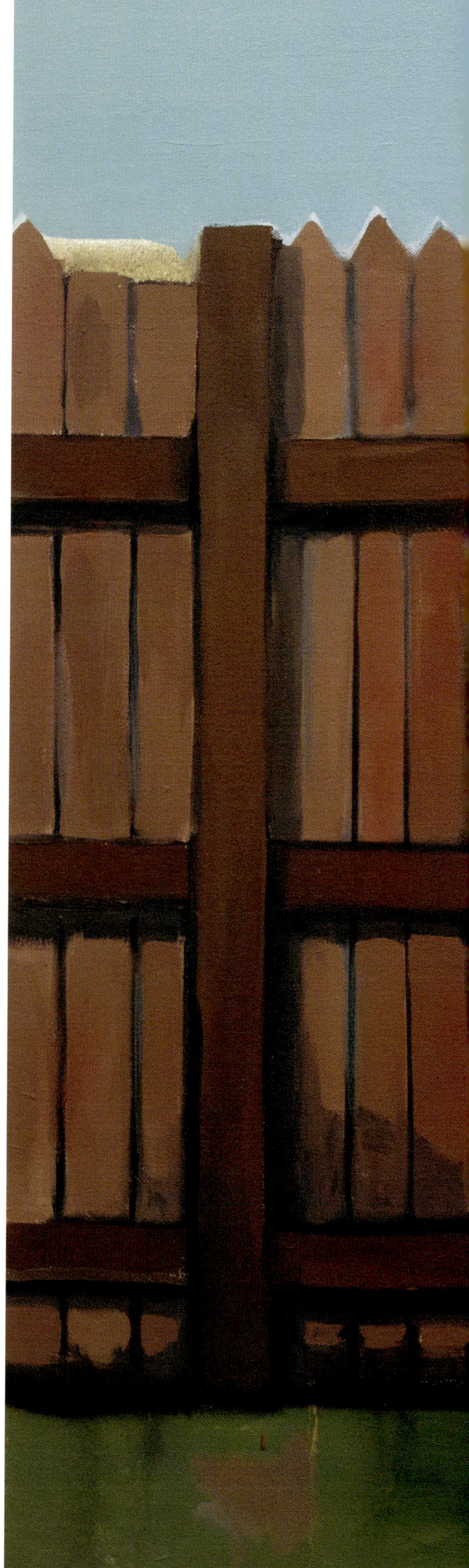

***The Other
Other Side***
Mixed media
on canvas
36 x 36 inches
2017

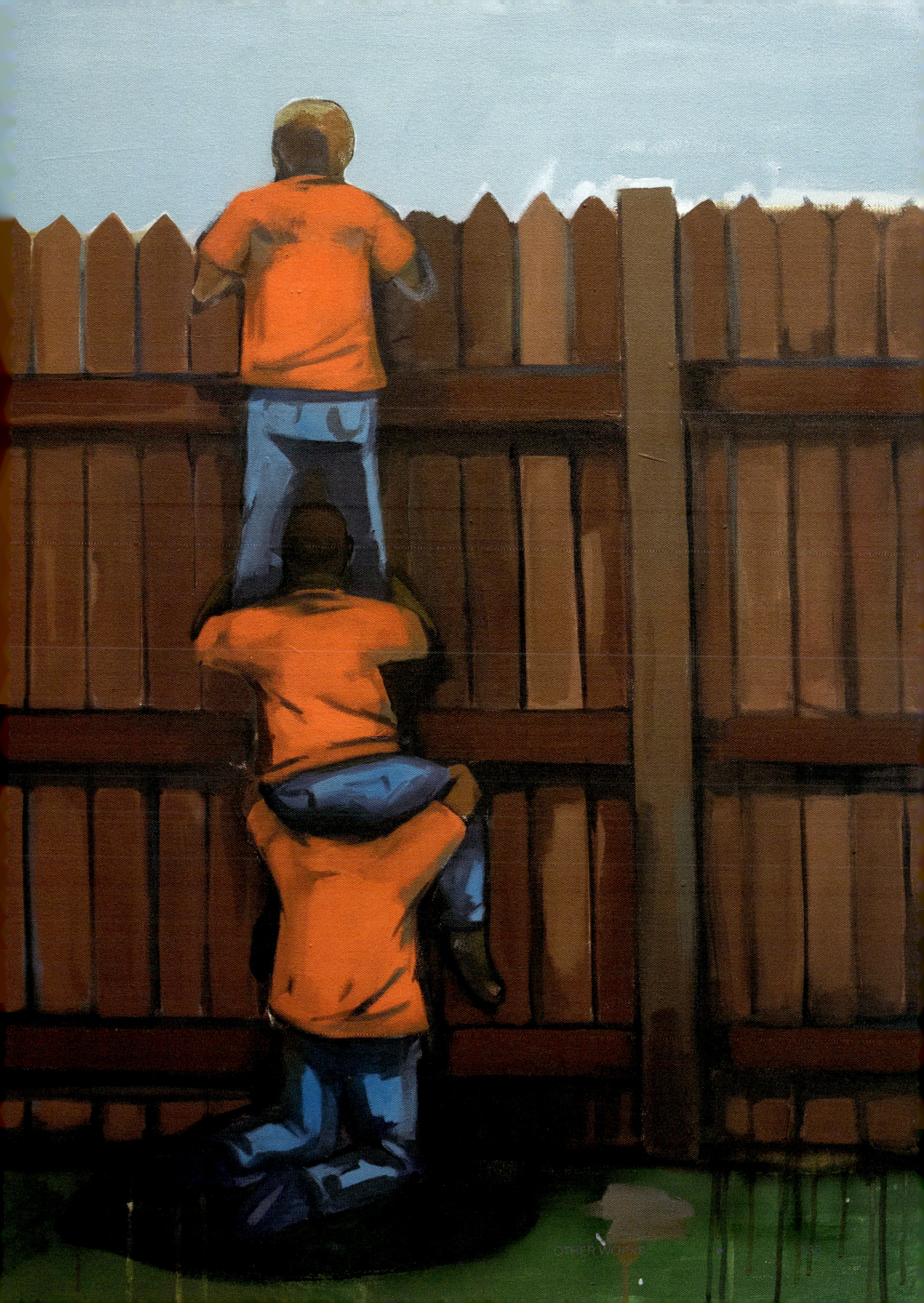

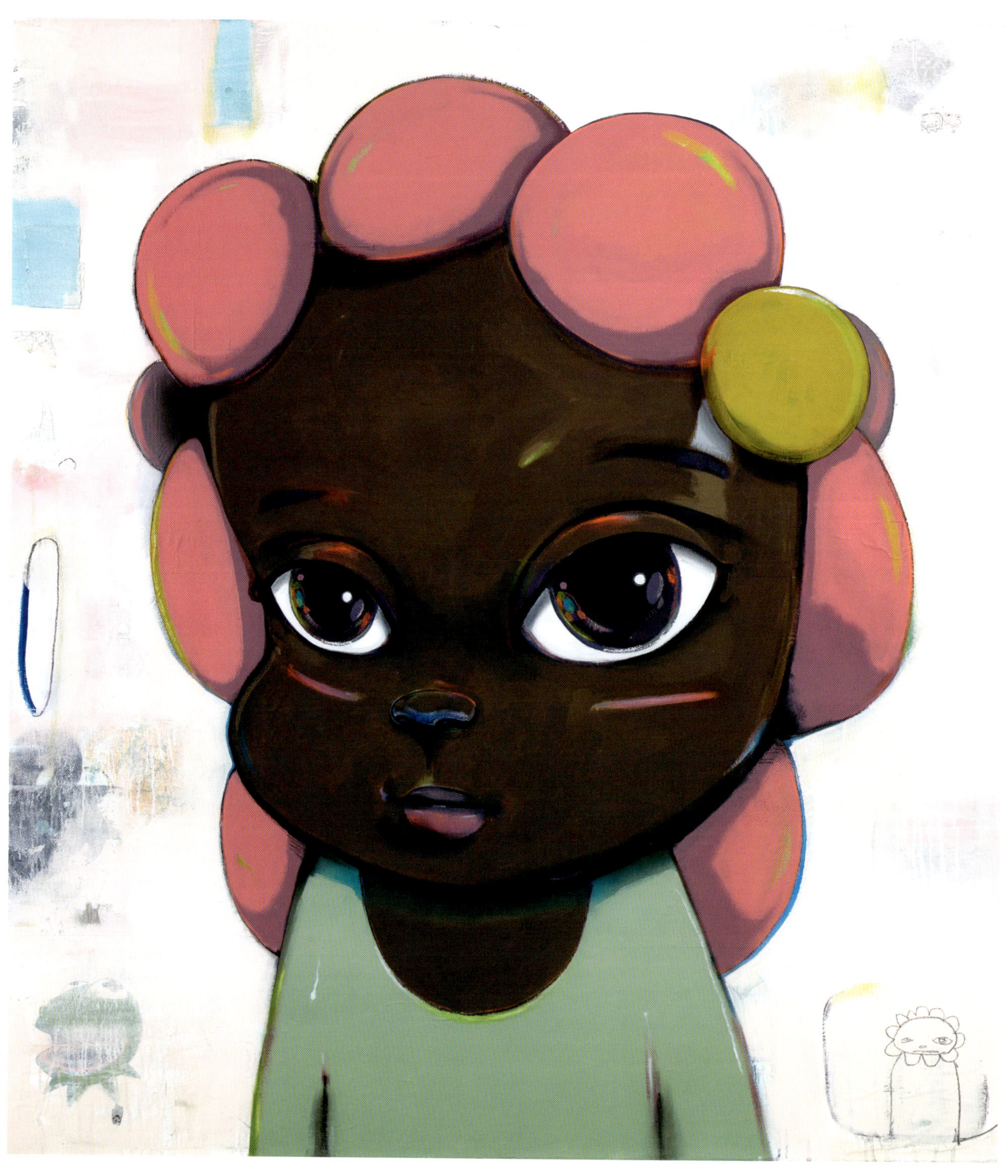

Budding Acrylic, pastel, and spray paint on canvas, 49 x 56 inches, 2017–2020

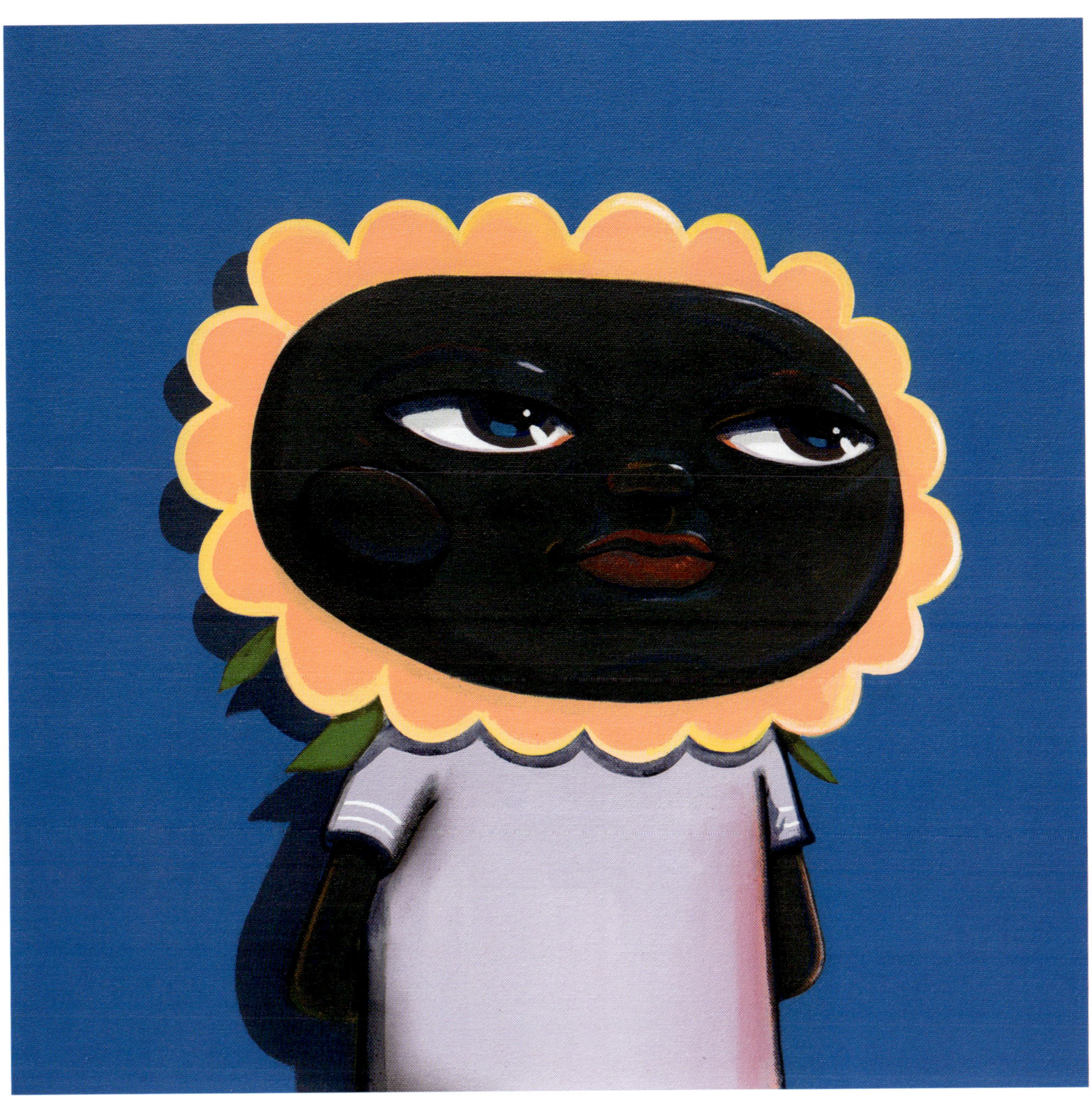

Peaceful Protest Mixed media on canvas, 20 x 20 inches, 2020

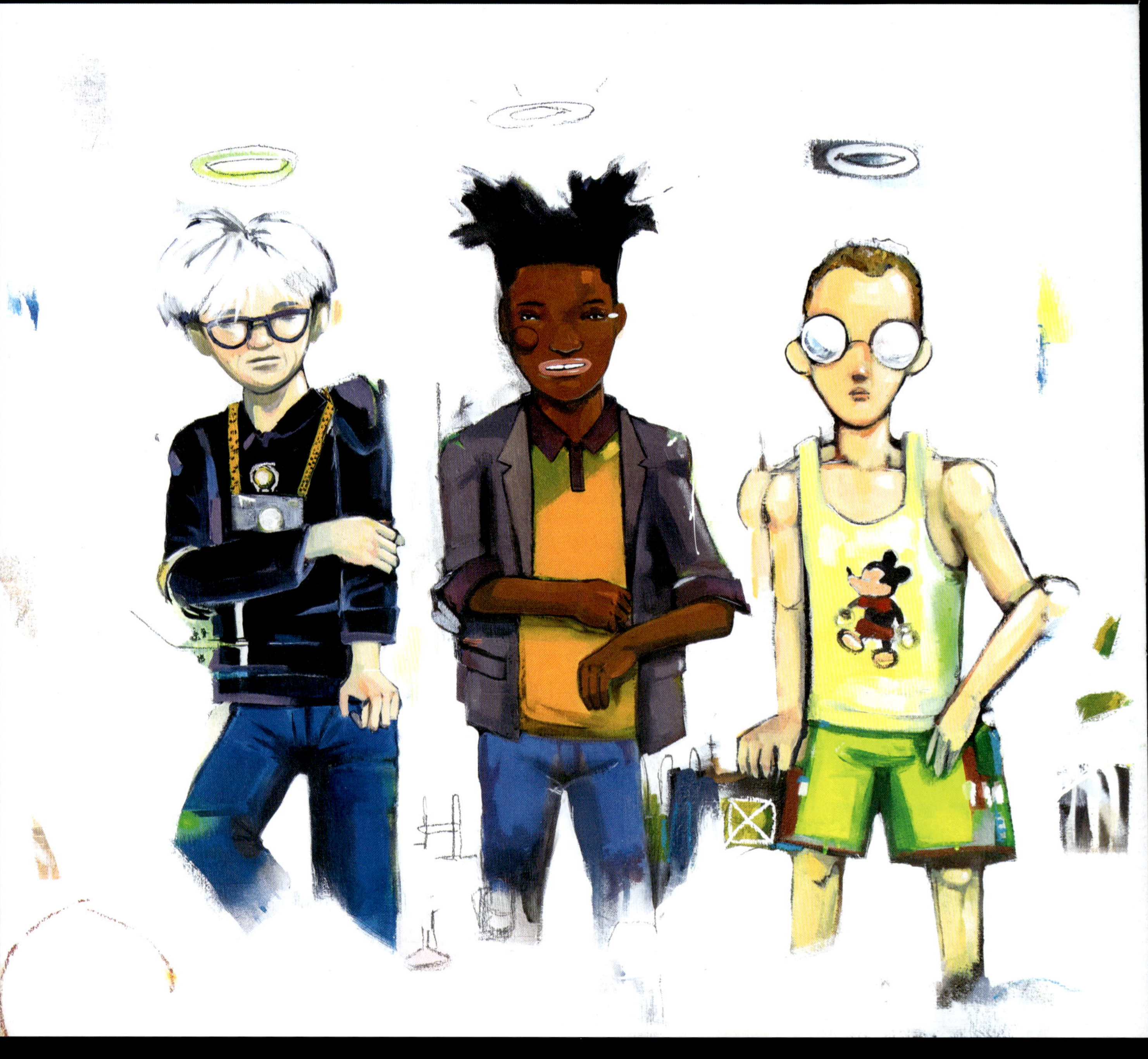

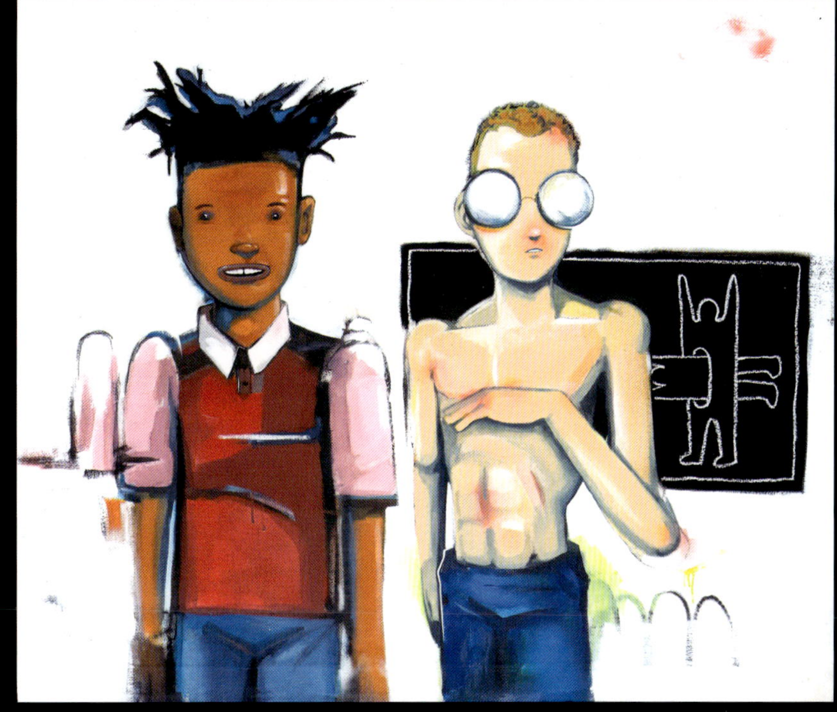

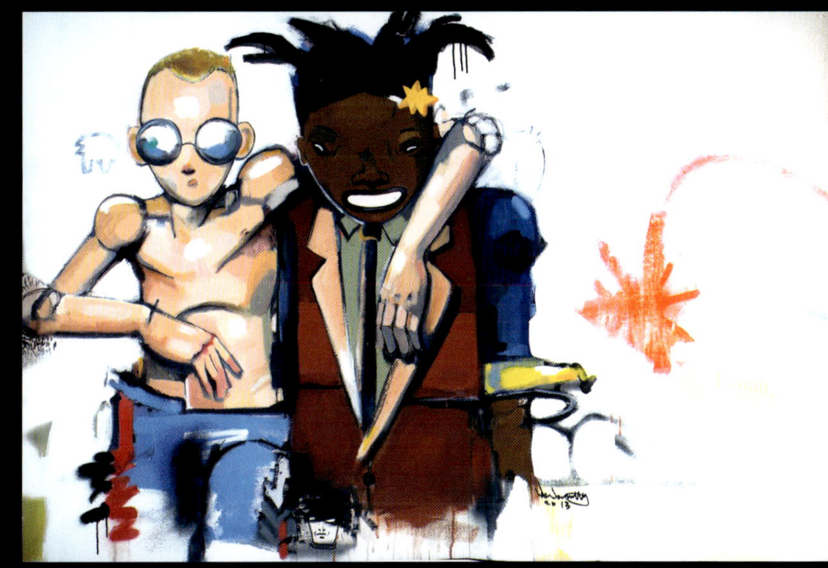

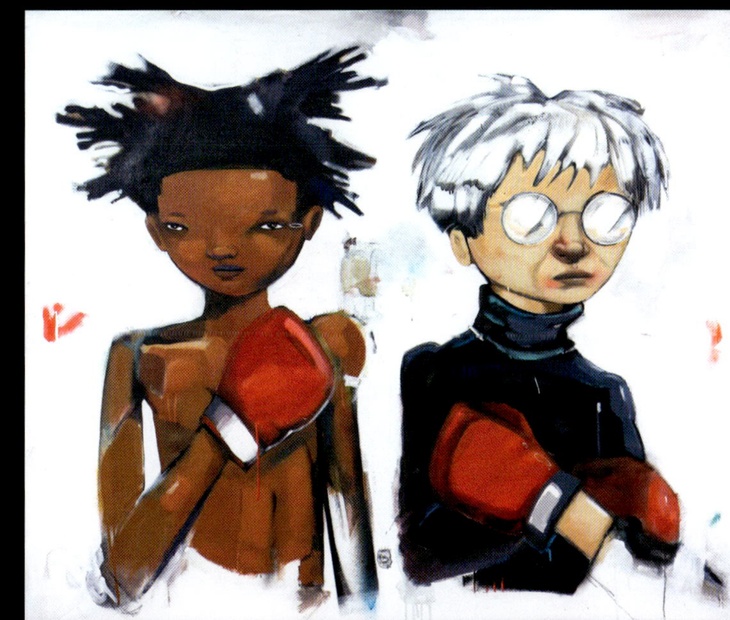

(From top)
The King and The Jester
Spray paint and acrylic on canvas
43 x 37 inches
2017

Untitled
Spray paint and acrylic on canvas
2013

No More Public Battles, Just Private Wars
Spray paint and acrylic on canvas
58 x 49 inches
2017

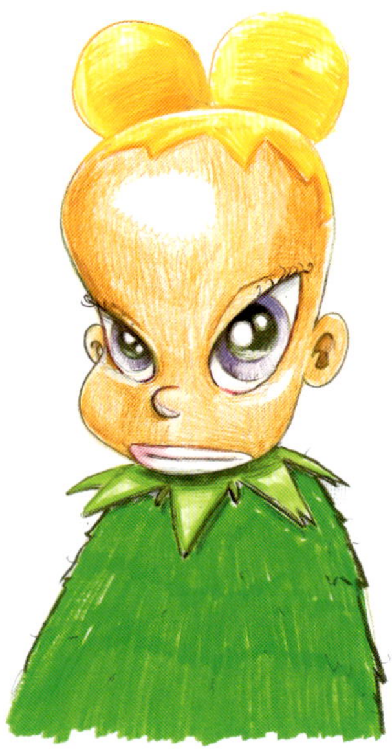

(Above)
Lu Lu
Colored pencil
on paper
11 x 14 inches
2021

(Right)
That Flower
N Word
Wax pastel,
colored pencil,
and paint marker
on paper
14 x 17 inches
2021

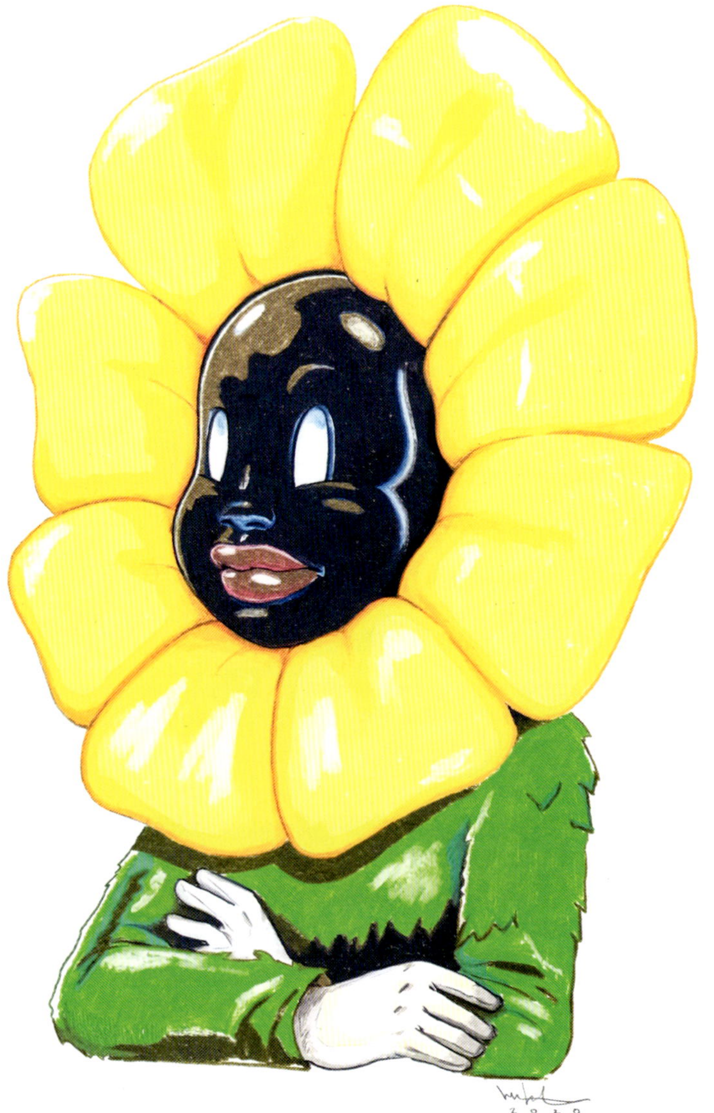

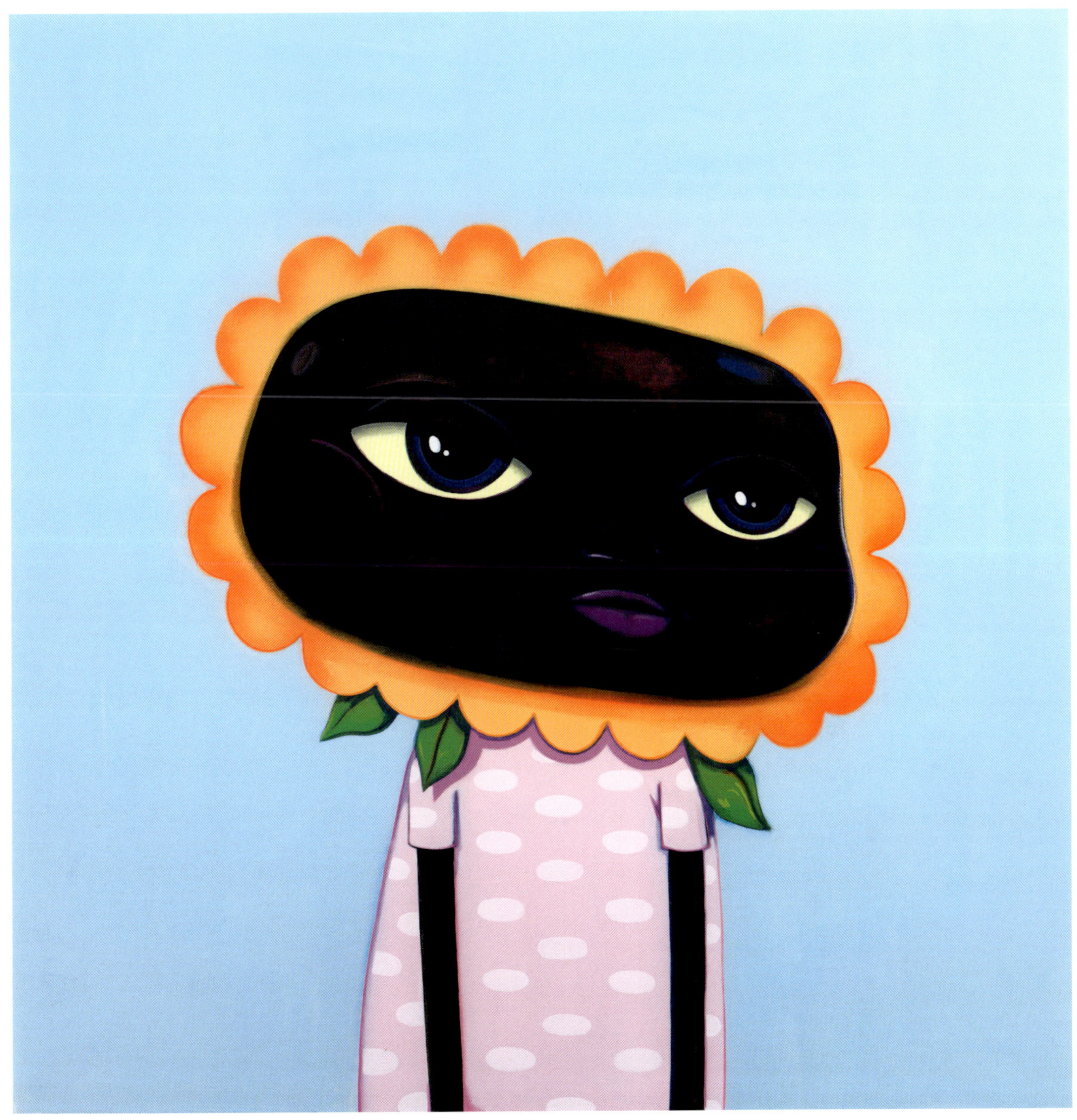

Smitten Acrylic, pastel, and spray paint on canvas, 48 x 50 inches, 2020

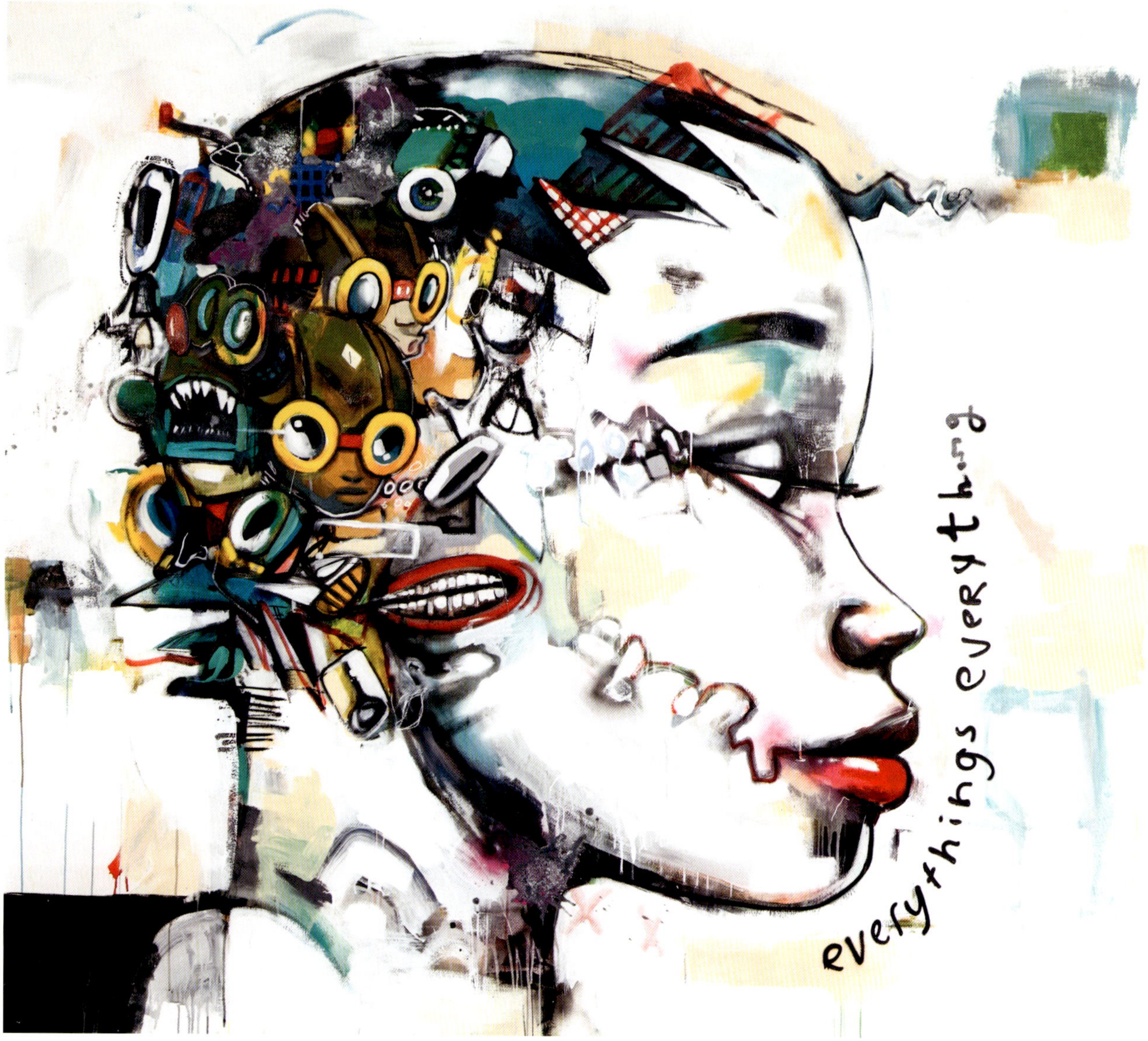

(Above)
Everything's Everything
Mixed media
on canvas
2012

(Right)
Untitled
Mixed media
on canvas
2012

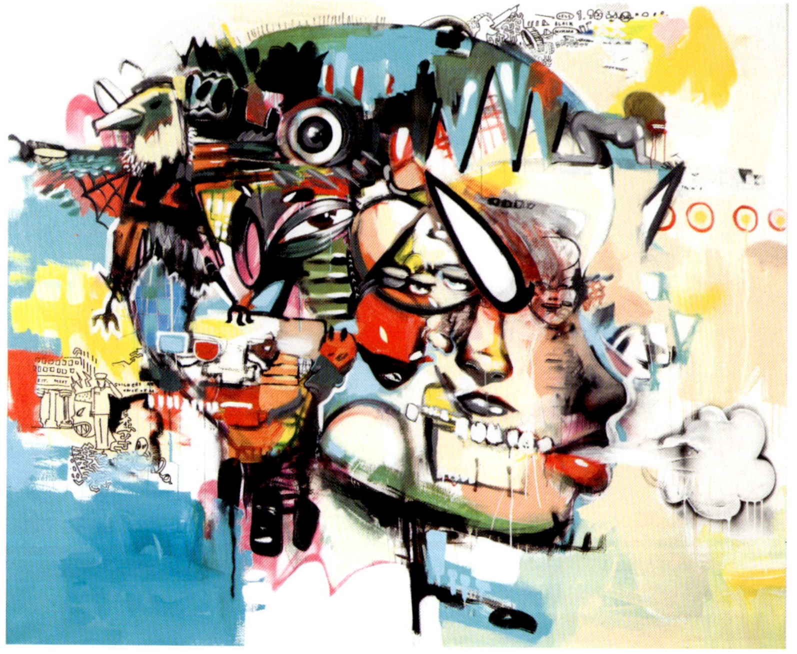

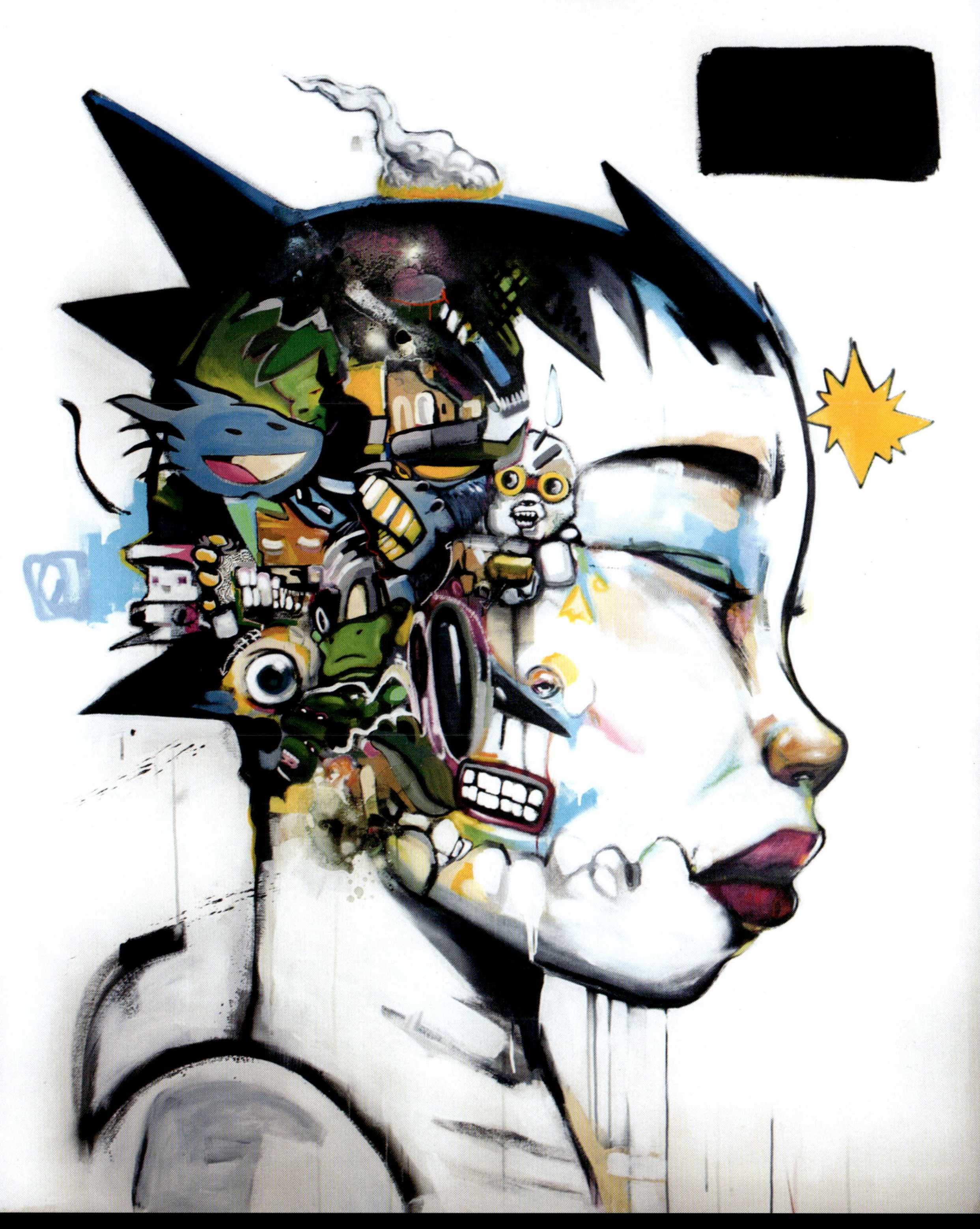

Astro Wifey
Mixed media
on canvas
58 x 71 inches
2014

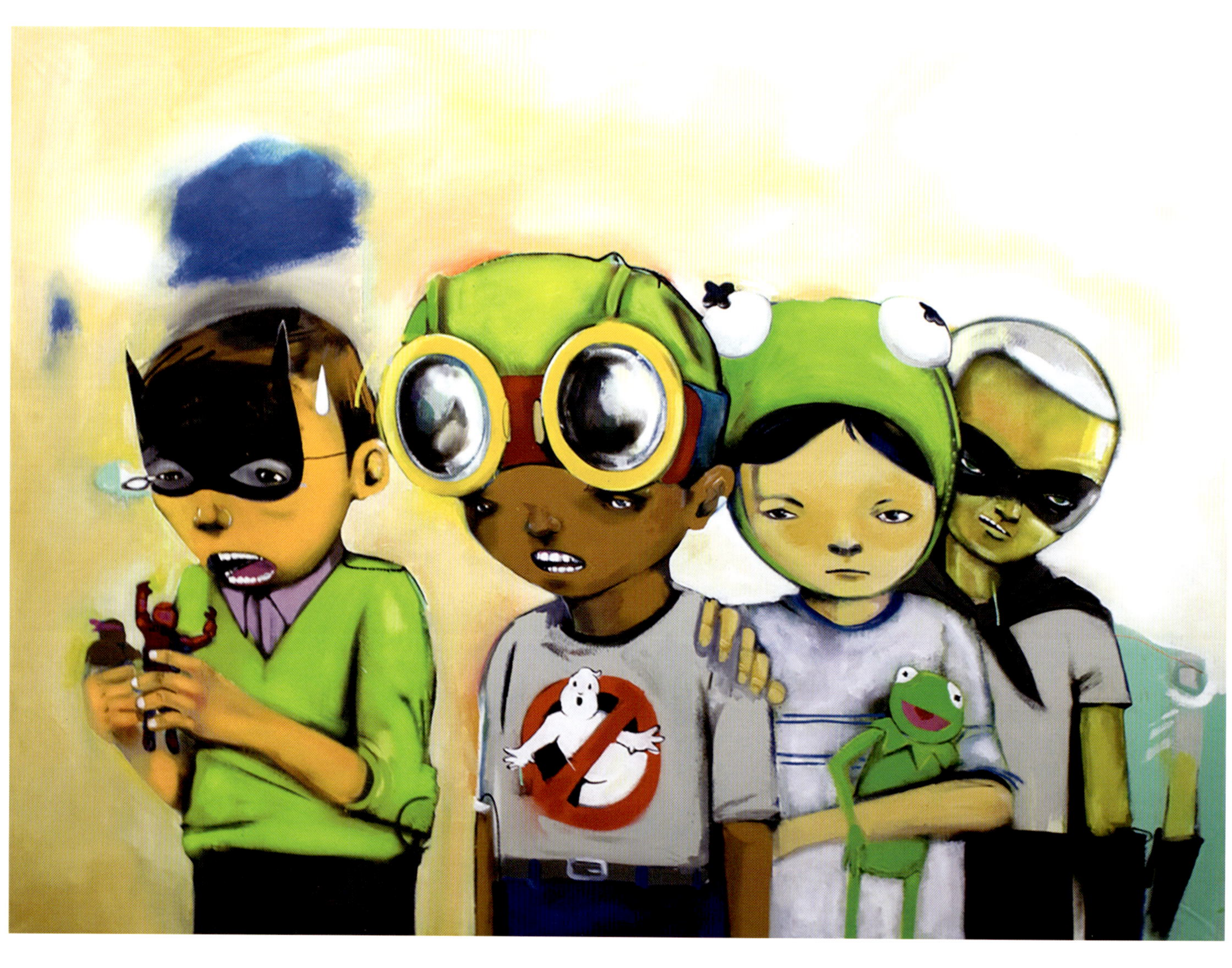

(Opposite)
Yesterday's Losers
Oil on canvas
2011

(Right)
That Girl Has A Walk That Suggest Head
Mixed media on canvas
48.5 x 72.25 inches
2017

(Below)
The Lizzies
Mixed media on canvas
2011

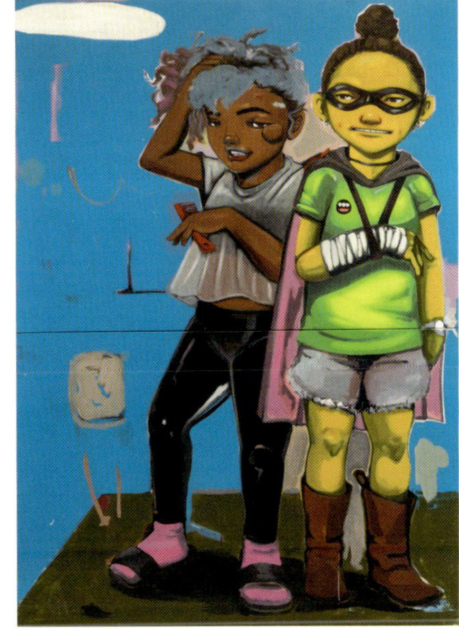

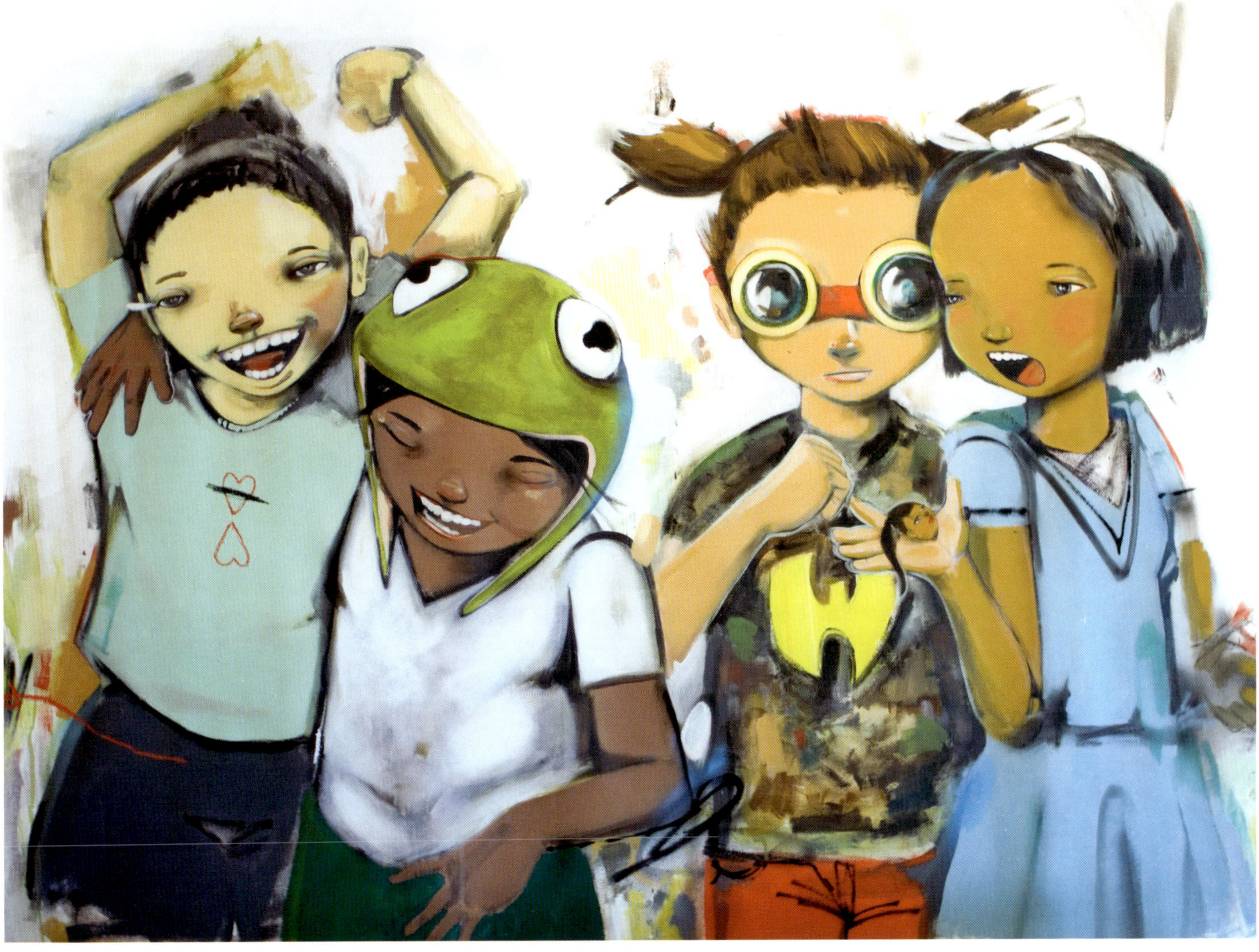

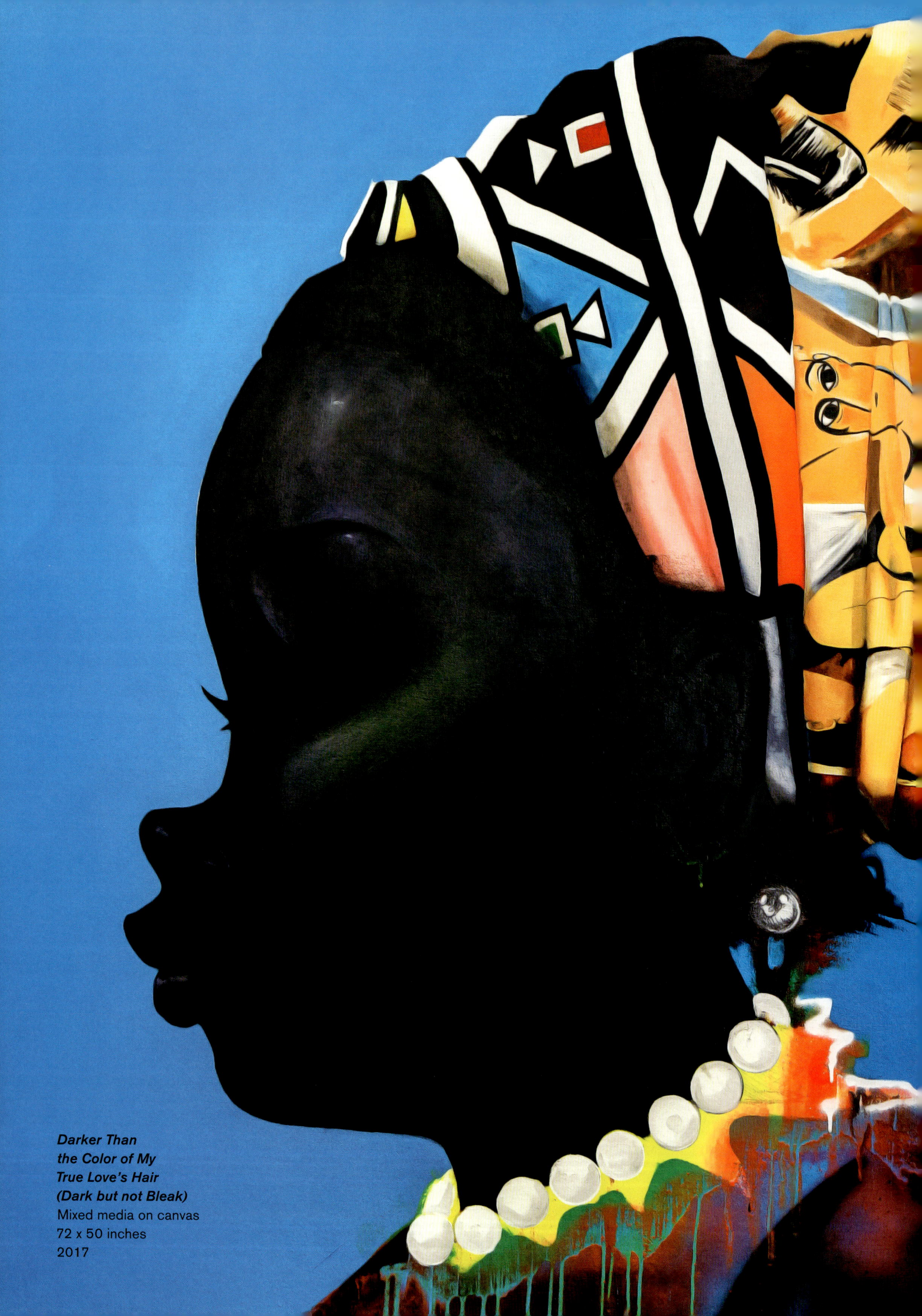

Darker Than the Color of My True Love's Hair (Dark but not Bleak)
Mixed media on canvas
72 x 50 inches
2017

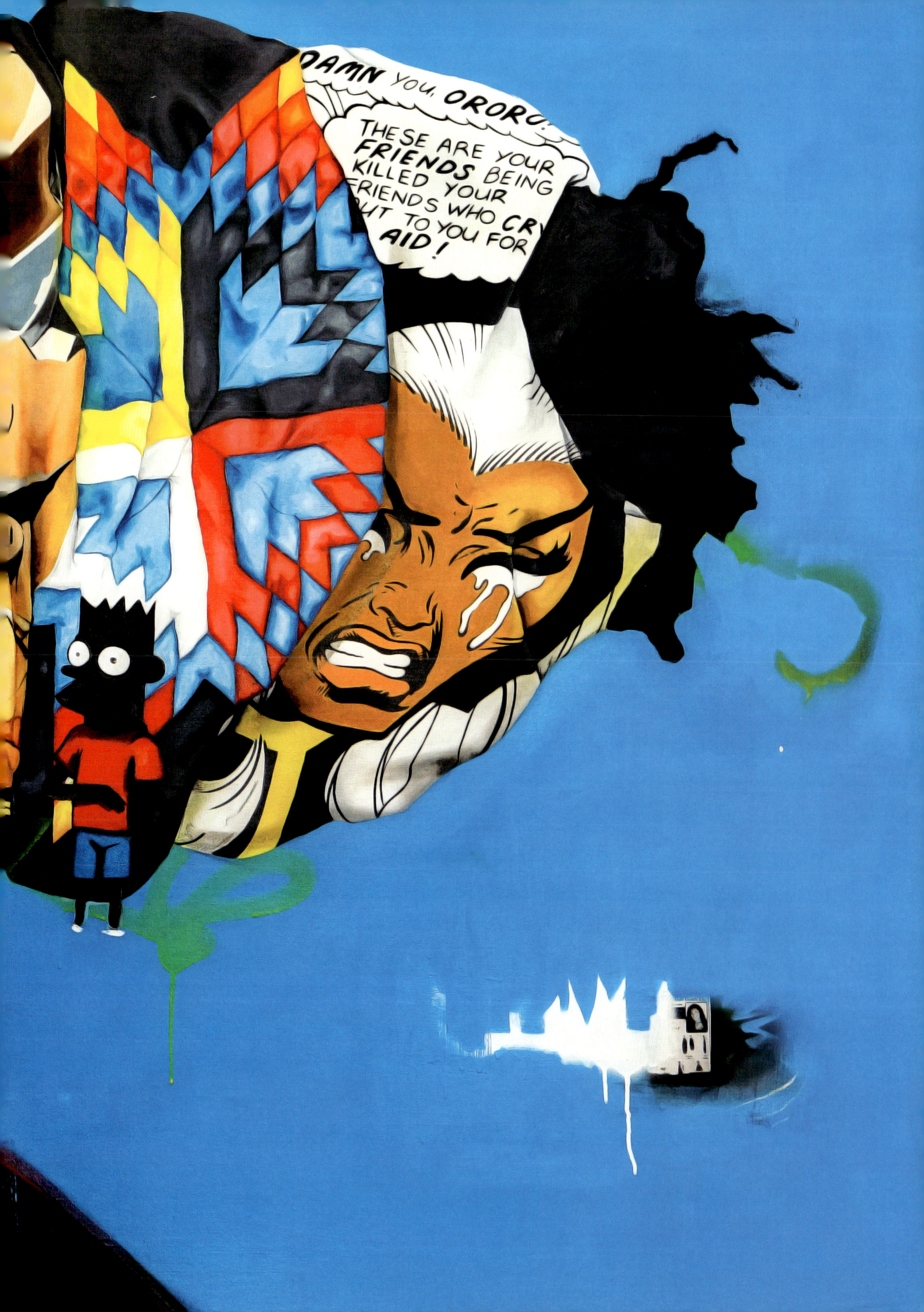
DAMN YOU, ORORO
THESE ARE YOUR FRIENDS BEING KILLED YOUR RIENDS WHO CR UT TO YOU FOR AID!

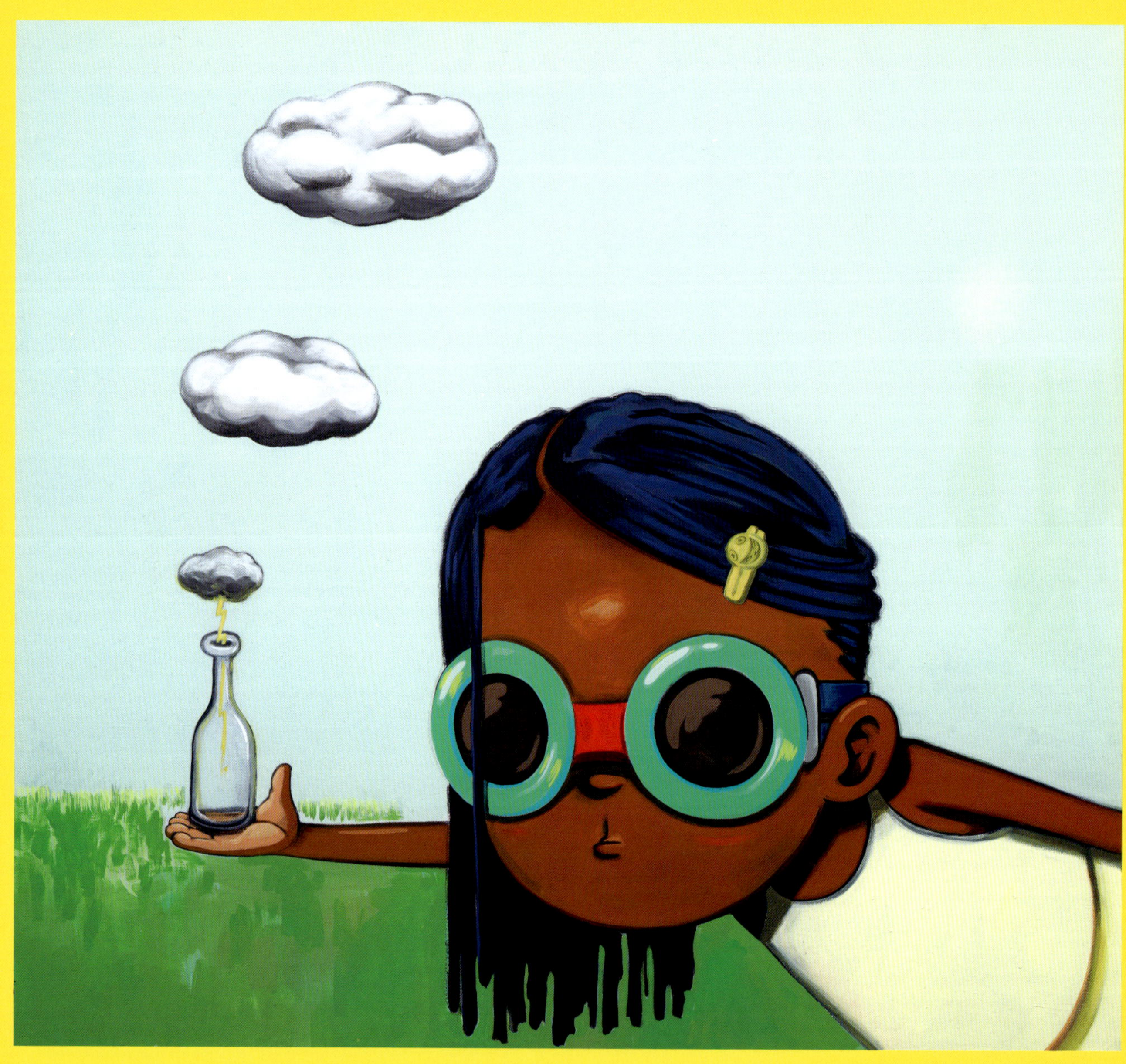

In the Bottle
Acrylic and pastel
on canvas
31 x 33 inches
2020

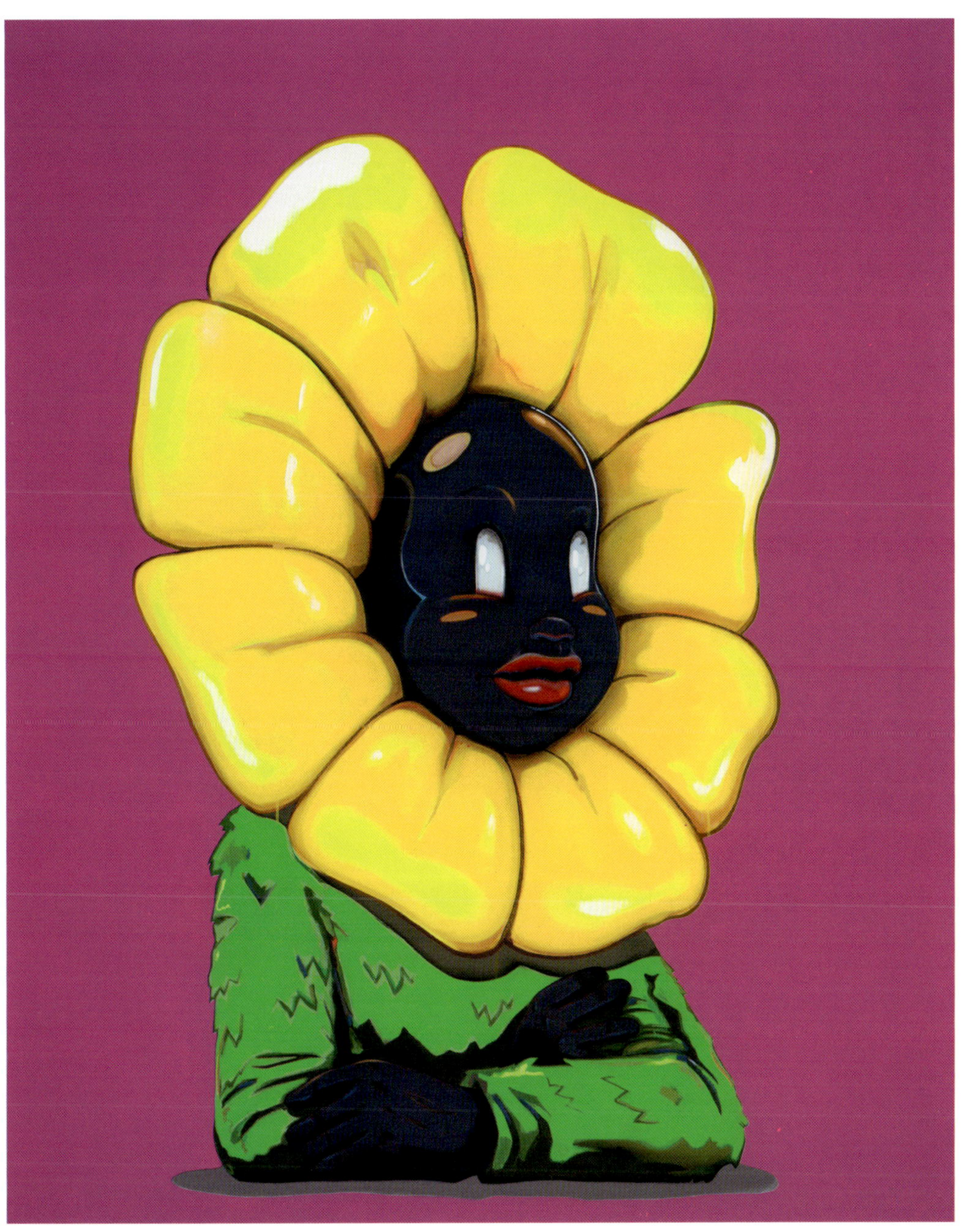

That Flower N Word
Acrylic, oil, and
spray paint on canvas
48 x 62 inches
2021

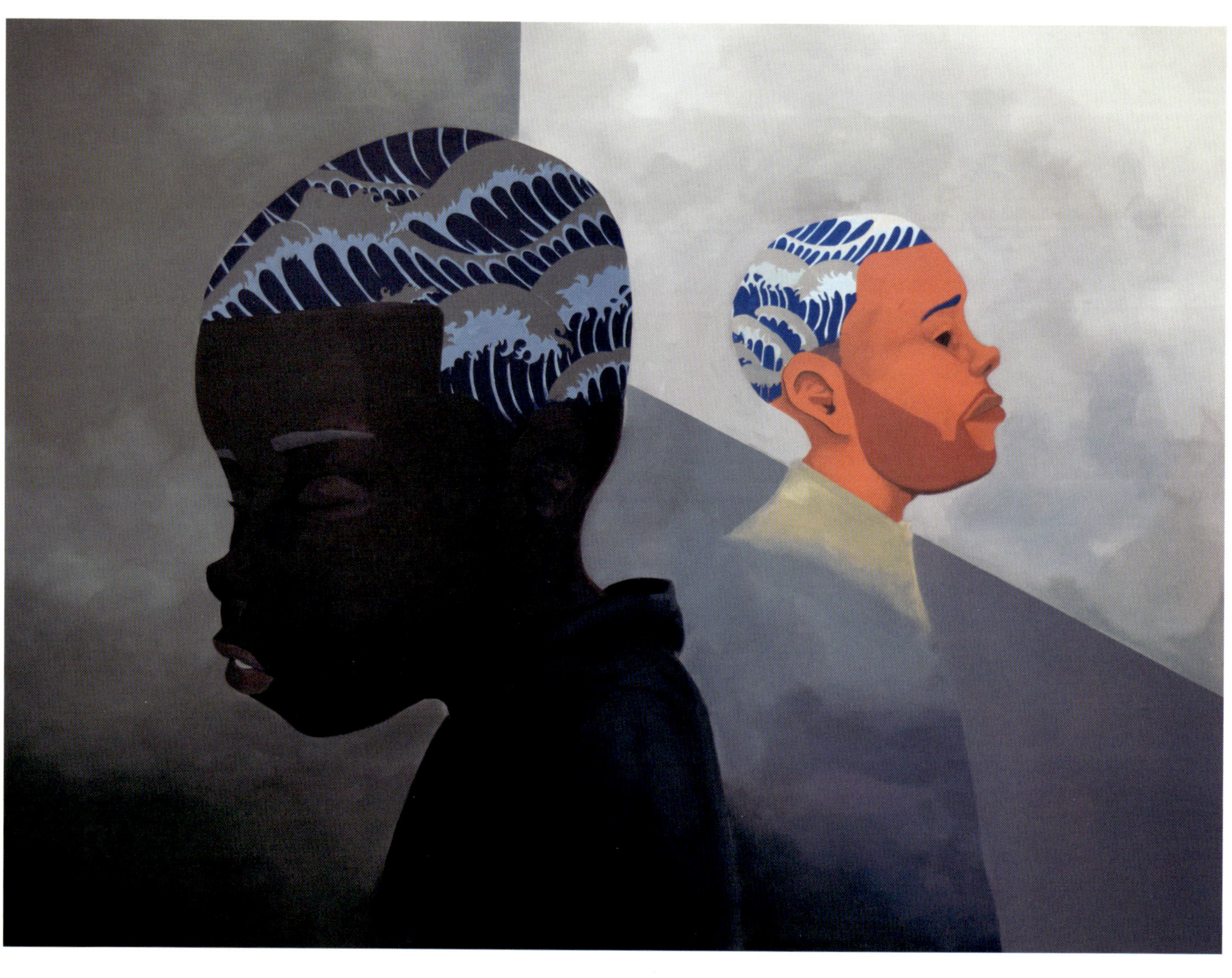

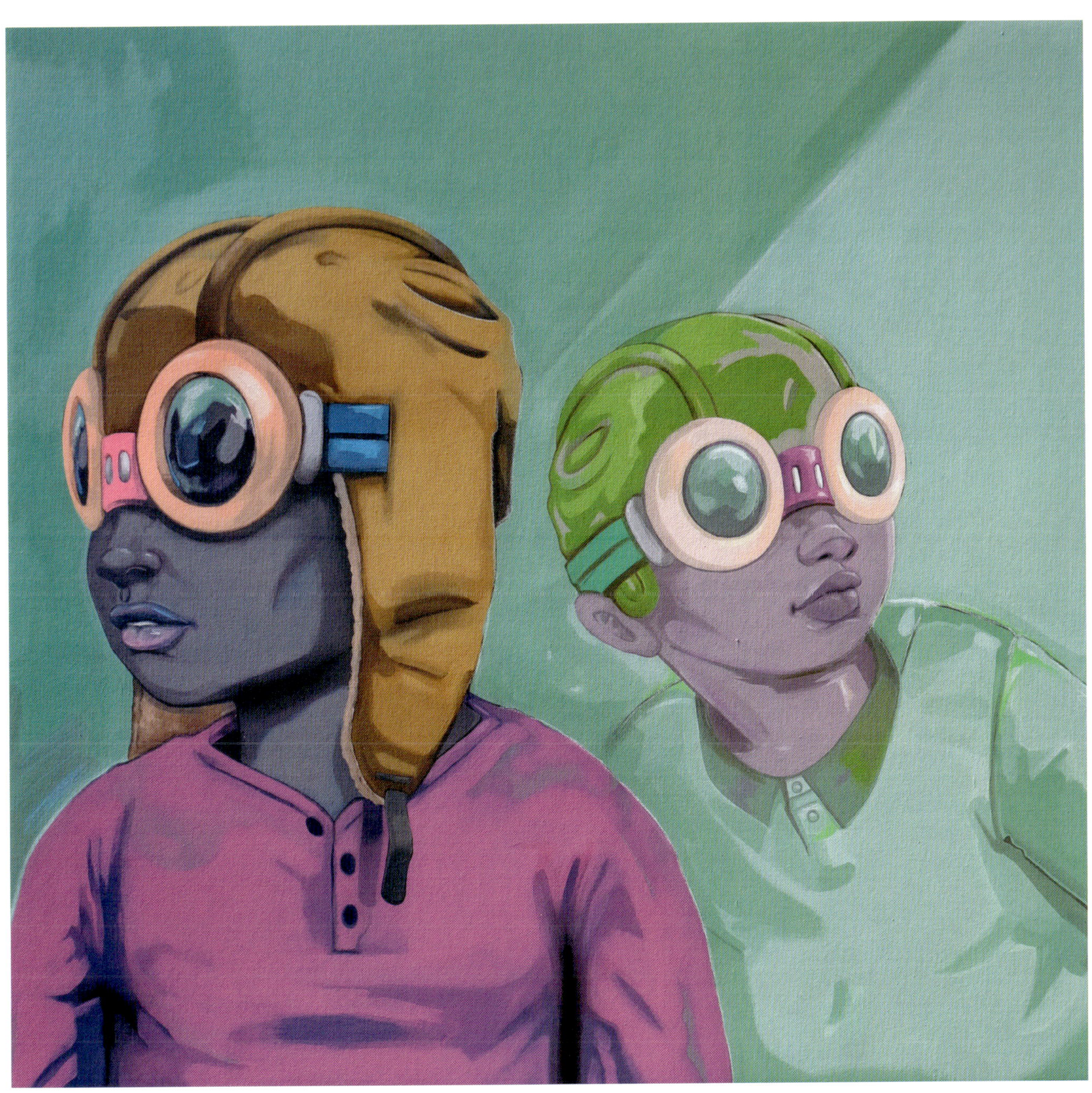

(Above)
Cousins
Mixed media
on canvas
38.5 x 38.5 inches
2020

(Opposite)
Two Men
Sporting Waves
Mixed media
on canvas
62.25 x 48 inches
2018

"I CONSIDER HEBRU BRANTLEY TO BE ONE OF THE VERY FEW VISUAL ARTISTS, THROUGH HIS MANY DIVERSE POINTS OF EXECUTION, TO SUCCESSFULLY TAP INTO AN ECLECTIC AUDIENCE."

—DERRICK ADAMS

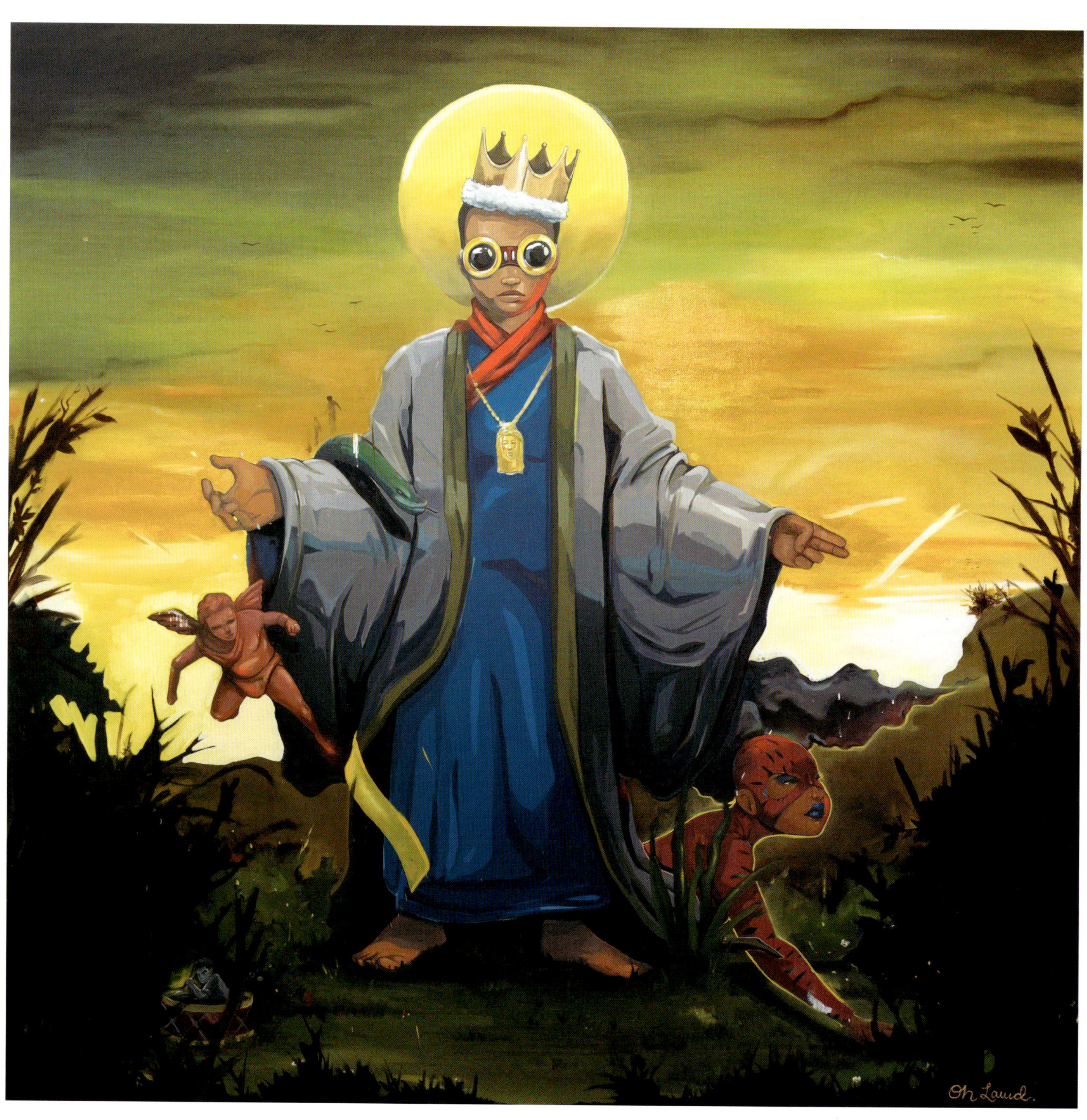

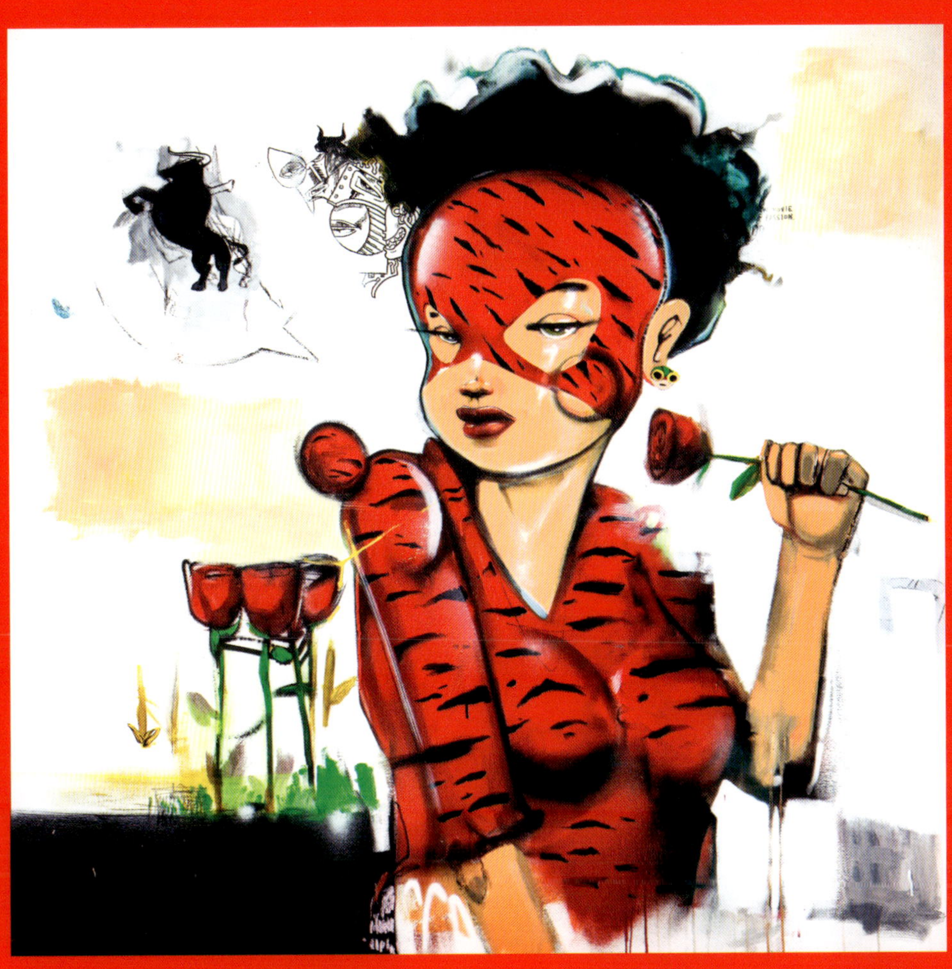

(Opposite)
No Church in the Wild
Mixed media on canvas
2016

(Above)
Heat of the Bull
Mixed media on canvas
2013

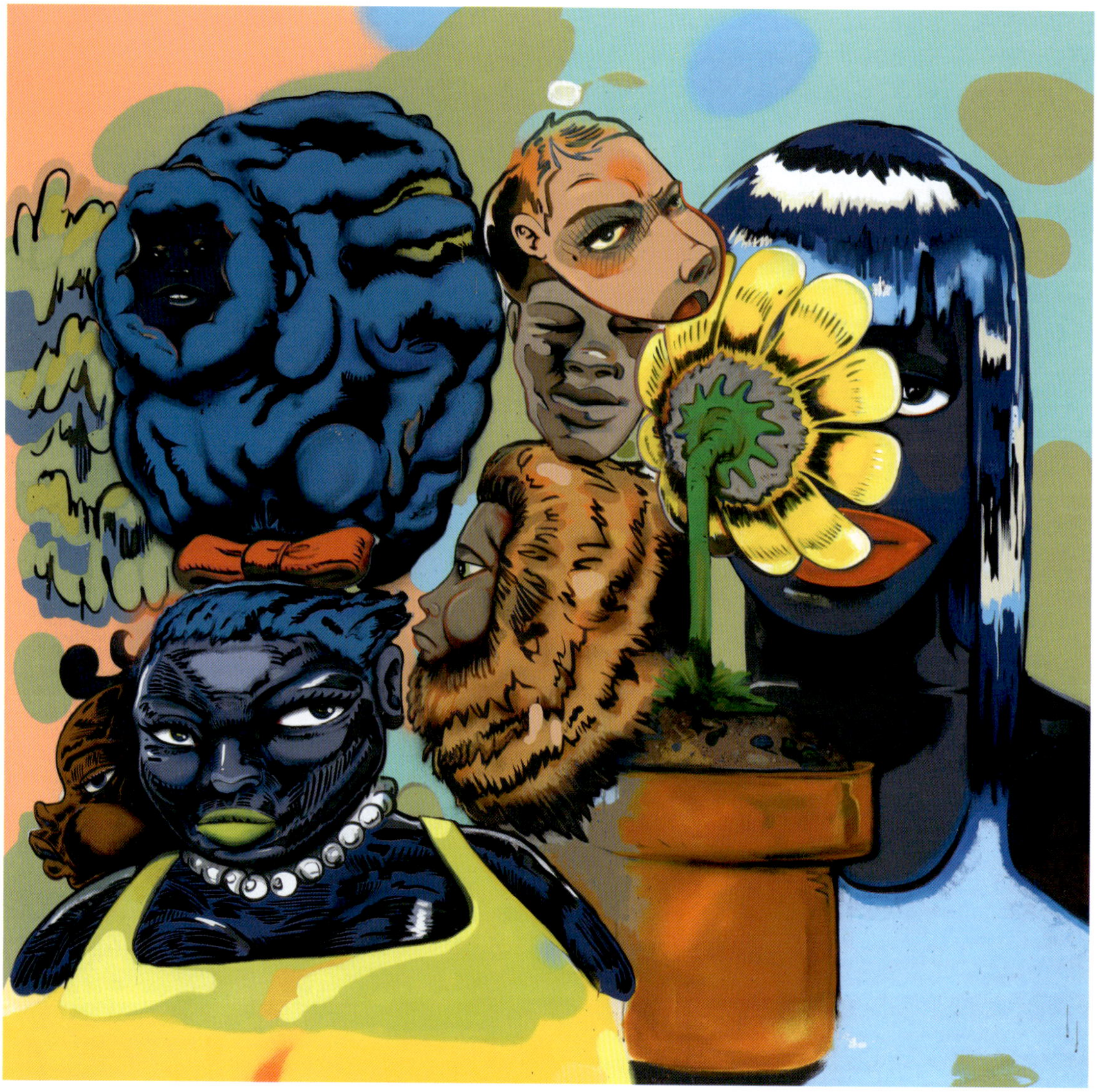

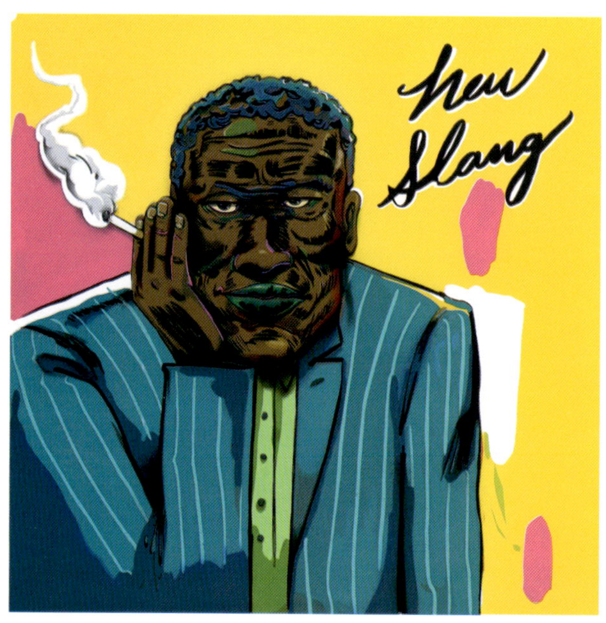

(Above)
They Try To Block My Sun
Mixed media on canvas
72 x 72 inches
2021

(Left)
Jazz Rebel
Mixed media on canvas
64 x 64 inches
2021

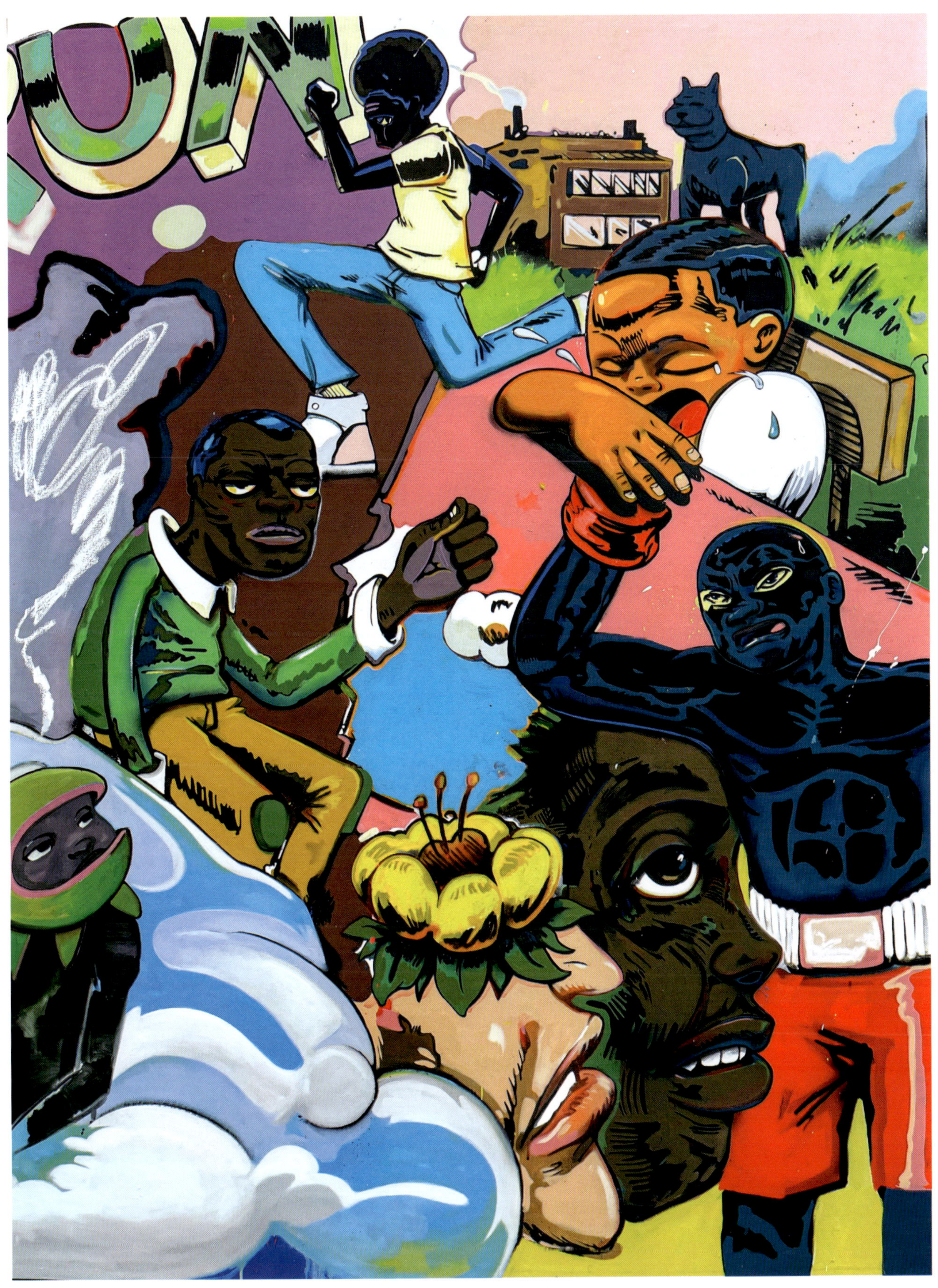

Baldwin's Truth Bombs
Mixed media on canvas
60 x 83 inches
2021

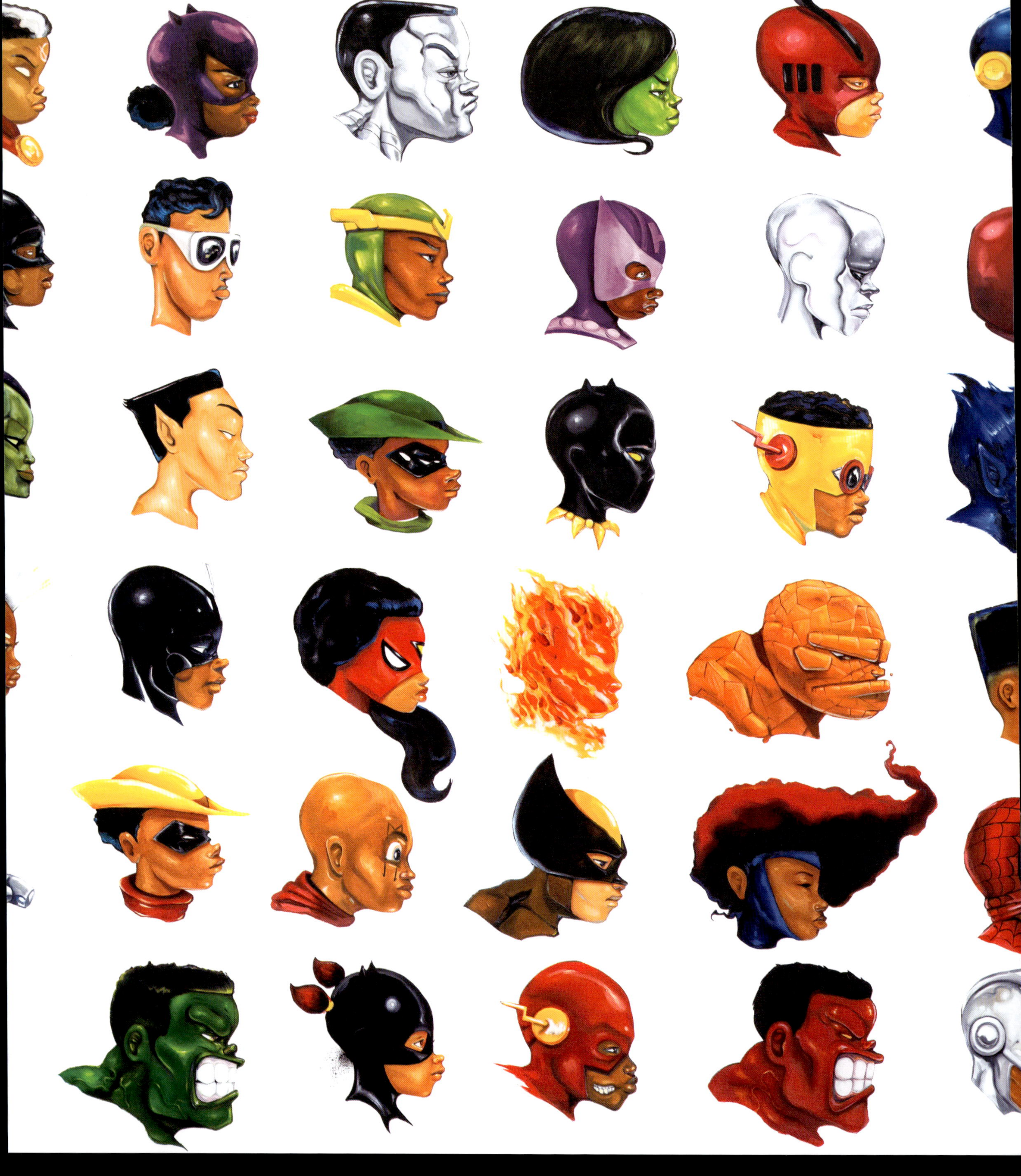

MYTHOS

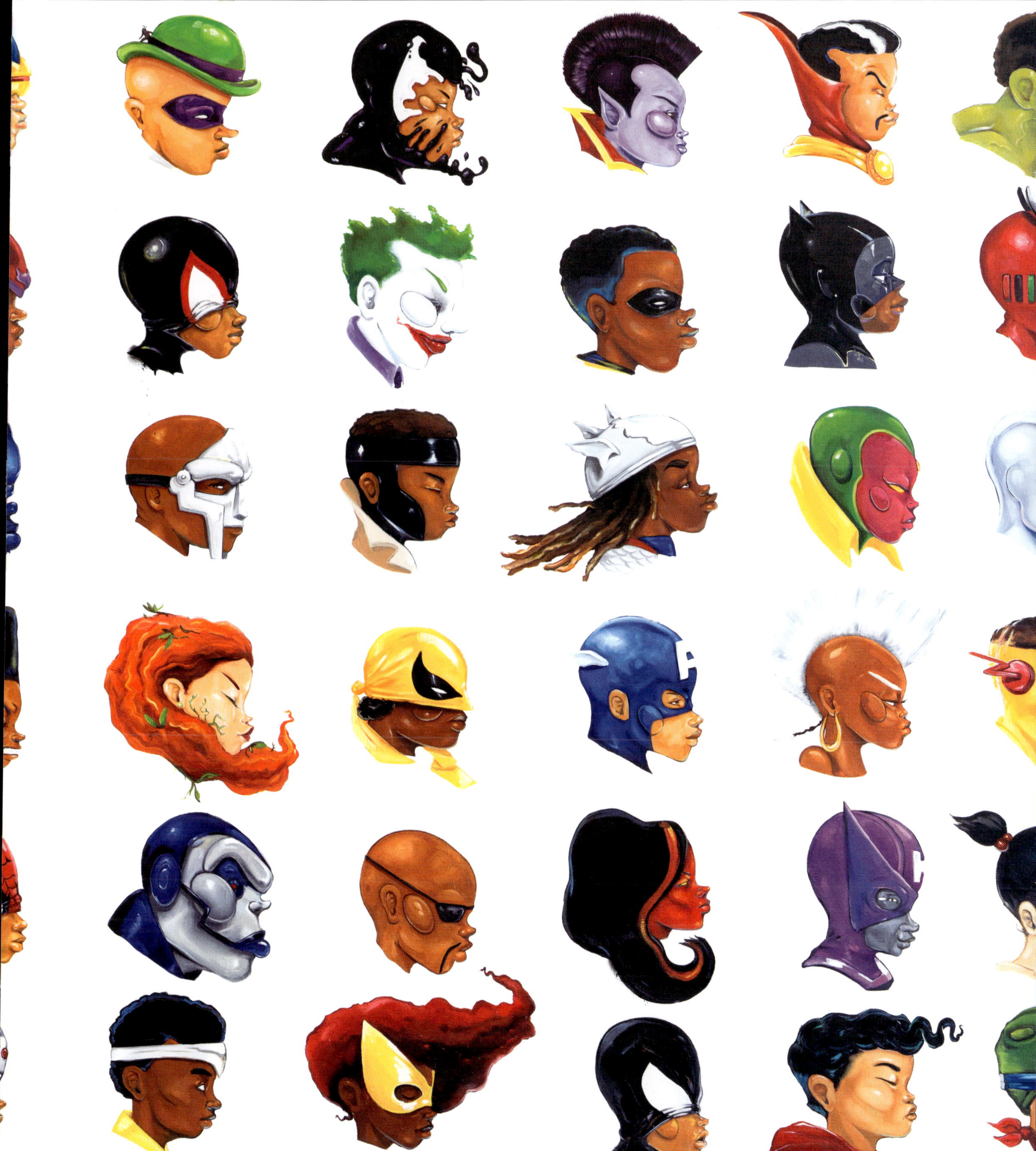

Negro Mythos Series: The Unabridged Version
Oil on canvas
135 x 85 inches
2016

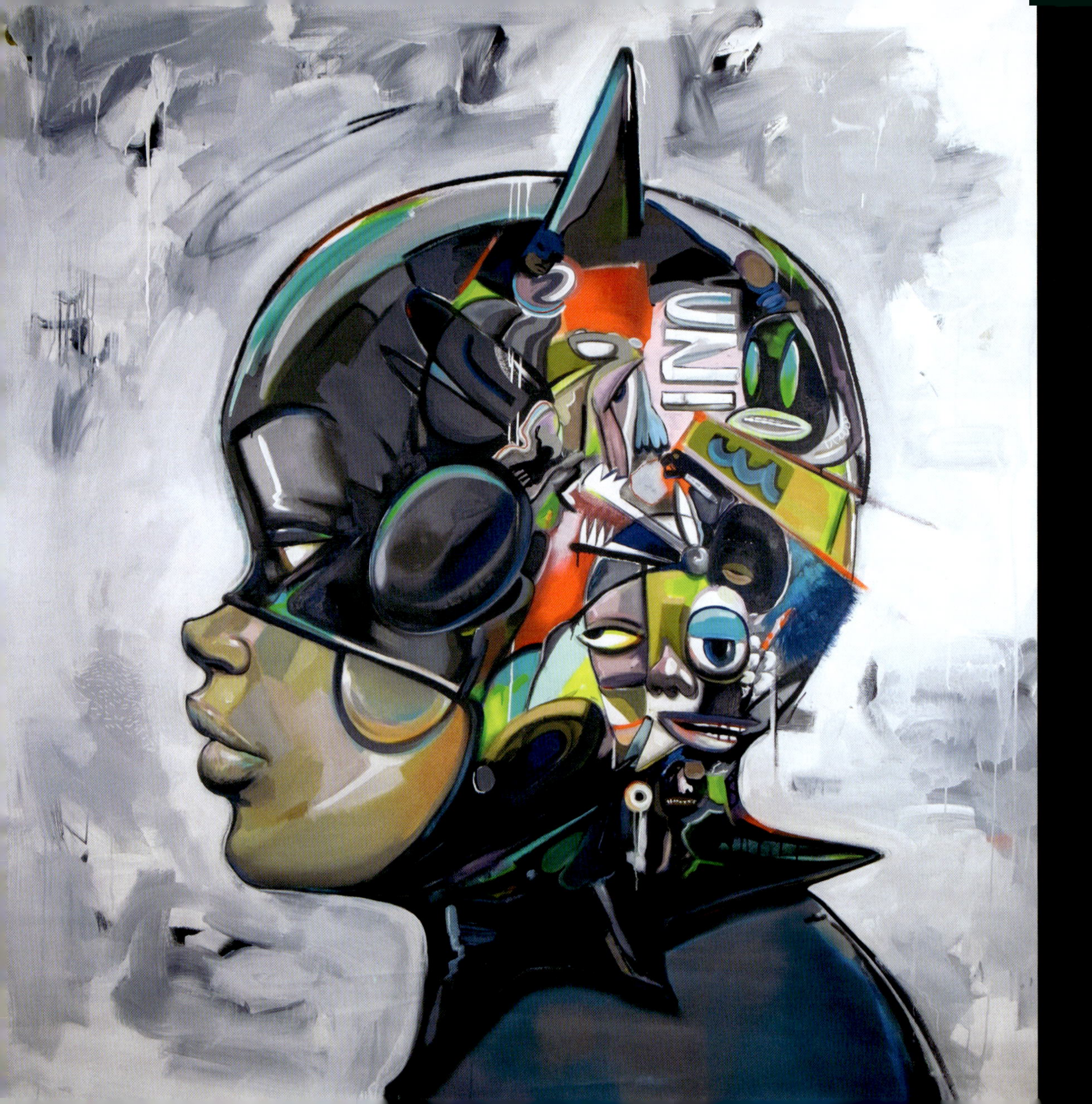

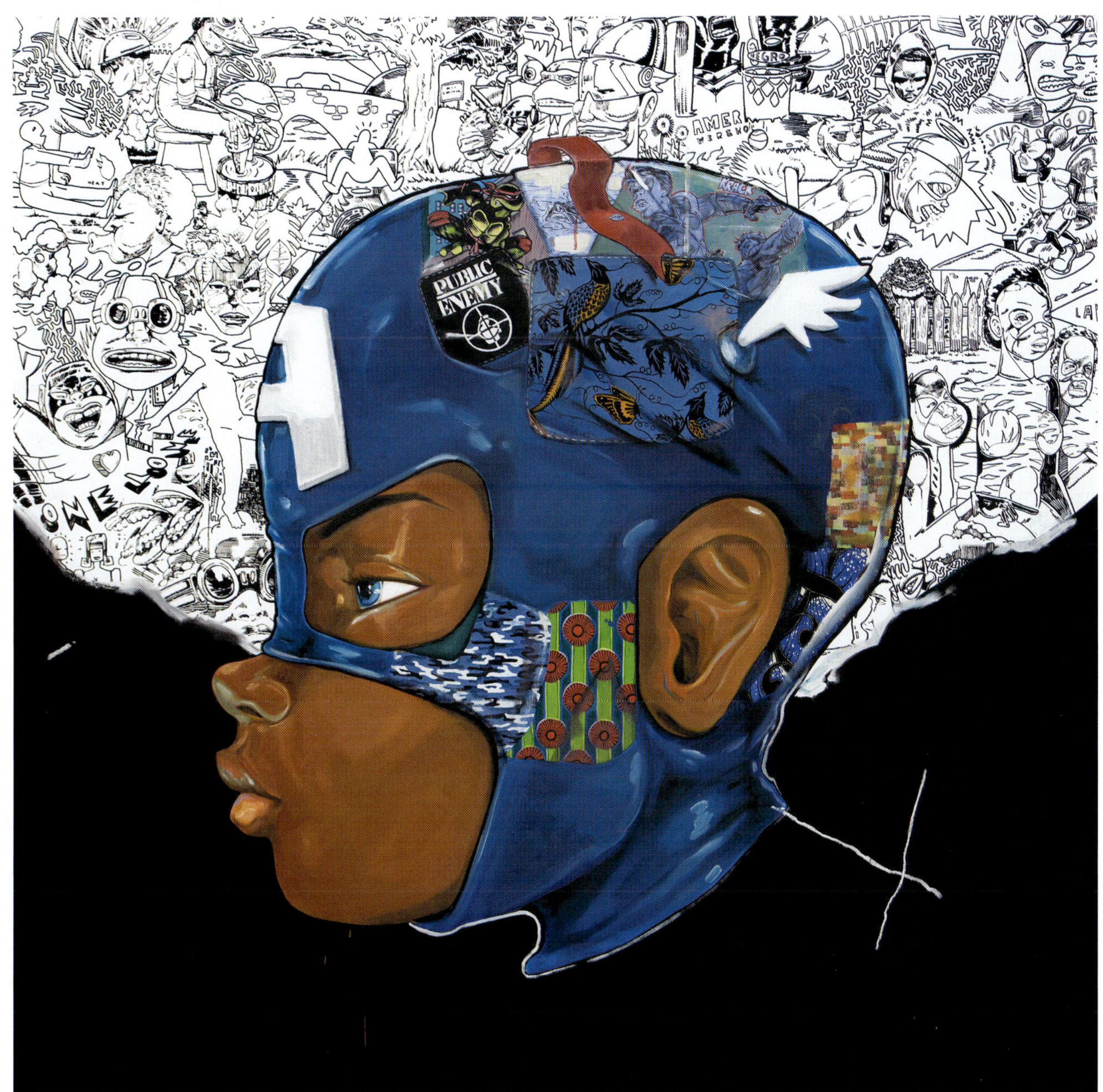

(Opposite)
Untitled: BAT
Mixed media
on canvas
66 x 72 inches
2019

(Above)
I Was Once A Misguided, Undereducated Rebel Soldier
Oil on canvas
74 x 75.25 inches
2015

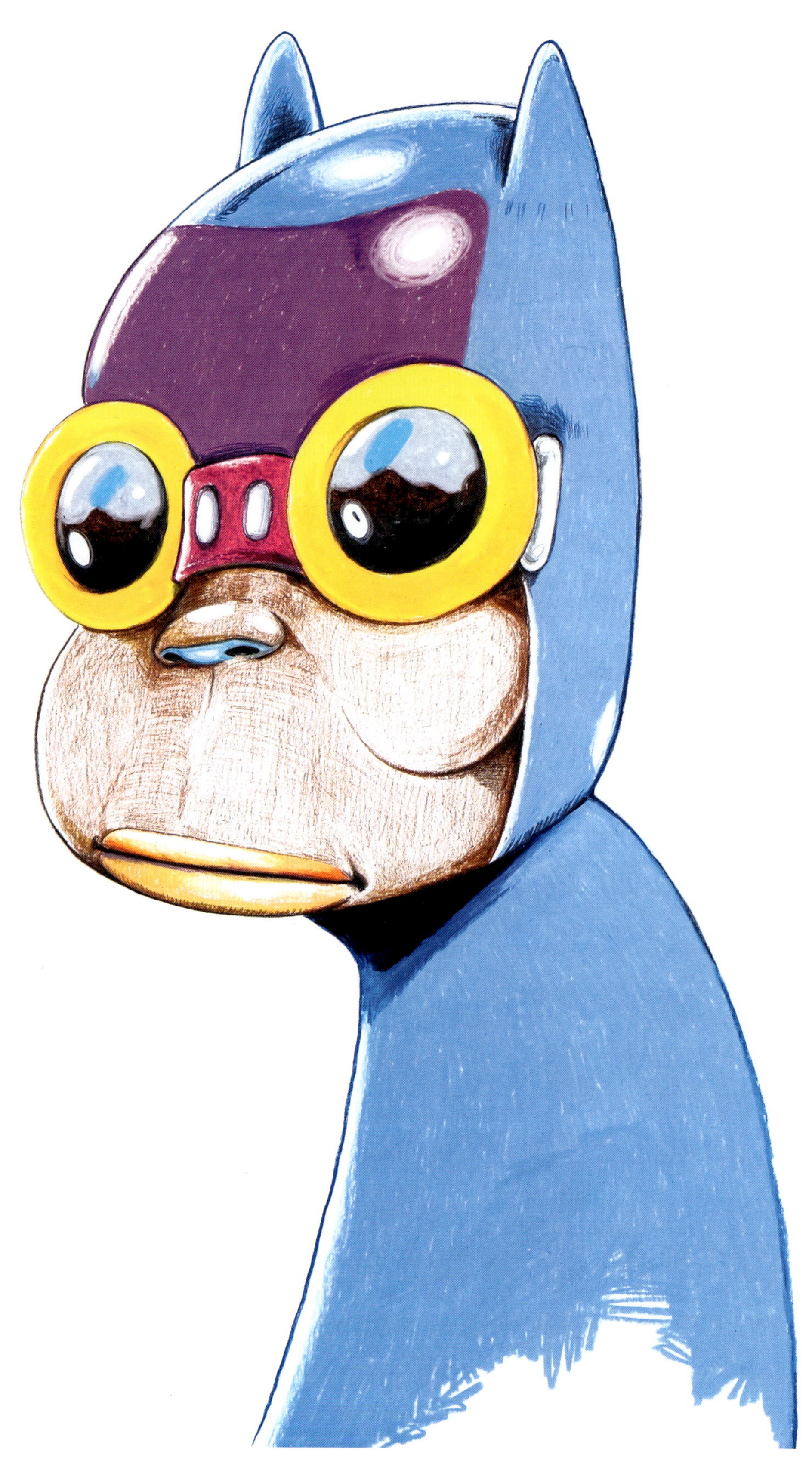

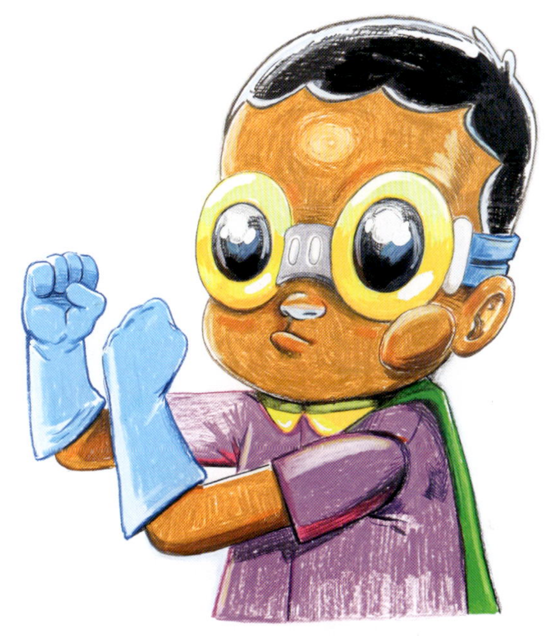

(Opposite)
Batboy Pt. 68
Wax pastel
on paper
19 x 24 inches
2021

(Above)
Fighting Stance
Wax pastel
and paint marker
on paper
19 x 24 inches
2021

(Right)
Batboy with Timberlands
Colored pencil
on paper
18 x 24 inches
2021

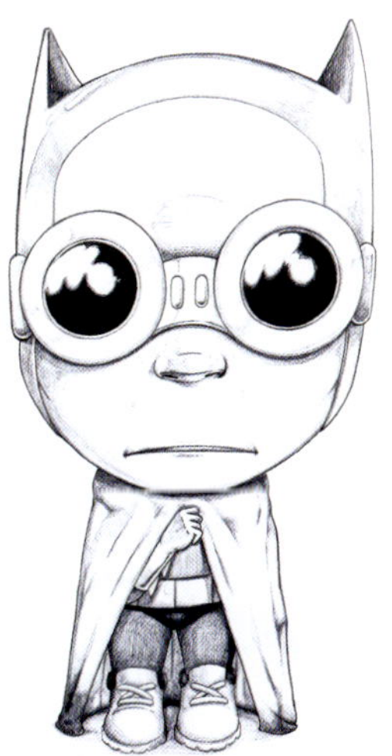

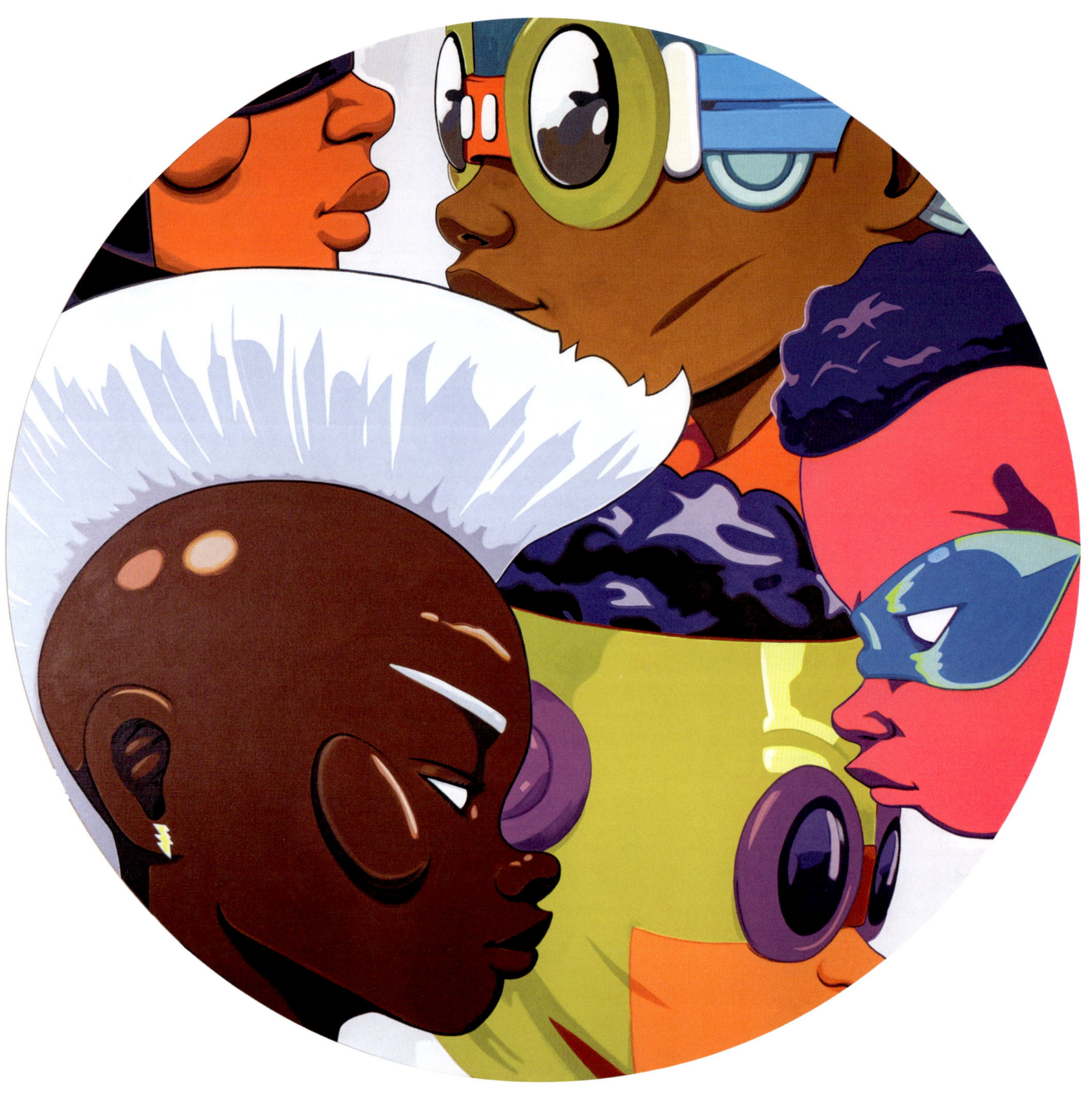

Neighbor Hood Watch Acrylic on canvas, 60 inches diameter, 2021

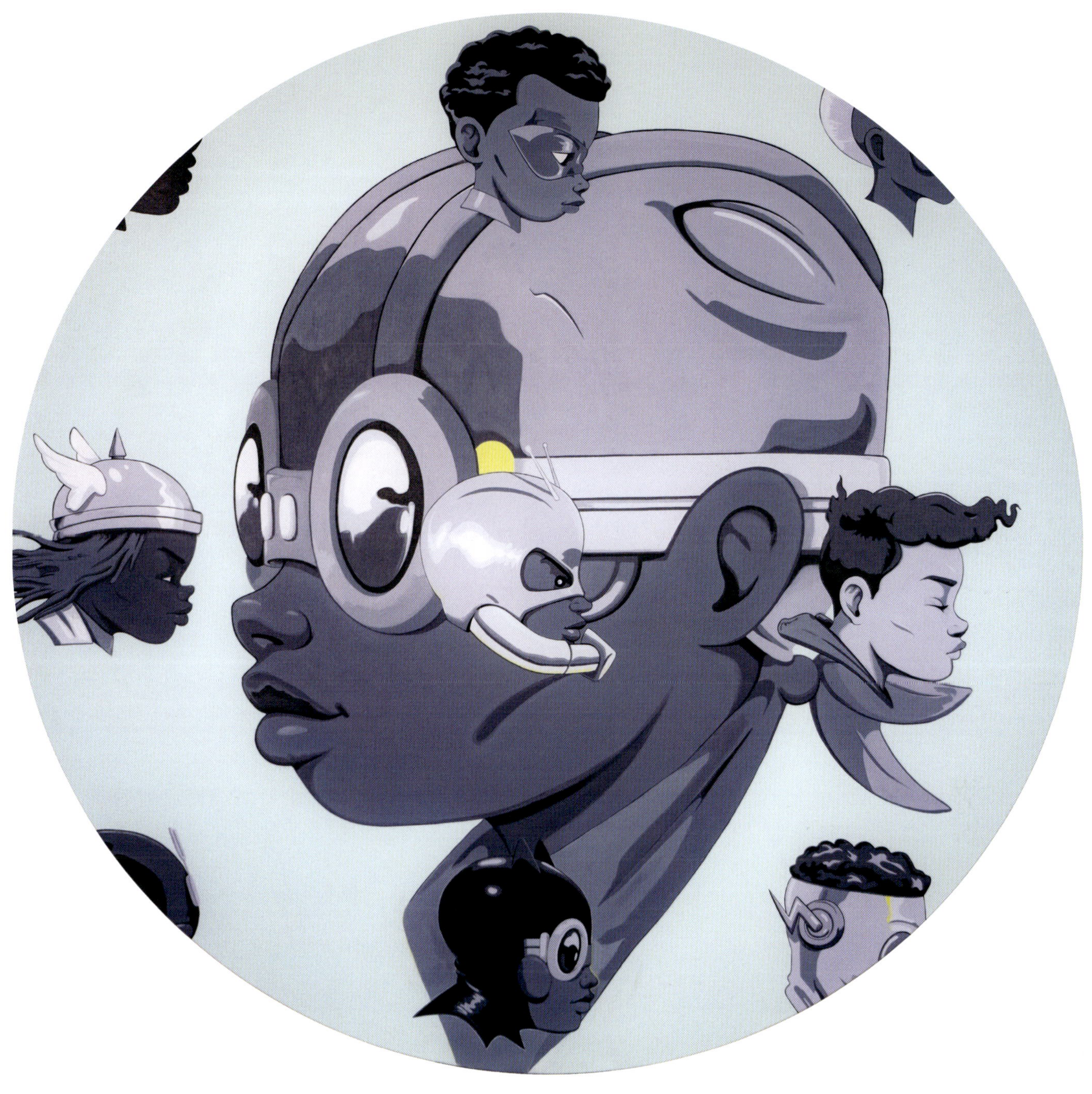

Taking No Mo Shit

Acrylic on canvas, 60 inches diameter, 2021

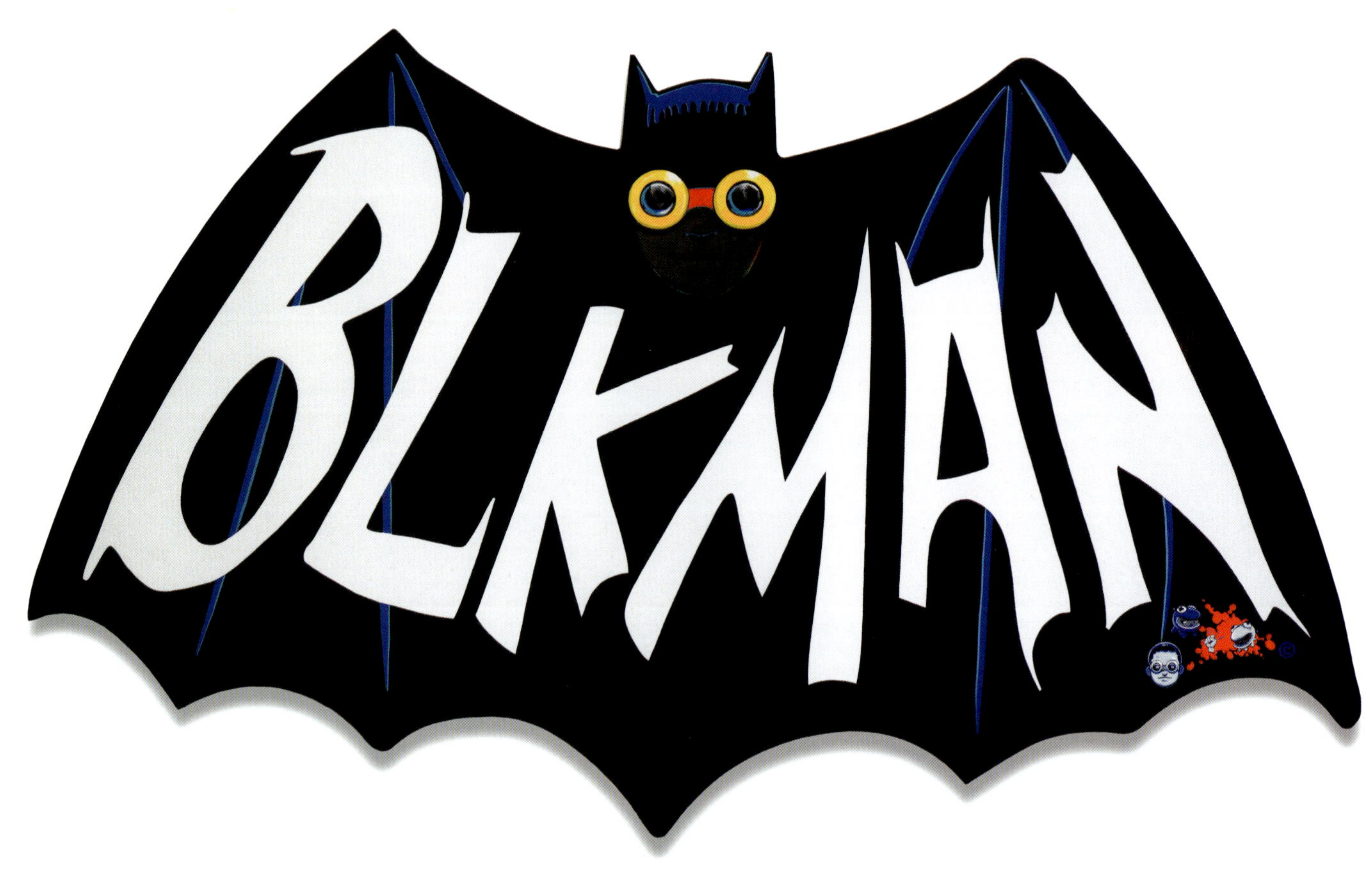

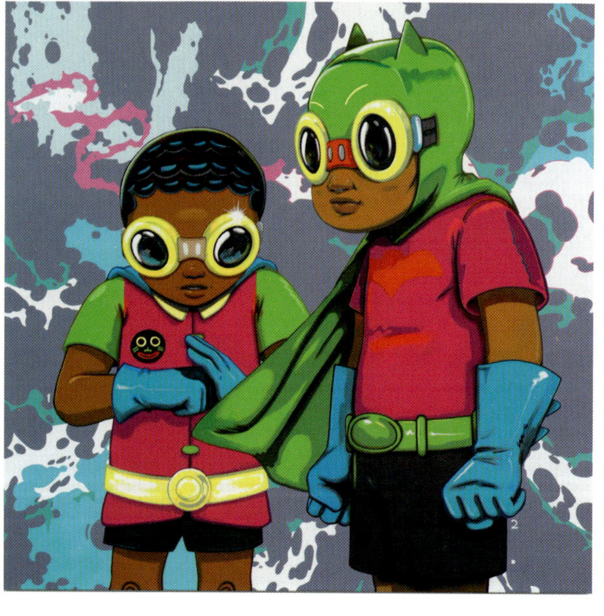

(Above)
Calling All Cars!
Acrylic on canvas
41.5 x 70 inches
2021

(Left)
Them / Both
Acrylic, spray paint, oil stick, and diamond dust on canvas
68 x 68 inches
2021

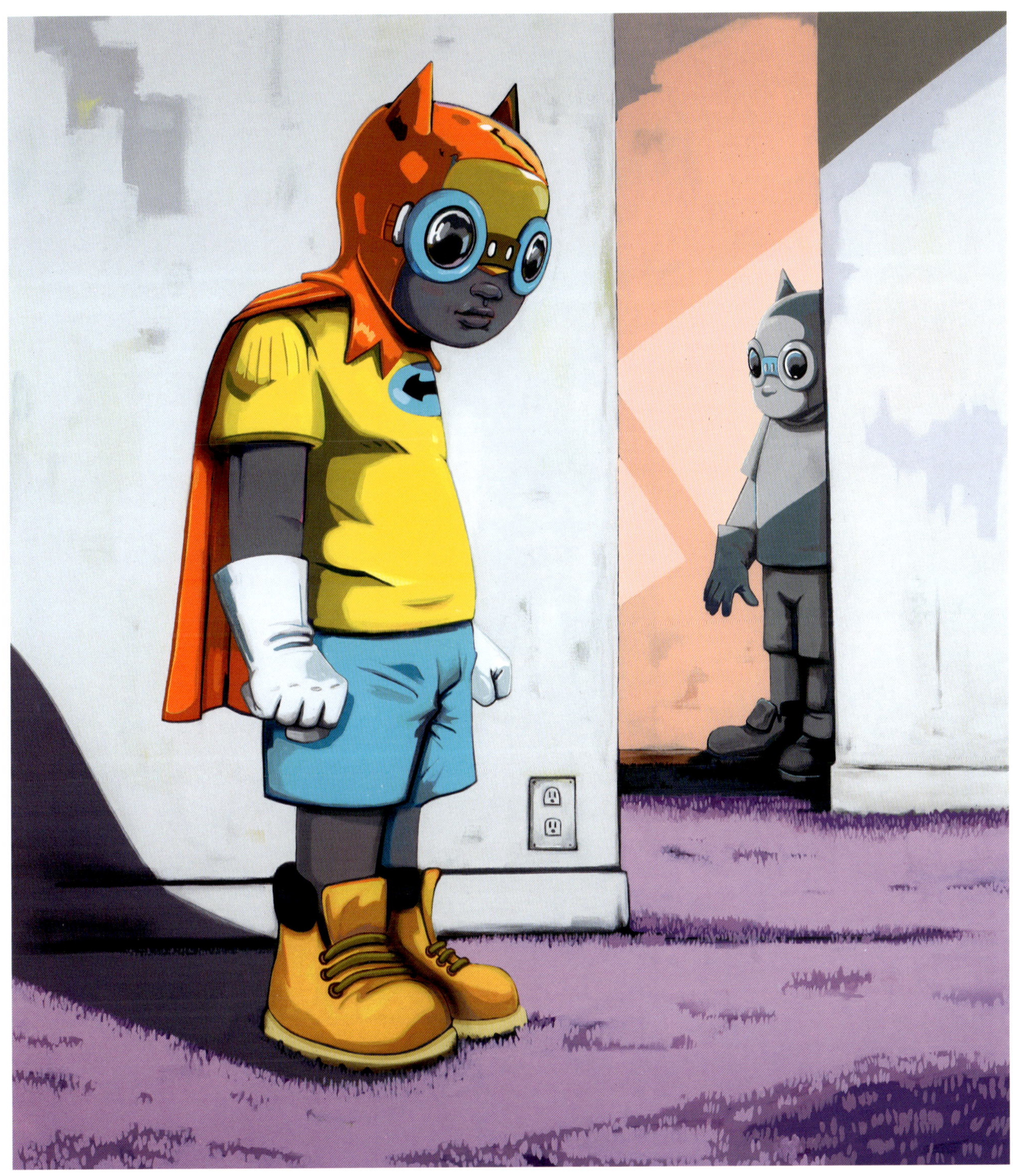

Imitation
Acrylic, pastel,
and spray paint
on canvas
60 x 70 inches
2019–2020

Flynamic Duo
Vinyl figures
Batboy, 16 inches
Sparrow, 13 inches
2021

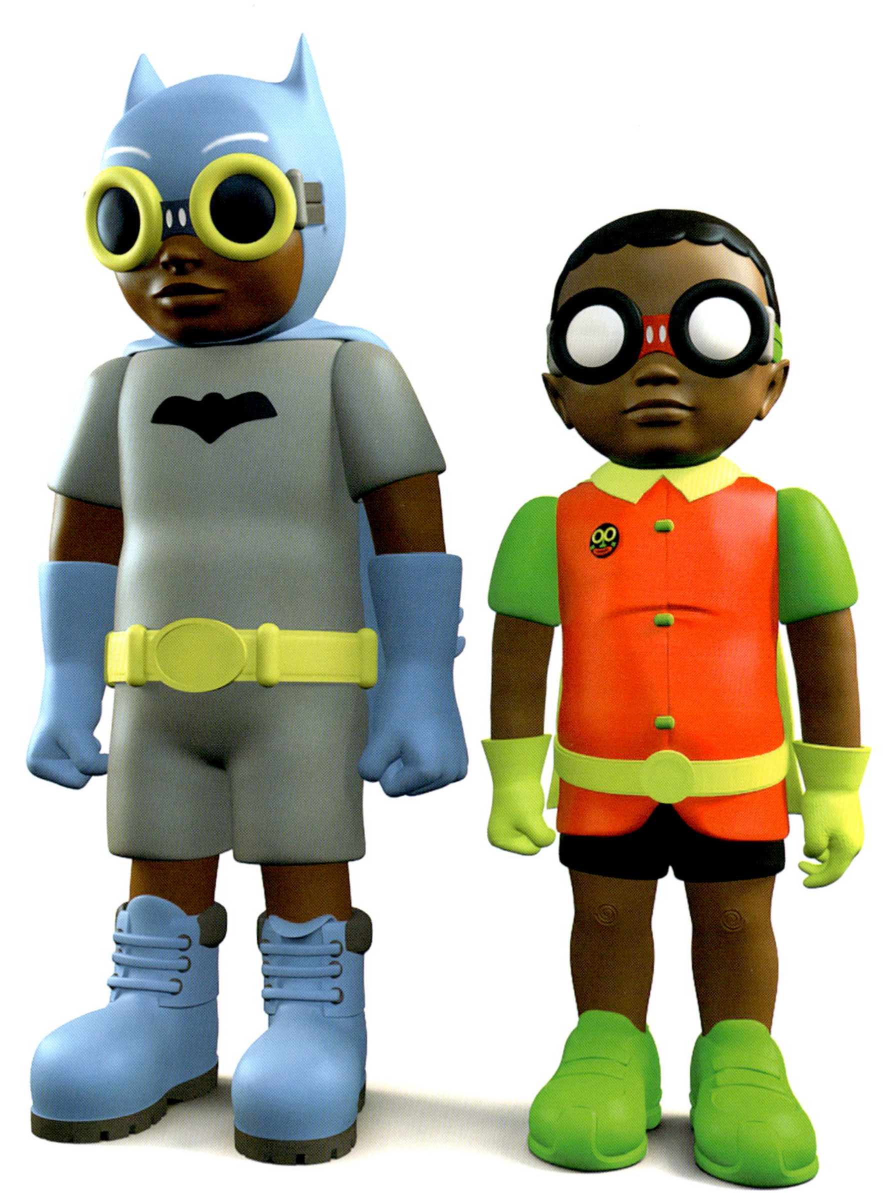

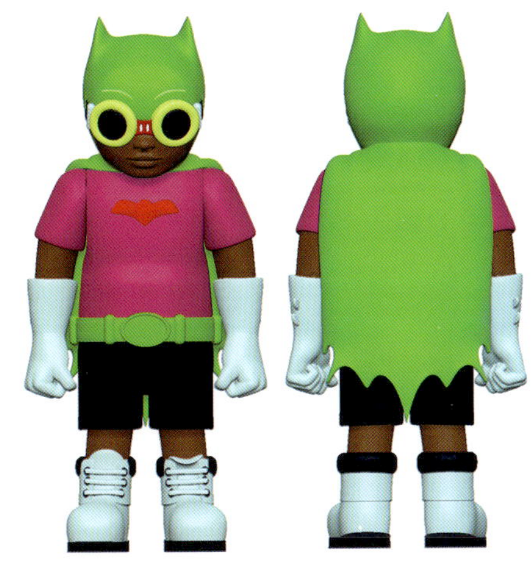

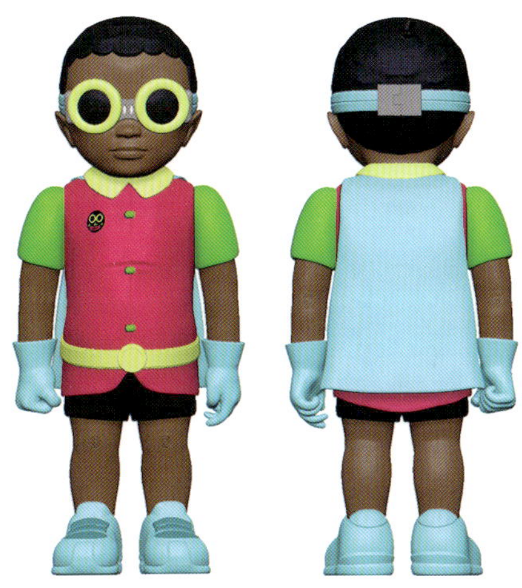

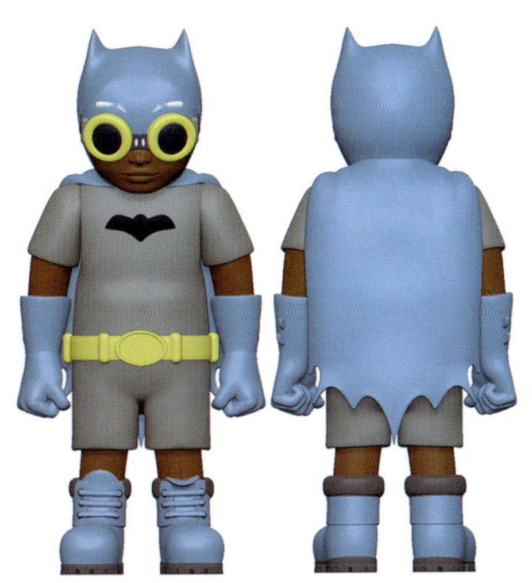

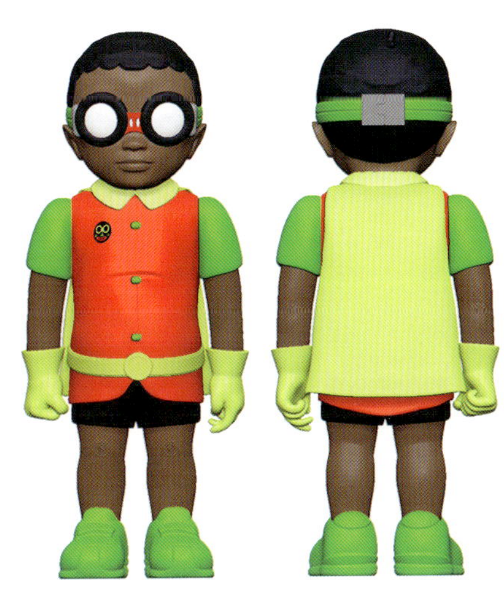

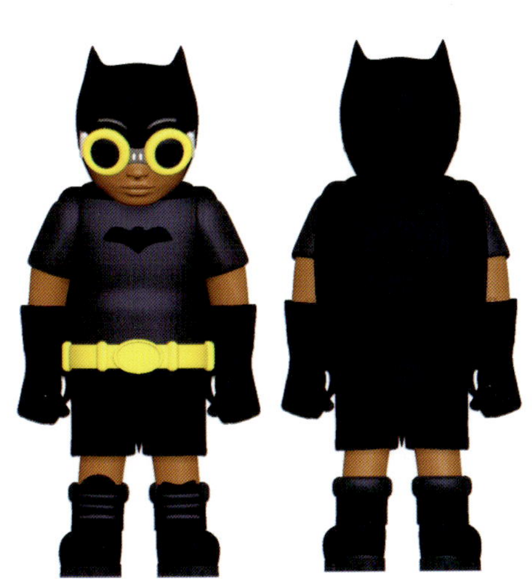

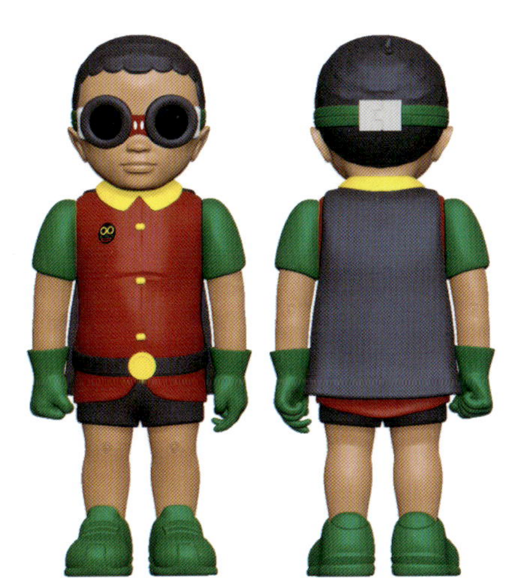

(Top left)
Flash
Acrylic on canvas
20 x 20 inches
2019

(Top right)
Untitled
Mixed media
on canvas
24 x 24 inches
2019

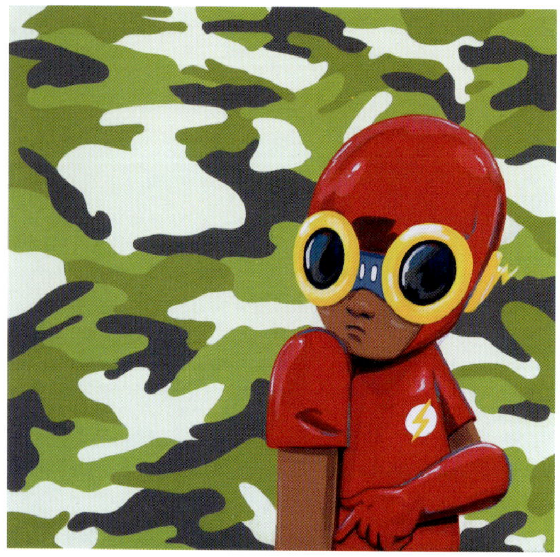

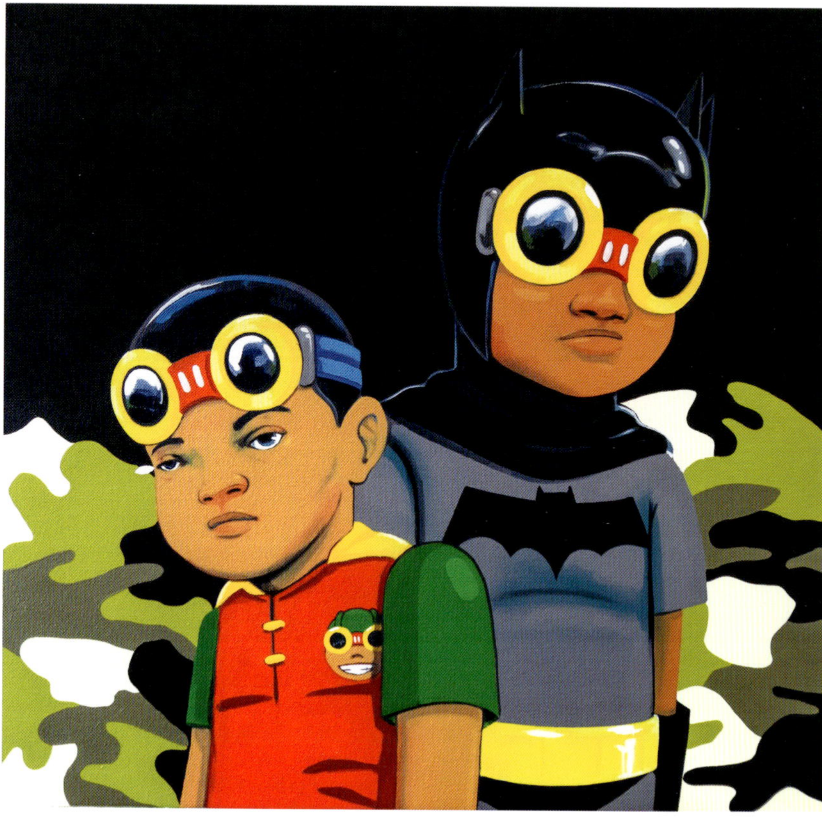

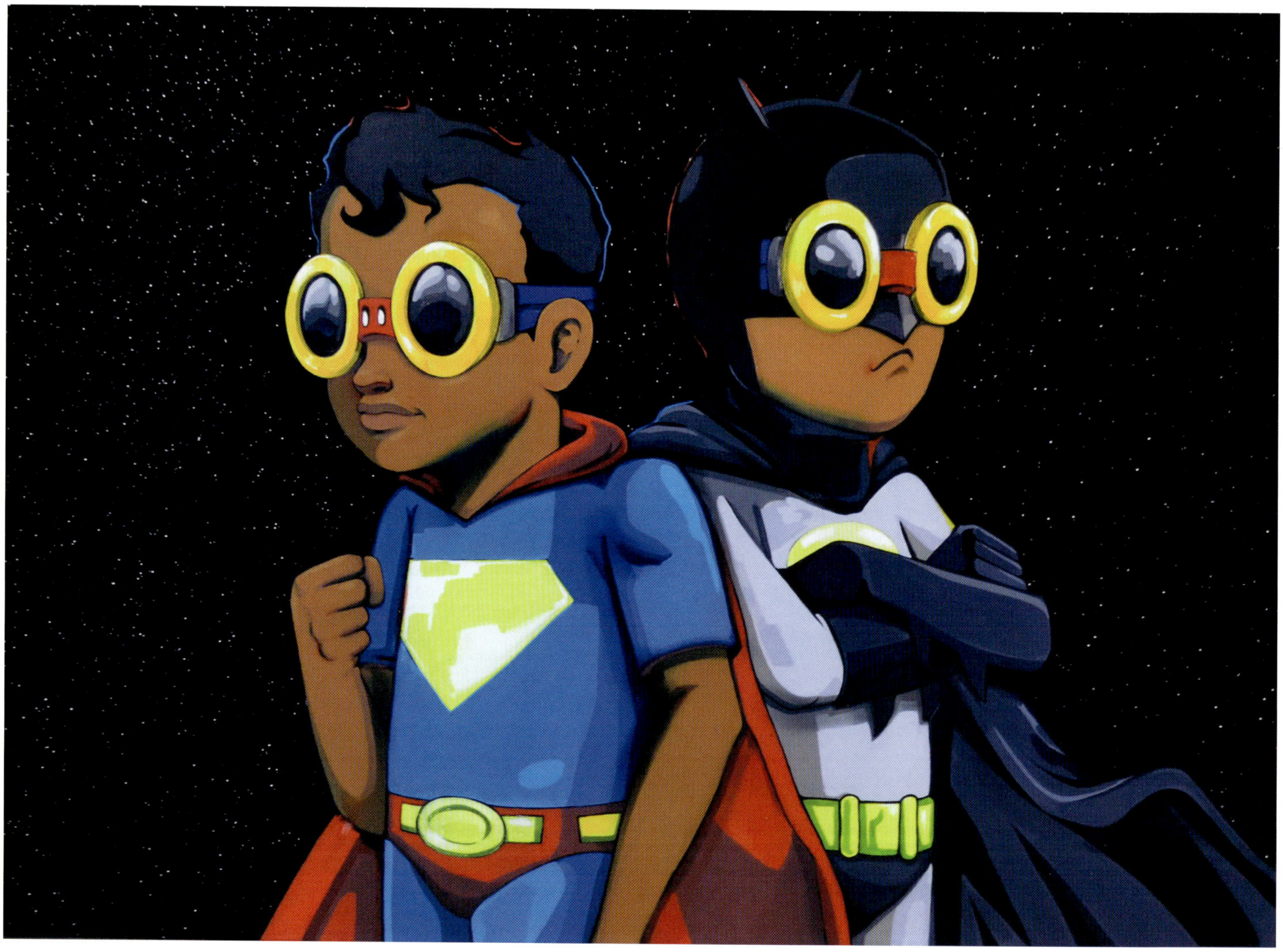

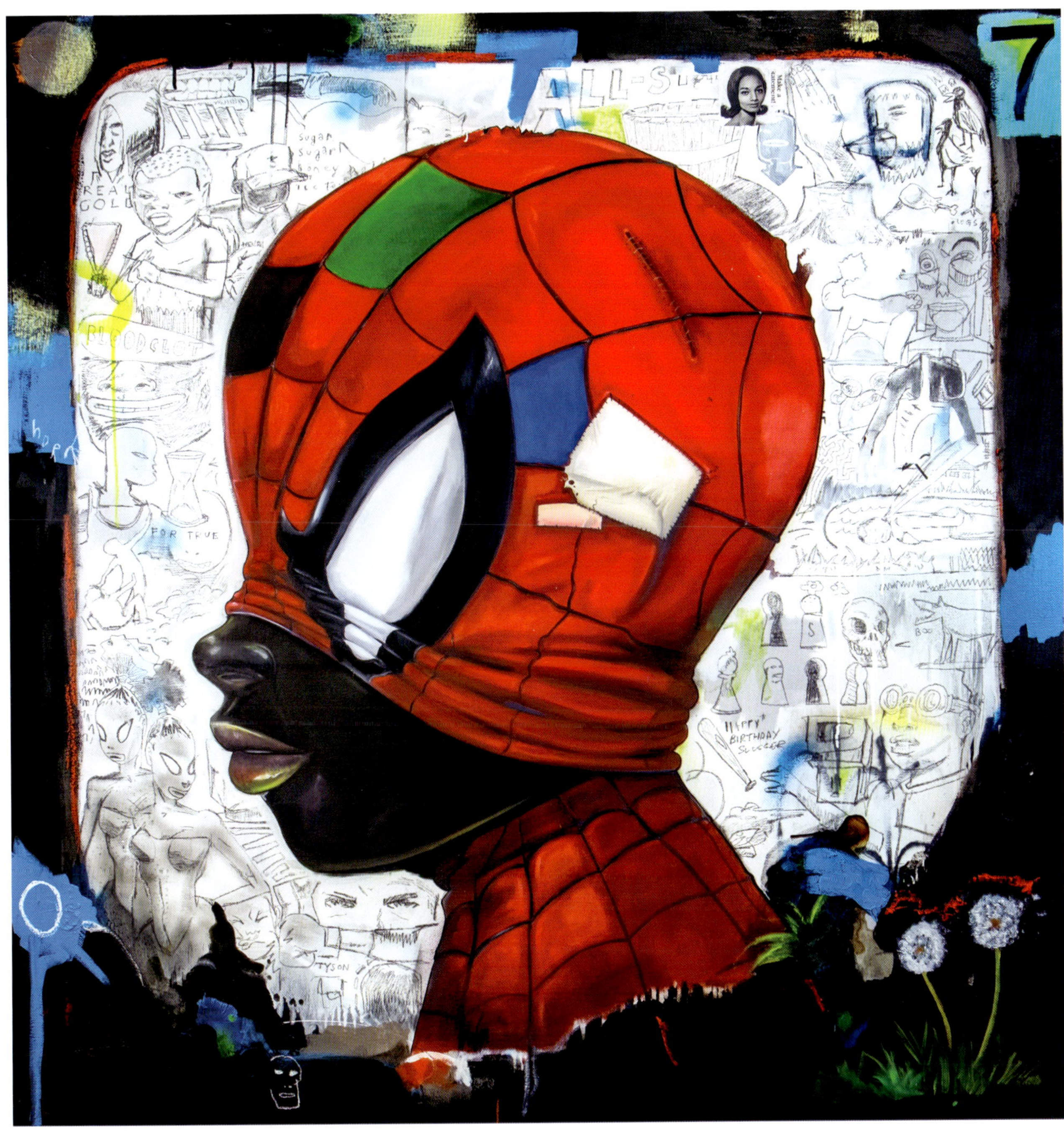

The Webs We Weave
MIxed media on canvas
58 x 62 inches
2019

(Opposite bottom)
The Night Show
Acrylic and diamond dust on canvas
24 x 18 inches
2015

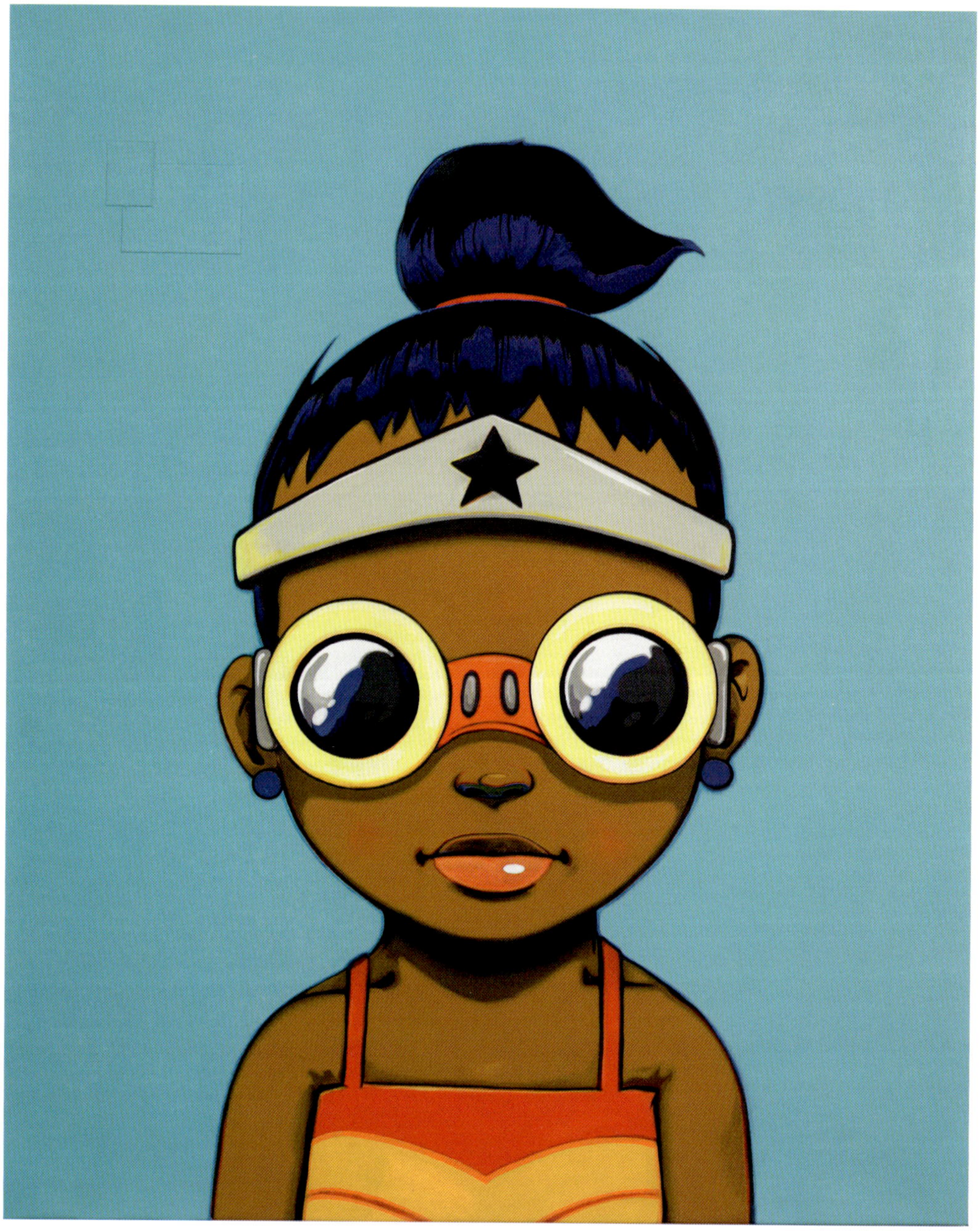

One of My Favorite Songs
Mixed media
on canvas
46 x 58 inches
2021

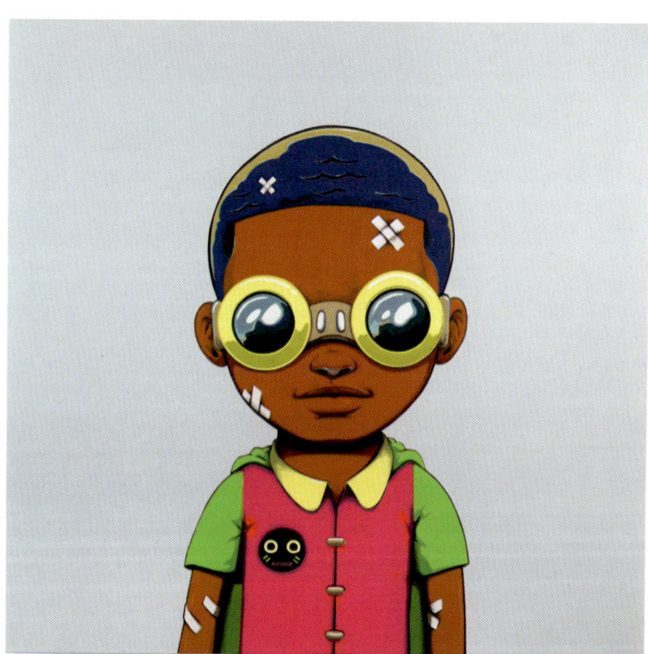

Sparrow
Mixed media
on canvas
58 x 58 inches
2021

(Opposite)
Girl with Flowers
Acrylic, spray
paint, and pastel
on canvas
54 x 77 inches
2020

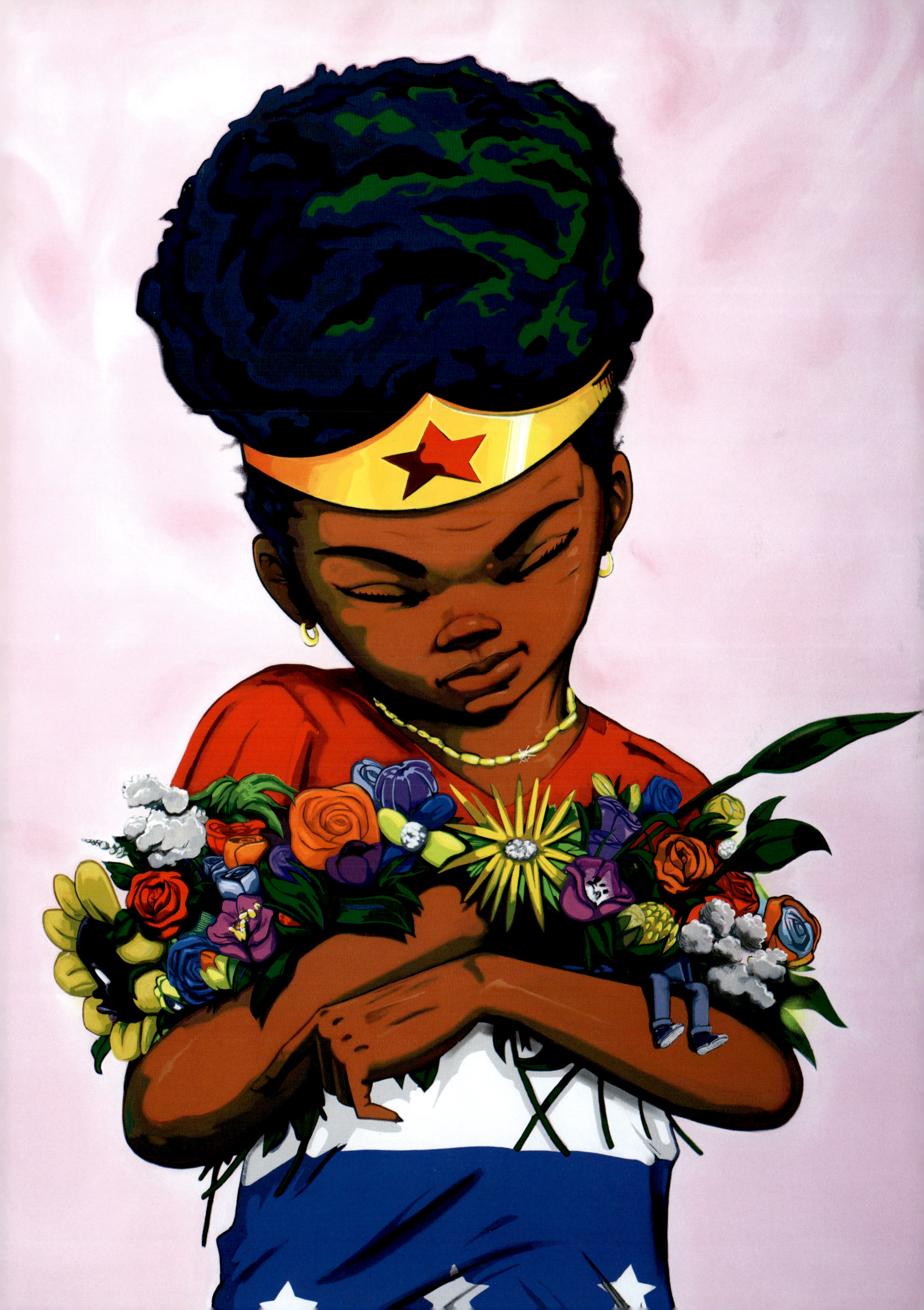

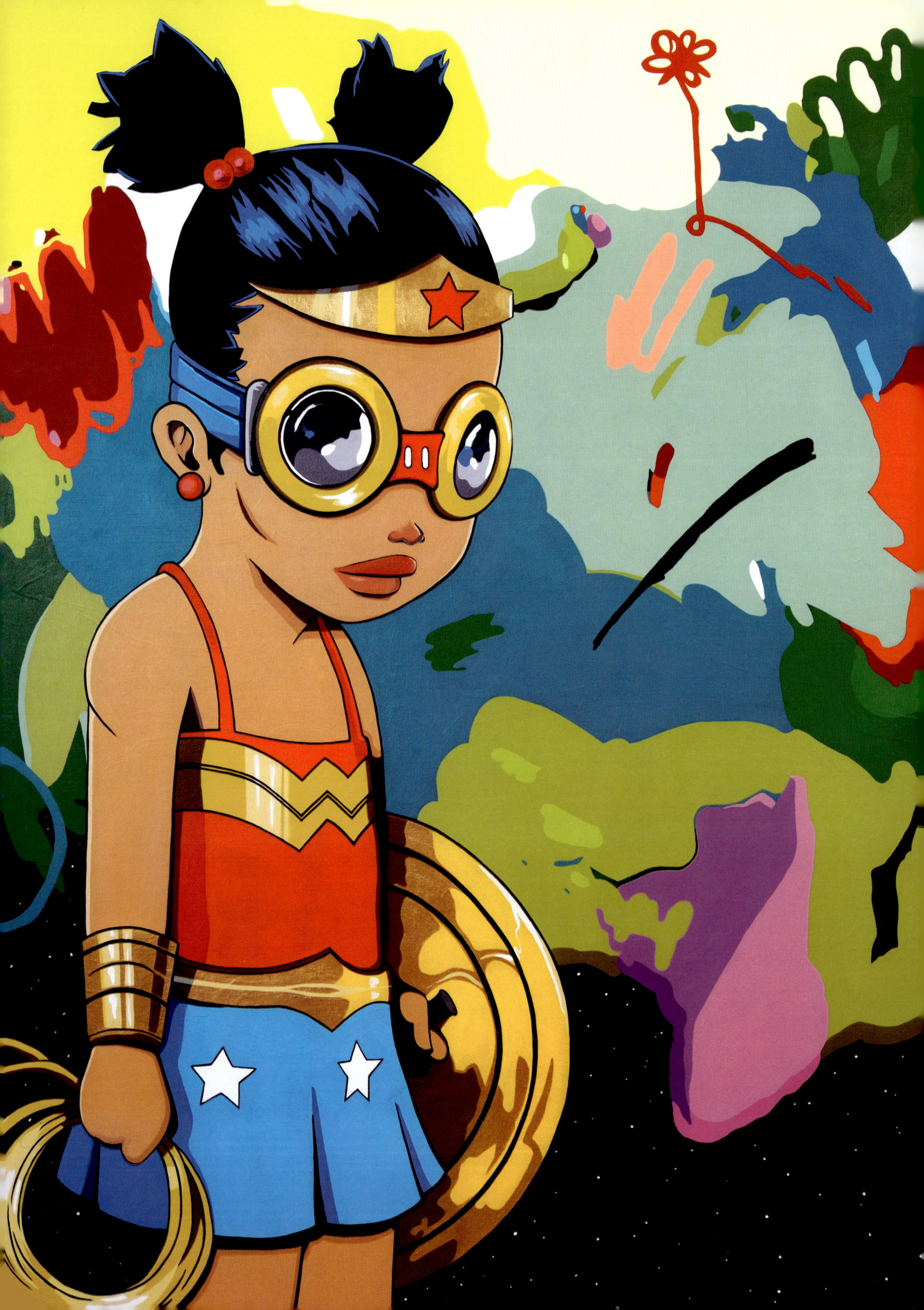

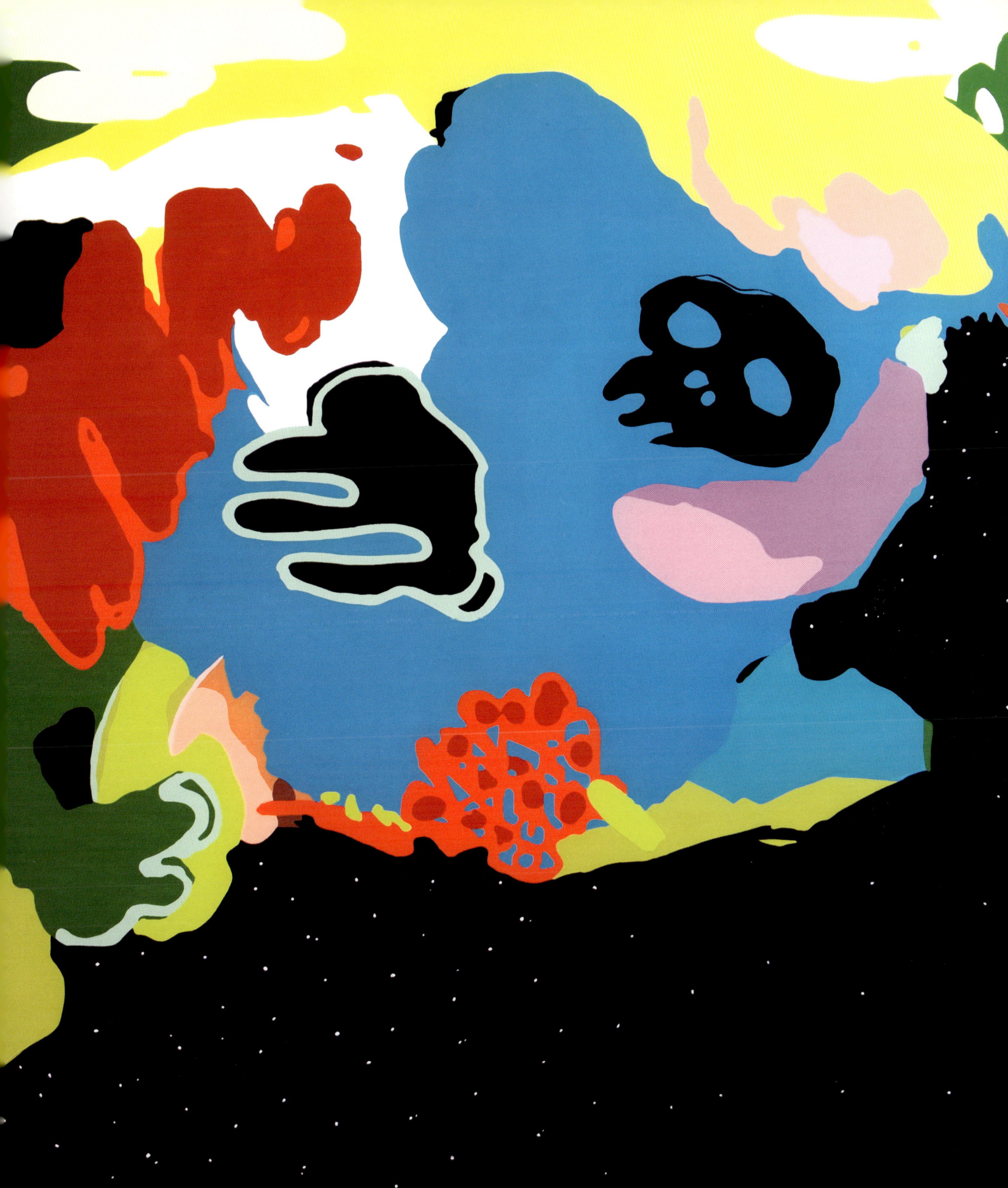

Untitled
(Wonder Study)
False camo
Mixed media
on canvas
36 x 48 inches
2018

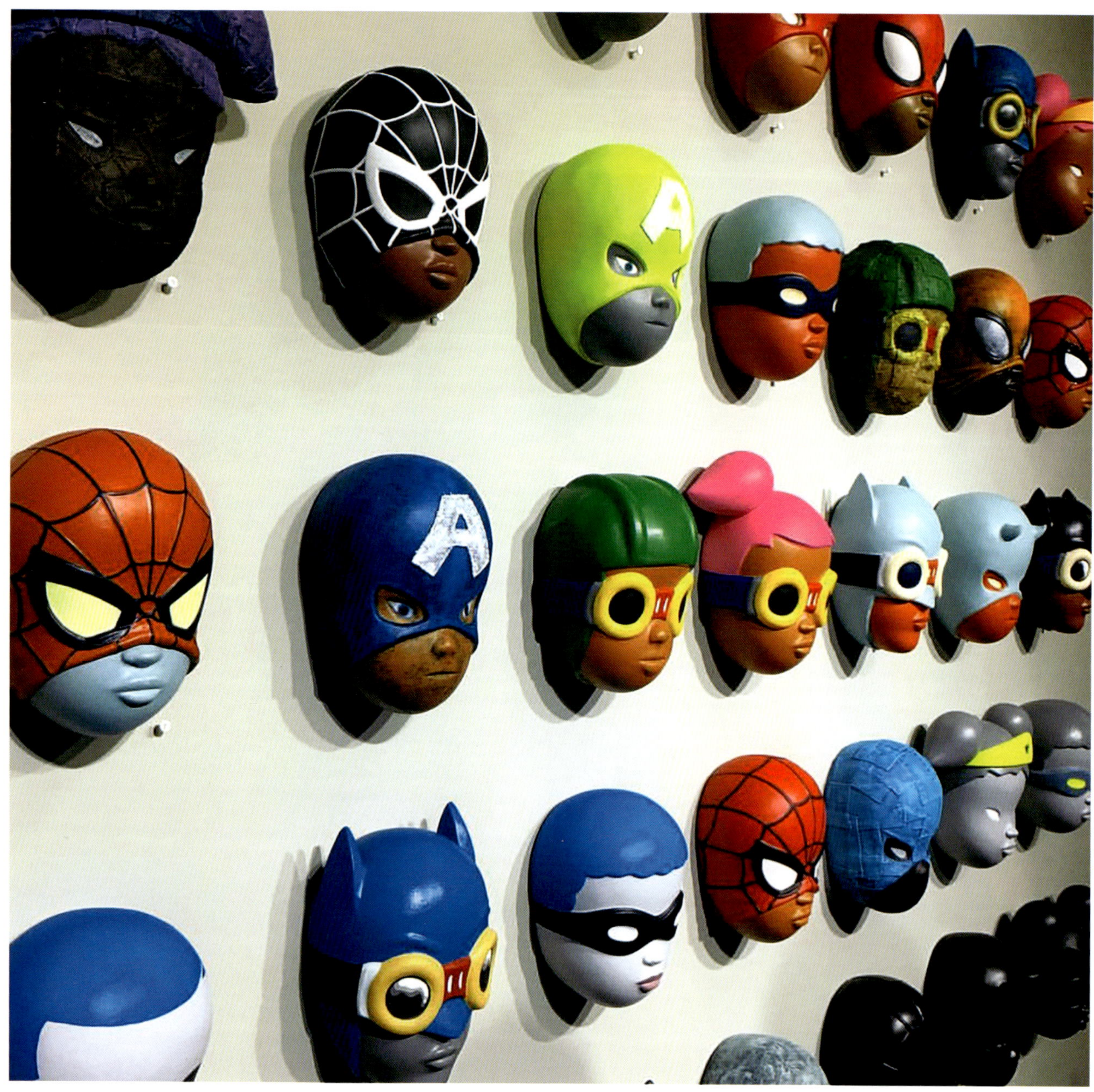

Sculpture Heads Acrylic, fiberglass and resin, 2016

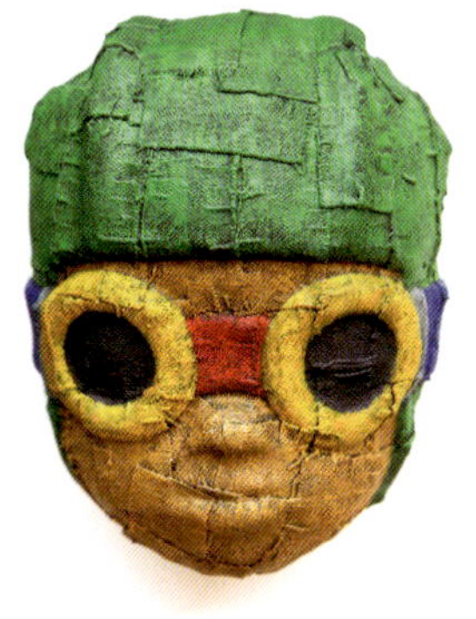
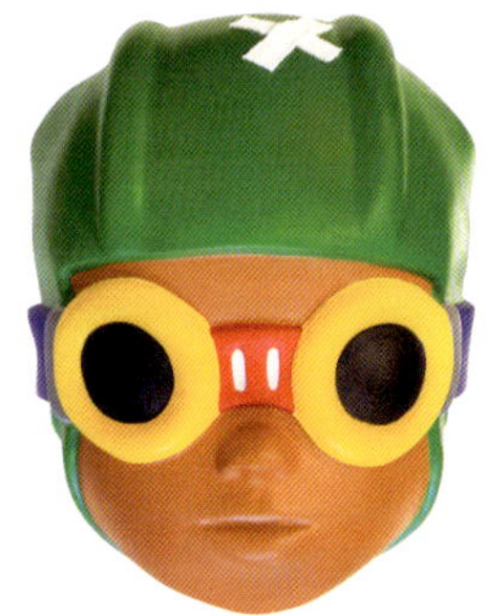
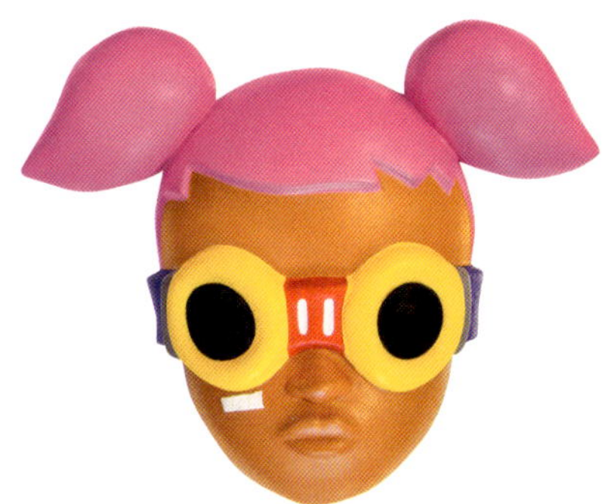
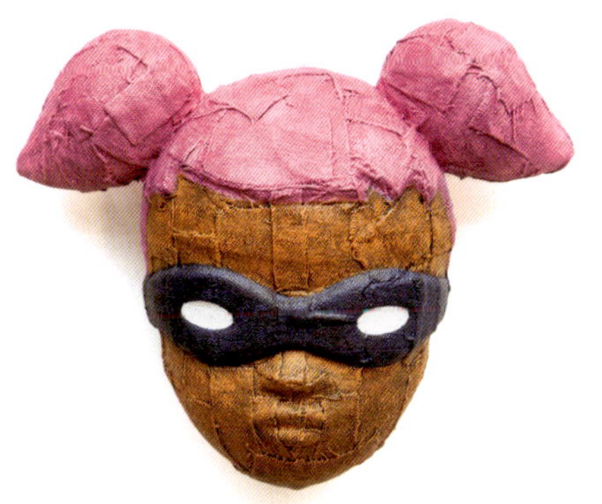
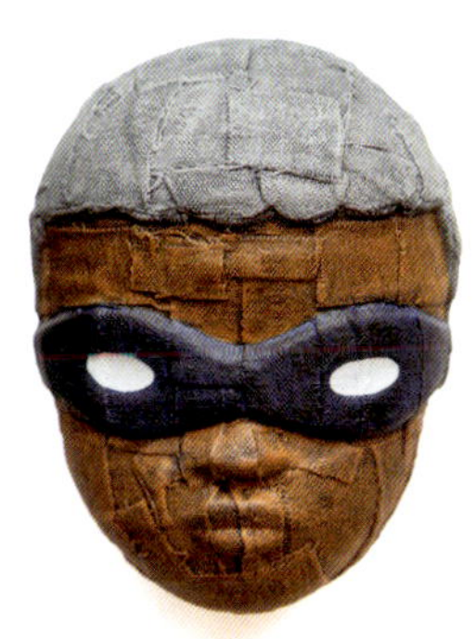
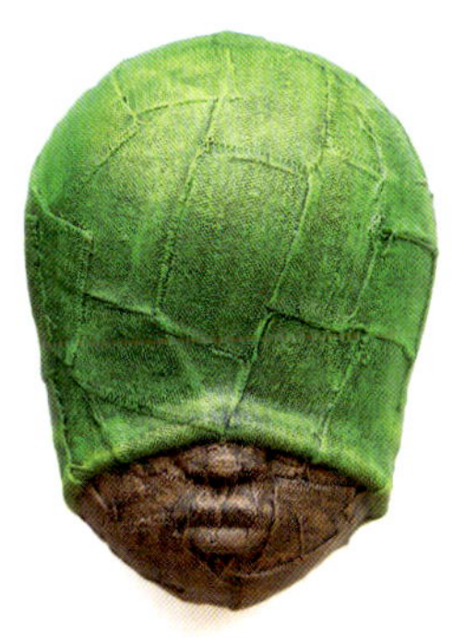
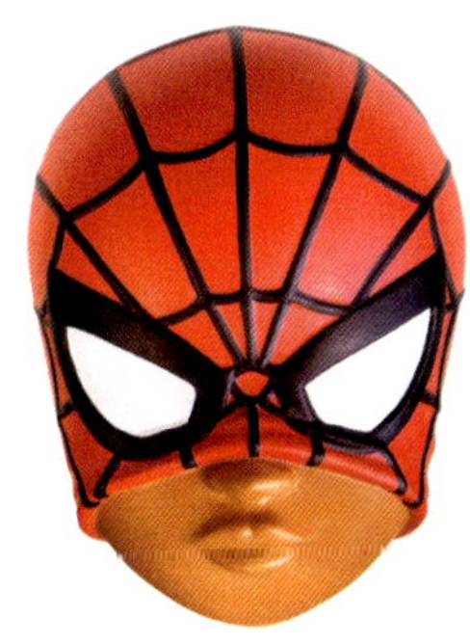
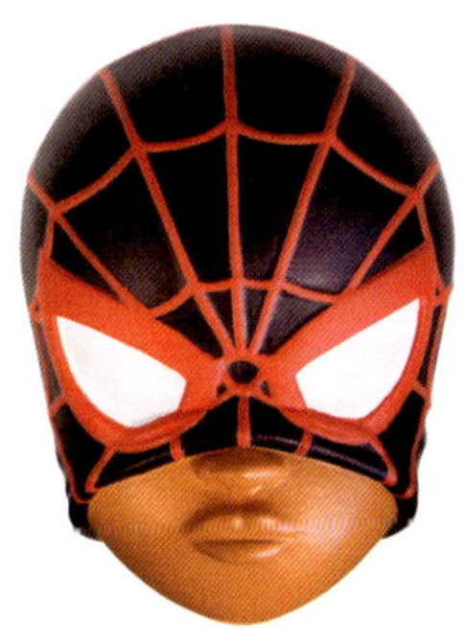
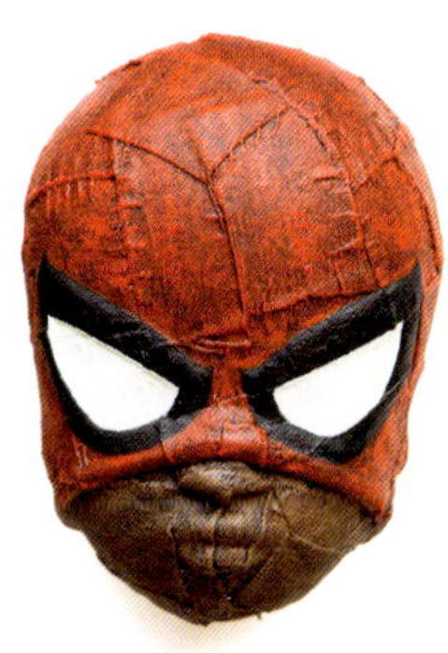

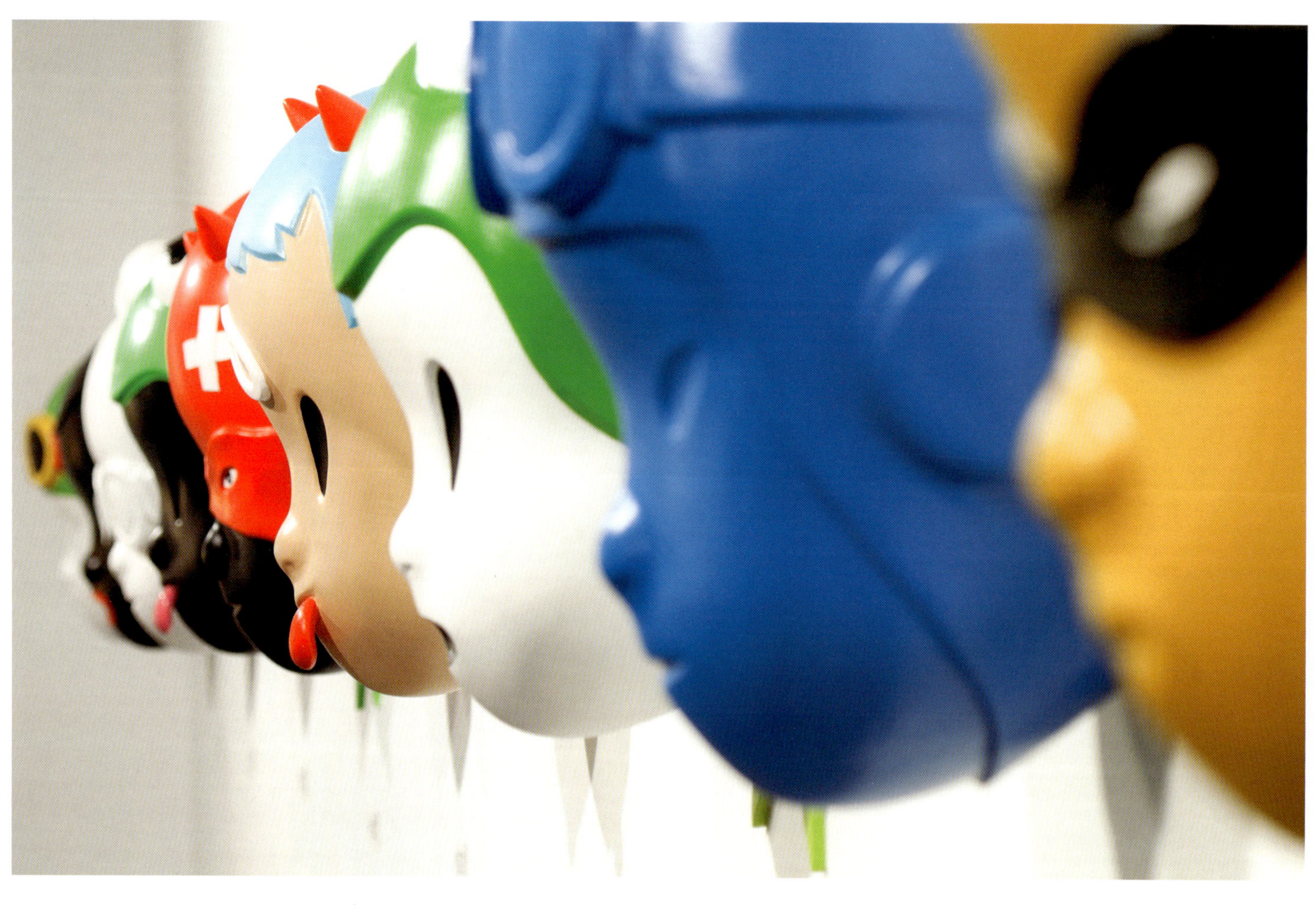

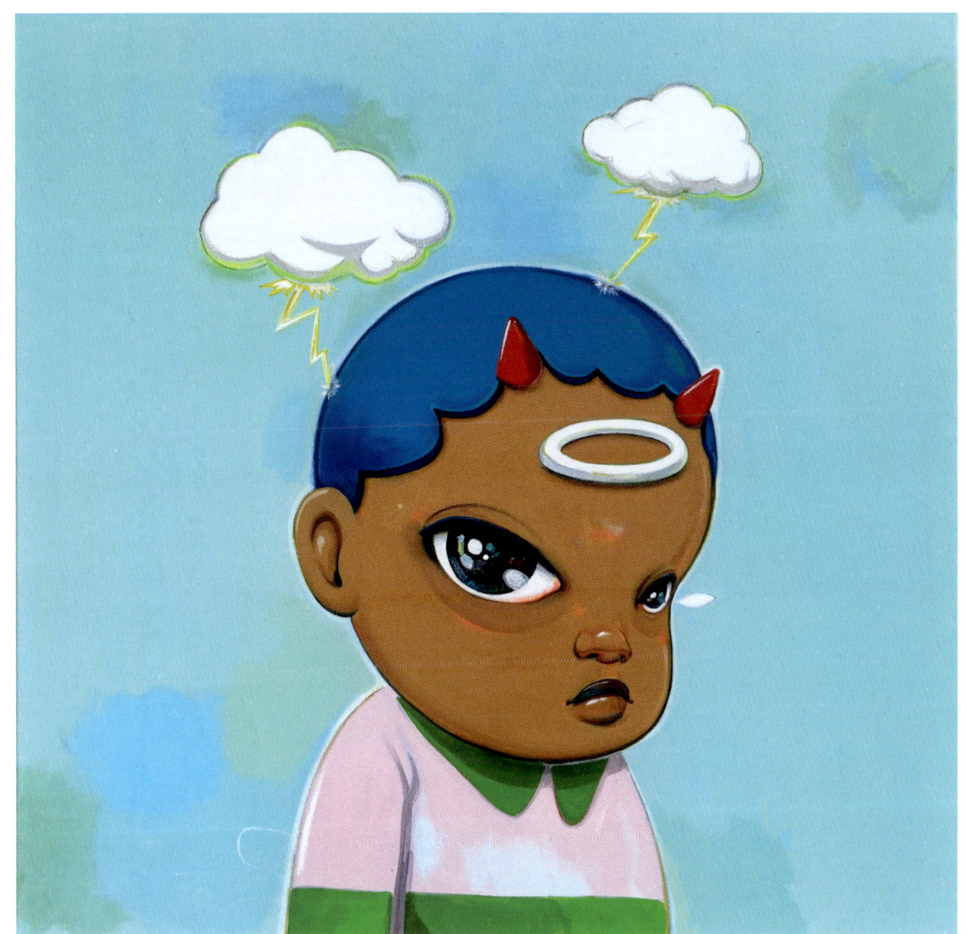

Both Are Him
Mixed media
on canvas
30 x 30 inches
2021

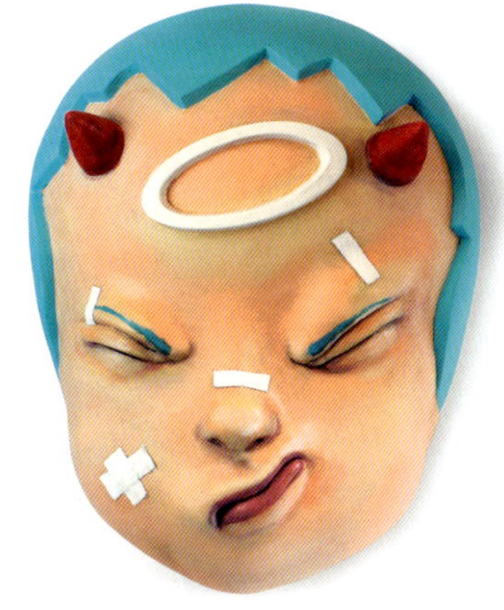

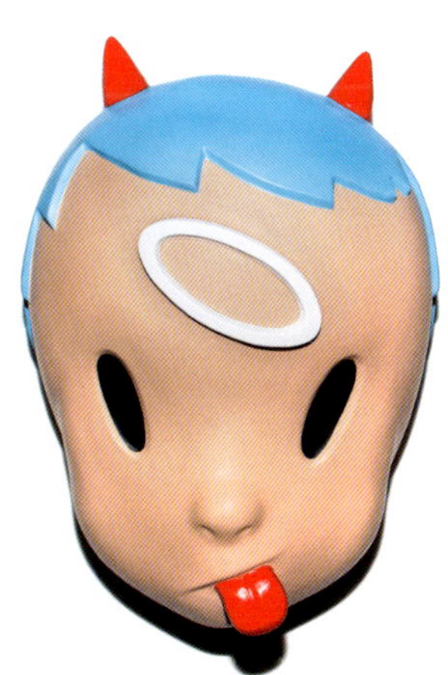

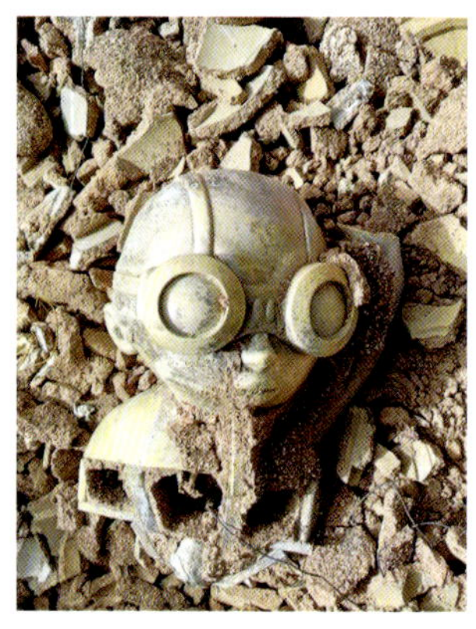

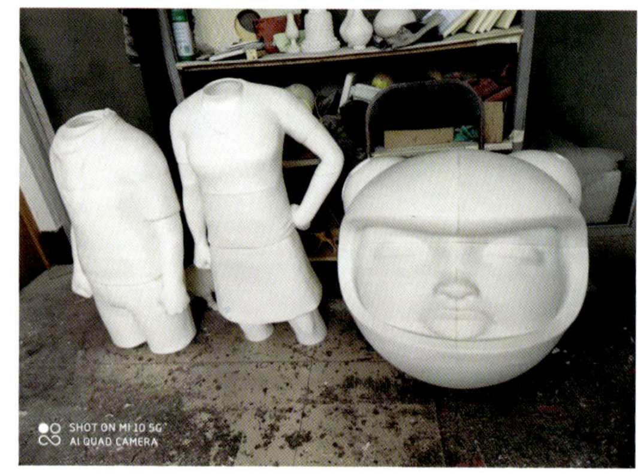
SHOT ON MI 10 5G
AI QUAD CAMERA

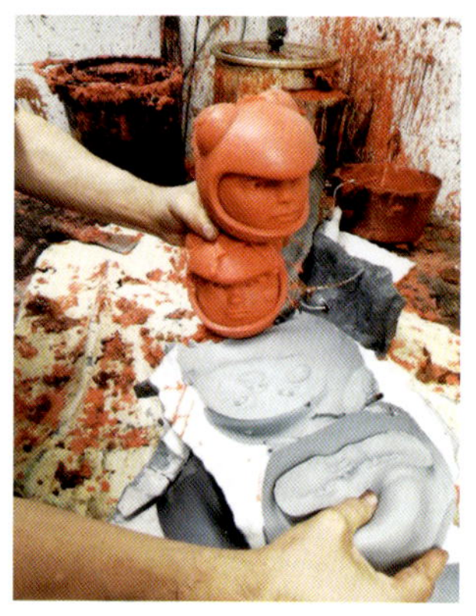

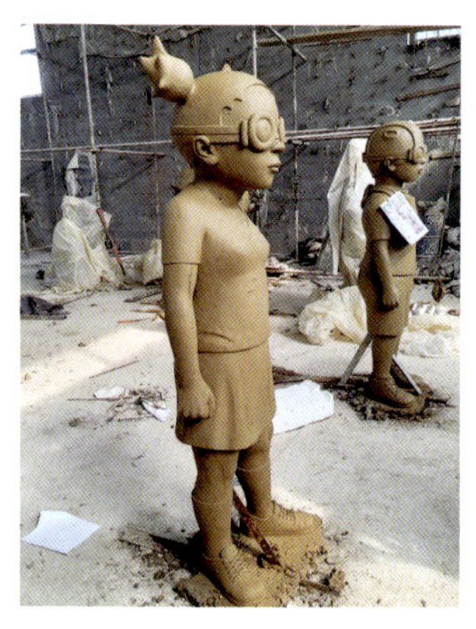

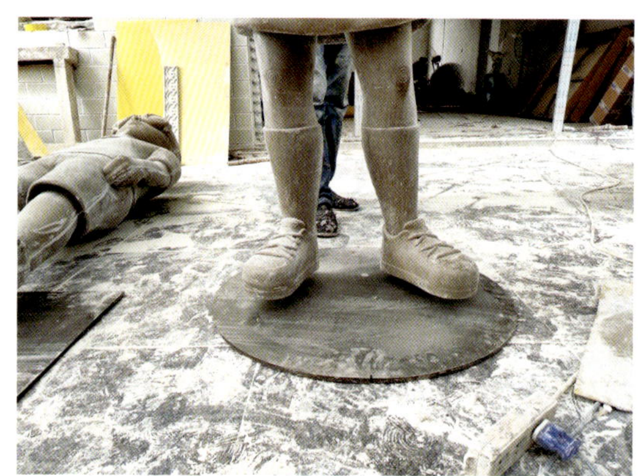

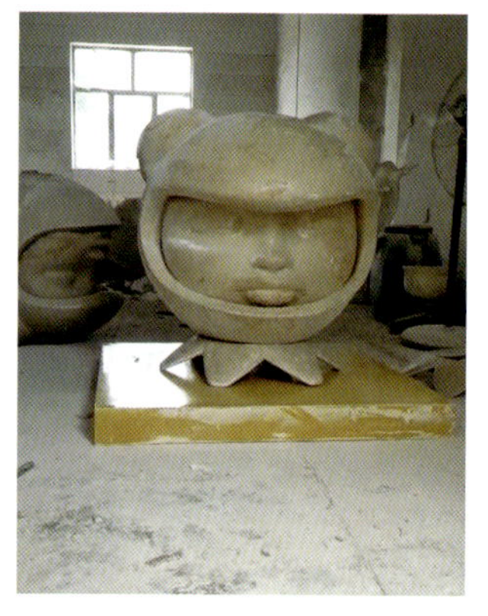

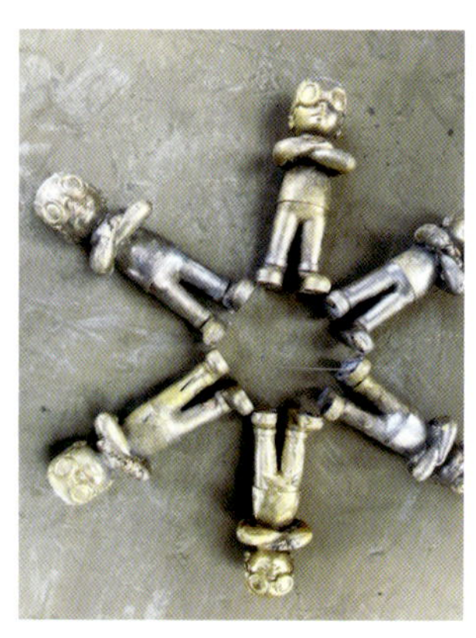

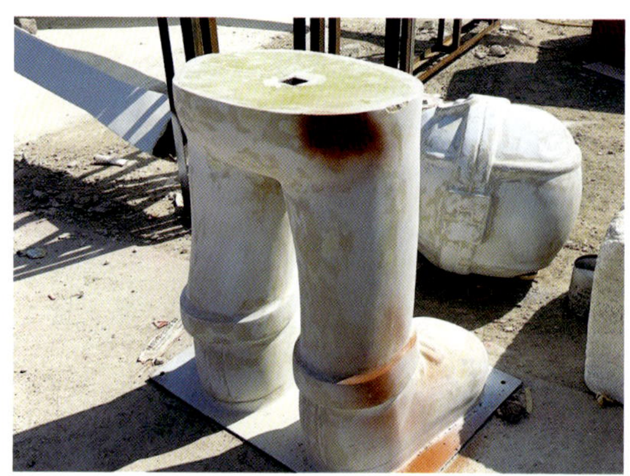

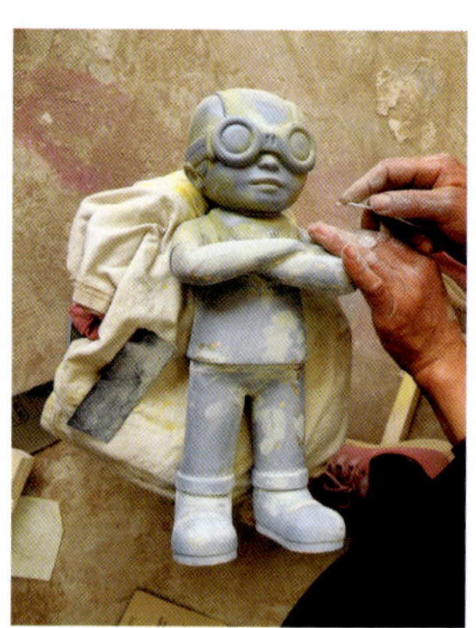

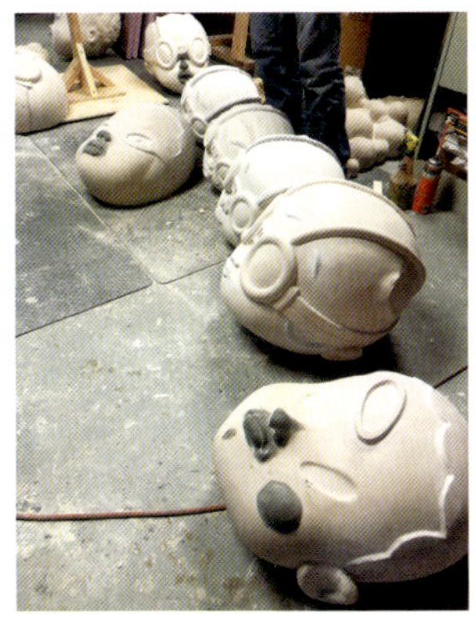
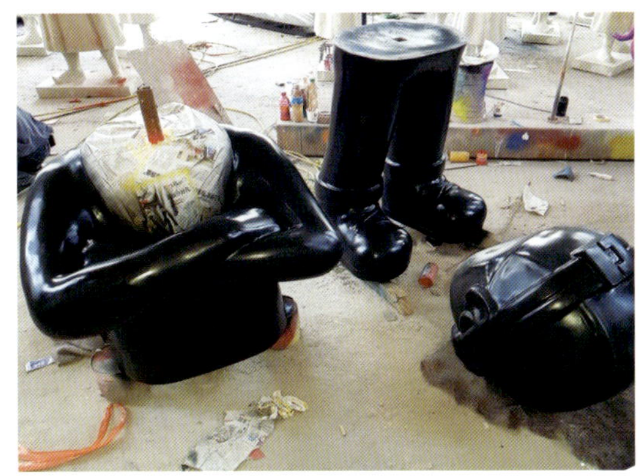
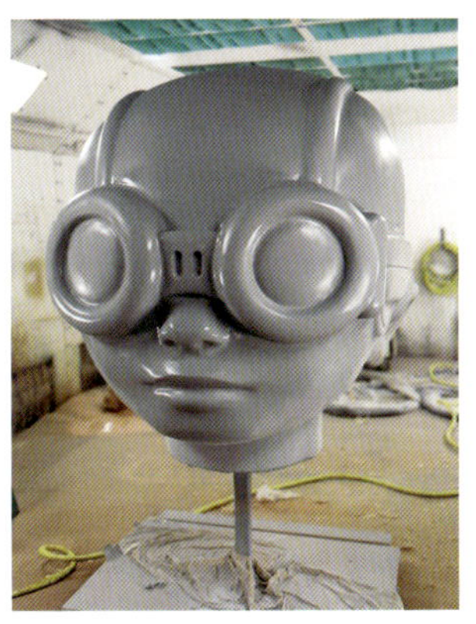
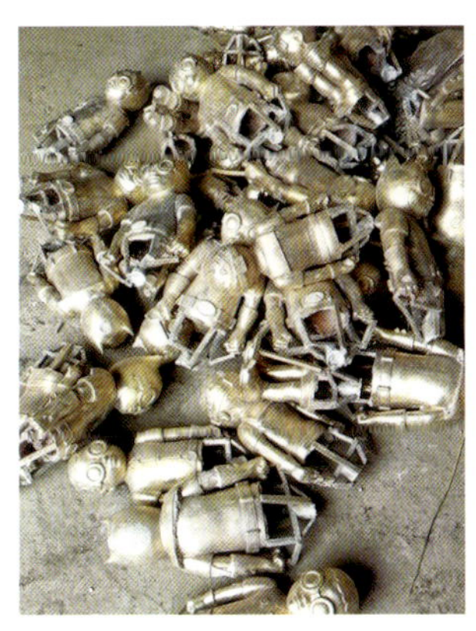
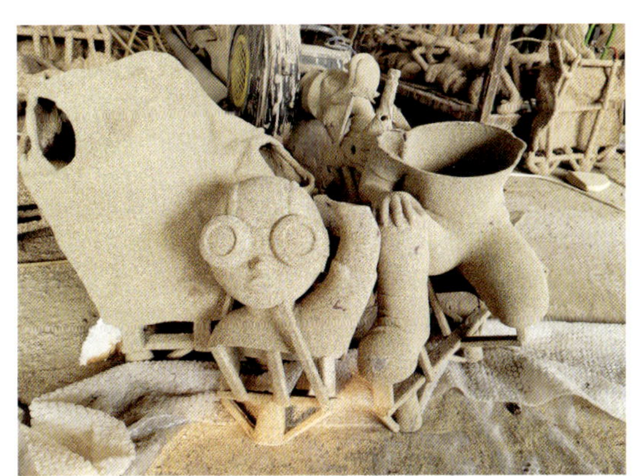
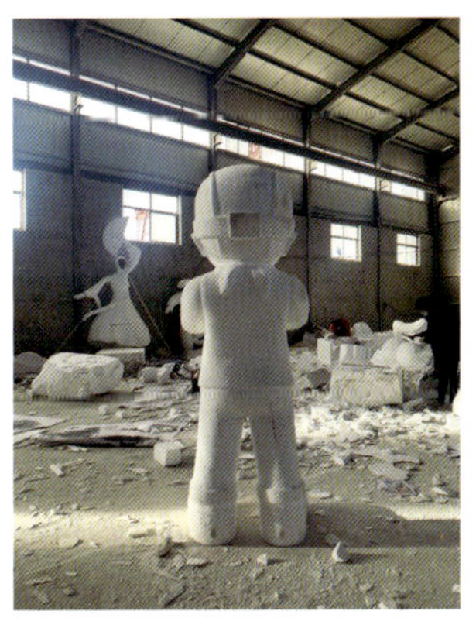
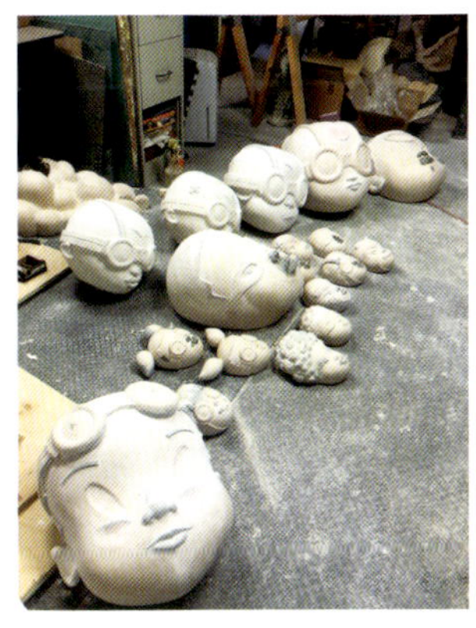
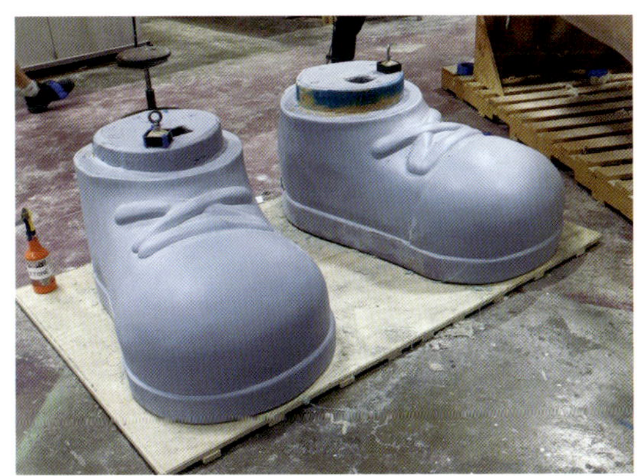
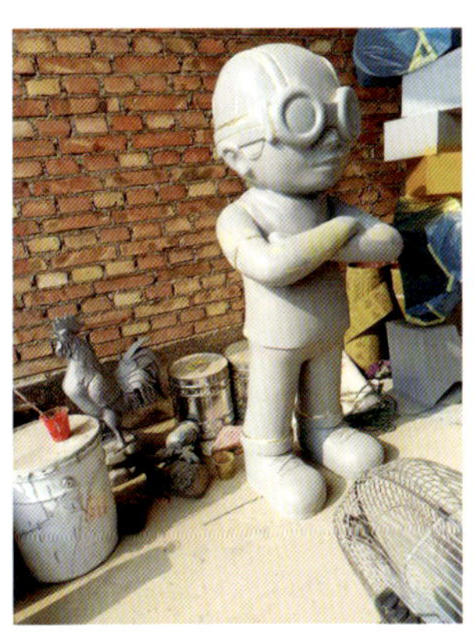

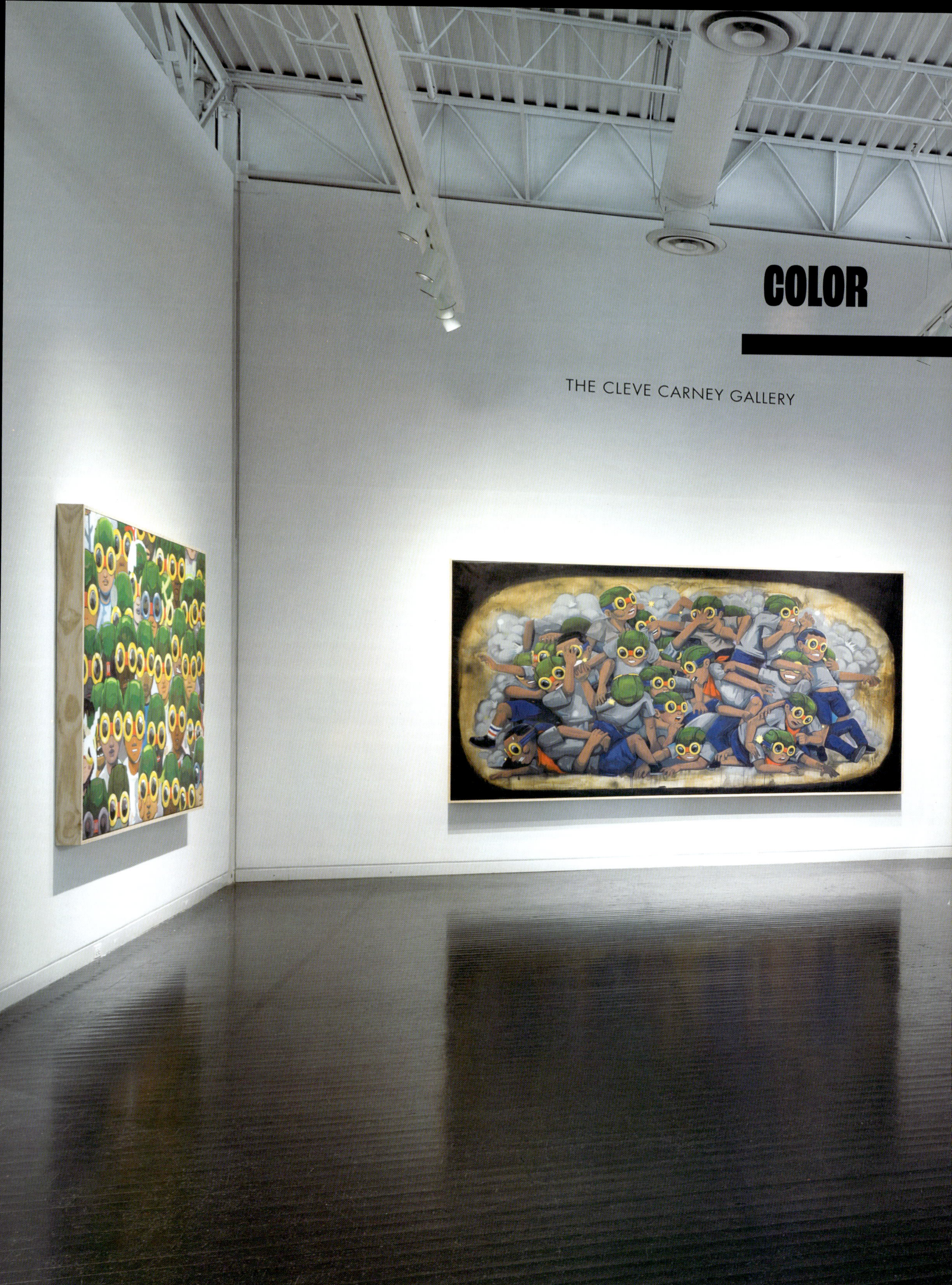
THE CLEVE CARNEY GALLERY

TWO:

EXHIBITIONS INSTALLATIONS COLLECTIONS

FORCED FIELD

Elmhurst Art Museum, Chicago, 2018

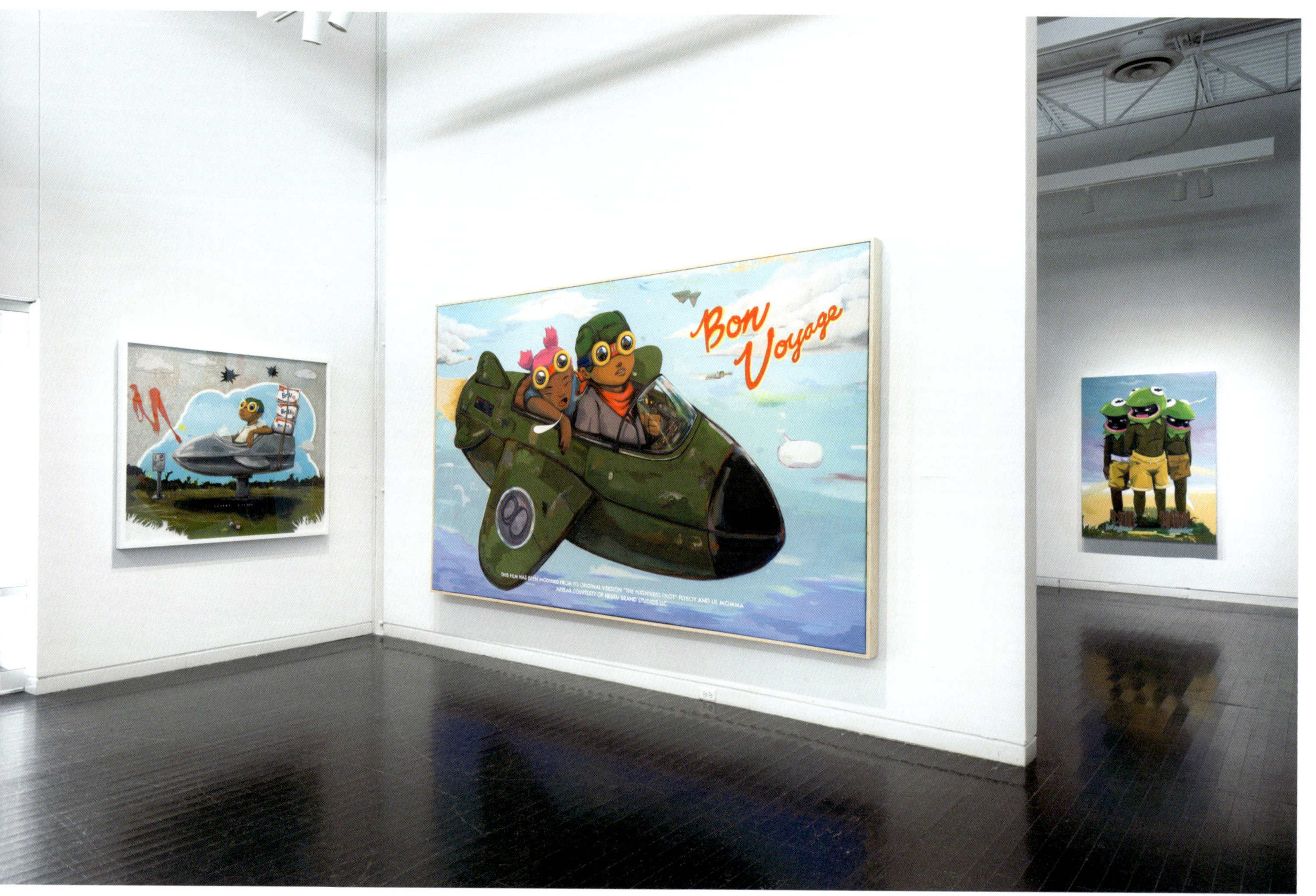

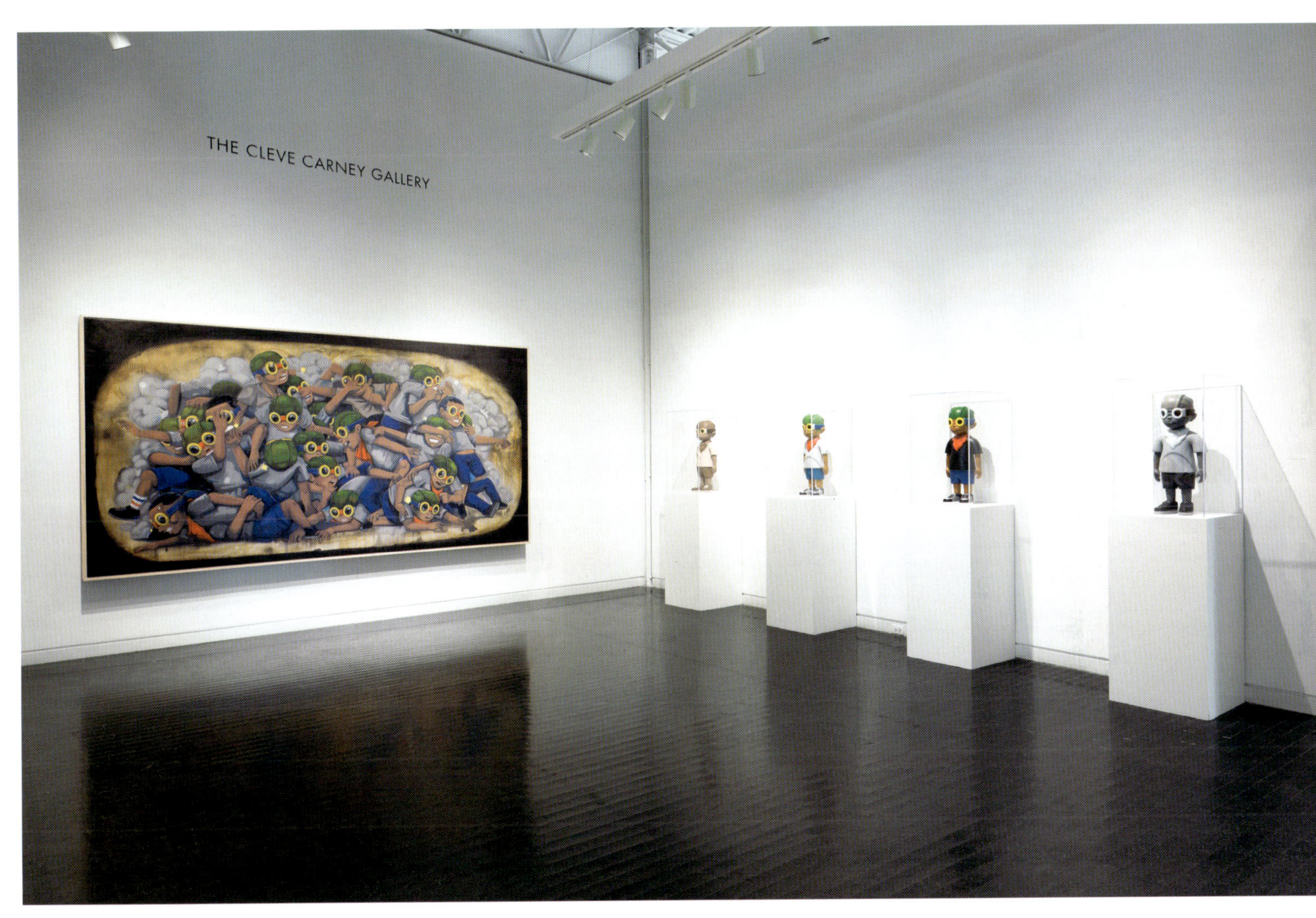
THE CLEVE CARNEY GALLERY

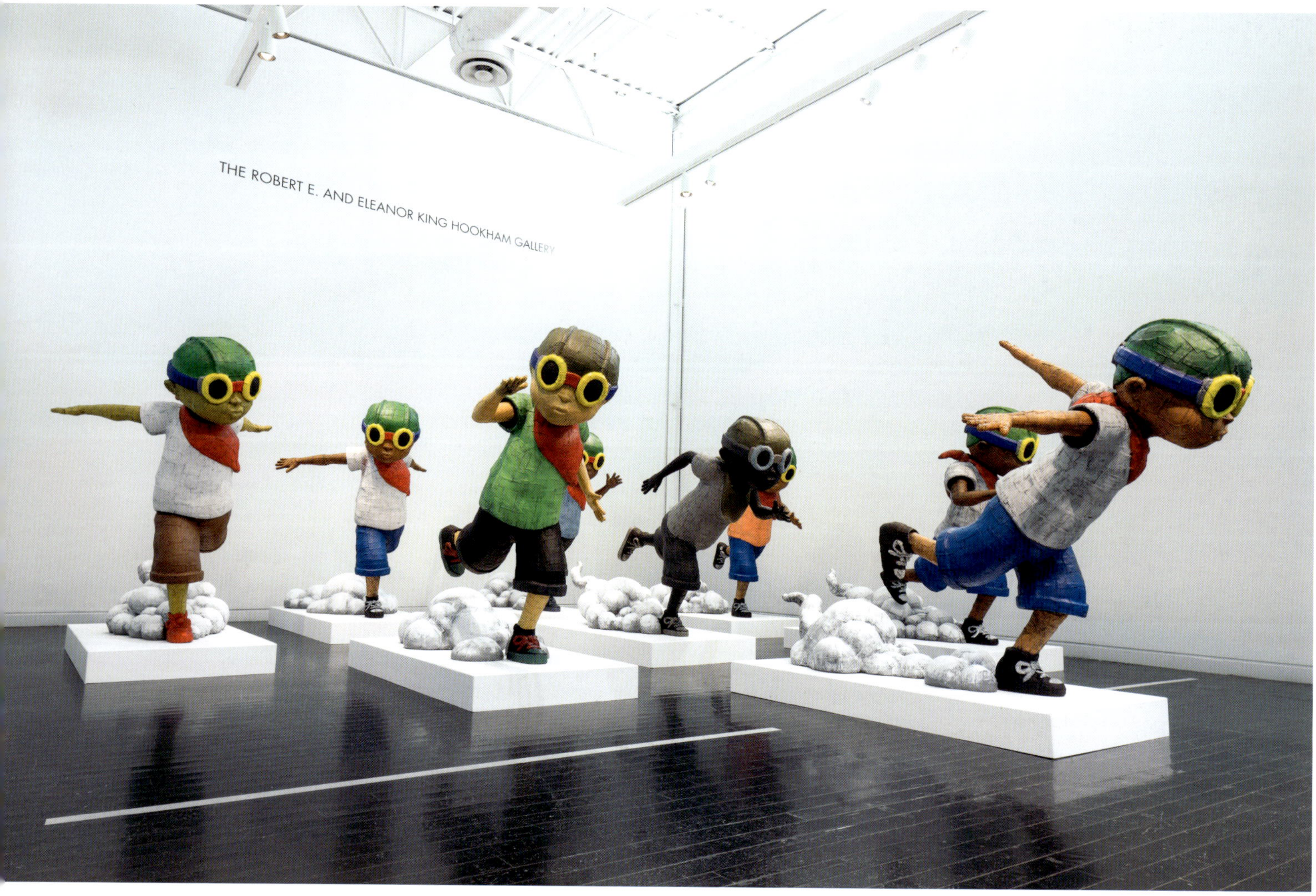

Boy Run
Canvas wrapped
fiberglass, resin,
and acrylic

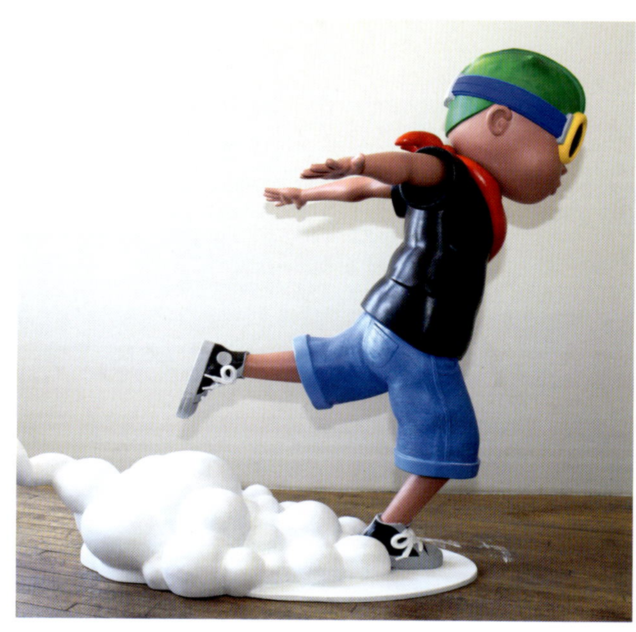

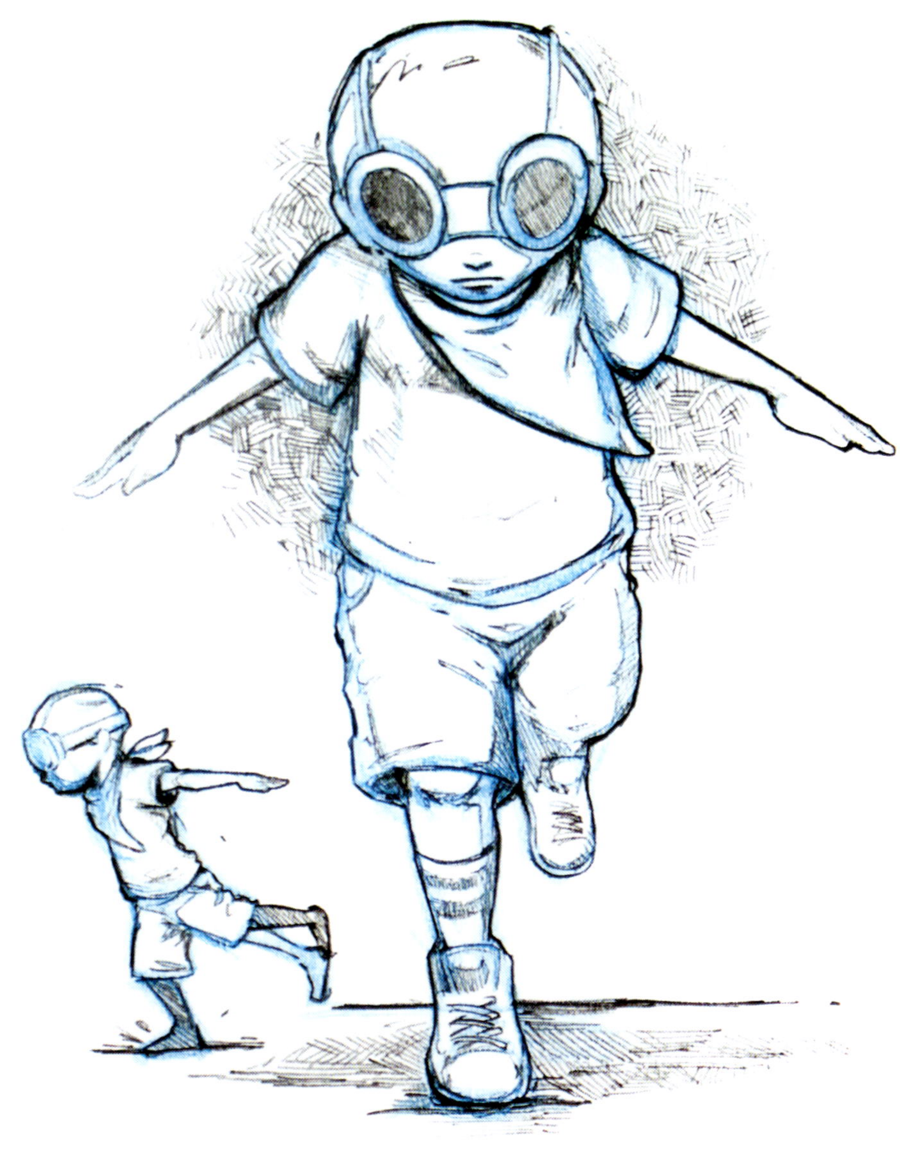

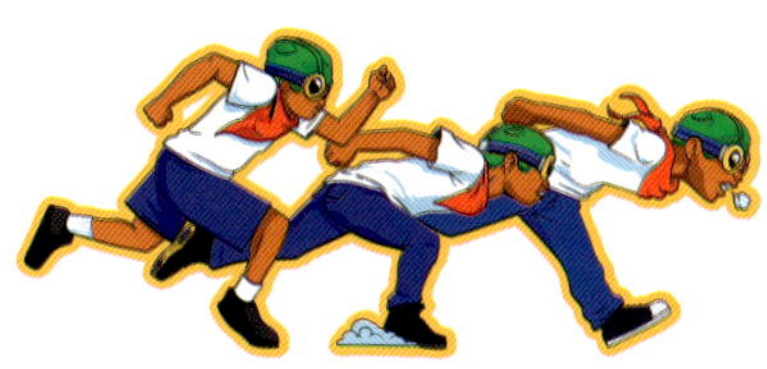

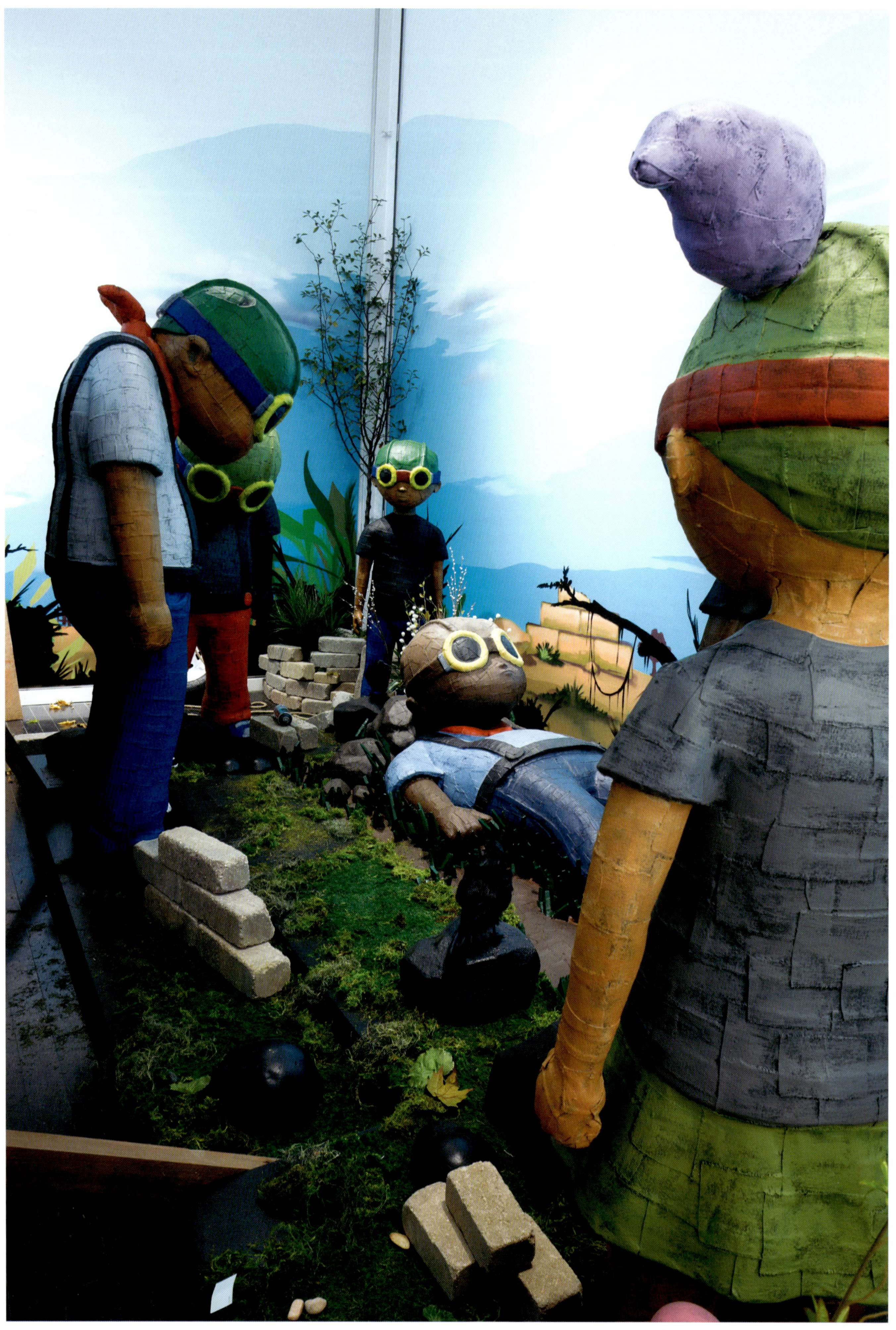

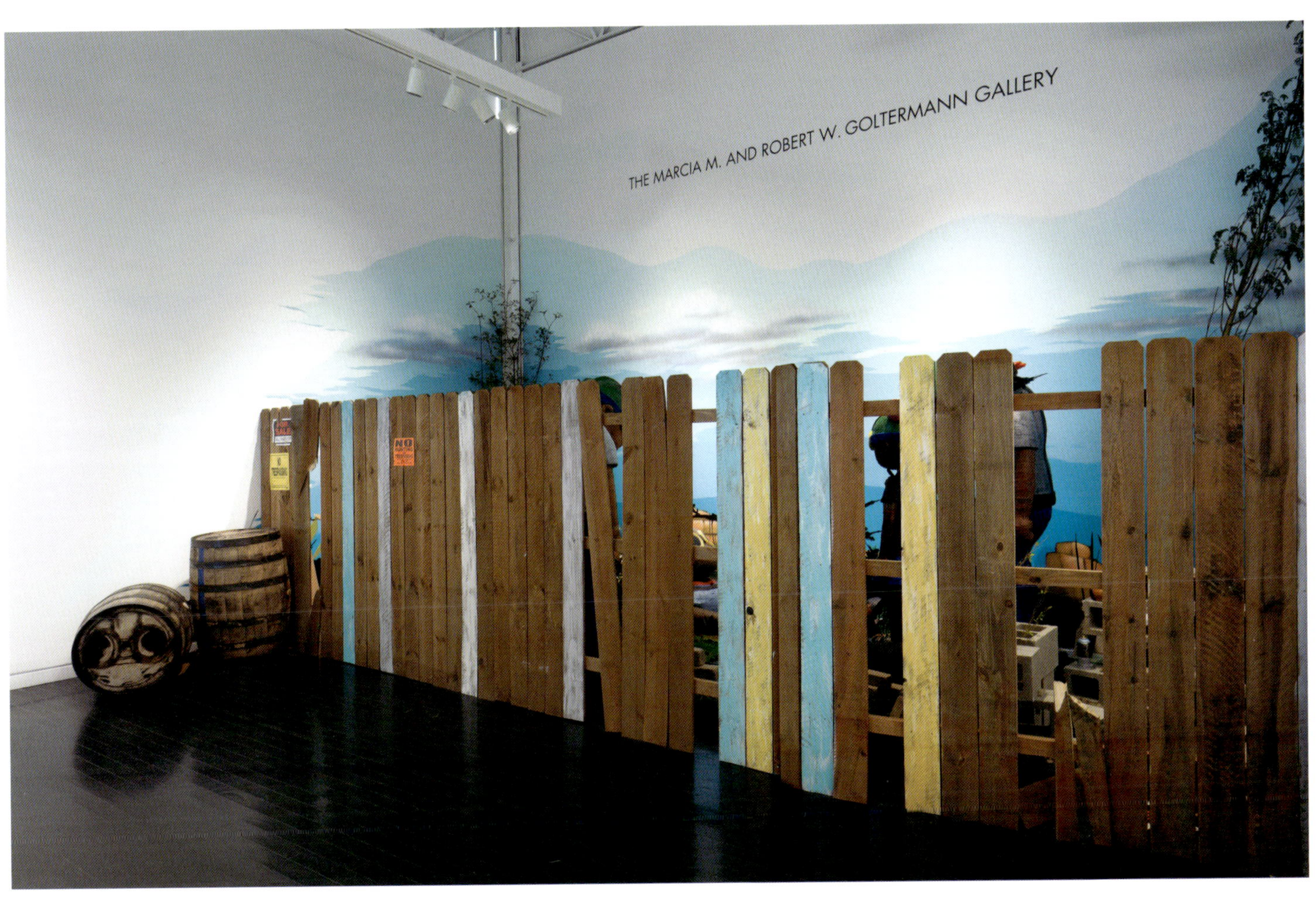

FORCED FIELD

Elmhurst Art Museum, Chicago, 2018

***Snow White*-inspired sculpture installation**
Canvas wrapped fiberglass, resin, and acrylic

CHICAGO IDEAS WEEK

Public art installation, 2013

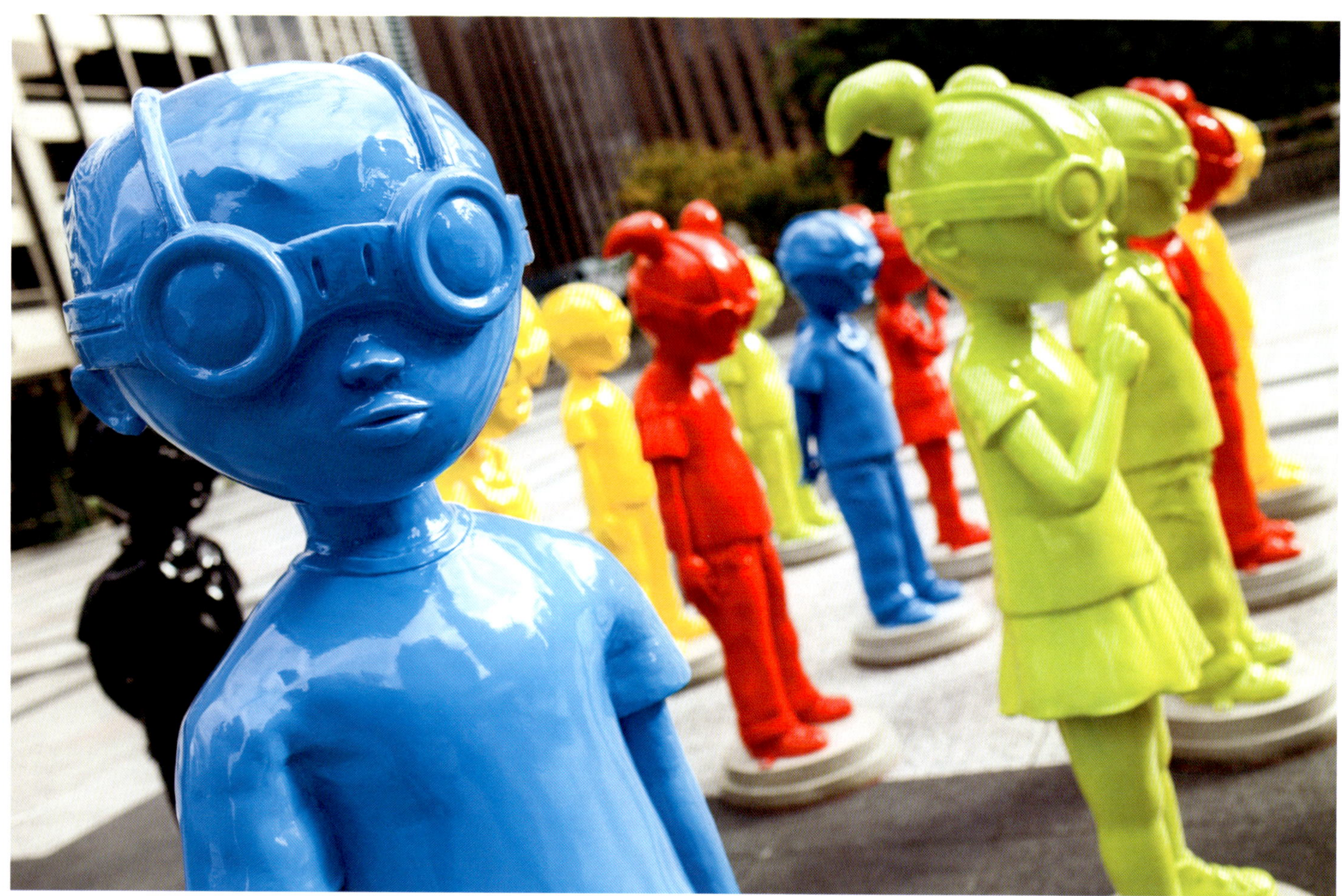

The Watch
Acrylic, fiberglass,
and resin

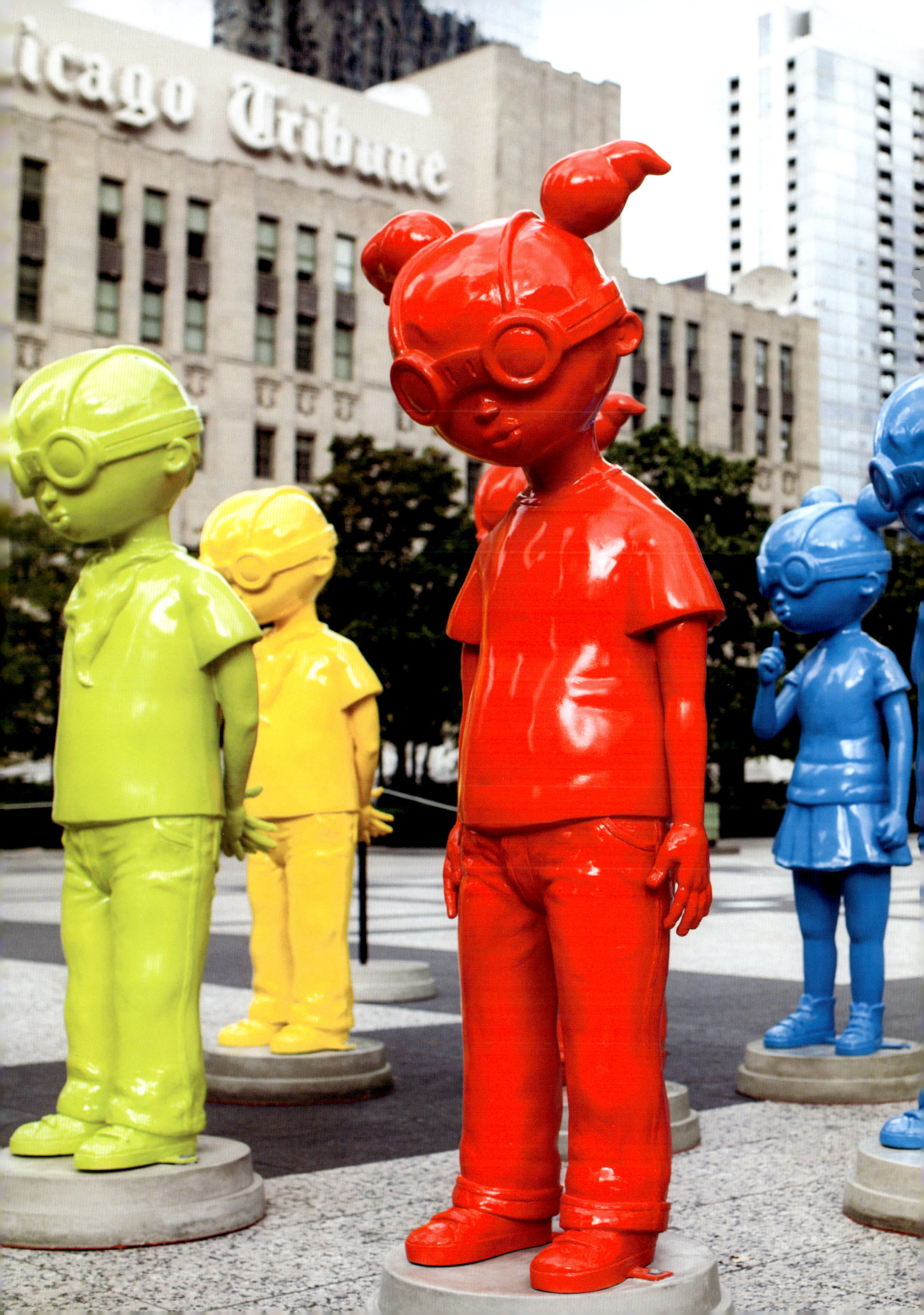
icago Tribune

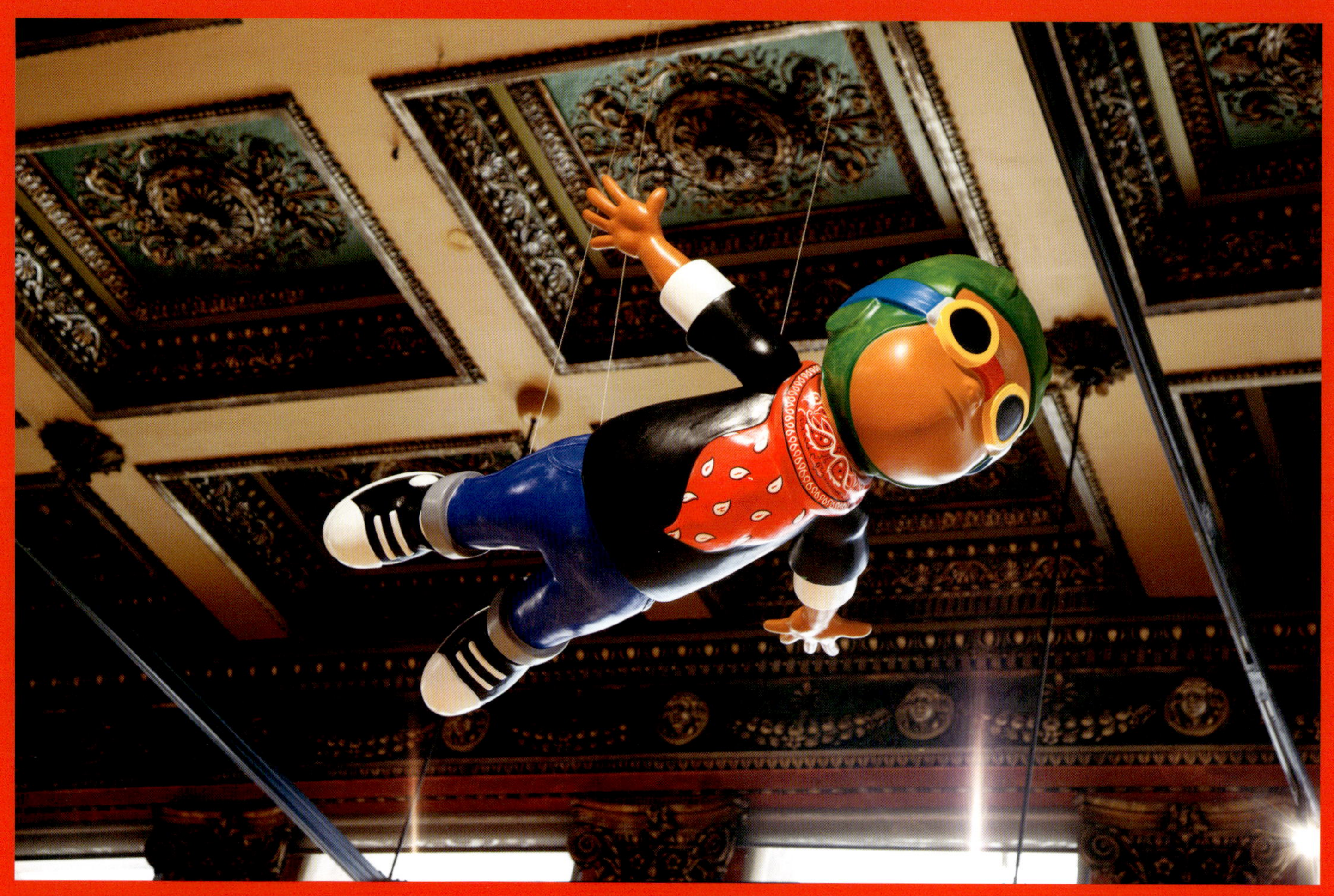

PARADE DAY RAIN

Chicago Cultural Center, 2014

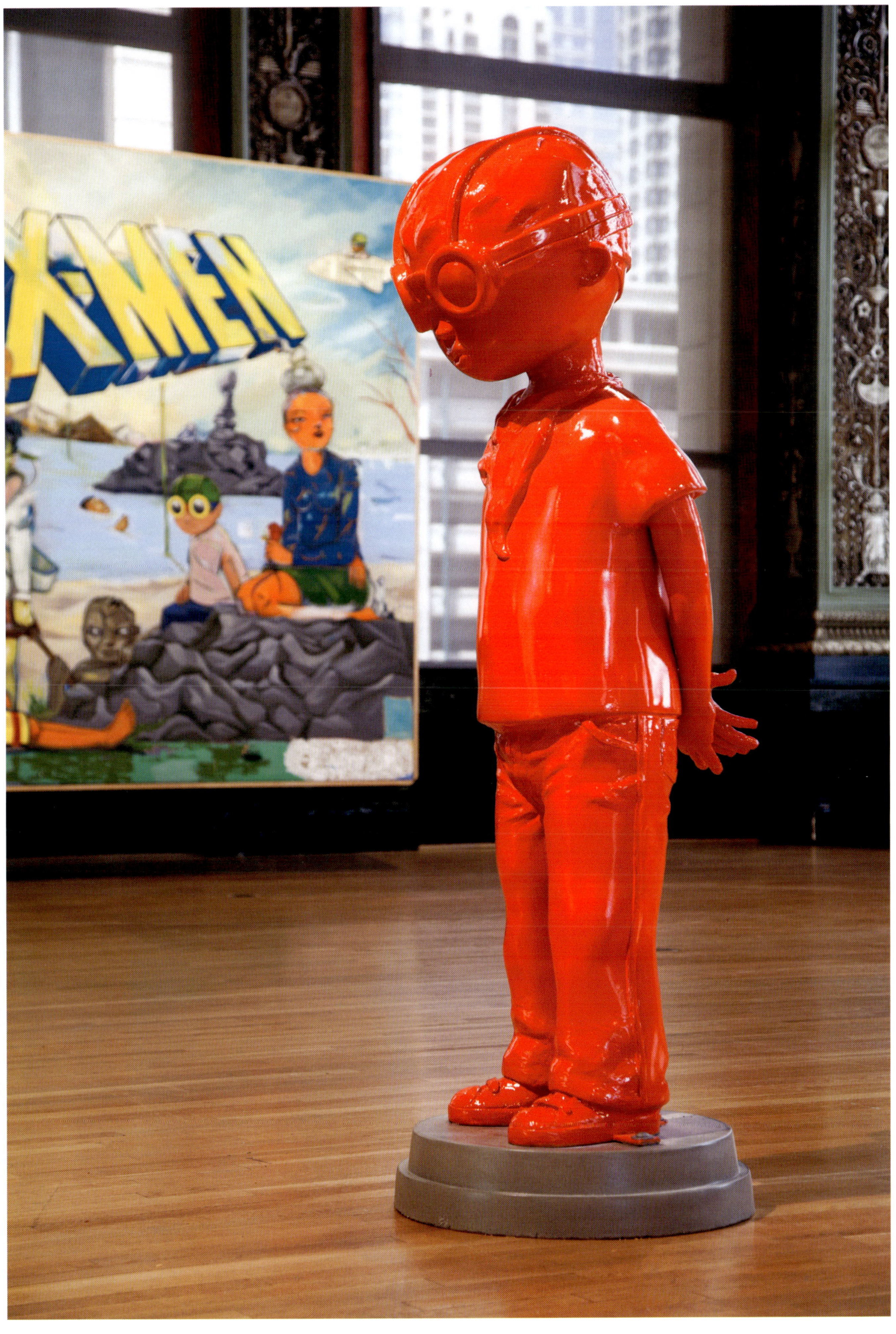
X-MEN

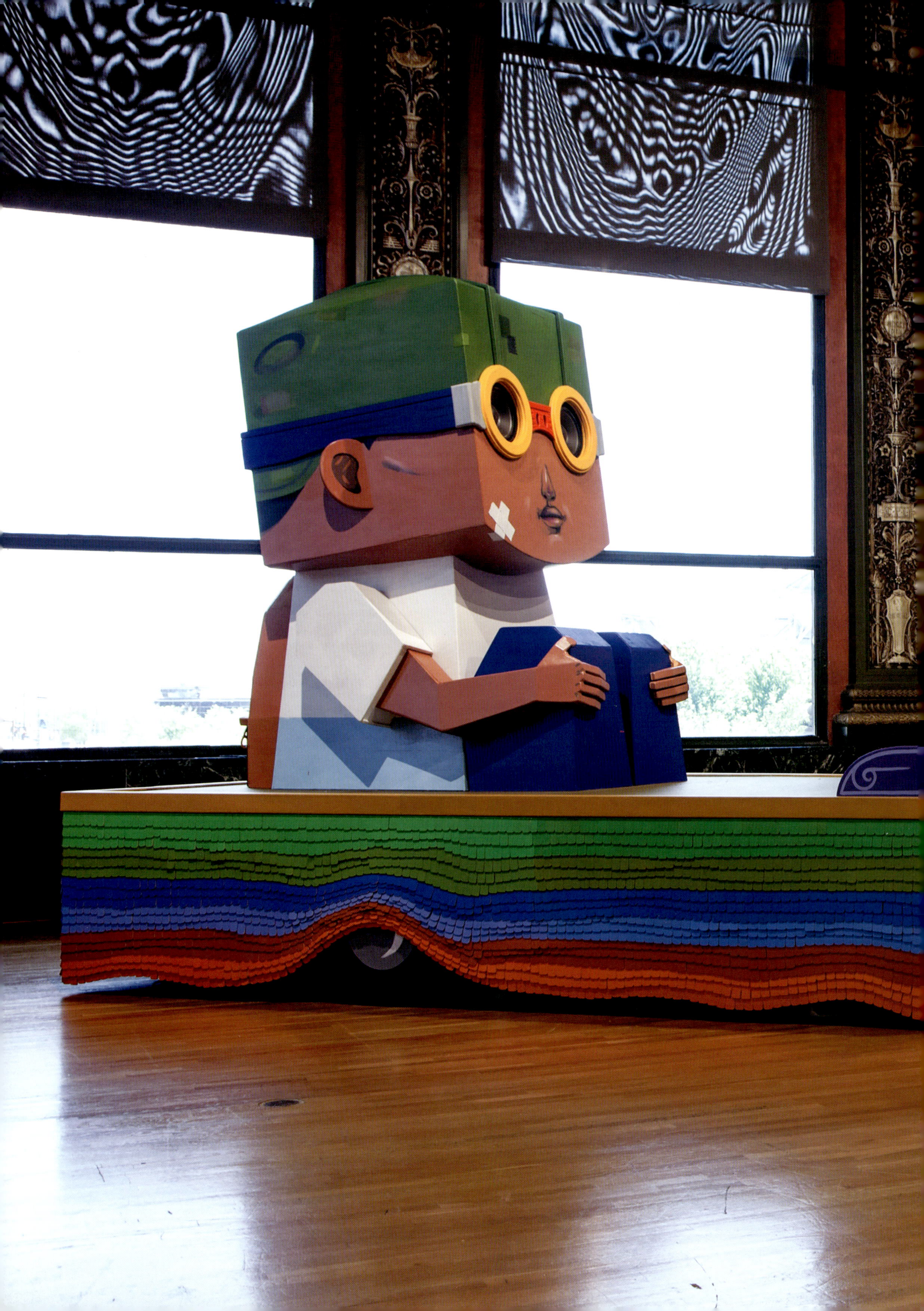

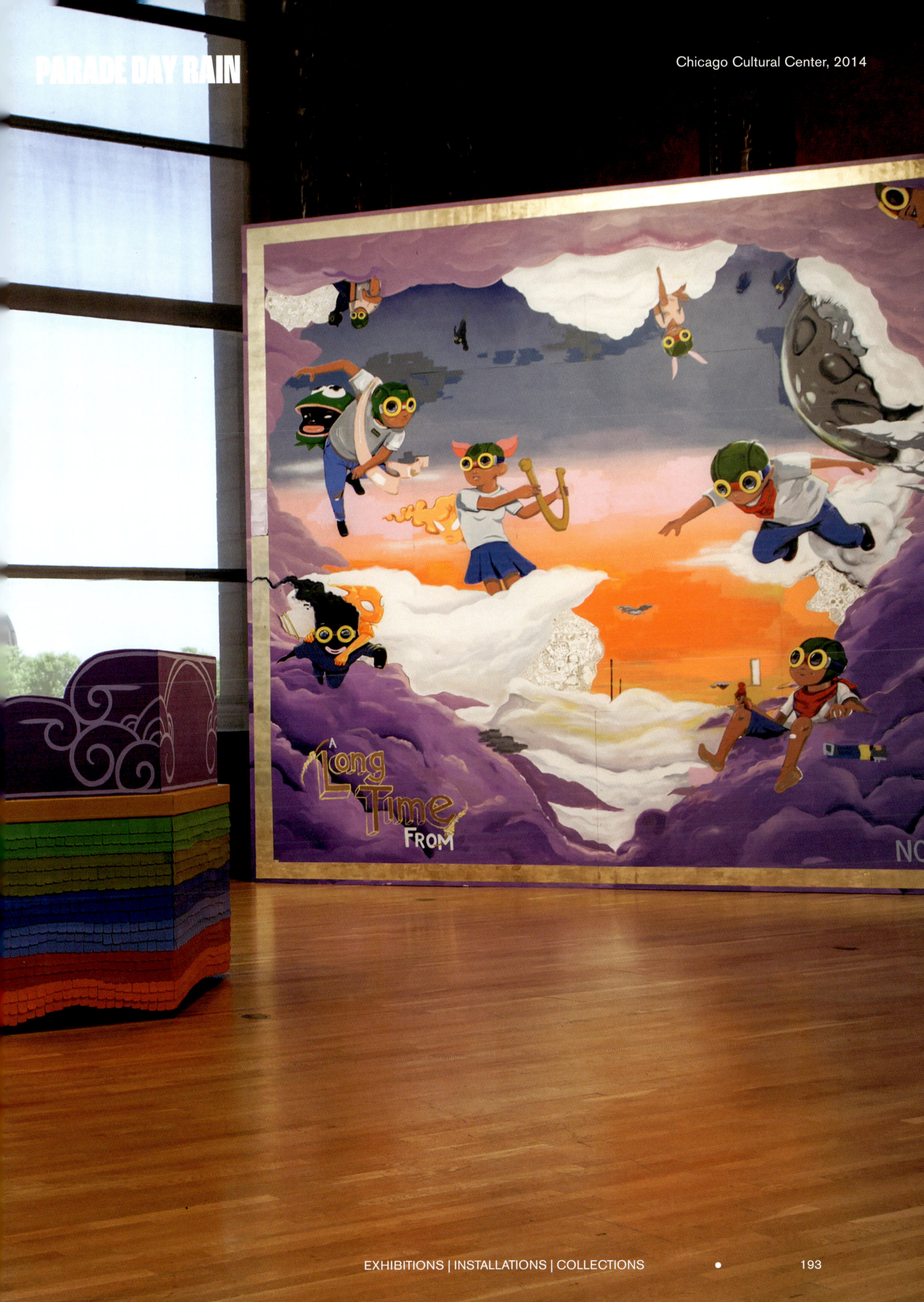
A
Long
Time
FROM

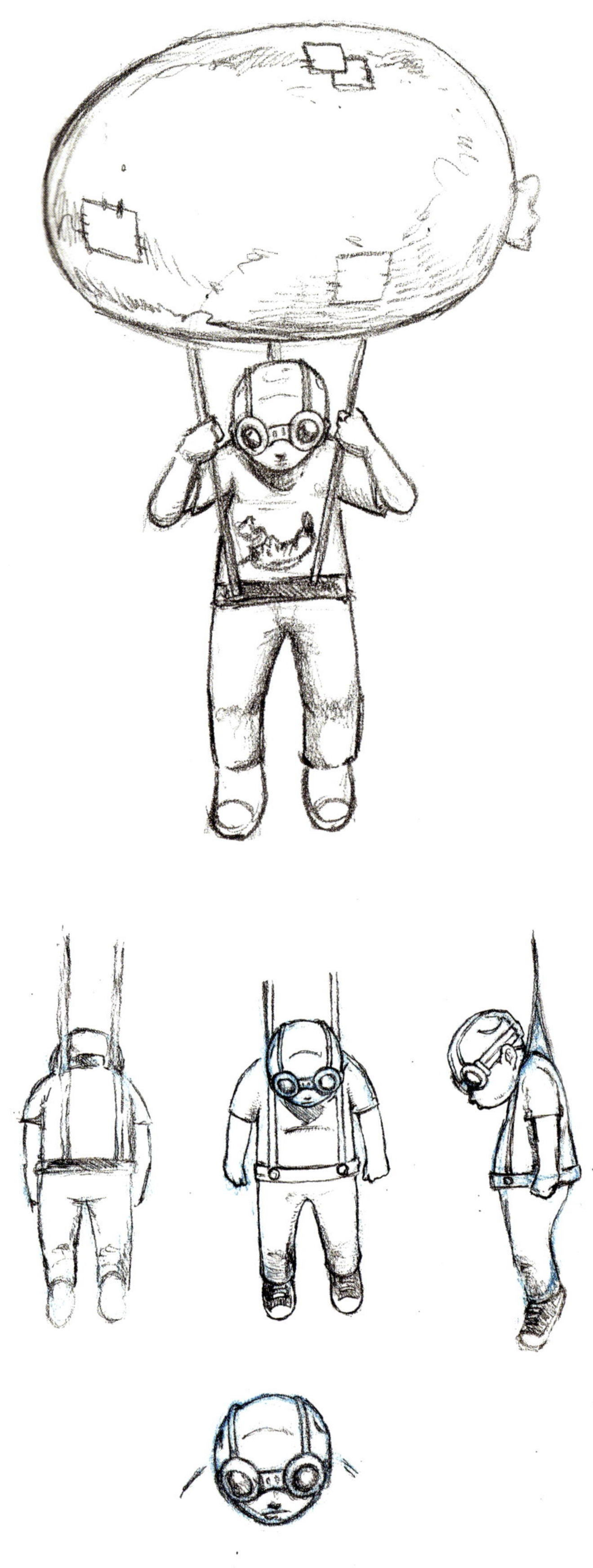

Impossible View
Acrylic, fiberglass,
and resin

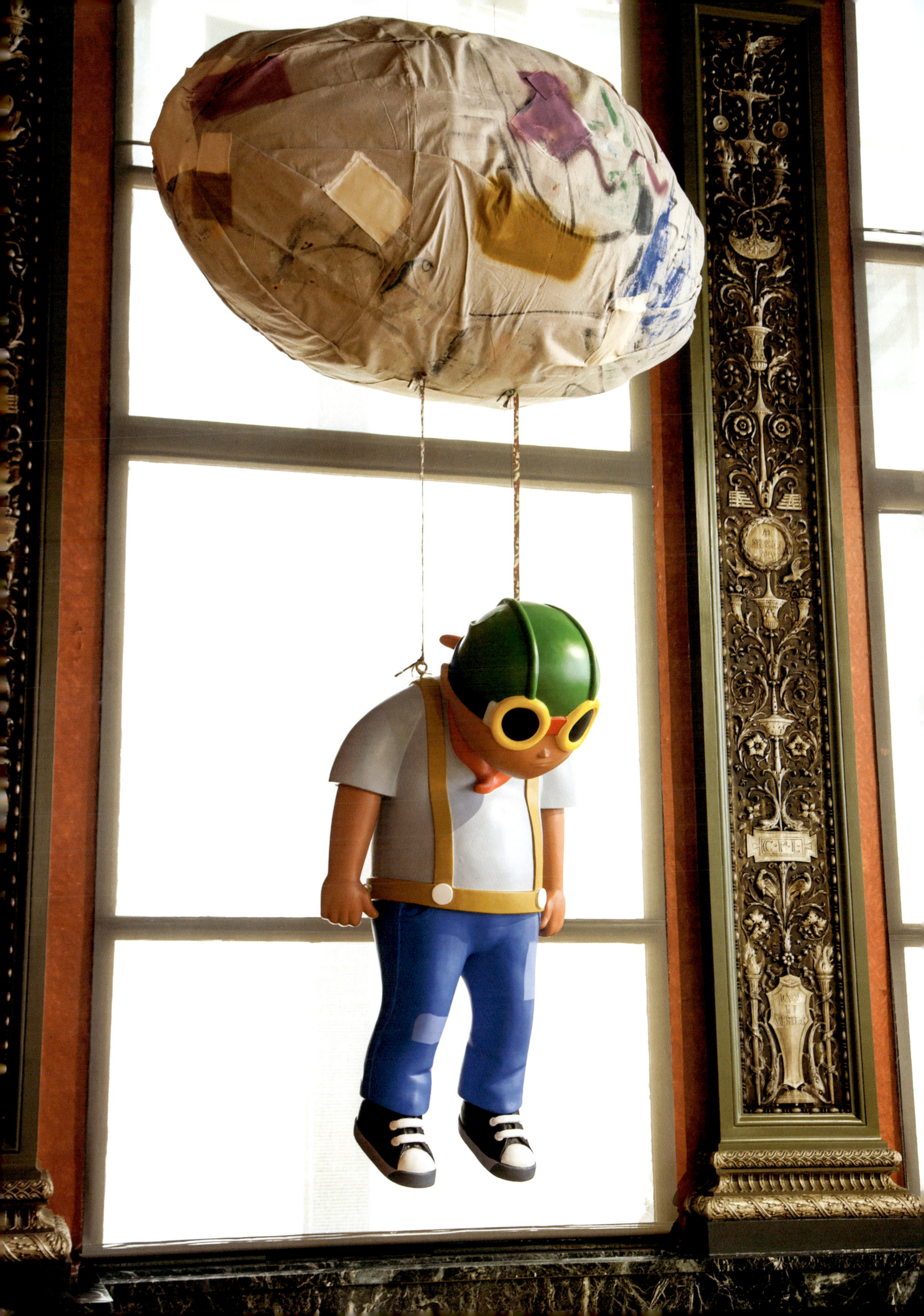

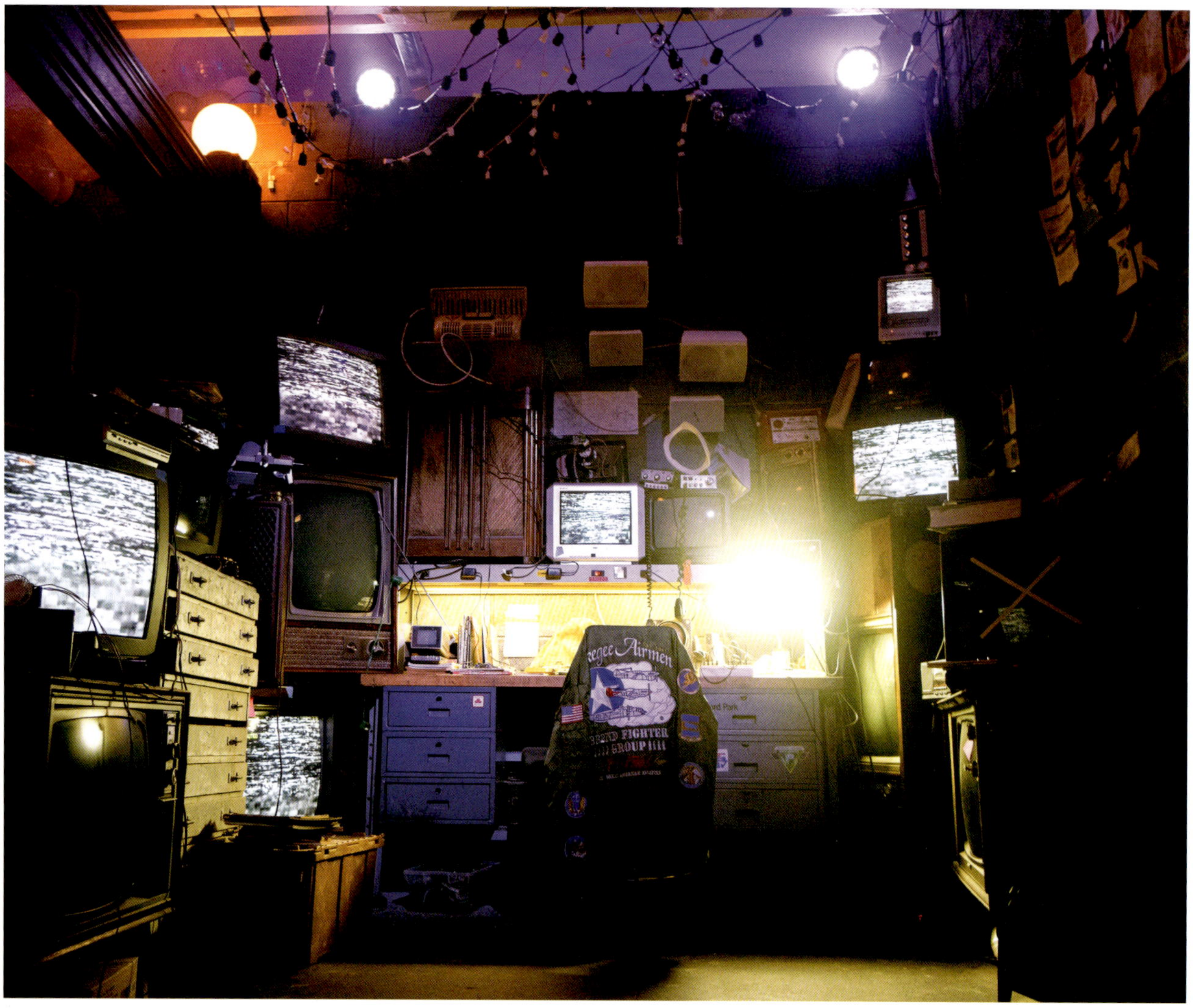

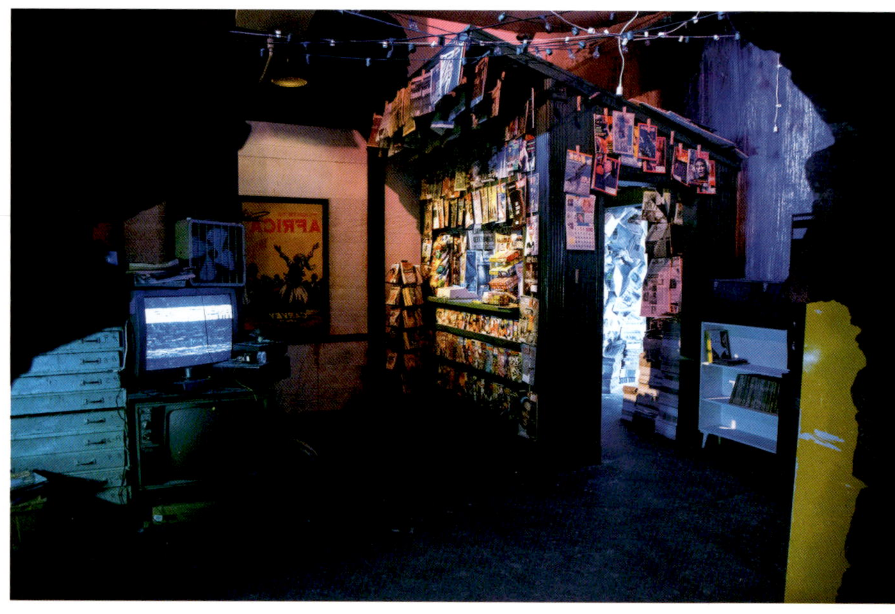

NEVERMORE PARK

Art installation
Chicago
2019

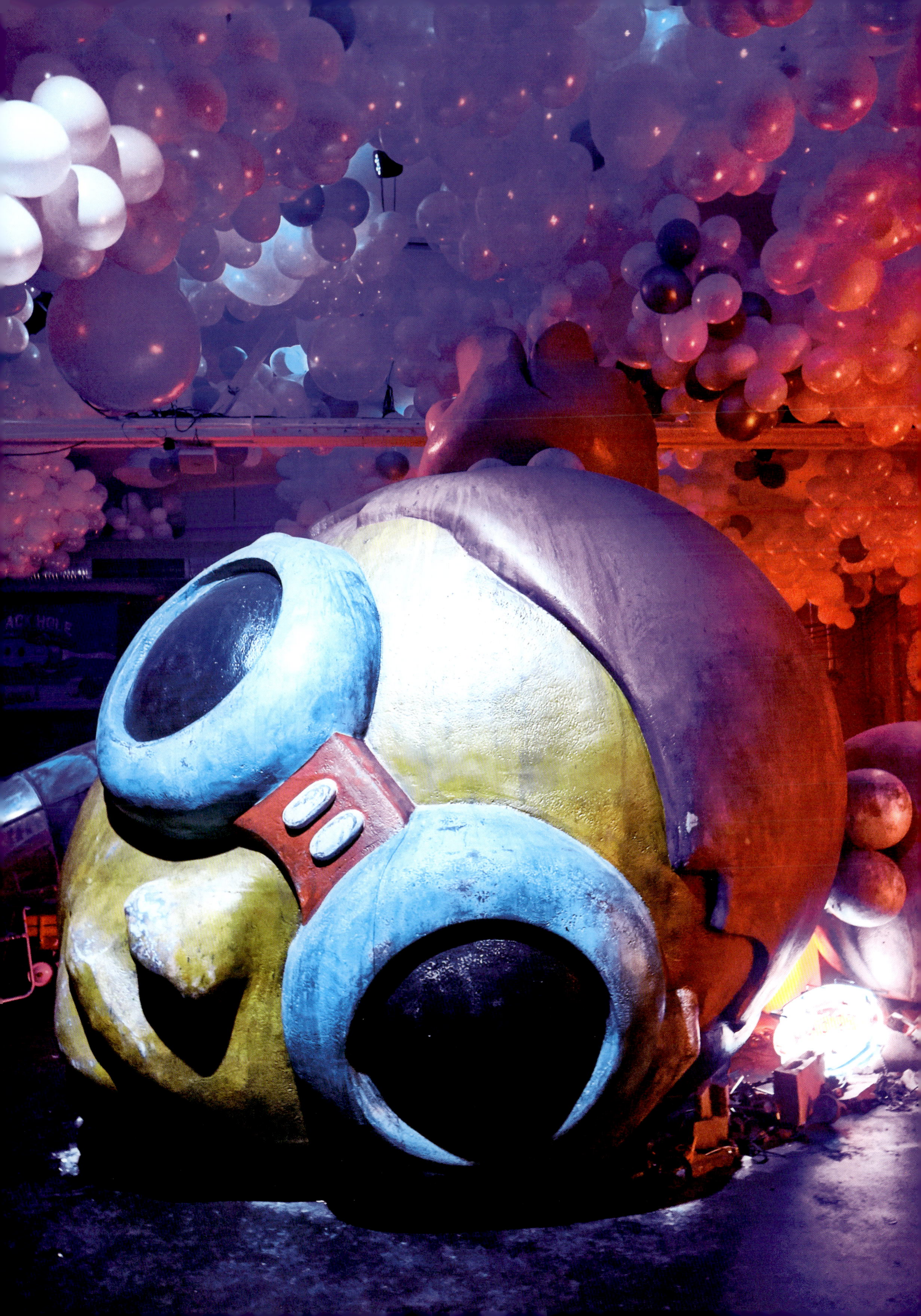

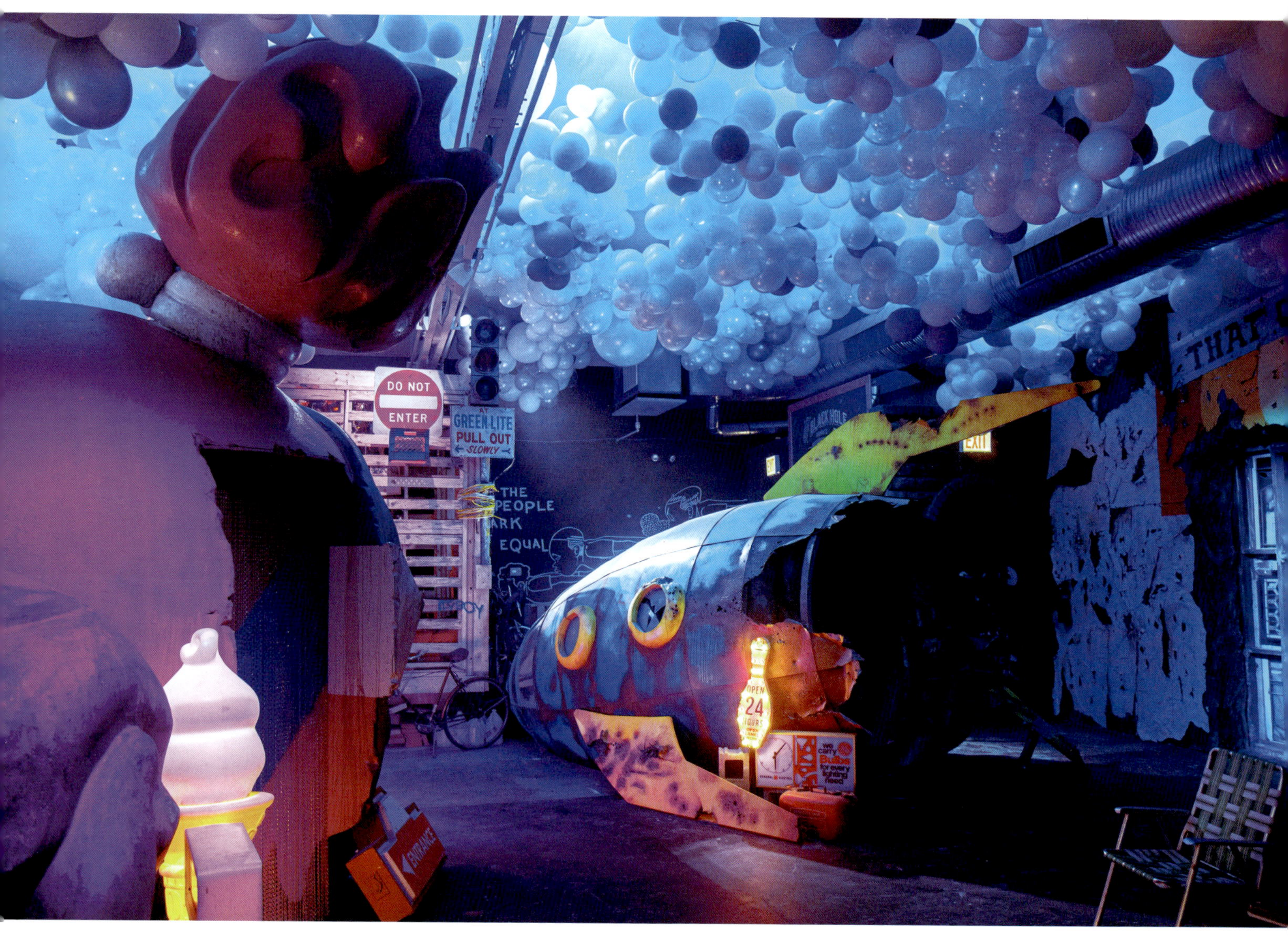

NEVERMORE PARK

Art installation, Chicago, 2019

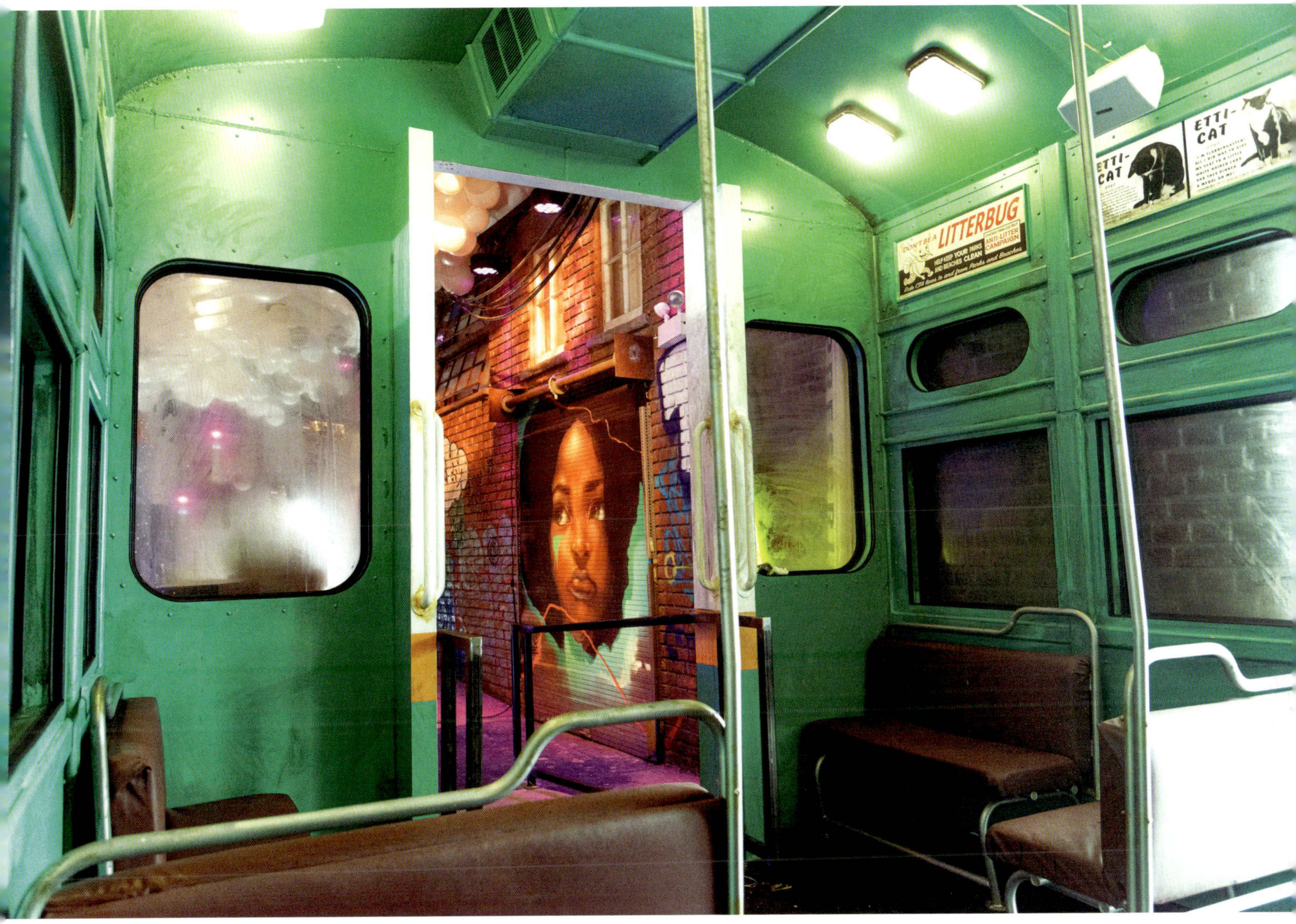

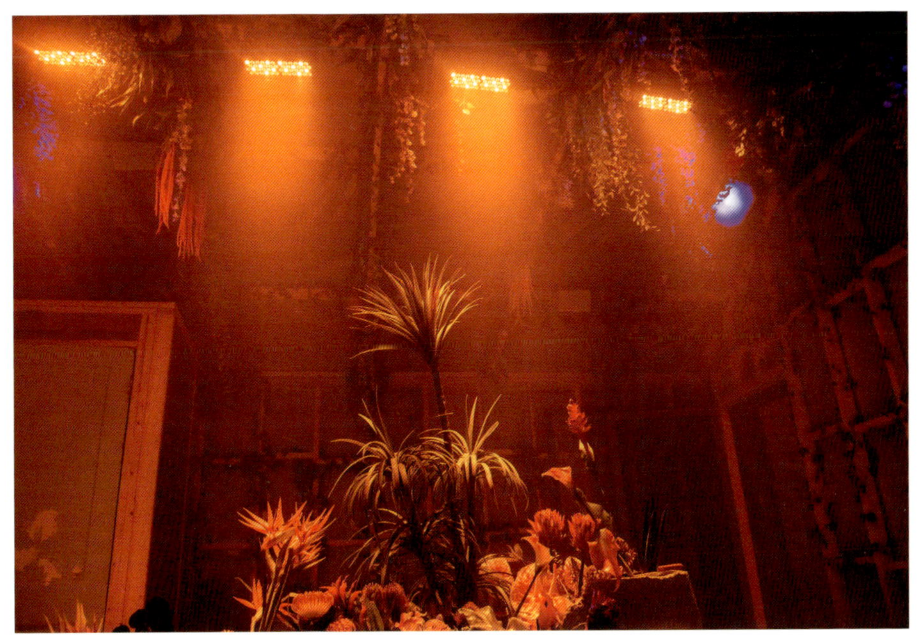

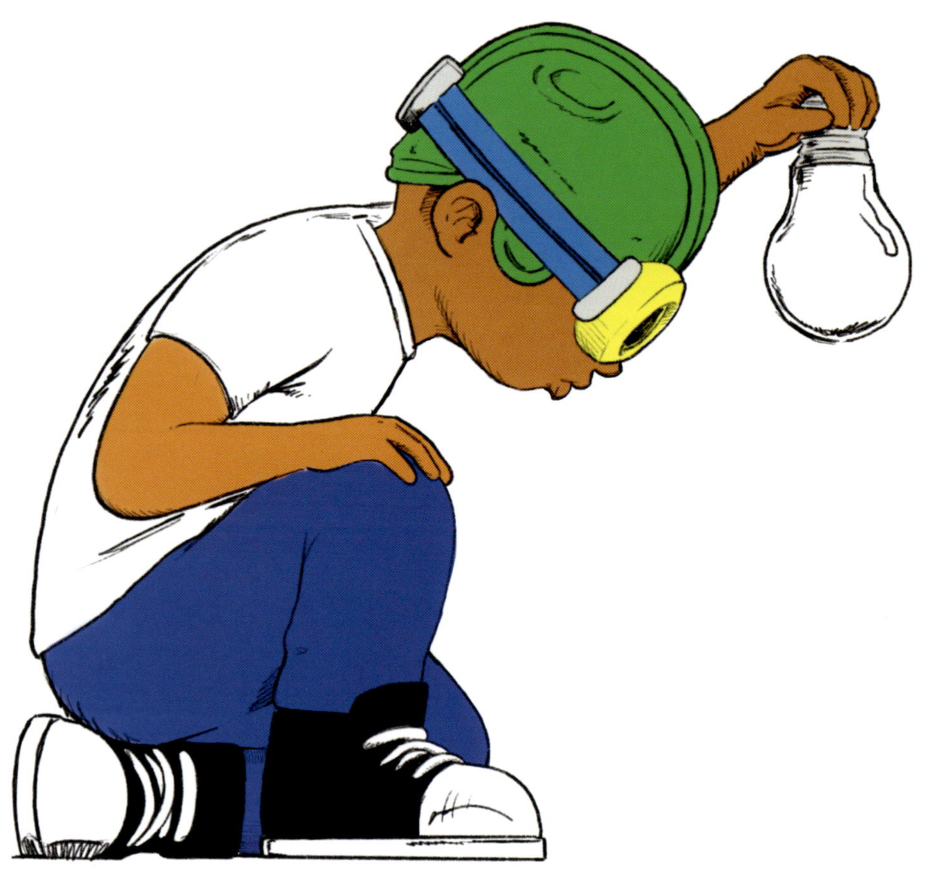

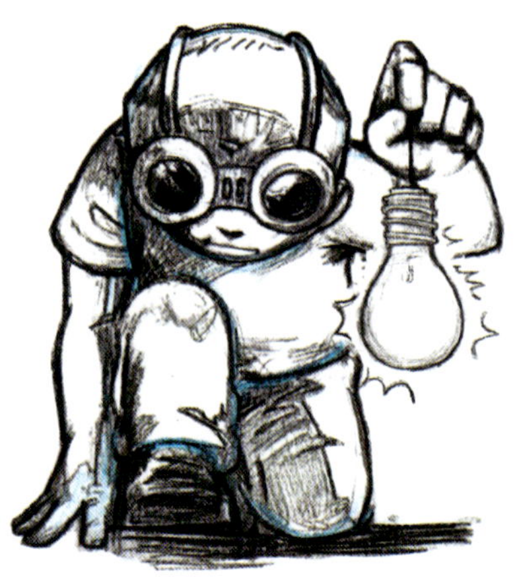

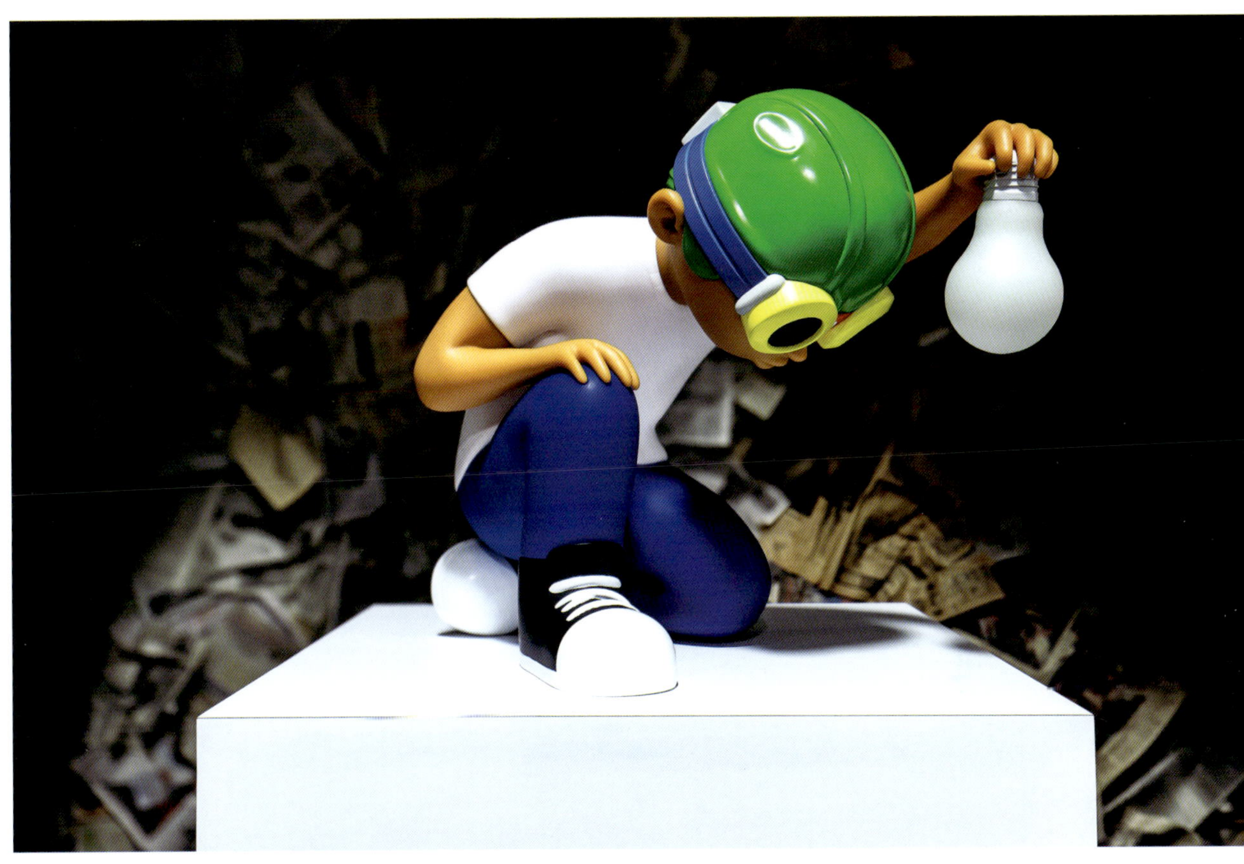

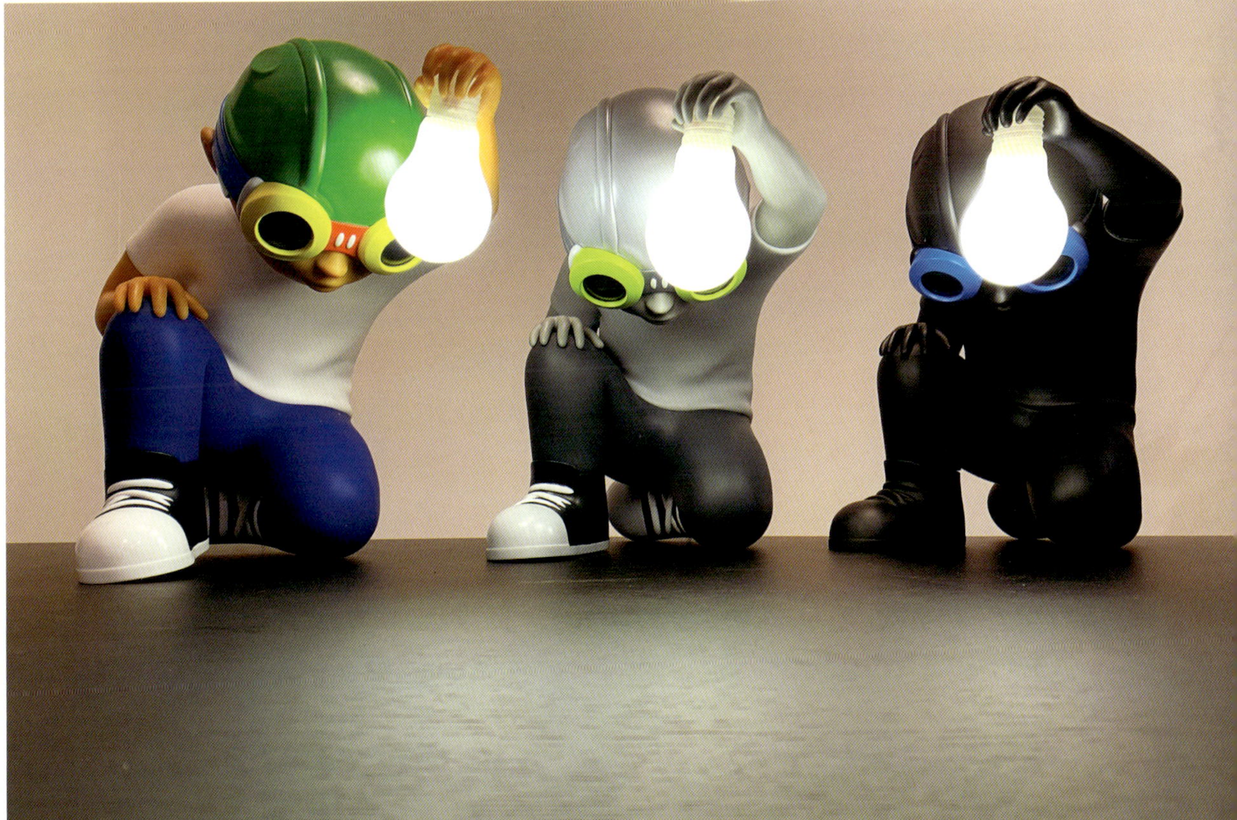

Ultra Lumen
Flyboy Lamp
2021

THE GRADUATE HOTEL

Roosevelt Island, New York, New York, 2020

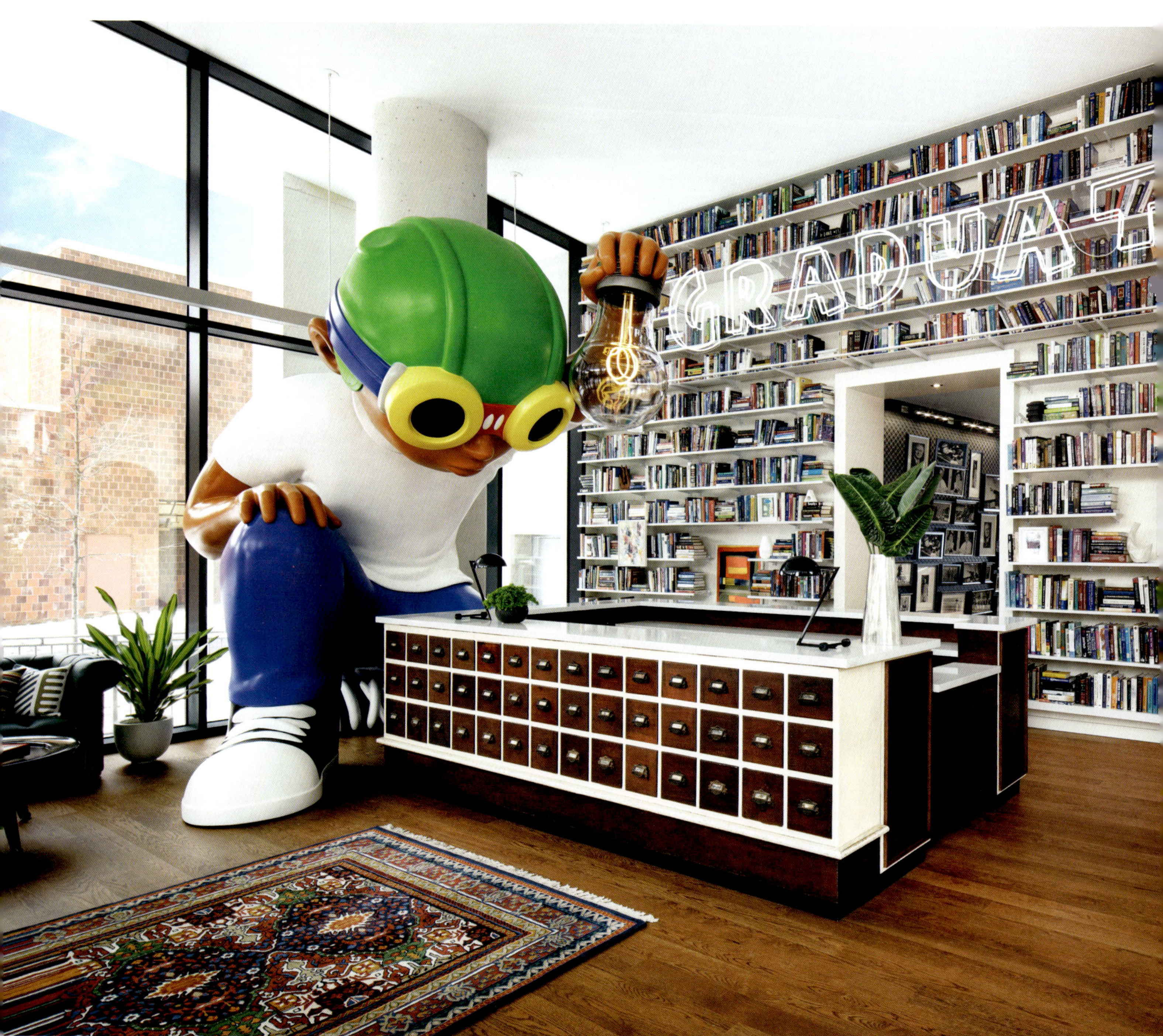

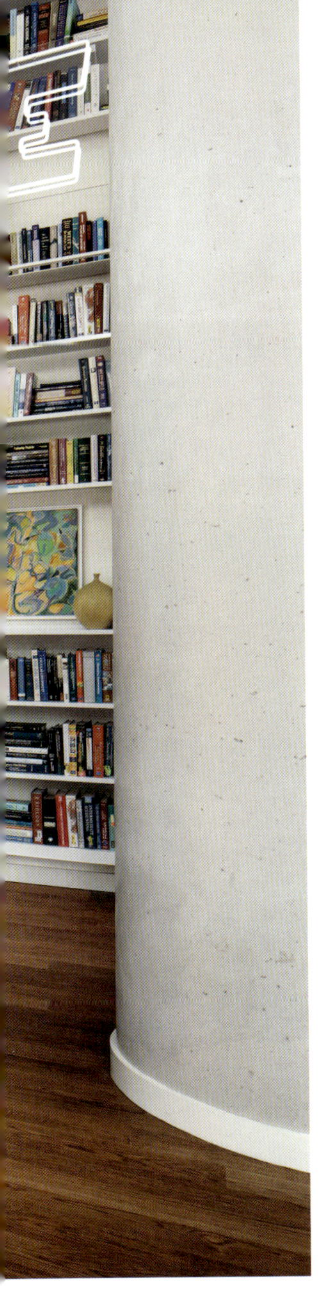

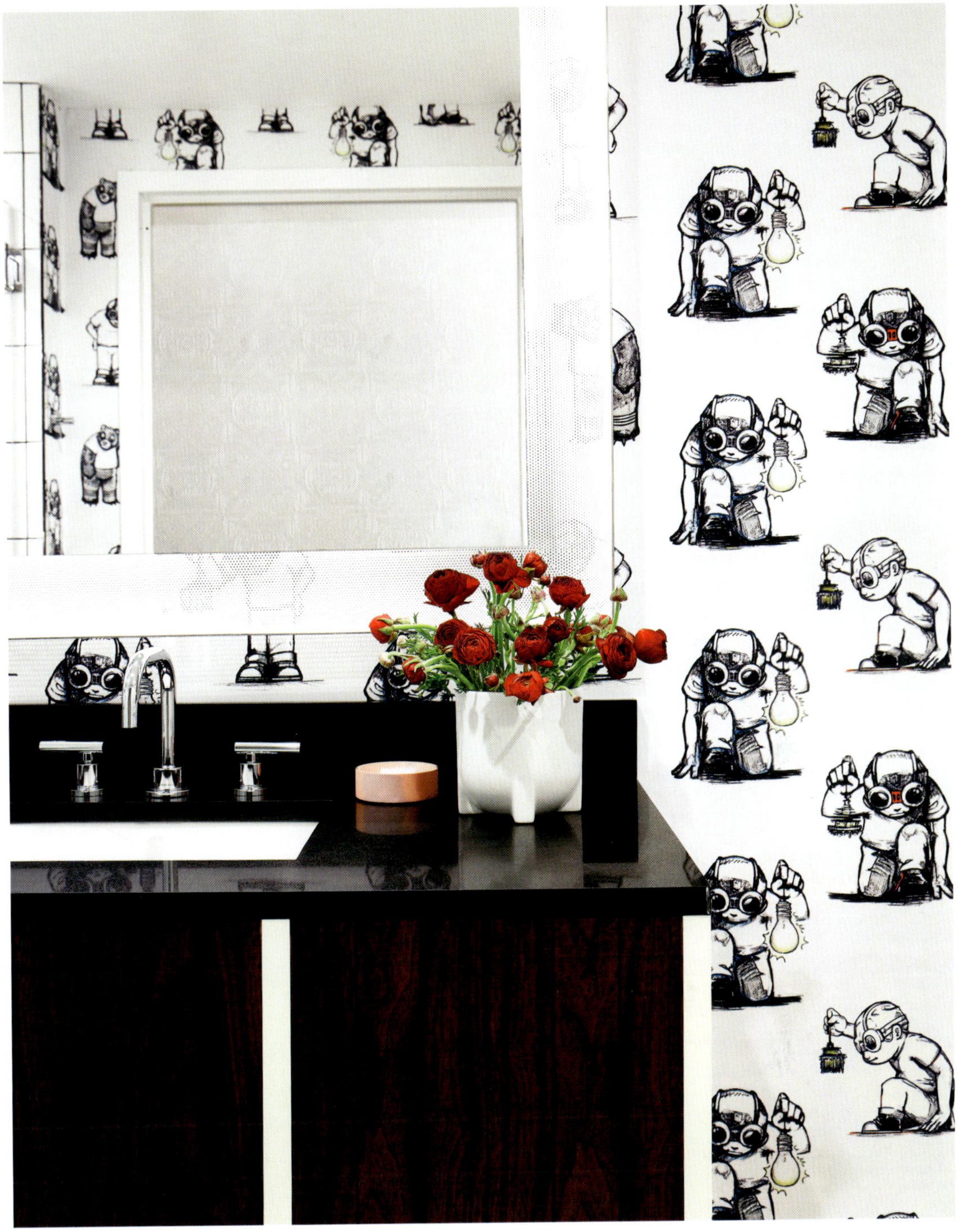

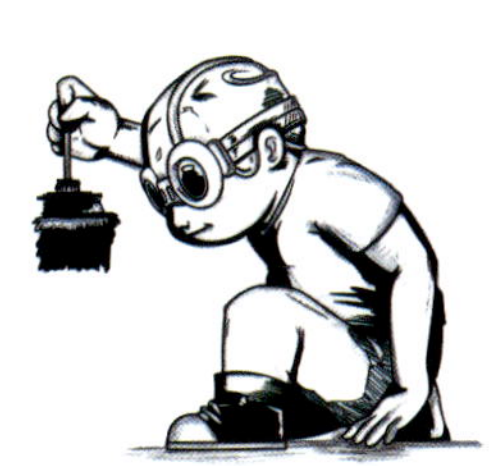

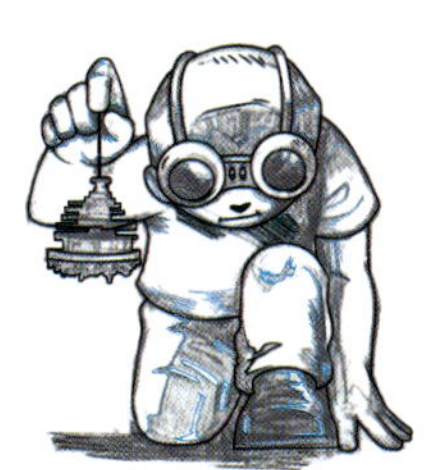

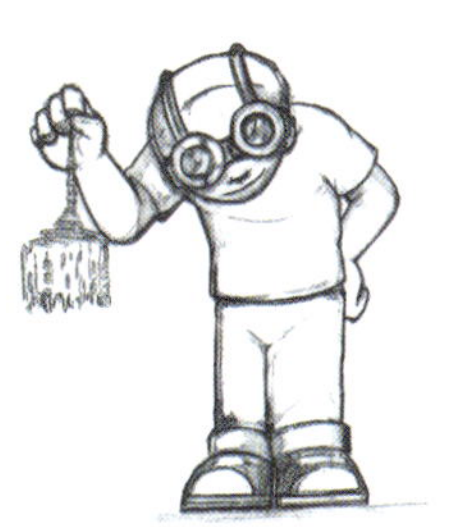

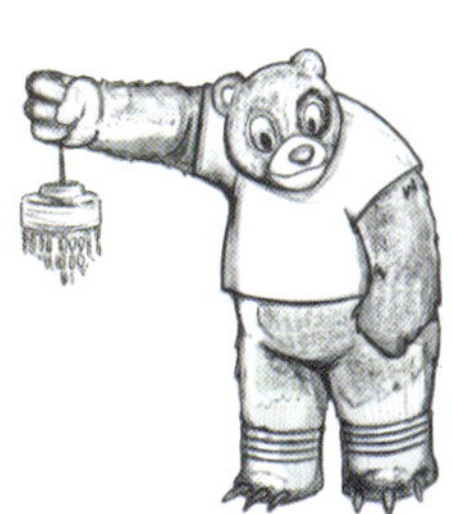

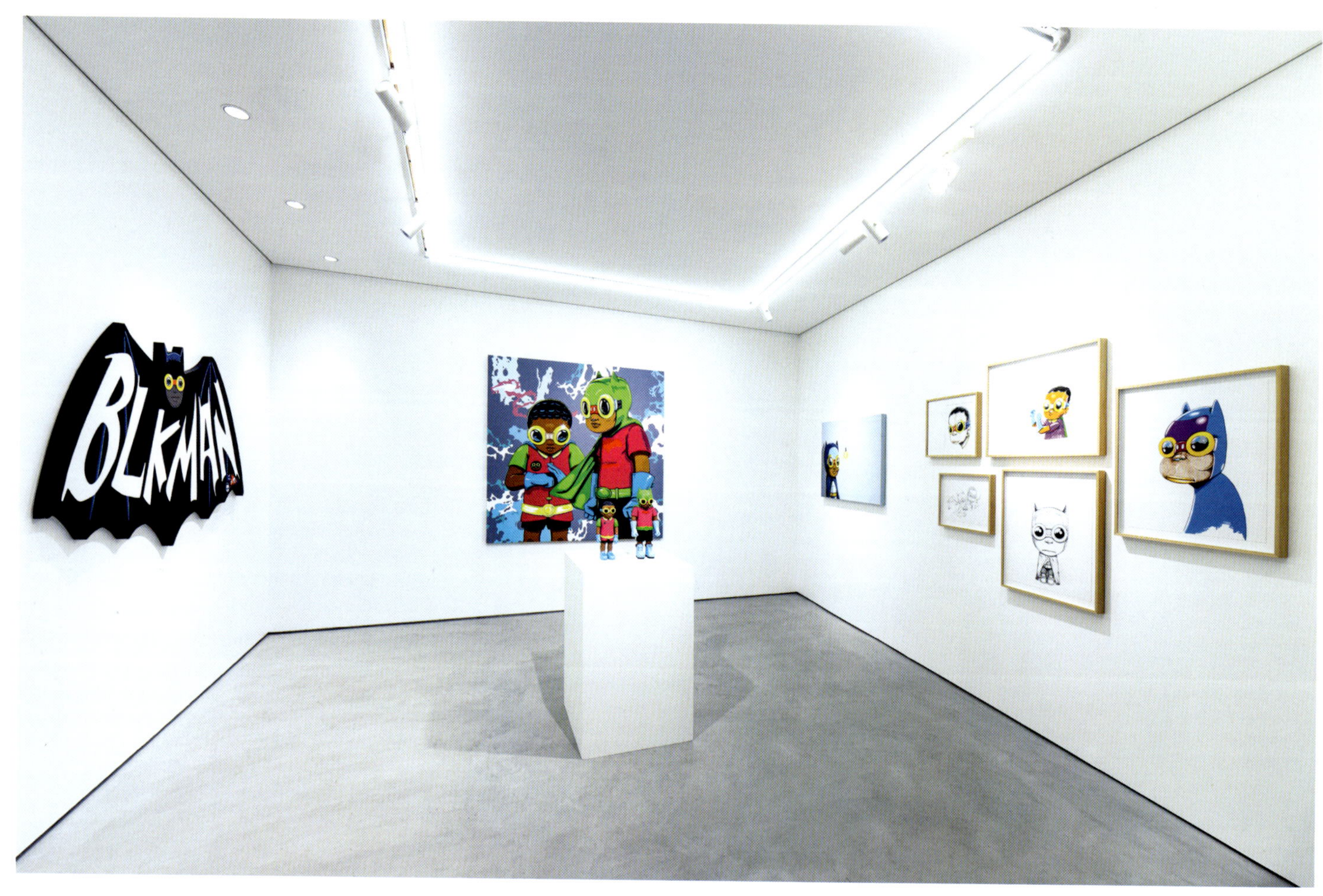

MYTHOS OPUS TWO

2G Nanzuka Gallery, Tokyo, 2021

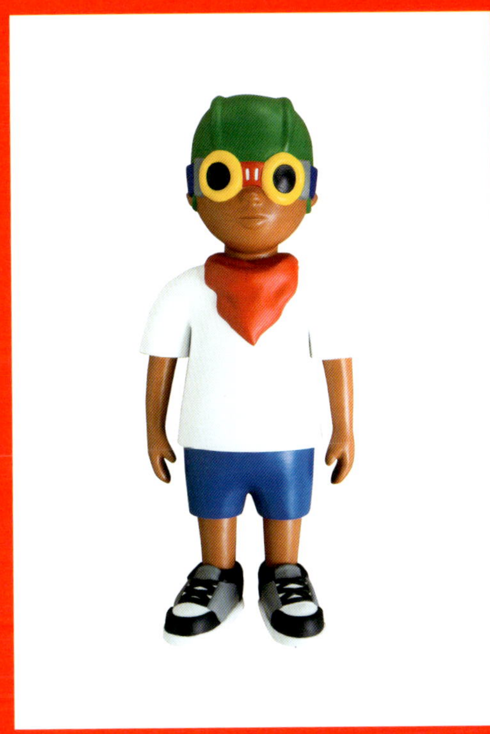

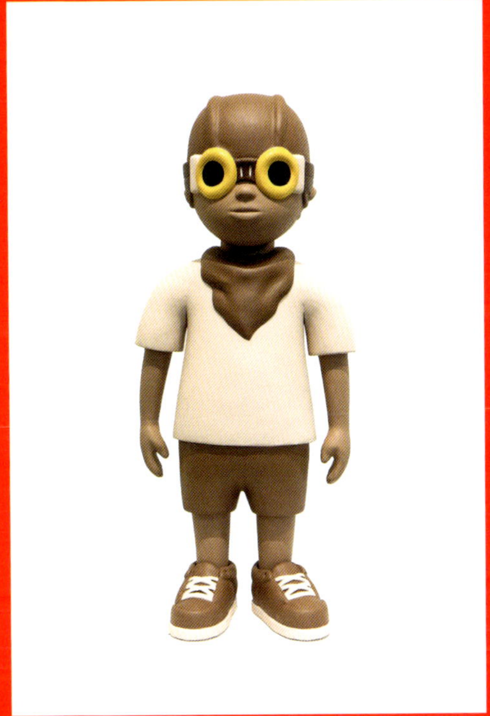

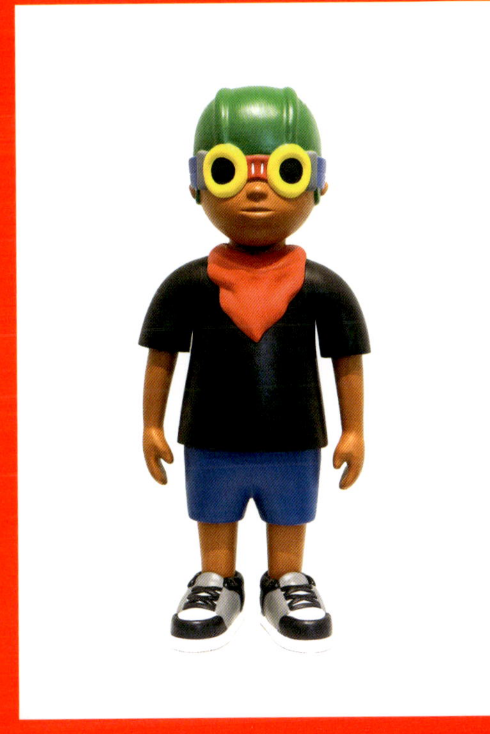

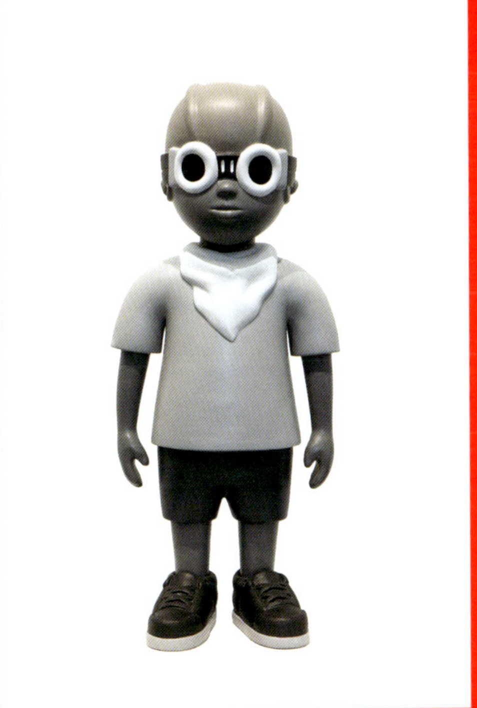

The Sophomores   Fiberglass, resin, and acrylic, 27 inches, 2018

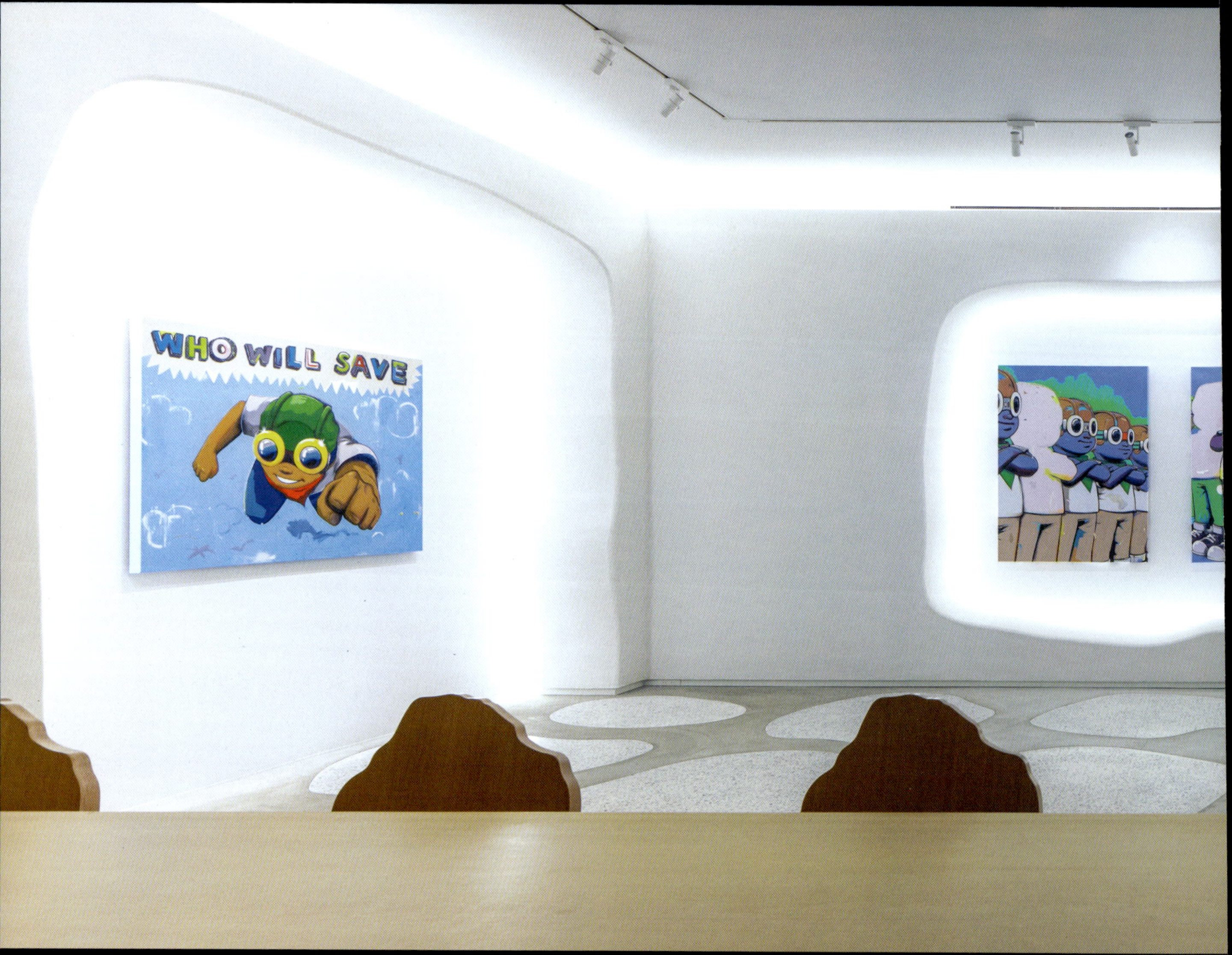

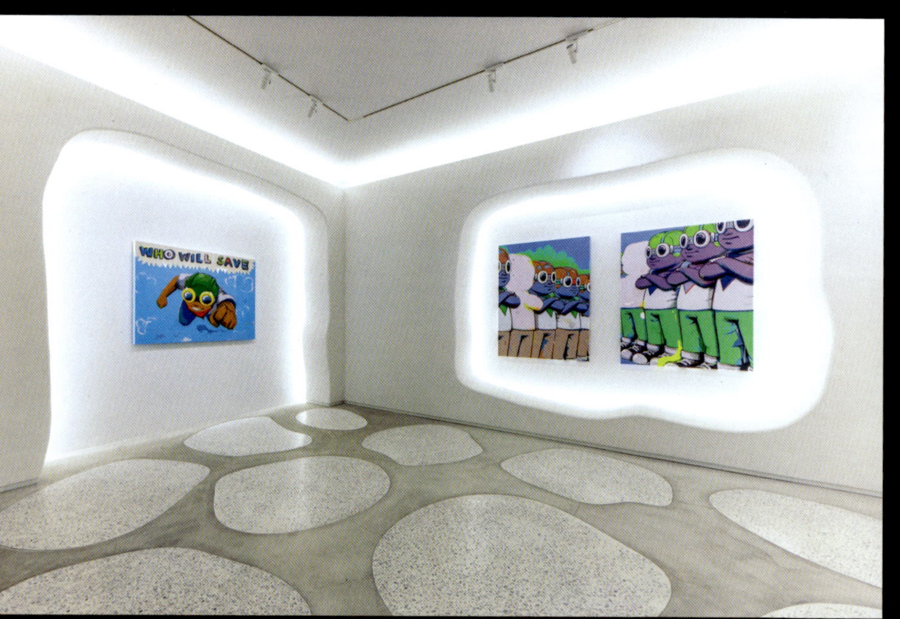

MYTHOS OPUS THREE

3110NZ by
LDH Kitchen
Tokyo
2021

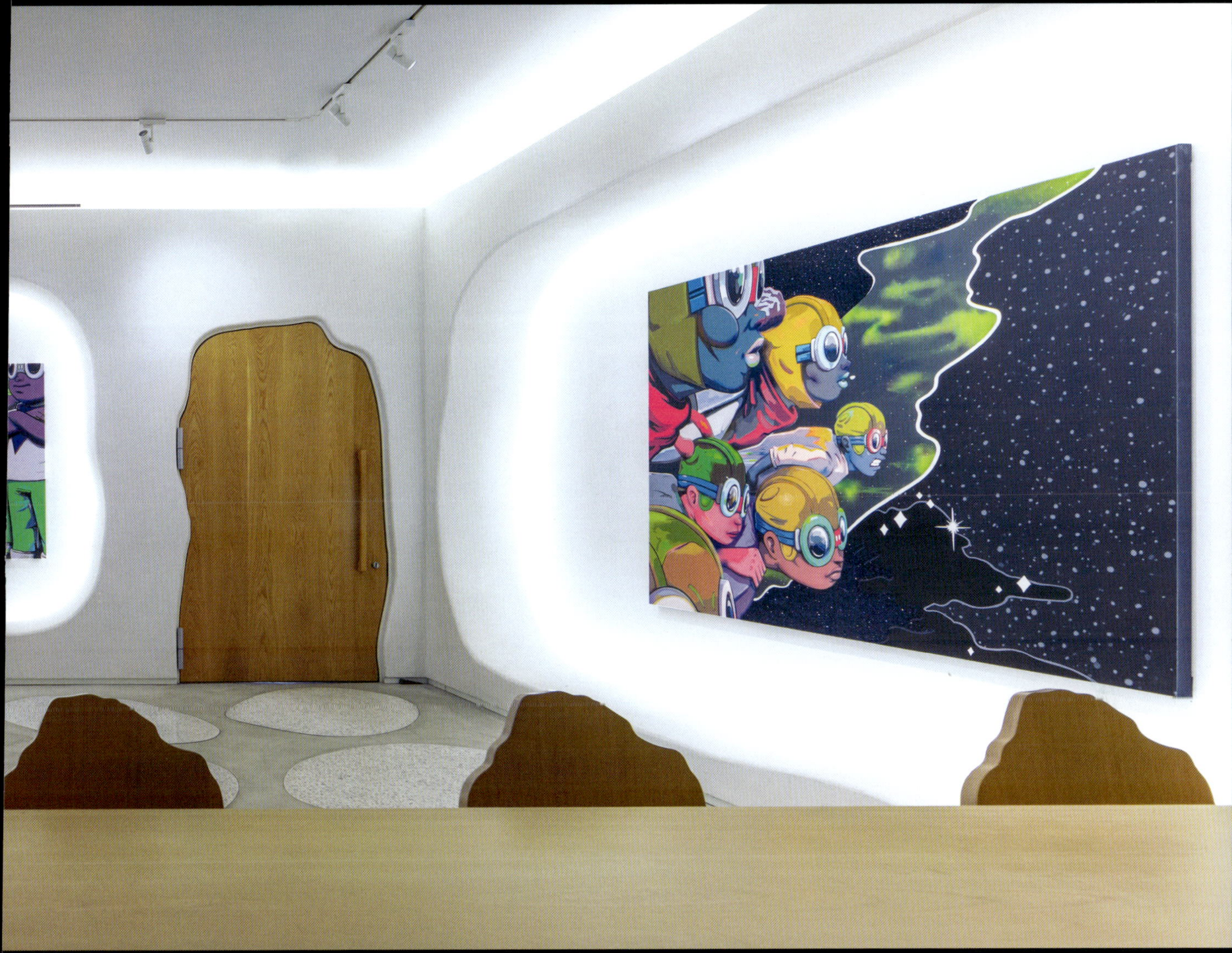

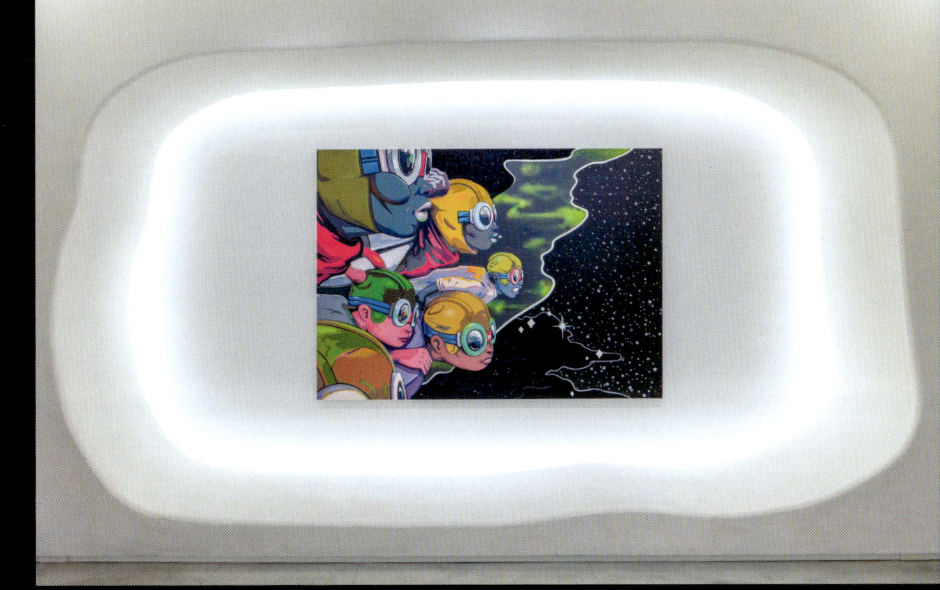

Megumi Ogita Gallery, Tokyo, 2021

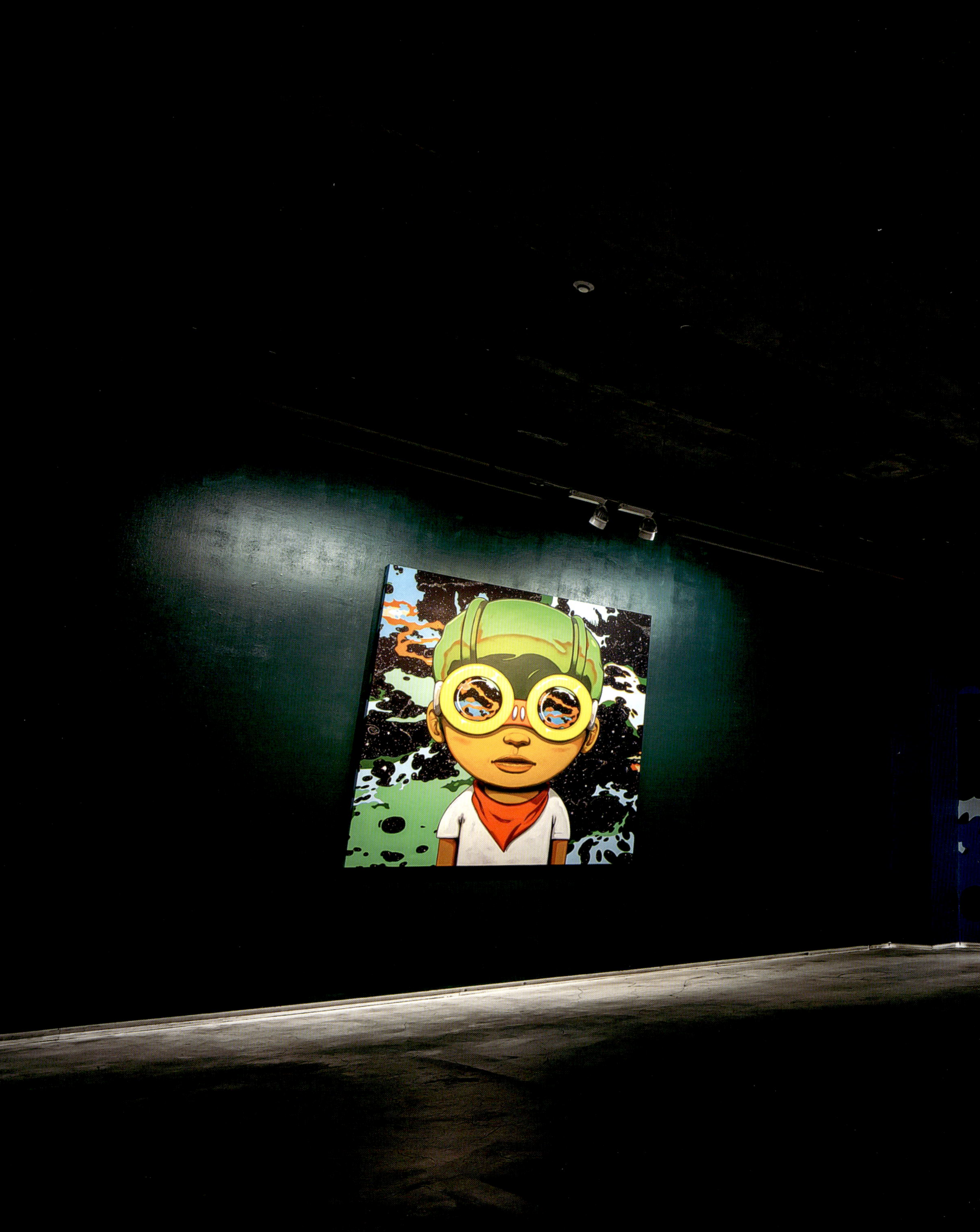

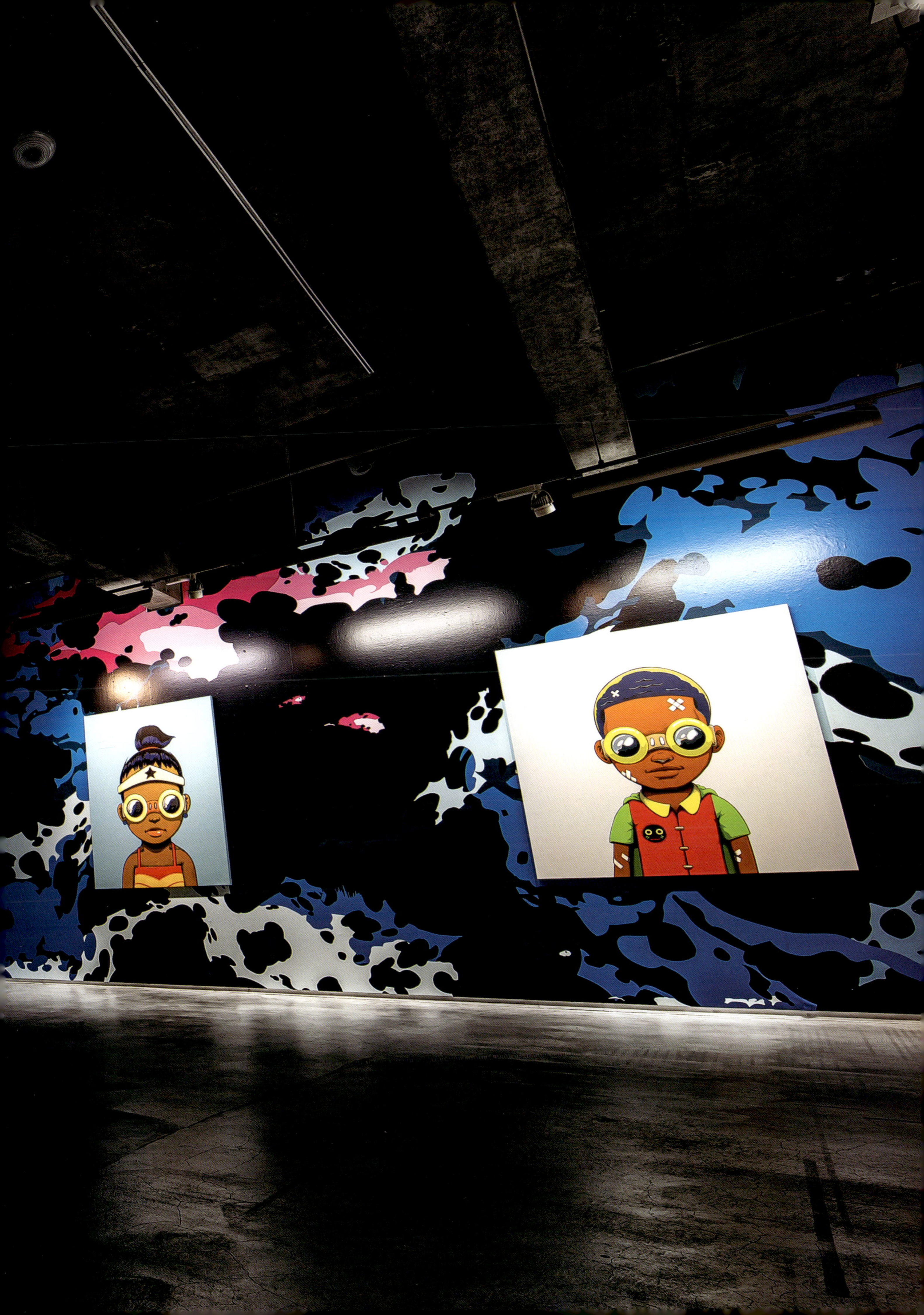

Untitled
Fiberglass, resin,
and acrylic
64 inches
2019

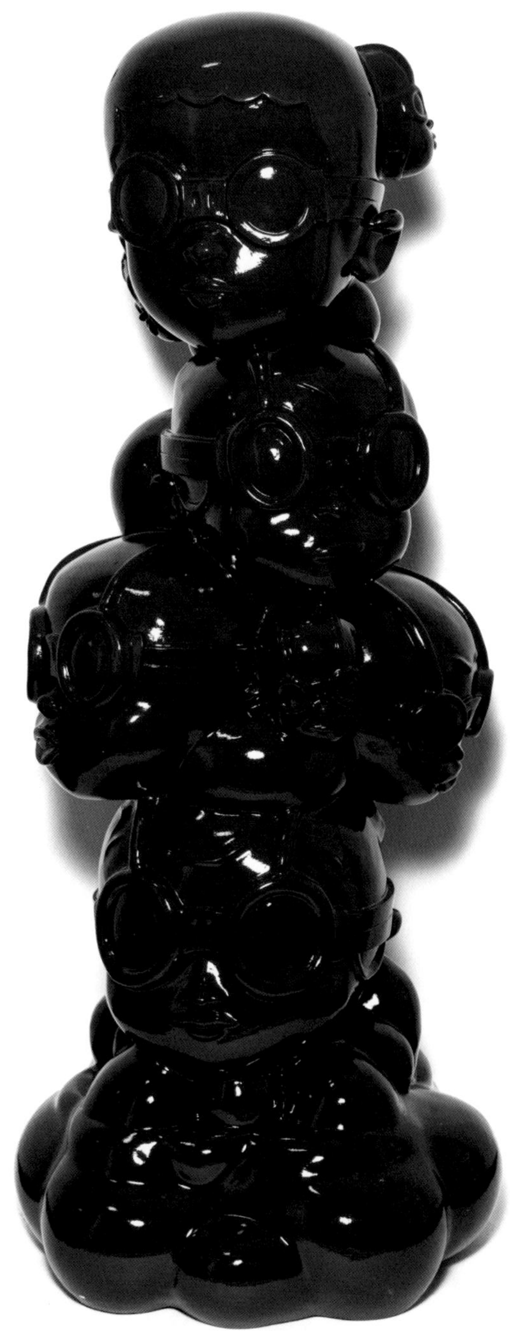

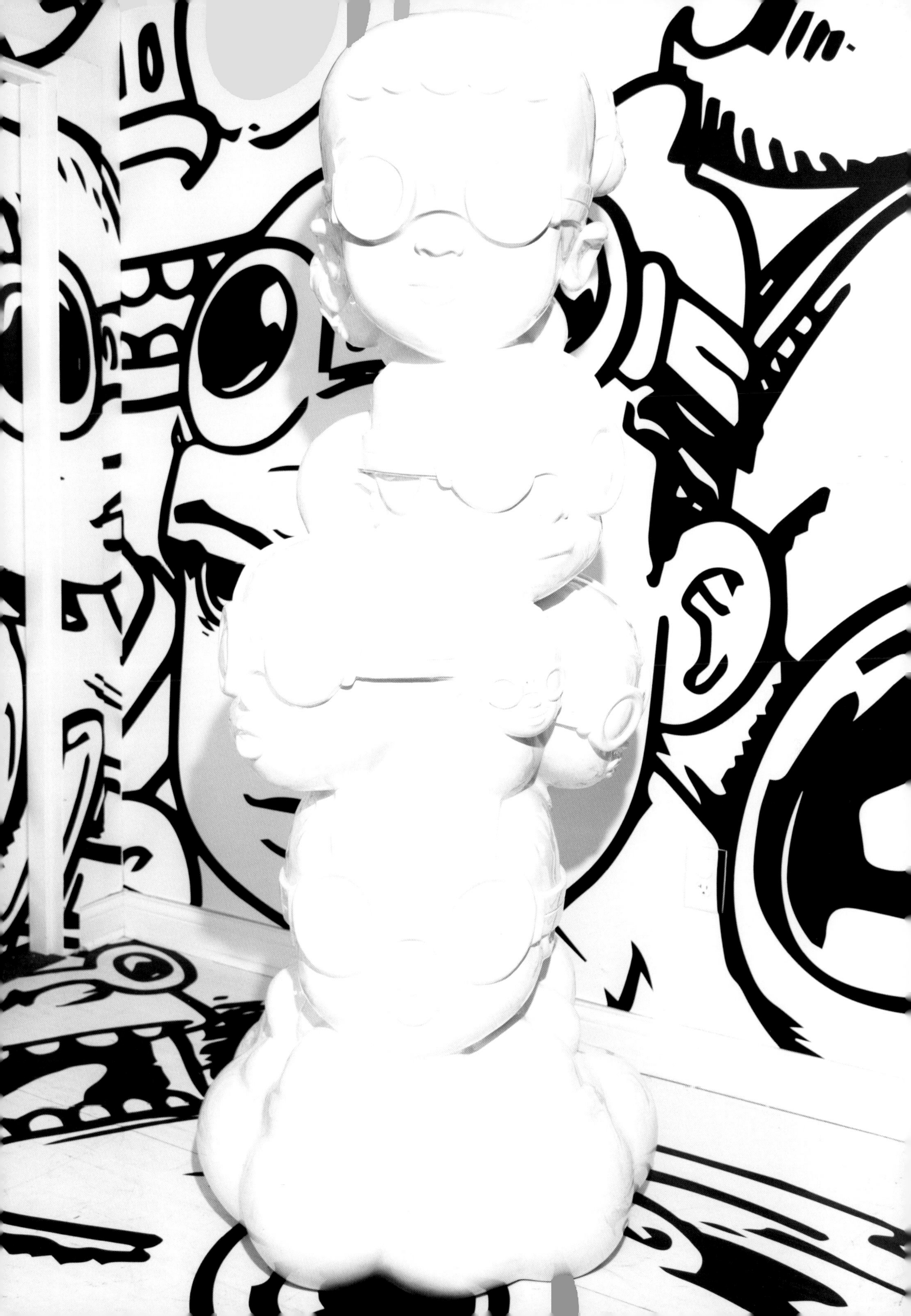

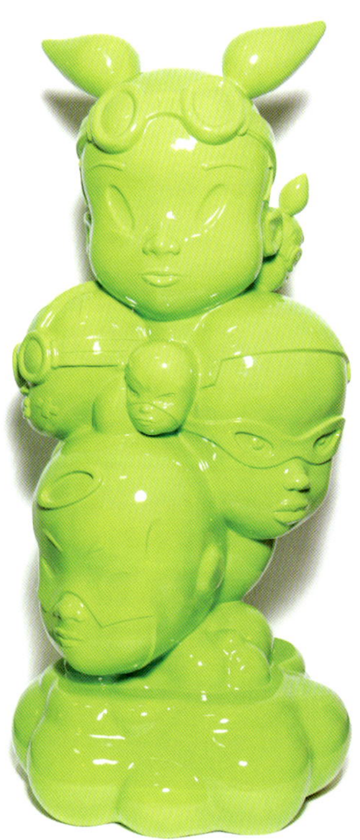

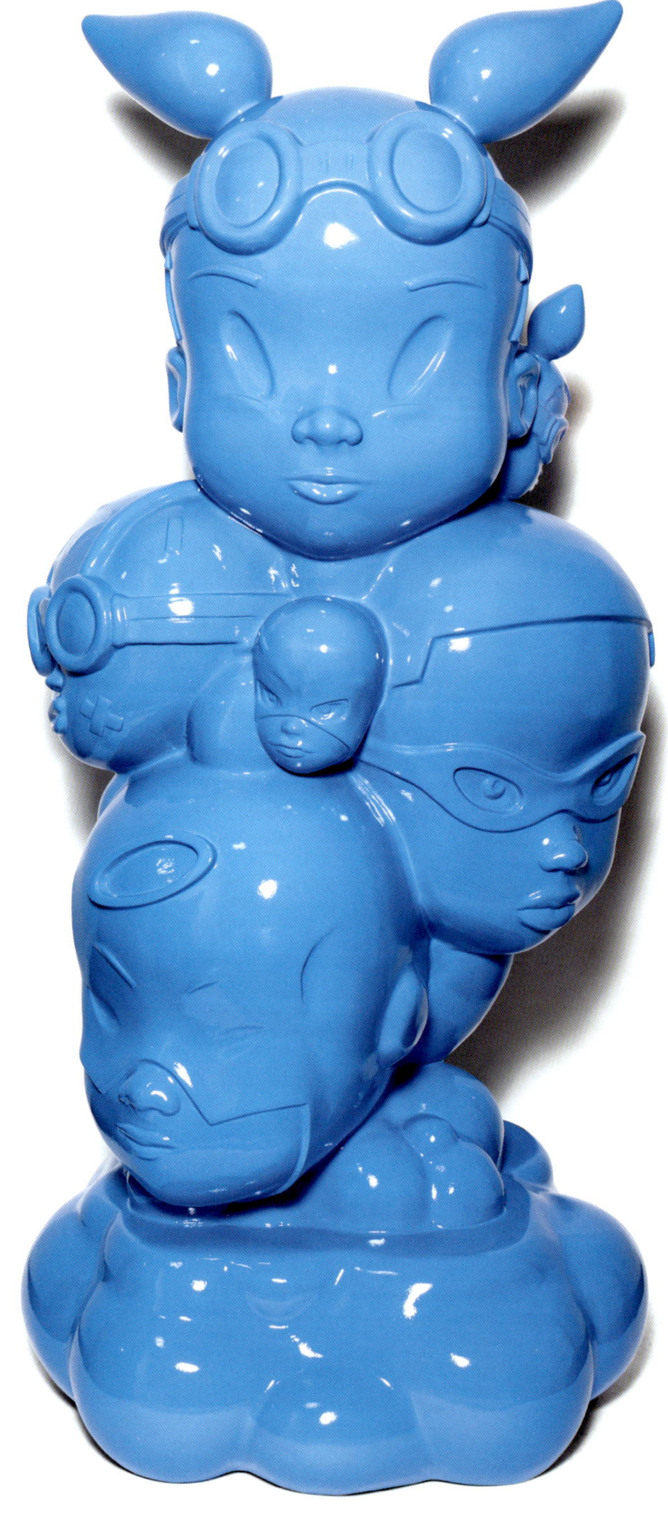

Untitled
Fiberglass, resin,
and acrylic
56 inches
2019

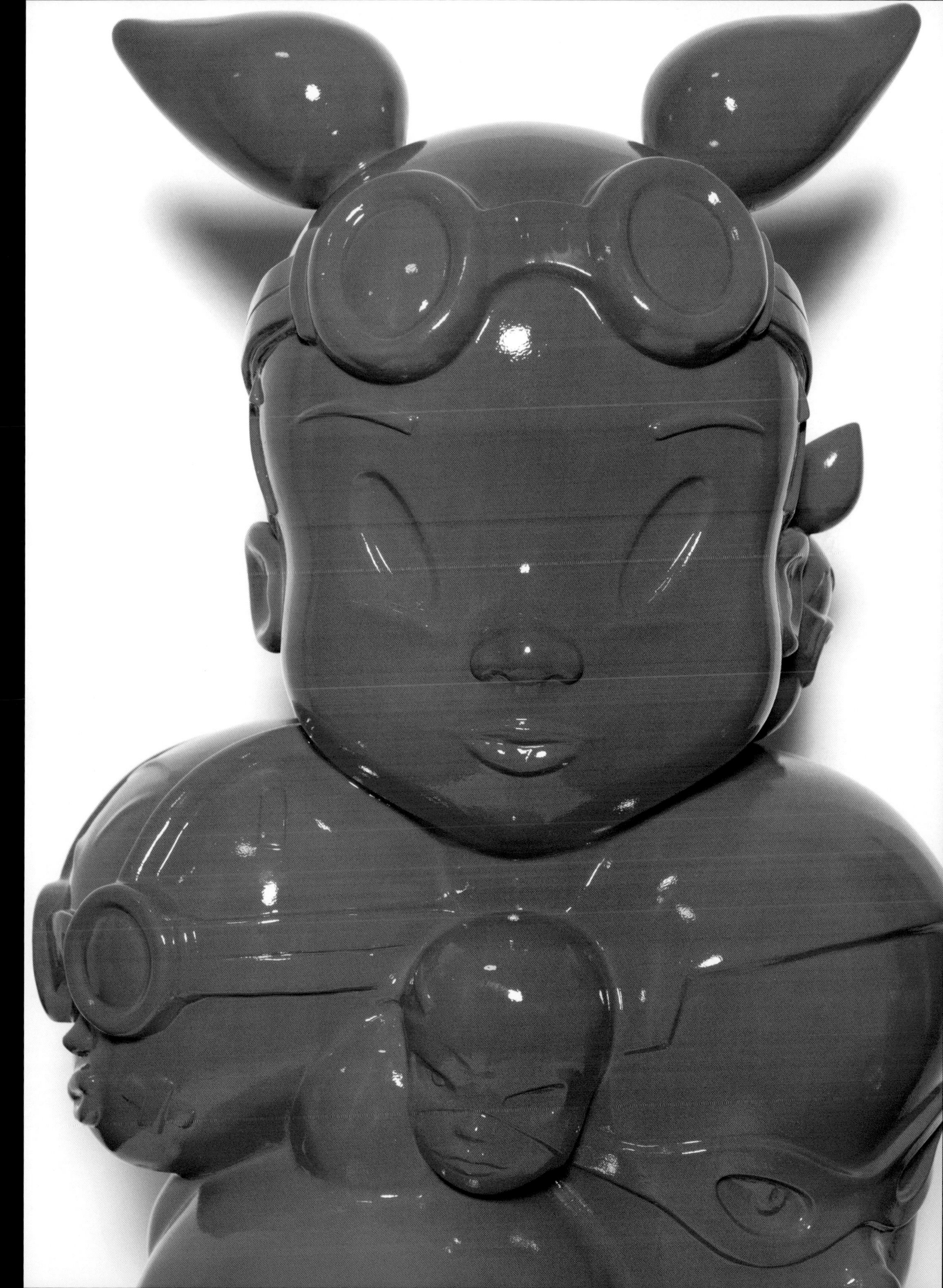

"AS AN ART HISTORIAN SPECIALIZING IN CONTEMPORARY ART, AND AS AN ART HISTORY PROFESSOR AND MUSEUM DIRECTOR FOR THIRTY-FIVE-PLUS YEARS, I'VE CHARTED AND GUIDED THE CAREERS OF QUITE A NUMBER OF EMERGING CONTEMPORARY ARTISTS. THAT SAID, WHEN MY RADAR PICKED UP ON HEBRU BRANTLEY'S WORK, THE ALERT ALARM BEEPED BEYOND ALL EXPECTATIONS. HEBRU INHALED EVERYTHING THAT ANDY WARHOL AND ROY LICHTENSTEIN BREATHED OUT AND TRANSFORMED IT INTO A WHOLE NEW FORM OF EXPRESSION THAT, FRANKLY, GAVE NEW LIFE TO EVERYTHING THE POP ART MOVEMENT WAS TRYING TO ACCOMPLISH. MORE THAN THAT, HEBRU IS A NEW GENRE UNTO HIMSELF. HIS SUBJECTS AND THEIR NARRATIVES SPEAK TO EACH OF US IN A MORE PERSONAL WAY THAN ANY OF THE POP ARTISTS EVER COULD HAVE IMAGINED. HEBRU BRANTLEY IS BOTH A CONTEMPORARY PIONEER AND A POWERHOUSE WHO IS PLAYING A LEADERSHIP ROLE IN CHALLENGING CONTEMPORARY ART TO STEP UP ITS GAME AND ONCE AGAIN PLAY A ROLE IN ADVANCING AMERICAN CULTURE."

—CHARLES SHEPARD, FORT WAYNE MUSEUM OF ART CEO

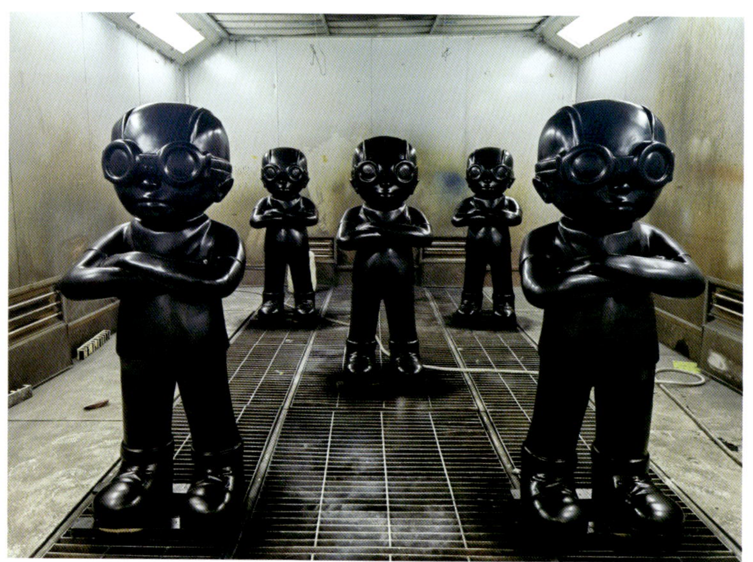

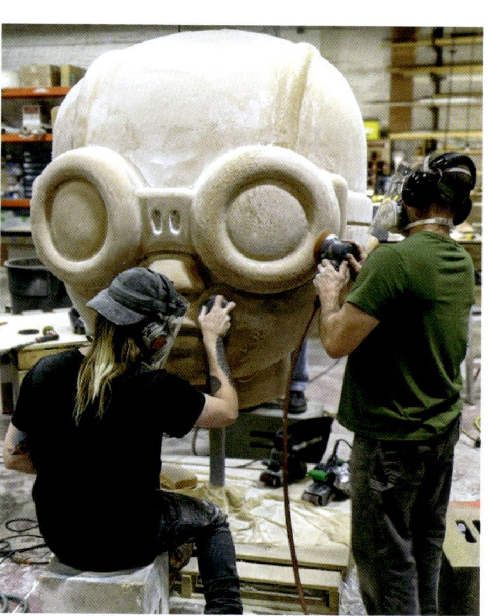

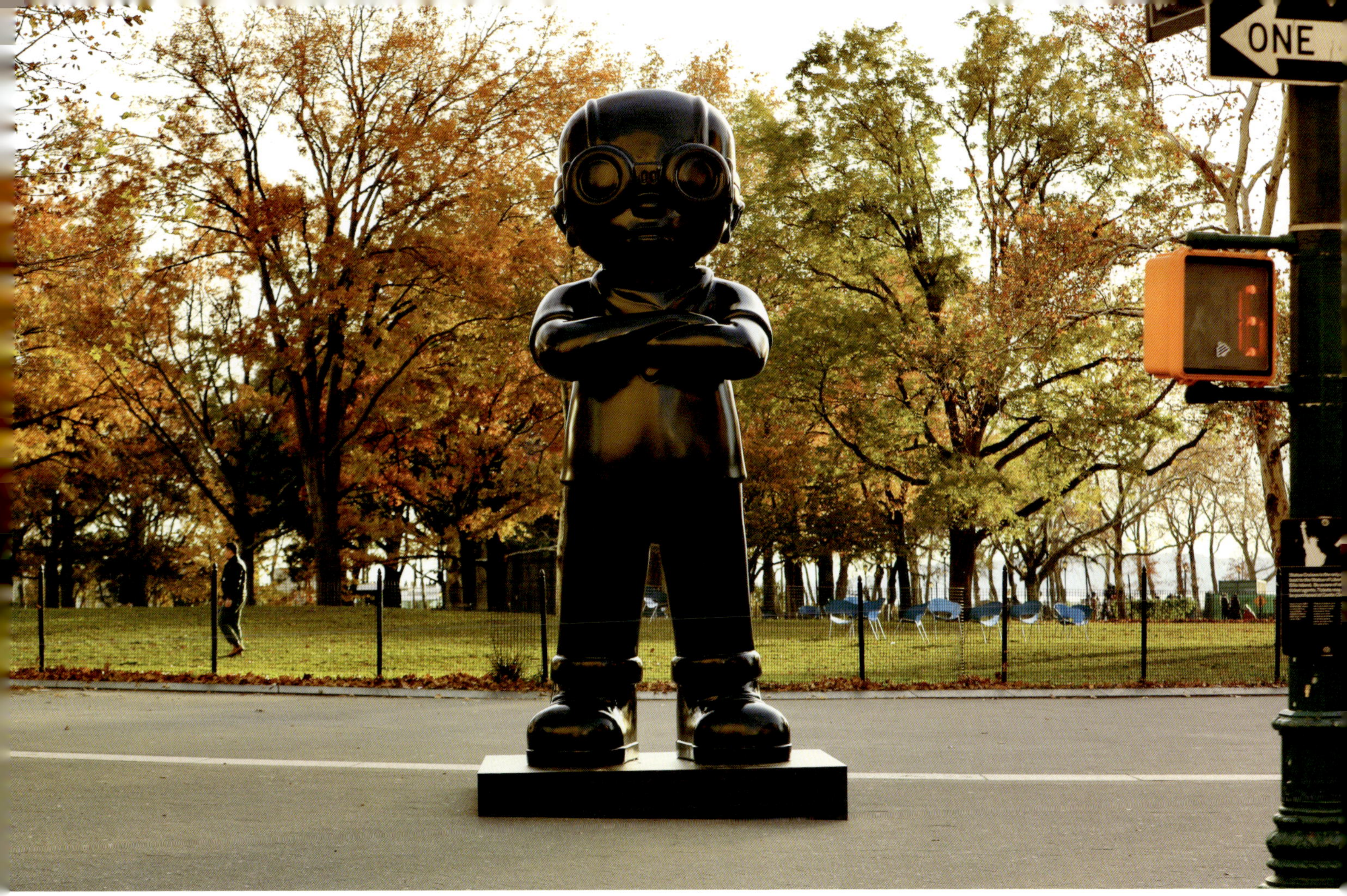

The Great Debate
The Battery
New York, New York
16 Feet
2021

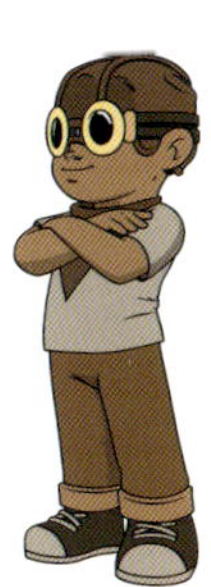

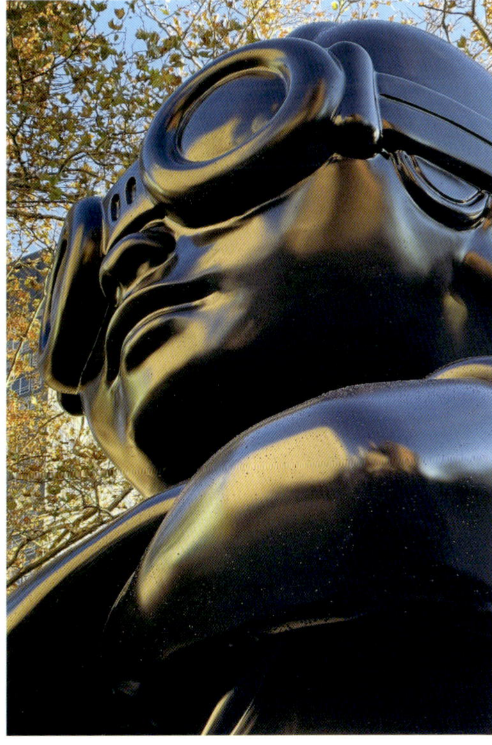

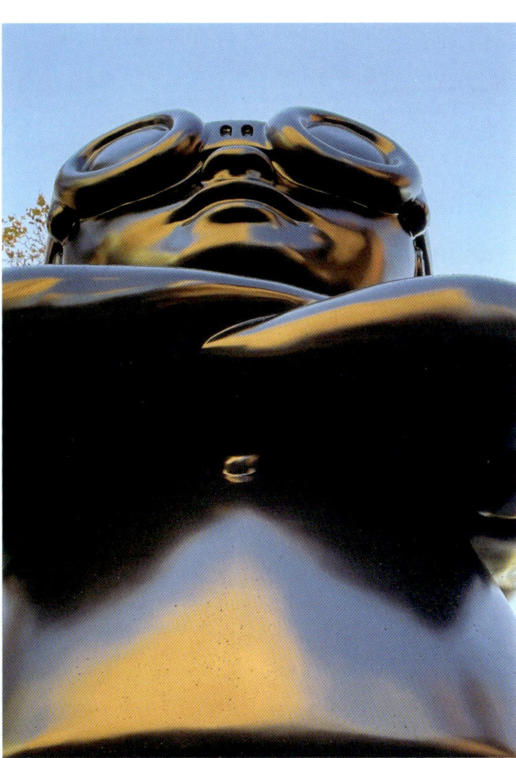

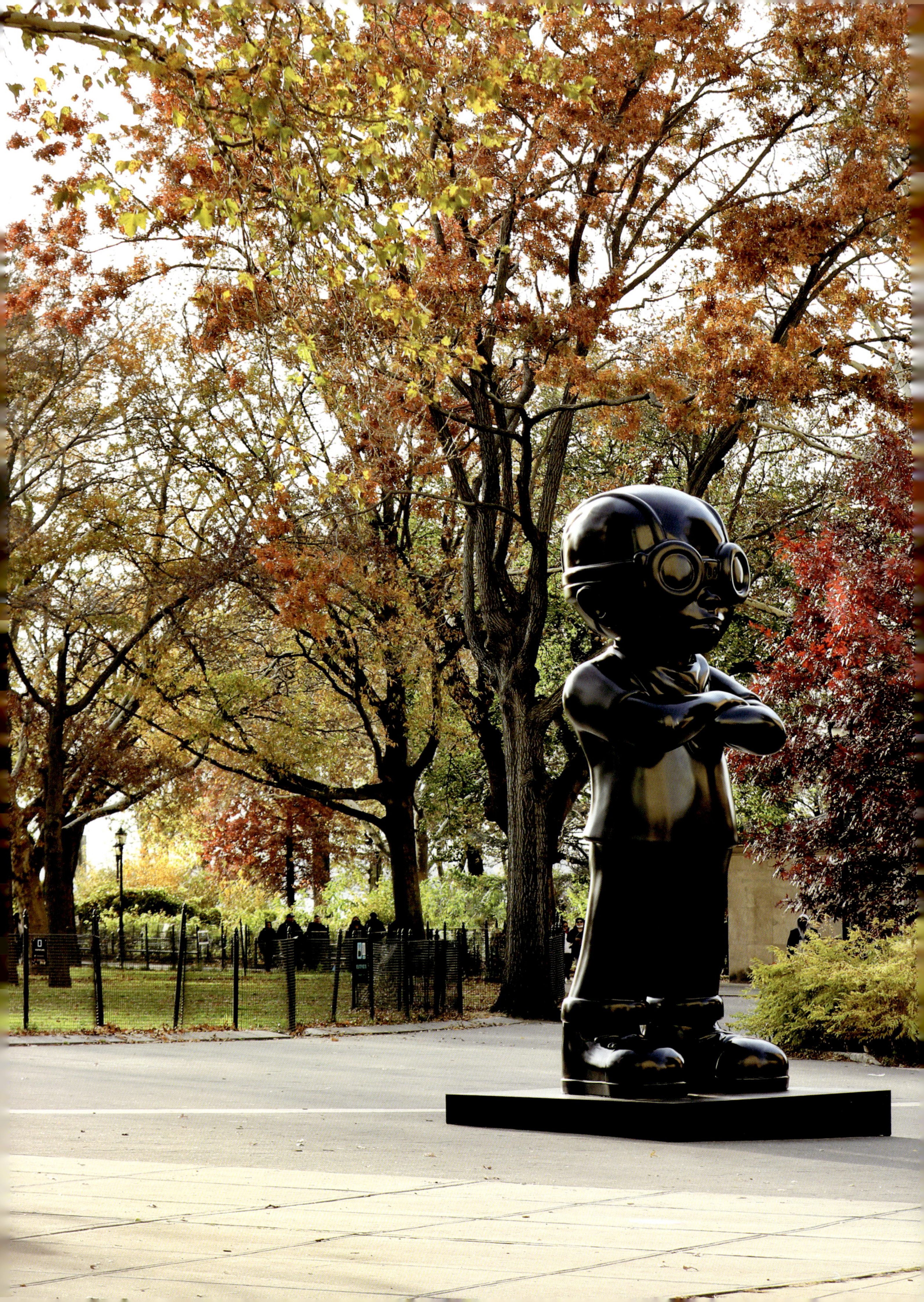

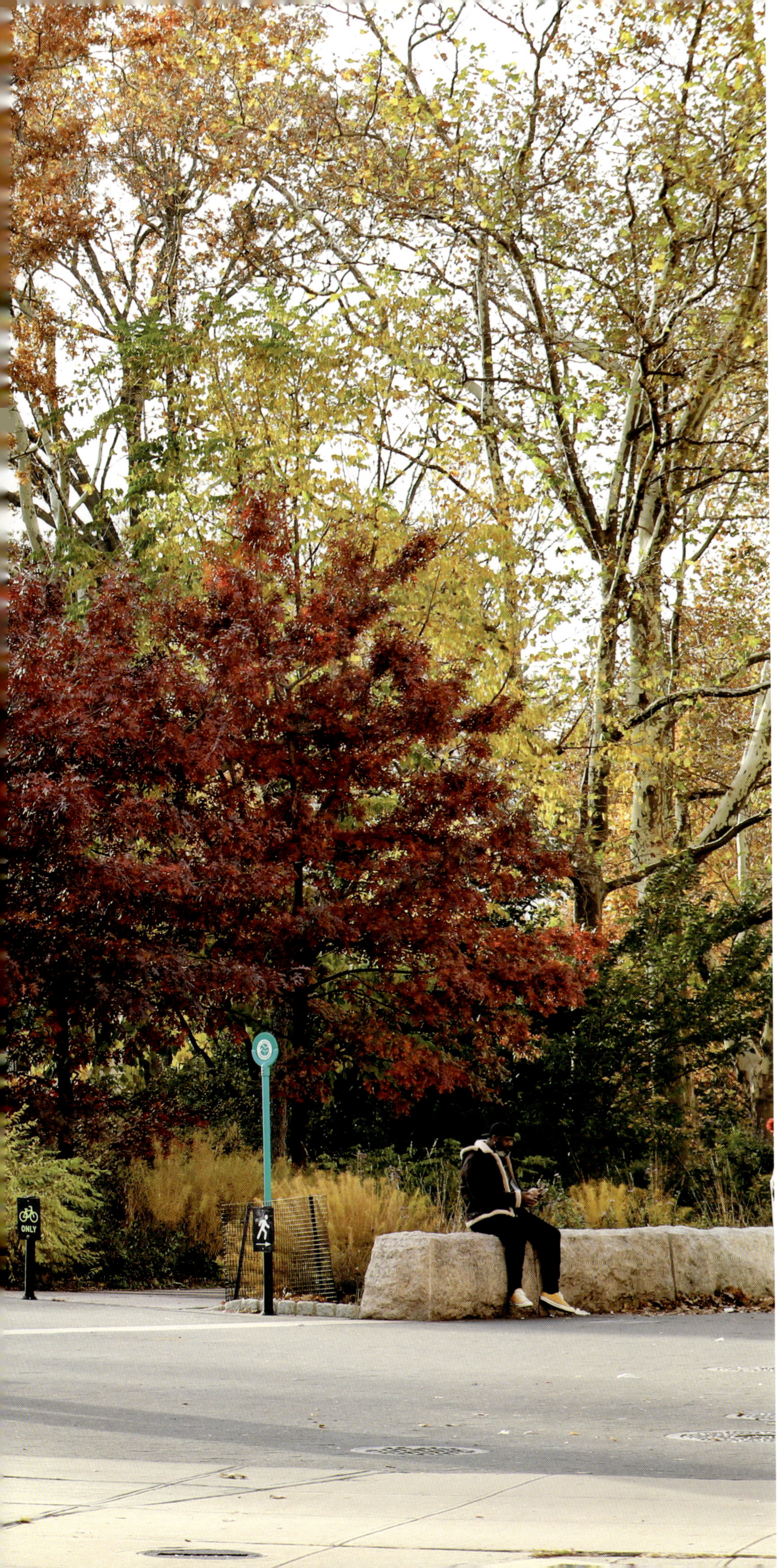
ONLY

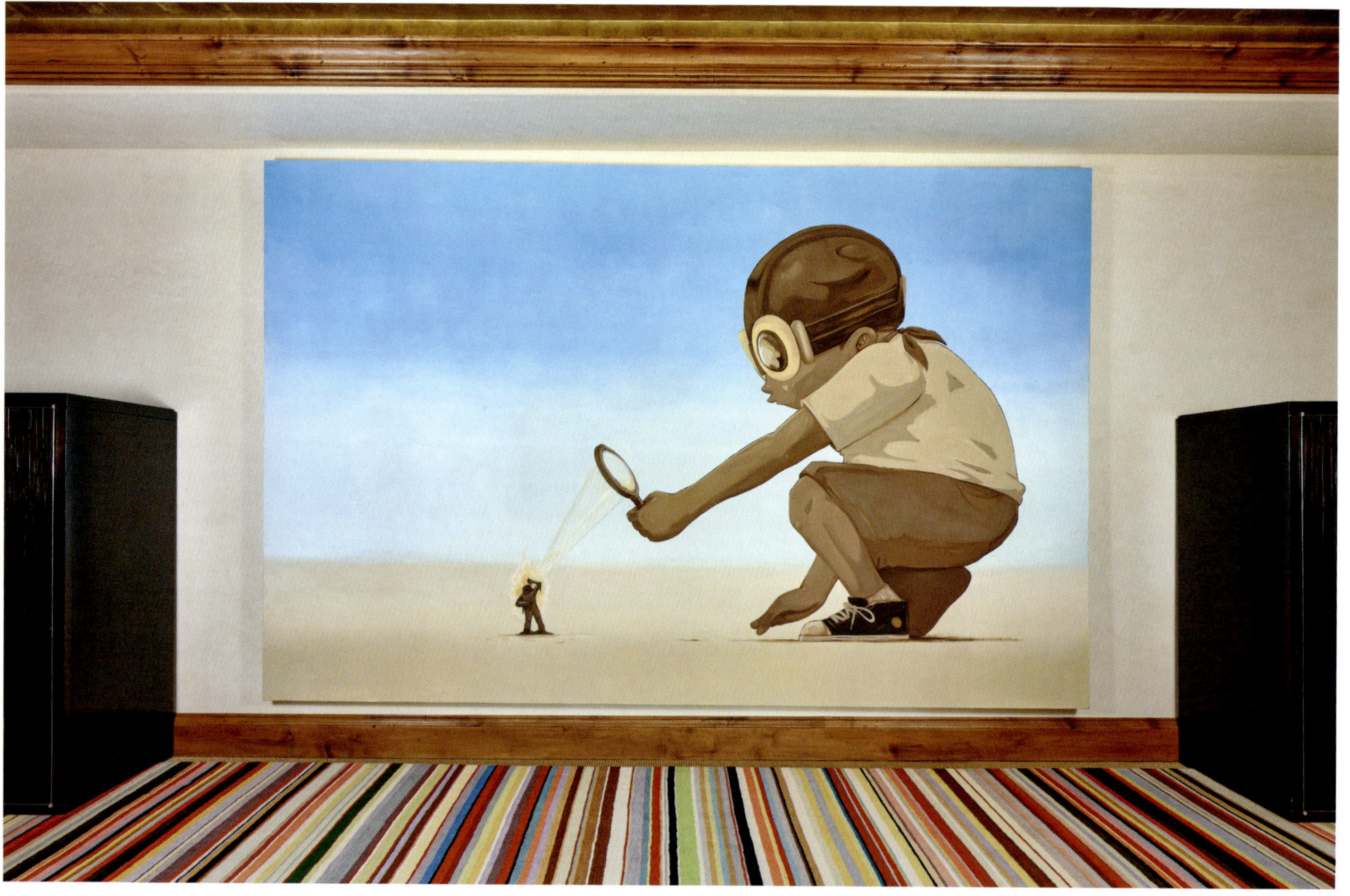

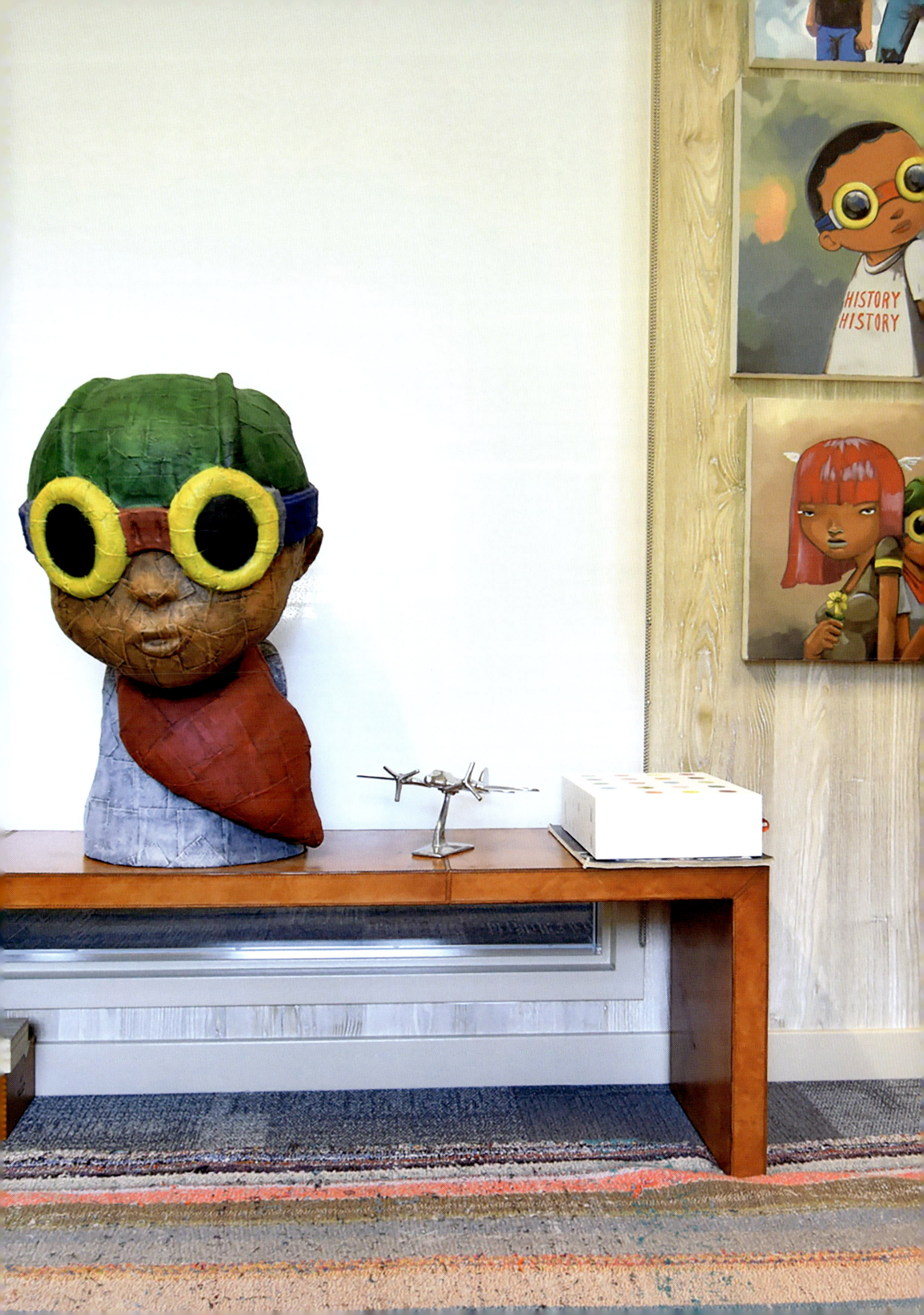
HISTORY
HISTORY

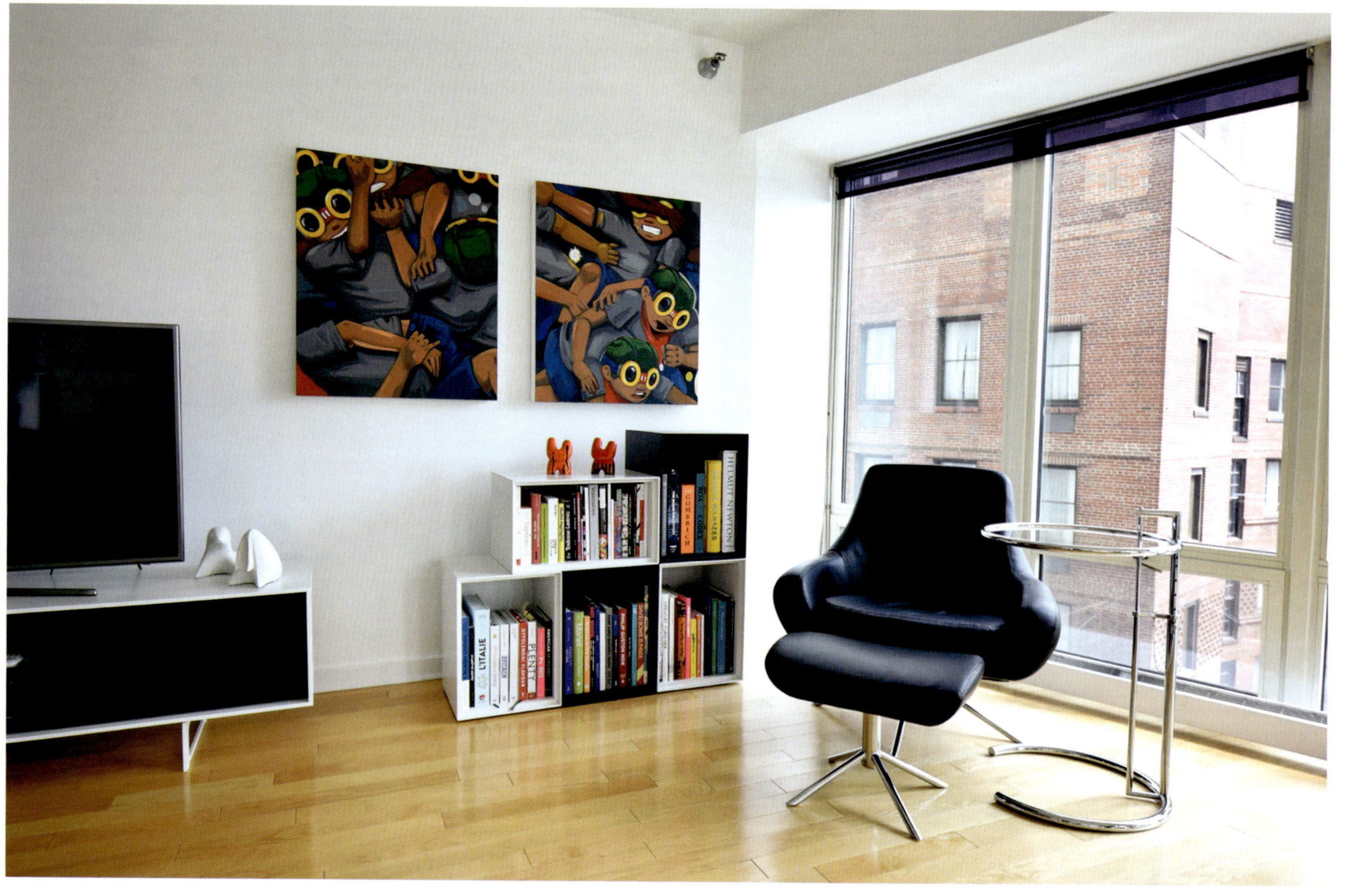
HELMUT NEWTON
L'ITALIE

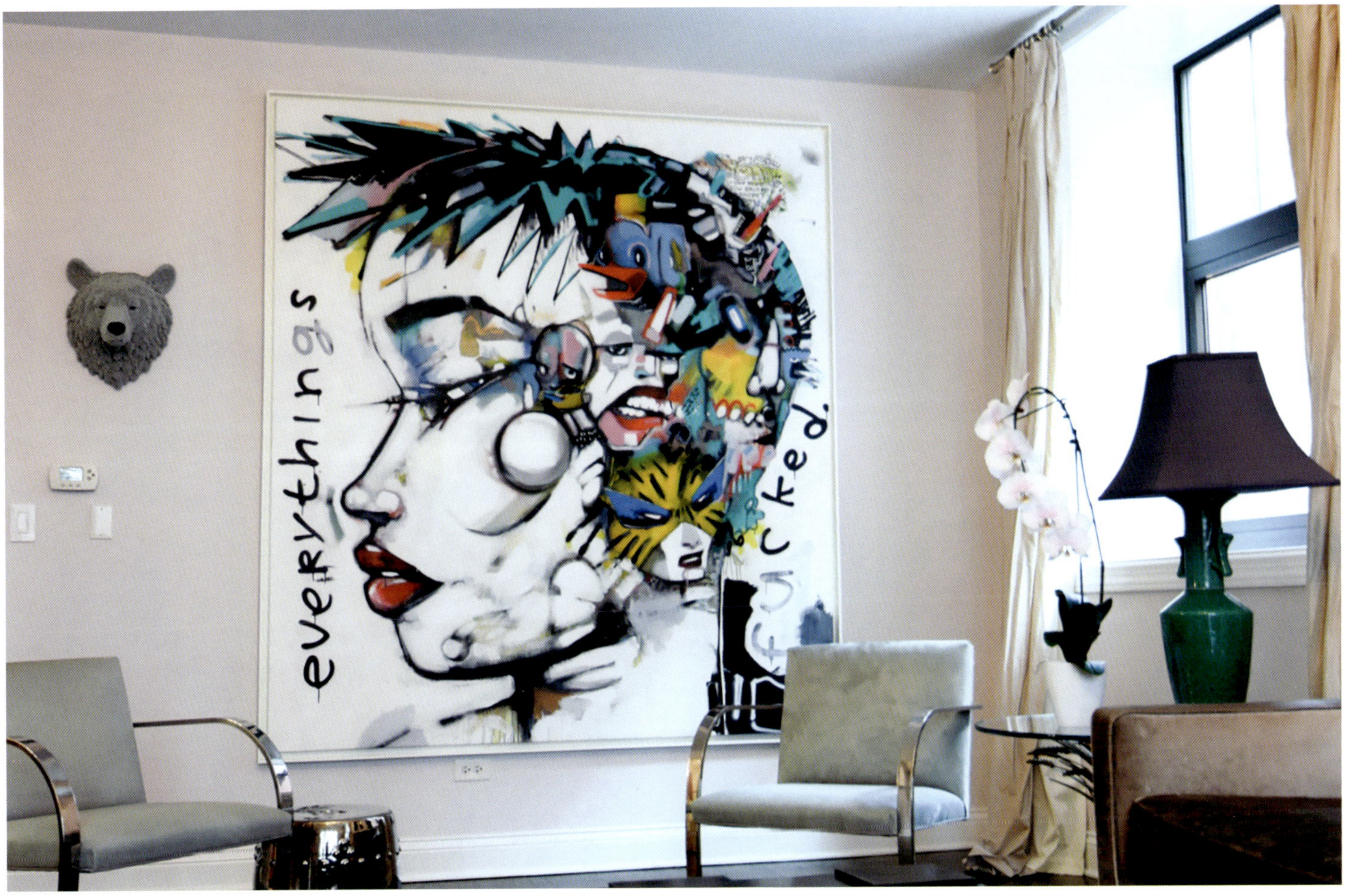

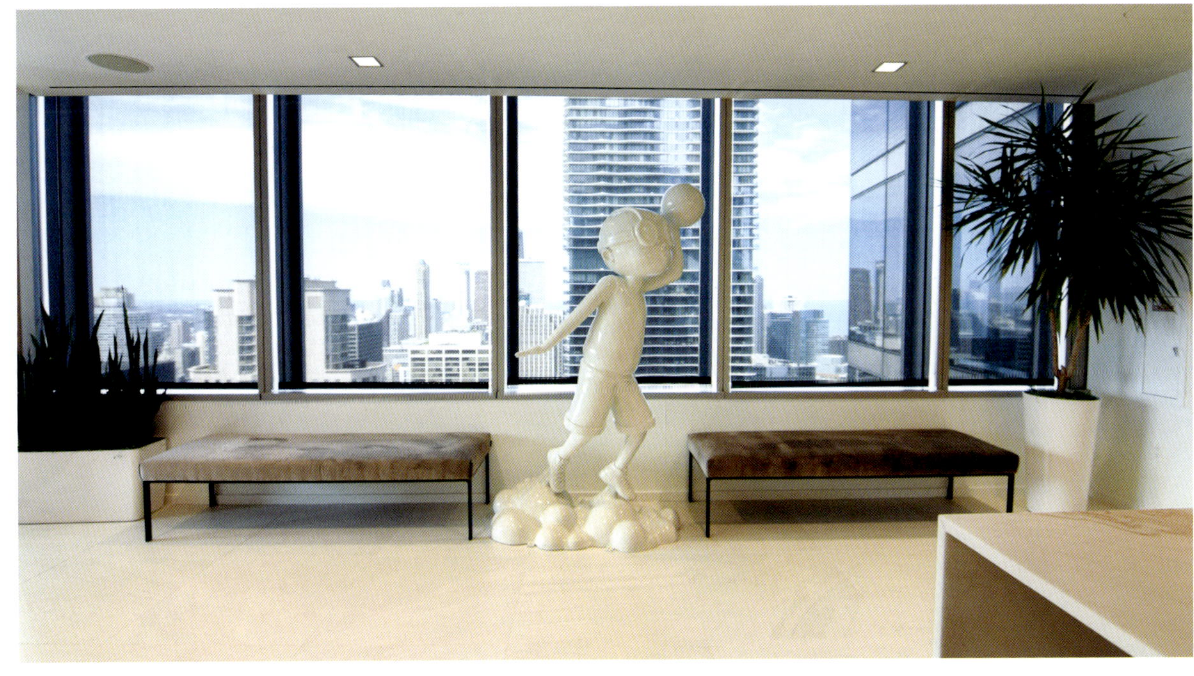

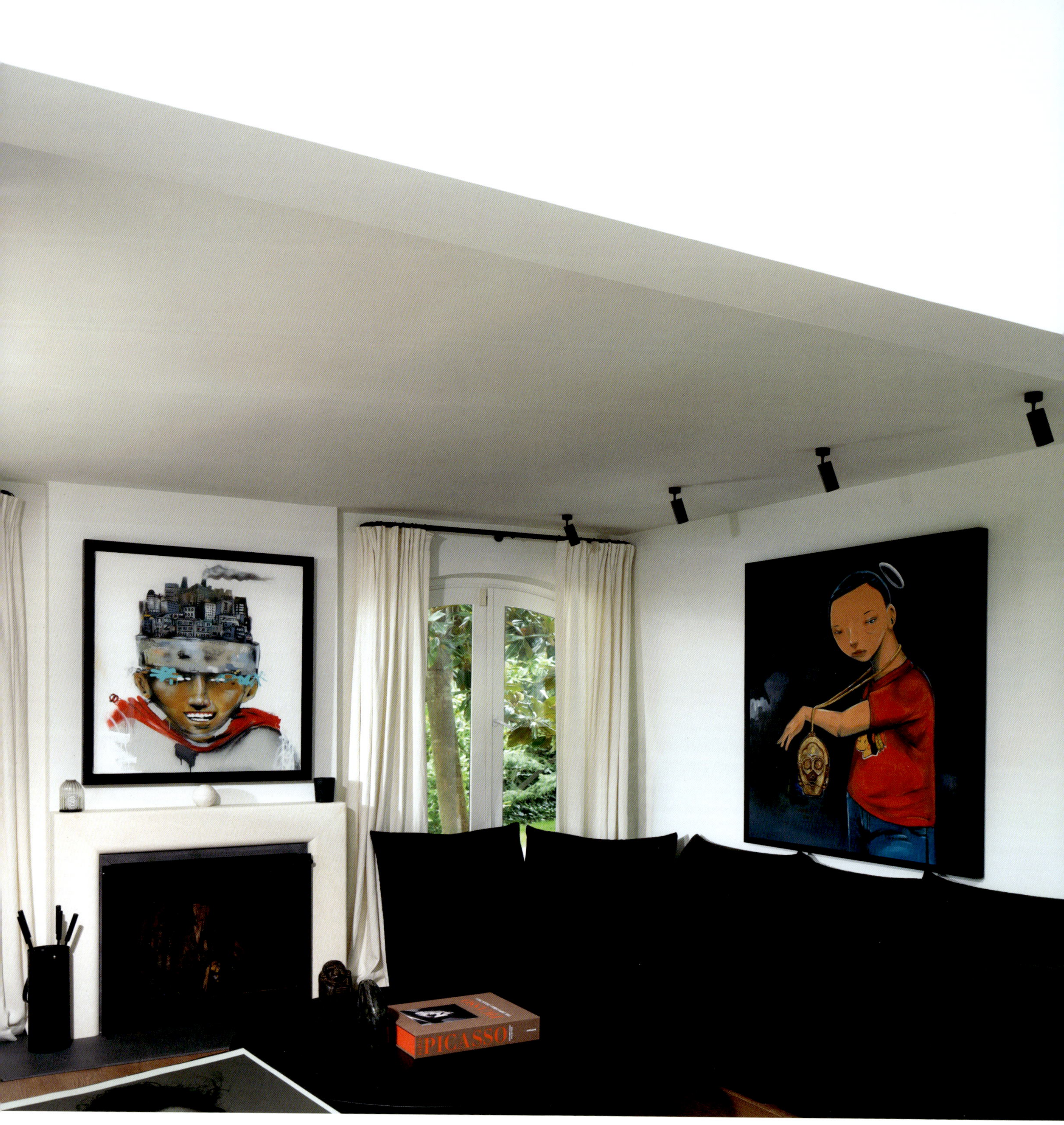
PICASSO

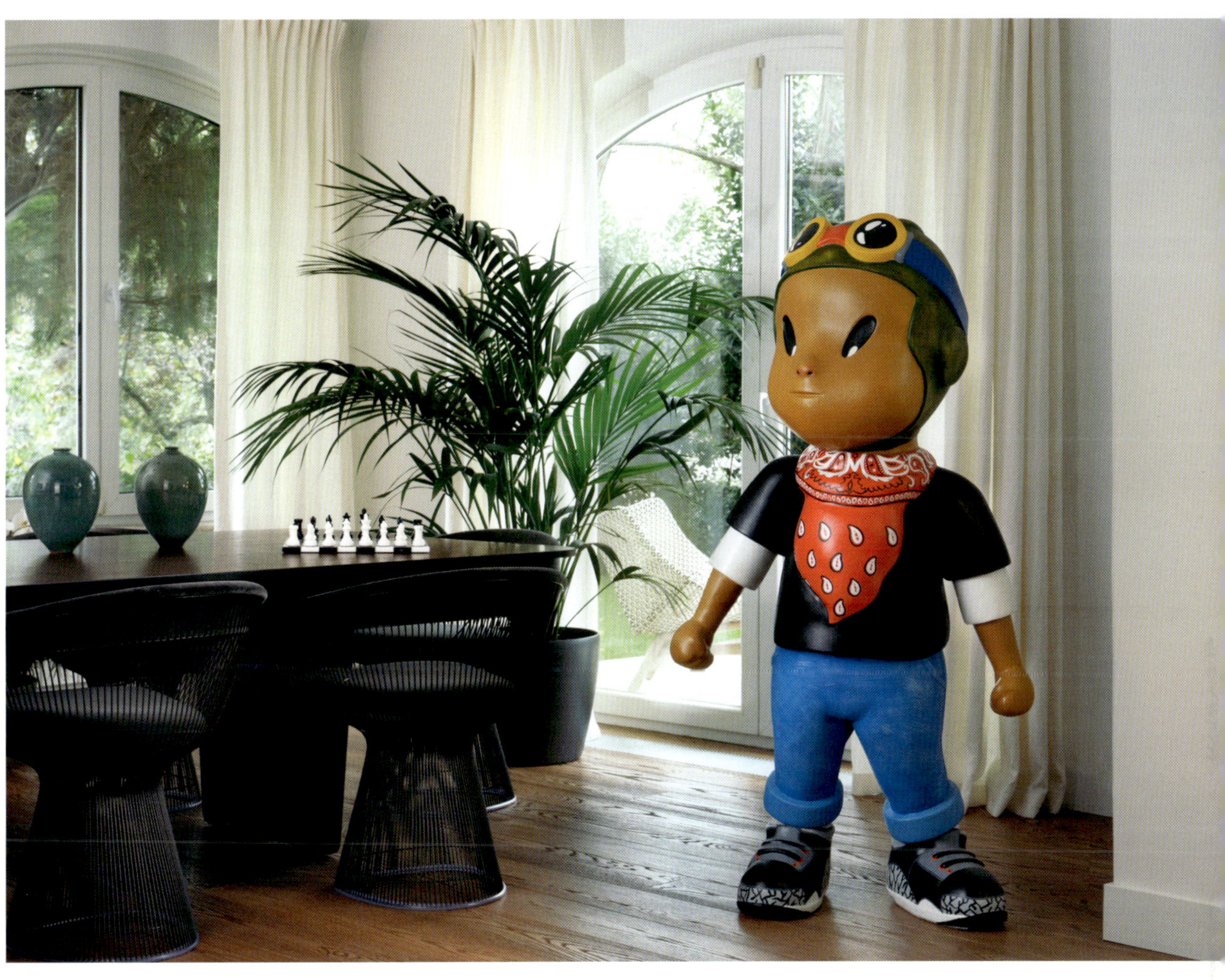

Private Collections

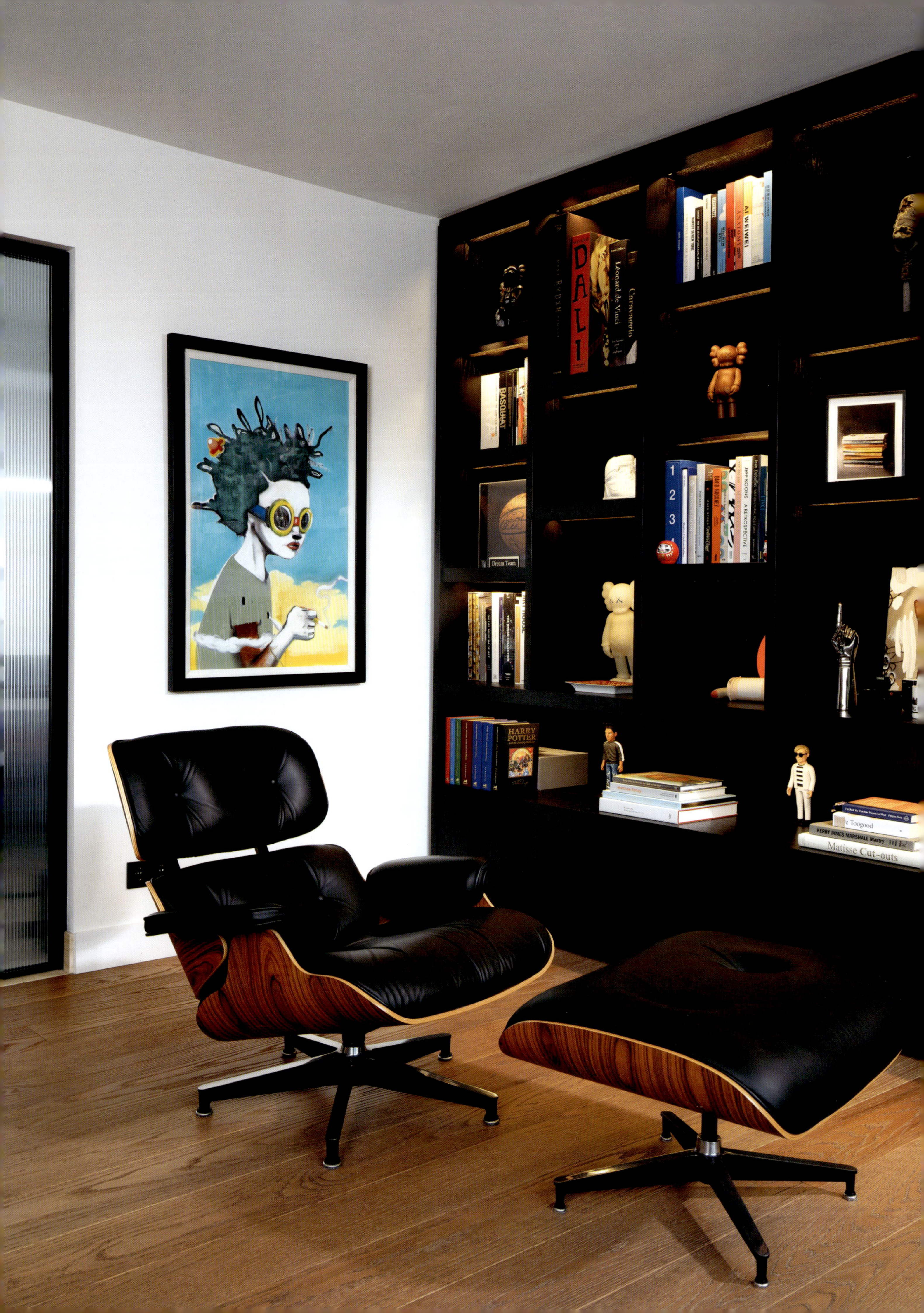

DALI
Léonard de Vinci
BASQUIAT
AI WEIWEI
JEFF KOONS A RETROSPECTIVE
DAVID HOCKNEY
Dream Team
HARRY POTTER
KERRY JAMES MARSHALL Mastry
Matisse Cut-outs

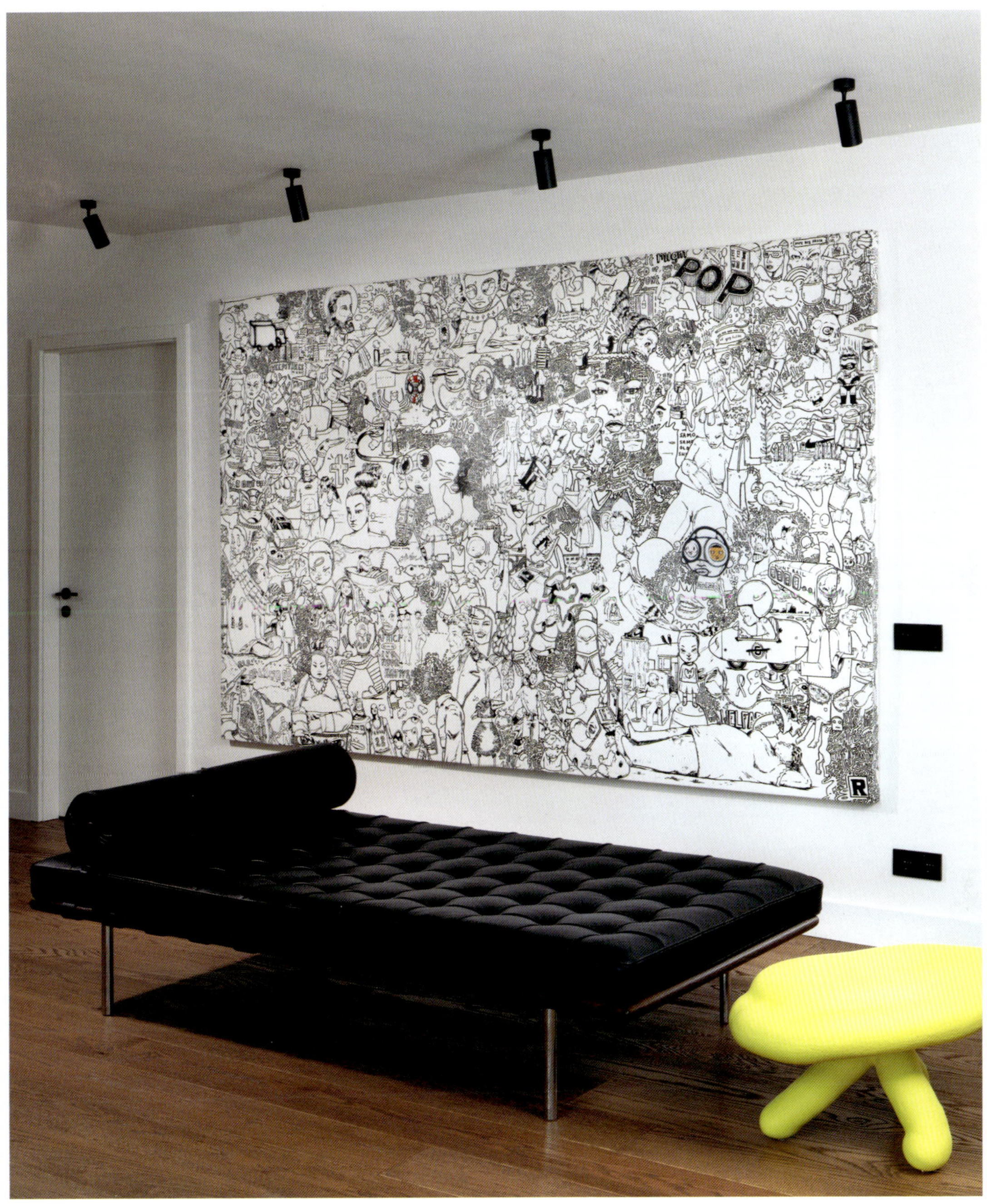

Private Collections

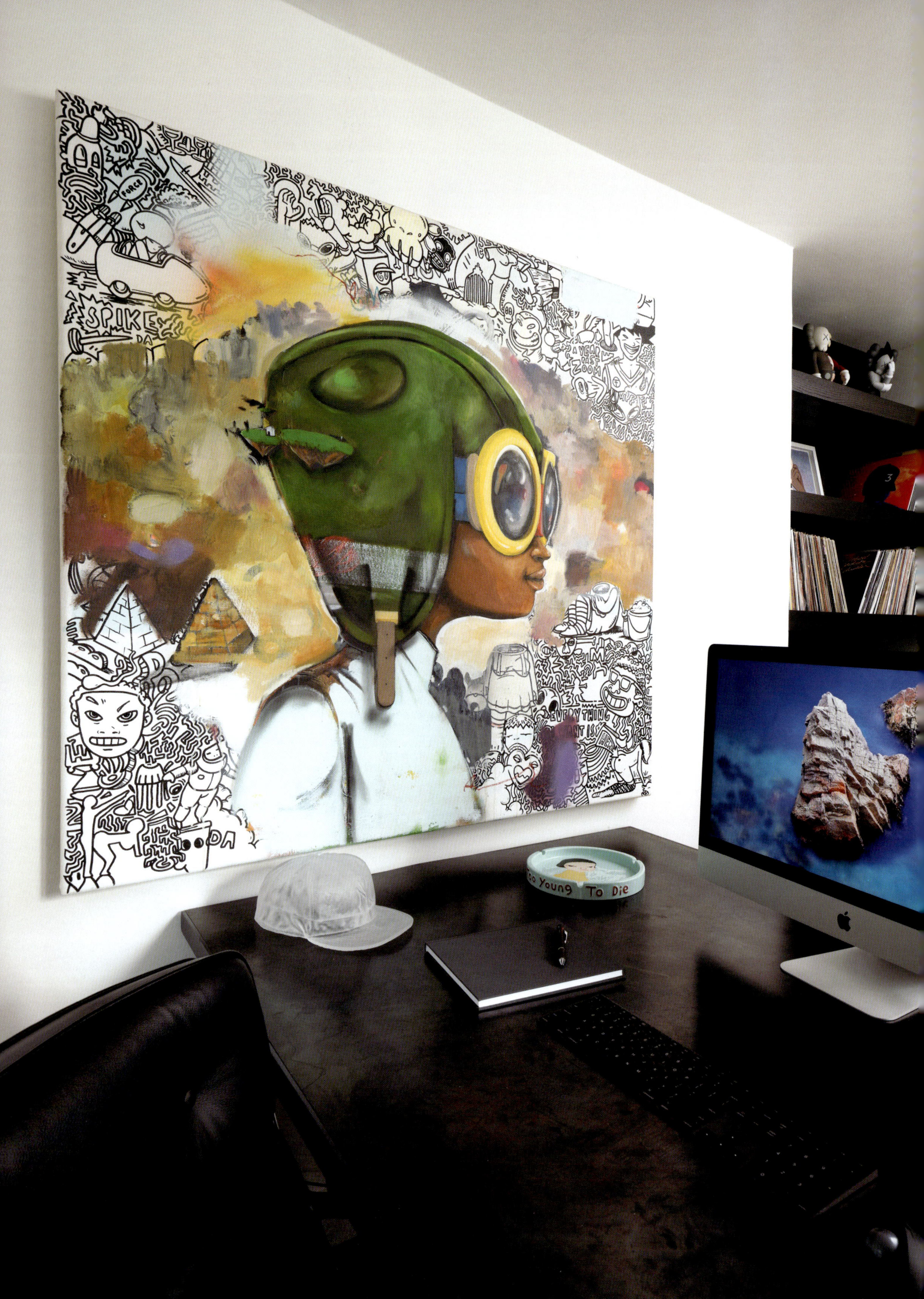
SPIKE
FORCE
oo Young To Die

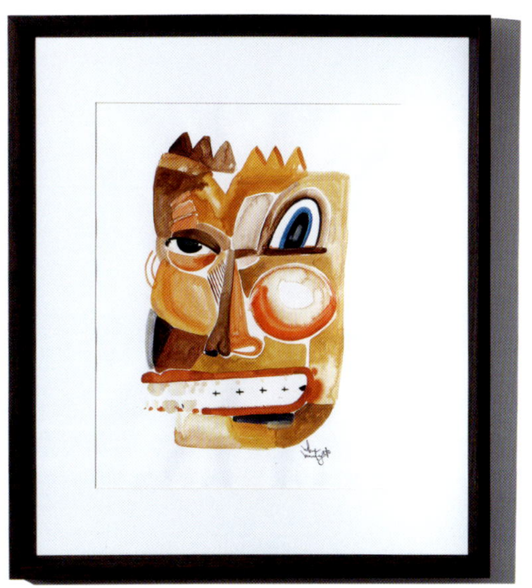

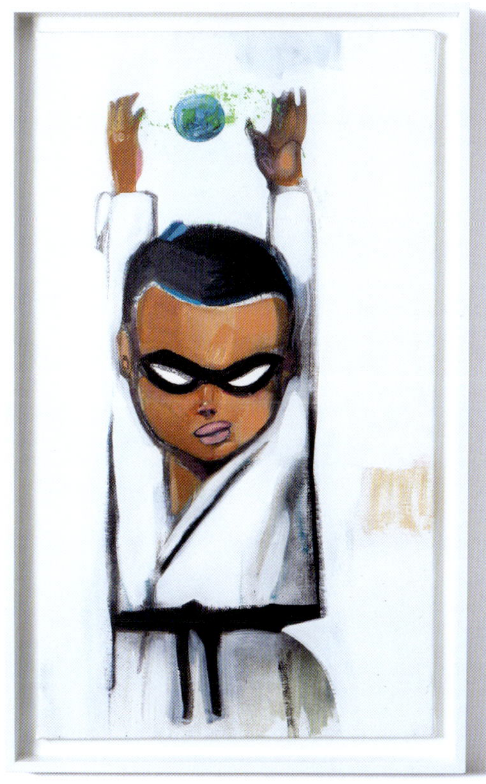

COLOR

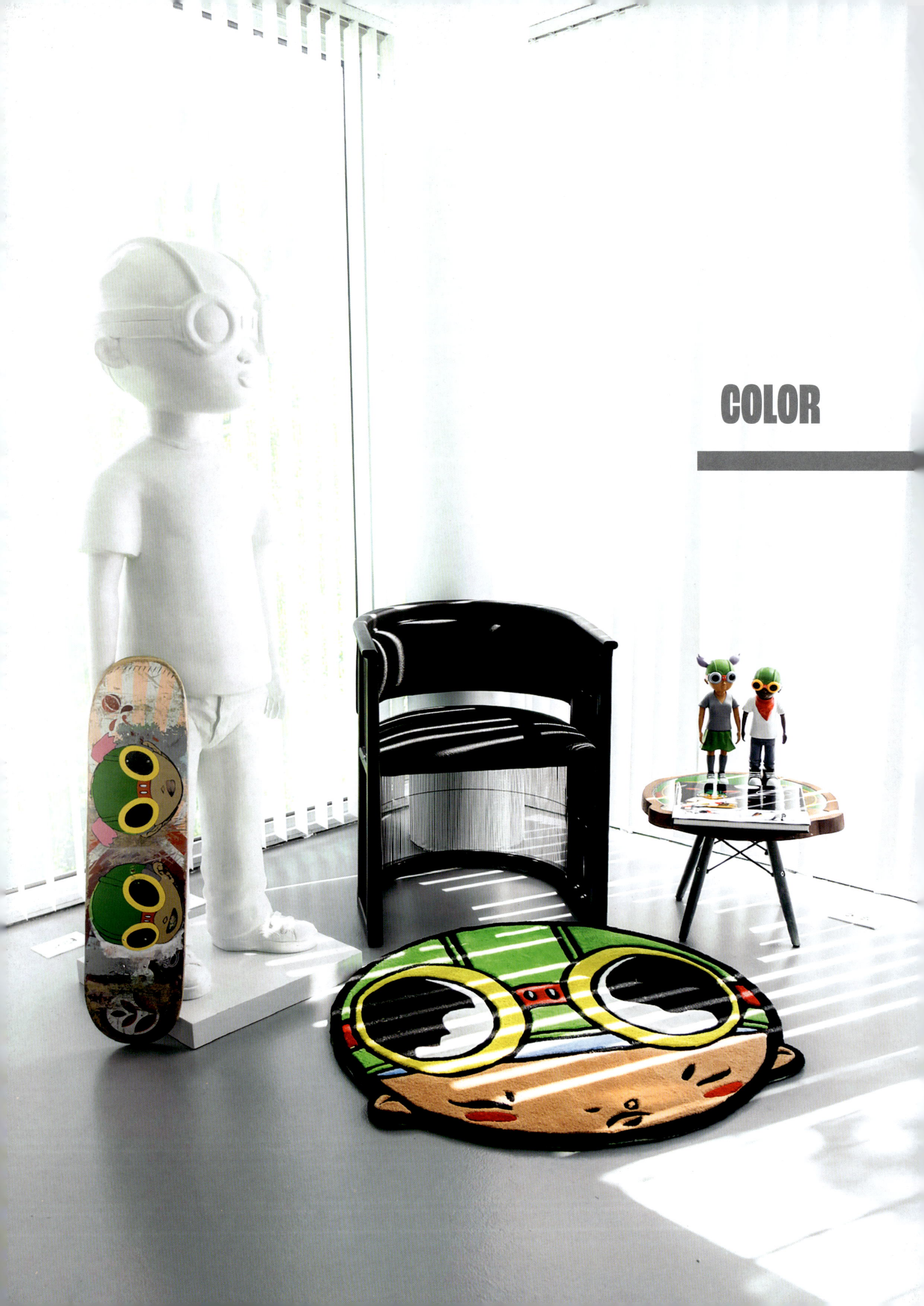

THREE:

COLLABORATIONS MERCHANDISE

(Below)
BAPE x Hebru Brantley
Flyboy Shark
full-zip hoodie
2018

(Opposite)
Bearbrick x Hebru Brantley
Flyboy Shark
bearbrick
2018

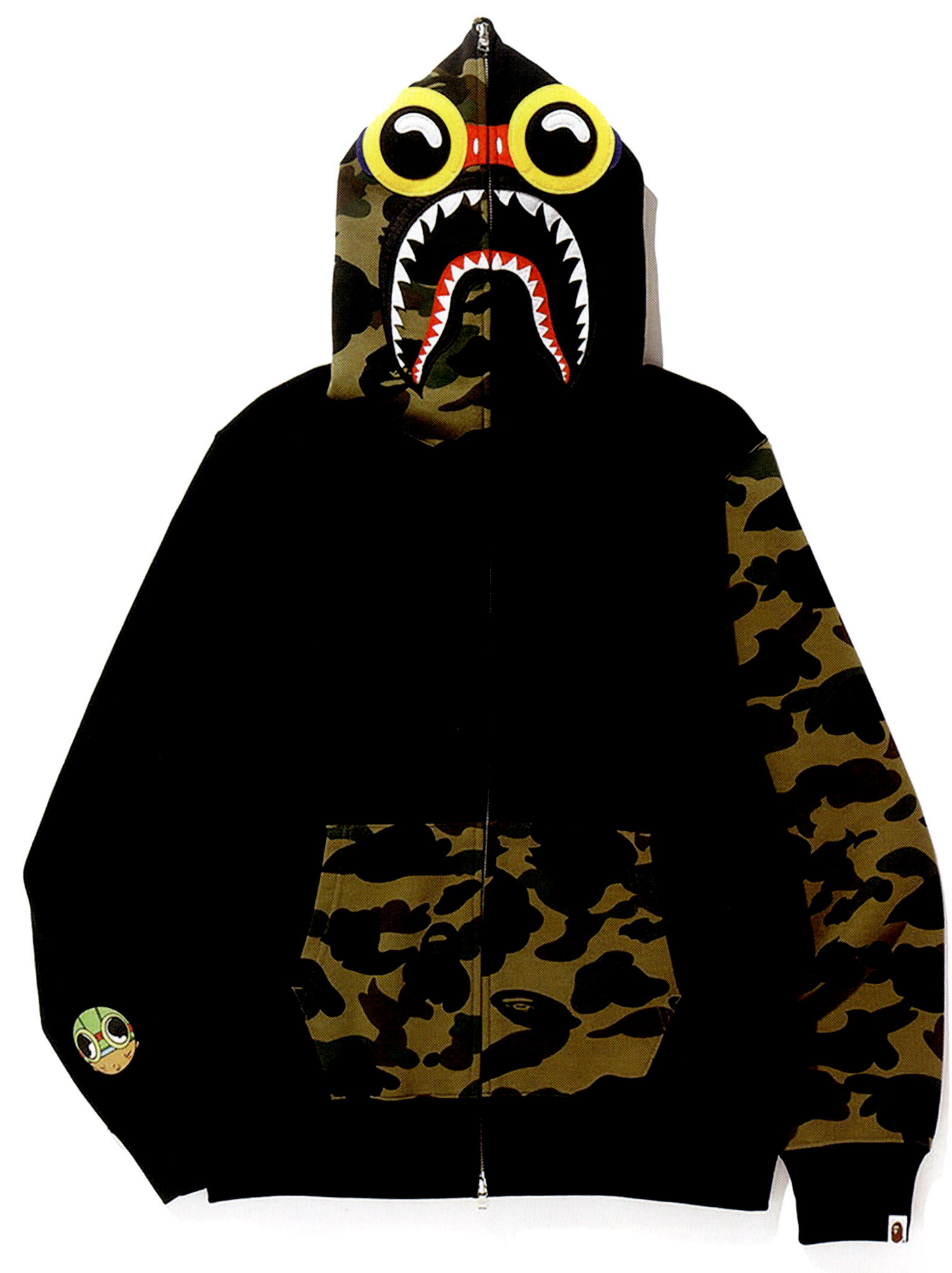

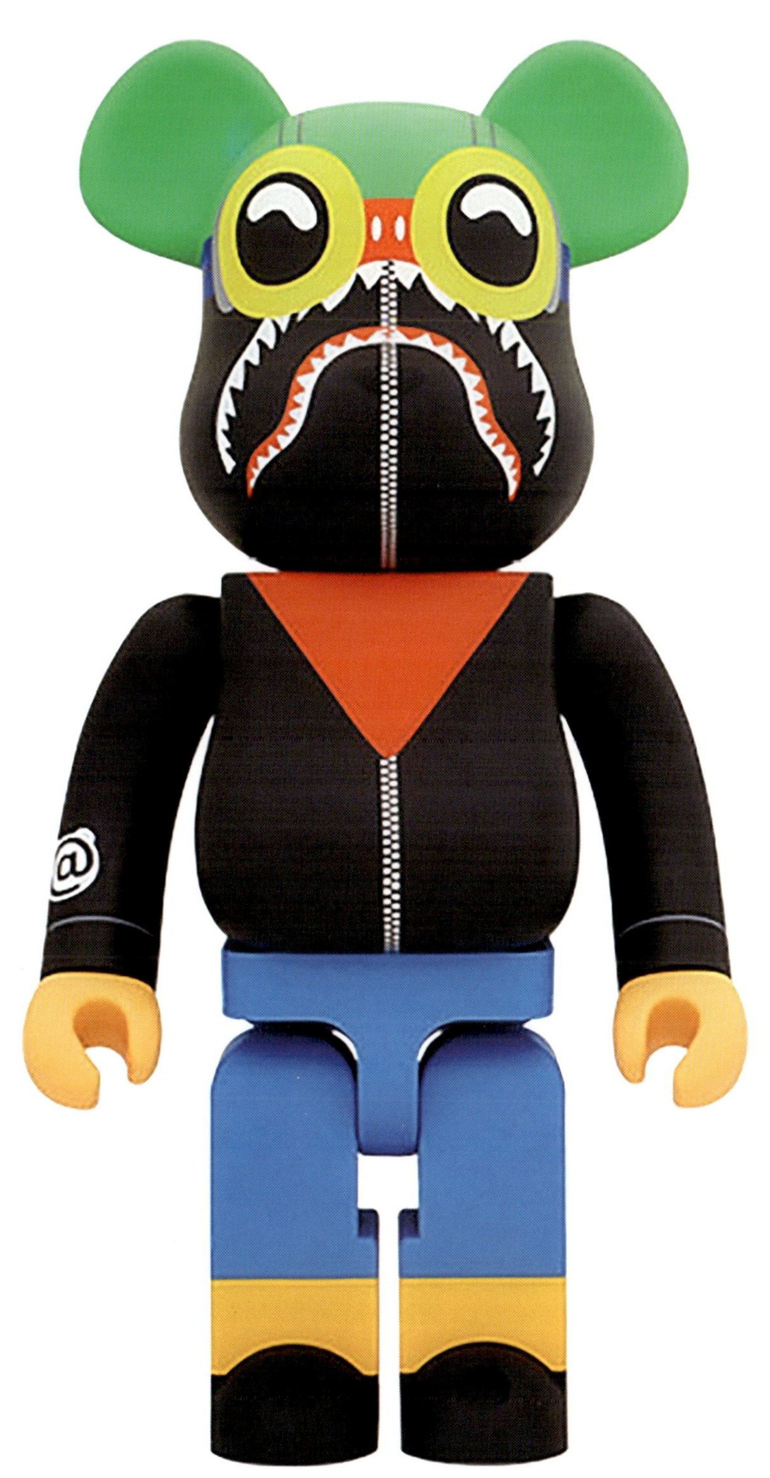

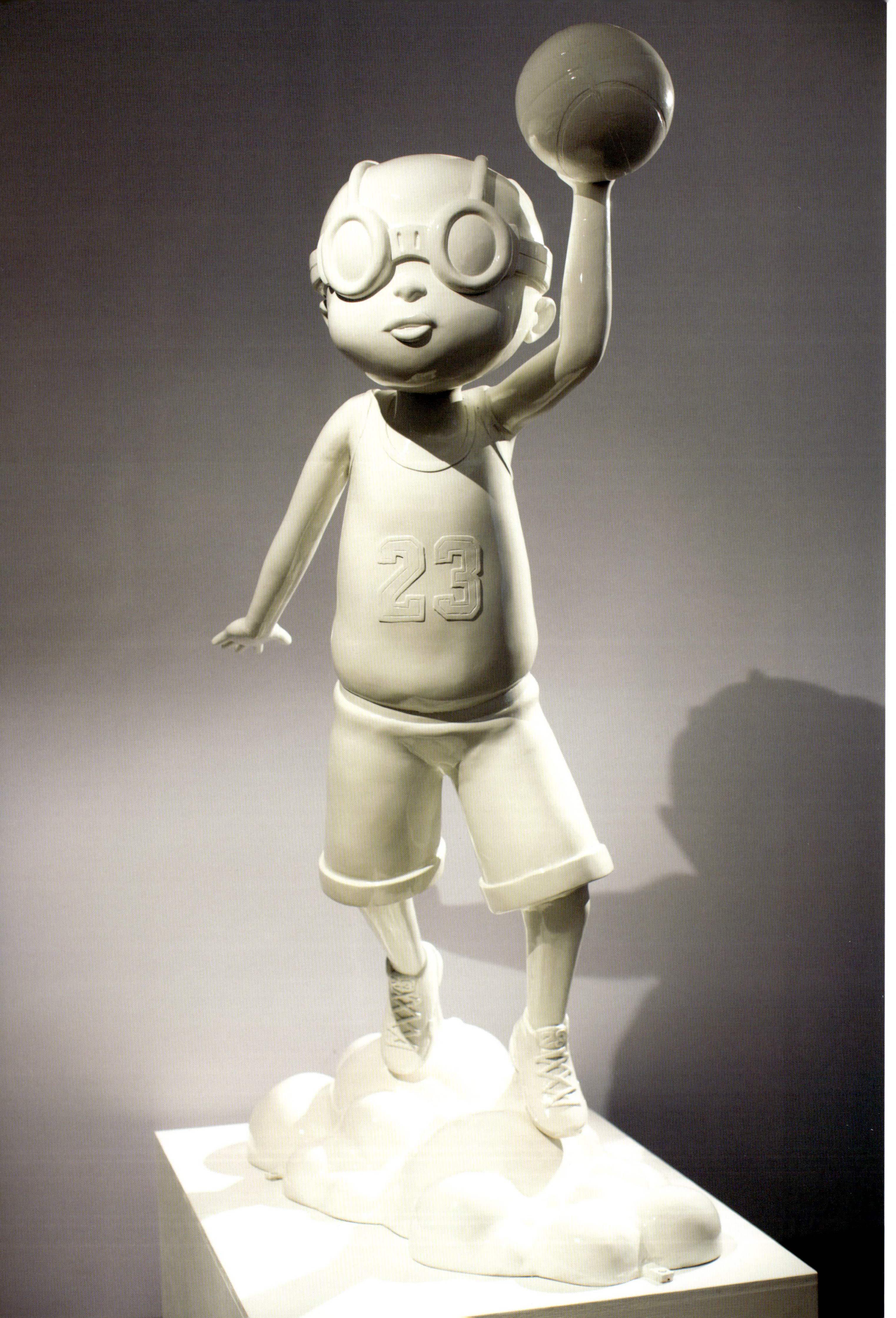
23

(Opposite)
Flyboy Jordan Sculpture
Acrylic, fiberglass, and resin
78 inches
2015

(Below)
Hebru Brantley x Mitchell & Ness
NBA branded apparel
2021

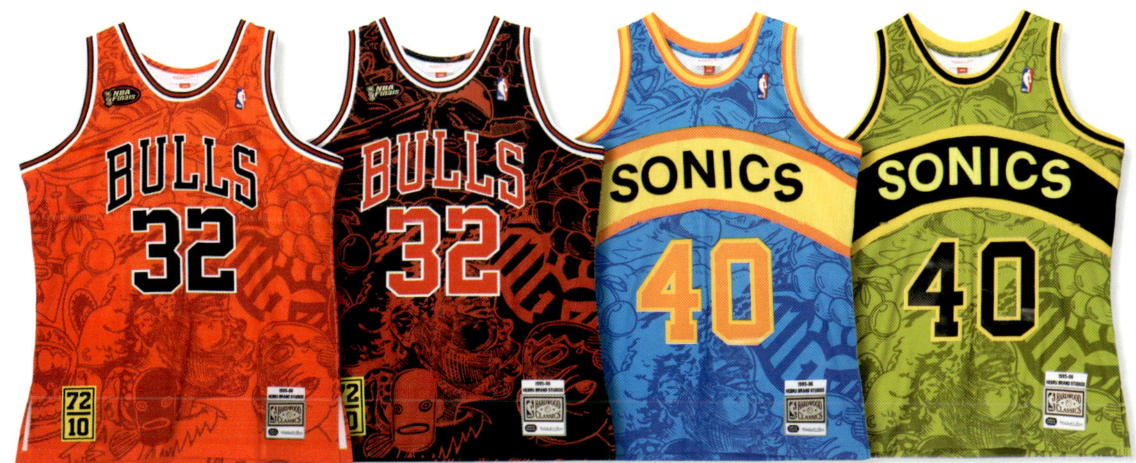

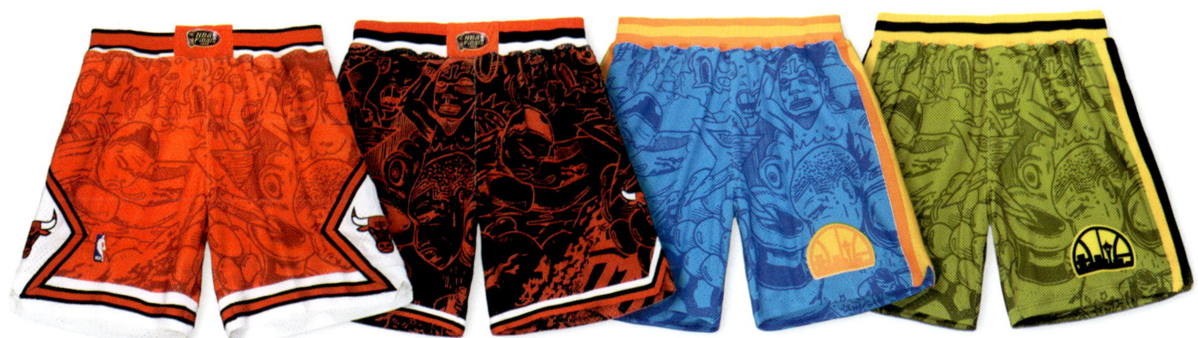

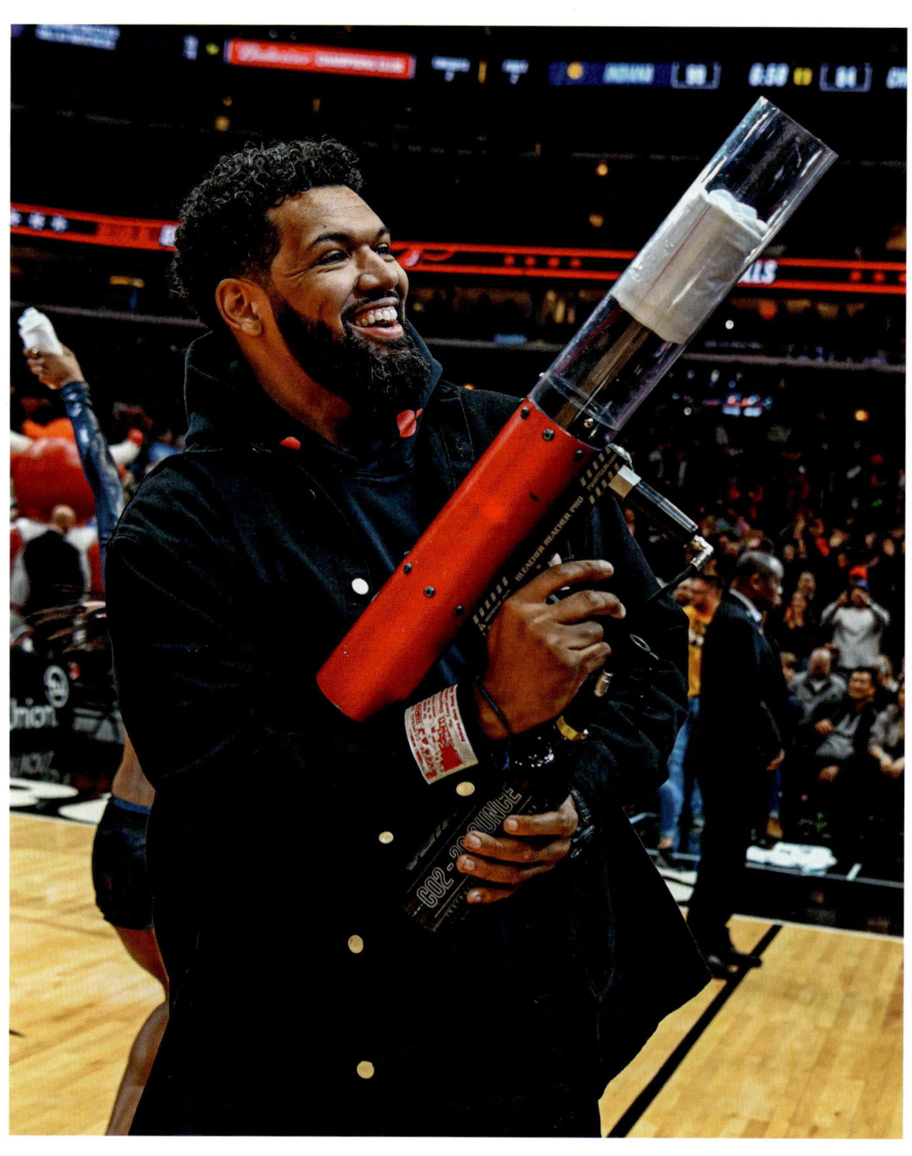

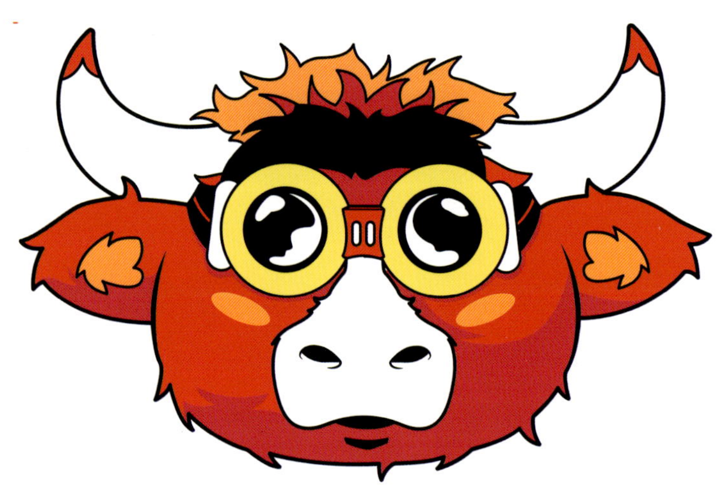

Chicago Bulls
Benny the Bull
Bobblehead
2020

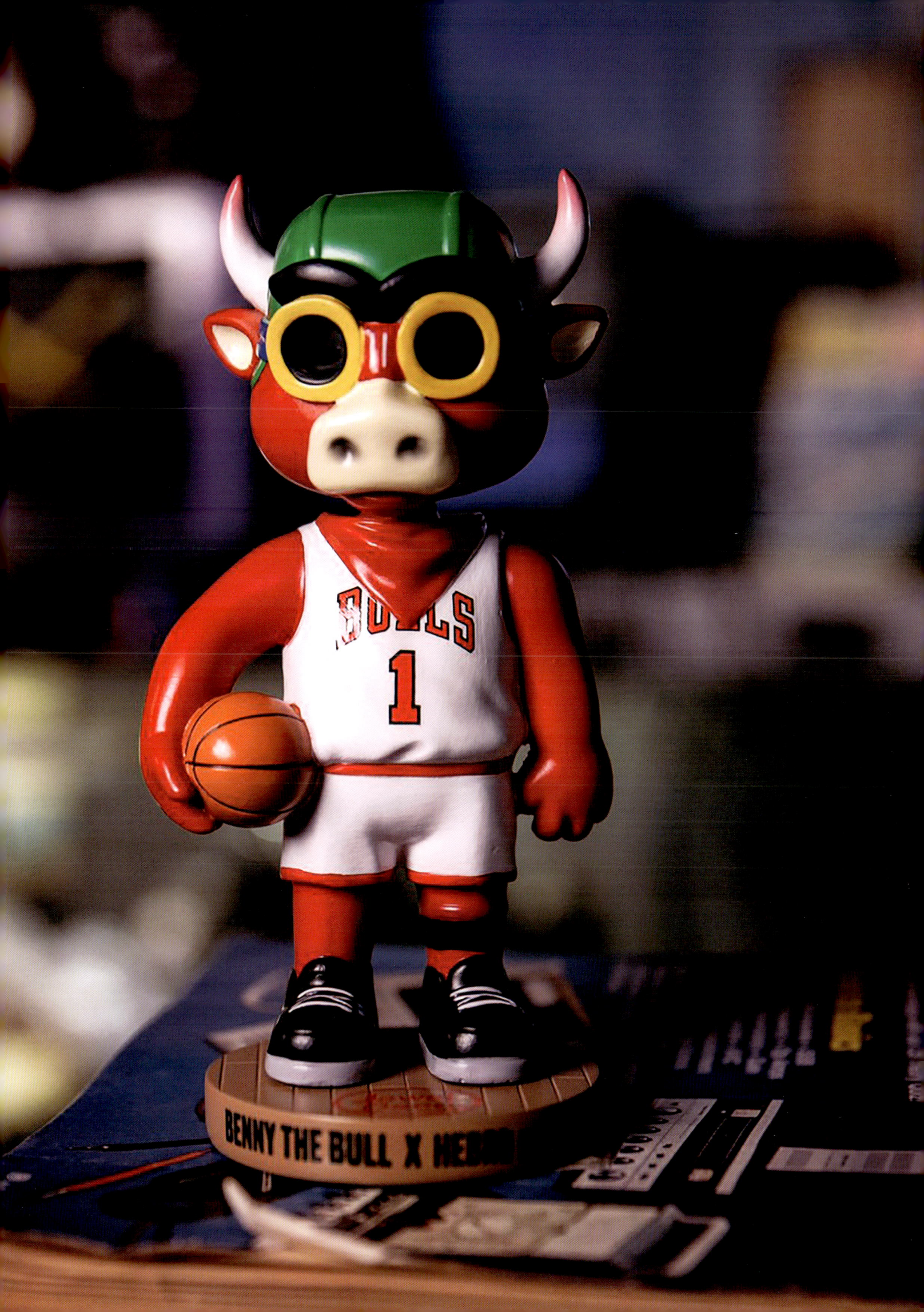
BULLS
1
BENNY THE BULL X

Melo M11 Hebru
Sneaker
2015

(Opposite)
Metcalfe Park Basketball Court
Chicago
2019

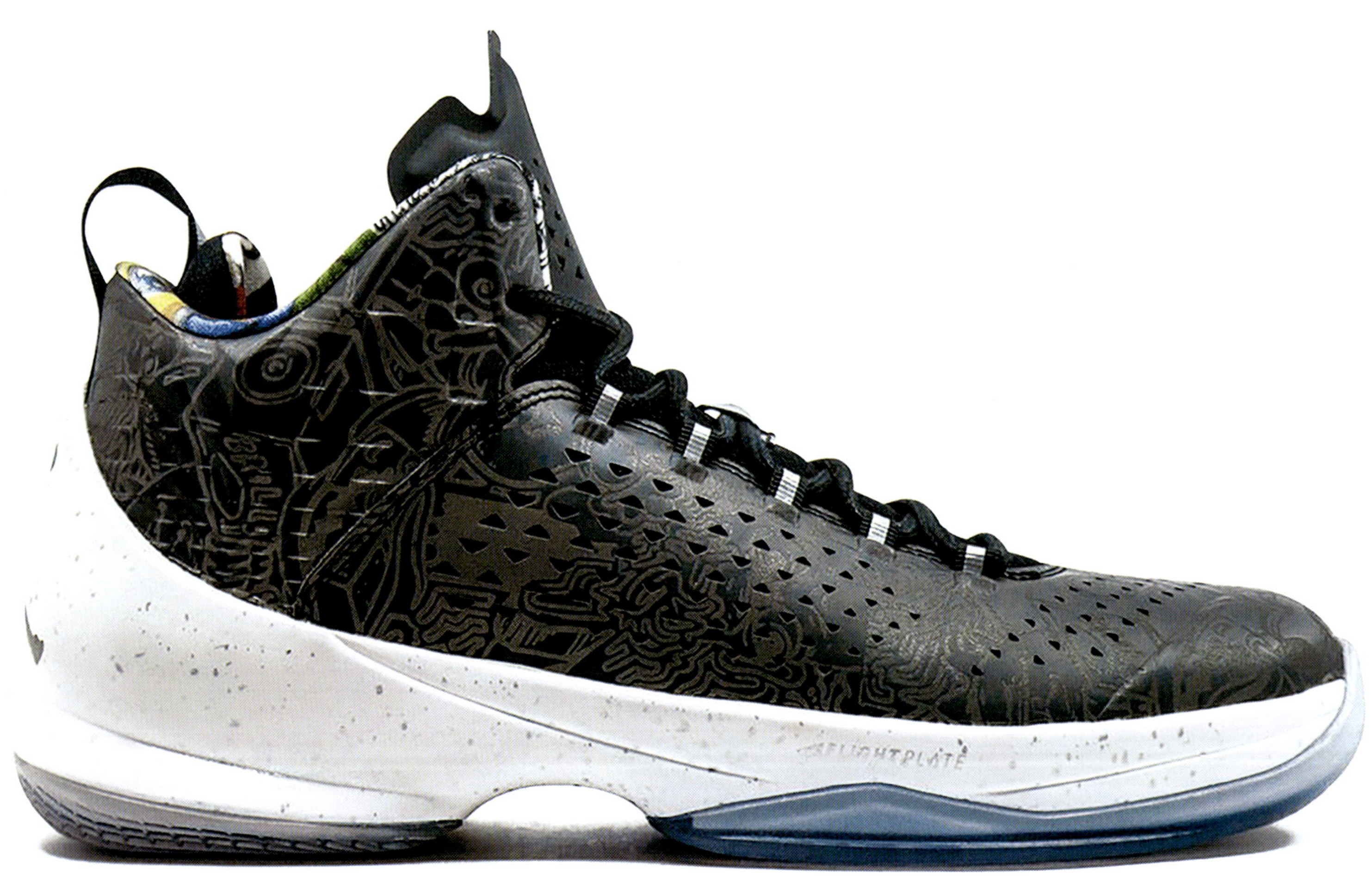

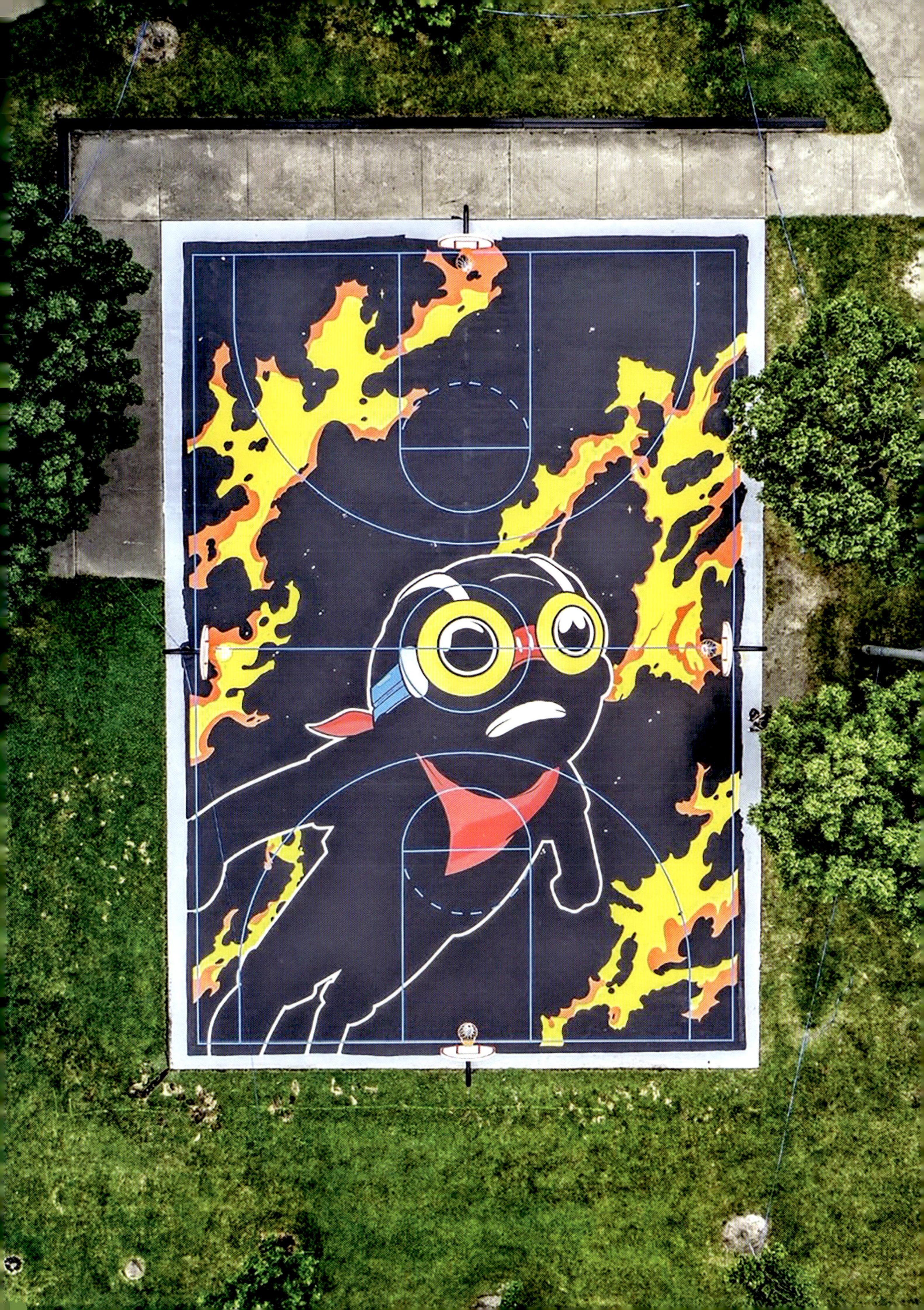

Hebru Brantley x Wilson Flyboy Basketball, 2019

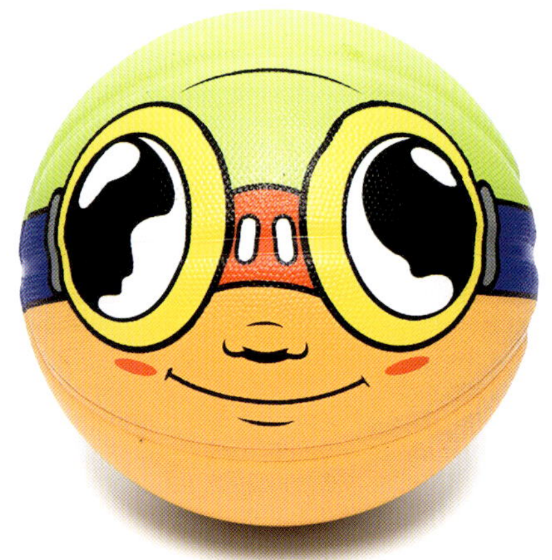

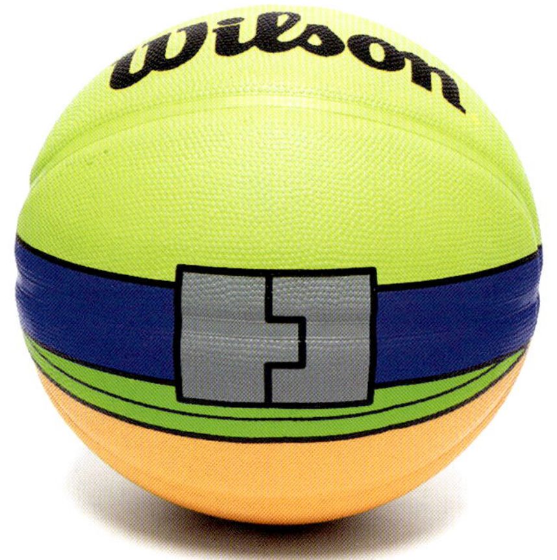

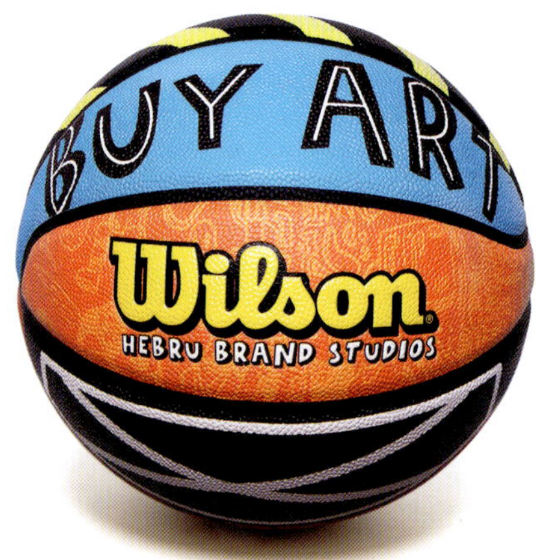

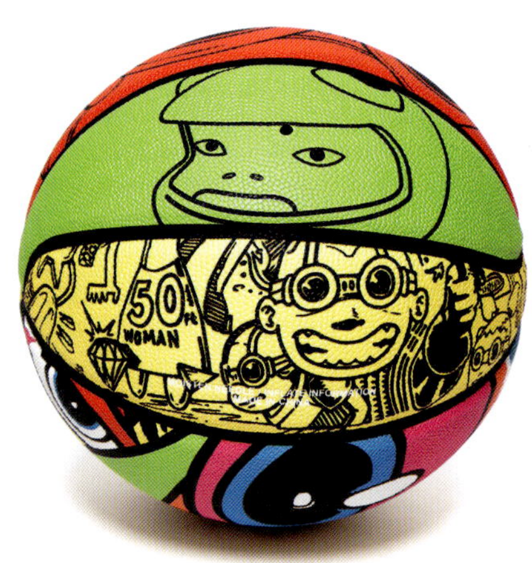

Wilson Champions Edition Basketball, 2020

Hebru Brantley x
Adidas Rivalry Hi
2019

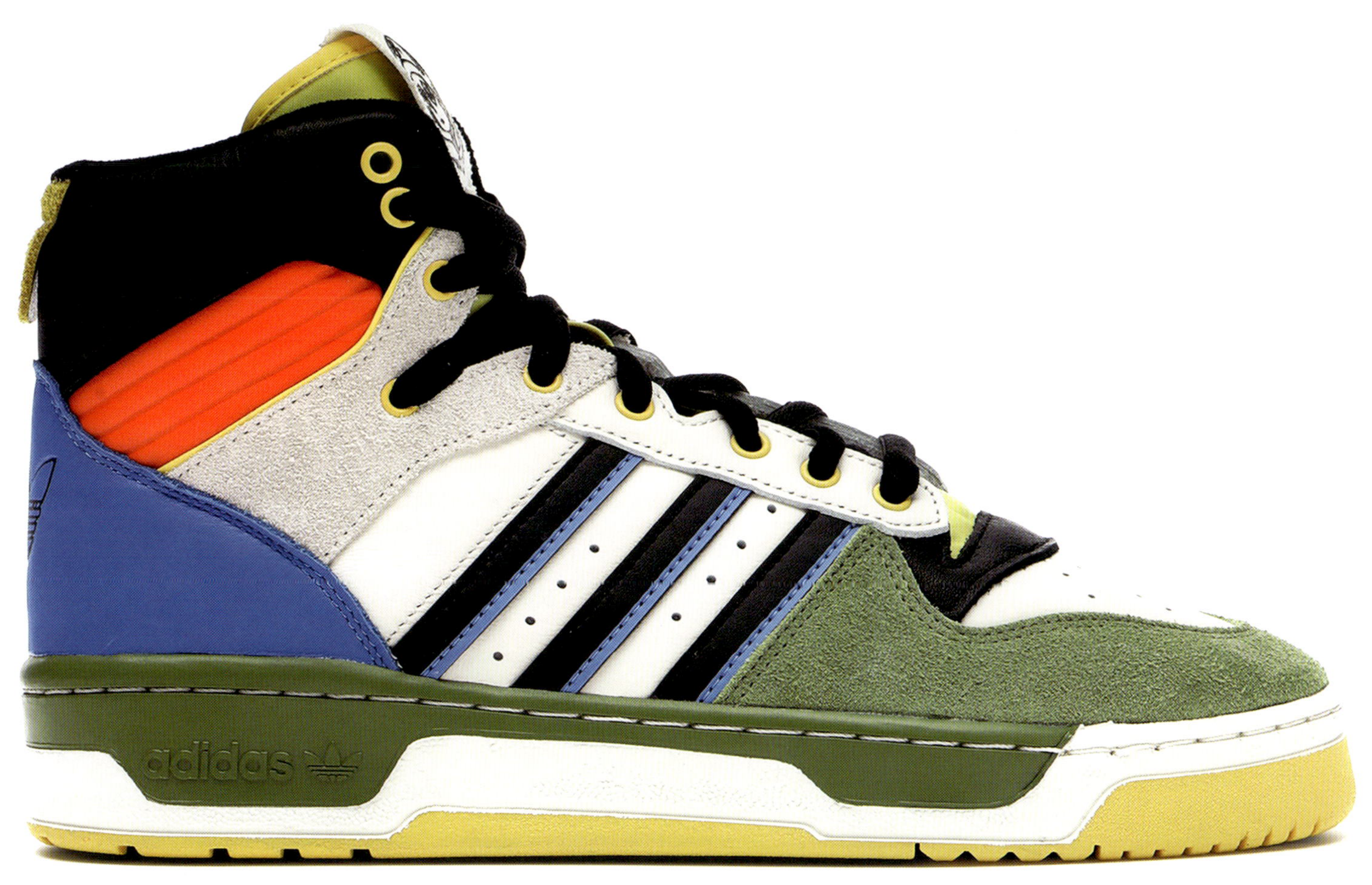

(Above)
Hebru Brantley x Adidas Forum Low
2022

(Below)
Hebru Brantley x Adidas Forum High
2022

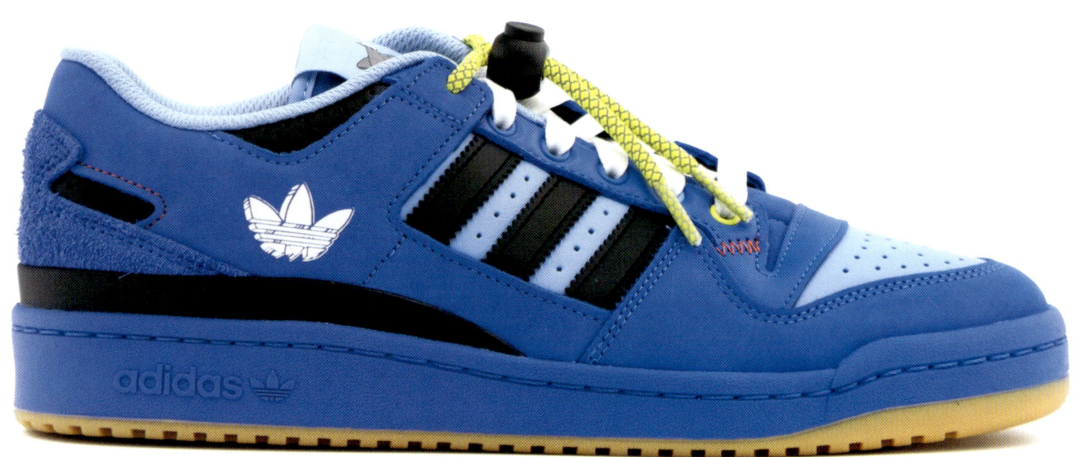

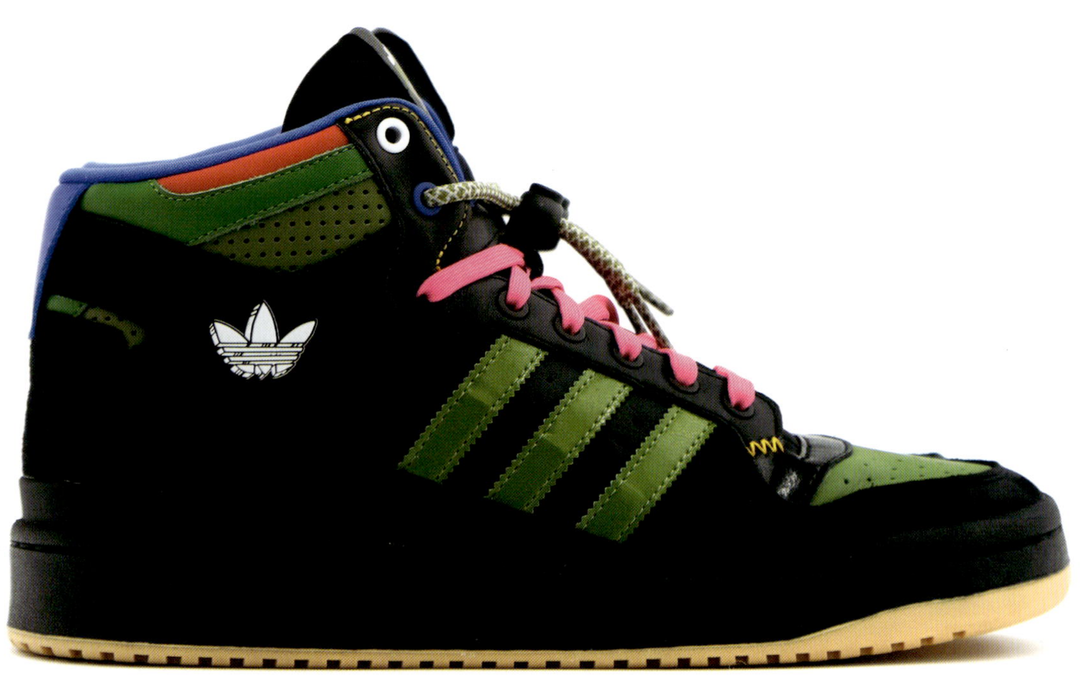

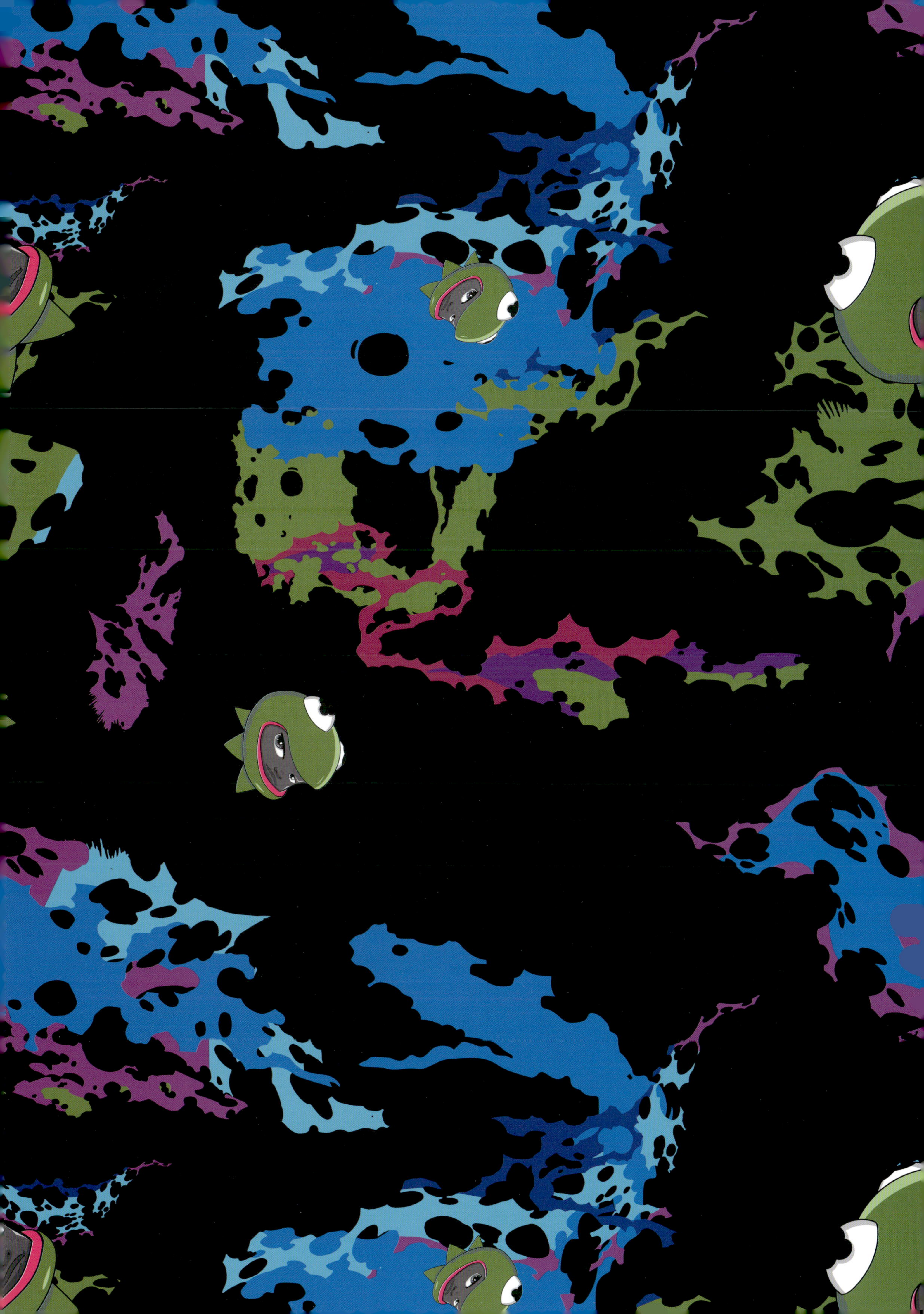

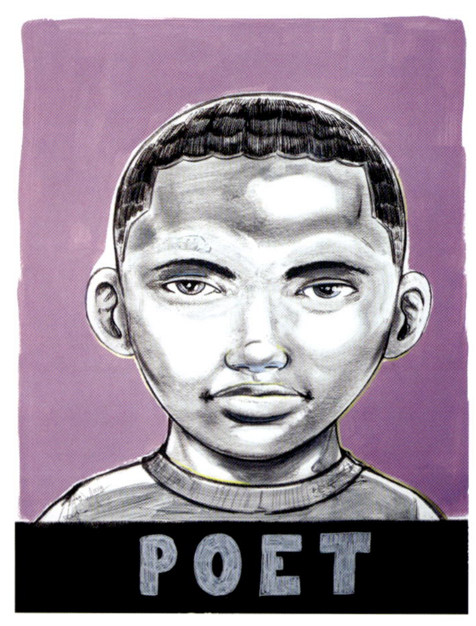

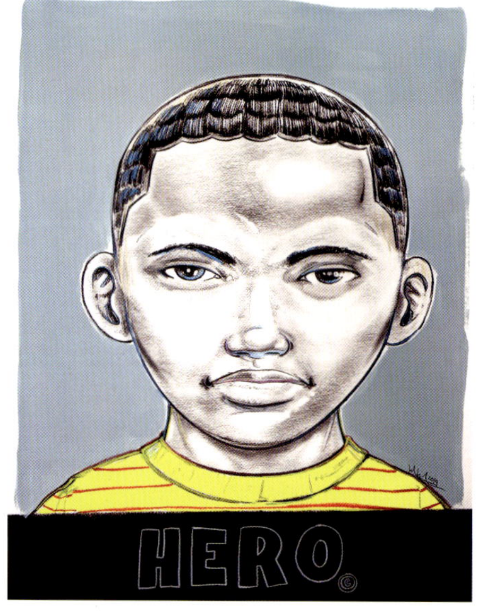

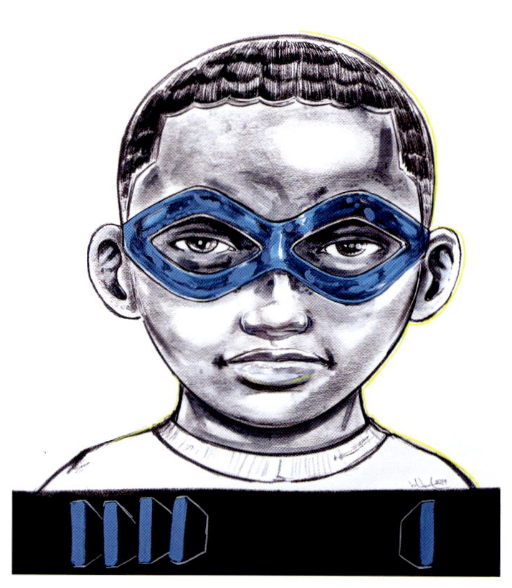

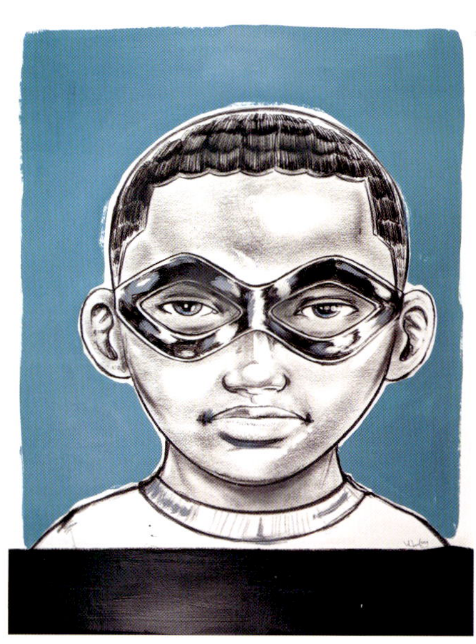

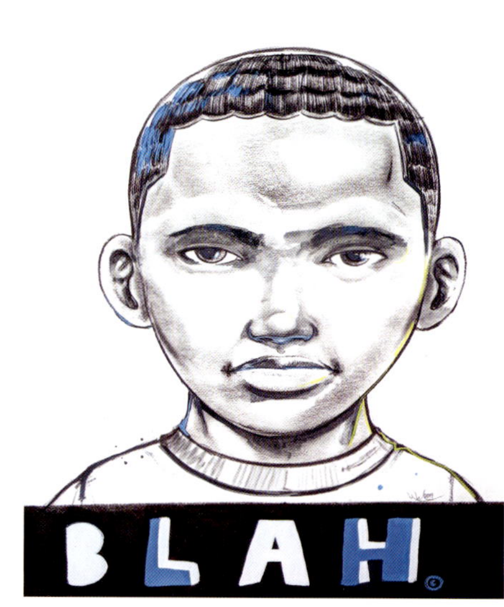

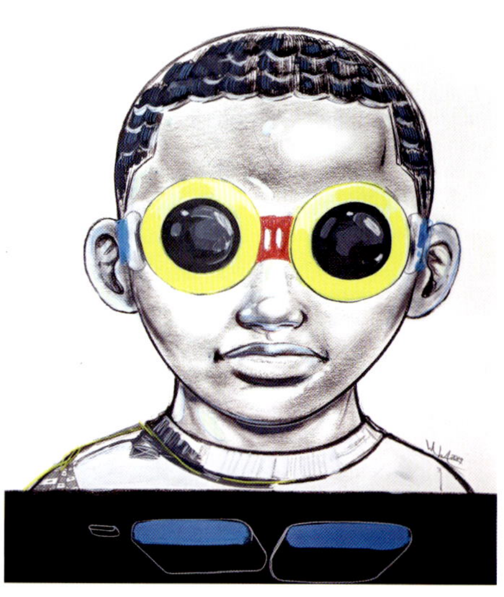

No ID Print Series
Hand-embellished
archival pigment print
18 x 24 inches
2019

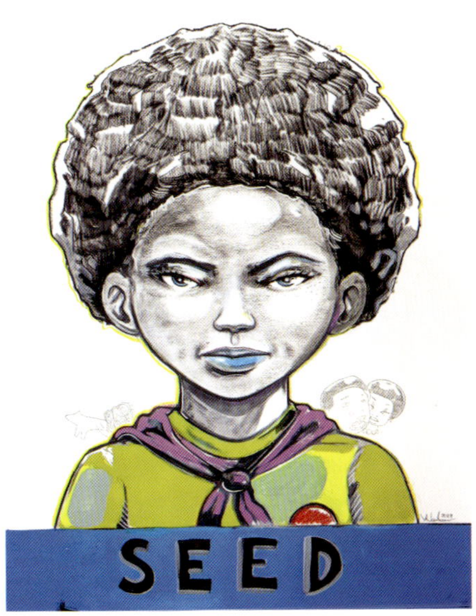
SEED

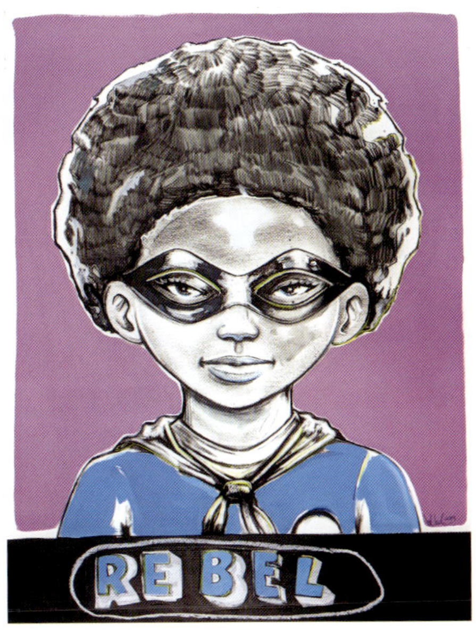
REBEL

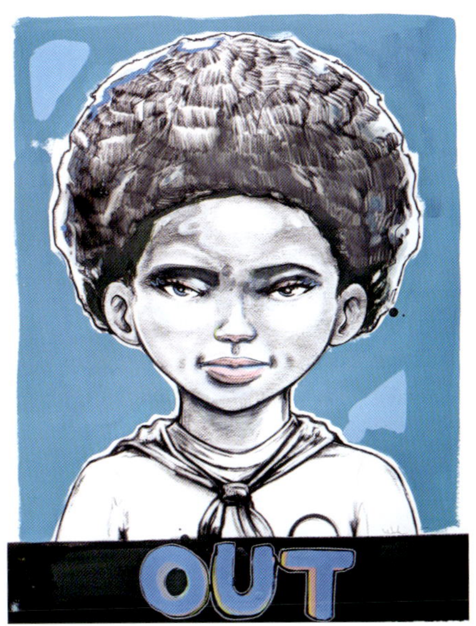
OUT

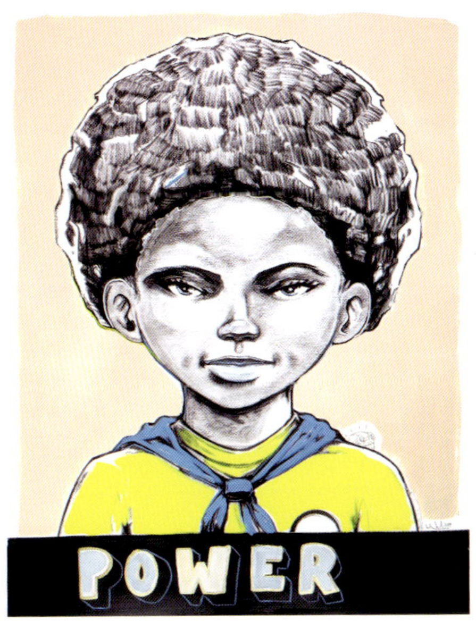
POWER

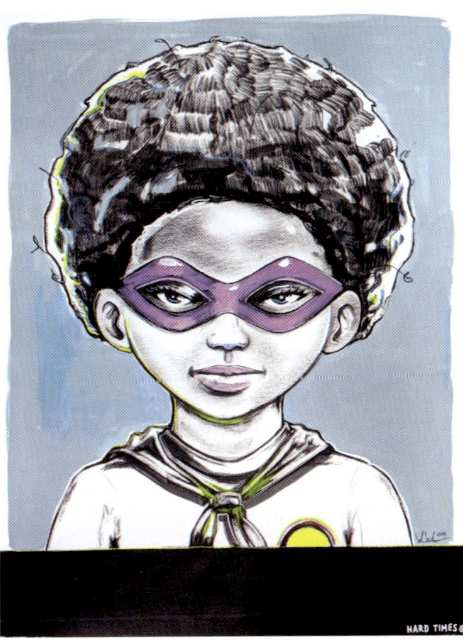
HARD TIMES

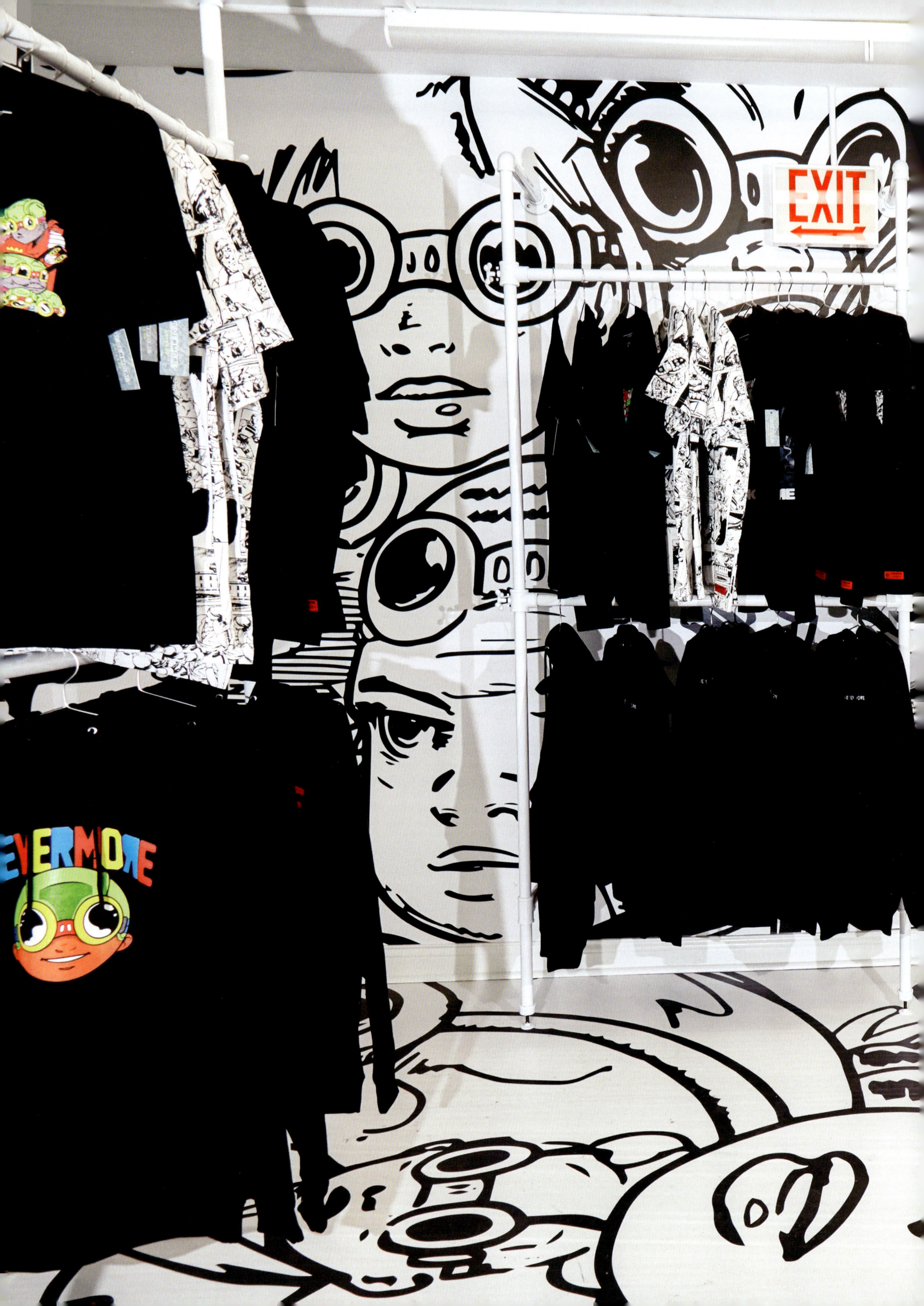
EXIT

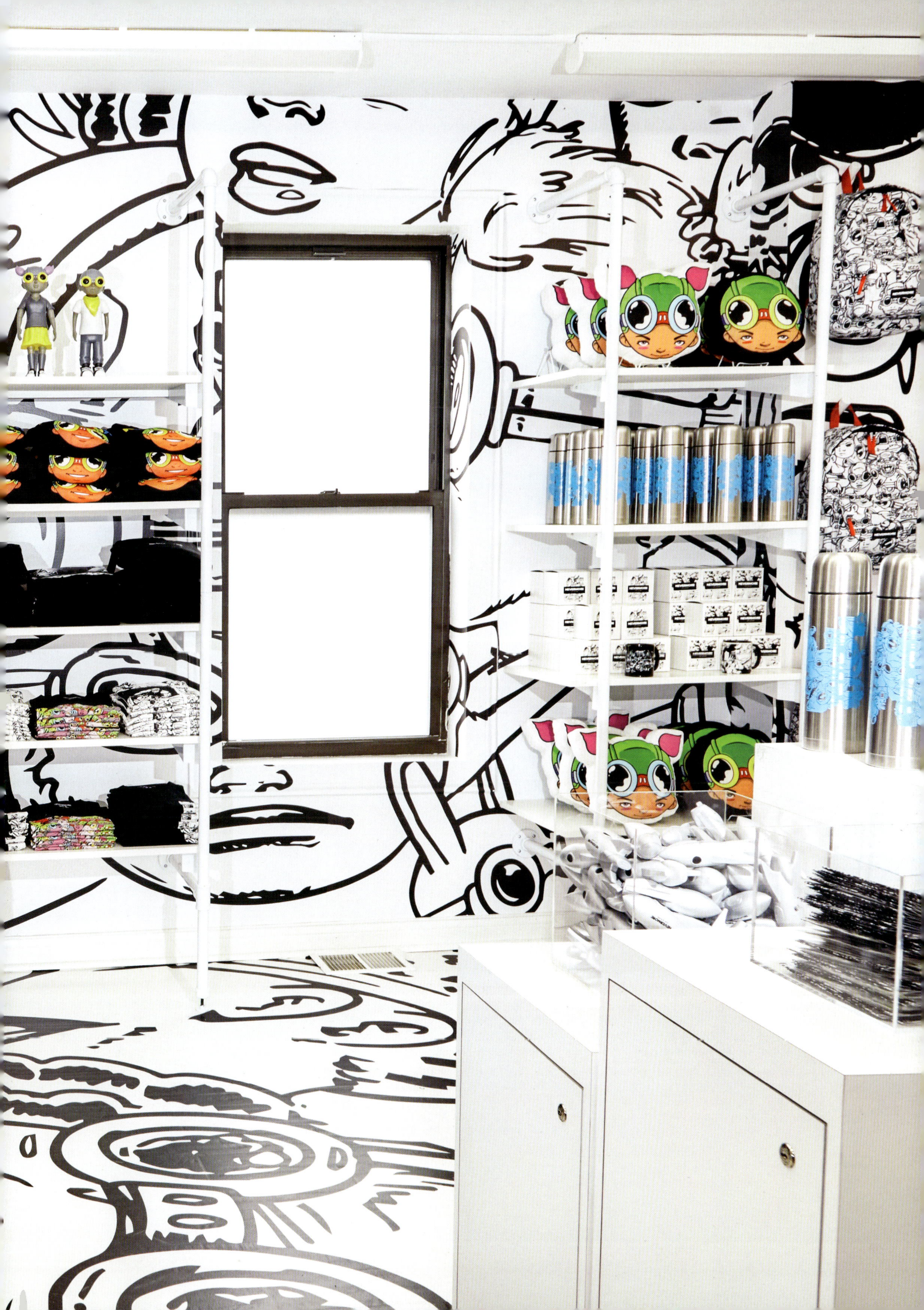

Flyboy and Lil Mama
Wool Rugs

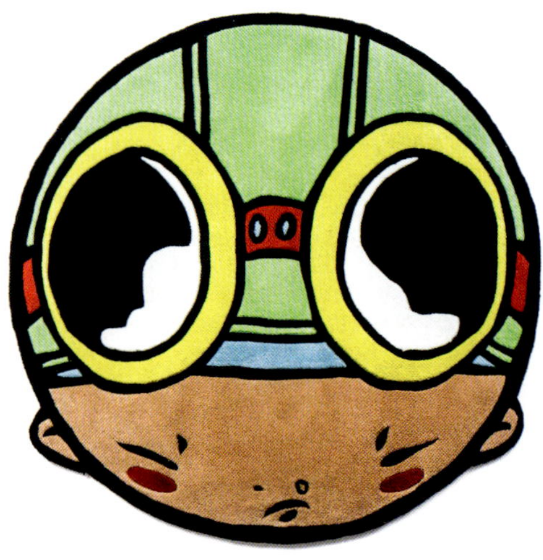

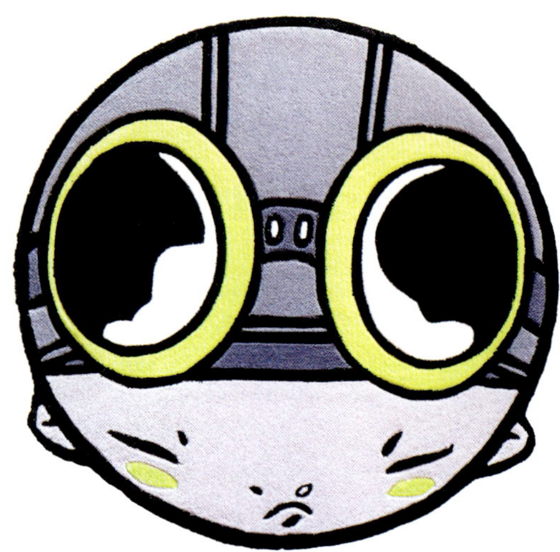

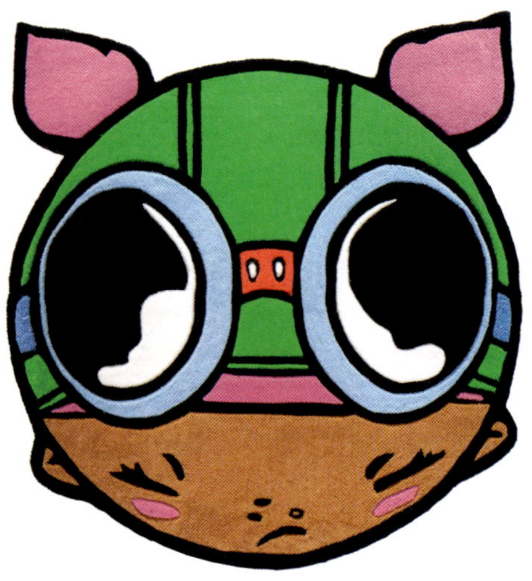

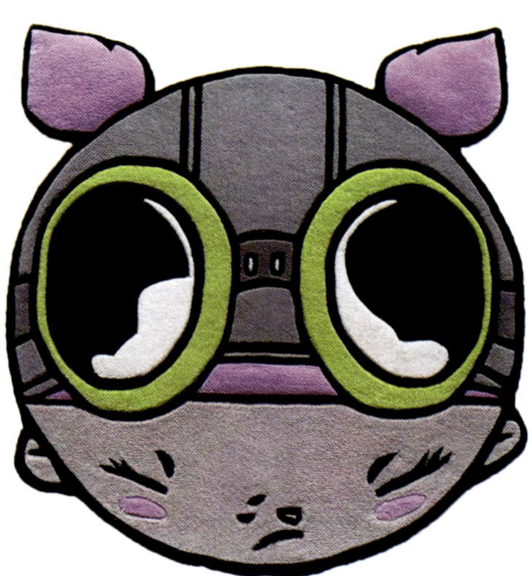

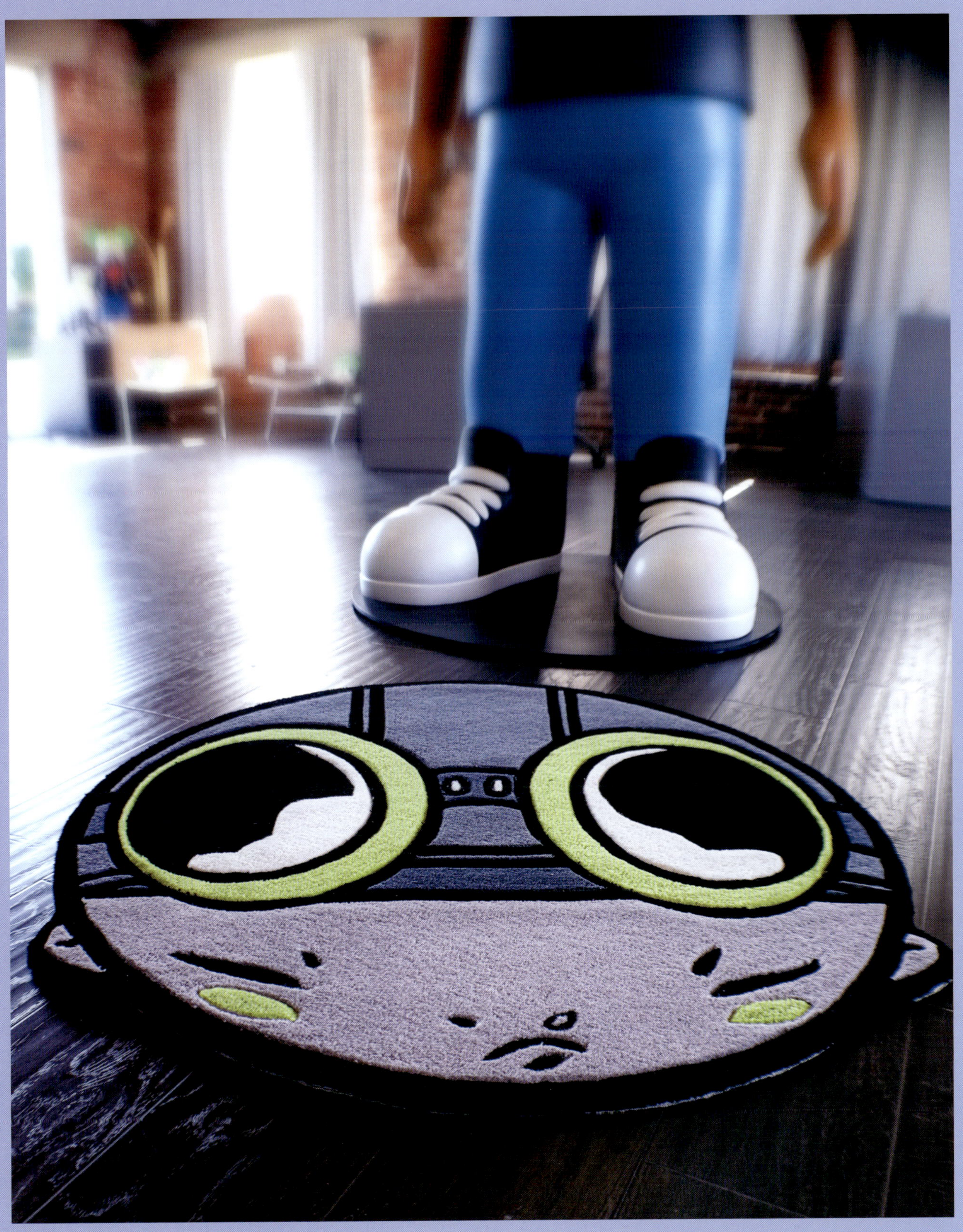

(Below)
Flyboy Skateboards

(Opposite)
Basketball Net
Printed leather-wrapped
board with copper

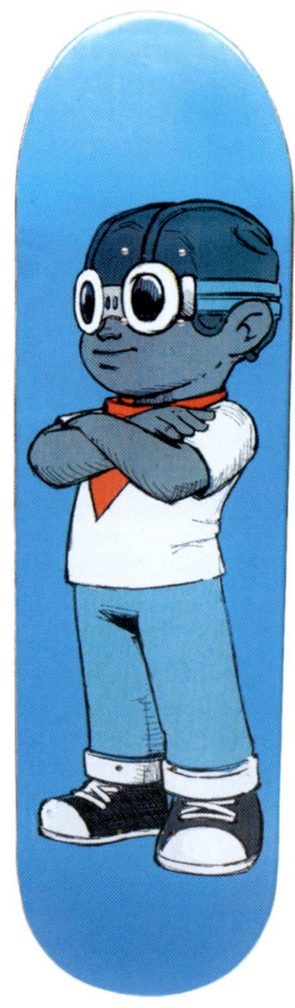

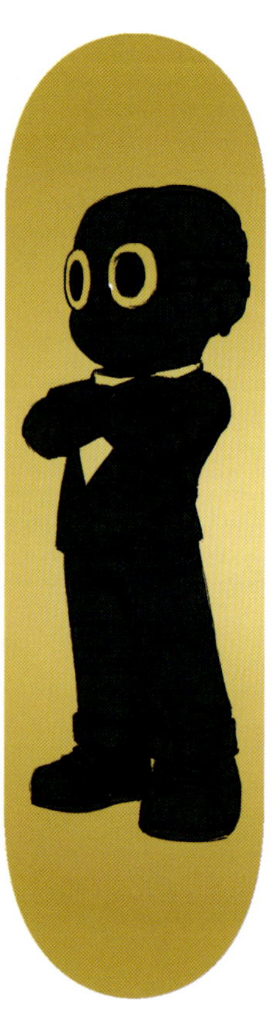

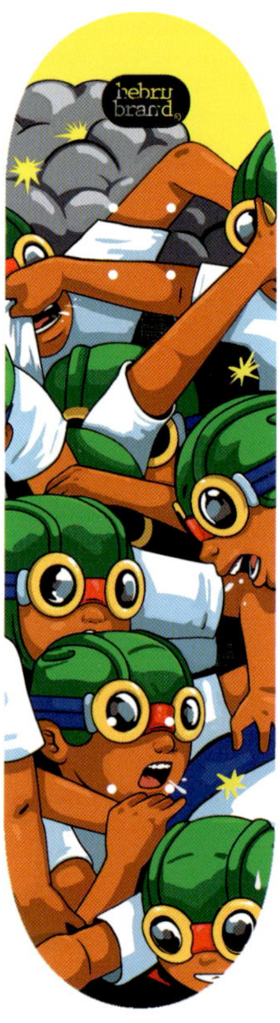

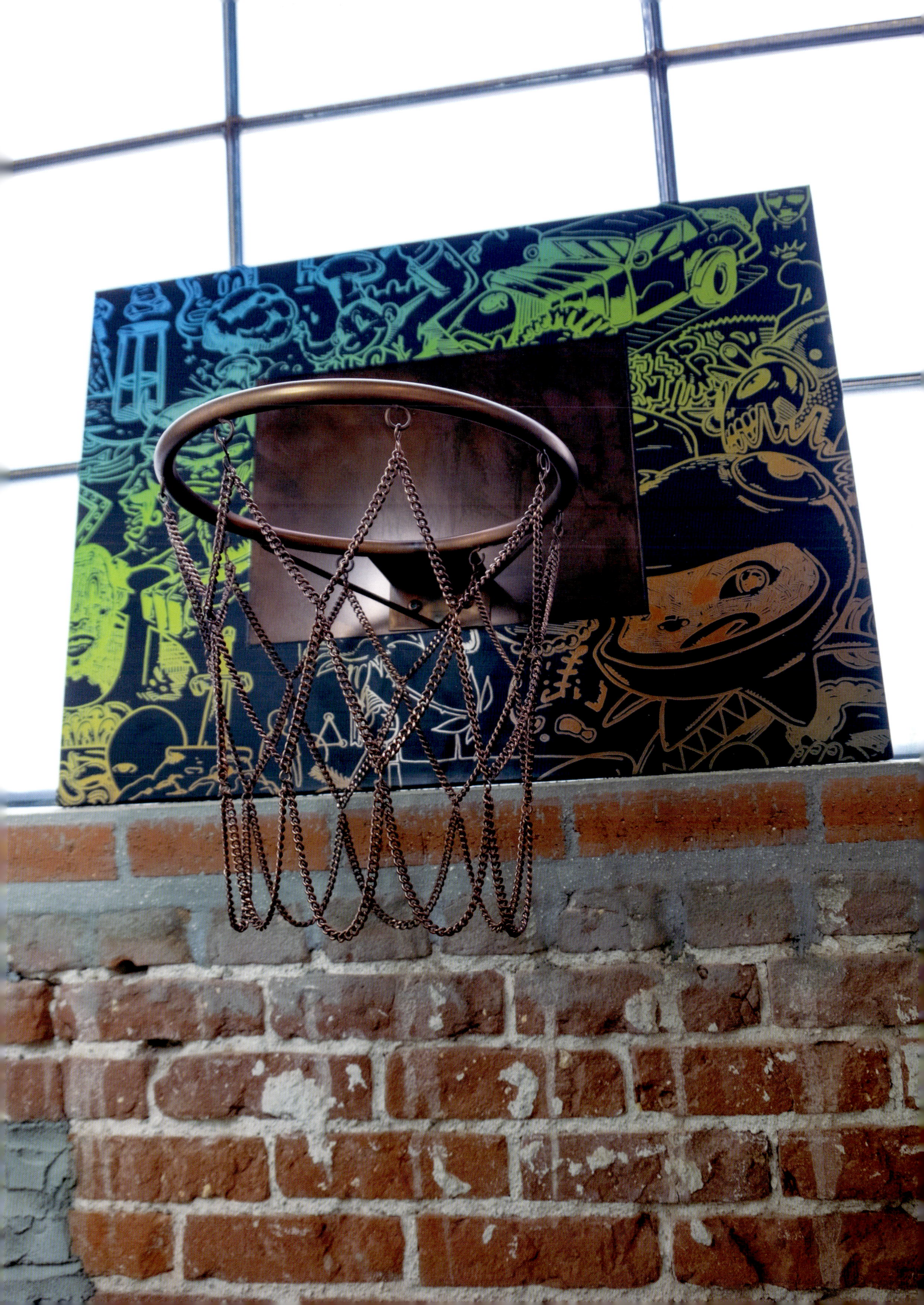

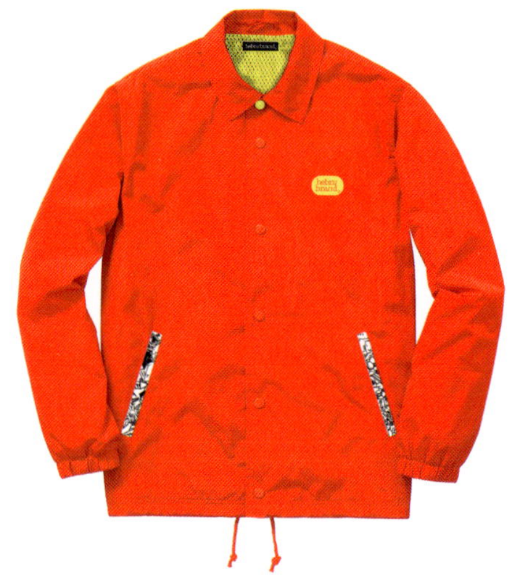

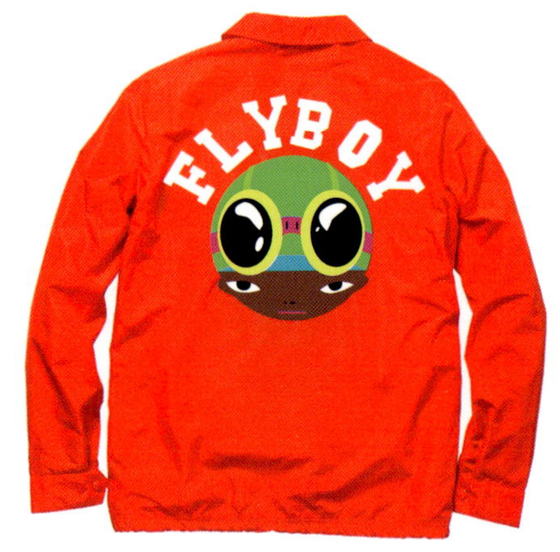
FLYBOY

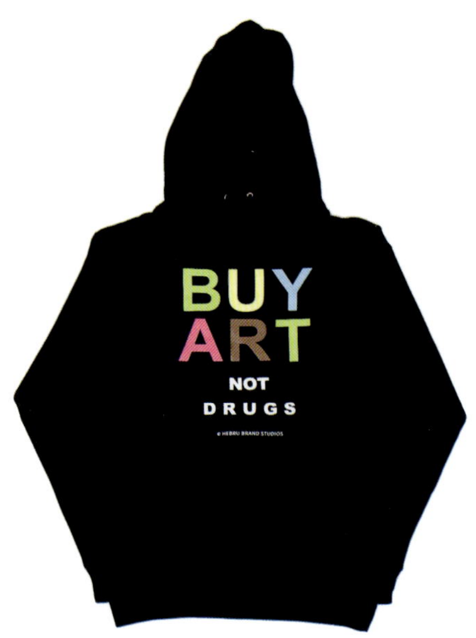
BUY
ART
NOT
DRUGS

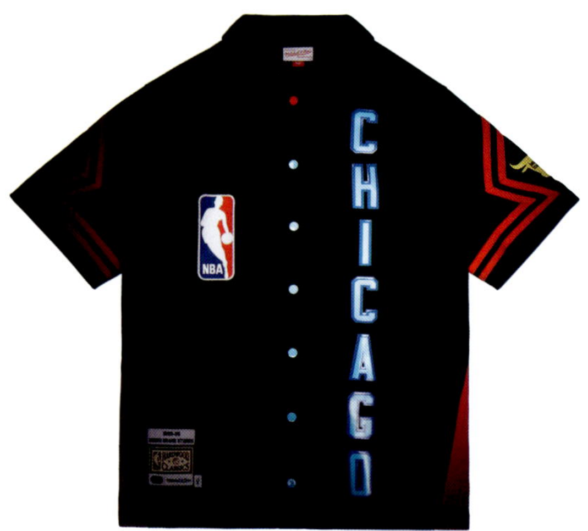
NBA
CHICAGO

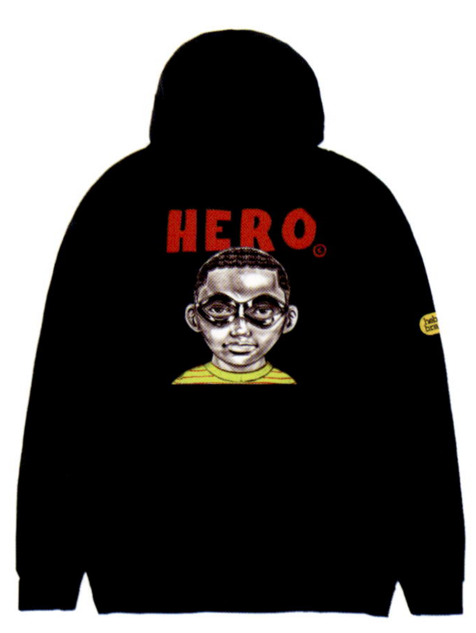
HERO

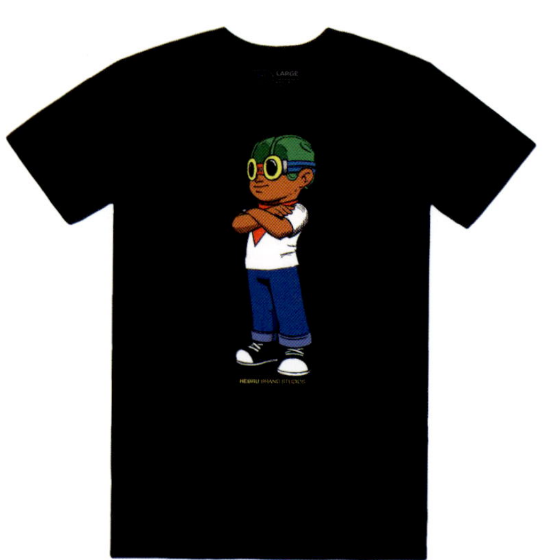

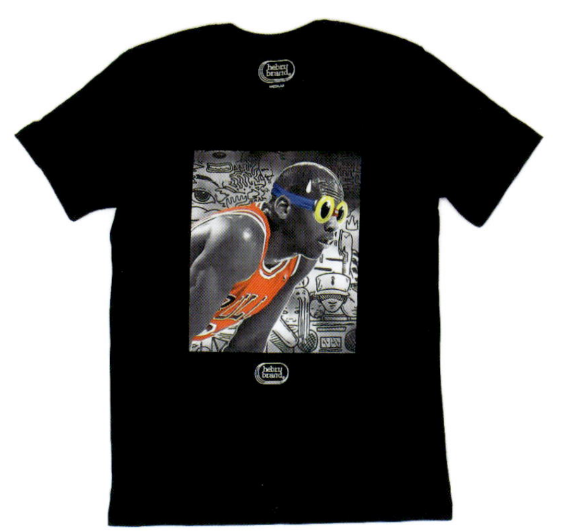

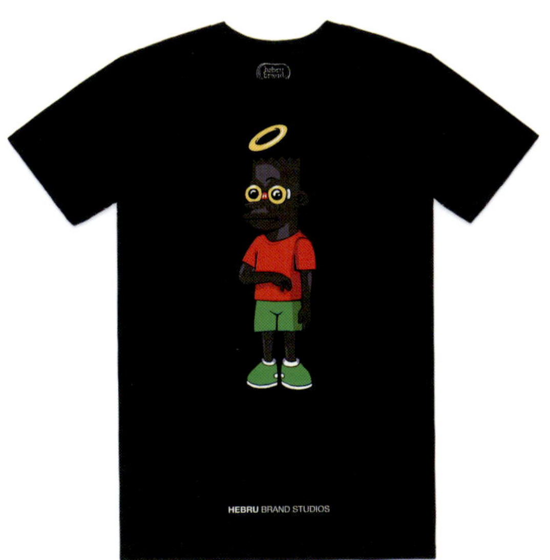
HEBRU BRAND STUDIOS

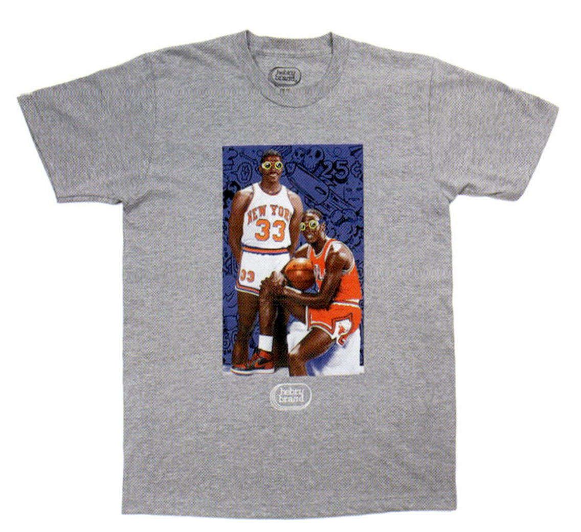
NEW YORK
33

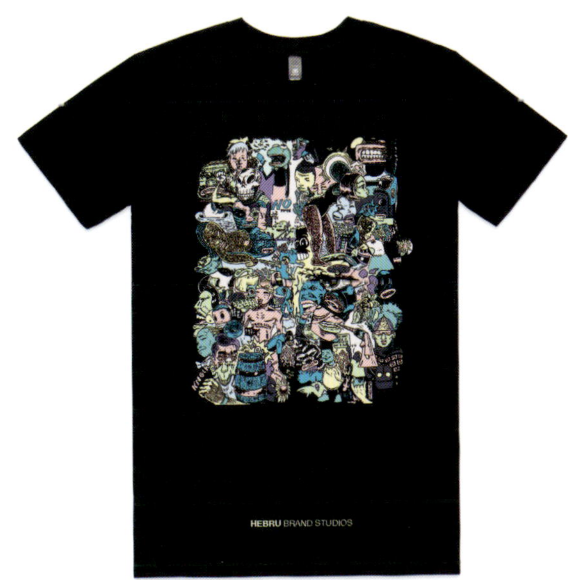
HEBRU BRAND STUDIOS

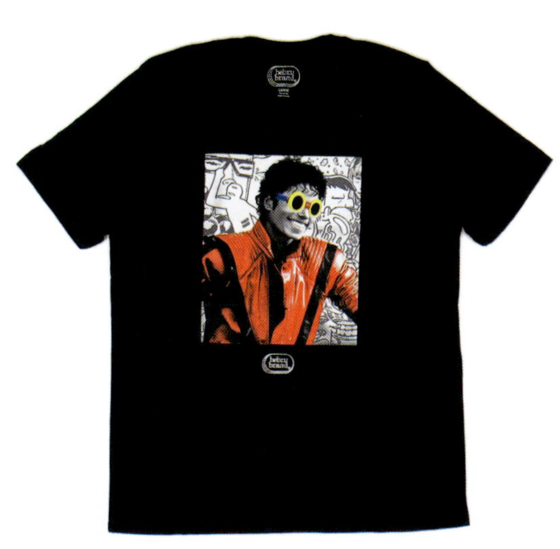

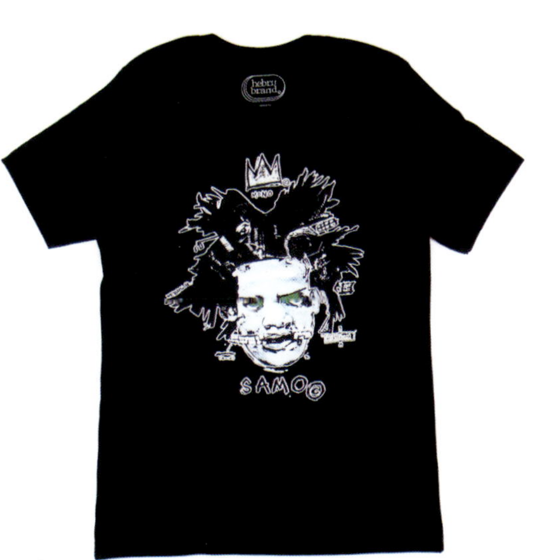
SAMO©

EPILOGUE

BY HEBRU BRANTLEY

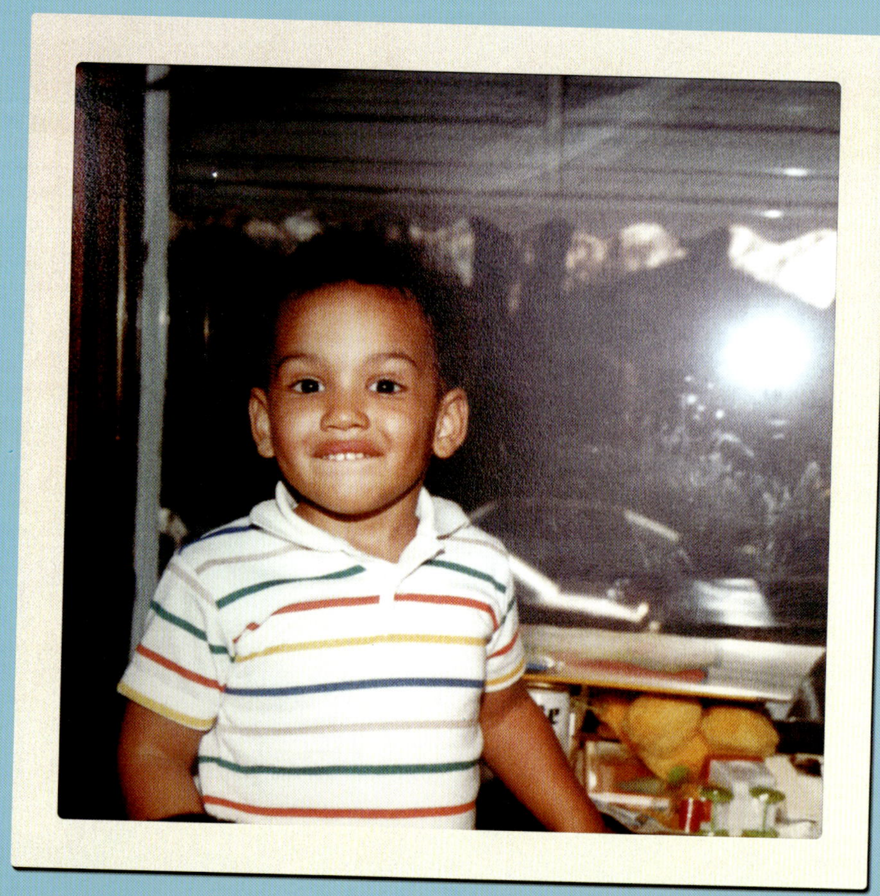

The process of compiling this book has allowed me, for the first time in a great while, to look back at the scope of work I've created over the years. As we wrap up the project, I find myself reminiscing about the point in time when I was a young college graduate—broke, living at my parents' house again after swearing that this would never be my reality. I was shiftless, not fully understanding what my next move would be. What was my next creation? What was my next big feat? What were my goals?

I zero in on the definitive moment when I happened upon a large, hardcover book that would forever change my creative path. It was a historical book with an in-depth look into WWII and its participants. This was not really my kind of go-to literature—I'm more of a graphic novel/magazine guy—but I found myself in need of some reading material for the office, a.k.a. the bathroom, as many do when nature calls. As I began to flip through the book, trying to avoid some of the graphic content one might find when dealing with the subject of war, I found a story about the Tuskegee Airmen. Here was a group of young brothers tasked to fight in a war for a country that didn't even grant them equal citizenship.

Although this book only supplied a bite-size account of their exploits, it got my wheels turning. I needed to learn more about who these men were and why they weren't more widely celebrated. I knew there was something there for me to possibly explore in my work. For days I couldn't shake the idea of these airmen; they stayed with me as I thought about my path, my significance, and what historical mark I wanted to leave on the world. I started to think about how heavy the world was for the Tuskegee Airmen at the time, as they were immersed in a war, fighting for a country that did not accept them. I saw real heroism in their actions, and in who these young men were. I knew at that moment, that was it, that was what I had been looking for: the perfect intersection between historic and heroic. I wanted to create something that not only encapsulated the valor of those men but told a story beyond it. It was more than 18 years ago that I stumbled upon the idea of Flyboy. Who would have thought my life's work would have been conceived while taking a shit? A concept that would shape the course of my artistic path, my life, my career—an idea that continues to motivate, inspire, and feed hope to those who come across these paintings, sculptures, and works across many different mediums.

You never know when you're going to be visited by the goddess Muse—when inspiration will find you—but the key is always being open to it, always being receptive and welcoming. I never set out to do the things I am doing now, but the best part of the adventure is when it finds you. Through this journey of creating these characters, I've seen both life and death. I've grown from a boy to a man, from a man to a father. These characters that I created have helped to shape me and helped me to gain a higher understanding of my place in this world, of who I am, and I am immensely grateful for that. Without them, I do not know where I would be. These are my children; they are my family. I hope that for years to come, far beyond when I still draw breath from this earth, this family can still have the same effect on others that it does today.

(Opposite)
Hebru Age 5

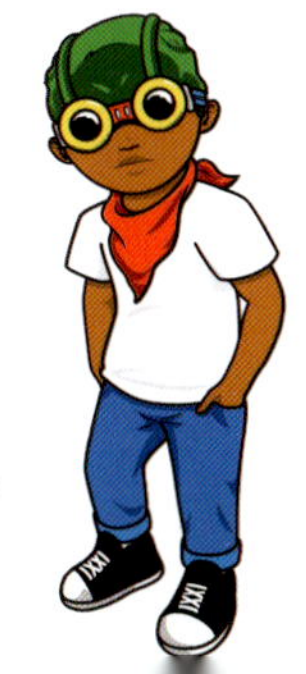

CREDITS

p. 12	Photographs by Ja Tecson, courtesy Keith Estiler/©HypeArt
p. 180–187	Installation photography by James Prinz and Allie Rowe
p. 196–199	Installation photography by Bianca Garcia
p. 201	Photography by Mike Patton
p. 204	Photo courtesy of Nanzuka Gallery
p. 206–207	Photo courtesy of Nanzuka Gallery
p. 208–209	Photo courtesy of Megumi Ogita Gallery
p. 214–217	Photography by David Lee (pixelatedstreets)
p. 218	Photography by Aubree Dallas
p. 219–221	Photography by Allie Rowe
p. 222–227	Photography by Müfit Çirpanli
p. 228	Photography by Bianca Garcia
p. 230–231	Photo courtesy of BAPE
p. 233	Photo courtesy of Mitchel & Ness
p. 234–235	Photo courtesy of the Chicago Bulls
p. 238	Photo courtesy of Wilson Basketball
p. 239	Photo courtesy of Adidas Originals
p. 244–245	Photography by Amy Lombard

ACKNOWLEDGMENTS

I would like to extend my gratitude to the following people, without whom we would not have been able to realize this survey of my work that I am so proud of.

Thank you.

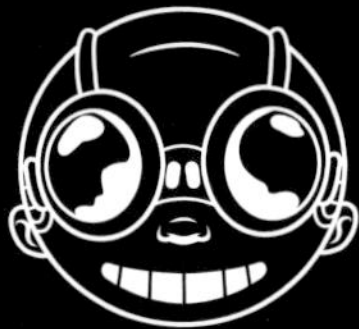

My family: My children Muse, Hero, Jayden and my wife Angela—my muses, my motivation, and my purpose. Rest in power Mom and Pops: Pamela and Terry. Ryan Glover and Shea Glover. Heather Williams, Sean Boston, Pamela Perrilliat, Javara Perrilliat, Joseph Stovall, Yahnomore

Rhea Fernandez, Janay Everett, Marika Shishido Dato, Noreen Otey,
Hebru Brand Studios and Angry Hero Entertainment
Ian Luna, Meaghan McGovern and Rizzoli Publications

Paul Spella and Oliver Munday
Carlo McCormick
Michael "Killer Mike" Santiago Render
Derek Collins
Derrick Adams
Bisa Butler
Don C
Charles Shepard
Lupe Fiasco
Coach K
Jenny Gibbs
Eric Phillips and the entire Phillips Clan
Chris, Rome, and Che
Swizz Beats
Chance the Rapper
Kendall Hurns
Enstrumental Drew
Yasiin Bey
Common
Sinan Uzan
Kevin Durant
Evan Turner
Juwan Howard
Joe Edery and Morris Missry
Randy Mims
Rich Paul
Lebron and Savannah James
Jay-Z
Shinji Nanzuka
Pharrell Williams
Lenny Santiago
Bianca Pastel
Alan Zhang
Troy Patterson
Fahamu Pecou
Theaster Gates
Monica Haslip
Anita Blanchard
Marty Nesbitt
Robbie and D'Rita Robinson
Patrick Mccoy
Patrick Hull
Max Sansing
Eve Ewing
Maya-Camille Brossard
Andrew Barber
The Cacciatore family
Chris Spurlock
Nito and Jewel
Mike Moore
Sean Brown
Pugz
Christophe Roberts
Michael B. Jordan
Clark Atlanta University
South Side of Chicago

I know I forgot a lot of people (sorry) but anyone else that has influenced me along this journey.

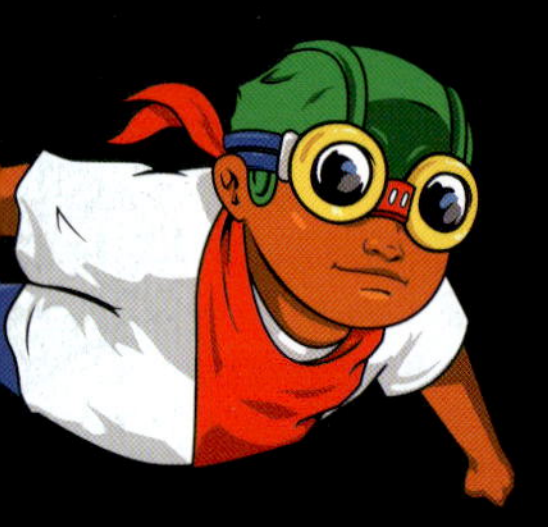

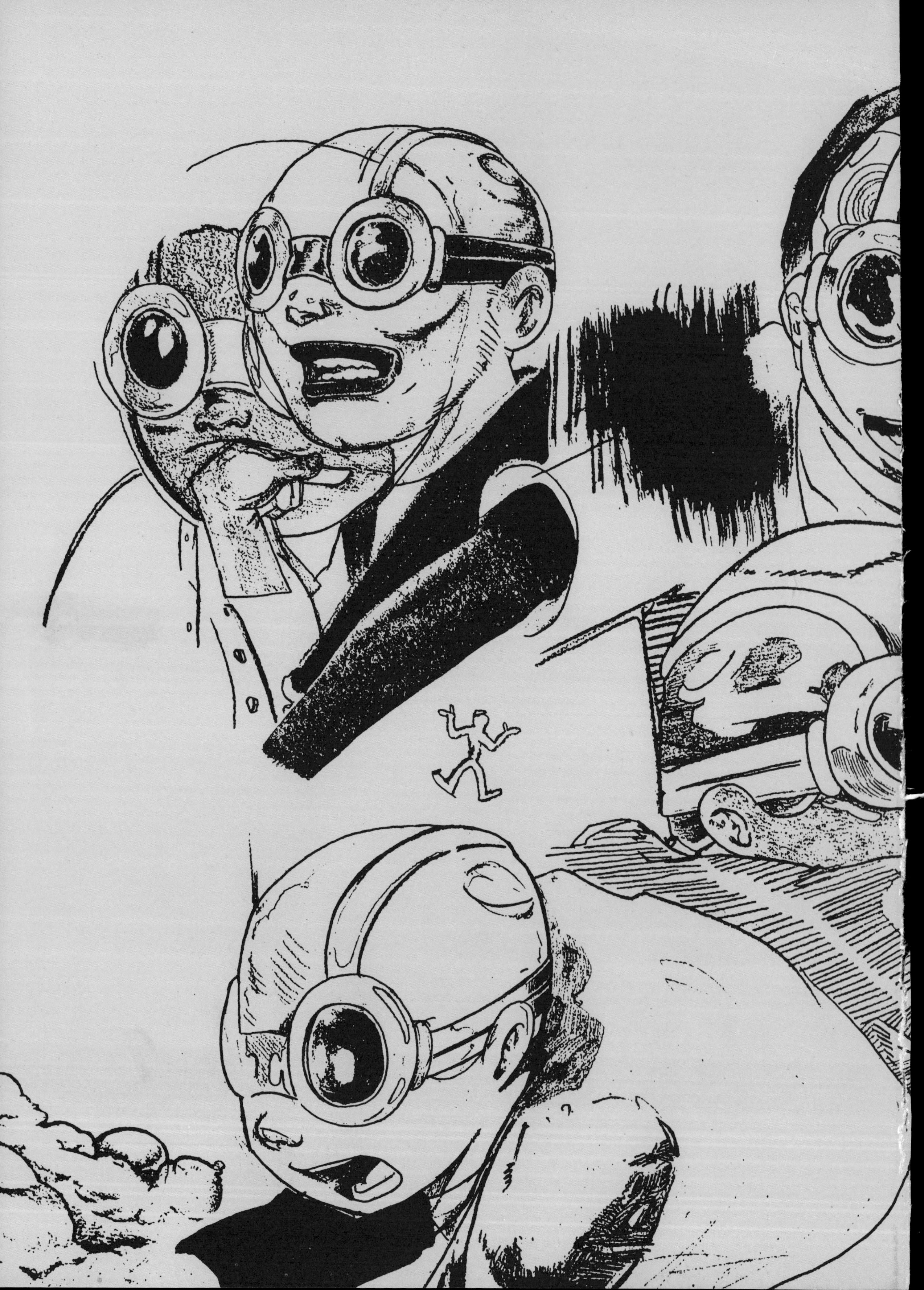